Lecture Notes in Computer Science

Commenced Publication in 1973
Founding and Former Series Editors:
Gerhard Goos, Juris Hartmanis, and Jan van Leeuwen

T0238035

Editorial Board

Mauro Barni   Jordi Herrera-Joancomartí
Stefan Katzenbeisser
Fernando Pérez-González (Eds.)

Information Hiding

7th International Workshop, IH 2005
Barcelona, Spain, June 6-8, 2005
Revised Selected Papers

 Springer

Volume Editors

Mauro Barni
Università di Siena
Dipartimento di Ingegneria dell'Informazione
Siena, Italy
E-mail: barni@dii.unisi.it

Jordi Herrera-Joancomartí
Universitat Oberta de Catalunya
Estudis d'Informàtica i Multimèdia
Barcelona, Spain
E-mail: jherreraj@uoc.edu

Stefan Katzenbeisser
Technische Universität München
Institut für Informatik
München, Germany
E-mail: katzenbe@in.tum.de

Fernando Pérez-González
Universidad de Vigo
Signal Processing in Communications Group
Vigo, Spain
E-mail: fperez@tsc.uvigo.es

Library of Congress Control Number: 2005936733

CR Subject Classification (1998): E.3, K.6.5, K.4.1, K.5.1, D.4.6, E.4, C.2, H.4.3, H.3, H.5.1

ISSN	0302-9743
ISBN-10	3-540-29039-7 Springer Berlin Heidelberg New York
ISBN-13	978-3-540-29039-1 Springer Berlin Heidelberg New York

Springer is a part of Springer Science+Business Media

springeronline.com

© Springer-Verlag Berlin Heidelberg 2005
Printed in Germany

Typesetting: Camera-ready by author, data conversion by Scientific Publishing Services, Chennai, India
Printed on acid-free paper   SPIN: 11558859   06/3142   5 4 3 2 1 0

Preface

It is our pleasure to present in this volume the proceedings of the 7th International Workshop on Information Hiding (IH 2005), held in Barcelona, Catalonia, Spain, during June 6–8, 2005. The workshop was organized by the Department of Computer Science and Multimedia, Universitat Oberta de Catalunya (UOC).

Continuing the tradition of previous workshops, we sought a balanced program, containing talks on various aspects of data hiding, anonymous communication, steganalysis, and watermarking. Although the protection of digital intellectual property has up to now motivated most of our research, there are many other upcoming fields of application. We were delighted to see that this year's workshop presented numerous new and unconventional approaches to information hiding.

The selection of the program was a very challenging task. In total, we received 90 submissions from 21 countries. At this point we want to thank all authors who submitted their latest work to IH 2005—and thus assured that the Information Hiding Workshop continues to be the top forum of our community. Each submission was refereed by three reviewers. Due to the space limitations of a single-track workshop, we could only accept 28 papers, keeping the high quality of previous workshops. We would like to thank all members of the Program Committee and all external reviewers for the enormous efforts they put into the review process. In addition to the regular presentations, an invited lecture entitled "On Joint Coding for Watermarking and Encryption" was given by Neri Merhav. Furthermore, to open the floor to additional ideas, we arranged a rump session.

Finally, we want to thank the Organizing Committee for handling all local organizational issues and the European Office of Aerospace Research and Development for their financial support.

We hope that you will enjoy reading these proceedings and that they will inspire your own research in the area of information hiding.

July 2005

Mauro Barni
Jordi Herrera Joancomartí
Stefan Katzenbeisser
Fernando Pérez-González

7th International Workshop on Information Hiding

June 6–8, 2005, Barcelona (Spain)

General Chairs

Jordi Herrera-Joancomartí, Universitat Oberta de Catalunya, Spain
Fernando Pérez-González, University of Vigo, Spain

Program Chairs

Mauro Barni, Università di Siena, Italy
Stefan Katzenbeisser, Technische Universität München, Germany

Program Committee

Ross J. Anderson, University of Cambridge, UK
Mauro Barni, Università di Siena, Italy
Jan Camenisch, IBM Zurich Research Laboratory, Switzerland
Christian Collberg, University of Arizona, USA
Ingemar J. Cox, University College London, UK
Jessica Fridrich, SUNY Binghamton, USA
Jordi Herrera-Joancomartí, Universitat Oberta de Catalunya, Spain
John McHugh, SEI/CERT, USA
Ira Moskowitz, Naval Research Laboratory, USA
Stefan Katzenbeisser, Technische Universität München, Germany
Darko Kirovski, Microsoft Research, USA
Richard C. Owens, University of Toronto, Canada
Fernando Pérez-González, University of Vigo, Spain
Andreas Pfitzmann, Dresden University of Technology, Germany
Michiel van der Veen, Philips Research, Netherlands

Local Organization

Joan Arnedo, Universitat Oberta de Catalunya, Spain
David Megías, Universitat Oberta de Catalunya, Spain
Julià Minguillón, Universitat Oberta de Catalunya, Spain
Emma Pedrol, Universitat Oberta de Catalunya, Spain
Jordi Serra, Universitat Oberta de Catalunya, Spain
Michael Tautschnig, Technische Universität München, Germany

External Reviewers

Michael A. Colón	Myong Kang	Elisa Sayrol
Andre Adelsbach	Andrew Ker	Dagmar Schönfeld
Farid Ahmed	Dogan Kesdogan	G.C.M. Silvestre
Felix Balado	Farinaz Koushanfar	Sandra Steinbrecher
Richard Bergmair	Thomas Kriegelstein	Kenneth Sullivan
Mike Bergmann	Ginger M. Myles	Ashwin Swaminathan
Rainer Böhme	John McDermott	Paul Syverson
Roberto Caldelli	Catherine Meadows	Cuneyt Taskiran
Mehmet Celik	David Megías	Clark Thomborson
R. Chandramouli	Nasir Memon	Roman Tzschoppe
Sebastian Clauss	Juliá Minguillón	José Emilio Vila-Forcén
Pedro Comesaña Alfaro	Steven Murdoch	Renato Villán
Scott Craver	Aweke N. Lemma	Changjie Wang
George Danezis	Jasvir Nagra	Ying Wang
Alessia De Rosa	Richard Newman	Brent Waters
Josep Domingo-Ferrer	Luis Perez-Freire	Andreas Westfeld
Sorina Dumitrescu	Alessandro Piva	Kevin Whelan
Hany Farid	Miodrag Potkonjak	Jennifer Wong
Elke Franz	Gang Qu	Min Wu
Shan He	Majid Rabbani	Li Wu Chang
Peter Hon Wah Wong	Victor Raskin	Yacov Yacobi
Mark Horgan	Ahmad-Reza Sadeghi	Hong Zhao
Neil Hurley	Phil Sallee	

Table of Contents

Invited Talk

Anonymity

Watermarking

Theory

Watermark Attacks

Steganography

Hiding in Unusual Content

Steganalysis

Software Watermarking

Fingerprinting

On Joint Coding for Watermarking
and Encryption

Neri Merhav

Department of Electrical Engineering,
Technion – Israel Instistute of Technology,
Technion City, Haifa 32000, Israel
`merhav@ee.technion.ac.il`

Abstract. In continuation to earlier works where the problem of joint information embedding and lossless compression (of the composite signal) was studied in the absence [6] and in the presence [7] of attacks, here we consider the additional ingredient of protecting the secrecy of the watermark against an unauthorized party, which has no access to a secret key shared by the legitimate parties. In other words, we study the problem of joint coding for three objectives: information embedding, compression, and encryption. Our main result is a coding theorem that provides a single–letter characterization of the best achievable tradeoffs among the following parameters: the distortion between the composite signal and the covertext, the distortion in reconstructing the watermark by the legitimate receiver, the compressibility of the composite signal (with and without the key), and the equivocation of the watermark, as well as its reconstructed version, given the composite signal. In the attack–free case, if the key is independent of the covertext, this coding theorem gives rise to a *threefold* separation principle that tells that asymptotically, for long block codes, no optimality is lost by first applying a rate–distortion code to the watermark source, then encrypting the compressed codeword, and finally, embedding it into the covertext using the embedding scheme of [6]. In the more general case, however, this separation principle is no longer valid, as the key plays an additional role of side information used by the embedding unit.

1 Introduction

It is common to say that encryption and watermarking (or information hiding) are related but they are substantially different in the sense that in the former, the goal is to protect the secrecy of the *contents* of information, whereas in the latter, it is the very *existence* of this information that is to be kept secret. In the last few years, however, we are witnessing increasing efforts around the *combination* of encryption and watermarking (WM), which is motivated by the desire to further enhance the security of sensitive information that is being hidden in the host signal. This is to guarantee that even if the watermark is somehow detected by a hostile party, its contents still remain secure due to the encryption. This combination of WM and encryption can be seen both in recently reported

M. Barni et al. (Eds.): IH 2005, LNCS 3727, pp. 1–10, 2005.

research work (see, e.g., [1],[2],[4],[5],[9],[11] and references therein) and in actual technologies used in commercial products with a copyright protection framework, such as the CD and the DVD.

This paper is devoted to the information–theoretic aspects of joint WM and encryption together with lossless compression of the composite signal that contains the encrypted watermark. Specifically, we extend the framework studied in [6] and [7] of joint WM and compression, so as to include encryption using a secret key. Before we describe the setting concretely, we pause then to give some more detailed background on the work reported in [6] and [7].

In [6], the following problem was studied: Given a covertext source vector $X^n = (X_1, \ldots, X_n)$, generated by a discrete memoryless source (DMS), and a message m, uniformly distributed in $\{1, 2, \ldots, 2^{nR_e}\}$, independently of X^n, with R_e designating the embedding rate, we wish to generate a composite (stegotext) vector $Y^n = (Y_1, \ldots, Y_n)$ that satisfies the following requirements: (i) Similarity to the covertext, in the sense that a distortion constraint, $Ed(X^n, Y^n) = \sum_{t=1}^{n} Ed(X_t, Y_t) \leq nD$, holds, (ii) compressibility, in the sense that the normalized entropy, $H(Y^n)/n$, does not exceed some threshold R_c, and (iii) reliability in decoding the message m from Y^n, in the sense that the decoding error probability is arbitrarily small for large n. A single–letter characterization of the best achievable tradeoffs among R_c, R_e, and D was given in [6], and was shown to be achievable by an extension of the ordinary lossy source coding theorem, giving rise to the existence of 2^{nR_e} *disjoint* rate–distortion codebooks (one per each possible watermark message) as long as R_e does not exceed a certain fundamental limit. In [7], this setup was extended to include a given memoryless attack channel, $P(Z^n|Y^n)$, where item (iii) above was redefined such that the decoding was based on Z^n rather than on Y^n. This extension required a completely different approach, which was in the spirit of the Gel'fand–Pinsker coding theorem for a channel with non–causal side information (SI) at the transmitter [3]. The role of SI, in this case, was played by the covertext.

In this paper, we extend the settings of [6] and [7] to include encryption. For the sake of clarity, we do that in several steps. First, we extend the attack–free setting of [6]: In addition to including encryption, we also extend the model of the watermark message source to be an arbitrary DMS, $U_1, U_2, \ldots$, independent of the covertext, and not necessarily a binary symmetric source (BSS) as in [6] and [7]. Specifically, we now assume that the encoder has three inputs: The covertext source vector, X^n, an independent (watermark) message source vector $U^N = (U_1, \ldots, U_N)$, where N may differ from n if the two sources operate in different rates, and a secret key (shared also with the legitimate decoder) $K^n = (K_1, \ldots, K_n)$, which, for mathematical convenience, is assumed to operate at the same rate as the covertext. It is assumed, at this stage, that K^n is independent of U^N and X^n. Now, in addition to requirements (i)-(iii), we impose a requirement on the equivocation of the message source relative to an eavesdropper that has access to Y^n, but not to K^n. Specifically, we would like the normalized conditional entropy, $H(U^N|Y^n)/N$, to exceed a prescribed threshold, h (e.g., $h = H(U)$ for perfect secrecy). Our first result is a coding theorem that gives a set of necessary and sufficient conditions, in terms of single–letter inequalities, such that a triple (D, R_c, h) is achievable, while maintaining reliable reconstruction of U^N at the legitimate receiver.

In the second step, we relax the requirement of perfect (or almost perfect) watermark reconstruction, and assume that we are willing to tolerate a certain distortion between the watermark message U^N and its reconstructed version $\hat{U}^N$, that is, $Ed'(U^N, \hat{U}^N) = \sum_{i=1}^{N} Ed'(U_i, \hat{U}_i) \leq ND'$. For example, if d' is the Hamming distortion measure then D', of course, designates the maximum allowable bit error probability (as opposed to the block error probability requirement of [6] and [7]). Also, in this case, it makes sense, in some applications, to impose a requirement regarding the equivocation of the *reconstructed* message, $\hat{U}^N$, namely, $H(\hat{U}^N | Y^n)/N \geq h'$, for some prescribed constant h'. The rationale is that it is $\hat{U}^N$, not U^N, that is actually conveyed to the legitimate receiver. For the sake of generality, however, we will take into account both equivocation requirements, with the understanding that if one of them is superfluous, then the corresponding threshold (h or h' accordingly) can always be set to zero. Our second result then extends the above–mentioned coding theorem to a single–letter characterization of achievable quintuples (D, D', R_c, h, h'). As will be seen, this coding theorem gives rise to a threefold separation theorem, that separates, without asymptotic loss of optimality, between three stages: rate–distortion coding of U^N, encryption of the compressed bitstream, and finally, embedding the resulting encrypted version using the embedding scheme of [6]. The necessary and sufficient conditions related to the encryption are completely decoupled from those of the embedding and the stegotext compression.

In the third and last step, we drop the assumption of an attack–free system and we assume a memoryless attack channel, in analogy to [7]. As it will turn out, in this case there is an interaction between the encryption and the embedding, even if the key is still assumed independent of the covertext. In particular, it will be interesting to see that the key, in addition to its original role in encryption, serves as SI that is available to both encoder and decoder. Also, because of the dependence between the key and the composite signal, and the fact that the key is available to the legitimate decoder as well, it may make sense, at least in some applications, to let the compressibility constraint correspond to the the the conditional entropy of Y^n given K^n. Again, for the sake of generality, we will consider both the conditional and the unconditional entropies of Y^n, i.e., $H(Y^n)/n \leq R_c$ and $H(Y^n | K^n)/n \leq R'_c$.

Our final result then is a coding theorem that provides a single–letter characterization of the region of achievable six–tuples $(D, D', R_c, R'_c, h, h')$. Interestingly, this characterization remains essentially unaltered even if there is dependence between the key and the covertext, which is a reasonable thing to have once the key and the stegotext interact anyhow.[1] In this context, the system designer confronts an interesting dilemma regarding the desirable degree of statistical dependence between the key and the covertext, which affects the

---

[1] In fact, the choice of the conditional distribution $P(K^n | X^n)$ is a degree of freedom that can be optimized subject to the given randomness resources.

dependence between the key and the stegotext. On the one hand, strong dependence can reduce the entropy of Y^n given K^n (and thereby reduce R'_c), and can also help in the embedding process: For example, the extreme case of $K^n = X^n$ (which corresponds to *private* WM since the decoder actually has access to the covertext) is particularly interesting because in this case, for the encryption key, there is no need for any external resources of randomness, in addition to the randomness of the covertext that is already available. On the other hand, when there is strong dependence between K^n and Y^n, the secrecy of the watermark might be sacrificed since $H(K^n|Y^n)$ decreases as well. An interesting point, in this context, is that the Slepian–Wolf encoder [10] is used to generate, from K^n, random bits that are essentially independent of Y^n (as Y^n is generated only after the encryption).

2   Results

We begin by establishing some notation conventions. Throughout this paper, scalar random variables (RV's) will be denoted by capital letters, their sample values will be denoted by the respective lower case letters, and their alphabets will be denoted by the respective calligraphic letters. A similar convention will apply to random vectors and their sample values, which will be denoted with same symbols superscripted by the dimension. Thus, for example, A^ℓ (ℓ – positive integer) will denote a random ℓ-vector $(A_1, ..., A_\ell)$, and $a^\ell = (a_1, ..., a_\ell)$ is a specific vector value in $\mathcal{A}^\ell$, the ℓ-th Cartesian power of $\mathcal{A}$. Sources and channels will be denoted generically by the letter P, or Q, subscripted by the name of the RV and its conditioning, if applicable, e.g., $P_U(u)$ is the probability function of U at the point $U = u$, $P_{K|X}(k|x)$ is the conditional probability of $K = k$ given $X = x$, and so on. Whenever clear from the context, these subscripts will be omitted. Information theoretic quantities like entropies and mutual informations will be denoted following the usual conventions of the Information Theory literature, e.g., $H(U^N)$, $I(X^n; Y^n)$, and so on. For single–letter information quantities (i.e., when $n = 1$ or $N = 1$), subscripts will be omitted, e.g., $H(U^1) = H(U_1)$ will be denoted by $H(U)$, similarly, $I(X^1; Y^1) = I(X_1; Y_1)$ will be denoted by $I(X; Y)$, and so on.

We now turn to the formal description of the problem setting for step 1, as described in the Introduction. A source P_X, henceforth referred to as the *covertext source* generates a sequence of independent copies, $\{X_t\}_{t=-\infty}^{\infty}$, of a finite–alphabet RV, $X \in \mathcal{X}$. At the same time and independently, another source P_U, henceforth referred to as the *message source* generates a sequence of independent copies, $\{U_i\}_{i=-\infty}^{\infty}$, of a finite–alphabet RV, $U \in \mathcal{U}$. The relative rate between the message source and the covertext source is λ message symbols per covertext symbol. This means that while the covertext source generates a block of n symbols, say, $X^n = (X_1, \ldots, X_n)$, the message source generates a block of $N = \lambda n$ symbols, $U^N = (U_1, \ldots, U_N)$. In addition to the covertext source and the message source, yet another source, P_K, henceforth referred to as the *key source*, generates a sequence of independent copies, $\{K_t\}_{t=-\infty}^{\infty}$, of a finite–

alphabet RV, $K \in \mathcal{K}$, independently[2] of both $\{X_t\}$ and $\{U_i\}$. They key source is assumed to operate at the same rate as the covertext source, that is, while the covertext source generates the block of length n, X^n, the key source generates a block of n symbols as well, $K^n = (K_1, \ldots, K_n)$.

Given n and λ, a block code for *joint WM, encryption, and compression* is a mapping $f_n : \mathcal{U}^N \times \mathcal{X}^n \times \mathcal{K}^n \rightarrow \mathcal{Y}^n$, $N = \lambda n$, whose output $y^n = (y_1, \ldots, y_n) = f_n(u^N, x^n, k^n) \in \mathcal{Y}^N$ is referred to as the *stegotext* or the *composite signal*, and accordingly, the finite alphabet $\mathcal{Y}$ is referred to as the *stegotext alphabet*. Let $d : \mathcal{X} \times \mathcal{Y} \rightarrow \mathbb{R}^+$ denote a single–letter distortion measure between covertext symbols and stegotext symbols, and let the distortion between the vectors, $x^n \in \mathcal{X}^n$ and $y^n \in \mathcal{Y}^n$, be defined additively across the corresponding components, as usual. An $(n, \lambda, D, R_c, h, \delta)$ code is a block code for joint WM, encryption, and compression, with parameters n and λ, that satisfies the following requirements: (1) $\sum_{t=1}^{n} Ed(X_t, Y_t) \leq nD$, (2) $H(Y^n) \leq nR_c$, (3) $H(U^N | Y^n) \geq Nh$, and (4) There exists a decoder $g_n : \mathcal{Y}^n \times \mathcal{K}^n \rightarrow \mathcal{U}^N$ such that $P_e \triangleq \Pr\{g_n(Y^n, K^n) \neq U^N\} \leq \delta$. For a given λ, a triple (D, R_c, h) is said to be *achievable* if for every $\epsilon > 0$, there is a sufficiently large n for which $(n, \lambda, D + \epsilon, R_c + \epsilon, h - \epsilon, \epsilon)$ codes exist. For simplicity, it is assumed[3] that $H(K) \leq \lambda H(U)$ as this upper limit on $H(K)$ suffices to achieve perfect secrecy. Our first coding theorem is the following:

Theorem 1. *A triple (D, R_c, h) is achievable iff the following conditions are satisfied: (a) $h \leq H(K)/\lambda$, and (b) There exists a channel $\{P_{Y|X}(y|x), x \in \mathcal{X}, y \in \mathcal{Y}\}$ such that: (i) $H(Y|X) \geq \lambda H(U)$, (ii) $R_c \geq \lambda H(U) + I(X;Y)$, and (iii) $D \geq Ed(X,Y)$.*

As can be seen, the encryption and the embedding and the compression do not interact at all in this theorem. There is a complete decoupling between them: While (a) refers solely to the key and the secrecy of the watermark, (b) is only about the embedding–compression part, and it is a replica of the conditions of the coding theorem in [6], where the role of the embedding rate, R_e is played by the product $\lambda H(U)$. This suggests a very simple separation principle, telling that in order to attain (D, R_c, h), first compress the watermark U^N to its entropy, then encrypt Nh bits (out of the $NH(U)$) of the compressed bit–string (by one–time padding with the compressed key), and finally, embed this partially encrypted compressed bit–string into the covertext, using the coding theorem of [6].

Turning to Step 2, we now relax requirement 4 in the above definition of an $(n, \lambda, D, R_c, h, \delta)$ code, and allow a certain distortion between U^N and its reconstruction $\hat{U}^N$ at the legitimate decoder. Precisely, let $\hat{\mathcal{U}}$ denote a finite alphabet, henceforth referred to as the *message reconstruction alphabet*. Let $d' : \mathcal{U} \times \hat{\mathcal{U}} \rightarrow \mathbb{R}^+$ denote a single–letter distortion measure between message symbols and message reconstruction symbols, and let the distortion between vectors $u^N \in \mathcal{U}^N$

---

[2] The assumption of independence between $\{K_t\}$ and $\{X_t\}$ is temporary and made now primarily for the sake of simplicity of the exposition. It will be dropped later on.

[3] At the end of Section 4 (after Theorem 4), we discuss the case where this limitation (or its analogue in lossy reconstruction of U^N) is dropped.

and $\hat{u}^N \in \hat{\mathcal{U}}^N$ be again, defined additively across the corresponding components. Finally, let $R_U(D')$ denote the rate–distortion function of the source P_U w.r.t. d'. It will now be assumed that $H(K) \leq \lambda R_U(D')$, for the same reasoning as before.

Requirement 4 is now replaced by the following requirement: There exists a decoder $g_n : \mathcal{Y}^n \times \mathcal{K}^n \to \hat{\mathcal{U}}^N$ such that $\hat{U}^N = (\hat{U}_1, \ldots, \hat{U}_N) = g_n(Y^n, K^n)$ satisfies: $\sum_{i=1}^N Ed'(U_i, \hat{U}_i) \leq ND'$. In addition to this modification of requirement 4, we add, to requirement 3, a specification regarding the minimum allowed equivocation w.r.t. the reconstructed message: $H(\hat{U}^N|Y^n) \geq Nh'$, in order to guarantee that the secrecy of the reconstructed message is also secure enough. Accordingly, we modify the above definition of a block code as follows: An $(n, \lambda, D, D', R_c, h, h')$ code is a block code for joint WM, encryption, and compression with parameters n and λ that satisfies requirements 1–4, with the above modifications of requirements 3 and 4. For a given λ, a quintuple (D, D', R_c, h, h') is said to be *achievable* if for every $\epsilon > 0$, there is a sufficiently large n for which $(n, \lambda, D+\epsilon, D'+\epsilon, R_c+\epsilon, h-\epsilon, h'-\epsilon)$ codes exist. Our second theorem extends Theorem 1 to this setting:

Theorem 2. *A quintuple (D, D', R_c, h, h') is achievable iff the following conditions are satisfied: (a) $h \leq H(K)/\lambda + H(U) - R_U(D')$, (b) $h' \leq H(K)/\lambda$, and (c) There exists a channel $\{P_{Y|X}(y|x), \ x \in \mathcal{X}, \ y \in \mathcal{Y}\}$ such that: (i) $\lambda R_U(D') \leq H(Y|X)$, (ii) $R_c \geq \lambda R_U(D') + I(X;Y)$, and (iii) $D \geq Ed(X,Y)$.*

As can be seen, the passage from Theorem 1 to Theorem 2 includes the following modifications: In condition (c), $H(U)$ is simply replaced by $R_U(D')$ as expected. Conditions (a) and (b) now tell us that the key rate (in terms of entropy) should be sufficiently large to satisfy both equivocation requirements. Note that the condition regarding the equivocation w.r.t. the clean message source is softer than in Theorem 1 as $H(U) - R_U(D') \geq 0$. This is because the rate–distortion code for U^N already introduces an uncertainty of $H(U) - R_U(D')$ bits per symbol, and so, the encryption should only complete it to h (see [12]). We also observe that the encryption and the embedding are still decoupled in Theorem 2, and that an achievable quintuple can still be attained by separation.

Finally, we turn to step 3, of including an attack channel. Let $\mathcal{Z}$ be a finite alphabet and let $\{P_{Z|Y}(z|y), \ y \in \mathcal{Y}, \ z \in \mathcal{Z}\}$ denote a set of conditional PMF's from $\mathcal{Y}$ to $\mathcal{Z}$. We now assume that Y^n is subjected to an attack modelled by the DMC $P_{Z^n|Y^n}(z^n|y^n) = \prod_{t=1}^n P_{Z|Y}(z_t|y_t)$. It is now assumed and that the legitimate decoder has access to Z^n, rather than Y^n (in addition, of course, to K^n). Thus, in requirement 4, the decoder is redefined again, this time, as a mapping $g_n : \mathcal{Z}^n \times \mathcal{K}^n \to \hat{\mathcal{U}}^N$ such that $\hat{U}^N = g_n(Z^n, K^n)$ satisfies the distortion constraint. As for the equivocation requirements, the conditioning will now be on both Y^n and Z^n, i.e., $H(U^N|Y^n, Z^n) \geq Nh$ and $H(\hat{U}^N|Y^n, Z^n) \geq Nh'$, as if the attacker and the eavesdropper are the same party (or if they cooperate), then s/he may access both. In fact, for the equivocation of U^N, the conditioning on Z^n is immaterial since $U^N \to Y^n \to Z^n$ is always a Markov chain, but it is not clear that Z^n is superfluous for the equivocation w.r.t. $\hat{U}^N$ since Z^n is one of the inputs to the decoder whose output is $\hat{U}^N$. Nonetheless, for the sake of uniformity and convenience, we keep the conditioning on Z^n in both equivocation criteria.

Redefining block codes and achievable quintuples (D, D', R_C, h, h') according to the modified requirements in the same spirit, we now have the following coding theorem, which is substantially different from Theorems 1 and 2:

Theorem 3. *A quintuple (D, D', R_c, h, h') is achievable iff there exist RV's V and Y such that $(K, X, V) \to Y \to Z$ is a Markov chain, $P_{KX}(k, x) = P_X(x)P_K(k)$, the alphabet size of V is bounded by $|\mathcal{V}| \leq |\mathcal{K}| \cdot |\mathcal{X}| \cdot |\mathcal{Y}| + 1$, and the following conditions are satisfied: (a) $h \leq H(K|Y)/\lambda + H(U) - R_U(D')$, (b) $h' \leq H(K|Y)/\lambda$, (c) $\lambda R_U(D') \leq I(V; Z|K) - I(V; X|K)$, (d) $R_c \geq \lambda R_U(D') + I(X; Y, V|K) + I(K; Y)$, and (e) $D \geq Ed(X, Y)$.*

First, observe that here, unlike in Theorems 1 and 2, it is no longer true that the encryption and the embedding/compression are decoupled. Note that now, although K is still assumed independent of X, it may, in general, depend on Y. On the negative side, this dependence causes a reduction in the equivocation of both the message source and its reconstruction, and therefore $H(K|Y)$ replaces $H(K)$ in conditions (a) and (b). On the positive side, this dependence introduces new degrees of freedom in enhancing the tradeoffs between the embedding performance and the compressibility. At first glance, it may appear intuitive that the best choice of RV's would be to keep (V, Y) independent of K: The expression $I(V; Z|K) - I(V; X|K)$ should certainly be maximized for such a pair (V, Y) since K conveys irrelevant additional SI, due to the independence between X and K and the conditional independence between Z and K given Y. It is not clear, however, that such a choice of (V, Y) would also be best for the compressibility condition (d). In other words, due to the *combination* of requirements, the dependence of (V, Y) on K may be needed, in order to obtain full generality of performance tradeoffs, and so, K now may have the additional role of symbolizing SI that is available to *both* encoder and legitimate decoder. In this sense, there is *no* longer a separation principle, in contrast to the attack–free case.

The achievability of Theorem 3 involves essentially the same stages as before (rate–distortion coding of U^N, followed by encryption, followed in turn by embedding), but this time, the embedding scheme is a conditional version of the one proposed in [7], where all codebooks depend on K^n, the SI given at both ends). An interesting point regarding the encryption is that one needs to generate, from K^n, essentially $nH(K|Y)$ random bits that are *independent* of Y^n (and Z^n), in order to protect the secrecy against an eavesdropper that observes Y^n and Z^n. Clearly, if Y^n was given in advance to the encrypting unit, then the compressed bitstring of an optimal lossless source code that compresses K^n, given Y^n as SI, would have this property (as if there was any dependence, then this bitstring could have been further compressed, which is a contradiction). However, such a source code cannot be implemented since Y^n itself is in turn generated from the encrypted message, i.e., *after* the encryption. In other words, this would have required a circular mechanism, which may not be feasible. A simple remedy is then to use a *Slepian–Wolf encoder* [10], that generates $nH(K|Y)$ bits that are essentially independent of Y^n (due to the same consideration), without the need to access the vector Y^n to be generated. For more details, see [8]. It is easy to see that in the absence of attack (i.e., $Z = Y$), Theorem 2 is obtained as a special case of Theorem 3 by choosing $V = Y$ and letting both be independent of K, a choice which is simultaneously the best for conditions (a)–(d) of Theorem 3.

Returning now to Theorem 3, as we observed, K^n is now involved not only in the role of a cipher key, but also as SI available at both encoder and decoder. Two important points are now in order, in view of this fact. First, one may argue that, actually, there is no real reason to assume that K^n is necessarily independent of X^n. If the user has control of the mechanism of generating the key, then s/he might implement, in general, a channel $P_{K^n|X^n}(k^n|x^n)$ using the available randomness resources, and taking (partial) advantage of the randomness of the covertext. Let us assume that this channel is stationary and memoryless, i.e., $P_{K^n|X^n}(k^n|x^n) = \prod_{t=1}^{n} P_{K|X}(k_t|x_t)$ with the single–letter transition probabilities $\{P_{K|X}(k|x) \ x \in \mathcal{X}, \ k \in \mathcal{K}\}$ left as a degree of freedom for design. While so far, we assumed that K was independent of X, the other extreme is, of course, $K = X$ (corresponding to private WM). Note, however, that in the attack–free case, in the absence of the compressibility requirement no. 2 (say, $R_c = \infty$), no optimality is lost by assuming that K is independent of X, since the only inequality where we have used the independence assumption, in the previous paragraph, corresponds to condition (d).

The second point is that in Theorems 1–3, so far, we have defined the compressibility of the stegotext in terms of $H(Y^n)$, which is suitable when the decompression of Y^n is *public*, i.e., without access to K^n. The legitimate decoder in our model, on the other hand, has access to the SI K^n, which may depend on Y^n. In this context, it then makes sense to measure the compressibility of the stegotext also in a *private* regime, i.e., in terms of the *conditional* entropy, $H(Y^n|K^n)$. Our last (and most general) version of the coding theorem below takes these two points into account. Specifically, let us impose, in requirement no. 2, an additional inequality, $H(Y^n|K^n) \leq nR'_c$, where R'_c is a prescribed constant, and let us redefine accordingly the block codes and the achievable region in terms of six–tuples $(D, D', R_c, R'_c, h, h')$. We now have the following result:

Theorem 4. *A six–tuple $(D, D', R_c, R'_c, h, h')$ is achievable iff there exist RV's V and Y such that $(K, X, V) \to Y \to Z$ is a Markov chain, the alphabet size of V is bounded by $|\mathcal{V}| \leq |\mathcal{K}| \cdot |\mathcal{X}| \cdot |\mathcal{Y}| + 1$, and the following conditions are satisfied: (a) $h \leq H(K|Y)/\lambda + H(U) - R_U(D')$, (b) $h' \leq H(K|Y)/\lambda$, (c) $\lambda R_U(D') \leq I(V; Z|K) - I(V; X|K)$, (d) $R_c \geq \lambda R_U(D') + I(X; Y, V|K) + I(K; Y)$, (e) $R'_c \geq \lambda R_U(D') + I(X; Y, V|K)$, and (f) $D \geq Ed(X, Y)$.*

The proof of Theorem 4 (which covers the previous theorems as special cases) appears in the full paper [8]. Note that the additional condition, (e), is similar to (d) except for the term $I(K; Y)$. It should be pointed out that with the new requirement regarding $H(Y^n|K^n)$, it is clear that introducing dependence of (V, Y) upon K is reasonable, in general. In the case $K = X$, the term $I(V; X|K)$, in condition (c), and the term $I(X; Y, V|K)$, in conditions (d) and (e), both vanish. Thus, both embedding performance and compression performance improve, like in private WM.

Finally, a comment is in order regarding the assumption $H(K) \leq \lambda R_U(D')$, which implies that $H(K|Y) \leq \lambda R_U(D')$. If this assumption is removed, Theorem 4 can be somewhat further extended. While h cannot be further improved if $H(K|Y)$ is allowed to exceed $\lambda R_U(D')$, there is still room for improvement in h': Instead of one rate–distortion codebook for U^N, we may have many *disjoint* codebooks. As was shown in [6], there are exponentially $2^{NH(\hat{U}|U)}$ disjoint codebooks, each covering the set of typical source sequences by jointly typical codewords. Now, if $H(K|Y) > \lambda R_U(D')$, we can use the $T = nH(K|Y) - NR_U(D')$ excess bits of the compressed key so as to select one of 2^T codebooks (as long as $T < NH(\hat{U}|U)$), and thus reach a total equivocation of $nH(K|Y)$ as long as $nH(K|Y) \leq NH(\hat{U})$, or equivalently, $H(K|Y) \leq \lambda H(\hat{U})$. for the original source). Condition (b) of Theorem 4 would now be replaced by the condition $h' \leq \min\{H(\hat{U}), H(K|Y)/\lambda\}$. But with this condition, it is no longer clear that the best test channel for lossy compression of U^N is the one that achieves $R_U(D')$, because for the above modified version of condition (b), it would be best to have $H(\hat{U})$ as large as possible (as long as it is below $H(K|Y)/\lambda$), which is in partial conflict with the minimization of $I(U;\hat{U})$ that leads to $R_U(D')$. Therefore, a restatement of Theorem 4 would require the existence of a channel $\{P_{\hat{U}|U}(\hat{u}|u),\ u \in \mathcal{U},\ \hat{u} \in \hat{\mathcal{U}}\}$ (in addition to the existing requirement of a channel $P_{VY|KX}$), such that the random variable $\hat{U}$ takes now part in the compromise among *all* criteria of the problem. This means that in conditions (a),(c),(d), and (e) of Theorem 4, $R_U(D')$ should be replaced by $I(U;\hat{U})$, and there would be an additional condition (g): $Ed'(U,\hat{U}) \leq D'$. Condition (b), in view of the earlier discussion above, would now be of the form: $h \leq \min\{H(U), H(K|Y)/\lambda + H(U) - I(U;\hat{U})\} \equiv H(U) - [I(U;\hat{U}) - H(K|Y)/\lambda]_+$, where $[z]_+ \stackrel{\Delta}{=} \max\{0, z\}$. Of course, under the assumption $H(K) \leq \lambda R_U(D')$, that we have used thus far, $H(\hat{U}) \geq I(U;\hat{U}) \geq R_U(D') \geq H(K)/\lambda \geq H(K|Y)/\lambda$, in other words, $\min\{H(\hat{U}), H(K|Y)/\lambda\}$ is always attained by $H(K|Y)/\lambda$, and so, the dependence on $H(\hat{U})$ disappears, which means that the best choice of $\hat{U}$ (for all other conditions) is back to be the one that minimizes $I(U;\hat{U})$, which gives us Theorem 4 as is. It is interesting to point out that this additional extension gives rise to yet another step in the direction of invalidating the separation principle: While in Theorem 4 only the encryption and the embedding interacted, yet the rate–distortion coding of U^N was still independent of all other ingredients of the system, here even this is no longer true, as the choice of the test channel $P_{\hat{U}|U}$ takes into account also compromises that are associated with the encryption and the embedding.

Note that this discussion applies also to the *classical* joint source–channel coding, where there is no embedding at all: In this case, X is a degenerate RV (say, $X \equiv 0$, if $0 \in \mathcal{X}$), and so, the mutual information terms depending on X in conditions (c), (d) and (e), all vanish, the best choice of V is $V = Y$ (thus, the r.h.s in condition (c) becomes the capacity of the channel $P_{Z|Y}$ with K as SI at both ends), and condition (f) may be interpreted as a (generalized) power constraint (with power function $\phi(y) = d(0, y)$).

Compulsion Resistant Anonymous Communications

George Danezis and Jolyon Clulow

University of Cambridge, Computer Laboratory,
William Gates Building, 15 JJ Thomson Avenue,
Cambridge CB3 0FD, United Kingdom
{George.Danezis, Jolyon.Clulow}@cl.cam.ac.uk

Abstract. We study the effect compulsion attacks, through which an adversary can request a decryption or key from an honest node, have on the security of mix based anonymous communication systems. Some specific countermeasures are proposed that increase the cost of compulsion attacks, detect that tracing is taking place and ultimately allow for some anonymity to be preserved even when all nodes are under compulsion. Going beyond the case when a single message is traced, we also analyze the effect of multiple messages being traced and devise some techniques that could retain some anonymity. Our analysis highlights that we can reason about plausible deniability in terms of the information theoretic anonymity metrics.

1   Introduction

Research on anonymous communication and mix networks has in the past concentrated on protecting users' anonymity against an eavesdropping adversary. Chaum in his seminal paper [7] argues that mix networks are secure against a global passive adversary, able to eavesdrop on all the communication links. Recent circuit based systems, such as Tarzan [16], MorphMix [22] and Tor [15], provide security against a partial passive adversary, that can only eavesdrop on part of the network. Some designs [12] additionally address active adversaries, that can modify data to gain information about the obscured routing of a message. Finally mix systems protect against corrupt intermediaries by distributing the mixing functionality across many nodes in the network.

Assuming a partial eavesdropping adversary, controlling only a small subset of network nodes one can show that very little information is leaked about the correspondence between actual senders and receivers of messages. It is often argued that such a threat model is more realistic than a global passive adversary, that is prohibitively expensive in a wide area network. On the other hand it does not encompass one of the most common threats, namely the *threat of compulsion of an honest node*.

M. Barni et al. (Eds.): IH 2005, LNCS 3727, pp. 11–25, 2005.

We will study the impact on anonymity if an adversary is able to ask for honest nodes' private keys or the decryption of arbitrary material. Such an adversary, if unbounded, would have a devastating effect on the security properties of a traditional mix network: they would be able to decrypt all layers of all packets and recover all hidden identity information. For this reason it is more instructive to think of such attacks in terms of the cost necessary to de-anonymize a message, *ie.* the number of honest nodes under compulsion necessary to achieve it.

In this work we introduce techniques to make compulsion attacks both more expensive, more visible and reduce the information they provide. The cost of compulsion attacks is raised by introducing some uncertainty, though multicasting steps, in the routing. Given that routing of messages is cheaper than compulsion attacks, this penalizes the adversary much more than it hinders the normal operation of the system. This technique bears some resemblance to source routed cover traffic.

Often it is assumed than an adversary is *shy* and would prefer the attack not to be known, particularly to the ultimate target. This is reasonable since advance warning of being under surveilance would allow one to destroy evidence, hide, or lie. We describe techniques that make it difficult to hide the fact that a packet is being traced, through using *compulsion traps*, loops in the routing that are designed to give advance warning of a successful attack.

Finally we make the results of an attack much less certain, by allowing both intermediate nodes to plausibly lie, and the final node to pretend to be merely an intermediary. An adversary is in these cases not able to find any bit string that would contradict these claims. This allows mix systems to provide initiator/receiver anonymity properties, and retain some anonymity, even if all nodes are under compulsion.

We used established research into measuring anonymity, and show that resistance to compulsion and plausible deniability can be measured within that framework. In other words compulsion is simply another form of attack that leads to the system providing varying degrees of anonymity depending on the intensity. We also show that traffic analysis, the tracing of multiple messages, has a devastating impact even against hardened systems. To protect against it we should question the conventional wisdom of relaying messages through completely random nodes.

2   The Compulsion Threat Model

The traditional anonymous communication threat model assumes an adversary that can eavesdrop or even modify traffic on a proportion of the network links. Furthermore it assumes that some proportion of the system nodes are subverted and directly controlled by the adversary. This threat model has been used in the context of cryptological research for some time, and can indeed express a wide spectrum of threats. On the other hand it suffers some biases from its military origins, that do not allow it to define some very important threats to anonymous communication systems.

Anonymous communication systems are often deployed in environments with a very strong imbalance of power. That makes each of the participants in a network, user or intermediary, individually vulnerable to *compulsion attacks*:

> A node under compulsion has to provide a service or information that is, to the adversary, indistinguishable from the genuine one. We will call protocols that allow a different service or information to be provided other than the one under normal operation, compulsion-resistant.

These compulsion attacks are usually expensive for all parties and cannot be too wide or too numerous.

A typical example of a compulsion attack would be a court order to keep and hand over activity logs to an attacker. Such a legal challenge led to the closure of the first remailer `anon.penet.fi` [18,19,17]. This can be targeted at particular intermediaries or can take the form of a blanket requirement to retain and make accessible certain types of data. Another example of a compulsion attack could be requesting the decryption of a particular ciphertext, or even requesting the secrets necessary to decrypt it. Both these could equally well be performed without legal authority by just using the threat of force.

Parties under compulsion could be asked to perform some particular task, which bears some similarity with subverted nodes. For example, this is an issue for electronic election protocols where participants might be coerced into voting in a particular way.

Note that compulsion and coercion cannot be appropriately modeled using the concept of subverted nodes from the traditional threat model. The party under compulsion is fundamentally honest but forced to perform certain operations that have an effect which the adversary can observe either directly or by requesting the information from the node under compulsion. The information or actions that are collected or performed under coercion are not as trustworthy, from the point of view of an adversary, as those performed by a subverted node since the coerced party can lie and deceive in an attempt not to comply. At the same time system designers should not assume that honest parties will always lie when under compulsion simply because they can – it is more prudent to assume that only nodes benefiting from deceiving the adversary are required to lie. Good compulsion-resistant designs will maintain their security properties even when all other, non-interested nodes, are cooperating with the adversary.

Election protocols [8,1] are specifically designed to allow voters to freely lie about how they voted, and *receipt-freeness* guarantees that there is no evidence to contradict them. Other protocols and systems attempt to provide *plausible deniability*, the ability to deceive the coercer and reveal partial or wrong information. Forward secure communications [6] guarantee the privacy of past conversations, by updating and deleting old keys. Forward secure signature schemes [2] make sure that signature keys leaked cannot be used to sign valid documents in past epochs. The steganographic file system [3] allows users to deny the existence of some stored files, while chaffinch allows users to deny the existence of some communication stream [9].

3   Introduction to Mix Systems

A mix, as introduced by David Chaum [7], is a network node that hides the correspondence between its inputs and outputs. It does that by receiving encoded inputs that it decodes using a private key, to outputs that are bitwise unlinkable with the inputs. Furthermore in order to disrupt the timing characteristics of traffic, several messages are batched together before being decoded and sent out in a random order.

In order to prevent a single corrupt mix compromising the anonymity of all messages traveling though it, a chain of mixes can be used. As long as one of them is honest, the message will be provided with some anonymity. The way one can select the series of mixes is called the topology of the network. If only one sequence is possible, we call such a network a cascade, and conversely if all possible sequences are permitted we call the network free route [4].

Technically a message to travel though a mix network has to be encoded using the public keys of all intermediate mix nodes. This is done by recursively encrypting the message in layers, starting with the last node in the path, and ending with the first. Each layer contains some routing information that allows the message at each intermediary to be routed to the next mix. It is also conventional to include a session key, and perform most cryptographic operations using symmetric primitives rather than asymmetric, and therefore expensive, operations.

Aside from the sender encoding messages to send them anonymously though the network, mix network can be used to route anonymous replies. In this case the sender includes a bit-string in the anonymous message that can be used by the receiver to send a message back. This process does not reveal any information about the identity of the original sender. We call these bit stings, anonymous reply blocks, and they are constructed in a similar way to messages, but with no payload. They contain the final address of their recipients, recursively encoded under the keys of intermediate mixes, with routing information in each layer. To route a message using a reply block, the message is appended to the block, and sent though the network. As it travels each intermediary mix decodes the reply block (with the last mix retrieving the final address), while at the same time encoding the reply message. This guarantees unlinkability, since both parts of the message are changed, and allows the final recipient, to decode the message since it knows the secret contained in the reply block, that he manufactured.

A good mix packet format would be expected, aside from providing bitwise unlinkability, to have a set of other properties. It should hide the total path length and the position on the path from intermediate mixes. It should also provide replies that are indistinguishable from other messages, and be resistant to tagging attacks. Both Mixminion [12] and the newer Minx [13] packet formats provide these properties.

Figure 1 illustrates the routing of normal sender anonymous messages, as well as anonymous replies. The notation $[x]_y$ means that message x is encoded under key y. The keys with capital letters subscripts $(K_A, \ldots, K_F)$ are the public keys of the corresponding nodes, while keys with lowercase subscripts

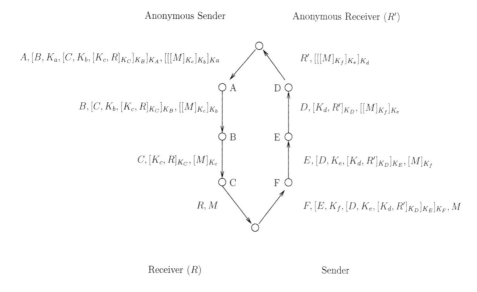

Fig. 1. Sending and replying to anonymous messages

$(K_a, \ldots, K_f)$ are symmetric session keys. The reply block, that the anonymous sender has constructed and included in the message M is the string: $F, [E, K_f, [D, K_e, [K_d, R']_{K_D}]_{K_E}]_{K_F}$. The figure abstracts away quite a few crucial details, such as the exact encoding scheme, the padding added to keep messages constant length, the duplicate detection mechanisms that discard already seen messages. The full details of how to engineer such schemes can be found in [12,13]. Nevertheless this simplified model allows us to describe the vulnerability to compulsion attacks, as well as ways of defending against them.

4   Using Compulsion to Attack Mix Systems

The security of mix systems relies on the correspondence between inputs and outputs of some mix on the message path to remain hidden. There is no cryptographic way of ensuring this (since it is impossible to prove that information was not leaked), and therefore some degree of trust is placed on the mixes. Even if these are not subverted and controlled by the adversary, an attacker can compel them to either decode a ciphertext or hand over any key material they possess.

Both types of compulsion attacks assume that the adversary is in possession of a ciphertext to decode. These can be intercepted by a global passive adversary, or even by a partial eavesdropping adversary that watches all anonymous messages sent by a particular user. Note that there is little value in intercepting messages in the middle of the network since they have already been stripped of information that could lead to their sender. Therefore an eavesdropper will try to intercept messages as close to their senders as possible, and then sequentially compel intermediate mixes to decode them. After a number of compelled mixes equal to the path length, an adversary will be able to link the targeted sender with the receiver of their messages.

Roger Dingledine [14] was first to point out that this mechanisms makes reply blocks more vulnerable to attack, than normal messages. The attacker has no need to eavesdrop on the network to get a first packet since the reply block is readily available and encodes all information needed to trace its creator. Therefore given a single use reply block and a number of compelled nodes equal to the path length, the identity of the user that has sent the message containing the reply block is revealed. Since this is the simplest and most devastating compulsion attack we will concentrate on making it more difficult.

Many stream based system such as Tor [15], MorphMix [22] and Cebolla [5], avoid using onion encrypted messages and reply blocks by recursively opening a bidirectional channel though the intermediaries. This architecture is very effective for supporting streams initiated by the anonymous client towards a server. It does not support very well streams initiated by a client towards an anonymous receiver, since the channel must be kept open (either using real network connection, or virtual labels and circuits), and connected to a well known public server. In particular Tor's implementation of 'Rendezvous point', are still susceptible to compulsion attacks. Since the connection though the tor network has to be kept alive all the time, an adversary only needs to compel each node in the route to reveal their predecessor, until the hidden service is uncovered.

We will see how to strengthen traditional mix systems against such compulsion attacks.

5   Protecting Mix Systems

In this section we present the technical details of the constructions we devised in order to strengthen mixed communications against compulsion attacks and in particular reply blocks, since they are the most vulnerable to this attack. We first consider the case of tracing a single reply block and then, in section 6, tracing multiple reply blocks. We will make some assumptions about the nature of the mix network, but present our solutions in the context of the abstract mix architecture of figure 1.

First we assume a peer-to-peer mix network, where all clients are also mix servers for other nodes. This is a challenging design for reasons not related to compulsion. The main difference from traditional, client-server, mix networks is the need to distribute the full list of all participating nodes and their keys at all times. A failure to distribute the whole list might result in attacks (as described in section 4.2.7 of [11].) Furthermore this has to be done in a way that is not manipulable by an adversary that tries to flood the network with corrupt nodes. Implementing such an infrastructure and key distribution in wide area networks are active, but separate, subject of research.

The abstract model of a mix net we use can in practise be implemented using the deployed Mixminion [12] or the proposed Minx [13] packet formats. These have been designed with some common requirements in mind: they allow multiple mix nodes to relay an encoded mix packet, making sure that the packet is cryptographically unlinkable at different hops. Single use reply blocks can be used to reply to anonymous senders, and their transport is indistinguishable from other packets. Both systems hide the total length of the chain of mixes, and the position of each mix node on the path of the message. Finally they are not vulnerable to tagging attacks – if a message is modified in an attempt to gain information it ends up getting discarded.

On the other hand the respective behavior of the two different, mixminion and minx, formats is different when it comes to discarding 'malformed' or potentially 'modified' messages. A mixminion node will discover that a message header is modified, using a message digest, and discard the message immediately. If the body of the message only has been modified then it will be forwarded, an all-or-nothing transform will take care of destroying the message contents, when it reaches a 'swap point'. On the other hand Minx nodes cannot tell if messages have been modified, since they do not contain any redundancy at all, and are indistinguishable from noise. The decoding procedure just ensures that modified messages turn into random bit-strings, and are therefore routed using a random walk around the network, until they are randomly discarded. Mixminion does never randomly route messages around since all routing information has to be well formed. These differences will have some impact on how the compulsion resistance mechanisms are implemented.

5.1   Multicast Steps

First we note the asymmetry between the cost of relaying a message and the cost of compelling a node to reveal secrets. Relaying consumes a bit of bandwidth and computation time. On the other hand compelling a node can only happen after a prolonged conflict, legal or physical, with a very high cost for all parties. We shall use this asymmetry to protect against compulsion.

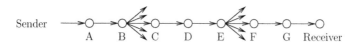

Fig. 2. Routing with multicast steps

A standard message travels through a mix network using a sequence of intermediate mix nodes. The routing information is encrypted to intermediary nodes, and they have to use their secrets in order to decrypt it. A way of pushing up the cost of compulsion would be to include some *multicast steps* into the routing, where the message is sent to a set of nodes at once. Only one of these nodes has the necessary secret to correctly decode the message, and continue routing it. The adversary, or even the node that is compelled to surrender the decoded message, has no way of knowing which of the nodes included in the multicast is the correct one. Therefore the adversary will have to try them one by one until a correct decryption is provided to trace that step.

In the case of Mixminion the nodes receiving a message that cannot be decrypted using their secrets will discard it immediately. As a result an adversary compelling them can be sure that they are not the nodes expected to route the message, since he can ask for all secrets and check for a well formed message. For each multicast step, multicasting the message to K nodes, the cost to the mix network during normal operation is $\mathcal{O}(K)$. On the other hand the adversary will have to query the multicast nodes one by one until one of them decodes the message correctly. This requires the adversary to query on average about $\frac{K}{2}$ nodes per multicast step until a correct decryption is provided.

If Minx is used to implement *multicast steps*, neither the nodes nor an adversary that compels them can tell if the message was intended for them. They will simply decode it and pass it along. This results in an exponential growth of the effort required to process the message, that makes this scheme impractical in the case of Minx. At the same time it also means that the adversary has to compel an enormous number of nodes, hoping that one of them will be the final node relaying the message.

5.2   Compulsion Traps

Some adversaries would prefer to trace messages using compulsion, without the ultimate recipient of the message knowing. Often this would allow the target to eliminate evidence, to destroy key material, and physically hide. We shall therefore assume that our adversary is *shy* and forces mix nodes not to hide whether they are under compulsion.

We modify the path selection procedure, that we use to select intermediary nodes in the mix network, to provide some advance warning of an attack. The sender of the message or reply block includes itself on the path that their own message is routed through – we call this a *compulsion trap*. As a result a reply block that is being traced back would require the attacker to compel the target to decode the message. The target can do this and provide a valid message, that still has to get routed to reach its ultimate destination. The adversary has no way of knowing which node on the path (aside from when it reaches the last) is the target, while the target gets some advance notice that tracing is taking place.

The overheads that this technique imposes on the system are negligible during the normal operation of the system. When a reply block and a message are being routed through the system, the receiver can decode the message the first time it sees it, since it can recognize the reply block as his. There is no need to route the actual message through the loop, since it eventually leads back to the same user. On the other hand if an adversary is tracing the message, the target node will

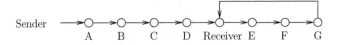

Fig. 3. Routing topology of a compulsion trap

provide a decryption, and force the adversary to compel more nodes, until he is eventually led back to the target. This means that more compulsion operations have to be performed by the adversary, than hops when honest nodes relay the message. During normal operation the message is not relayed for more hops than a message that is not using this scheme, and therefore the latency of messages is also not affected by this scheme.

5.3   Plausibly Deniable Routing

Compulsion traps might give an advance warning of a compulsion attack being performed against the network, but do not allow the ultimate recipient of a traced reply block to remain anonymous in the long run. As we have seen the normal operation of the mix network does not require the reply message to travel through all nodes specified, but only until the first occurrence of the recipient node. The question then arises: why including the same node again further down in the path? There is no reason, and one can include a random selection of other nodes instead.

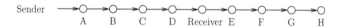

Fig. 4. Plausibly deniable recipient

The resulting construction, of including in the routing information a tail of random nodes, provides *plausible deniability*. That means that the adversary cannot determine with certainty that a particular node in the path was the intended recipient of the message. All nodes can provide a plausible theory to explain why they have been involved in relaying the message: most can claim that they were merely relaying the message. The last node can explain that they were just selected at random – which is true, and plausible given this strategy in known to be used. Note that the only node to be lying is the actual receiver and there is no information held by the adversary, that can contradict the false claim that the message is merely being relayed at this point[1].

Plausible deniability was introduced by Michael Roe [23], as the property that is complementary to non-repudiation, the inability to deny something. Early work has assumed that unless something is digitally signed, it is plausibly deniable. This is not quite true since other evidence, such as logging or the use of a time stamping service, can still produce a very high degree of confidence in an action or a sequence of events, that will make it difficult to deny it.

At the same time little effort has been made to quantify the degree of plausible deniability. When it comes to an actor trying to deny they performed

---

[1] Showing that a node is the actual receiver of the message would involve proving that they know a subset of the symmetric keys K_f, K_e, K_d, R' of figure 1. These can be generated on the fly using a master passphrase, and unless they are stored the claim will be difficult to prove. This assumption does not require the use of secure hardware for the receiver or any other nodes.

an action, plausible deniability can be measured using established measures of anonymity [24]. Therefore the plausible deniability property proposed can be analyzed as an anonymity property. We can at each stage of the compulsion attack assign a probability to each actor in the network of being the receiver. Then we use the established measure of anonymity, which is the entropy of this probability distribution, to assess how much plausible deniability is provided [24].

We shall compute the anonymity of the proposed scheme as a function of the compulsion effort of the adversary. We denote the number of hosts under compulsion as k. We assume there are N participants, in a peer-to-peer mix network. To simplify things we also assume that the total route length is of a fixed size l. The real recipient of the message was an equal probability of being at any position, while the other relays are chosen at random.

After k mixes have been forced to decode the reply block, and provide the adversary with the next recipient, the adversary knows k candidates that are equally likely to be the receiver. All other $N - k$ nodes also have an equal probability of being the receivers in case he is not in the set of nodes under compulsion. This is the case with probability $\frac{l-k}{l}$, namely the probability the target has chosen a position on the route further away from the part that has been traced back. The probability distribution that describes how likely each node is to be the receiver is the following (after k nodes under compulsion):

$$\Pr[i|k] = \begin{cases} \frac{k}{l}\frac{1}{k} & \text{if } i \text{ in the compelled set} \\ \frac{l-k}{l}\frac{1}{N-k} & \text{otherwise} \end{cases} \tag{1}$$

We can easily calculate the entropy $(\mathcal{H})$ of this distribution ($U(x)$ denotes the uniform distribution over x elements).

$$\mathcal{H}(\Pr[i|k]) = \mathcal{H}\left(\frac{k}{l}, \frac{l-k}{l}\right) + \frac{k}{l}\mathcal{H}(U(k)) + \frac{l-k}{l}\mathcal{H}(U(N-k)) \tag{2}$$

$$= \log l + \left(\frac{l-k}{l}\right)\log\frac{N-k}{l-k} \tag{3}$$

This formula is in line with our intuitions. When there is no compulsion $(\mathcal{H}(\Pr[i|0]))$ then the effective anonymity set size is equal to $\log N$, since all the network participants are equally likely to have been the receiver. The adversary is missing $\log N$ bits of information to uniquely identify the receiver. When all nodes in the route have been compelled we have $\mathcal{H}(\Pr[i|l]) = \log l$, since only the compelled nodes are equally likely to be the ultimate receivers of the message. Note that even when all participants are under compulsion, there is still some anonymity left.

6   From Single Message Tracing to Traffic Analysis

We have looked in detail how tracing a single message would be more expensive if our countermeasures are used, and calculated the anonymity that would remain.

Serious traffic analysis usually tries to infer the identity, or other characteristics, of communicating parties using repeated patterns of communication. We therefore need to assess the security of the proposed countermeasures against a compelling adversary that traces back multiple reply blocks.

Like in Crowds [21] allowing the actual receiver to be present at any position of the path opens the *compulsion trap* and *plausibly deniable routing* to predecessor attacks as first presented by Wright et al. [26] and analyzed further by Shmatikov [25]. Since mixing is taking place, one could try to skew the probability distribution describing the placement of the receiver on the path to gain some security against this attack. This would not add any security against compulsion attacks (beyond making compulsion slower to the same degree as the latency increases), and therefore we shall not discuss this countermeasure any further. Instead we will analyze the security of the base scheme and present in section 6.1 an alternative solution that relies on routing amongst a fixed set of 'friends'.

In the case of the *multicast steps* and the *compulsion trap* constructions, and adversary that compels enough nodes will eventually reach and identify the ultimate recipient. Therefore traffic analysis of multiple reply blocks can only be expected to yield a performance benefit (minimize the effort of the attacker).

In the case of multicast steps there is no such performance benefit for the attacker, and the optimal strategy is to trace a single block until the final node, which will also be the receiver. When attacking a compulsion trap based system tracing two single use reply blocks in parallel might prove to be cheaper. Assuming that all relay nodes are chosen at random, and the receiver will appear on both paths, a node that appears in both paths is the receiver with a very high probability.

We shall use the setup of figure 3, to illustrate how an adversary should decide between tracing one reply block until the end, or tracing two in parallel, when compulsion traps are used. We will assume that all reply blocks have a total path length of l, and the compulsion trap, the position in the route where the receiver node insert itself, is $k \in [1, l-1]$ (node that in figure 3 the last node is always the receiver), and it follows a uniform distribution over all positions $k \sim U(1, l-1)$ and therefore $\Pr[k] = \frac{1}{l-1}$. On average the compulsion trap point k, where the receiver has included himself in the path, will be at:

$$E[k] = \sum_{k=1}^{k=l-1} k \Pr[k|k \sim U(1, l-1)] = \frac{1}{l-1} \sum_{k=1}^{k=l-1} k = \frac{l-1}{2} \tag{4}$$

An attacker tracing two reply blocks in parallel will expect to have to compel $K_1 + K_2$ nodes, where both are independent random variables that follow the uniform distribution above, until it reaches the same recipient node, in both paths. Since $E[K_1 + K_2] = 2E[k] = l - 1$, a attacker will do marginally better by tracing two reply blocks in parallel. Tracing a single reply blocks is guaranteed to pay off after l compulsion steps. This slight efficiency improvement might be offset by the possible false positives, that would be the result of the same node appearing randomly in the two paths without being the receiver. This probability, in our example, equals (from section 2.1.5 of [20], that uses the notation $m^{(n)} = m(m-1)\ldots(m-n+1)$):

$$P_{\text{false}} = 1 - \frac{N^{(2k)}}{\left[N^{(k)}\right]^2} \tag{5}$$

Note how the probability of false positives goes quickly towards zero as N grows.

The method we presented that provides *plausible deniability* guarantees some anonymity even when all nodes on the path of one reply have been compelled. When two reply blocks to the same receivers are available an adversary reduces greatly the anonymity of the receiver. A second couple of nodes, one in each path, that are the same is extremely unlikely as N grows:

$$P_{\text{false}} = 1 - \frac{N^{(2(l-1))}}{\left[N^{(l-1)}\right]^2} \tag{6}$$

We should conclude that given the above models a mix system, even if it implements our countermeasures, can be subject to traffic analysis attacks to uncover the ultimate receiver of reply blocks. Therefore we must modify the way nodes are selected on the path to recover some plausible deniability and some anonymity even when faced with overwhelming compulsion. There are two ways in which one can select nodes to include in the path to enhance anonymity, the first is to route amongst a smaller group of friends, the second is to setup stings, that look to an attacker performing traffic analysis like the final receiver.

6.1 Routing Amongst Friends

As the network of mix participants (and therefore nodes) grows, traffic analysis attacks become more certain. The probability a random node is on the path of a reply block twice, becomes smaller, and as a result the probability of the attacker observing a false positive decreases quickly to zero. In order to strengthen the network against such attacks it might be worthwhile to form routes in a non random manner. The objective being to maximize the number of common nodes in the paths of different reply blocks.

First note that a particular node choosing routes that always include a fixed set of nodes foils the traffic analysis attacks. These set nodes can be arranged in a cascade but this is not necessary: they simply need to be present at some point, before or after the receiver, on the path.

To avoid the attacks against route selection described in section 4.2.7 of [11] the choice of the fixed set must remain private to the creator of the reply block. Care should also be taken for the set not to be inferred easily by corrupt nodes or an observer (although this goes beyond the strict compulsion threat model).

One way of inferring the set of 'friends' used is to observe the destination of messages sent by the user, or the origin of those received. Nodes that are always used will appear with much higher frequency than other ones. This can allow an adversary to infer the membership of this set. In turn this allows corrupt nodes on the network to infer that connection between these nodes are very likely to be carrying messages to the particular receiver.

A mixed approach, where a set of fixed nodes is used in conjunction with random nodes seems preferable. The reply block paths are constructed in such a way that between each node from the fixed 'friends' set there is a randomly chosen node. This prevents an observer or a corrupt node from trivially inferring the membership of the fixed set.

Using a fixed set of nodes of size F, guarantees that under any circumstances, including the tracing of multiply reply blocks, the effective anonymity set size will be at least $-\log(F+1)$. An attacker will not be able to distinguish between the actual receiver and the fixed set of nodes that is always used to route traffic. The additional security provided does not come for free: all F nodes must be on the path, along with another F random nodes. Therefore the latency will be on average proportional to the minimum degree of anonymity required. This fact might influence the design decisions behind systems that aim to prevent compulsion to provide less mixing (less latency per mix) and opt for longer routes instead.

6.2   Setting Someone Else Up

An attacker that naively relies on compulsion in order to infer the final recipient of a reply block must be very cautious. In the case of *compulsion traps* construction, where the final receiver is meant to be twice on the path of the message, it is easy to incriminate another node. A user can create a path that contains a loop at a different position than itself. For example the path [A, B, C, D, Receiver, E, F, D], contains a loop, that might look to the adversary as a compulsion trap when actually node D is unaware that the message is traveling twice through it (since it does not know all the keys that are necessary to decode the reply block and recognize it at each phase).

For each technique that the adversary could use for tracing a reply block (except the traffic analysis of different reply blocks), the adversary could create such a structure to convince the adversary that someone else is the receiver. This provides even more plausible deniability if the adversary does trace the message using compulsion and makes an inference as above.

7   Conclusions

We have presented the effects that compulsion powers might have in undermining the security of a mix network. Our analysis is based on an abstract model of how a mix network works and should be applicable to a large variety of architectures.

Three concrete techniques were presented to make such attacks more expensive for the adversary, tracing the especially vulnerable anonymous reply blocks. Introducing *multicast steps* in the routing increases the number of nodes that have to be compelled to trace, but also makes normal routing more expensive. *Compulsion traps* allow a user to get advance warning of a reply block being

traced, and might allow them to eliminate evidence or make tracing more difficult by deleting key material necessary for further tracing [10]. Finally *plausibly
deniable routing* provides some anonymity even though all nodes on the path of
the reply block have been compelled.

Conceptually we have shown that plausible deniability properties can, when
they describe uncertainty about identity, be quantified using the established
anonymity metrics. As an example we have calculated the remaining anonymity
after a compulsion attack against a plausibly deniable routing scheme. Furthermore we have challenged the optimality of choosing random routes through the
network, since it maximizes the effectiveness of traffic analysis, and opted for
routing amongst a set of 'friends'. All the techniques we have presented, can be
combined to provide a strengthened mix network against compulsion.

The anonymity provided by mix systems is crucially dependent upon trusting
third parties. Therefore quantifying the effects of an adversary with compulsion
powers against honest nodes is necessary. Other security protocols, or whole
systems, that rely on trusting third parties might benefit from such an analysis:
how much security can be retained even when trusted players are all forced to
turn bad?

Acknowledgements. The authors would like to express their gratitude to the
anonymous reviewers for their valuable comments and corrections.

References

1. Alessandro Acquisti. Receipt-free homomorphic elections and write-in ballots.
   Technical Report 105, International Association for Cryptologic Research, May
   2 2004.
2. Ross Anderson. Two remarks on public-key cryptology. Available at
   http://www.cl.cam.ac.uk/ftp/users/rja14/forwardsecure.pdf, 1997. Invited
   Lecture, ACM-CCS '97.
3. Ross Anderson, Roger Needham, and Adi Shamir. The steganographic file system.
   In David Aucsmith, editor, *Information Hiding (IH'98)*, volume 1525 of *LNCS*,
   pages 73–82, Portland, Oregon, USA, 15-17 April 1998. Springer-Verlag.
4. Rainer Bohme, George Danezis, Claudia Diaz, Stefan Kopsell, and Andreas Pfitzmann. Mix cascades vs. peer-to-peer: Is one concept superior? In *Privacy Enhancing Technologies (PET 2004)*, Toronto, Canada, May 2004.
5. Zach Brown. Cebolla – pragmatic IP anonymity. In *Ottowa Linux Symposium*,
   June 2002.
6. Ran Canetti, Shai Halevi, and Jonathan Katz. A forward-secure public-key encryption scheme. In Eli Biham, editor, *EUROCRYPT*, volume 2656 of *Lecture
   Notes in Computer Science*, pages 255–271. Springer, 2003.
7. David Chaum. Untraceable electronic mail, return addresses, and digital
   pseudonyms. *Communications of the ACM*, 24(2):84–88, February 1981.
8. David Chaum. Secret-ballot receipts: True voter-verifiable elections. *RSA Laboratories Cryptobytes*, 7(2):14–27, Fall 2004.

9. Richard Clayton and George Danezis. Chaffinch: Confidentiality in the face of legal threats. In Fabien A. P. Petitcolas, editor, *Information Hiding workshop (IH 2002)*, volume 2578 of *LNCS*, pages 70–86, Noordwijkerhout, The Netherlands, 7-9 October 2002. Springer-Verlag.

10. George Danezis. Forward secure mixes. In Jonsson Fisher-Hubner, editor, *Nordic workshop on Secure IT Systems (Norsec 2002)*, pages 195–207, Karlstad, Sweden, November 2002.

11. George Danezis. Designing and attacking anonymous communication systems. Technical Report UCAM-CL-TR-594, University of Cambridge, Computer Laboratory, 2004.

12. George Danezis, Roger Dingledine, and Nick Mathewson. Mixminion: Design of a Type III Anonymous Remailer Protocol. In *IEEE Symposium on Security and Privacy*, Berkeley, CA, 11-14 May 2003.

13. George Danezis and Ben Laurie. Minx: A simple and efficient anonymous packet format. In *Workshop on Privacy in the Electronic Society (WPES 2004)*. ACM, October 2004.

14. Roger Dingledine. Personal communication, 2003.

15. Roger Dingledine, Nick Mathewson, and Paul Syverson. Tor: The second-generation onion router. In *Proceedings of the 13th USENIX Security Symposium*, August 2004.

16. Michael J. Freedman and Robert Morris. Tarzan: A peer-to-peer anonymizing network layer. In Vijayalakshmi Atluri, editor, *ACM Conference on Computer and Communications Security (CCS 2002)*, pages 193–206, Washington, DC, November 2002. ACM.

17. Johan Helsingius. Johan helsingius closes his internet remailer. http://www.penet.fi/press-english.html, August 1996.

18. Johan Helsingius. Johan helsingius gets injunction in scientology case privacy protection of anonymous messages still unclear. http://www.penet.fi/injunc.html, September 1996.

19. Johan Helsingius. Temporary injunction in the anonymous remailer case. http://www.penet.fi/injuncl.html, September 1996.

20. Alfred J. Menezes, Paul C. Van Oorschot, and Scott A. Vanstone. *Handbook of Applied Cryptography*. CRC Press, 1996. ISBN: 0-8493-8523-7.

21. Michael Reiter and Aviel Rubin. Crowds: Anonymity for web transactions. *ACM Transactions on Information and System Security (TISSEC)*, 1(1):66–92, 1998.

22. Marc Rennhard and Bernhard Plattner. Introducing MorphMix: Peer-to-Peer based Anonymous Internet Usage with Collusion Detection. In *Workshop on Privacy in the Electronic Society (WPES 2002)*, Washington, DC, USA, November 2002.

23. Michael Roe. *Cryptography and Evidence*. PhD thesis, University of Cambridge, Computer Laboratory, 1997.

24. Andrei Serjantov and George Danezis. Towards an information theoretic metric for anonymity. In Roger Dingledine and Paul Syverson, editors, *Privacy Enhancing Technologies workshop (PET 2002)*, volume 2482 of *LNCS*, pages 41–53, San Francisco, CA, USA, 14-15 April 2002. Springer-Verlag.

25. Vitaly Shmatikov. Probabilistic analysis of anonymity. In *Computer Security Foundations workshop (CSFW-15 2002)*, pages 119–128, Cape Breton, Nova Scotia, Canada, 24-26 June 2002. IEEE Computer Society.

26. Matthew Wright, Micah Adler, Brian Neil Levine, and Clay Shields. An analysis of the degradation of anonymous protocols. In *Network and Distributed Security Symposium (NDSS '02)*, San Diego, California, 6-8 February 2002.

Provable Anonymity for Networks of Mixes[*]

Marek Klonowski and Mirosław Kutyłowski

Institute of Mathematics and Computer Science, Wrocław University of Technology,
ul. Wybrzeże Wyspiańskiego 27, 50-370 Wrocław, Poland
{Marek.Klonowski, Miroslaw.Kutylowski}@pwr.wroc.pl

Abstract. We analyze networks of mixes used for providing untraceable communication. We consider a network consisting of k mixes working in parallel and exchanging the outputs – which is the most natural architecture for composing mixes of a certain size into networks able to mix a larger number of inputs at once. We prove that after $\mathcal{O}(1)$ rounds the network considered provides a fair level of privacy protection for any number of messages n. Number of required rounds does not dependent on number of mixes provided that $n \gg k^2$. No mathematical proof of this kind has been published before. We show that if at least one of server is corrupted we need substantially more rounds to meet the same requirements of privacy protection.

Keywords: anonymity, mix network, Markov chain, rapid mixing, coupling.

1 Introduction

Providing anonymity becomes one of the key security problems of electronic communication today. There growing dangers both for the private sphere, business communication and information security on a national level.

Many anonymity systems have been proposed - for a collection of papers see [7]. Most anonymity schemes are based on a MIX - a cryptographic primitive introduced by David Chaum [8].

1.1 Mixes

A MIX-server processes many encrypted messages at once: it recodes them cryptographically and outputs the re-coded messages in a random order. The purpose of these operations is that no relation between input and output can be established by an adversary that can see the input and the output of a mix.

For instance, a mix described in [8] works as follows (see Fig.1): assume that users $1, 2, \ldots, n$ want to publish anonymously messages $m_1, m_2, \ldots, m_n$. The users submit their messages to the mix encrypted with the public key k of the mix server: $E_k(m_1), E_k(m_2), \ldots, E_k(m_n)$. The mix server decrypts them with its private key, chooses a permutation π uniformly at random, and outputs $m_{\pi(1)}, m_{\pi(2)}, \ldots, m_{\pi(n)}$.

In fact, some additional precautions are necessary: encryption scheme should be probabilistic, duplicates should be removed ... . Necessary properties may be implemented in many ways – for example by slightly modified onions [15] or Universal

---

[*] Partially supported by KBN grant 3T11C 011 26.

M. Barni et al. (Eds.): IH 2005, LNCS 3727, pp. 26–38, 2005.

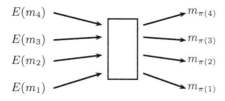

Fig. 1. Batch of messages processed by single MIX-server by using random permutation π

Re-Encryption [9]. For more details see [8] and other papers available in the collection of papers [7].

For a proper design, a mix server provides perfect anonymity – after entering the mix messages become indistinguishable, as long as the encryption scheme applied has not been broken. Unfortunately, there are serious drawbacks of a single mix solution. First, we have to trust the server. There are also scalability problems, since every participant has to use the same server. Also, any server failure (random or caused by an adversary through a DoS attack) has severe consequences.

1.2 Networks of Mixes

In order to avoid the problems mentioned, many authors propose mixing structures consisting of many MIX-servers interconnected, called *MIXing networks*. The messages entering a network of mixes must visit the MIX-servers in an appropriate order to get to the final destination. At each MIX-server visited a message is recoded appropriately. Of course, encoding scheme must take into account the route of a message.

If a user may distrust certain MIX-servers, then it is reasonable to apply a cascade of mixes: if k MIX-servers are available, then they are pipelined so that the output of server i is the input of server $i + 1$. However, if a mix cannot process all messages at once, a natural solution is a "parallel mix cascade" (see Fig. 2): let us assume that we

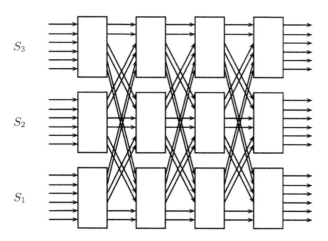

Fig. 2. Parallel MIX-cascade with $n = 18$ messages and $k = 3$ mix servers during $T = 4$ steps

have MIX–servers $S_1, S_2, \ldots, S_k$ ($k > 1$) and n messages to be mixed. The protocol consists of T phases (parameter T has to be chosen sufficiently large). During a round n/k messages are submitted to each MIX-server. Each server recodes the messages submitted, permutes the results at random, and sends n/k^2 messages to the each server. In particular, n/k^2 messages remain at this server.

Details of this protocol may differ slightly in various proposals. For instance, the next MIX-server for each message can be chosen uniformly at random, independently from other messages, instead of directing a fixed fraction to each server. For the rest of the paper we shall consider the former scenario.

2   Problem Statement – Anonymity Guarantees

Perfect mixing by the MIX-servers in a MIXing network do not guarantee that all messages get mixed properly. An extreme case of this problem is when each mix gets two inputs at a time – then we have to do with a switching network where switches are set at random. In this case designing a good architecture with quality guarantees remains an unsolved problem. An existing solution [5] with a provable level of anonymity has polylogarithmic depth (i.e., the number of rounds T is a bounded by a polynomial in $\log n$, where n is the total number of messages processed), but the exponent is too high and excludes any practical application.However,the situation we are dealing with is not that extreme – we are interested in the case that $n \gg k^2$.

The general strategy is as follows: in order to permute n messages at random we split the messages into k groups, permute randomly each group separately, re-arrange the groups, permute at random each group, re-arrange the groups, and so on. The main question here is how to arrange the groups. Is the parallel mix cascade the best possible architecture? How many rounds are necessary until we approach a random permutation of (encoded) messages?

Still there is no general answer to the question how to permute n elements at random if we have components that may permute n/k elements in one round. There are at least two general approaches: one represented by the parallel mix cascade, and one in which we arrange growing groups of well mixed elements. The main part of such algorithms is a shuffling procedure that take two groups and merges them.

We assume that there is an adversary trying to trace messages going through a MIX-network. He knows the algorithm but cannot break the cryptographic scheme used. We can also consider a situation that an adversary controls certain mixes and therefore knows the permutations applied by these mixes.

2.1   Previous Work

The very first paper introducing MIXes as a tool for enhancing anonymity level was published by David Chaum [8]. He also proposed pipelining of several MIX-servers that form a "MIX-cascade". In [15] Rackoff and Simon presented a very significant extension of Chaum's scheme – in this protocol the route of a message is determined by a sender and the message is encoded in a structure resembling an onion. A similar approach was used later by many authors (e.g. [16,13]), but progress in estimating the runtime such that a good level of anonymity is achieved, was quite slow. The topology of parallel mix cascade that we consider in this paper was described for instance in [13].

The first paper with an anonymity proof of a mixing protocol was published by Rackoff and Simon [15]. Further results about the same protocol under a different adversary model have been obtained recently [3,12].

None of these results applies to the situation considered in this paper – the main focus of these papers is on how much information is granted to the adversary through traffic information. In our case the communication is oblivious and does not depend on how the messages are mixed. A recent paper [10] considers anonymity of a protocol closely related to parallel mix cascade. Some estimations for weak anonymity measures are provided there.

2.2 New Results

We provide a detailed analysis of parallel mix cascades and estimate how many rounds are necessary until the probability distribution over possible mappings between the messages entering the network and those leaving the network becomes close to uniform. It turns out that this number does not depend on the number of messages and on the number of mixes, provided that there are much more messages than mixes! In this case the adversary cannot link the decoded messages that leave the network with the messages submitted by the users – the probabilities are close to the case of the uniform probability distribution. This result is given by Theorem 1.

Our result is based on *delayed path coupling* - a technique introduced in [6], which is an extension of path coupling [1]. In fact, there are some traces of the current technical approach in our former paper [11].

2.3 Paper Organization

In Section 3 we consider adversary and the definition of anonymity that we use. We discuss very quickly why this definition provides better anonymity guarantees than some other definitions used in the literature. Section 4 is devoted to the main result. We start it with a description of mathematical tools necessary to analyze mix networks. In Section 5 we analyze the situation in which one of the MIX-servers is corrupted (i.e. reveals its permutation to the adversary in order to make traffic analysis easier).

3 Mixing Network and Anonymous Communication

Adversary Model. There are substantially different models of an adversary trying to establish relation between messages entering a MIX-system and the messages leaving this system. Many papers deal with so–called a *global passive adversary*. This adversary can just observe the traffic on some number of links and servers (in our case the traffic on the links is oblivious, so the traffic on the links is of no use). The most common model assumes that an adversary can eavesdrop all links but none of servers. If a server reveals permutation that it use to an adversary we call it *corrupted* or *dishonest*.

An active adversary can add, remove, replace, duplicate messages at certain nodes or links. This turns out to be very dangerous and there are several papers dealing with these issues – for example [9,14].

Our main result refers to the model with a global passive adversary with no control over the servers. In Section 5 we consider the case of dishonest servers.

Anonymity Definition. Anonymity is a vague notion that can be formalized in various ways. Since our goal is to provide some security *guarantees*, we consider one of the strongest notions.

A relation between n messages entering and leaving the whole mixing structure can be described by a permutation of elements $\{1, \ldots, n\}$. An adversary wants to reveal (at least partially) this permutation using information at hand or at least to know that some permutations are much more probable than the others.

Already applying a few mixes the number of possible permutations is quite a big one. So an adversary can consider the permutation of messages $\{1, \ldots, n\}$ as a random variable with some probability distribution Π_t depending on the traffic information gained by the adversary. Of course, we would wish that Π_t is a uniform distribution μ_U. Unfortunately, in many systems it is impossible due to simple divisibility reasons. In particular, it cannot happen for a parallel MIX cascade for any number of rounds.

On the other hand, stochastic process Π_t converges to the uniform distribution over $\mathbb{S}_n$ in respect to the metrics *total variation distance*. Recall that for random variables Γ_1 and Γ_2 with a finite set of values $\mathcal{Y}$ variation distance between Γ_1 and Γ_2 is defined by the formula:

$$\text{TVD}(\Gamma_1, \Gamma_2) = \tfrac{1}{2} \sum_{y \in \mathcal{Y}} |\Pr(\Gamma_1 = y) - \Pr(\Gamma_2 = y)| .$$

Let Π_U be denote a random variable with a uniform distribution on the set of permutations of n elements. We say that the parallel mix cascade provides anonymity after t_0 steps if

$$\text{TVD}(\Pi_U, \Pi_t) < 1/c$$

or every $t \geq t_0$. Parameter c is usually $1/n^\alpha$.

This definition takes into account not only distribution of a single message, but also correlations between them. This is very important, for instance in the case when mixes are used for electronic voting [11].

The anonymity definition considered is equivalent to a definition based on information theory [3]. Some other papers use yet another substantially weaker definitions like cardinality of so-called *anonymity set* (see for example [14]). They might be useful and suffice in concrete situations. On the other hand, since we prove a bound for a strong definition, our result applies also to the weaker ones.

4   Coupling Proof of the Main Result

It is intuitively obvious for the parallel mix cascade that the distribution of Π_t converges to the uniform distribution. We use a standard convergence measure called *mixing time*:

$$\tau_{\text{M}}(\varepsilon) = \min \{T : \forall t \geq T \ \text{TVD}(\Pi_t, \Pi_U) \leq \varepsilon\}$$

In this section we formally prove that distribution of Π_t converges very quickly to uniform distribution. For this purpose we use *delayed path coupling* technique described below.

Delayed Path Coupling. Delayed Path Coupling [5] is a tool for proving convergence rate of a homogeneous Markov chain. It is an extension of Path Coupling [4] and the generic coupling method. Let us recall it briefly. Let $\mathbf{M} = \{\mathcal{Y}_t\}_{t \in \mathbb{N}}$ be a discrete-time Markov chain with a finite state space $\mathbf{S}$ that has a unique stationary distribution μ. A *coupling* for a Markov chain $\{\mathcal{Y}_t\}_{t \in \mathbb{N}}$ is a stochastic process $\{(Y_t, Y_t^\star)\}_{t \in \mathbb{N}}$ on the space $\mathbf{S} \times \mathbf{S}$ such that processes $\{Y_t\}_{t \in \mathbb{N}}$ and $\{Y_t^\star\}_{t \in \mathbb{N}}$ considered separately are faithful copies of $\{\mathcal{Y}_t\}_{t \in \mathbb{N}}$. In other words, $\Pr(\mathcal{Y}_{t+1} = y | \mathcal{Y}_t = x) = \Pr(Y_{t+1} = y | Y_t = x) = \Pr(Y_{t+1}^\star = y | Y_t^\star = x)$ for each $x, y \in \mathbf{S}$.

We assume that there is a metric $\Delta : \mathbf{S} \times \mathbf{S} \longrightarrow \mathbb{N} \cup \{0\}$; let D be the largest distance according to metrics Δ. Further, let

$$\Gamma = \{(Y_{t\delta}, Y_{t\delta}^\star) \in \mathbf{S} \times \mathbf{S} : \Delta(Y_{t\delta}, Y_{t\delta}^\star) = 1\} \ .$$

Further, we need to assume that for all $(Y_{t\delta}, Y_{t\delta}^\star) \in \mathbf{S} \times \mathbf{S}$, if $\Delta(Y_{t\delta}, Y_{t\delta}^\star) = r$, then there exist a sequence (a "path") $Y = \Lambda_0, \Lambda_1, \ldots, \Lambda_r = Y^\star$ with $(\Lambda_{i-1}, \Lambda_i) \in \Gamma$ for $0 \leq i < r$. No we can formulate the main technical result on delayed path coupling:

Lemma 1 (Delayed Path Coupling Lemma). *Assume that there exist a coupling* $(Y_{t\delta}, Y_{t\delta}^\star)$ *for a process* $\{\mathcal{Y}_t\}_{t \in \mathbb{N}}$ *such that for some real* $\beta < 1$ *and positive integer* δ *we have* $\mathbf{E}[\Delta(Y_{(t+1)\delta}, Y_{(t+1)\delta}^\star)] \leq \beta$ *for all* $(Y_{t\delta}, Y_{t\delta}^\star) \in \Gamma$ *and for all* $t \in \mathbb{N}$. *Then,*

$$\tau_{\mathbf{M}}(\varepsilon) \leq \delta \cdot \lceil \ln(D\varepsilon^{-1}) / \ln \beta^{-1} \rceil \ .$$

For further details on delayed path coupling see [5,4]. By Lemma 1, in order to estimate the total variation distance between probability distribution describing the state of a process after step t and its stationary distribution it suffices to construct an appropriate coupling. We should stress that processes $\{Y_t\}_{t \in \mathbb{N}}$ and $\{Y_t^\star\}_{t \in \mathbb{N}}$ are usually dependent – constructing a proper dependence between them is the tricky part of the proof.

4.1   Main Result

Theorem 1 (Main Result) *For a parallel MIX cascade* $TVD(\Pi_U, \Pi_t) = \frac{1}{n}$ *for* $t > T$, *where* $T = \mathcal{O}(1)$ *and does not depend on either the number of messages* n *or the number of mix-servers* k *provided that* $n \gg k^2$.

Preliminaries. At the beginning we observe that $\{\Pi_t\}_{t \in \mathbb{N}}$ is a symmetric and ergodic Markov chain. So the uniform distribution is its unique stationary distribution.

The second key observation is that after mixing in the first step we can confine ourselves to permutations of n balls colored with k different colors - n/k balls of each color. We say that a ball has color i, if it is processed by server i in the first step of the protocol. So the process $\{\Pi_t\}_{t \in \mathbb{N}}$ has values in a space of all placements of such balls on n positions. We denote this space by $\mathbf{S}$.

For $y_1, y_2 \in \mathbf{S}$ we define $\Delta(y_1, y_2)$ to be the minimal number of transpositions necessary to get from state y_1 to y_2. Of course, Δ is a metric and $D = \max_{y_1, y_2} \Delta(y_1, y_2) = n(k-1)/k$.

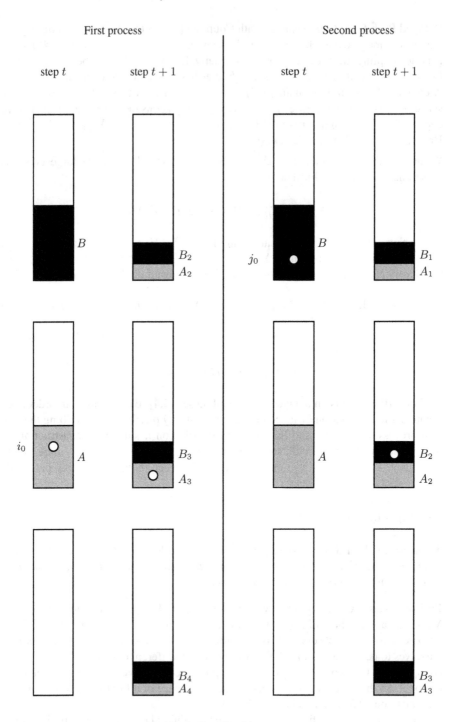

Fig. 3. Coupling idea

Construction of Coupling. Let processes $\{\Upsilon_t\}_{t \in \mathbb{N}}, \{\Upsilon_t^\star\}_{t \in \mathbb{N}}$ differ on one position at time t. Let i_0 and j_0 be the positions at which the configurations $\Upsilon_t, \Upsilon_t^\star$ do not match, say the first process has a white ball at position i_0 and a black ball at position j_0, while for the second process the roles are reversed: a black ball is at i_0 and a white ball is at i_0.

We shall talk about an "extra white ball" for each process. This is the white ball that originally stands at position i_0 for the first process and ball at position j_0 for the second process. This terminology refers to the fact that if we replace them by black balls, then the states of both processors become the same. In our approach we take into account black balls and the extra white balls of each process. The remaining balls go to the same positions for both processes.

Since the remaining positions are left for the black balls and for the extra white balls, the configuration of each process is determined by the placement of the extra white ball on the positions that are left.

Let $S_1, S_2, \ldots, S_k$ denote sets of positions corresponding, respectively to mixes 1, 2, $\ldots$, k. Let $\Psi(i)$ be the position occupied by a ball from position i in the previous step. Observe that if the extra white balls from both processes are placed in the same server, i.e. $\Psi(i_0) \in S_l$ and $\Psi(j_0) \in S_l$ for an $l \leq k$, then we can couple the processes. Namely, the second process uses the same permutation π for S_l as the first process but composed with a transposition concerning the positions of the extra white balls (the transposition is applied before π). It is easy to see that this operation does not change the marginal probability distribution of the second process, because π has the uniform distribution and so composition of a fixed transposition and of π yields a uniformly distributed permutation. Unfortunately, the situation described has a low probability, namely $1/k$. For this reason a more sophisticated strategy is necessary.

For presenting coupling construction we need some notations. Let $i_0 \in S_i$ and $j_0 \in S_j$. Let A and B be the set of positions occupied by the black balls and the extra white balls in S_i and S_j. Let $A_i = \Psi(A) \cap S_i$ and $B_i = \Psi(B) \cap S_i$. That is, A_i (B_i) is the set of positions occupied in step $t+1$ in server i by balls that were at positions from set A (B, respectively) at step t. Further, let: $a = |A|$, $a_i = |A_i|$, $b = |B|$, and $b_i = |B_i|$. Let $I_A = \{i \mid \frac{a_i}{a} > \frac{b_i}{b}\}$ and $I_B = \{1 \ldots k\} \setminus I_A$.

Coupling Definition.

1. We let the first process to place all balls except these starting from positions in set $A \cup B$. The second process places the corresponding balls in exactly the same way.
2. Now the extra white ball (of the first process) from position i_0 is placed uniformly at random on one of the positions that are left – i.e. $\Psi(A \cup B)$.
   Now let us assume that $\Psi(i_0) \in S_h$. We define how to place the second extra white ball. Let $U = \sum_{i \in I_B} (\frac{b_i}{b} - \frac{a_i}{a})$. (So $U = \sum_{i \in I_A} (\frac{a_i}{a} - \frac{b_i}{b})$, as well.)
   Case 1 – $h \in I_B$: in this case we put the extra white ball of the second process on a position chosen uniformly at random from the set B_h.
   Case 2 – $h \in I_A$: we toss an asymmetric coin:
   – with probability $\frac{b_h}{b} / \frac{a_h}{a} = \frac{b_h \cdot a}{b \cdot a_h}$ we place the extra white ball of the second process on randomly chosen position from set B_h,
   – with probability $1 - \frac{b_h \cdot a}{b \cdot a_h}$, we choose a position at random: we put the extra white ball into set B_l with probability

$$\frac{(b_l/b) - (a_l/a)}{U}$$

for $l \in I_B$. The choice of position within B_l is uniform.

3. We are left with black balls only. Each process simply places them at the remaining unoccupied positions.

If the extra white balls fall into the same server at step $t + 1$, then in the next step we couple successfully the processes as it was described above.

Correctness of Coupling. Now we have to show that the procedure described above is a proper coupling - that is the second process has appropriate probability distribution of transitions. Obviously, it is enough to show that the extra white ball from the second process will be placed in each set B_h with probability $\frac{b_h}{b}$. We consider two cases:

Case 1 – $h \in I_B$: In this case the extra white ball had to fall into the set A_h and we had a "positive" result of tossing the coin. So probability of this even is

$$\frac{a_h}{a} \cdot \left(\frac{b_h \cdot a}{b \cdot a_h}\right) = \frac{b_h}{b} .$$

Case 2 – $h \in I_B$: In this situation the extra white ball from the second process could be placed in set B_h in two situations. Either the extra white ball from the first process falls into set A_h or it falls into some of the sets $A_i, i \in I_A$. Events leading to these situations are disjoint. So:

$$\Pr(\Psi(j_0) \in B_h) = \frac{a_h}{a} + \sum_{i \in I_A} \frac{a_i}{a} \cdot \left(1 - \frac{b_i \cdot a}{b \cdot a_i}\right) \cdot \frac{b_h/b - a_h/a}{U} =$$

$$\frac{a_h}{a} + \frac{b_h/b - a_h/a}{U} \cdot \sum_{i \in I_A} \frac{a_i}{a} \left(1 - \frac{b_i}{b} \cdot \frac{a}{a_i}\right) = \frac{a_h}{a} + \frac{b_h/b - a_h/a}{U} \cdot U = \frac{b_h}{b} .$$

Success Probability of Coupling Strategy. Now we estimate probability of the event that the processes get coupled in two steps. As we have seen, it happens at the beginning of step $t + 2$ if at the end of step $t + 1$ the extra white balls get into the same server.

As before, we consider two cases with respect to the position of the extra white ball of the second process at step $t + 1$. Let $\Psi(i_0) \in S_h$.

Case $h \in I_A$: the processes get coupled with probability $\frac{b_h \cdot a}{b \cdot a_h}$. So this contributes $\frac{a_h}{a} \cdot \frac{b_h \cdot a}{b \cdot a_h} = \frac{b_h}{b}$ to the overall probability of successful coupling.

Case $h \in I_B$: the processes get coupled with probability 1. So this contributes $\frac{a_h}{a}$ to the overall probability of successful coupling.

Hence:

$$\Pr(\Upsilon_{t+2} = \Upsilon_{t+2}^\star) = \sum_{i \in I_A} \frac{b_i}{b} + \sum_{i \in I_B} \frac{a_i}{a} = \sum_{i=1}^{k} \min\left\{\frac{a_i}{a}, \frac{b_i}{b}\right\} .$$

Now our goal is to estimate $\frac{a_i}{a}$ and $\frac{b_i}{b}$.

Lemma 2. *Starting at any situation in our model after one step each server contains at least $n/16k^2$ balls of each color with probability greater then $1 - \exp(-n/32k^2)$*

Sketch of the proof. Without loss of generality, we consider the black balls and server S_1, only. Let us assume that in the first step we have x_i black balls in the server S_i. So $x_1 + x_2 + \ldots + x_k = n/k$. Let y_i be the number of black balls that goes from server S_i in the first step to server S_1 in the second step. Of course $y_i \le x_i$. We are interested in estimating $y = y_1 + y_2 + \ldots + y_k$.

We consider two cases:

$x_i \le n/2k^2$: then we can estimate y_i from below by x_i independent Bernoulli trials each with probability $1/2k$.

$x_i > n/2k^2$: in this case we can estimate from below y_i by $n/4k^2$ Bernoulli trials each with probability of success $x_i k/2n$.

Indeed, if $x_i > n/2k^2$, then probability of assigning the jth position connecting S_j with S_1 to a black ball after making decisions about positions 1 through $j-1$ is at least

$$(x_i - (j-1))/(n/k) \ge (x_i - n/4k^2)/(n/k) > (x_i/2)/(n/k) = x_i k/2n .$$

Without loss of generality let us assume that exactly the first l servers belongs to the first category – they have $x_i \le n/2k^2$ black balls at first step. The remaining $k - l$ servers belong to the second category. Then

$$E(y) \ge (x_1 + \ldots + x_l)\tfrac{1}{2k} + \tfrac{n}{4k^2}\tfrac{x_{l+1}k}{2n} + \ldots + \tfrac{n}{4k^2}\tfrac{x_k k}{2n} \ge$$
$$= (x_1 + \ldots + x_k)\tfrac{1}{8k} = \tfrac{n}{8k^2} .$$

We use Chernoff bound in the following form: if X is a sum of independent random variables, then $\Pr(X \le (1-\delta)E(X)) \le \exp(-\delta^2 E(X))$ for each $0 < \delta < 1$. So for $\delta = 1/2$ and the previous estimations we get that $\Pr(y \le \tfrac{n}{16k^2}) \le \exp(-n/32k^2)$. $\square$

Let us recall the following lemma (see [2]):

Lemma 3. *Let us assume that we choose βN balls at random from set of αN black balls and $(1 - \alpha)N$ white balls without replacing. Let X be the number of black balls chosen. Then for $\gamma > 0$*

$$\Pr(|X - \alpha\beta N| > \sqrt{2\beta\gamma N}) \le 2\exp(-\gamma) .$$

Now we can estimate the values a_i/a and b_i/b. We use Lemma 3 with the parameters $N = n/k$, $\alpha = ak/n$ and $\beta = 1/k$. We get:

$$\Pr\left(|a_i - \tfrac{a}{k}| > \sqrt{2\gamma n}/k\right) < 2\exp(-\gamma) .$$

Of course it implies

$$\Pr\left(a_i < \tfrac{a}{k} - \sqrt{2\gamma n}/k\right) < 2\exp(-\gamma) .$$

So by dividing by a we get

$$\Pr\left(\frac{a_i}{a} < \frac{1}{k} - \frac{\sqrt{2\gamma n}}{ka}\right) < 2\exp(-\gamma) .$$

By Lemma 2 applied to a in expression written above and using very rough estimation of probabilities we have for $\gamma = n^{0.4}$:

$$\Pr\left(\frac{a_i}{a} < \frac{1}{k} - \sqrt{2} \cdot \frac{16k}{n^{0.3}}\right) < 2\exp(-n^{0.4}) + \exp(-n/32k^2) .$$

Note that analogous formulas hold for a_i/a as well as b_i/b for all $0 < i \le k$. Thereby

$$\Pr(\Upsilon_{t+2} = \Upsilon^\star_{t+2}) = \sum_{i=1}^{k} \min\left\{\frac{a_i}{a}, \frac{b_i}{b}\right\}$$
$$> k\left(\frac{1}{k} - \sqrt{2} \cdot \frac{16k}{n^{0.3}}\right) - 2k(2\exp(-n^{0.4}) + \exp(-n/32k^2)) .$$

For sufficiently large n we can estimate the expression above by $1 - 23k^2/n^{0.3}$.

Stopping Time.   Now we have all factors necessary to evaluate formula of Delayed Path Coupling. Since in our coupling the distance cannot increase we have:

$$\beta = E(\Delta(\Upsilon_{t+2}, \Upsilon^\star_{t+2})) = \Pr(\Upsilon_{t+2} \ne \Upsilon^\star_{t+2}) < 23k^2/n^{0.3}$$

By our construction, $\delta = 3$. Since $D = n(k-1)/k$ we get finally

$$\tau_M(\varepsilon) \le 3 \left\lceil \frac{\ln n(k-1)k^{-1}\varepsilon^{-1}}{0.3\ln n - 2\ln 23k} \right\rceil .$$

So for a standard value $\varepsilon = 1/n$ used in the literature we have $\tau_M = \mathcal{O}(1)$, which is $\mathcal{O}(1)$ with respect to the number of messages n and number of mix-servers k.

Remark about the result.   Let us emphasize that this result does not mean that number of necessary steps of protocol is independent on parameters n and k for any k and n. Indeed, we assumed that $n \gg k^2$. This assumption is important, since in Lemma 1 $\beta < 1$ is required. In Subsection 4.1 we estimated β by $23k^2/n^{0.3}$. For that reason the shall assume that $k < n^{0.15}/\sqrt{23}$. If this relation between n and k would not hold, the number of required steps of protocol depends on parameter k.

5   Dishonest Server Case

In this section we compare the results obtained in the previous section with the case in which at least one server is dishonest (i.e. reveals permutations used to an adversary), and show that we need significantly more steps to achieve the same level of anonymity. Namely, this number of steps becomes a function of n, which is a significant difference with the previous case.

First observe that if the exact position of at least one message after mixing process is known - i.e. $\widehat{\Pi}_T(i) = j$ for certain i, j, then

$$\mathrm{TVD}(\widehat{\Pi}_T, \Pi_U) \ge 1 - 1/n .$$

(This shows how sensitive is total variation distance as a measure of anonymity.) Obviously, the variation distance considered reaches a minimum if $\widehat{\Pi}_T$ maps all messages (except i) uniformly at random on positions $\{1, \ldots, n\} \setminus \{j\}$. In this case

$$\text{TVD}(\widehat{\Pi}_T, \Pi_U) = \frac{1}{2} \left((n-1)! \left| \frac{1}{(n-1)!} - \frac{1}{n!} \right| + (n! - (n-1)!) \left| 0 - \frac{1}{n!} \right| \right) = 1 - 1/n \ .$$

Now we check that if a dishonest server permanently reveals how it permutes the messages, then with a constant probability the route of some message will be revealed for $T = \Theta(\log n / \log k)$ steps. After the first step exactly n/k^2 messages remain at the dishonest server. We choose $n/2k^2$ of them and for each of them estimate the chance that it will remain at the dishonest server all the time. In order to analyze a single step we assume that the distinguished messages choose the output position of the mix at random: the first message can choose an arbitrary output position, the next message chooses at random from all output positions of this mix except the one occupied by the first message, the third message chooses among n/k-2 positions, and so on. In any case each of the distinguished messages has probability at least $\frac{n/k^2 - n/(2k^2)}{n/k} = 1/2k$ to remain at the dishonest server, hence at least $(1/2k)^T$ within T steps, no matter what happens with the remaining distinguished messages. Hence the probability that at least one message stays at the same dishonest server is greater than

$$1 - \left(1 - \left(\tfrac{1}{2k} \right)^T \right)^{n/2k^2} \ .$$

So if $T = \Theta(\log n / \log k)$, then with a constant probability an adversary can trace the whole route of some message.

6   Conclusions and Open Problems

We have shown an interesting phenomenon that if all servers of parallel mix cascade are honest, the number of steps necessary to achieve good provable anonymity does not depend on the number of messages, while it is not true if a single mix is dishonest.

It is still an open question how many steps we do need for other mix-network topologies and what is the optimal topology. The case when k is close to n remains also to be considered.

References

1. Aldous, D.: *Random Walks of Finite Groups and Rapidly Mixing Markov Chains*. In: Azéma, J., Yor, M. (eds.): Séminare de Probabilités XVII 1981/82. Lecture Notes in Mathematics 986, Springer-Verlag, 243-297
2. Auletta, V., Caragiannis, I., Kaklamanis, C., Persiano, P.: *Randomized Path Coloring on Binary Trees*. APPROX'2000, LNCS 1913, Springer-Verlag, 60-71
3. Berman, R., Fiat, A., Ta-Shma, A.: *Provable Unlinkability Against Traffic Analysis*. Financial Cryptography 2004, LNCS 3110, Springer-Verlag, 266-280
4. Bubley, B., Dyer, M.: *Path Coupling: A Technique for Proving Rapid Mixing in Markov Chains*. 38 ACM-SIAM FOCS, 1997, 223-231

5. Czumaj, A., Kanarek, P., Kutyłowski, M., Loryś, K.: *Switching Networks for Generating Random Permutations*. In: Switching Networks: Recent Advances. Kluwer Academic Publishers, 2001, ISBN 0-7923-6953-X, 25-61

6. Czumaj, A., Kutyłowski, M.: *Delayed Path Coupling and Generating Random Permutations*. Random Structures and Algorithms, 2000, 17(3-4): 238-259

7. Dingledine, R.: Anonymity Bibliography http://freehaven.net/anonbib/

8. Chaum, D.: *Untraceable Electronic Mail, Return Addresses, and Digital Pseudonyms*. CACM , 1981 , 24(2): 84-88

9. Golle, P., Jakobsson, M., Juels, A., Syverson, P.: *Universal Re-encryption for Mixnets*. RSA-CT'04, LNCS 2964, Springer-Verlag, 163-178

10. Golle, P., Juels, A.: *Parallel Mixing*. ACM Conference on Computer and Communications Security (CCS) '2004, 220-226

11. Gomułkiewicz, M., Klonowski, M., Kutyłowski, M.: *Rapid Mixing and Security of Chaum's Visual Electronic Voting*, ESORICS'2003, LNCS 2808, Springer-Verlag, 132-145

12. Gomułkiewicz, M., Klonowski, M., Kutyłowski, M.: *Provable Unlinkability Against Traffic Analysis Already After $\mathcal{O}(\log(n))$ Steps!*. Information Security Conference (ISC)'2004, LNCS 3225, Springer-Verlag, 354-366

13. Gülcü, C., Tsudik, G.: *Mixing E-mail with BABEL*. ISOC Symposium on Network and Distributed System Security, IEEE 1996, 2-16

14. Kesdogan, D., Egner, J., Büschkes, R.: *Stop-and-Go-MIXes Providing Probabilistic Anonymity in an Open System*. Information Hiding '98, LNCS 1525, Springer-Verlag, 83-98

15. Rackoff, C., Simon, D.R.: *Cryptographic Defense Against Traffic Analysis*. ACM Symposium on Theory of Computing25, 1993, 672-681

16. Syverson, P. F., Reed, M. G., Goldschlag, D. M.: *Anonymous Connections and Onion Routing*. IEEE Journal on Selected Areas in Communication, 1998, 16(4):482-494

On Blending Attacks for Mixes with Memory

Luke O'Connor

IBM Research, Switzerland
oco@zurich.ibm.com, luke.oconnor@swissonline.ch

Abstract. Blending attacks are a general class of traffic-based attacks, exemplified by the $(n-1)$-attack. Adding memory or pools to mixes mitigates against such attacks, however there are few known quantitative results concerning the effect of pools on blending attacks. In this paper we give a precise analysis of the number of rounds required to perform an $(n-1)$-attack on the pool mix, timed pool mix, timed dynamic pool mix and the binomial mix.

1 Introduction

Mixes, first proposed by Chaum [3], are a means of providing unlinkability between a set of messages received and subsequently forwarded by the mix. This is typically achieved through a combination of cryptographic techniques and traffic manipulation such as delaying, padding and re-ordering. The original proposal of Chaum, referred to as a *threshold mix*, has been extended and improved by many authors (see [12,11,7] for surveys). Anonymous remailer systems such as Mixmaster [10], and its successor Mixminion [4], are embodiments of (and improvements to) the principles originally presented by Chaum. Anonymity systems are subject to a wide variety of threats including attacks pertaining to replay, blending, pseudospoofing, tagging, intersection and timing [4]. The threat that such attacks pose against a given anonymity system will depend on the system design and its operational characteristics, as well as the control that an attacker can can exert on the mix, or its environment, to mount the attack.

In this paper we will be mainly concerned with *blending attacks*, which refer to a general class of attacks based on manipulating network traffic to compromise the anonymity of one or several messages sent to a mix [12]. The attacker is assumed to be a *global active attacker*, who is able to monitor all communication links, delete and delay legitimate message traffic, and insert arbitrary amounts of spurious traffic. The best known blending attack is the $(n-1)$-*attack*, where the traffic to a mix is manipulated so that it contains a message batch of size n that consists of a target message m^* and $n-1$ spurious messages generated by the attacker. When the mix is a standard threshold mix, the target message is guaranteed to be included in the next set of flushed messages, and can therefore be isolated and traced by the attacker. For standard threshold mixes, the $(n-1)$-attack requires just two rounds: one round to wait for the current mix contents to be flushed, and then one additional round to flush the target message while blocking other legitimate message traffic. The $(n-1)$-attack can always be

M. Barni et al. (Eds.): IH 2005, LNCS 3727, pp. 39–52, 2005.

attempted given a sufficiently powerful attacker, and the authors of [2] remark that there is "no general applicable method to prevent this attack".

A general strategy that mitigates against blending attacks is to introduce memory into a mix, referred to as the *pool*. A pool permits messages to be retained in the mix for several rounds before being forwarded, which increases the message delay but also mixes messages within larger message sets. With respect to the $(n-1)$-attack, the attacker must then first replace the current pool of legitimate messages in the mix with spurious messages, then submit the target message, and finally keep submitting more spurious messages until the target message is flushed. Therefore when a mix is equipped with a pool, the attacker will be required to control the mix for more rounds to arrange the circumstances for a successful $(n-1)$-attack as compared to a threshold mix.

If a mix designer is to validate their choice a system parameters (such as the batch size, pool size, or timing threshold) then a thorough understanding of the trade-off between these parameters and their influence on the success of blending attacks is required. For example, the timed dynamic pool mix is used in the recent design of the Mixminion remailer [4], and while the authors state that their batching strategy will force an attacker to spend multiple time intervals to complete an $(n-1)$-attack, no specific analysis is presented. The main reference on analysing blending attacks is [12], later revised and extended in [11]. While many cogent remarks concerning mix designs are made in [12,11], accurate expressions for the number of rounds required to complete the $(n-1)$-attack on the basic threshold pool mix and the timed dynamic pool mix are not given.

Our main result is to derive the probability distribution for the number of rounds required to complete an $(n-1)$-attack against several types of mixes with memory. In particular we consider the pool mix, the timed pool mix, the timed dynamic pool mix and the binomial mix [12,8]. Our analysis is based on a steady-state strategy where the attacker keeps the number of messages entering and leaving the mix constant over the rounds of the attack, which is true of the pool mix by design.

An outline of this paper can be given as follows. In §2 we introduce basic concepts and notations for mixes with memory used throughout the paper. In §3 we give an overview of blending attacks, and then elaborate on the steady-state strategy for blending attacks in §3.1. The basic threshold pool mix is analyzed in §4, and that analysis is then extended to the timed pool mix in §5, and the timed dynamic pool mix in §6. Finally, the binomial mix is discussed in §7, and our conclusions are presented in §8.

2   Mixes with Memory

As with memoryless mixes, mixes with memory operate over a series of *rounds*. At the beginning of round $r \geq 1$, the mix contains a message pool P_r of size $|P_r|$, that consists of the messages retained in the mix from round $r-1$. It is assumed that P_1 consists of dummy messages generated by the pool mix itself, denoted by the set B_0. The set of messages collected by the mix over the course of round r will be denoted by B_r, referred to as r-th batch set. Round r is terminated when the *batching condition* is satisfied. Let $S_r = (P_r \cup B_r)$ denote the set of messages resident in the mix when the batching condition is satisfied, referred to as the *selection set*. The mix then uses a *flushing rule* to select a subset F_r of messages from S_r to be flushed (forwarded), referred to as the *flush set*. Each message $m \in F_r$ is flushed, and the pool for the next round is then defined as $P_{r+1} = (S_r - F_r)$. The batching condition and flushing rule are collectively referred to as the *batching strategy* for the mix.

Mixes with memory can be parameterized to support a large variety of batching strategies (see [12,11,7] for extensive surveys). A basic design principle is whether the batching condition is threshold-based, time-based, or potentially a combination of both. The batching condition of a threshold mix is satisfied when $|B_r| = n$, and n is referred to as the *threshold parameter*. For threshold mixes the round structure is then defined as intervals over which the mix receives n messages. On the other hand, the flushing condition of time-based mixes is satisifed every t time units, where t is called the *mixing interval*. In this case the round structure is defined as the series of mixing intervals of length t. Another basic design distinction is whether the pool size is static or dynamic. For mixes with static pools, $|P_r| = N$ for all $r \geq 0$, while for dynamic pools, $|P_r|$ is a function of $|S_{r-1}|$, the number of messages in the mix at time $r - 1$. These two properties can be combined to produce different variants on mixes mixes with memory including the pool mix, the timed pool mix, the threshold or timed pool mix, and so on. We also assume that in practice each mix has two additional integer parameters, $N_{\min}$ and $N_{\max}$, to handle boundary cases. When $|B_r| < N_{\min}$ the mix retains the current batch in the pool but does not flush any messages. On the other hand, when the mix receives a large number of messages it restricts the size of the batch to be less than $N_{\max}$ to avoid overflow conditions.

3   Blending Attacks

Blending attacks refer to a class of attacks where an attacker is able to manipulate the messages entering the mix, typically through a combination of trickling and flooding operations [12]. The $(n-1)$-attack can be generalized to mixes with memory, and consists of two phases: *pool flushing* and *target flushing*. The object of pool flushing is to replace the current pool set P_r by spurious messages generated by the attacker. Once P_r has been flushed, the attacker can submit the target message m^*, and then submit additional spurious messages until the target message is flushed.

We note that the attacker can verify when the pool flushing is complete if they have knowledge of the internal parameters of the mix. For example, assume that the attacker knows the size N of the pool in a threshold pool mix. The attacker can then block legitimate traffic and submit batches of spurious messages until the observed difference between the number of messages sent to, and flushed by, the mix is N.

For a typical parameter selection, the number of rounds required to complete the attack is dominated by the pool flushing, since flushing the target message from the mix can be viewed as special case of flushing a pool set of size one. Our analysis therefore concentrates on the number of rounds required to flush a general pool size of $N \geq 1$.

3.1   The Steady-State Strategy

Various strategies could be pursued by an attacker to flush the current pool from the mix. Our analysis will be with respect to a particular strategy that we will refer to as the *steady-state strategy* [1]. In this strategy the attacker observes and/or manipulates a mix for some number of rounds, say up to and including round $r - 1$, where $|F_{r-1}|$ messages were flushed from the mix. Assume that the attacker wishes to flush P_r from the mix. The attacker then blocks all legitimate message traffic to the mix and submits k batches $B_r, B_{r+1}, \ldots, B_{r+k-1}$ of size $|F_{r-1}|$ to the mix, which forces $|F_{r+j}| = |F_{r-1}|$ for $0 \leq j < k$. The batching rule is satisfied at each of these rounds (as it was at round $r - 1$) and the mix will either flush immediately or when the next time interval completes.

Let $\Delta(P_r)$ be the random variable which describes the minimum number of rounds required to flush the pool set P_r, assuming that the mix is in a steady-state during these rounds. If $\Delta(P_r) = k$, for some $k \geq 1$, then $P_r \cap P_{r+k} = \{\emptyset\}$, and $P_r \cap P_{r+j} \neq \{\emptyset\}$ for $1 \leq j < k$, In other words, at least one message $m_i \in P_r$ was retained in the mix until the beginning of round $r + k - 1$, but all such remaining messages are then included in the set of flushed messages F_{r+k-1} for that round.

We will determine $\Pr(\Delta(P_r) > k)$ for $k \geq 1$, where the probabilities are defined by choices of the flush set F_r at each round. Thus when $\Pr(\Delta(P_r) > k) < \epsilon$, for some suitably small ϵ, the attacker has the assurance that P_r was flushed from the mix in k rounds or less with probability $1 - \epsilon$. If $\Pr(\Delta(P_r) = k)$ is desired, then for $k > 1$ this probability can be determined via

$$\Pr(\Delta(P_r) = k) = \Pr(\Delta(P_r) > (k - 1)) - \Pr(\Delta(P_r) > k). \tag{1}$$

Equation (1) cannot be use to determine $\Pr(\Delta(P_r) = 1)$, but this probability can typically be calculated directly from the context of the attack.

4   The Threshold Pool Mix

The threshold pool mix is defined by two parameters: the threshold n, and the pool size N. Each round r is defined by collecting a message batch B_r of size n such that the contents of the mix are then $S_r = (B_r \cup P_r)$. The flush set F_r is then selected as random subset of S_r of size n. The messages of F_r are forwarded and the pool for round $r + 1$ is set to $P_r = (S_r - F_r)$. The values of n and N are

---

[1] The steady-state strategy was described in [12], and we introduce the term here only as a convenient shorthand.

static over all rounds, so that for $r \geq 0$, $|B_r| = |F_r| = n$, $|S_r| = N+n$, $|P_r| = N$. In the remainder of this section we will use the term 'mix' to mean a threshold pool mix.

Following the discussion of §3.1, the threshold pool mix is in a steady-state by definition since the threshold and pool size are fixed. We now consider the number of rounds $\Delta(P_r)$ required to flush the pool P_r. The probability of flushing P_r in a single round is

$$\Pr(\Delta(P_r) = 1) = \frac{\binom{n}{n-N}}{\binom{N+n}{n}}. \tag{2}$$

For $k > 1$, we will calculate $\Pr(\Delta(P_r) > k)$ by decomposing this probability into events concerning the individual messages from P_r. If we let $P_r = \{m_1, m_2, \ldots, m_N\}$, then for $1 \leq i \leq N$, let $A_{i,k}$ denote the event that $m_i \in P_{r+k}$, meaning that m_i was not flushed from the mix after k consecutive rounds. We will write $A_{i,1}$ as A_i, which is the event that m_i is not flushed after one round. By definition

$$\Pr(\Delta(P_r) > k) = \Pr\left(\bigcup_{j=1}^{N} A_{i,k} \right) \tag{3}$$

and the union operation of the RHS of (3) may be expanded using the inclusion-exclusion principle (IEP) [9]. To apply the IEP, various intersections (joint events) between the $A_{i,k}$ events must be computed. Conveniently the intersections of these events exhibit considerable symmetry when the mix is in a steady-state.

Theorem 1. For $N, n, k \geq 1$,

$$\Pr(\Delta(P_r) > k) = \binom{N+n}{n}^{-k} \cdot \sum_{j=1}^{N} \binom{N}{j}\binom{N+n-j}{n}^{k}(-1)^{j+1}. \tag{4}$$

Proof. We first note that $A_1 A_2 \cdots A_j$ is the event that *at least* the j messages $m_1, m_2, \ldots, m_j$ are retained in the mix. The probability of this event is then

$$\Pr(A_1 A_2 \cdots A_j) = \frac{\binom{N+n-j}{n}}{\binom{N+n}{n}} \tag{5}$$

which only depends on j, and thus $\Pr(A_1 A_2 \cdots A_j) = \Pr(A_{i_1} A_{i_2} \cdots A_{i_j})$ for all choices $1 \leq i_1 < i_2 < \cdots < i_j \leq N$. Since the flush set is chosen uniformly and independently at each round, it follows that

$$\Pr(A_{i_1,k} A_{i_2,k} \cdots A_{i_j,k}) = (\Pr(A_1 A_2 \cdots A_j))^{k}. \tag{6}$$

Now consider the following derivation of $\Pr(\Delta(P_r) > k)$

$$\Pr(\Delta(P_r) > k) = \Pr\left(\bigcup_{j=1}^{N} A_{i,k}\right) \tag{7}$$

$$= \sum_{j=1}^{N} \sum_{1 \le i_1 < \cdots < i_j \le N} \Pr\left(A_{i_1,k} A_{i_2,k} \cdots A_{i_j,k}\right) \cdot (-1)^{j+1} \tag{8}$$

$$= \sum_{j=1}^{N} \binom{N}{j} \cdot (\Pr(A_1 A_2 \cdots A_j))^k \cdot (-1)^{j+1}. \tag{9}$$

Equation (8) is simply the IEP expansion of (7), and (9) is derived by simplifying (8) using (6). Finally, the theorem follows from substituting (5) into (9). □

Let S_j be the sum of the first j terms of the RHS of (4), for $1 \le j \le N$. The Bonferroni inequalities [9] state that for $1 \le j < N$,

$$S_{j+1} \le \Pr(\Delta(P_r) > k) \le S_j. \tag{10}$$

Setting $j = 1$ yields that $S_2 \le \Pr(\Delta(P_r) > k) \le S_1$ where

$$S_1 = N \cdot \left(\frac{N}{N+n}\right)^k. \tag{11}$$

$$S_2 = S_1 - \binom{N}{2} \cdot \left(\frac{N(N-1)}{(N+n)(N+n-1)}\right)^k,$$

$$= S_1 \left(1 - \left(\frac{N-1}{2}\right) \cdot \left(\frac{N-1}{N+n-1}\right)^k\right). \tag{12}$$

Here $S_1 = N \cdot (\Pr(A_1))^k$ is well-known as Boole's inequality, and is often referred to as the union bound. We see that S_1 is a good approximation to $\Pr(\Delta(P_r) > k)$ as k increases, since the inner term of (12) is tending to 1 as a function of k.

Table 1 shows Theorem 1 evaluated for several choices of n and N. For example, when $n = 160, N = 100$ then with probability better than a half, more than 5 rounds will be required to flush the pool; but the probability that more 15 rounds are required is 0.596×10^{-4}. The values given in Table 1 were computed using Maple [1], and required about 20 seconds of computation time on a moderately fast laptop. Computing that $\Pr(\Delta(P_r) > 30) = 0.217 \times 10^{-7}$ for $n = 1000$ and $N = 800$ was also quickly determined. Thus a mix designer can easily evaluate the effect of various choices of n and N against the the number of rounds to flush a given pool P_r.

We recall that the $(n-1)$-attack has two phases: flushing the current pool P_r, followed by submitting and flushing the target message m^*. For a mix with given parameters n' and N', we simply apply Theorem 1 with $N = 1$, and $n = n' + N' - 1$ to determine the number of rounds required to flush m^*.

Table 1. Example bounds on $\Pr(\Delta(P_r) > k)$ derived from Theorem 1

n	N	$k, \Pr(\Delta(P_r) > k)$				
100	80	(3, 0.999)	(5, 0.761)	(10, 0.238×10^{-1})	(15, 0.417×10^{-3})	(15, 0.723×10^{-5})
100	160	(5, 0.999)	(10, 0.719)	(20, 0.966×10^{-2})	(30, 0.755×10^{-4})	(40, 0.588×10^{-6})
160	100	(3, 0.999)	(5, 0.575)	(10, 0.706×10^{-2})	(15, 0.596×10^{-4})	(20, 0.501×10^{-6})
200	160	(5, 0.943)	(10, 0.047)	(15, 0.834×10^{-3})	(20, 0.145×10^{-4})	(25, 0.250×10^{-6})

Example 1. Consider a threshold pool mix with threshold $n = 160$ and a pool size $N = 100$. If an attacker undertakes steady-state strategy to flush the pool P_r at some round r, then from Table 1 this will require less than 15 rounds with probability $1 - 0.596 \times 10^{-4}$, and less than 20 rounds with probability $1 - 0.501 \times 10^{-6}$. If the attacker knows the value of N then they can verify the success of the pool flushing by submitting spurious batches until the difference between the number of message submitted and the flushed is N. There is less than 1 chance in a million that this phase will require more than 20 rounds. Once the pool has been flushed the attacker then submits the target message m^*, along with another batch of $n - 1$ spurious messages. The number of rounds required to flush the target message is given by Theorem 1 after setting $N = 1$ and $n = 160 + 100 - 1$, which corresponds to flushing a pool of size 1. Again the success of this phase can be verified by the attacker. Evaluating Theorem 1 with these parameters shows that 3 or less rounds are required to flush the target message with probability $1 - 0.531 \times 10^{-7}$. Thus the attack can be undertaken is 23 rounds or less with high probability. □

Undertaking an attack for 23 rounds may seem unrealistic, however since the mix is threshold-based, the attacker is able to flush the mix at will by submitting batches of size n. Such a lengthy attack would be more difficult to mount on a timed pool mix.

4.1   Estimating the Pool Size

Theorem 1 is derived assuming a knowledge of n and N, which will be true for the system designer, but may not be the case for the attacker. Of course, n will always be known since each flush set F_r is of size n, and may be passively observed by the attacker. The attacker can also obtain a accurate estimate of N by passively 'sampling' the behaviour of the mix. The probability that a given message $m \in S_r$ is included in F_r at round r is easily shown to be $p = n/(N+n)$. Since n is known, the attacker can approximate the pool size given a sufficiently accurate estimator $\hat{p}$ for p. Assume that the attacker submits one (distinguished) message m_i to the mix for s rounds, $1 \leq i \leq s$. Let $X_i = 1$ if m_i was flushed at round i, and let $X_i = 0$ otherwise. Then $\hat{p} = (\sum_{i=1}^{s} X_i)/s$ is a normally distributed estimator of p.

Example 2. Let $n = 160$ and let $N = 100$. We have used Maple to generate 500 random bernoulli samples with parameter $p = 160/(100 + 160) = 0.6154$, of which 318 were successes, yielding that $\hat{p} = 318/500 = 0.636$. This corresponds to an attacker submitting 500 messages to the mix in 500 different rounds, and observing that a message was flushed at the same round it was received with probability 0.636. Using the normal distribution, the true value of p lies in the interval $0.594 \le p \le 0.637$ with 95% confidence. Solving for N given that $p = n/(N + n)$ yields that N lies in the range $91.216 \le N \le 109.42$ with 95% confidence. Increasing the number of samples to 1000 yields improves the interval to $93.706 \le N \le 106.615$.

We note that it is relatively simple for the attacker to obtain a large number of samples from the mix since the attacker can passively obtain the samples. Since the mix is threshold-based, samples can be obtained rapidly in times or high or even moderate traffic. Further since n and N are fixed parameters, the attacker can take the samples over a potentially long period and then later mount an $(n-1)$-attack using the steady-state strategy.

5   The Timed Pool Mix

In this variant of the pool mix, batches are defined by fixed mixing intervals of time t, with a fixed number of messages retained at each round. If the message batch B_r collected during the r-th time period is of size n_r, then P_{r+1} is selected as a random subset of size N from $S_r = (P_r \cup B_r)$, and the flush set is defined as $F_r = (S_r - P_{r+1})$. If $n_r = 0$ then $P_{r+1} = P_r$ and no messages are flushed. For any given round r, this construction is equivalent to the threshold pool mix with a threshold of $n = n_r$. Example parameters were given in [6–p.311], where the following rule ensures that $N = 20$: if $n_r \le 20$ then $|F_r| = 0$; otherwise $|F_r| = (1 - 20/n_r) \cdot |S_r|$.

The steady-state strategy for the attacker is similar to the threshold pool mix, except that the attacker is able to increase the batch size in an effort to reduce the number of required flushing rounds. In practice the attacker cannot increase the batch size arbitrarily and the mix will have an internal limit N_{max} on the number of messages that the mix can hold. In any case, N_{max} may still be large enough relative to N so that the current pool can be flushed quickly. Since the pool size N is fixed, we then assume that $N_{\max}$ can be written as $N_{\max} = N + n_{\max}$ where $n_{\max}$ is the maximum batch size. We now outline a design strategy which mitigates against the attacker attempting to flood the mix and quickly flush the current pool.

5.1   A Design Strategy

The designer begins by selecting a maximum batch size $n_{\max}$ that is to be accepted at each round, perhaps based on expected traffic statistics. Let us assume that the mix is also designed so that with high probability an attacker blocking all legitimate traffic can be detected in at most k consecutive intervals with high probability, say $1 - \epsilon$, for some appropriately small choice of ϵ. The system may be designed, for example, using the heartbeat traffic suggested in [5]. Given, $n_{\max}, k$ and ϵ the designer can now use Theorem 1 to find a pool size N so that $\Pr(\Delta(P_r) > k) > (1 - \epsilon)$. The analysis assumes that the attacker is submitting

$n_{\max}$ messages per batch in the stead-state strategy, but even if the attacker actually submits less messages, then $\Pr(\Delta(P_r) > k)$ upper bounds the success of flushing the pool.

Example 3. As an example, assume that the designer decides that the mix should accept no more than $n_{\max} = 500$ messages per interval, and that the system can (should!) confidently detect steady-state attacks after 3 rounds with probability $1 - 10^{-4}$. Then using Theorem 1, selecting a pool of size $N = 250$, guarantees that for the steady-state strategy $\Pr(\Delta(P_r) > 3) > (1-10^{-4})$. Further increasing N to 270 ensures that $\Pr(\Delta(P_r) > 3) > (1 - 10^{-5})$. On the other hand, if the maximum batch size is increased to $n_{\max} = 1200$, then Theorem 1 yields that $\Pr(\Delta(P_r) > 3) > (1 - 10^{-4})$ when $N = 450$ and $\Pr(\Delta(P_r) > 3) > (1 - 10^{-5})$ when $N = 480$.   □

If the mix can accept large batch sizes relative to N, then the attacker may be able to flush the current pool before the attack is detected by the mix. The approach outlined above mitigates against this possibility by starting with an upper limit in the batch size to be accepted, and then deriving a pool size N which defeats the steady-state strategy for a given number of intervals k with a given probability $1 - \epsilon$.

6   The Timed Dynamic Pool Mix

The threshold and timed pool mixes considered previously have a pool size that is constant over each round. A dynamic pool mix determines the size of pool $|P_{r+1}|$ to be retained for the next round as a function of the number of messages $|S_r|$ currently in the mix. In this section we consider timed dynamic pool mixes, since these are of practical interest [10,4]. Typically a dynamic pool mix is characterized by three parameters:

- The mixing interval t.
- The minimal size of the pool $N_{\min}$.
- The fraction $\alpha < 1$ of the messages to be flushed (subject to $N_{\min}$).

At the end of the r-th mixing interval, the mix considers its contents S_r. If $|S_r| \leq N_{\min}$ then $|F_r| = 0$ and no messages are flushed. Otherwise, let $|F_r| = \min(|S_r| - N_{\min}, \lfloor \alpha \cdot |S_r| \rfloor)$ and construct F_r as a random subset of S_r of size $|F_r|$.

Example 4. An example parameterization of $\alpha = 0.65, N_{\min} = 45$ was considered in [7], which defines the following rules for the number of messages to be flushed:

- If $0 < |S_r| \leq 45$ then $|F_r| = 0$;
- If $46 \leq |S_r| \leq 129$ then $|F_r| = |S_r| - 45$;
- If $|S_r| \geq 130$ then $|F_r| = \lfloor \alpha \cdot |S_r| \rfloor$.

Thus, when the mix contains 130 messages or more the pool size at the next round is then $|P_{r+1}| = |S_r| - \lfloor \alpha \cdot |S_r| \rfloor$.   □

6.1   The Steady-State Strategy

We now derive the success of the steady-state strategy, assuming that the objective is to flush P_r and that the values of $N = |S_{r-1}|$ and α are known. In the next section we discuss how the attacker can determine a good estimate of α, and hence $|S_r|$ at any round. The attacker selects a round $r-1$ where the observed traffic has been sufficiently high to expect that $|F_{r-1}| = \lfloor \alpha \cdot |S_{r-1}| \rfloor$, or the attacker injects a moderate number of spurious messages to force this condition with high probability.

Theorem 2. If $|F_{r-1}| = \lfloor \alpha \cdot |S_{r-1}| \rfloor$ and $|S_{r-1}| = N$, then for $k \geq 1$,

$$\Pr(\Delta(P_r) > k) = \binom{N}{\lfloor \alpha N \rfloor}^{-k} \cdot \sum_{j=1}^{N - \lfloor \alpha N \rfloor} \binom{N - \lfloor \alpha N \rfloor}{j} \binom{N - j}{\lfloor \alpha N \rfloor}^k (-1)^{j+1}.$$

Proof. The proof is a direct adaption of Theorem 1 by observing that $|P_r| = N - \lfloor \alpha N \rfloor$ and

$$(\Pr(A_1 A_2 \cdots A_j))^k = \binom{N - j}{\lfloor \alpha N \rfloor}^k. \tag{13}$$

$\square$

Example 5. Let $\alpha = 0.6$, which is the default value for timed dynamic pool mix of Mixminion [4], and let there be $N = 200$ messages in the mix at round $r-1$. Then $|F_{r-1}| = \lfloor 0.6 \cdot 200 \rfloor = 120$. Given these parameters, $\Pr(\Delta(P_r) > k)$ is calculated in Table 2 for several values of k. $\square$

Table 2. Example bounds on $\Pr(\Delta(P_r) > k)$ derived from Theorem 2

α N	$k, \Pr(\Delta(P_r) > k)$				
0.6 200	(3, 0.996)	(5, 0.556)	(10, 0.835×10^{-2})	(15, 0.859×10^{-4})	(20, 0.879×10^{-6})

As with the time pool mix, the steady-state strategy may not have a sufficient number of rounds to succeed if the designer incorporates specific measure to detect the blocking of legitimate traffic.

6.2   Estimating the Value of α

The value of α may not be know to the attacker, but a good estimate of α can be obtained as follows. Assume that under normal operation the attacker observes that the mix at round r flushes $|F_r|$ messages where $|F_r| = \lfloor \alpha N \rfloor$ where $N = |S_r|$. If the attacker blocks legitimate messages during round $r+1$, and submits $2 \cdot |F_r|$ spurious messages then $|F_{r+1}| = \lfloor \alpha(N + \lfloor \alpha N \rfloor) \rfloor$. It follows that $|F_{r+1}|/|F_r|$ is a good approximation to $1 + \alpha$ since

$$\frac{|F_{r+1}|}{|F_r|} \approx \frac{\alpha(N + \alpha N)}{\alpha N} = 1 + \alpha. \tag{14}$$

If we define α^* as $F_{r+1}/|F_r|-1$ then $N^* = \lfloor |F_r|/\alpha^* \rfloor$ is a good approximation to N. For example, if $\alpha = 0.6$ and $N = 397$, then $\alpha^* = .600840336$ and $N^* = 396$. The attacker can now mount a steady-state attack using these estimates.

This (attack) method for estimating α assumes that $|F_r| = \alpha \cdot |S_r|$, and therefore that $(|S_r| - N_{min}) > \alpha \cdot |S_r|$. In practice, we expect this condition to be satisfied when the mix contains as few as several hundred messages. The condition for the example rule given above with $\alpha = 0.65, N_{min} = 45$ is 130 messages. If the attack is mounted during a period of low traffic to the mix then the attacker will need to send several hundred spurious messages to prime the mix for the attack.

7   The Binomial Mix

The binomial mix was introduced in [8], and was further elaborated upon in [11–p.77]. The distinguishing property of these mixes is the use of a *flushing probability function* $f : \mathbb{N} \rightarrow [0,1]$ to determine the set of messages to be flushed. Binomial mixes are timed, and at the r-th interval f is evaluated to yield $f(|S_r|) = p_r$. Each message $m \in S_r$ is then included in F_r independently with probability p_r, and thus $|F_r|$ follows the binomial distribution with parameter p_r.

Potentially many functions could be used as a flushing probability function. In [8] the suggested function is the normal distribution[2]

$$\Phi_{\mu,\sigma}(s) = \frac{1}{\sigma\sqrt{2\pi}} \int_{-\infty}^{s} e^{-\frac{(t-\mu)^2}{2\sigma^2}} dt \tag{15}$$

so that $p_r = \Phi_{\mu,\sigma}(|S_r|)$ at round r. No values for μ and σ were suggested in [8], but later in [11–p.80], there is graphical comparison between the Cottrell mix with $\alpha = 0.8$ and the binomial mix with $\mu = 100, \sigma = 40$. [3]

7.1   The Steady-State Strategy

We first derive a bound on the steady-state strategy, assuming that all relevant parameters are known. Consider a steady-state attack at round r such that $|F_{r-1}|$ was observed by the attacker, and let Let $p_{r-1} = f(|S_{r-1}|)$ and $N = |P_{r-1}|$. Adapting Theorem 7 with $\Pr(A_1 A_2 \cdots A_j))^k = (1 - p_{r-1})^{jk}$, and letting $q = 1 - p_{r-1}$, yields

$$\Pr(\Delta(P_r) > k) = \sum_{j=1}^{N} \binom{N}{j} q^{jk} \cdot (-1)^{j+1}$$

---

[2] In [8] the authors refer to the normal distribution as the cumulative normal distribution, but the former term is correct.

[3] Figure 5.6 [11–p.80] seems to be incorrect since it shows $\Phi_{100,40}(s)$ to be converging to 0.8, when in fact it must be converging to 1.

$$= -\sum_{j=1}^{N} \binom{N}{j}(-q^k)^j$$
$$= -((1-q^k)^N - 1)$$
$$= 1 - (1-q^k)^N, \tag{16}$$

which simply states that $\Pr(\Delta(P_r) > k) = 1 - \Pr(\Delta(P_r) \leq k)$ when messages are selected for flushing independently. Also from (1) it follows that $\Pr(\Delta(P_r) = k) = (1-q^k)^N - (1-q^{k-1})^N$ for $k > 1$. Letting $k = \lceil \log_{\frac{1}{q}} N - \log_{\frac{1}{q}} \epsilon \rceil$ for some suitably small $\epsilon < 1$, consider the following bound

$$(1-q^k)^N \leq \exp\left\{-Nq^k\right\}$$
$$\leq \exp\left\{-q^{-\lceil \log_{1/q} \epsilon \rceil}\right\}$$
$$\leq \exp\left\{-\epsilon\right\}$$
$$= 1 - \epsilon + O(\epsilon^2), \tag{17}$$

where we have used the bounds $\ln(1 - x) < -x$ and $e^{-x} = 1 - x + O(x^2)$ for $x < 1$. It follows from (17) that

$$\Pr(\Delta(P_r) > k) = \epsilon + O(\epsilon^2). \tag{18}$$

The $O(\epsilon^2)$ term can be improved to $\epsilon^2 \cdot e^{-\epsilon}/2$ since

$$e^{-\epsilon} = 1 - \epsilon + \frac{\epsilon^2}{2}\sum_{i \geq 0}(-\epsilon)^i/i! = 1 - \epsilon + \frac{\epsilon^2 \cdot e^{-\epsilon}}{2}.$$

The number of rounds k required for the steady-state strategy to succeed with the error bound given in (18) is then $\lceil \log_{\frac{1}{q}}(N/\epsilon) \rceil$.

7.2   The Robustness of Parameter Selection

In [8] it is stated that binomial mixes make blending attacks more probabilistic since the attacker becomes less certain of the number of messages which are retained in the mix from one round to the next. This is true, but the success of the steady-state strategy outlined above is quite robust against possible choices for N and $q = 1 - p_{r-1}$, as we now argue.

We first note that when $N \geq \mu$ then $p_{r-1} \geq \frac{1}{2}$, which for the example parameters above is satisfied when the mix has 100 messages or more. In this case, $q \leq \frac{1}{2}$ and $k = \lceil \log_2(N/\epsilon) \rceil$ steady-state rounds produce an error bound equal to or less than that of (18). So if the attacker overestimates N with $\hat{N}$, such that $\hat{N}/N = d$ then an additional $\lceil \log_2 d \rceil$ rounds will be added to achieve the error bound of (18) using $\hat{N}$, as compared to using the actual value of N. Thus overestimating N by a factor of 8 will only add 3 additional rounds to the attack as compared to using the exact value of N.

In this discussion we have assumed that $p_{r-1} \geq \frac{1}{2}$, which is true when $N = |S_{r-1}| \geq \mu$. Arranging this condition through flooding does not appear to be too difficult a task for for the attacker. No general theory for the optimal selection of μ and σ was presented in [8] or [11–p.77], but based on other mixes, we would expect μ to be less than 1000. Thus it seems quite feasible for the attacker to create a steady-state where $p_{r-1} \geq \frac{1}{2}$.

8   Conclusion

In this paper we have presented a general method for analysing the success of the $(n-1)$-attack using the steady-state strategy against a variety of mixes with memory (pools). This permits a mix designer to analyse parameters choices with respect to their effect on mitigating against the $(n-1)$-attack. Our analysis methods also permits an attacker to evaluate their success in undertaking a blending attack, assuming relevant parameters are known or can be estimated.

Our results indicate that the threshold pool mix is particularly susceptible to blending attacks since it can be rapidly flushed by an attacker, and its pool size can be accurately estimated if it is not known. The timed pool mix, and its dynamic variant, are more resistant to blending attacks since the mixing interval limits the speed with which an blending attack can be mounted. We introduced a design strategy where the designer can select the pool size and the maximum batch size so that a blending attack is unlikely to succeed before it is detected. This strategy is not possible for the threshold pool mix since the attacker can flush the mix at will.

An original design goal of the binomial mix is to frustrate blending attacks by reducing the knowledge that the attacker has concerning the size of the pool N that must be flushed. However we have shown that the exact value of N is not required to complete the attack with high probability. Our analysis cannot be taken further at this point without a general theory on parameter selection for the binomial mix.

There are several limitations on the analysis that has been presented, which we now discuss. Throughout the paper the attacker is assumed to be a global active attacker, who is able to monitor all communication links, delete and delay legitimate message traffic, and insert arbitrary amounts of spurious traffic. Such attackers are very powerful and designing explicit defenses against such attackers might seem unnecessary The analysis of the pool mixes considered in this paper is simplified by assuming such an attacker, and we may treat the results as lower bounds on the capabilities of less powerful adversaries. However it appears that the $(n-1)$-attack cannot be mounted (with certainty) by an attacker who is not globally active.

Another limitation of the analysis presented is the absence of considerations concerning traffic rates, dummy traffic, the length of mixing intervals, and a host of other practical considerations. For example we have simply assumed that an attacker can block all traffic to a mix for 20 rounds, which may correspond to an elapsed 10 hour time period in practice, and is very likely to be noticed by the mix owner. We stress however that the results of this paper are mainly aimed at the mix designer, who can then select parameters to provide security guarantees, both based on practical consideration and the analysis provided here. Previous to our work, there was no accurate basis for predicting the success of blending attacks.

References

1. See the Maple homepage at http://www.maplesoft.com.
2. Oliver Berthold, Andreas Pfitzmann, and Ronny Standtke. The disadvantages of free MIX routes and how to overcome them. In H. Federrath, editor, *Proceedings of Designing Privacy Enhancing Technologies: Workshop on Design Issues in Anonymity and Unobservability*, pages 30–45. Springer-Verlag, LNCS 2009, July 2000.
3. David Chaum. Untraceable electronic mail, return addresses, and digital pseudonyms. *Communications of the ACM*, 4(2), February 1981.
4. George Danezis, Roger Dingledine, and Nick Mathewson. Mixminion: Design of a Type III Anonymous Remailer Protocol. In *Proceedings of the 2003 IEEE Symposium on Security and Privacy*, May 2003. Additional information on the Mixminion remailer can be found at http://mixminion.net.
5. George Danezis and Len Sassaman. Heartbeat traffic to counter (n-1) attacks. In *Proceedings of the Workshop on Privacy in the Electronic Society (WPES 2003)*, Washington, DC, USA, October 2003.
6. Claudia Díaz and Bart Preneel. Reasoning about the anonymity provided by pool mixes that generate dummy traffic. In *Proceedings of 6th Information Hiding Workshop (IH 2004)*, LNCS, Toronto, May 2004.
7. Claudia Díaz and Bart Preneel. Taxonomy of mixes and dummy traffic. In *Proceedings of I-NetSec04: 3rd Working Conference on Privacy and Anonymity in Networked and Distributed Systems*, Toulouse, France, August 2004.
8. Claudia Díaz and Andrei Serjantov. Generalising mixes. In Roger Dingledine, editor, *Proceedings of Privacy Enhancing Technologies workshop (PET 2003)*. Springer-Verlag, LNCS 2760, March 2003.
9. W. Feller. *An Introduction to Probability Theory and its Applications*. New York: Wiley, 3rd edition, Volume 1, 1968.
10. Ulf Möller, Lance Cottrell, Peter Palfrader, and Len Sassaman. Mixmaster Protocol — Version 2. Draft, July 2003.
11. A. Serjantov. On the anonymity of anonymity systems. Technical Report UCAM-CL-TR-604, Computer Laboratory, University of Cambridge, 2004. Available at http://www.cl.cam.ac.uk/TechReports/UCAM-CL-TR-604.html.
12. Andrei Serjantov, Roger Dingledine, and Paul Syverson. From a trickle to a flood: Active attacks on several mix types. In Fabien Petitcolas, editor, *Proceedings of Information Hiding Workshop (IH 2002)*. Springer-Verlag, LNCS 2578, October 2002.

Pervasive Random Beacon in the Internet for Covert Coordination

Hui Huang Lee, Ee-Chien Chang, and Mun Choon Chan

School of Computing, National University of Singapore
{leehuihu, changec, chanmc}@comp.nus.edu.sg

Abstract. A random beacon periodically outputs a random number and was introduced by Rabin[12] to secure remote transaction. We consider a random beacon that is *pervasive* in the sense that, it is available everywhere, and accesses to the beacon blends with normal activities. With a pervasive beacon, it is difficult to disrupt the beacon and detect accesses to it. As a result, the pervasiveness of the beacon can facilitate covert coordination, whereby a large collection of agents covertly decide on a common action. In this paper, we discuss the desirable properties of a pervasive random beacon which can be used for covert coordination, and describe how such a beacon can be found in the Internet based on major stock market indices closing values. We also investigate how such a covert coordination can be used, in particular, in coordinating distributed denial of service (DDoS) attacks. Finally, we explore ways to, in a limited manner, disrupt the beacon.

1 Introduction

A random beacon periodically outputs random bits and was introduced by Rabin [12] to secure remote transactions such as contract signing. Since then, a number of other applications of random beacons have been proposed. For example, Bennett et. al. proposed using a random beacon to authenticate video recording[2]. Aummann and Rabin [1] also proposed using higher bandwidth beacon to achieve unconditional security with respect to eavesdroppers with limited storage. Mossel and O'Donnell investigated methods of obtaining a random beacon from a noisy source[10]. Additional discussions on random beacons can be found in [3, 6].

In this paper, we introduce an additional requirement of *pervasiveness*, and give a construction of pervasive random beacon by using information available in Internet, namely major stock market indices closing values. The advantages of using this random source is that it is widely available and replicated on many web servers. Furthermore, there are enormous accesses of this information from vastly different URLs. As a result, it is difficult to distinguish accesses to the beacon from normal web activities. Disrupting access to the beacon is also difficult without substantial disruption to normal web accesses.

As an application of such a pervasive random beacon, we demonstrate how it can be used to coordinate DDoS attacks. In a distributed denial of service

M. Barni et al. (Eds.): IH 2005, LNCS 3727, pp. 53–61, 2005.

attack (DDoS), an attacker employs multiple machines (also known as agents or zombies) to attack a victim, preventing it from providing services to legitimate clients.

Existing coordination models in DDoS attacks can be grouped into three categories: *manual, semi-automatic* or *automatic* [8]. In a manual or semi-automatic attack, the attacker (or master) send the attack parameters such as the network address of the victim and the time of attack to the agents (or zombies). The attacker can directly send his commands to the agents, or the communication can be indirect through another layer of proxies. One weakness of the manual and semi-automatic attacks is that the discovery of one entity may lead to the discovery of the DDoS network.

Alternatively, a DDOS attack can be automated by avoiding communication among the agents and attacker altogether, and thus reduces the risk of detection. However, the parameters of an attack, including start time, attack type, target, are preprogrammed in the code. As a result, once a copy of the agents is captured and examined, parameters of the attack will be known, and usually well in advance of the attack.

In view of the above, we look into whether other models of covert coordination can be employed by the attackers, such that the discovery of an agent will not reveal the attack parameters, and hence will not compromise the DDoS network. It turns out that this can be easily achieved if a pervasive random beacon is available.

In the rest of this paper, we will investigate a method that uses stock closing indices to provide a pervasive random beacon. In Section 2, we discuss various desirable properties of a pervasive random beacon. In Section 3, we describe implementation issues in using the stock closing indices. A survey on current DDoS coordination models is given in Section 4. An alternative model is proposed in Section 5. In Section 6, we describe a few potential methods to disrupt such a beacon.

2   Pervasive Random Beacons

A random beacon periodically outputs random bits. There are a few formal formulations of randomness. In this paper, we take an informal description: the outputs cannot be computationally distinguishable from an uniform distribution. In addition, the output has to remain unpredictable, until the time the random number is revealed. Hence, a secure pseudo random number generator by itself is not sufficient to be a random beacon. An additional infrastructure is required to ensure that the random numbers are honestly and periodically generated, for example, a trusted provider that periodically outputs a random bit using a secure pseudo random number generator, can be a random beacon.

In this paper, we consider random beacons that are pervasive. There are two additional requirements:

High Availability: We require that the outputs of the random beacon can be easily obtained most of the time. Hence, a trusted provider that outputs random bits may not be pervasive if it is the only source. On the other hand, if the outputs from the provider are extensively replicated and the copies are publicly available, the beacon can be pervasive.

Blended Access: We require that accesses to the beacon can be blended with normal activities, making it difficult to distinguish beacon accesses from normal activities.

When a beacon is available in many locations to provide high availability, accesses to the beacon can also be distributed over a large number of servers. Together with the ability to blend with normal activities, it is very difficult to identify beacon accesses or disrupt the beacon. These properties facilitate covert operations.

3   WWW Content as Pervasive Random Beacon

To find a pervasive random beacon in the Internet, we look in the WWW and consider content-based random sources, for example lottery results, political events and sport events. After exploring various possibilities, we found that the stock closing indices are good candidates for the beacon. First, they are replicated all over the WWW and widely accessed. Furthermore, it is well-accepted that a stock index can be used as a random source, for example, there are also other works that use stock index as random seed[5].

A stock market index is calculated using a certain number of stocks from its stock market. For example, the Dow Jones Industrial Average (DJIA) is a price-weighted average of 30 blue-chip stocks that are typically traded on the New York Stock Exchange. During trading period, the value of an index fluctuates, and the reported value can be inconsistent among different service providers at any time. On the other hand, the daily closing index is static and consistent throughout the market's closing period. Since different stock markets around the world have different closing times, by using several indices from different stock markets, we can obtain several random bits, each at a different time of the day.

After deciding on using the stock indices, there are two implementation issues. Firstly, how many random bits can be extracted from a stock index. Secondly, how should the beacons be accessed. We will discuss these issues in the rest of this section.

3.1   Stock Indices as Random Beacon

Since different stock markets around the world have different closing times, by using several indices from different stock markets, we can obtain several random bits, each at a different time of the day. As an illustration, we can use the following 4 indices (All times stated will be in Coordinated Universal Time (UTC)):

1. Dow Jones Industrial Average (DJIA): The DJIA comprises of 30 components and is from the New York Stock Exchange (closing period is from 21:00 to 14:30 when daylight saving time is not in effect and from 20:00 to 13:30 if daylight saving time is in effect)
2. Nikkei 225 (N225): The N225 comprises of 225 components and is from the Tokyo Stock Exchange (closing period is from 06:00 to 00:00)
3. Straits Times Index (STI): The STI comprises of 45 components and is from the Singapore Stock Exchange (closing period is from 09:00 to 01:00)
4. FTSE 100: The FTSE 100 comprises of 102 components and is from the London Stock Exchange (closing period is from 16:30 to 08:30 when daylight saving time is not in effect and from 15:30 to 07:30 if daylight saving time is in effect)

Figure 1 show the closing period of the 4 stock exchanges. Closing stock quotes for major indices are stored and available on the web, e.g. DJIA is available starting Oct 1, 1928 from quote.yahoo.com. Hence, it is not necessary to get them during the closing period.

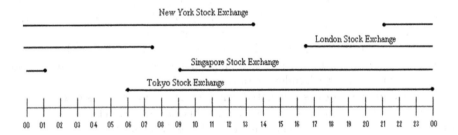

Fig. 1. Closing hours of the 4 stock exchanges

From an index, a mixing function is applied to extract a few bits. An example of a mixing function is a series of XOR operations on the binary representation. Ideally, the number of bits extracted should be the entropy of the closing index. In order to obtain an estimate of the entropy value, we use a publicly available random tester **ent** [14], which provides an estimate of the entropy of a given set of input data.

The test is performed on DJIA closing index (round to 2 decimal places) for the past 30 years. Only the 15 least significant bits are used in the test. The random tester **ent** determines that the entropy is about 13 bits. More random bits can be obtained by considering individual stock or other indices in the same market.

3.2   Accessing the Beacon

Major stock market closing indices can be found on many online newspapers as well as websites of financial organizations. In an implementation, a list of websites can be preprogrammed. For each access, a website is chosen and its web-pages is parsed to obtain the necessary information. To ensure consistency, two or more websites can be visited and parsed. A more sophisticated access mechanism may use web indexing services or web-search engine to update the preprogrammed list.

In order to evade detection, access to the beacon has to be camouflaged and blended into normal network activities. One way to achieve that is to mimic normal web-surfing behavior. In our implementation, randomness is introduced into the access pattern. For instance, each agent will prefer a particular website, but it will also access the information on some other randomly chosen websites with certain probability.

4   Coordination Model in DDoS

There are several methods an attacker can use to coordinate a DDoS attack. Based on their communication models, current methods can be grouped into three categories: *manual, semi-automatic* or *automatic* [8].

In a manual or semi-automatic attack, the attackers send the attack parameters such as the victim and attack time to the agents. The attacker can directly send his commands to the agents, or the communication can be indirect. In the handler-agent model, the attacker sends his commands to a few handler machines which will then relay them to the agents. For example, DDoS tools such as Stacheldraht and Trin00 employ such indirect communications.

One weakness of the manual and semi-automatic attacks is that the discovery of one entity may lead to the discovery of the DDoS network. If a copy of an IRC based tool is captured and examined, the name and password of the IRC channel used by the attacker and agents for communication can be revealed. The network traffic of the captured agents can also be monitored to expose the identity of other agents or handlers. In addition, communication may generates suspicious traffic. For instance, the packets used could be of a specific protocol (E.g. TCP or UDP) and specific port numbers, and the payload of the packets will likely contain strings conforming to a specific syntax. Detection of such suspicious communications among the agents can also lead to the discovery of the network.

An automatic attack avoids communication among the agents and attacker altogether, and thus reducing the risk of detection. However, the parameters of the attack, including start time, attack type, target, are preprogrammed in the code. Examples of such predetermined attacks include the Blaster worm and the Code Red worm (see [4, 11]). Once a copy of the agents is captured and examined, parameters of the attacks will be known. In practice, such discovery usually happens well in advance of the attack. Hence, appropriate countermeasures such as employing extra physical resources (e.g. extra servers or high bandwidth links), or deploying experts at the victim site, can be carried out to mitigate the effects of the attack. For instance, it was discovered on 11th August 2003 that the Blaster worm had been preprogrammed to attack Microsoft's Windows Update website starting from 16th August 2003, thus giving Microsoft ample time to react[7].

Note that although the attacks are preprogrammed, usually a backdoor is still left open for further modification of the code. Nevertheless, communication will be much lower compared to the manual and semi-automatic method.

5   Covert Coordination in DDoS

A DDoS attack based on *covert coordination* would be much harder to defend against. In a covert coordination, a large collection of agents decide when to carry out a synchronized action, and the action to be performed. The coordination is covert in the following ways. (1) Activities, in particular communication among the agents, should be hidden and difficult to distinguish from normal activities. (2) The capture of one agent will not expose the identity of the other agents. (3) Finally, if an agent is captured, the action to be performed, and the time to carry out the action, will not be revealed.

A covert coordination can be achieved by using a pervasive random beacon. The coordination of DDoS can be carried out in the following way. Periodically, the agents obtain two random number r_1 and r_2. Within a weekday, except holiday, 4 random numbers corresponding to 4 major stock markets can be obtained. It is not necessary for the agents to access the beacon at the same time, since archive of the stock indices are readily available. From r_1 and possibly other parameters like the date, the agents determine whether to commence an attack. If an attack is to be launched, using r_2 and a predefined table, the actual time of the attack t, the attack type and the victim are determined.

The total number of random bits per beacon access depends on the design of r_1 and r_2. There is no need for a lot of bits. About 13 bits is sufficient, with 9 allocated to r_1 and 4 allocated to r_2. From the test described in Section 3, the DJIA alone provides 13 bits. If more bits are required, the other market indices can be used as well.

Independent Agents: Since each agent does not communicate with other agents or handlers, even if some of them are discovered, no information (e.g. IP addresses) that lead to the discovery of other agents will be revealed. Taking a few discovered agents offline will at most reduce the number of agents available for attacks, and will in no way disable the DDoS network.

Furthermore, the attacker's job is finished after the agent code is installed on the compromised machines. Thereafter, the attacker and the agents do not communicate with each other and hence is virtually impossible to trace based on the network traffic.

Agents Remain Hidden: Due to the pervasiveness of the beacon, it is difficult to distinguish an agent's beacon accesses from normal web-activities. During the coordination process, the only incoming and outgoing traffic used by agents are normal, well-formed HTTP requests and HTTP replies.

Detecting such activities could be easier in the agents' end, for instance, by an intrusion detection system in or near an agent. Furthermore, it is also easier to detect the agents by scanning the compromised hosts. Note that typically, DDoS attacks are carried out by agents who live in less secure hosts.

However, at the web-server, or any intermediate gateway in an Internet Service Provider(ISP), distinguishing such activities among legitimate usages would be difficult, even with the collaboration of several ISPs. Since the agents cannot be confidently identified, it is difficult to preempt the attack by blocking their web accesses.

Probabilistic Attack Parameters: If an agent is captured and its program is analyzed, the actual algorithm that determines the attack parameters (the attack time and type) will be revealed. However, the attack parameters will still remain probabilistic, since the beacon is unpredictable. Even if the beacon is closely monitored, the defenders will still have limited time to react. Such uncertainty places the defenders in a stressful situation. For instance, the additional hardwares and experts have to be on standby and be readily deployable for an extended period.

On the other hand, since the attack parameters are probabilistic, the attackers also do not have direct control over the agents and the actual DDoS attacks may not be successful. However, in the context of DDoS, the defenders generally suffer more than the attackers since the defenders have to be prepared for the worst case scenario. For example, the attacker may assign a small probability, say 2^{-11} of commencing attack in the earlier phase. The probability is small so as to provide sufficient time for the DDoS network to grow. Nevertheless, there is still a small possibility that an attack commences early. When the attack is launched too quickly, the chances that sufficient agents have been recruited might be low. When the existence of the agents and risks are known, even though the likelihood and damage may be low, the victims will still have to react immediately to prepare for the small chance that a successful DDoS attack could be launched.

6   Disrupting and Influencing the Beacons

In this section, we look at some mechanisms that disrupt the beacons.

6.1   Targeting the Reporting Services

It is well-accepted that it is difficult to manipulate or predict the stock indices. Furthermore, recall that a mixing function is applied to each index to obtain the random bits. This makes manipulation or prediction even more difficult, since a small perturbation of an index would lead to a different output.

While it is difficult to influence stock indices, it is relatively easier to influence the reporting of the indices. For instance, with sufficient incentive, a financial information provider may migrate its services to other web-sites and purposely provide wrong information in the original site. However, this measure is drastic and difficult to realize. Firstly, the provider may not be directly affected by the beacon and hence does not have strong motivation to make the change. Secondly, migrating the services will also disrupt business activities, and providing wrong information affects the provider's credibility and may create legal issues.

6.2   Misleading the Parser

If the actual program that accesses the beacon is made available, or in the context of DDoS, a copy of the agent is captured, then it can be analyzed for weaknesses. In particular, the preprogrammed parser that extracts the required information can be analyzed to find ways to mislead it, while keeping the content of the site unchanged. For example, it is possible that the parser may be unable to handle slight changes in reporting format, for instance, a change from "DJIA 10427.20" to "DJIA 10,427.20".

Another method is to craft the html page such that the preprogrammed parser will not only fail to obtain the required information, but obtain wrong information. For instance, placing false information in a commented section of the html page may mislead some parsers, but does not change the content presented to the human eye.

Since the above methods do not change the content of the web-pages, it may be easier to convince the service providers to collaborate in disrupting a particular way of beacon access. On the other hand, it is easy to improve the reliability of beacon access by simply using more than one website. Hence, many providers have to be convinced to implement the changes. This is not an easy task if numerous service providers are involved.

6.3   Using Hard AI to Disrupt the Beacon

Instead of storing and displaying the indices explicitly, they can be stored and displayed in a form that is easily recognized by human, but not by current computer programs. This is similar to the use of hard AI [13] and graphical Turing test [9] in securing web-access, where the decimal figures are displayed as a spatially "warped" or "distorted" image.

Another effective method stores the actual indices in a transformed form, and use a script to reconstruct it. For example, the string may be stored in a reversed order and it is reconstructed during display. Note that the reconstruction script has to be made available to the public including the agents, and hence it is still possible to obtain the information. Nevertheless, the burden of program flow analysis is passed to the access program, who has to be generic enough to obtain the correct information.

Although the above two methods are effective, they generate overhead in network delay and processing, and may be unable to serve some legitimate users due to browser's compatibility or users who turn off certain browser's capabilities. With the use of hard AI, the distorted image may also appear strange to the users. Such inconveniences could turn away users. Hence, these methods are not desirable for providers in a competitive business environment.

7   Conclusion

In this paper, we describe a pervasive random beacon that is based on the closing indices of major stock markets. Such a random beacon meets the requirements of being random, unpredictable, is highly available and allows covert access. We demonstrate how such a random beacon can be constructed and present a use of the beacon for covert coordination of DDoS attack. Finally, we also present ways where the operation of beacon can be disrupted.

References

[1] Y. Aumann and M.O. Rabin. Information theoretically secure communication in the limited storage space model. *CRYPTO 1999*, pages 65–79, 1999.

[2] C.H. Bennett, D.P. DiVincenzo, , and R. Linsker. Digital recording system with time-bracketed authentication by on-line challenges and method for authenticating recordings. *US Patent 5764769*, 1998.

[3] Charles H. Bennett and John A. Smolin. Trust enhancement by multiple random beacons. *The Computing Research Repository(CoRR) cs.CR/0201003*, 2002. `http://xxx.lanl.gov/archive/cs/intro.html`.

[4] Drew Copley, Riley Hassell, Barnaby Jack, Karl Lynn, Ryan Permeh, and Derek Soeder. Blaster worm analysis. *eEye Digital Security*, 2003. `http://www.eeye.com/`.

[5] Donald E. Eastlake. Rfc 2777: Publicly verifiable nomcom random selection. *Internet RFC/STD/FYI/BCP Archives*, 2000.

[6] U.M. Maurer. Conditionally-perfect secrecy and a provably secure randomized cipher. *Journal of Cryptology*, 5:53–66, 1992.

[7] Ellen Messmer. Update: Blaster worm infections spreading rapidly. *Network World Fusion*, 2003. `http://www.nwfusion.com/`.

[8] Jelena Mirkovic and Peter Reiher. A taxonomy of ddos attack and ddos defense mechanisms. *ACM SIGCOMM Computer Communications Review*, 34(2):39–54, 2004.

[9] William G. Morein, Angelos Stavrou, Debra L. Cook, Angelos D. Keromytis, Vishal Misra, and Dan Rubenstein. Using graphic turing tests to counter automated ddos attacks against web servers. *10th ACM Int. Conf. on Computer and Communications Security*, pages 8–19, 2003.

[10] Elchanan Mossel and Ryan O'Donnell. Coin flipping from a cosmic source: On error correction of truly random bits. To appear in Random Structures and Algorithms, 2004.

[11] Ryan Permeh and Marc Maiffret. ida "code red" worm analysis. *eEye Digital Security*, 2001. `http://www.eeye.com/`.

[12] M.O. Rabin. Transaction protection by beacons. *J. Computer and System Sciences*, 27(2):256–267, 1983.

[13] Luis von Ahn, Manuel Blum, Nicholas J. Hopper, and John Langford. Captcha: Using hard ai problems for security. *EUROCRYPT*, 2003.

[14] John Walker. ent. *Fourmilab Switzerland*, 1998. `http://www.fourmilab.ch/`.

Censorship Resistance Revisited*

Ginger Perng, Michael K. Reiter, and Chenxi Wang

Carnegie Mellon University, Pittsburgh PA, USA

Abstract. "Censorship resistant" systems attempt to prevent censors from imposing a particular distribution of content across a system. In this paper, we introduce a variation of censorship resistance (CR) that is resistant to selective filtering even by a censor who is able to inspect (but not alter) the internal contents and computations of each data server, excluding only the server's private signature key. This models a service provided by operators who do not hide their identities from censors. Even with such a strong adversarial model, our definition states that CR is only achieved if the censor must disable the entire system to filter selected content. We show that existing censorship resistant systems fail to meet this definition; that Private Information Retrieval (PIR) is necessary, though not sufficient, to achieve our definition of CR; and that CR is achieved through a modification of PIR for which known implementations exist.

1 Introduction

Digital censorship resistance, as defined by Danezis and Anderson [11], is the ability to prevent a third-party from imposing a particular distribution of documents across a system. Following the original work of Eternity service [2], a number of proposals have appeared in the literature to implement censorship resistant information services, including Tangler [27], Freenet [9], and Freehaven [12]. However, the term "censorship resistance" has never been formally defined. The most common definition is a variation of "Our system should make it extremely difficult for a third party to make changes to or force the deletion of published materials" [28]. What is meant by "extremely difficult" is subject to interpretation. As a result, it is challenging to precisely evaluate and compare the effectiveness of the various proposals.

In this paper, we present one possible formal definition of *censorship susceptibility*, the dual of censorship resistance. Informally, we define censorship susceptibility as the likelihood a third-party can restrict a targeted document while allowing at least one other document to be retrieved. Both our definition, and the threat model that it permits, refine various prior discussions of censorship resistance. First, while some prior works have included availability of the service as a necessary condition for censorship resistance (e.g., [2]), our definition decouples these notions (as does, e.g., Dagster [24]). As defined here, censorship susceptibility measures the extent to which an adversary can prevent *selected* content from being distributed. A service with low censorship susceptibility thus leaves the adversary only the option of completely shutting down the

---

* This research was supported in part by National Science Foundation Grant No. 0208853 and the NSF Graduate Research Fellowship.

service. While high availability, in a technical sense, is one approach to preventing this, it is not the only one; others include defeating efforts to shut down the service in court[1] and extreme social opposition[2]. As such, we find it useful to decouple the notions of censorship resistance and high availability.

A second distinction of our work is that the threat model we adopt grants the adversary more capabilities than prior works, and in this sense is conservative. First, we permit the adversary to identify the server(s); unlike many prior works in censorship resistance, we do not employ anonymization mechanisms, or, if they are employed, we presume that the adversary can break them (e.g., [17,25,29]) and discover the servers. Second, we permit the adversary to inspect every request to and response from the server, and even a transcript of the server's processing steps on the request, in order to reach a decision as to whether to filter (drop) the response. The *only* secret that the server is permitted to keep from the adversary is a digital signing key, which we argue is a necessity to keep the adversary from simply impersonating and effectively replacing the service to all clients. The only other limitation is that the adversary is not permitted to modify the server's contents. We are primarily interested in censorship resistance for documents which are legal to possess (and so it is not lawful for the adversary to remove them), but the distribution of which may be restricted; Church of Scientology scriptures and other lawfully purchased but copyrighted works are but two examples.

In this context, we conduct a foundational study of censorship susceptibility in an effort to relate it to known cryptographic primitives. Our primary results are as follows:

- Censorship Resistance (CR) implies Private Information Retrieval (PIR) [10,8,6]. That is, in order to implement CR (or more specifically, low censorship susceptibility), it is necessary to implement PIR.
- PIR does not imply CR. That is, not any implementation of PIR satisfies our definition of CR.
- CR can be achieved through a simple modification of PIR using digital signatures.

PIR is a cryptographic primitive that allows a user to query a database without revealing the index of the queried item. Our study shows that censorship resistance, as defined here, cannot be achieved with primitives weaker than PIR. Additionally, we show that PIR achieves a set of properties that are not sufficient to implement CR services, but that are sufficient when combined with digital signatures.

The rest of the paper is structured as follows: in Section 2, we discuss related work, in Section 3 we describe the system model and give a formal definition of censorship susceptibility. We analyze existing CR approaches using the definition in Section 4. We show a reduction from general CR to PIR in Section 5 and prove that PIR is not sufficient for CR in Section 6. In Section 7 we describe a system that implements CR. We conclude in Section 8.

---

[1] An example is the April 2003 U.S. federal court decision that file-sharing services Grokster and StreamCast networks were not culpable for illegal file trading over their networks, citing substantial uses in addition to copyright-infringing ones.

[2] The Chinese media control department, in 2001, reversed its prior decision to censor a Taiwanese TV series due to extreme popular demand.

2   Related Work

Our model of censorship resistance is similar to the all-or-nothing integrity (AONI) model proposed by Aspnes *et al* [3]. AONI is the notion of *document dependency* where the corruption of one document leads to the corruption of other documentsin the system. Their definition leads to an analysis of classes of adversaries in which AONI is not possible. Ours is a different formulation that more readily allows a reduction of CR to other cryptographic primitives (e.g., PIR). This allows us to make precise statements about the hardness of the problem and delineate the necessary cryptographic primitives to build a system that is indeed CR.

Danezis and Anderson proposed an economic model to evaluate censorship resistance of peer-to-peer systems [11]. They analyzed the effect of resource distribution schemes (random vs. discretionary) on the system's ability to resist censorship. Their model focuses on the economic values of censoring and anti-censoring. While the findings in [11] are interesting and can help shape future designs of censorship resistant systems, the goal of our study is somewhat different. We strive to understand the fundamental relationships between censorship resistance (as per the assumptions of our model) and other known cryptographic primitives as to permit the derivation of a formal security argument.

There exist numerous implementations of censorship resistant services [2,4,5,9,12,26,24,28,27]. We defer our discussion of those schemes to Section 4.

3   System Model and Definitions

In this section, we describe a formal definition of censorship susceptibility. We begin by describing the model of an information system to frame our discussion.

3.1   System Components and Interface

An information system, sys, includes the following components:

1. **Server:** A server is an entity that stores and responds to requests for (perhaps in conjunction with other servers) data. The server uses a signing oracle that encapsulates it private signature key.
2. **Document store:** A document store ds is a collection of servers that jointly provides information services. ds has a public key pk_{ds} such that pk_{ds} is the union of all servers' public keys.
3. **Client:** A client c is a process that queries the document store for documents.

Note that the private signature key is used solely for authentication. We discuss the ramifications of the private signature key in Section 3.2.

We now describe the system interface for information retrieval. We assume that there is a finite and static set of documents, DOC, in the system and that each document, $doc \in DOC$, is associated with some descriptive $name$ that uniquely identifies doc. The format of $name$ and the mapping between $name$ and doc is left intentionally undefined. We further assume a client, c executes an information retrieval function get such that

$$doc \leftarrow \mathsf{get}^{ds}(pk_{ds}, name)$$

to retrieve the document doc identified by $name$ from ds. We assume that ds signs all responses to queries, and as part of the get function, $\mathsf{get}(\cdot)$ verifies the response from ds with public key pk_{ds}.

3.2 Adversarial Model

A censorship resistance adversary $\mathcal{A}_{CR}$ wishes to remove a targeted document. $\mathcal{A}_{CR}$ is composed of two algorithms:

1. **Generator:** A generator G is an algorithm that outputs the $name$ of a targeted document and some state s to send to the filter.
2. **Filter:** A filter $f(\cdot)$ is an algorithm imposed upon a document store ds. $f(\cdot)$ takes in state s from G as input. $f(\cdot)$ may intercept, modify, or drop queries for and responses from ds. $f(\cdot)$ is allowed to examine the internal transcripts of the servers in the document store, but it cannot modify the state of the servers or the client side algorithm.

Note that $f(\cdot)$ models our adversary of interest. We assume that $f(\cdot)$ runs on each information server and the servers readily subject themselves to the filter's inspection. We assume that filters have full access to the server's communication and work logs. Modeling the server and the adversary in such a manner allows the conceptual formulation of a law-compliant server that willingly turns over all internal states to a third party censor (a filter). The only exception is the server's private signing key; the signing operation is modeled by a signature oracle whose internal state is hidden from outside view. We note that allowing the server to keep its signature key private is a reasonable assumption as it is used solely as an authentication mechanism. Furthermore, the disclosure of the signature key would allow the adversary to impersonate the server to clients using the service, thus defeating any other mechanisms to resist censorship.

We now discuss the changes in the $\mathsf{get}(\cdot)$ protocol when an adversarial filter $f(\cdot)$ is placed upon a document store ds. We define ds' as ds installed with the filter, $f(\cdot)$. More specifically, $ds' = f(\cdot)^{ds}$ where $f(\cdot)$ uses ds as an oracle to answer queries. The $\mathsf{get}(\cdot)$ function between client c and ds' is modified as follows:

1. $\mathsf{get}^{ds'}(pk_{ds}, name)$ constructs a query, $\mathsf{q}(name)$ and sends the query to ds'.
2. ds' receives the query from c. If the query is passed onto ds, ds performs some computations in response to the query (e.g, searching for the document, signing the response using its oracle, etc.), all of which are logged and viewable by $f(\cdot)$. ds' may or may not respond to $\mathsf{get}(\cdot)$.
3. If $\mathsf{get}(\cdot)$ receives an answer, it authenticates the response using pk_{ds} and performs the necessary client-side computation before outputting the document to c.

3.3   Definition

Informally, we define censorship susceptibility as the probability that an adversary can block a targeted document while allowing at least one other document to be retrieved. A system has low censorship susceptibility if the maximum *advantage* of any censorship resistance (CR) adversary is small. More formally:

Definition 1. *Let $A_{CR} = \langle G, f(\cdot) \rangle$ be a CR adversary. Let Name be the set of descriptive names that retrieve documents in ds, and $\perp$ be defined as an undefined or incorrect result. Name and pk_{ds} are public knowledge. A_{CR}'s advantage is:*

$$\mathbf{Adv}_{sys}^{CR}(A_{CR}) = \Pr[\perp \leftarrow \mathbf{get}^{ds'}(pk_{ds}, name) \mid (name, s) \leftarrow G^{ds}; \, ds' \leftarrow f(s)^{ds}] \, -$$
$$\min_{name' \in Name} [\Pr[\perp \leftarrow \mathbf{get}^{ds'}(pk_{ds}, name') \mid (name, s) \leftarrow G^{ds}; \, ds' \leftarrow f(s)^{ds}]]$$

The censorship susceptibility of a system is thus defined as:

$$\mathbf{Adv}_{sys}^{CR}(t, q) \overset{\text{def}}{=} \max_{A_{CR}} \{ \mathbf{Adv}_{sys}^{CR}(A_{CR}) \}$$

where the maximum is taken over all adversaries that run in time t and make at most q queries to its oracle, ds.

This definition states that for a system to be CR, there cannot exist an adversary who can block a certain document while allowing another to be retrieved. More specifically, generator G outputs the *name* of the *doc* it wishes to censor and passes s to $f(\cdot)$. Given a system *sys* with its document store installed with filter $f(s)$, *sys*'s censorship susceptibility is based on the probability that the filter successfully blocks *name* while not blocking some *name'*. If *sys* has low censorship susceptibility, then the adversary's only viable option is to institute a complete shut down of the service.

For the remainder of this paper, we omit specifications of t and q, as these values will be clear from context.

4   Analysis of Current CR Schemes

In this section we analyze current implementations of CR schemes based on the model described in Section 3. We briefly describe each mechanism first and then analyze its capability to resist censorship. Some of the interface descriptions are abbreviated as we only describe the parts that are integral to the discussion. In the discussions that follow, we loosely categorize the different CR proposals into four categories: data replication, anonymous communication, server deniability, and data entanglement.

4.1   Data Replication

Eternity Service: Eternity Service [2] provides censorship resistance through anonymous communication and data replication across multiple jurisdictions. The underlying premise is that a universal injunction across all jurisdictions is unlikely.

Freenet: Freenet [9] consists of volunteer servers that provide a document store. A document in Freenet is encrypted with a descriptive name as its key and requested using

Freenet's get($name$) interface where $name$ is its content key. Queries are forwarded to servers hosting names which offer the closest match to $name$. If the document is found, the server reverse-routes doc back to the client, and each server on the return route caches a copy of the document.

Gnutella: Gnutella [26] also uses data replication to resist censorship. Data replication in Gnutella is achieved primarily in a discretionary manner—data is replicated to users who request the data.

These schemes rely on replicating data either arbitrarily across the system or in some structured way (as in Freenet) to thwart a censor authority in its effort to locate and destroy all copies. While data replication will likely increase the cost of censorship [11], it is insufficient against the attacker model we described in Section 3.

Recall that we permit an adversarial filter to observe and inspect communications and internal processings of each information server. In effect, one can view the filters as the result of a universal injunction; thus, systems that rely solely on replication are not sufficient. In the case of Freenet, documents are referenced by a publicly known $name$. The filter can simply block any query with a particular $name$, thereby achieving censorship. We can calculate the censorship susceptibility of Freenet using the definition in Section 3.3; as each $name$ is uniquely mapped to a single document, the censorship susceptibility of Freenet by our definition is equal to 1. The censorship susceptibility of Gnutella and Eternity Service is similar.

In addition, censorship against both Freenet and Gnutella can be achieved without significant effort on the part of the censor. In Freenet, documents are only replicated along the retrieval route; if a document is not particularly popular, then its number of replicas will be limited. In peer-to-peer systems such as Gnutella that rely solely on discretionary replication, it has been shown that the system degenerates into a client-server model where most documents are replicated only on a subset of the peers [1]. As such, the cost of censorship can be significantly less than what is required to procure a universal injunction.

4.2 Anonymous Communication Systems

Many CR implementations rely on anonymous communication channels [7,13,20,21]. We discuss two such systems here.

Free Haven: Free Haven [12] is a peer-to-peer network that provides anonymity and document persistence. In Free Haven, each stored document is divided into shares that are signed with the document's private key. The shares are stored on a server along with the hash of the corresponding public key. Clients retrieve documents with a get($name$) interface where $name$ is the hash of the document's public key. A request is broadcast to the entire network; servers holding the matching key hash respond with the stored shares. The client recreates the file upon receiving a sufficient number of shares.

Anonymizing Censorship Resistant Systems: Serjantov [22] describes a peer-to-peer system that provides censorship resistance using Onion Routing [14]. Each peer in the system can act as a server, forwarder, or decrypter. Each stored document is divided into encrypted blocks and placed on multiple servers. A forwarder acts as an intermediary between the servers and a client; only a forwarder knows the mapping between the data blocks and the servers that store them. A decrypter is responsible for decrypting data blocks but does not have knowledge of the data-server mapping. In this system, *name* in the get(*name*) function encodes the set of forwarders and the labels of the encrypted blocks. All communications in this system are carried out on top of anonymous channels.

Both Free Haven and Serjantov's system rely on anonymous communication channels (e.g, [14], [18]) to resist censorship. Free Haven additionally migrates document shares periodically among servers to offer another level of protection [12]. Serjantov's system also uses data encryption to protect servers; the intuition is that if servers cannot decrypt the blocks they store, they cannot be prosecuted for storing certain data.

Unfortunately, in Free Haven one can easily identify the target document in a query using well known public keys. In Serjantov's system, the identities of the forwarders are in the public *name* of the document. A third party filter can easily deny queries associated with a particular key or in the latter case, simply deny queries to the particular forwarders found in *name*, thus achieving selective filtering. Similar to prior discussions, the censorship susceptibility of both systems is thus equal to 1.

We note that attacks against anonymous communication channels have been demonstrated (e.g., [17,19,25,29]). It is feasible that a censor authority could possess the resources to undermine current anonymous communication technology and discover the locations of the servers in the system.

4.3 Server Deniability

Publius: Publius [28] consists of a static set of servers hosting encrypted documents. The encrypted documents are stored onto multiple servers, each with a share of the document key. Because servers do not store the entire key for a particular document, and documents are stored encrypted, Publius suggests that it achieves *server deniability*, the ability for a server to deny knowledge of the hosted documents' contents. To retrieve *doc*, a Publius client use the get(*name*) function, where *name* is the Publius URL that encodes the hosting servers and the target document. A subset of those servers respond with the encrypted document and their key shares, the latter of which the client uses to reconstruct the key to decrypt the document.

Publius claims to be censorship resistant because servers cannot determine the content of its storage. However, since the Publius *name* (e.g., the URL) for a document is well known, a censor authority can easily locate the servers and filter the requests associated with a particular *name*.

4.4 Data Entanglement

Tangler: Tangler [27] is a network of servers that provide data storage. Censorship resistance is provided by "entangling" documents such that the removal of one document will result in the removal of other documents. In Tangler, each document is divided into blocks, each of which is *entangled* (using Shamir secret sharing [23]) with two arbitrary blocks in the system. Each entanglement creates two new blocks in addition to the two existing ones. A threshold number of entangled blocks reconstruct the original block. To retrieve a document, a client uses the get(*name*) function where *name* identifies the necessary blocks to reconstruct the document. Tangler servers periodically move blocks from server to server using consistent hashing [15].

Dagster: Dagster [24] is a single-server system with a similar goal to Tangler: prevent censorship resistance by "entangling" different documents. In Dagster, data is entangled in such a manner that the removal of a document results in the unavailability of the documents entangled with it.

Both Tangler and Dagster use data entanglement to offer protection against censorship. However, because only a limited number of blocks are used in a particular entanglement, an adversary can institute the removal of a document without visibly affecting the overall availability of the remaining documents. Per our definition in Section 3.3, the system censorship susceptibility is equal to 1.

4.5   Discussion

We note that our threat model grants the adversary more capabilities than prior work in that we allow the adversary power to impose universal policies across the system and capability to inspect internal server states. In situations where these assumptions do not hold, that is, servers do not voluntarily cooperate or jurisdiction boundaries prevent universal censor policies, the mechanisms analyzed in this section would offer certain protection against censorship. In those cases, the economic model [11] can be used to reason about their abilities to resist censorship.

5   CR Implies PIR

In this section, we show that CR implies Private Information Retrieval (PIR). This implication states that CR systems cannot be constructed with primitives weaker than PIR. We first introduce the PIR primitive. We then prove that CR implies PIR.

5.1   Preliminaries

Private Information Retrieval: A private information retrieval (PIR) scheme [6,8,10,16] is an interactive protocol between two entities: a database, DB, and a user, U. The goal of a PIR protocol is to allow U to query DB without revealing to DB the index of the queried item. DB holds a n-bit string $x \in \{1, 0\}^n$ which is indexed by $i \in \{1, ..., n\}$. U construct queries, $q(i)$, to retrieve the i-th bit, x_i, from DB. At the end of the protocol, two properties must hold:

1. Correctness: U has the correct value for x_i, and
2. User Privacy: DB has no knowledge of the retrieved index, i.

The user privacy of a PIR may be modeled as the advantage a PIR adversary has against the scheme. More formally, the advantage of a PIR adversary is defined as:

Definition 2. *The advantage an adversary, A_{PIR} has against a PIR protocol, P, is defined as:*

$$\mathbf{Adv}_{\mathrm{P}}^{\mathrm{PIR}}(A_{\mathrm{PIR}}) = \max_{i,j}[\Pr[A_{\mathrm{PIR}}(q(i)) = 1] - \Pr[A_{\mathrm{PIR}}(q(j)) = 1]]$$

where $i, j \in \{1 \ldots n\}$ are indices into the database. The advantage of the PIR protocol is thus defined as:

$$\mathbf{Adv}_P^{PIR}(t) \stackrel{\text{def}}{=} \max_{A_{PIR}}[\mathbf{Adv}_P^{PIR}(A_{PIR})]$$

where the maximum is taken over all adversaries that run in time t.

In the remainder of this paper, we omit the specifications of t, as its value will be clear from context.

Informally, the user privacy of a PIR protocol is modeled as the probability that an adversary can distinguish between queries for two different indices.

In the discussion below, we assume a PIR protocol similar to those in [8,10]. These protocols retrieve a block of bits per query, which permits us to draw a parallel between a document from a CR system and a block of bits from a PIR database.

5.2   CR Implies PIR

In this section, we construct a PIR protocol from a generic CR system. We define a PIR protocol built on top of a secure CR system, *sys*, as PIR-*sys*. We show that if there exists a PIR adversary against PIR-*sys* with significant advantage, then there exists a CR adversary against *sys* with significant advantage. More formally:

Theorem 1. $\forall A_{PIR}, \exists A_{CR} : \mathbf{Adv}_{sys}^{CR}(A_{CR}) \geq \mathbf{Adv}_{PIR\text{-}sys}^{PIR}(A_{PIR}).$

Proof. We prove the above theorem by constructing the PIR protocol, PIR-*sys*, from a generic CR system, *sys*.

A PIR protocol has two parties: a user U, and a database DB. To create the PIR protocol, we map the CR document store (ds) to DB, and allow U access to all of the functions available to the CR client. The set of retrievable documents in a CR system can be indexed from 1 to n, where $n = |DOC|$. We view this enumerated set of documents as the PIR data-string held by DB.

Recall from Section 3.1 that documents in the CR system are retrieved using descriptive names. Because a descriptive name uniquely identifies a document, we can map the set of descriptive names associated with a document to an index in the PIR database. A PIR query for index i, $q(i)$, simply becomes a combination of a lookup function to find a descriptive name that corresponds to the document at i and a call to the CR query function with the given descriptive name. The protocol for the PIR protocol is as follows:

1. U wishes to retrieve the document indexed at i from DB. He calls the mapping function, map(i), to get a descriptive name, $name$, corresponding to the document.
2. U uses $name$ to outputs a query, q$(name)$, using the query function of the CR system. Specifically, U performs get$^{ds}(pk_{ds}, name)$.
3. Upon receiving the query, ds performs its normal computations to return a response to U.
4. U performs the CR computations to reconstruct the document from the response.

We denote the described protocol as PIR-*sys*. We now prove that the two properties of PIR, correctness and user privacy, indeed hold for the resulting PIR protocol.

Correctness: Follows directly from the CR system. The PIR query is essentially a CR query.

User Privacy: To prove that our PIR scheme satisfies the property of user privacy, we show that the existence of a PIR adversary, A_{PIR}, implies the existence of a CR adversary, A_{CR} with at least the same advantage. Let us assume that there indeed exists an A_{PIR} that distinguishes between two indices with advantage, $\mathbf{Adv}^{PIR}_{PIR\text{-}sys}(A_{PIR})$. From A_{PIR}, we can build a CR adversary A_{CR}, whose advantage $\mathbf{Adv}^{CR}_{sys}(A_{CR})$ is at least that of A_{PIR}. Recall that $A_{CR} = \langle G, f(\cdot) \rangle$. The CR adversary works as follows:

1. A_{PIR} has two indices, i and j, where the PIR advantage is maximized. Namely,

$$\mathbf{Adv}^{PIR}_{PIR\text{-}sys}(A_{PIR}) = \Pr[A_{PIR}(q(i)) = 1] - \Pr[A_{PIR}(q(j)) = 1] \quad (1)$$

2. G designates i to be the target document *doc* and uses $\mathsf{map}(i)$ to find *name* such that $doc \leftarrow \mathsf{get}^{ds}(pk_{ds}, name)$.
3. G creates some state s to pass to $f(\cdot)$. For every query, $f(s)$ will function as follows:
   (a) $f(s)$ sends the received query q to A_{PIR}.
   (b) If A_{PIR} returns 1, $f(s)$ denies the query. Otherwise, $f(s)$ passes the query to ds.
4. G outputs $(name, s)$.

Recall from Section 3 that the goal of the CR adversary is to block a targeted document while allowing at least one other document to be retrieved. The CR adversary's advantage is calculated as:

$$\mathbf{Adv}^{CR}_{sys}(A_{CR}) = \Pr[\bot \leftarrow \mathsf{get}^{ds'}(pk_{ds}, name) \mid (name, s) \leftarrow G^{ds}; ds' \leftarrow f(s)^{ds}] -$$
$$\min_{name' \in Name} [\Pr[\bot \leftarrow \mathsf{get}^{ds'}(pk_{ds}, name') \mid (name, s) \leftarrow G^{ds}; ds' \leftarrow f(s)^{ds}]]$$

We label the two events in this advantage calculation as "A_{CR} block targeted" and "A_{CR} block not targeted" respectively. From our construction of PIR from CR, we see that

$$\Pr[A_{CR} \text{ block targeted}] = \Pr[A_{PIR}(q(i)) = 1] \quad (2)$$
$$\min_{name' \in Name} [\Pr[A_{CR} \text{ block not targeted}]] \leq \Pr[A_{PIR}(q(j)) = 1] \quad (3)$$

Thus, we have the following reduction:

$$\mathbf{Adv}^{CR}_{sys}(A_{CR}) = \Pr[A_{CR} \text{ block targeted}] - \min_{name' \in Name} [\Pr[A_{CR} \text{ block not targeted}]]$$
$$\geq \Pr[A_{PIR}(q(i)) = 1] - \Pr[A_{PIR}(q(j)) = 1]$$
$$\geq \mathbf{Adv}^{PIR}_{PIR\text{-}sys}(A_{PIR}) \quad (4)$$

This proof shows that CR implies PIR. Since the CR system sys is secure, and the PIR adversary's advantage is bound from above by the advantage of the CR advantage against sys, the PIR protocol, PIR-sys is secure. Thus, this theorem states that CR implies PIR. Consequently, CR systems cannot be built with primitives weaker than PIR.

6   PIR Does Not Implement CR

In this section, we sketch a proof of why PIR does not implement CR. In this proof, we use a specific implementation of computational PIR based on the Quadratic Residuosity Assumption [16]. We first describe the PIR implementation; we then show that using this PIR implementation trivially as the CR mechanism results in high censorship susceptibility.

6.1   PIR Scheme

The parties in the PIR protocol from [16] are identical to the generic PIR protocol described in Section 5.1. However, in this implementation, we view the database as a $s \times t$ matrix of bits (denoted by M). The target document is thus $M_{(a,b)}$, where a and b are the row and column indices, respectively. The following notation is used in describing the protocol:

- N is a natural number.
- $\mathbb{Z}_N^* \equiv \{x \mid 1 \leq x \leq N, \gcd(x, N) = 1\}$
- $H_k \equiv \{N | N = p_1 \cdot p_2 \text{ where } p_1, p_2 \text{ are } k/2\text{-bit primes}\}$
- $Q_N(y)$ denotes the quadratic residuosity predicate such that $Q_N(y) = 0$ if $\exists w \in \mathbb{Z}_N^* : w^2 = y \mod N$ and $Q_N(y) = 1$ otherwise.
- y is a QNR if $Q_N(y) = 1$, otherwise y is a QR.
- $J_N(y)$ denotes the Jacobi symbol of $y \mod N$. Note that if $J_N(y) = -1$, then y is QNR, and if $J_N(y) = 1$, then y can be QNR or QR.
- $\mathbb{Z}_N^1 \equiv \{y \in \mathbb{Z}_N^* | J_N(y) = 1\}$

The PIR protocol for U interested in $M_{(a,b)}$ is as follows:

1. U begins by picking a random k-bit number $N \in H_k$.
2. U selects t random values $y_1, ... y_t \in \mathbb{Z}_N^1$ such that y_b is a QNR and y_j is a QR for $j \neq b$. U sends $(y_1, ..., y_t, N)$ to DB and keeps N's factorization secret.
3. DB computes, for every row r, a number $z_r \in \mathbb{Z}_N^*$, as follows: It first computes $w_{r,j}$ such that $w_{r,j} = y_j^2$ if $M_{r,j} = 0$, and $w_{r,j} = y_j$ otherwise. It then computes

$$z_r = \prod_{j=1}^t w_{r,j}.$$

4. DB sends $z_1, ..., z_s$ to U.
5. U only considers z_a. Because $Q_N(xy) = Q_N(x) \oplus Q_N(y)$, z_a is QR iff $M_{(a,b)} = 0$. Since U knows the factorization of N, she can check whether z_a is a QR and thus retrieve bit $M_{(a,b)}$.

This protocol has been shown to be a secure PIR protocol under the Quadratic Residuosity Assumption[16]. In the discussion below, we denote this PIR protocol as QRA.

6.2   PIR Does Not Implement CR

We now show how the PIR scheme, QRA, does not implement CR. Consider a system that is a straightforward implementation of the PIR protocol, QRA. Namely, interpreting the PIR protocol as the CR system: the CR document store consists of one-bit documents, the "descriptive names" of the documents are the indices into the data string, and the CR get($\cdot$) function is the PIR query function. Let n be the size of the PIR database. We have the following theorem:

Theorem 2. $\exists\, DB\; :\; \mathbf{Adv}^{CR}_{QRA}(A_{CR}) = 1$

Proof. Assume that the CR adversary wishes to censor the document, $M_{(a,b)}$. As described in Section 3, the filter, $f(\cdot)$, may modify the query, but it may not change the retrieval algorithm of the server. We show an implementation of $f(\cdot)$ that modifies client queries to censor $M_{(a,b)}$. The filter works as follows:

1. $f(\cdot)$ receives query $(y_1, ..., y_t, N)$. $f(\cdot)$ creates a $y' = z^2$ where $z \leftarrow_R \mathbb{Z}_N^*$.
2. $f(\cdot)$ replaces y_b (where b is the column that holds the bit the filter wishes to censor) with y'.
3. $f(\cdot)$ forwards the modified query, $(y_1, ...y', ..., y_t, N)$ to DB.

We now calculate the censorship susceptibility of the system. Let us assume that the PIR database holds the value 0 for all indices other than (a, b). For the bit $M_{(a,b)}$, the value is 1. Recall that an adversary's censorship susceptibility advantage is calculated as follows:

$$\mathbf{Adv}^{CR}_{sys}(A_{CR}) = \Pr[A_{CR}\text{ block targeted}] - \min_{name' \in Name} \Pr[A_{CR}\text{ block not targeted}].$$

where $sys = $ QRA. From the filter we created, the probability of "A_{CR} block targeted" is calculated as:

$$\Pr[A_{CR}\text{ block targeted}] = \Pr[M_{(a,b)} = 1] \tag{5}$$

The filter algorithm replaces y_b with y' for every query that it sees. Because y' is guaranteed to be a QR, regardless of the value stored on the database, the modified query result always returns a QR, effectively returning a 0. Since our database is such that $M_{(a,b)} = 1$, this modification guarantees that the client is unable to retrieve the correct bit. Therefore, the probability that the filter blocks the targeted bit is equal to 1.

Using a similar argument, we can calculate $\Pr[A_{CR}\text{ block not targeted}]$. Let $M_{(a',b')}$ be the bit the client wishes to retrieve. If $b' = b$, then the filter's modification of y_b to y' results in $M_{(a',b')}$ being returned as a 0. Since the database values have been chosen such that only $M_{(a,b)}$ equals 1, a modification of y_b to y' does not affect results for $M_{(a',b)}$ since $M_{x,y} = 0\; \forall x \neq a, y \neq b$. In this case, $\Pr[A_{CR}\text{ block not targeted}]$ is equal to 0.

From our calculations, the censorship susceptibility of this CR protocol is 1. Thus, PIR does not trivially implement CR.

Combining the result of this theorem with Theorem 5.2, we have shown that PIR is necessary but not sufficient to implement CR.

7   A CR Implementation

In this section, we show a CR implementation by modifying any generic PIR protocol.

In Section 6, we showed that PIR does not implement CR. A filter can simply modify client queries to censor a targeted document. We show a modification of the PIR protocol such that client queries cannot be altered without detection.

A client, c, can detect if her request has been altered if ds simply includes c's request in its reply to c. ds can digitally sign each message with its response and c's request. Thus, c's get$(\cdot)$ verifies that the request it generated is unaltered and that the response comes from ds. If the query has been altered, then get$(\cdot)$ fails to retrieve the document. We denote this new CR system as sys+S.

For the following theorem, we implement the CR system, sys, using a generic PIR protocol, P. Our modification leads us to the following theorem:

Theorem 3. $\forall A_{CR}, \exists A_{PIR} : \mathbf{Adv}_P^{PIR}(A_{PIR}) \geq \mathbf{Adv}_{P+S}^{CR}(A_{CR}).$

Proof. Recall the document retrieval protocol from Section 3. $f(\cdot)$ may modify the query before it invokes ds for a response, and $f(\cdot)$ may drop the query after ds finishes computing its answer for the query. However, because ds includes c's query in its digitally signed response, $f(\cdot)$ is unable to modify the query without c detecting the modification. Thus, $f(\cdot)$'s only viable option is to drop queries. Given that the CR system, P+S, uses a generic PIR protocol, P, as its underlying retrieval protocol, we prove that if A_{CR} has some advantage, $\mathbf{Adv}_{P+S}^{CR}(A_{CR})$, then there exists a PIR adversary with advantage, $\mathbf{Adv}_P^{PIR}(A_{PIR})$ against P.

Similar to Section 6, we assume that documents in the CR system are one-bit documents, and the "descriptive names" of the documents are the indices for a PIR datastring. The PIR adversary works as follows:

1. Given $(name, s) \leftarrow G$, A_{PIR} finds the corresponding index, i, that maps to $name$.
2. For any query q, A_{PIR} passes q to $f(s)$. If $f(s)$ drops the request or response, A_{PIR} outputs 1. Otherwise, A_{PIR} outputs 0.

Recall from Section 5 that the CR adversary's advantage is calculated as:

$$\mathbf{Adv}_{P+S}^{CR}(A_{CR}) = \Pr[A_{CR} \text{ block targeted}] - \min_{name' \in Name} [\Pr[A_{CR} \text{ block not targeted}]] .$$

Recall that the PIR adversary's advantage is defined as:

$$\mathbf{Adv}_P^{PIR}(A_{PIR}) = \max_{i,j} [\Pr[A_{PIR}(q(i)) = 1] - \Pr[A_{PIR}(q(j)) = 1]] .$$

We can see from our construction of the PIR adversary that:

$$\Pr[A_{PIR}(q(i)) = 1] = \Pr[A_{CR} \text{ block targeted}]$$

$$\exists j : \Pr[A_{PIR}(q(j)) = 1] = \min_{name' \in Name} \Pr[A_{CR} \text{ block not targeted}]$$

Thus, we have the following reduction:

$$\mathbf{Adv}_P^{PIR}(A_{PIR}) = \max_{i,j} [\Pr[A_{PIR}(q(i)) = 1] - \Pr[A_{PIR}(q(j)) = 1]]$$

$$= \Pr[A_{CR} \text{ block targeted}] - \min_{name' \in Name} \Pr[A_{CR} \text{ block not targeted}]$$

$$= \mathbf{Adv}_{P+S}^{CR}(A_{CR}) \tag{6}$$

8 Conclusion

In this paper, we introduced a formal definition for censorship susceptibility. Intuitively a system with low censorship susceptibility is censorship resistant. Our definition provides a framework with which to evaluate different designs of censorship resistant information services. In this work, we adopt an aggressive threat model, allowing the possibility of a universal injunction and voluntary cooperation of servers with external censor authorities. We show that many current implementations of CR services do not satisfy censorship resistance under this threat model.

Our model allows us to prove intrinsic relationships between the property of censorship resistance and the cryptographic primitive of Private Information Retrieval (PIR). We show that PIR is necessary for censorship resistance, but does not trivially implement CR. We then show an implementation using PIR that does meet our definition of censorship resistance.

References

1. E. Adar and B. A. Huberman. Free Riding on Gnutella. *First Monday*, **5**(10), October 2004.
2. R. J. Anderson. The Eternity Service. *Pragocrypt*, 1996.
3. J. Aspnes, J. Feigenbaum, A. Yampolskiy, and S. Zhong. Towards a Theory of Data Entanglement. *European Symposium on Research in Computer Security*, September 2004.
4. A. Back. The eternity service. *Phrack Magazine*. *http://www.cypherspace.org/ adam/eternity/phrack.html.*, 7:51, 1997.
5. T. Benes. The strong eternity service. *Information Hiding Workshop*, April 2001.
6. C. Cachin, S. Micali, and M. Stadler. Computationally Private Information Retrieval with Polylogarithmic Communication. *Eurocrypt*, 1999.
7. D. Chaum. Untraceable electronic mail, return addresses, and digital pseudonyms. *Communications of the ACM*, **24**(2):84-88. ACM Press, 1981.
8. B. Chor and N. Gilboa. Computationally Private Information Retrieval. *Symposium on Theory of Computing*, 1997.
9. I. Clarke, O. Sandberg, B. Wiley, and T. W. Hong. Freenet: A distributed anonymous information storage and retrieval system. *Workshop on Design Issues in Anonymity and Unobservability*, 2000.
10. D. A. Cooper and K. P. Birman. Preserving Privacy in a Network of Mobile Computers. *IEEE Symposium on Security and Privacy*, 1995.
11. G. Danezis and R. Anderson. The Economics of Censorship Resistance. *Workshop on Economics and Information Security*, 2004.
12. R. Dingledine, M. J. Freedman, and D. Molnar. The Free Haven project: distributed anonymous storage service. *Workshop on Design Issues in Anonymity and Unobservability*, 2001.
13. M. J. Freedman and R. Morris. Tarzan: A Peer-to-Peer Anonymizing Network. *ACM Conference on Computer and Communications Security*, 2002.
14. D. Goldschlag, M. Reed, and P. Syverson. Onion Routing for Anonymous and Private Internet Connections. *Communications of the ACM*, **42**(2):39-41. ACM Press, 1999.
15. D. Karger, E. Lehman, T. Leighton, M. Levine, D. Lewin, and R. Panigraphy. Consistent Hashing and Random Trees: Distributed Caching Protocols for Relieving Hot Spots. *ACM Symposium on Theory of Computing*, 1997.
16. E. Kushilevitz and R. Ostrovsky. Replication Is Not Needed: Single Database, Computationally-Private Information Retrieval. *IEEE 38th Annual Symposium on Foundations of Computer Science*, 1997.

17. B. N. Levine, M. K. Reiter, C. Wang, and M. Wright. Timing Attacks in Low-Latency Mix Systems. *Financial Cryptography*, 2004.
18. D. Mazieres and M. F. Kaashoek. The Design and Operation of an E-mail Pseudonym Server. *ACM Conference on Computer and Communications Security*, 1998.
19. J.-F. Raymond. Traffic Analysis: Protocols, Attacks, Design Issues, and Open Problems. *Workshop on Design Issues in Anonymity and Unobservability*, 2000.
20. M. G. Reed, P. F. Syverson, and D. M. GoldSchlag. Proxies for anonymous routing. *12th Annual Computer Security Applications Conference*, 1996.
21. M. K. Reiter and A. D. Rubin. Crowds: Anonymity for Web Transactions. *ACM Transactions on Information and System Security*, 1(1):66–92.
22. A. Serjantov. Anonymizing censorship resistant systems. *International Workshop on Peer-to-Peer Systems*, 2002.
23. A. Shamir. How to share a secret. *Communications of the ACM*, **22**(11):612-613. ACM Press, 1979.
24. A. Stubblefield and D. S. Wallach. *Dagster: Censorship-Resistant Publishing Without Replication*. Technical Report TR01-380. Rice University, July 2001.
25. P. Syverson, G. Tsudik, M. Reed, and C. Landwehr. Towards an Analysis of Onion Routing Security. *Workshop on Design Issues in Anonymity and Unobservability*, 2000.
26. Gnutella. http://gnutella.wego.com.
27. M. Waldman and D. Mazieres. Tangler: A Censorship Resistant Publishing System Based on Document Entanglement. *ACM Conference on Computer and Communication Security*, 2001.
28. M. Waldman, A. D. Rubin, and L. F. Cranor. Publius: A robust, tamper-evident, censorship-resistant web publishing system. *USENIX Security Symposium*, 2000.
29. M. Wright, M. Adler, B. N. Levine, and C. Shields. An Analysis of the Degradation of Anonymous Protocols. *ISOC Network and Distributed Security Symposium*, 2002.

Optimal Embedding for Watermarking
in Discrete Data Spaces

Stéphane Bounkong, Borémi Toch, and David Saad

Aston University, Neural Computing Research Group, Information Engineering,
Birmingham B4 7ET, United Kingdom
{bounkons, tochb, d.saad}@aston.ac.uk
http://www.ncrg.aston.ac.uk/

Abstract. In this paper, we address the problem of robust information embedding in digital data. Such a process is carried out by introducing modifications to the original data that one would like to keep minimal. It assumes that the data, which includes the embedded information, is corrupted before the extraction is carried out. We propose a principled way to tailor an efficient embedding process for given data and noise statistics.

1 Introduction

In this work, we assume that the original host data to be modified is represented as a random vector C of N i.i.d.[1] scalars denoted c_j with $j \in [1, N]$. Each scalar c_j is an integer in $I_n = [1, n]$. Let us denote p_i the probability for an element c_j to be equal to i with $i \in I_n$,

$$p_i = P(c_j = i). \tag{1}$$

The information to be embedded refers to the message and is represented by a bit string

$$M = \{m_1, m_2, \ldots, m_j, \ldots\}, \text{ with } m_j \in \mathscr{M} \text{ and } \mathscr{M} = \{-1, 1\}. \tag{2}$$

For simplicity, we assume that the scalars c_j are modified independently of each other and that a single message bit m_j is embedded per scalar. Thus, the length of the message M is equal to the length N of the digital data C. As shown later, this simplification is in no way restricting the approach presented. An extension of the proposed approach to a more general case is outlined in Sect. 5. We assume furthermore that $m_j = 1$ and $m_j = -1$ are equally likely and that m_j is independent of c_j.

We denote $Q : \mathscr{M} \times I_n \to I_n$, the embedding process of a message bit m_j in the data c_j, $A : I_n \to I_n$, the corruption process which is assumed to be stochastic, and $W : I_n \to \mathscr{M}$, the extraction process. In the following sections,

---

[1] Independent identically distributed.

M. Barni et al. (Eds.): IH 2005, LNCS 3727, pp. 77–90, 2005.

we focus on finding an efficient embedding Q given the corruption process A, the probability distribution p_i and a fixed extraction process W. The extraction process W considered is deterministic and independent of the corruption process A. It can be characterised by the set $\mathcal{U}$ composed of the elements of I_n such that $\forall a \in \mathcal{U}, W(a) = 1$. The complementary set of $\mathcal{U}$ is denoted $\tilde{\mathcal{U}}$ and $\forall b \in \tilde{\mathcal{U}}, W(b) = -1$.

In this work, the performance of the embedding process Q and the distortion it introduces are quantified respectively by the probability of the extracted information $\hat{m}_j$ to be equal to the embedded information m_j,

$$P(\hat{m}_j = m_j), \text{ with } \hat{m}_j = W(A(Q(m_j, c_j))) \tag{3}$$

and

$$\hat{\mathcal{D}}(Q) = \sum_{c_j \in I_n} p_{c_j} D(c_j, Q(m_j, c_j)), \tag{4}$$

where D is an arbitrary symmetric definite positive scalar distortion measure such that

$$\left(\hat{\mathcal{D}}(Q) = 0\right) \Rightarrow \left(\forall (m_j, c_j) \in \mathcal{M} \times I_n, Q(m_j, c_j) = c_j\right). \tag{5}$$

1.1   Related Work

In the past few years, several studies were devoted to information embedding processes. Related work on quantisation based embedding techniques can be found in [1,2,3,4,5].

The basic approach relies on disjoint quantisation grids, which are regular in most of these studies. Each of them corresponds to a different message to be embedded, such as -1 and 1 in the case of binary messages. Then, the embedding process consists of two steps: first, select the quantisation grid corresponding to the message to be embedded, and then map the data c_j to the nearest quantisation point of the chosen grid. The extraction process is relatively straightforward: find the nearest quantisation point[2] to the data c_j (in which information has been embedded); the information associated to the chosen grid gives the extracted message.

Such an approach is quite efficient, when the noise level is low compared to the characteristic size[3] Δ of the quantisation grids, and has been shown to be asymptotically optimal in [3]. Moreover, this technique does not need the original data to extract the embedded data. Only knowledge of the quantisation grids[4] is required for the embedding and the extraction processes.

However, the performance of this approach degrades significantly as the ratio between Δ and the noise level decreases. The use of a larger Δ increases this

---

[2] Among all quantisation points of all grids.
[3] Which usually corresponds to the minimum distance between two quantisation points of two different grids.
[4] Which is limited to Δ and a reference point of each grid if the grids are regular.

ratio, but it also increases the distortion introduced by the embedding process Q. Thus, to keep the distortion constant, one has to give up the naive mapping of data c_j to the grid's quantisation points as in [3,4,5]. These new techniques, based on an ad-hoc mapping, show significantly improved results. However, due to the heuristic nature of their design, their performance could easily be improved further as shown in [1,2].

1.2   Relation to This Work

Here, we would like to stress the similarity between the suggested framework and that of the techniques presented earlier. In both frameworks, the choice of quantisation grids usually determines completely the extraction process W and its two characteristic sets $\mathcal{U}$ and $\widetilde{\mathcal{U}}$ in the case of a binary message. The extraction process W is therefore known beforehand and can be taken into account in the design of the embedding process Q; this facilitates the approach we are suggesting.

Furthermore, the techniques of [3,4] typically include a parameter, which is tuned with respect to the noise properties. Such optimisation allows to choose the best embedding process Q within a given family. Here, we argue that if noise properties are known in advance, we might as well look for the optimal embedding process Q without restricting it to a predefined family of embedding processes. Note that in most practical cases, the noise properties are not known beforehand, it is therefore important to examine the performance of embedding techniques, when the actual noise is different from the expected one.

In this paper, we present a principled method to find the optimal embedding process Q. We also show that its application to practical cases results in an improved extraction performance compared to existing approaches.

2   Embedding Process

In order to find an optimal embedding process, we propose an iterative and constructive algorithm. This algorithm is guaranteed to converge after a certain number of iterations that depends on p_i, the distortion measure D (see Eq. (4)) and the allowed embedding distortion denoted by $\mathcal{D}$. Since statistical properties of the message m_j and of the data c_j are identical for all indices j, these indices will be omitted in all notations, thus $m = m_j$, $\hat{m} = \hat{m}_j$ and $c = c_j$. The embedding process result $Q(m, c)$ depends on the message to be embedded m and the data value c. In the following, the algorithm is presented for a given value of m and the associated quantisation grid. In order to obtain the full embedding process Q, the algorithm has to be applied to all possible values of the message m.

2.1   Intuitive Explanation

A complete and rigorous proof of optimality of this algorithm can be found in Appendix A or in [1]. Here, we shall only give an intuitive explanation to motivate the procedure.

In this algorithm, we start with an embedding process Q equal to the identity function and try to improve it at each iteration with respect to $P(\hat{m} = m)$. The allowed embedding distortion limits the possible modifications of Q, which need to be chosen with care. Therefore, only modifications, which increase $P(\hat{m} = m)$, are of interest as specified in Eq. (7) below. Furthermore, we would like to optimise the modification with respect to the additional embedding distortion introduced. In other words, among all possible modifications of Q, we want to select the one with the best ratio between the improvement of $P(\hat{m} = m)$ and the additional embedding distortion introduced as given in Eq. (6), referring to the explicit expressions detailed in Sec. 2.2.

If such modification does not exist, then the algorithm stops. If this modification exists but results in an embedding distortion greater than $\mathscr{D}$, a probabilistic mapping is used as in Eq. (10), which also terminates the algorithm. Otherwise, the modification is carried out as in Eq. (9) and the procedure is repeated from step 2.

The convergence of the algorithm is straightforward since the embedding distortion is strictly increasing at each iteration by at least $\min_{c \neq c'} D(c', c)$ and is upper bounded by $\mathscr{D}$. An upper bound to the number of iterations for the procedure can also be easily obtained as a function of $\mathscr{D}$, $\min_i p_i$ and of $\min_{c \neq c'} D(c', c)$, as in [1].

2.2   Optimisation Algorithm

1. First, set $Q(m, c) = c$ for all $c \in I_n$, thus $\hat{\mathscr{D}}(Q) = 0$.
2. Then, find the couple (c_*, c'_*) such that

$$(c_*, c'_*) = \underset{(c,c') \in I_n^2}{\operatorname{argmax}} \left(\frac{P(W(A(c')) = m) - P(\hat{m} = m)}{D(c', c) - D(Q(m, c), c)} \right) \qquad (6)$$

such that
$$P(W(A(c'_*)) = m) - P(\hat{m} = m) > 0, \qquad (7)$$

where $\hat{m} = W(A(Q(m, c)))$.
3. If no such couple is found the algorithm terminates. If such a couple is found and

$$\hat{\mathscr{D}}(Q) + p_{c_*}(D(c'_*, c_*) - D(Q(m, c_*), c_*)) \leq \mathscr{D}, \qquad (8)$$

then we modify Q by setting

$$Q(m, c_*) = c'_*, \qquad (9)$$

and the algorithm repeats from step 2. Finally, if such a couple is found but Eq. (8) is not satisfied, this means that the remaining distortion allowed is insufficient to proceed as in Eq. (9). Thus, we modify Q by setting

$$Q(m, c_*) = \begin{cases} c'_*, & \text{with probability } p, \\ d, & \text{otherwise,} \end{cases} \qquad (10)$$

where d is the value of $Q(m, c_*)$ at the previous iteration and where the probability p is the ratio between the remaining embedding distortion allowed and the distortion difference between a mapping to c'_* and d,

$$p = \frac{\mathscr{D} - \hat{\mathscr{D}}(Q)}{D(c'_*, c_*) - D(d, c_*)} . \tag{11}$$

This also terminates the algorithm.

3   An Example

In this section, the proposed algorithm is applied to a practical case. We assume that the extraction is based on two[5] disjoint regular grids such that the distances of a grid point to the points immediately greater and lower on the other grid are equal. The extracted message $\hat{m}_j$ is given by the nearest grid point message as described in Sect. 1.1.

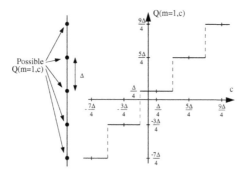

Fig. 1. The DM embedding function [3] for $m = 1$. For $m = -1$, the embedding functions obtained are slightly shifted towards the left by $-\Delta/2$.

An example of two well-known embedding functions [3] is given by

$$Q_{DM}(m, c) = \left\{ \mathrm{round}\left(\frac{c}{\Delta} - \frac{m}{4} \right) + \frac{m}{4} \right\} \Delta , \tag{12}$$

for Dither Modulation (DM) embedding function and by

$$Q(m, c) = \alpha Q_{DM}(m, c) + (1 - \alpha)c . \tag{13}$$

for Distortion Compensated DM (DC-DM) function. Both are represented in Fig. 1 and Fig. 2. These embedding functions[6] based on regular quantisation grids, are Δ-periodic up to a shift on the y-axis. Due to the regularity of the

---

[5] One for each of the possible messages $m_j \in \mathscr{M}$.
[6] Which correspond to the description given in Sect. 1.1.

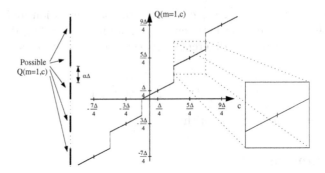

Fig. 2. The DC-DM embedding function [3] for $m = 1$. For $m = -1$, the embedding functions obtained are slightly shifted towards the left by $-\Delta/2$.

extraction process W, the embedding processes Q derived from the application of the proposed algorithm are also regular. Thus, we shall plot only a reduced part as framed in Fig. 2 for the DC-DM technique.

Now, the task is to find an optimal embedding process Q for a given noise model. In the following example, a discrete Gaussian noise distribution of mean 0 and of standard deviation σ is used. Quantisation grids of two different minimum distance values Δ have been tested. The embedding distortion measure used is given by

$$\hat{\mathscr{D}}(Q) = \sum_{c \in I_n} p_c \big(Q(m,c) - c \big)^2, \tag{14}$$

while the watermark to noise ratio (WNR) in decibel (dB), which quantifies the relative strength between the watermark and the noise distortion, is given by

$$WNR = 10 \log_{10} \left(\frac{\hat{\mathscr{D}}(Q)}{\sigma^2} \right). \tag{15}$$

The resulting optimised embedding processes are plotted in Fig. 3 and Fig. 4 for various watermark-to-noise ratios. Although they may look quite different,

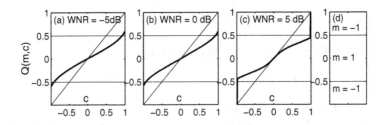

Fig. 3. Optimised embedding functions for $m = 1$, $\Delta = 2$, $\mathscr{D} = 1/12$ and various WNR. The plain thick line represents the embedding function while the identity function is given as reference by the plain thin line. The extraction areas are also given in (d).

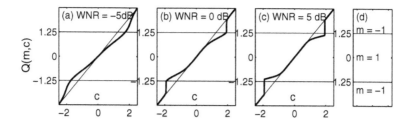

Fig. 4. Optimised embedding functions for $m = 1$, $\Delta = 5$, $\mathscr{D} = 1/12$ and various WNR. The plain thick line represents the embedding function while the identity function is given as reference by the plain thin line. The extraction areas are also given in (d).

some insights can be derived from their similarities and differences. First, note that the result of the embedding process $Q(m = 1, c)$ is always closer to the centre 0 of the area associated to $m = 1$ than the original data c. This can be explained by the Gaussian noise probability density function, which is bell shaped and centred at 0.

Then, note that if the original data c is closer to 0 than the original data c', then so will $Q(m = 1, c)$ with respect to $Q(m = 1, c')$. This can be explained by two factors: the bell shape of the noise distribution and the quadratic nature of the embedding distortion measure given in Eq. (14). Indeed, as $Q(m = 1, c)$ is getting closer to 0, the additional improvement of the extraction in the sense of $P(\hat{m} = m)$ decreases. Moreover, as the distance between $Q(m = 1, c)$ and c increases, the additional embedding distortion also increases.

When the allowed embedding distortion $\mathscr{D}$ is limited, these two factors usually result in a reduced embedding distortion when c is either close to 0 as in Fig. 3 and Fig. 4 or very far to 0 as in Fig. 4. Note that the distortion always appears where it is more effective in improving $P(\hat{m} = m)$, such as at the borders of the extraction areas.

Compared to the embedding functions presented in Fig. 1 and Fig. 2, the embedding processes we obtained in Fig. 3 and Fig. 4 use more efficiently the embedding distortion allowance $\mathscr{D}$. Indeed, in the DM and DC-DM techniques, significant amounts of this allowance is wasted for data far from 0. The consequences of these differences are discussed in the following section.

4   Performance Comparison

As mentioned previously, the DC-DM technique are based on a real parameter $\alpha \in [0, 1]$ that can be optimised with respect to the noise properties (for any WNR value). Moreover, one can define this parameter α as a function of the quantisation grid size Δ and of the embedding distortion $\mathscr{D}$ as

$$\alpha = \frac{\sqrt{12\mathscr{D}}}{\Delta}. \tag{16}$$

When the optimal α is used for the embedding, the DC-DM technique is also referred to the SCS embedding[7] [4]. Similarly, given a noise model, our algorithm can be used with different quantisation grid size Δ, resulting in an optimised embedding process for each Δ. When the optimal Δ is used for the embedding, the embedding process derived by our algorithm is termed Discrete Embedding Scheme (DES).

4.1 Capacity

In this section, the capacities of the SCS and DES schemes are considered. Both schemes are based on scalar quantisers and parameterised by Δ and/or α, which are related for a fixed distortion as shown in Eq. (16). From the general expression of the capacity for communication with side information found in [6], it can be derived that the capacity of the SCS and DES schemes is expressed as follows [4]

$$C = \max_{\Delta} I\big(A(Q(m,c)), m\big), \tag{17}$$

where $I(A(Q(m,c)), m)$ is the mutual information [7] between the received data $A(Q(m,c))$ and the embedded message m.

In the case where the decoding process W consists in decoding to the nearest grid point, the maximal mutual information is given by

$$K = \max_{\Delta} I(\hat{m}, m), \tag{18}$$

where $\hat{m} = W(A(Q(m,c)))$ is the decoded message. This decoding is clearly suboptimal, but it is nevertheless a very simple technique which is widely used and its investigation provides useful insight into the performance of the various methods.

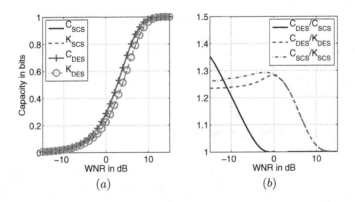

Fig. 5. Capacity of the QIM, SCS and DES embedding processes against a Gaussian noise for various WNR values

---

[7] Scalar Costa Scheme.

The capacity C and the maximal mutual information K for the SCS and DES schemes are plotted in Fig. 5a, while various ratios between these measures are presented in Fig. 5b. These figures show that for positive WNR values, the DES and SCS schemes have very similar capacity values. They also reveal that the SCS scheme is outperformed for negative WNR values.

Both figures also confirm that decoding to the nearest quantisation grid point is suboptimal except for very large WNR values (above 12 dB). As shown in Fig. 5b, the discrepancy between C and K is fairly important for negative WNR values. Hence, significant improvement might be achievable by an optimised decoder.

It can also be noticed that for negative WNR values, this decoding provides higher performance for the DES scheme than for the SCS scheme. This improvement is most likely due to the fact that the DES embedding process is optimised for this decoding, while the SCS embedding function is not.

4.2   Decoding Error Probability

In this section, both DES and SCS are optimised with respect to the decoding error probability.

The performance of the DM, SCS and DES embedding processes are plotted in Fig. 6 for a Gaussian noise model and various WNR values. As seen in Fig. 6, the DM embedding function is significantly outperformed by both the SCS and the DES embedding processes, while the latter is only slightly better than SCS. That basically means that, for this noise model and range of parameters used, one degree of freedom is sufficient for the DC-DM method to achieve very good results, when it can adapt to the actual noise.

However, as we suggested it earlier, this is not a practical case. In most cases, the actual noise characteristics are unknown at the embedding stage. Thus, the performance of an embedding technique has to be tested for a range of noise properties beyond those it has been tuned for. For instance, the quantisation grid size Δ cannot be adapted to the actual noise. Indeed, the embedding occurs before the transmission and hence before any transmission corruption.

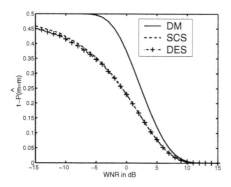

Fig. 6. Performance of the DM, SCS and DES embedding processes against a Gaussian noise for various WNR values

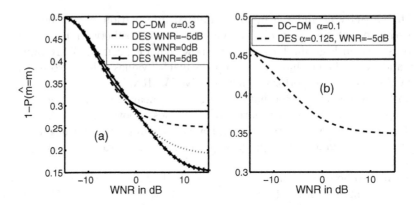

Fig. 7. Performance of the DC-DM and DES embedding processes against a Gaussian noise for various WNR values and fixed parameters

In the following experiments, we simulate such practical cases. Both schemes are given a set of fixed parameters, which are optimal for a WNR value, and compared on the whole range of WNR values.

In the first experiment described in Fig. 7a, both DC-DM and DES schemes are optimised for a WNR value of -5 dB. The optimal α is 0.3 for both. Moreover, for comparison purpose, the performance of the DES scheme for $\alpha = 0.3$ and expected WNR values of 0 dB and 5 dB are also plotted. When the DES scheme is optimised with expected WNR values of -5 dB or 0 dB, it has the same performance as the DC-DM scheme for an actual WNR of -5 dB. However, if the actual WNR is greater than -5 dB, the DC-DM scheme is clearly outperformed.

In the second experiment described in Fig. 7b, the DC-DM scheme is optimised for a WNR value of -15 dB. The optimal α is 0.1. We found here that the DES scheme optimised for an expected WNR value of -5 dB with $\alpha = 0.125$ has the same performance as the DC-DM scheme for a WNR value of -15 dB but performs significantly better for larger WNR values.

In practical scenarios, when the noise property is unknown at the embedding, watermarking techniques need to be tuned for the worst relevant case. However, such tuning may limit the performance of the scheme when the Gaussian noise is not as strong as expected. Simulation shows that the DES scheme performs generally better than the DC-DM scheme when dealing with such a noise.

5   Conclusion

In this paper, we proposed a principled way to derive an efficient embedding process. The derivation relies on an optimisation algorithm of the embedding scheme with respect to the extraction error. Although, this algorithm has to be applied for a given noise model, we have found out that the embedding processes obtained, termed DES, performs fairly well for different values of the noise parameters, unlike existing embedding functions such as DM and DC-DM.

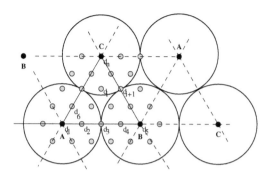

Fig. 8. Two dimensional data space with an hexagonal lattice and three different messages denoted 'A', 'B', and 'C'. The lattice points are marked with black dots,while normal data points labelled d_i are marked with grey dots.

Moreover, the proposed algorithm can be used in a more general framework than the simplified version used here for the demonstration. For instance, let us assume a two dimensional space with a hexagonal lattice and three different messages as depicted in Fig. 8. Here, the embedding process will also be regular due to the lattice structure. As shown in the figure, the working space is a triangle instead of a line segment, and the data point can be labelled from d_1 to d_n replacing the values of I_n. The proposed algorithm can be similarly applied with these new settings.

Further work on an algorithm which can cope with different noise models at the same time is currently carried out.

Acknowledgements

Support from EU-FP6 IP EVERGROW (SB, DS) and EU-FP5 Human Potential Programme HPRN-CT-2002-00319, STIPCO (DS) is gratefully acknowledged.

References

1. Bounkong, S.: Digital Image Watermarking. PhD thesis, Aston University (2004)
2. Bounkong, S., Toch, B., Saad, D., Lowe, D.: Structured codebooks for SCS watermarking. In: Proceedings of the Signal Processing, Pattern Recognition, and Applications Conference, ACTA Press (2003) 77–81
3. Chen, B., Wornell, G.: Quantization index modulation: a class of provably good methods for digital watermarking and information embedding. IEEE Transactions on Information Theory **47** (2001) 1423–1443
4. Eggers, J., Bauml, R., Tzschoppe, R., Girod, B.: Scalar costa scheme for information embedding. IEEE Transactions on Signal Processing **51** (2003) 1003–1019
5. Ramkumar, M.: Data hiding in multimedia - theory and applications. PhD thesis, New Jersey Institute of Technology (2000)

6. Heegard, C., Gamal, A.A.E.: On the capacity of computer memory with defects. IEEE Transactions on Information Theory **29** (1983) 731–739
7. Cover, T., Thomas, J.: Elements of information theory. John Wiley and Sons, New York (1991)

A   Proof

As stated at the beginning of Sect. 2, the algorithm has to be performed for all possible value of the message m. Thus, the proof considers m as given. The following notation is introduced to simplify the subsequent equations. For a given decoding and its corresponding characteristic set $\mathscr{U}$, we define the characteristic function

$$\forall c_i \in I_n, \quad \delta_{\mathscr{U}}(c_i) = \begin{cases} 1 \text{ if } c_i \in \mathscr{U}, \\ 0 \text{ otherwise.} \end{cases} \tag{19}$$

If the corruption process A is applied to c_i, the probability of its output to belong to a given subset $\mathscr{U}$ is denoted

$$\forall c_i \in I_n, \quad E_{c_i} = \int_{\mathscr{U}} P\big(A(c_i) = z\big)\, dz. \tag{20}$$

When $\mathscr{U}$ corresponds to the embedded message and c_i is the output of the embedding process, E_{c_i} corresponds to the probability of successful decoding (PSD). The optimality of the returned function will be proved by induction, based on the successive steps of the algorithm. Let us prove that for any distortion $\hat{\mathscr{D}} \in [0, \mathscr{D}]$, the proposed algorithm results in an optimal embedding function.

Initial step: For $\hat{\mathscr{D}} = 0$, there exists one and only one possibility for Q : the identity function. Hence, it is clearly optimal. We name it Q_0.

Induction step: Let us assume that the algorithm returns the optimal function, in terms of the PSD, for any distortion $\hat{\mathscr{D}} \in [0, \hat{\mathscr{D}}_n]$. The function returned by the algorithm for a distortion $\hat{\mathscr{D}}(Q_n) = \hat{\mathscr{D}}_n$ is denoted Q_n. This is our induction hypothesis.

Now let us define Q_{n+1} as

$$\forall c_i \in I_n, \quad Q_{n+1}(m, c_i) = \begin{cases} c'_* & \text{if } c_i = c_*, \\ Q_n(m, c_i) & \text{otherwise,} \end{cases} \tag{21}$$

where (c_*, c'_*) is as defined in Eq. (6), and the associated maximum ratio in the argument of Eq. (6) is denoted M_{n+1}. We have

$$\hat{\mathscr{D}}(Q_{n+1}) = \hat{\mathscr{D}}(Q_n) + p_{c_*}\Big(D\big(c_*, c'_*\big) - D\big(c_*, Q_n(m, c_*)\big)\Big). \tag{22}$$

Let Q be an embedding process, inducing a distortion $\hat{\mathscr{D}}(Q) \in [\hat{\mathscr{D}}_n, \hat{\mathscr{D}}_{n+1}]$. Its corresponding PSD can be written as

$$E_Q = \sum_{(c_i, c_j) \in I_n^2} P\big(Q(m, c_i) = c_j \,\big|\, c_i\big)\, p_{c_i} E_{c_j}. \tag{23}$$

Let us prove that Q is a suboptimal embedding function. It is trivially the case if $E_Q \leq E_{Q_n}$. We now consider the case where $E_Q > E_{Q_n}$. Hence,

$$E_Q - E_{Q_n} = \sum_{(c_i, c_j) \in I_n^2} p_{c_i} R_{c_i, c_j} S_{c_i, c_j} , \tag{24}$$

where

$$S_{c_i, c_j} = D(c_i, c_j) - D(c_i, Q_n(m, c_i)) \tag{25}$$

and

$$R_{c_i, c_j} = \frac{P(Q(m, c_i) = c_j | c_i) E_{c_j} - \delta(Q_n(m, c_i), c_j) E_{Q_n(m, c_i)}}{S_{c_i, c_j}} . \tag{26}$$

The notation $\delta(., .)$ is the Kronecker delta. Let us now consider a partition of I_n^2,

$$\Gamma = \{(c_i, c_j), \text{ such that } R_{c_i, c_j} > 0\} , \tag{27}$$

$$\Theta = \{(c_i, c_j), \text{ such that } R_{c_i, c_j} \leq 0\} . \tag{28}$$

Note that Γ and Θ implicitly depend on Q. Since $E_Q > E_{Q_n}$ by definition, we get

$$\left| \sum_{(c_i, c_j) \in \Theta} p_{c_i} R_{c_i, c_j} S_{c_i, c_j} \right| < \sum_{(c_i, c_j) \in \Gamma} p_{c_i} R_{c_i, c_j} S_{c_i, c_j} . \tag{29}$$

Thus, there exists $\gamma \in [0, 1]$ such that

$$\sum_{(c_i, c_j) \in \Theta} p_{c_i} R_{c_i, c_j} S_{c_i, c_j} + \gamma \sum_{(c_i, c_j) \in \Gamma} p_{c_i} R_{c_i, c_j} S_{c_i, c_j} = 0 . \tag{30}$$

Eq. (24) can be rewritten as

$$E_Q - E_{Q_n} = \sum_{(c_i, c_j) \in \Theta} p_{c_i} R_{c_i, c_j} S_{c_i, c_j} + \gamma \sum_{(c_i, c_j) \in \Gamma} p_{c_i} R_{c_i, c_j} S_{c_i, c_j} +$$
$$(1 - \gamma) \sum_{(c_i, c_j) \in \Gamma} p_{c_i} R_{c_i, c_j} S_{c_i, c_j} . \tag{31}$$

The first two terms correspond to a probabilistic embedding process $\underline{Q}$ defined as

$$\forall c_i \in I_n, \quad \underline{Q}(m, c_i) = \begin{cases} c_j & \text{if } (c_i, c_j) \in \Theta, \text{ with probability } q_{ij} \\ c_k & \text{if } (c_i, c_k) \in \Gamma, \text{ with probability } q_{ki} \\ c_i & \text{otherwise,} \end{cases} \tag{32}$$

where

$$q_{ji} = P(\underline{Q}(m, c_i) = c_j | c_i) \quad \text{and} \quad q_{ki} = P(\underline{Q}(m, c_i) = c_k | c_i) . \tag{33}$$

By construction, $E_{\underline{Q}} - E_{Q_n} = 0$ as in Eq. (30). Given the induction hypothesis, Q_n is optimal, thus

$$\hat{\mathscr{D}}(\underline{Q}) \geq \hat{\mathscr{D}}(Q_n) = \hat{\mathscr{D}}_n . \tag{34}$$

Consequently, Eq. (24) can be rewritten as

$$E_Q - E_{Q_n} = (1 - \gamma) \sum_{(c_i, c_j) \in \Gamma} p_{c_i} S_{c_i, c_j} R_{c_i, c_j} \tag{35}$$

$$\leq (1 - \gamma) \sum_{(c_i, c_j) \in \Gamma} p_{c_i} S_{c_i, c_j} M_{n+1}, \tag{36}$$

by definition of M_{n+1} in Eq. (21). Let us consider the embedding process $Q^\star$, constructed as the algorithm does according to Eq. (10):

$$\forall c_i \in I_n, \ Q^\star(m, c_i) = \begin{cases} Q_{n+1}(m, c_i) = c'_\star & \text{if } c_i = c_\star, \text{ with probability } q, \\ Q_n(m, c_i) & \text{otherwise,} \end{cases} \tag{37}$$

where

$$q = \frac{\sum_{(c_i, c_j) \in \Gamma} (1 - \gamma) S_{c_i, c_j}}{\hat{\mathscr{D}}_{n+1} - \hat{\mathscr{D}}_n}. \tag{38}$$

The embedding process Q can thus be decomposed as $\underline{Q}$, which has the same good decoding probability as Q_n but induces a larger distortion given Eq. (34), and an embedding process causing the same distortion as $Q^\star$, with a lower good decoding probability according to Eq. (36). Hence, the embedding process $Q^\star$ returned by the algorithm has a higher good decoding probability and creates a lower distortion than any function Q with $\hat{\mathscr{D}}(Q) \in [\hat{\mathscr{D}}_n, \hat{\mathscr{D}}_{n+1}]$. It proves the optimality of the solution returned by the algorithm, which concludes the induction step, and consequently the optimality proof.

A Spread Spectrum Watermarking Scheme Based on Periodic Clock Changes for Digital Images

Vincent Martin[1], Marie Chabert[1], and Bernard Lacaze[2]

[1] ENSEEIHT/IRIT, National Polytechnic Institute of Toulouse,
2 Rue Camichel, BP 7122, 31071 Toulouse Cedex 7, France
[2] INSA/IRIT
vincent.martin@enseeiht.fr

Abstract. This paper proposes a spread spectrum watermarking scheme based on periodic clock changes (PCC) for digital images. The PCC spreading properties and applications in multiuser communications are recalled. This alternative spread spectrum technique is compared with a classical Direct Sequence (DS) method in terms of robustness to attacks and noise, secret message bit rate and multiple watermarking performance. PCC proves to be a simple alternative to pseudo-noise modulation spreading methods, that provides similar performance.

1 Introduction

Property and integrity protection of digital images, sounds and videos is currently of great commercial interest. Watermarking proposes to embed an imperceptible mark in the digital data. This mark allows data authentication or ownership evidence. Multiple marks can be used to identify the sellers and buyers and hence illegal copy sources in the fingerprinting application. Watermarks must be detectable and readable by their encoder, unnoticeable for the public and robust to malicious attacks or innocent signal processing operations. Watermarks are inserted in the perceptible components rather than in the file headers to be independent of the transmission formats. For instance, digital image watermarking modifies either the pixel luminance or colors.

Let consider the insertion of J marks M_j, $j = 1, ..., J$ ($J > 1$ in the case of multiple watermarking) in the image pixel luminance I. First M_j is transformed according to a secret key into the watermark W_j. Binary antipodal messages are considered for simplicity. Second, W_j is inserted in I providing the watermarked image pixel luminance I_W. These quantities are either handled as matrices or as vectors built by taking the rows in successive order as follows:

$$M_j = [m_j(l)]_{l \in \{1,...,L\}}, W_j = [w_j(n)]_{n \in \{1,...,N\}}$$
$$I = [i(n)]_{n \in \{1,...,N\}} \text{ and } I_W = [i_W(n)]_{n \in \{1,...,N\}} . \quad (1)$$

L is called the payload. This study focuses on additive embedding of simultaneous watermarks in the spatial and DCT domains and their decoding:

$$I_W = I + W \text{ or } I_W = \text{IDCT}(\text{DCT}(I) + W), \text{ where } W = \alpha \sum_{j=1}^{J} W_j . \quad (2)$$

M. Barni et al. (Eds.): IH 2005, LNCS 3727, pp. 91–105, 2005.

DCT and IDCT denote the 8x8 block two-dimensional Discrete Cosine Transform and Inverse Discrete Cosine Transform respectively. The masking factor α trades off watermark decoding performance and imperceptibility [1]. α can be replaced by a pixel dependent perceptual mask $[\alpha(n)]_{n\in\{1,...,N\}}$ taking into account the individual perceptual impact of each pixel or transformed domain coefficient. Note that the insertion can be as well multiplicative [2] or performed in any transformed domain (full-frame DCT [3], time-scale [4]...).

The watermarked image I_W is transmitted and possibly attacked, leading to the image I'_W. A classification of attacks can be found in [1]. A single noise source $B = [b(n)]_{n\in\{1,...,N\}}$ can model the distortions introduced as well by the transmission channel and by the so-called waveform attacks. Under the assumption of mild attacks, the noise model amounts to the widespread additive white Gaussian channel model:

$$I'_W = I_W + B \text{ where: } B \sim \mathcal{N}(0, \sigma_B^2) \ . \tag{3}$$

When more severe attacks occur, the noise model may be more sophisticated with possibly non-Gaussian distribution. Such attacks may lead to intractable derivation of the watermarking performance. In such case, the performance is studied through simulations only. The distortion introduced by an attack is measured by the Peak Signal to Noise Ratio (PSNR):

$$\text{PSNR} = \frac{Nmax^2}{\sum_{n=1}^{N}(i'_W(n) - i(n))^2} \ , \tag{4}$$

where max is the maximum value attainable by I.

The watermark decoding step aims at recovering M from I'_W knowing the secret key. In the widespread blind public watermarking scheme, I is not required for decoding. The decoding performance is measured through the bit error rate (BER): BER=P$[d_j(l) \neq m_j(l)]$, where $D_j = [d_j(l)]_{l\in\{1,...,L\}}$ is the final hard decision on the message estimate. The BER is estimated in the simulations by

$$\hat{\text{BER}} = \frac{\sum_{j=1}^{J}(1 - \sum_{l=1}^{L}\delta(d_j(l), m_j(l)))}{JL} \ , \tag{5}$$

where δ denotes the Kronecker symbol.

For the public, W is a low-level noise. For the encoder, W is the signal of interest. Thus, the watermarking scheme amounts to the transmission of W through a highly noisy channel. This noise model includes both B and I contributions and the usual image distributions prevent from Gaussian noise assumption. Denoting $\mathcal{P}_I = \frac{\sum_{n=1}^{N} i(n)^2}{N}$ the power of a given image I and σ_W^2 the variance of W, let define the document to watermark ratio (DWR) and the watermark to noise ratio (WNR):

$$\text{DWR} = \frac{\mathcal{P}_I}{\sigma_W^2}, \ \text{WNR} = \frac{\sigma_W^2}{\sigma_B^2} \ . \tag{6}$$

DWR measures W imperceptibility with respect to the host image. WNR measures transmission noise and attack influence.

This formulation as a transmission problem has inspired watermarking methods based on communication theory. In particular, a great interest has been devoted to spread spectrum techniques due to their security, their robustness to interference as well as their possible use for multiple access. Spread spectrum watermarking has been used for digital images [3], audio [5] and video [1]. Direct Sequence (DS) spread spectrum is the most commonly used method. M_j is modulated by a pseudo-random sequence providing a noise-like watermark W_j. The use of several orthogonal sequences allows for multiple watermarking. Many other spread spectrum methods have been studied in a communication framework: orthogonal Walsh functions can replace pseudo-random sequences, time or frequency division multiple access are rather based on multiplexing [6]. This study proposes the Periodic Clock Changes (PCC) as an alternative spread spectrum watermarking technique. DS and PCC multiuser communications have been compared in [7]. However, watermarking involves different noise models and performance criteria.

Section 2 recalls DS spread spectrum watermarking. Section 3 presents PCC general principle and proposes a PCC-based watermarking scheme. Section 4 compares the DS and PCC watermarking decoding performance with respect to noise, current signal processing operations and various attacks through simulations (the detection is not adressed).

2 Direct Sequence Spread Spectrum Watermarking

DS spread spectrum multiple watermarking modulates the jth message M_j by a zero-mean P-periodic pseudo-random sequence $C_j = [c_j(p)]_{p \in \{1,...,P\}}$ with:

$$c_j(p) = \pm 1, p \in \{1, ..., P\},$$
$$< C_j, C_k > = 0 \text{ for } j \neq k, j, k \in \{1, ..., J\} , \tag{7}$$

where $<, >$ denotes the inner product. These J orthogonal sequences act as secret keys. Each message bit $m_j(l)$ is associated to a symbol $\underline{w}_j^l$ of P samples such as:

$$\underline{w}_j^l = [w_j(k)]_{k \in \{(l-1)P+1,...,lP\}} = m_j(l)C_j . \tag{8}$$

Let P and L values verify $N = PL$ for further watermark insertion. The spreading factor P is a redundancy factor related to the message bit rate defined by $R = L/N = 1/P$ in bit/pixel. The watermark $W_j = [\underline{w}_j^l]_{l \in \{1,...,L\}}$ exhibits a spread spectrum. Given a vector X of length $N = LP$, $\underline{x}^l$ denotes $[x(k)]_{k \in \{(l-1)P+1,...,lP\}}$ in the following. The larger P, the better the sequence spreading properties. The family of Gold codes provides long orthogonal pseudo-random sequences [6]. The resulting watermarked image I_W given by (2) is then transmitted leading to I'_W given by (3). The decoding derives $d_j(l) = [\text{sgn}(\hat{m}_j(l))]_{l \in \{(1,...,L\}}$ where $\text{sgn}(x) = 1$ for $x > 0$ and $\text{sgn}(x) = -1$ for $x < 0$. In the case of spatial embedding:

$$\hat{m}_j(l) = \frac{1}{\alpha P} < \underline{i'_W}^l, C_j > , \tag{9}$$

and assuming perfect synchronization between $\underline{i'_W}^l$ and C_j as well as perfect sequence orthogonality:

$$\hat{m}_j(l) = m_j(l) + \frac{1}{\alpha P} < \underline{i}^l + \underline{b}^l, C_j > . \tag{10}$$

The scalar product derivation in (10) amounts to a noisy host image spreading. It consists in an element-by-element multiplication of $(\underline{i}^l + \underline{b}^l)$ and C_j followed by the summation of the resulting samples. For a given image I and for large P, these samples are supposed independent and identically distributed [8], C_j being the only random variable. The Central-Limit theorem states that

$$< \underline{i}^l + \underline{b}^l, C_j > \sim \mathcal{N}(0, \sigma^2) \text{ with } \sigma^2 = \sum_{k=1}^{P}(\underline{i}^l(k) + \underline{b}^l(k))^2 \ . \tag{11}$$

As the luminance is bounded, $\lim_{P \to \infty} \frac{\sigma}{P} = 0$ and the additive Gaussian noise influence on detection performance is reduced for large αP. However, as α increases the watermark imperceptibility decreases and P is limited by the relation $N = PL$. The same properties hold when I is replaced by its block DCT coefficients and α by a perceptual mask.

DS can be hardly considered as a standard spread spectrum watermarking technique as few papers investigate the spectrum spreading in itself. The pseudo-noise generation and the modulation technique may differ depending on the algorithm. For instance, Hernández and Pérez-González propose a 2D pseudo-random pulse modulating a set of pixels scattered on the whole image [8]. For a payload of L bits, other algorithms use multiple watermarking and embed the superposition of L orthogonal pseudo-noises. However, DS remains the most commonly used and as such may provide a reference for the performance study of new alternative techniques.

3   Periodic Clock Changes

3.1   Definition and Properties

A linear periodic time varying (LPTV) filter is a filter whose impulse response is a T-periodic function $h(n, k)$ of the time indexed by $n \in \mathbb{N}$. Let $x(n)$, $y(n)$ the input (resp. the output) of the filter:

$$y(n) = \sum_{k=-\infty}^{+\infty} h(n, k)x(n-k), \qquad h(n+T, k) = h(n, k) \ . \tag{12}$$

Its transfer function $H_n(\omega)$ is defined by:

$$H_n(\omega) = \sum_{k=-\infty}^{+\infty} h(n, k)e^{-ik\omega}, \qquad H_n(\omega) = H_{n+T}(\omega) \ . \tag{13}$$

LPTV have been successfully used for interleaving, blind equalization and spread spectrum communications [9].

Let $f : \mathbb{N} \to \mathbb{N}$ be a T-periodic function of n. In a stochastic framework, a Periodic Clock Change (PCC) transforms a stationary process $Z = \{Z(n), n \in \mathbf{Z}\}$ in the process

$$U(n) = Z(n - f(n)), \qquad f(n) = f(n + T) \ . \tag{14}$$

PCC are particular LPTV filters $(H_n(\omega) = e^{-i\omega f(n)})$. For such a digital sequence Z, PCC amounts to a sample permutation. If Z is zero mean, the output U is zero mean and cyclostationary [10]. Let $V(n) = U(n + \phi)$ a stationarized version of U (where ϕ is a uniformly distributed random variable on $\{0, 1, ..., T - 1\}$).

Now consider $f(n)$ as a T-periodic random permutation and let $f^{-1}(n)$ denote the PCC of the inverse permutation:

$$f(n) = \underline{n} - q_{\underline{n}}, \qquad f^{-1}(n) = \underline{n} - q_{\underline{n}}^{-1} , \tag{15}$$

where q is a permutation of $(0, 1, 2, ..., T - 1)$ and $\overline{n}$ and $\underline{n}$ are respectively the quotient and the remainder of the division of n by T ($n = \overline{n}T + \underline{n}$). Then for T large enough, V spectrum approaches a white noise spectrum [11].

PCC multiuser communications transmit a particular random permutation f_j of each message. The successive application of any two PCC $f_i \circ f_j$ is a PCC and spreads the spectrum. Only the inverse PCC f_j^{-1} allows to retrieve the input spectrum. This property is to be linked with DS spread spectrum orthogonality [7].

PCC and DS multiuser communication performance has been compared with respect to the number of users. The BER estimations show that PCC and DS perform similarly for a large number of users while PCC performs better for a small one [7]. However, the simulation parameter values (particularly the SNR range) reflected a multiuser communication environment but were unrealistic for the watermarking application.

3.2 Application to Watermarking

LPTV designed for a watermarking framework must be whitening, invertible, cryptographically secure and optionally form an orthogonal set for multiple embedding. Periodic random permutations meet all these hypotheses for a low computational cost.

LPTV and PCC have not been previously used in the literature as spreading techniques in a watermarking scheme. However, the particular case of random permutations can be found at various levels of some watermarking schemes. Numerous authors use permutations as a message interleaver for security improvement [8][5] in a pseudo-noise modulation spreading scheme. Hsu and Wu use the non-additive embedding of a permutation of a visually recognizable pattern (logo) in the middle frequencies of the block DCT [12]. In a spreading purpose, Furon and Duhamel propose to interleave a spectrally colored information representing a 1-bit payload for an asymmetric audio watermarking scheme [13]. The literature does not provide any comparison between random permutations as a spread spectrum technique and the most commonly used DS method nor any consideration of the spreading properties in a theoretic framework.

One-Dimensional Periodic Clock Changes (1D-PCC): 1D-PCC performs on vectorial format (1). To reach a reasonable BER in the watermarking SNR conditions, redundancy is first introduced by means of repetition. The resulting message M_j' is the concatenation of P replicas of M_j (recall that P is such that $N = LP$):

$$m_j'(l + (p - 1)L) = m_j(l), l \in \{1, ..., L\}, p \in \{1, ..., P\} . \tag{16}$$

The payload L is thus supposed large enough to guarantee a diversity in M_j' between the $+1$ and -1 bits. W_j is obtained by applying a T_{1D}-periodic PCC f_j (the secret key) to M_j'. The first decoding step applies the inverse PCC f_j^{-1} to I_W'. The second step averages the P samples corresponding to each bit of the initial message

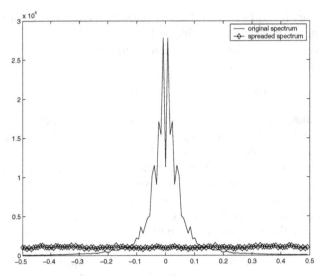

Fig. 1. PCC spreading properties (Lena)

$$\hat{m}_j(l) = \frac{1}{\alpha P} \sum_{p=1}^{P} (f_j^{-1}(i'_W))(l + (p-1)L)$$

$$= m_j(l) + \frac{1}{\alpha P} \sum_{p=1}^{P} (f_j^{-1}(i+b))(l + (p-1)L) \ . \tag{17}$$

Let $\mu(I_W) = \frac{1}{N} \sum_{n=1}^{N} I_W(n)$ denote the mean of I_W. Since f_j^{-1} spreads I spectrum for large P values (Fig.1 displays the effect of random permutation on Lena image spectrum), the permuted samples are independent and identically distributed and the Central-Limit theorem allows Gaussian assumption on $\hat{M}_j$ with $E[\hat{M}_j] = M_j + \mu(I_W)$. The decoding derives $D_j = [\text{sgn}(\hat{m}_j(l)) - \mu(I_W))]_{l \in \{(1,\dots,L)\}}$.

Two-Dimensional Periodic Clock Changes (2D-PCC): 2D-PCC performs on matrix format. The spread spectrum watermark results from successive column-wise f_j^1 and row-wise f_j^2 permutations of the redundant message. The insertion and decoding follow the same principle as 1D-PCC. 2D-PCC is expected to perform similarly with smaller periods: the association of two PCC at the decoding should efficiently remove the spatial correlation between pixels or transform domain coefficients.

4 Direct Sequence and Periodic Clock Changes Watermarking Performance Comparison

4.1 Implementation

Embedding Domain: W can be embedded in the luminance I or in any invertible transform of I (DFT, DCT, Wavelet transform...). DS and PCC have been compared in the spatial (or luminance) domain (L-DS, L-PCC) and in the 8x8-block DCT domain (DCT-DS, DCT-PCC), that is the most popular transform domain since it is used in the JPEG compression format.

Perceptual Masking: Embedding in the 8x8-block DCT domain (DCT-DS, DCT-PCC) benefits from research on perceptual analysis developed in image compression, since it is used in the JPEG format. The perceptual mask inspired from the work of Ahumada and Peterson [14] and used for instance by Hernandez and Pérez-González [8] has been chosen in the DCT domain. It consists in embedding W in 22 out of 64 mid-frequencies DCT coefficients. $\alpha(k)$ is derived from a *visibility threshold* (which gives the maximum amplitude of a modification of the coefficient under the imperceptibility constraint) and a *contrast-masking effect* (which takes into account the amplitude of the coefficient itself).

Prefiltering at the Detector: The statistical properties of I allow for the use of optimum embedding and decoding strategies [8].

In the spatial domain, only local moments are available since I is non-stationary. Hernández and Pérez-González propose the use of a Wiener filtering [8] in order to obtain an estimate $\hat{I}$ of the original image at the decoder. The prefiltered image is $I''_W = I'_W - \hat{I}$ and (11) becomes

$$\sigma^2 = \sum_{k=1}^{P}((\underline{i}^l(k) - \hat{\underline{i}}^l(k)) + \underline{b}^l(k))^2 , \tag{18}$$

thus considerably reducing the power of the host image noise. This prefiltering provides a better BER for a given DWR or improves DWR for a given BER, thus allowing to strictly respect the imperceptibility constraint. It has been discarded in the following simulations for computational reasons since it does not interfere in the comparison of the spreading techniques.

Each coefficient of a block in the 8x8 DCT domain follows a generalized Gaussian distribution. Maximum Likehood decoding provides an optimum decoding strategy under this assumption [8]. It has not been implemented in this study, since it is expected to enhance the BER for a given DWR for both spreading methods whithout interfering in the comparison.

4.2 Parameters of the Simulations

This section compares DS, 1D-PCC and 2D-PCC watermarking decoding performance through simulations. BER is estimated under various classical attacks as a function of DWR, WNR, R (message bit rate) or J (number of watermarks).

Since the perceptual mask in the DCT domain determines a threshold of maximum alteration, a theoretical value of the threshold of imperceptibility DWR_{imp} can be computed for each image ($DWR_{imp} = 35.8$ dB is a mean value for the image set). Empirically, a less demanding threshold of $DWR_{emp} = 30$ dB is often sufficient. It is to be noted that the use of Wiener prefiltering in the spatial domain allows for good decoding performance under the theoretical imperceptibility constraint. The attacks follow the same constraint of imperceptibility. In the following, using the empirical threshold, it will be assumed that the attack is perceptible, thus inefficient, if PSNR < 35.2 dB.

For an accurate BER estimation, messages are randomly generated until at least 100 erroneous bits have been observed. For computational reasons, the computed BER is sometimes poor (BER$= 10^{-2}$). It could be improved by decreasing L (more redundancy) or increasing DWR (provided that the imperceptibility constraint is respected). The simulations provide the averaged performance on the test image set composed of Lena, Baboon, Fishingboat, Pentagon and Peppers[1]. Unless otherwise stated, the parameter values are: $L = 100$ bits (message length), $N = 2^{18}$ pixels (image length) and $J = 1$ (single watermark). For simulations involving a fixed value, DWR$= 30$ dB offers the best decoding performance under the empirical imperceptibility constraint. $T_{1D} = 2^{12}$ (1D-PCC period) and $T_{2D} = 2^6$ (2D-PCC period) trade off imperceptibility, decoding performance and computational cost on this image set.

4.3   PCC: Choice of the Permutation Period and the Message Length

When the permutation period T increases, the properties of whitening and orthogonality are expected to increase. It is the case for T_{1D} in both spatial and DCT domain. However, in the spatial domain, L-2D-PCC performs better for small values of T_{2D} (Fig.2). It is due to the spatial correlation between pixels, in blocks corresponding to the objects of the image, that are interleaved by the PCC. In the DCT domain, the data in more noise-like and the influence of T_{2D} is reduced. As good compromises between performance, security and whitening, $T_{1D} = 2^{12}$ and $T_{2D} = 2^6$ have been set as default values.

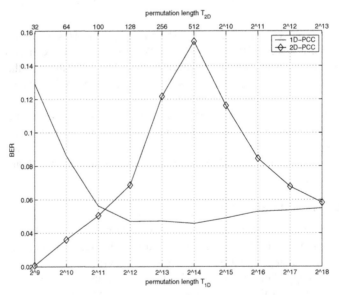

Fig. 2. PCC decoding performance with respect to T (spatial domain)

A side effect of the repetition of the message introduced in 2D-PCC before spreading is the dependence of its performance on the least common multiple between N_1 and

---

[1] http://www.petitcolas.net/fabien/watermarking/image_database/

L (if N_1 is multiple of L, the effect of one of the permutations might be cancelled). An intermediate value of $L = 100$ bits has therefore been set as default message length.

4.4 Attacks to Security

As opposed to the attacks to robustness studied in the following, which aim at increasing the BER of the watermarking channel, attacks to security aim at discovering the secret key K from a vector $\boldsymbol{I_W}^{N_o}$ of N_o observations [15]. Cayre, Fontaine and Furon [16] present a theoretic framework for the study of watermarking security, as well as practical algorithms for the estimation of K. Comesaña et al. [15] use the mutual information between I_W and K to measure information leakages. Moreover, if K is a discrete variable, the remaining uncertainty about K after N_o observations is the equivocation

$$h(K|\boldsymbol{I_W}^{N_o}) = h(K) - h(\boldsymbol{I_W}^{N_o}) + h(\boldsymbol{I_W}^{N_o}|K) , \qquad (19)$$

where h denotes the differential entropy ($h(X) = -\sum_x p(x)\log_2 p(x)$).

As there exists $T!$ permutations q of period T, the entropy of the key is $h(q) = \log_2(T_{1D}!)$ for 1D-PCC and $h(q^1, q^2) = 2\log_2(T_{2D}!)$ for 2D-PCC. The use of 2D-PCC reduces the entropy of the key, since $T_{2D} << T_{1D}$. This is to be compared with $h(C) = N$ for DS if C is pseudo-random as in [8]. For the considered parameter values ($N = 2^{18}, T_{1D} = 2^{12}$), DS slightly outperforms 1D-PCC in terms of entropy of the key, but as soon as $T_{1D} > N/8$, 1D-PCC is better.

Further research will investigate the impact of PCC's on $h(\boldsymbol{I_W}^{N_o}|K)$.

4.5 Robustness with Respect to Noise

Recall that the watermark is submitted to different noise sources: the host image and additive or multiplicative noises modelling current signal processing or malicious attacks. Fig.3 displays the decoding performance as a function of DWR. Redundancy and averaged decoding provide DS, 1D-PCC and 2D-PCC similar robustness to the host image noise. Fig.4 (resp. Fig.5) shows that detection performance of the three algorithms are not altered by an acceptable additive (resp. multiplicative) noise. An higher noise variance leads to an image deterioration confirmed by the PSNR criterion.

4.6 Message Bit Rate Influence and Multiple Watermarking

DS, 1D-PCC and 2D-PCC decoding performance is first estimated as a function of the message redundancy $P = 1/R$. The decoding performance is expected to increase with P. For instance, for $P = 1$ (no redundancy), a poor BER (BER= 10^{-2}) is hardly obtained at the expense of the image deterioration (DWR=5 dB is required). Fig.6 shows that DS and PCC behave similarly when R increases, whith a light superiority of 2D-PCC in the spatial domain.

Multiple ($J > 1$) watermarking offers another way to transmit a given number of bits. Fig.7 displays the performance with respect to J in the case of multiple watermarking. Tests are performed with $J = 2$ to 14 messages. The multiple bit rate defined by $R_J = JL/N$ increases proportionally. The algorithms perform similarly when R_J increases.

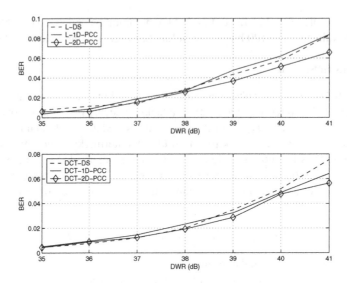

Fig. 3. Decoding performance with respect to DWR

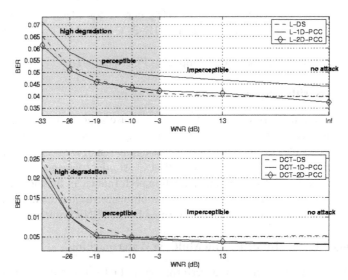

Fig. 4. Robustness to additive noise attack

4.7   Robustness to Sophisticated Attacks

This subsection compares DS, 1D-PCC and 2D-PCC performance when subjected to more sophisticated attacks. The DWR range used in these simulations has been chosen in order to obtain a significant BER comparison with the simple insertion method considered in this study. Since the considered attacks are very efficient, the DWR range in this subsection is above the limit of perceptibility.

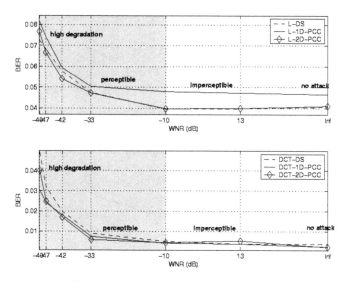

Fig. 5. Robustness to multiplicative noise attack

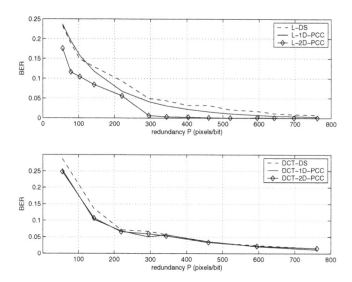

Fig. 6. Decoding performance with respect to P

Desynchronizing attacks (such as cropping, translation or rotation [1]) are not considered since they lead to catastrophic BER for the three considered algorithms in their basic form. Indeed the inner product derivation for DS or the inverse permutation for PCC yield totally erroneous results when derived on slightly shifted vectors or matrices. Several solutions (which are outside the scope of this study) use the insertion in appropriate transformed domains [17] or insertion of a synchronizing signal (template) [18]. Both methods can be applied to PCC as well as DS. However, an efficient synchroniz-

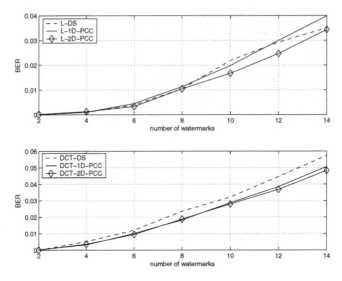

Fig. 7. Decoding performance with respect to J

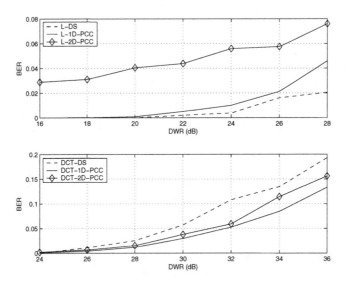

Fig. 8. Robustness to scaling

ing method robust to local, non-affine geometric tranforms and to template removal is still to be found.

Scaling: The image is shrunk by a factor S and then re-scaled to its original size by the nearest-neighbors method. The attack is very efficient, though nearly perceptible (PSNR= 28.3 dB in average). L-2D-PCC is less robust to this attack than the other methods (Fig.8). DCT-DS and DCT-PCC are more robust than L-DS and L-PCC.

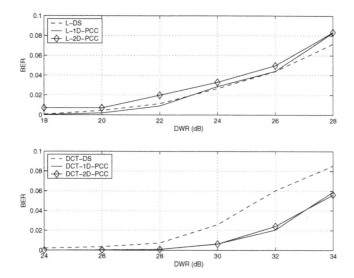

Fig. 9. Robustness to Wiener filtering

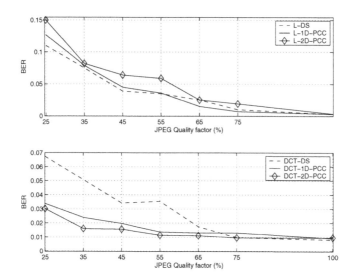

Fig. 10. Robustness to JPEG compression

Wiener Filtering: Wiener filter is an image-dependent filter derived from moment estimates to eliminate additive noise (as a difference from Wiener prefiltering at the decoding, W is here considered as the noise and I as the original signal). The Wiener filtering attack aims at removing the watermark. The simulations (Fig.9) show a high degradation of the performance for a light deformation (PSNR= 37.8 dB in average). DCT-DS is less robust to this attack than DCT-PCC (Fig.8). DCT-DS and DCT-PCC are more robust than L-DS and L-PCC.

JPEG Compression: I_W is JPEG compressed with a given compression rate. Although the visual deformation is very light (PSNR= 39.7 dB in average for a 75% quality factor), the attack is very efficient on the three algorithms in the spatial domain. Embedding in the DCT domain allows for a good robustness to JPEG compression (Fig.10), since the JPEG compression algorithm involves a progressive quantification of the 8x8 block DCT with small impact on the middle frequencies coefficients.

5   Conclusion

DS spread spectrum communications have inspired many watermarking schemes. Random permutations have been used at various levels of the watermarking process. This study has proposed to use random permutations in the PCC theoretic general framework. A PCC spread spectrum watermarking scheme has been proposed and compared to the classical DS algorithm in the spatial domain and in the block DCT domain. PCC and DS performance are globally similar and consistent with those expected for spread spectrum techniques: a high robustness to additive and multiplicative noise but vulnerability to desynchronizing attacks. As expected, embedding in the DCT domain allows for a better robustness to sophisticated attacks. 2D-PCC would be preferred to 1D-PCC for its lower computational cost and better performance provided a good choice of the permutation length.

This study concludes at a general equivalence between PCC spreading and classical spreading techniques using random pseudo-noise modulation, thanks to theoretical and experimental arguments. It justifies also the use of random permutations as an alternative spreading technique in existing algorithms. Random-permutation based PCC is very simple in its concept, implementation and computation and can be embedded in various watermarking schemes concerning different transform domains. The use of PCC spreading could also be advised to watermarking documents such as audio and video, where the redundancy would be greater and the periodicity would be better exploited. The spreading properties of more general LPTV's, that allow to perform simultaneously spectral shaping and whitening, are under study.

References

1. Hartung, F.: Digital Watermarking and Fingerprinting of Uncompressed and Compressed Video. Shaker Verlag, Aachen, Germ. (99)
2. Piva, A., Barni, M., Bartolini, F., Cappellini, V.: DCT-based watermark recovering without resorting to the uncorrupted original image. ICIP'97, Proc. 1 (1997) 520–523
3. Cox, I., Kilian, J., Leighton, F., Shamoon, T.: Secure spread spectrum watermarking for multimedia. Image Processing, IEEE Transactions on 6 (1997) 1673–1687
4. Kundur, D., Hatzinakos, D.: Digital Watermarking Using Multiresolution Wavelet Decomposition. IEEE ICASSP'98 5 (1998) 2659–2662
5. Kirovski, D., Malvar, H.: Spread-spectrum watermarking of audio signals. IEEE Trans. on Signal Processing 51 (2003) 1020–1033
6. Proakis, J.: Digital Communications. 4th edn. McGraw, NY (2001)
7. Roviras, D., Lacaze, B., Thomas, N.: Effects of Discrete LPTV on Stationary Signals. IEEE ICASSP'02, Proc. 2 (2002) 1127–1220

8. Hernández, J., Pérez-González, F.: Statistical analysis of watermarking schemes for copyright protection of images. IEEE Proc., Special Issue on Identification and Protection of Multimedia Information **87** (1999) 1142–1166

9. McLernon, D.: One-dimensional Linear Periodically Time-Varying structures: derivations, interrelationships and properties. IEE Proc.-Vis. Image Signal Proc. **146** (1999) 245–252

10. Gardner, W.A.: Cyclostationarity in Communications and Signal Processing. New York: IEEE Press (94)

11. Lacaze, B., Roviras, D.: Effect of random permutations applied to random sequences and related applications. Signal Processing **82** (2002) 821–831

12. Hsu, C.T., Wu, J.L.: Hidden Digital Watermarks in Images. IEEE Transactions on Image Processing **8(1)** (1999) 58–68

13. Furon, T., Duhamel, P.: An asymmetric watermarking method. IEEE. Trans. on Signal Proc. **51** (2003) 981–995

14. Ahumada, A., Peterson, H.: Luminance-model-based DCT quantization for color image compression. Proc. SPIE on Human Vision, Visual Proc., and Digital Display III **1666** (1992) 365–374

15. Comesaña, P., Pérez-Freire, L., Pérez-González, F.: An information-theoretic framework for assessing security in practical watermarking and data hiding scenarios. 6th International Workshop on Image Analysis for Multimedia Interactive Services (2005)

16. Cayre, F., Fontaine, C., Furon, T.: Watermarking security : Theory and practice. IEEE Transactions on Signal Processing, Special Issue on Content Protection **to appear** (2005)

17. J.J.K. Ó Ruanaith, Pun, T.: Rotation, scale and translation invariant spread spectrum digital image watermarking. Signal Proc. **66** (1998) 303–317

18. Pereira, S., Pun, T.: Fast robust template matching for affine resistant image watermarking. IEEE Transactions on signal proc. **51** (2003) 1045–1053

A Quantization Watermarking Technique Robust to Linear and Non-linear Valumetric Distortions Using a Fractal Set of Floating Quantizers

Patrick Bas

CNRS,
Laboratoire des Images et des Signaux de Grenoble,
961 rue de la Houille Blanche Domaine universitaire,
B.P. 46 38402, Saint Martin d'Hères cedex, France
and
Laboratory of Computer and Information Science,
Helsinki University of Technology, P.O. Box 5400, FI-02015 Hut, Finland

Abstract. This paper presents an extension of the classical Quantization Index Modulation (QIM) data-hiding scheme in the context of valumetric distortions. This scheme uses a fractal quantization structure during the detection but also a content dependent quantization grid to achieve both global constant robustness and the ability to recover the watermark after non-linear valumetric distortions. Previous works are first presented. Then the construction of a floating quantizer that addresses the problem of non-linear transformations is introduced. The embedding and detection schemes for digital image watermarking are afterward introduced, the main characteristic of this scheme is the fact that the detection scheme can use a hierarchical set of quantizers to deal with non-linear valumetric transforms while preserving an average constant quantization step. Finally the performance of this scheme and the comparison with other robust quantization schemes considering valumetric transforms and noise addition are presented.

1 Introduction

Quantization watermarking techniques[1], first introduced by Chen and Worwell [1] are widely used in watermarking applications because they provide both robustness to the AWGN channel and high capacity capabilities while preserving the fidelity of the host document. Basically, the Quantization Index Modulation (QIM) scheme uses one different quantizer for each code word that is transmitted and the set of quantizer is span on the range of possible values that can be taken by each sample. For example, using a two stages codeword (e.g. a bit of information) requires two disjoints quantizers. The embedding rule of a bit b in a coefficient C is the following:

---

[1] The work described in this paper has been supported (in part) by the European Commission through the IST Programme under Contract IST-2002-507932 ECRYPT and the National French project Fabriano.

M. Barni et al. (Eds.): IH 2005, LNCS 3727, pp. 106–117, 2005.

$$\text{If } b[k] = 1 : C_w = 2\Delta\mathcal{E}\left(\frac{C + \Delta/2}{2\Delta}\right) - \Delta/2$$
$$\text{If } b[k] = 0 : C_w = 2\Delta\mathcal{E}\left(\frac{C - \Delta/2}{2\Delta}\right) + \Delta/2$$

(1)

Where Δ represents the distance between one quantized value and the next one, and $\mathcal{E}(x)$ is the integer part of x. For security issues, it is also possible to add a key-dependant random signal on the future quantized sample before performing the quantization step and to remove the random signal (call the dither signal) on the quantized value. Chen *et. al* have first introduced such a method called dither modulation (DM) and have combined it with a distortion compensation module.

However the usage of quantization techniques such as QIM or DM are not straightforward in real application scenarios such as video watermarking where valumetric distortions are often present during the broadcasting process.

1.1   QIM/DM and Valumetric Distortions

A valumetric distortions can be defined by any function $f(p)$ that modifies the value of the original pixel p. In practical cases, $f()$ can be either linear (e.g. $f(p) = \alpha(p)$) and represents a gain, or non-linear to represents more widely used distortions. For example, the gamma correction function $\Gamma_\gamma(p)$, which has to be especially considered in video watermarking applications when the watermarked signal has to suffer DA/AD conversions, is given by:

$$\Gamma_\gamma(p) = p_{MAX}\left(\frac{p}{p_{MAX}}\right)^\gamma$$

where p_{MAX} is the maximum value of a pixel. A valumetric transform will consequently alter the quantized value in such a way that, if $p_w - f(p_w) > \Delta/2$, the decoding step will probably lead to an error. Such an effect is depicted on Fig. 1 which outlines the displacement of the different quantized values after linear and non-linear valumetric transforms.

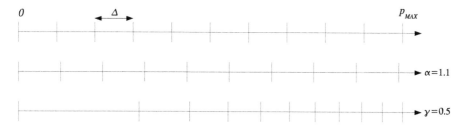

Fig. 1. Effects of valumetric transforms on quantized values: the initial quantization grid (first axis) cannot be used to decode the watermark neither after a linear transform (second axis) nor after a non linear transform such as the Gamma transform (third axis). In many cases, the decoding will lead to erroneous results.

1.2   Previous Works

The goal of this subsection is to present a brief overview of the other works that address the problem of QIM/DM detection in presence of valumetric distortions.

Histogram analysis: Eggers *et. al* have presented a scheme to address the case of an affine valumetric distortion $f(p) = \alpha p + \beta$ [2]. This method is based on the analysis of a two-dimentional probability density function (pdf) that depends on the received sample r and the range of the possible deviations for one secret key k. The resulting pdf presents periodical components for each deviation and the period is proportional to $\alpha \Delta$. Consequently the authors propose to apply a DFT and a phase shift function for each deviation of the two-dimensional PDF before summing the spectra of the pdfs on the k axis. The maximum of the overall spectrum reveals then the term α and the term β is derived from the phase at the location of the maxima. In [3] the authors have also addressed the problem of the non-linear gamma transform by trying to invert the gamma transform before the estimation of α and β but this method need a full search of the γ parameter and consequently increase the complexity of the algorithm.

ML estimator: Lagendijk *et. al* have proposed a similar approach than the previous one that also uses the Fourier transform of the histogram to estimate α [4]. They also have presented in [4] and [5] an estimation of parameter α that is based on the Maximum Likelihood (M.L.) estimator. The pdf of the watermarked image after scaling and noise addition is first expressed as $f(p, \alpha, \sigma_n^2)$ where σ_n^2 denotes the noise variance. The estimates $\hat{\alpha}$ and $\hat{\sigma}_n^2$ parameters are calculated performing a search on the Likelihood function:

$$(\hat{\alpha}, \hat{\sigma}^2) = \arg\max_{\alpha, \sigma_n^2} L(\alpha, \sigma_n^2) = \arg\max_{\alpha, \sigma_n^2} \log f_p(p, \alpha, \sigma_n^2)$$

It is important to notice that the likelihood function is expressed for an host signal and a noise that have both gaussian distributions. The model of the host signal does not represent typical distributions of natural images. This can be seen as a limitation of this approach. Moreover this approach is based on a fixed valumetric distortion model (in this case linear), and the use of ML estimator for nonlinear functions is not straightforward.

Host proportional embedding: Another way to deal with the problem of valumetric transforms is to use a quantification step Δ_p that is constructed in such a way that it is *proportional* to a valumetric feature of the signal. Pérez-Gonzaález *et. al.*[6] have proposed to use a function $g(\mathbf{p})$ which has the property that $g(\alpha \mathbf{p}_i) = \alpha g(\mathbf{p}_i)$ as a weighting function of the initial quantization step[2]. This function can be for example the l_n vector norm given by:

$$g(\mathbf{p}_i) = \left(\frac{1}{L} \sum_{j=i-L}^{i-1} |p_j|^n \right)^{1/n}$$

---

[2] $\mathbf{p}_i$ represents a vector composed by i neighbour pixel values that have been centered.

For example if $n = 1$ and $p_j \geq 0$ for all j, the quantization step is proportional to the mean of the vector $\mathbf{p}_i$. If $n = 2$, it is then proportional to the standard deviation of $\mathbf{p}_i$. The authors give the proof that when $L \to +\infty$, the presented scheme, called Rational Dither Modulation, is equivalent to the classical dither modulation scheme presented by Eggers. Another similar scheme has been also proposed at the same time by Oostveen *et. al*[7], in this scheme the proportional function is chosen as the averaging[3] function ($n = 1$).

As we will see in section 3, host proportional embedding is adapted for linear valumetric functions when L is large enough. Nevertheless the performances of proportional embedding quantization schemes are poor for non-linear transforms beacause the function $g(\mathbf{p})$ has not special properties to cope with a nonlinearity). Additionally for affine transforms, such schemes cannot handle the addition of an offset value. Another important drawback of proportional embedding schemes is the fact that the quantization step Δ is not constant. If $L \ll +\infty$ and $n = 2$ for example, the quantization step is less important in homogeneous areas than in textured areas. This last point can be a serious handicap considering addition of noise because homogeneous areas will be more sensitive to provide detection errors than textured areas.

2   A Floating Quantization Scheme with a Fractal Structure

As we have mentioned previously, the presented schemes have several drawbacks: *histogram analysis* enables to identify a linear distortion but its extension to non linear distortions is not straightforward, *ML estimator* depends both on a host model and a distortion model, *host proportional embedding* is adapted for linear distortion but not to affine or non linear distortions and moreover the quantization step Δ_p is constant only for stationary iid images.

The objectives of the presented scheme are twice, the first is to provide a quantization scheme that is robust both to linear and non-linear distortions and the second is to provide a constant quantization step for each watermarked coefficient, or at least to bound the range of values that can be taken by the quantization step Δ.

In this paper, we propose first to use a floating quantization grid that is based on the local features of the host coefficient to provide robustness to both linear and non linear transforms. A nearly constant quantization step is secondly guaranteed using a fractal set of quantizers. These ideas are presented in the following sections.

2.1   Dealing with Non-linear Distortions

A classical solution to cope with a non-linear distortion $f(p)$ is to locally approximate the function $f()$ by a linear function whose the slope is an approximation

---

[3] In this work, the authors do not use the absolute value term because they only consider pixel (positive) values otherwise the two schemes can be considered as similar.

of the derivate of $f(p)$. To estimate this derivate, we have can use the fact that images are not idd signals but are more often highly correlated. For example adjacent pixels of an image have highly similar values. We choose in this paper the two neighbours of a given pixel because these three values are often highly similar for natural images. The quantization step Δ_f is afterward constructed by taking the minimum p_{Min} and the maximum pixel p_{Max} of these three values respectively as the lower and upper bounds of the quantization grid. Because such a grid relies on the host signal and is specific for each pixel, we have named it a floating quantization grid. The embedding of one bit of information is after done quantizing the middle value p_{Mid}. Fig.2 depicts the principle of the floating quantizer. For clarity purposes only two quantized values p_1 and p_0 are used in this figure. We can notice that if the distorted values p_1' and p_0' are reliable approximations of their equivalent linear transformations, the respective approximation errors ϵ_1 and ϵ_2 are small under the condition that the nonlinearity is not too important.

A floating quantizer has however to deal with several limitations that have to be addressed.

The first one in the fact that the embedding rate is limited to one third of the total number of sample in the host signal. This is due to the fact that three samples are needed to embed one bit.

The second point to adress is the case where $p_{Max} = p_{Min}$. It is however easy to solve this issue by increasing p_{Max} or decreasing p_{Min} in such a way that $p_{Max} - p_{Min} = \Delta_{min}$.

The last limitation of this proposal is the fact that the resilience against additive noise is not constant because we choose a quantization step Δ_f that is

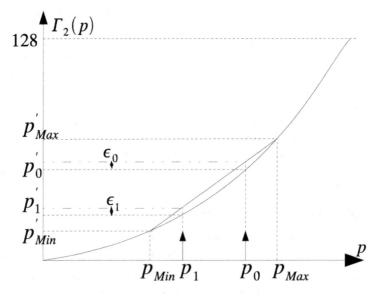

Fig. 2. Effect of a floating quantizer with the function $\Gamma()$ considering $\gamma = 2$

proportional to the range distance $r = p_{Max} - p_{Min}$. This fact is by nature contradictory with the essence of a quantization based-scheme which aims to give an equal quantization step for each watermarked coefficient. We have consequently decided to adopt a specific quantization rule $\mathcal{R}$ that is chosen according to the value of the quantization step r: $\Delta_f = \mathcal{R}(r)$. This last point is addressed in the next subsection.

2.2   Using a Fractal Quantization Structure

The main idea is to build a set of N hierarchiezed quantizers $Q = \{Q_1, ..., Q_N\}$ such that it is possible to have a bijection between one quantizer and one specific value r. In order to have a nearly constant quantization step Δ_f for each quantizer one might fix the minimum and maximum possible values of Δ_f by setting $\alpha_1 \Delta \leq \Delta_f \leq \alpha_2 \Delta$ where $\alpha_1 \leq 1$, $\alpha_2 \geq 1$ and Δ is an arbitrary fixed quantization step. To guaranty that there are no overlapping or impossible affectation between on quantizer and its adjacent quantizers these parameters are naturally linked by the relation $\alpha_2 = 2\alpha_1$. The choice of α_1 depends of different kinds of applications. For example if we want to guarantee a minimum quantization step Δ, this leads to $\alpha_1 = 1$. On the other hand, if we consider an uniform host distribution and want an average quantization step equal to Δ, we then have to choose $\alpha_1 = 0.66$. The value of the floating quantization step Δ_f is given by the relation:

$$\Delta_f = \frac{r}{2^{N(r)}} \quad \text{if} \ \ N(r) > 0 \tag{2}$$

$$\Delta_f = \Delta \ \ \text{if} \ \ N(r) = 0 \tag{3}$$

where the power function $N()$ is given using the positive integer part function $\mathcal{E}_+()$:

$$N(r) = \mathcal{E}_+ \left(\log_2 \left(\frac{r}{\alpha_1 \Delta} \right) \right)$$

The calculus of Δ_f naturally leads to the construction of the set of quantizers Q because each different value of $N(r)$ is associated to a number of quantization values. Fig. 3 depicts the set of quantizers which mainly presents a fractal structure: the basic quantization pattern Q_1 is repeated on Q_2, Q_3 and Q_4 using a contraction factor respectively equal to $1/2$; $(1/2)^2$ and $(1/2)^3$. Only the quantizer Q_0 is not a member of the fractal set and this quantizer can be additionally used when initially $p_{Max} = p_{Min}$. This fractal structure has the main advantage to avoid to have different quantization cells on the same location on the different axes. Fig. 4 represents the repartition of the set of quantizer Q in function of the range value r. We have decided to note each upper border of the quantizer Q_i by q_i. Note also that the quantizer Q_0 corresponds to the case where $N(r) = 0$ and in this case, because the value of r is considered as too small, the quantizer step is forced to be equal to Δ.

2.3   Embedding Scheme

Based on the building of the specific floating quantizer, we can afterward apply a classical quantization scheme. The presented scheme is basic but it can be

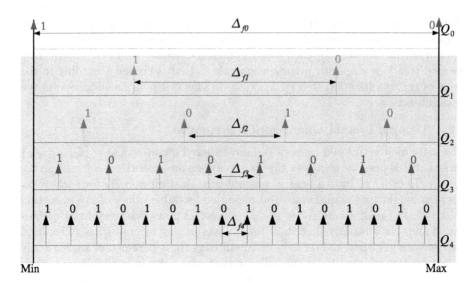

Fig. 3. Building of the set of quantizers. Quantizers that are in the gray area represent a fractal structure. The choice of the quantizer is determined by the value of r.

Fig. 4. Repartition of Q in function of r for $\alpha_1 = 1$

easily improved by using a dither signal or a distortion compensation module as proposed by Chen. The embedding of a message $b(k)$ of size N is done by embedding one bit b for each triplet of the original image. The main steps of the embedding procedure are listed below:

- Select a triplet of pixels (p_i, p_j, p_k). Note that better performance for non-linear distortion will be obtained if this triplet corresponds to adjacent pixels.
- Order the triplet in $(p_{Min}, p_{Mid}, p_{Max})$ and compute $r = p_{Max} - p_{Min}$, Δ_f from (2) and (3) that will provide Q_i.
- If $Q_i \neq Q_0$ quantize p_{Mid} according to Q_i and b.
- Else quantize both p_{Mid} and p_{Min} for $b = 0$ or p_{Mid} and p_{Max} for $b = 1$.
- Select another triplet that was not selected before and embed another bit b.

2.4   Detection Scheme

The detection procedure has to consider that the received image has undergone a valumetric transform $f()$. This implies that a given pixel that has been quantized using quantizer Q_i may be decoded using another quantizer. To deal with this issue we have first to constrain the possible variations of $f()$ assuming that $\beta_1 \leq f'(p) \leq \beta_2$. Assuming that $(\beta_1, \beta_2) \in [1/2; 1] \times [1; 2]$, the pixels that are watermarked using a given quantizer Q_i may be decoded using Q_i and Q_{i-1} or Q_i and Q_{i+1}. Note that in these particular cases, because we use a set a 2 quantizers, the robustness may be divided by 2 or 4. Therefore we can also consider another alternate decoding scheme that consists in using only the decoder Q_i. This is due to the fact that after a valumetric distortion, an initial pixel watermarked using Q_i may still be decoded using Q_i if the value of r has not changed of quantization cell. The differences between these two decoders will be assessed in the next section. Finally, the different steps of the decoding algorithm are listed below:

- Select (p_i, p_j, p_k).
- Compute r and Δ_f.
- Using the fractal detection: if $r > \beta_1 q_{i-1}$ perform the detection using both Q_i and Q_{i-1} and choose the nereast quantization cell considering the two quantizers.
- Using the fractal detection: if $r < \beta_2 q_{i+1}$ perform the detection using both Q_i and Q_{i+1} and choose the nereast quantization cell considering the two quantizers.
- Else or for the classical floating quantizer: perform the detection using Q_i.

3   Results and Comparisons

In this section we outline the capability of the presented scheme to achieve robustness for linear and non-linear distortions and noise addition. We also compare these performances with classical and proportional QIM/DM embedding and detection schemes. In each cases, $1/3$ of the pixels are watermarked for both the lena image and baboon image. This is done to achieve the same capacity of embedding. For proportional quantization, we have chosen to use a proportional function that skips the future quantized coefficients to improve the estimation of quantization step. Note that in [6], the authors compute the function $g(\mathbf{p}_i)$ using watermarked samples which is an equivalent way to cope with this problem. We have tested two neighbourhood size: $N = 10$ and $N = 100$ pixels and we also used $n = 2$ which means that the quantization step is proportional to the standard deviation of the selected samples. The floating quantization scheme is tested using both a fractal decoder with $\beta_1 = 0.7$ and $\beta_2 = 1.42$ and a non-fractal decoder.

Fig. 5 and Table. 1 presents the performances of the floating quantization scheme to non-linear distortions (gamma correction and histogram equalization) for different Document to Watermark Ratios.

In Fig. 5, we can notice that the possibility to use multiple quantizers (named in the figure by Fractal quantizer) improve the decoding performances comparing to only one quantizer. Moreover this figure illustrates the fact that the proportional embedding is not adapted to non linear distortions even for little neighbourhood size. In this last case, this is mainly due to the fact that the quantization step of proportional schemes can be too small. For example,

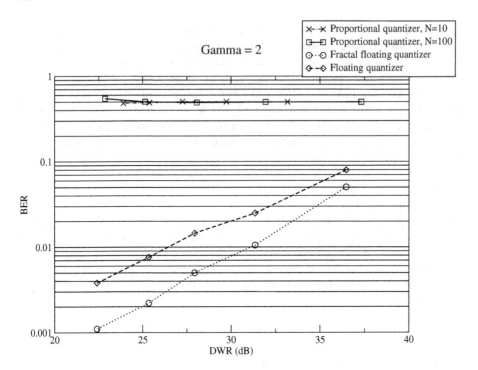

Fig. 5. BER results after gamma correction $\gamma = 0.5$ for the lena image

Table 1. BER results after histogram equalization for two different images (WDR=27db, neighbourhood size=200)

BER (%)	fractal	non fractal	proportional
lena	3.0	3.0	36.2
baboon	12.3	15.5	58.8

if the neighbourhood represents a constant portion of the image, the distance between watermarked samples representing 0 and 1 will be null and will consequenlty lead to decoding errors. The effect of the used valumetric distortion is illustrated in Fig. 8.

Table 1 presents the robustness of the floating quantization scheme after histogram equalizations that are equivalent to an image dependent nonlinear transform. Fig. 9 represents these functions for the two images and Fig. 8 shows the result on the *Lena* image. We can notice that the performance of the floating quantization is once again superior to the use of proportional embedding but also depends of the nature of the image. For example, the baboon image, which is more textured than the lena image, offer weaker performance: as mentioned before, this is due to the fact that the linear approximation is not reliable when r is too important, e.g. when the triplet belong to a textured area.

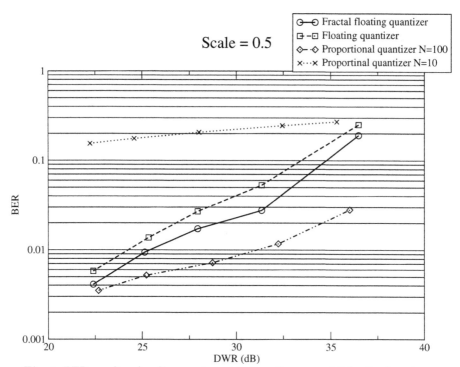

Fig. 6. BER results after linear valumetric transform $\alpha = 0.5$ for the lena image

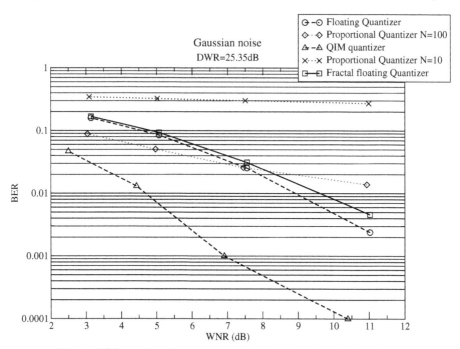

Fig. 7. BER results after gaussian noise addition for the lena image

Original lena   lena after Gamma transform ($\gamma = 2$)

Fig. 8. Effects of the gamma transform for the presented tests images

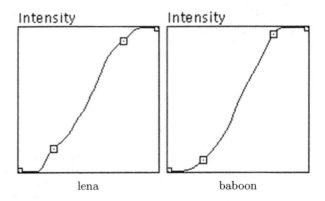

lena   baboon

Fig. 9. $f(p)$ for histogram equalization on two images

Fig. 6 presents the performance of the different schemes when the valumetric transform is linear for different $DWRs$. A scaling factor equal to 0.5 has been applied on the pixels of the watermarked image and no noise is added. Here the proportional quantization scheme can outperform the floating quantization scheme if the size of the neighbourhood is important enough ($N = 100$). Note however that contrary to floating quantization, proportional quantization is robust to an affine transform $f(x) = ax + b$ only when $b = 0$.

Fig. 7 compare the robustness after Gaussian noise addition for a DWR equal to $25.35dB$. In this case, we can see that the classical QIM/DM scheme outperforms all the other schemes, and that the floating quantization scheme is weaker than the proportional quantization scheme for a large neighbourhood size ($N = 100$). This is due to the fact that Δ_f is proportional to r that is also subject to noise. When the neighbourhood size is not enough important however, the proportional quantizer scheme is less efficient that the floating quantizer because a minimum quantization step is not guaranteed with the first solution.

4   Concluding Remarks and Perspectives

We have presented in this paper a practical implementation of a quantization watermarking scheme that is more robust to non-linear distortions than previous proposed schemes. This performance gain is mainly due to the use of a floating quantizer and the adoption of a fractal set of quantizers.

Future works will address the capacity limitation of this scheme by performing an iterative embedding on each sample to achieve a capacity equal to one bit per sample.

References

1. Chen, B., Wornell, G.W.: Quantization index modulation: A class of provably good methods for digital watermarking and information embedding. IEEE Transactions on Information Theory **47** (2001) 1423–1443
2. Eggers, J.J., Buml, R., Tzschoppe, R., Girod, B.: Scalar costa scheme for information embedding. IEEE Trans. on Signal Processing **51** (2003) 1003–1019
3. Eggers, J.J., Bauml, R., Girod, B.: Estimation of amplitude modifications before scs watermark detection. In: Proceedings of SPIE, Security, Steganography and Watermarking of Multimedia Contents IV, San Jose, USA (2002)
4. Shterev, I., Lagendijk, R., Heusdens, R.: Statistical amplitude scale estimation for quantization-based watermarking. In: Proceedings of SPIE, Security, Steganography and Watermarking of Multimedia Contents VI, San Jose, USA (2004)
5. Lagendijk, R.L., Shterev, I.D.: Estimation of attacker's scale and noise variance for qim-dc watermark embedding. In: Proc. if ICIP, Singapore (2004)
6. Perez-Gonzalez, F., Barni, M., Abrardo, A., Mosquera, C.: Rational dither modulation: a novel data-hiding method robust to value-metric scaling attacks. In: IEEE International Workshop on Multimedia Signal Processing, Siena, Italy (2004)
7. Oostveen, J., Kalker, T., Staring, M.: Adaptive quantization watermarking. In: Proceedings of SPIE, Security, Steganography and Watermarking of Multimedia Contents VI, San Jose, USA (2004)

Efficient Steganography with Provable Security Guarantees

Aggelos Kiayias*, Yona Raekow, and Alexander Russell**

University of Connecticut, Storrs, CT

Abstract. We provide a new provably-secure steganographic encryption protocol that is proven secure in the complexity-theoretic framework of Hopper et al. The fundamental building block of our steganographic encryption protocol is a "one-time stegosystem" that allows two parties to transmit one-time steganographic messages of length shorter than the shared key with *information-theoretic* security guarantees. The employment of a pseudorandom number generator (PRNG) allows the transmission of longer messages in the same way that such a generator allows the use of one-time pad encryption for messages longer than the key in symmetric encryption. The advantage of our construction compared to that of Hopper et al. is that it avoids the use of a pseudorandom function family and instead relies (directly) on a PRNG in a way that provides a linear versus constant improvement in the number of applications of the underlying (say) one-way permutation per bit transmitted. This advantageous trade-off is achieved by substituting the pseudorandom function family employed in the previous construction with an appropriate combinatorial construction that has been used extensively in derandomization, namely almost *t*-wise independent function families.

1 Introduction

In steganography, Alice and Bob wish to communicate securely in the presence of an adversary called the "Warden" that monitors whether they exchange "conspicuous" messages. In particular Alice and Bob may exchange messages that adhere to a certain channel distribution that represents "inconspicuous" communication. By controlling the kind of messages that are transmitted over such a channel (that is assumed to have sufficient entropy) Alice and Bob may exchange messages that cannot be detected by the Warden. There have been two approaches in formalizing Steganography, one based on information theory [1,2,3] and one based on complexity theory [4]. The latter approach is more specific and has the potential of allowing more efficient constructions. Most steganographic constructions that come with provable security guarantees are instantiations of the following basic procedure (which has been also called "rejection-sampling"):

---

* Supported by NSF CAREER grant CNS-0447808.
** Supported by NSF CAREER grant CCR-0093065, and NSF grants CCR-0121277, CCR-0220264, CCR-0311368, and EIA-0218443.

M. Barni et al. (Eds.): IH 2005, LNCS 3727, pp. 118–130, 2005.

there is a family (or channel distribution) that provides a number of possible options for a so-called "covertext" to be transmitted. The sender and the receiver possess some sort of function that is private (e.g. a keyed hash function, MAC, or other similar function) that maps to a single bit or a short sequence of bits. The sender applies the function to the covertext and checks whether it happens to produce the stegotext it wishes to transmit. If this is the case, the covertext is transmitted. In case of failure, a second covertext is drawn, etc. While this is a fairly specific procedure, there are a number of choices to be made and these are of both practical and theoretical concern. From the security viewpoint one is primarily interested in the choice of the function that is shared between the sender and the receiver. From a practical viewpoint one would be interested in how the channel is implemented and whether it conforms to the various constraints that are imposed on it by the steganographic protocol specifications (e.g., are independent draws from the channel allowed? does the channel remember previous draws? etc.). As mentioned above, the security of a stegosystem can be naturally phrased in information-theoretic terms (cf. [1]) or in complexity-theoretic terms [4]. Informally, the latter approach considers the following experiment for the warden-adversary: the adversary selects a message (or messages) to be embedded and receives either the covertexts that embed the stegotexts or covertexts simply drawn from the channel distribution (without any embedding). The adversary is then asked to distinguish between the two cases. Clearly, if the probability of success is very close to $1/2$ it is natural to claim that the stegosystem provides security against such (eavesdropping) adversarial activity. Formulation of stronger attacks such as active attacks is also possible. Given the above framework, Hopper et al. [4] provided a provably secure stegosystem that pairs rejection sampling with a pseudorandom function family. Given that rejection sampling, when implemented properly and paired with a truly random function, is indistinguishable from the channel distribution, the security of their construction followed from the pseudorandom function family assumption. From the efficiency viewpoint this construction required about 2 evaluations of the pseudorandom function per bit transmission. Constructing efficient pseudorandom functions is possible either generically [5] or, more efficiently, based on specific number-theoretic assumptions [6]. Nevertheless, pseudorandom function families are a conceptually complex and fairly expensive cryptographic primitive. For example, the evaluation of the Naor-Reingold pseudorandom function on an input x requires $O(|x|)$ modular exponentiations. Similarly, the generic construction [5] requires $O(k)$ PRNG doublings of the input string where k is the length of the key. In this article we take an alternative approach to the design of provably secure stegosystems. Our main contribution is the design of a building block that we call a *one-time stegosystem*: this is a steganographic protocol that is meant to be used for a single message transmission and is proven secure in the information-theoretic sense provided that the key that is shared between the sender and the receiver is of sufficient length (this length analysis is part of our result). In particular we show that we can securely transmit ν bits with a key of length $O(\ell(\nu) + \log|\Sigma|)$ where $\ell(\cdot)$ is the stretching function of an appropriate error-correcting code and Σ is the size of the channel alphabet (see Section 3.4 for more details regarding the exact formulation). Our basic building block is a natural analogue of a one time-pad for steganography. It is based on the rejection sampling technique outlined above in combination with a combinatorial construction that is a function family that is almost t-wise independent [7]. We note that such combinatorial constructions have been extremely useful for derandomization methods and here, to the best of our knowledge, are employed for the first time in the design of steganographic protocols. Given a one-time stegosystem, it is fairly straightforward to construct provably secure steganographic encryption for longer messages by using a pseudorandom number generator (PRNG) to stretch a random seed that is shared by the sender and the receiver to sufficient length. The resulting stegosystem is provably secure in the computational sense of Hopper et al. [4] and is in fact much more efficient: in particular, while the Hopper, et al. stegosystem requires 2 evaluations *per bit* of a pseudorandom function, amounting to a linear (in the key-size) number of applications of the underlying PRNG (in the standard construction for pseudorandom functions of [5]), in our stegosystem we require *per bit* a constant amount of PRNG applications. The reason for this improvement is that in our case we do not perform per bit pseudorandom function evaluations because we rely on the combinatorial constructions of function families with good randomization properties that are extremely efficient.

2   Definitions and Tools

The channel which will be used for transmission of data is abstracted as a family of probability distributions $\{\mathcal{C}_h\}_{h \in \Sigma^*}$ with support $\Sigma = \{c_1, c_2, \ldots, c_n\}$. A communication according to $\mathcal{C}_h$ can be viewed as drawing elements (we call them covertexts) from Σ for a history h.

Definition 1. *Let $M = \{0,1\}^\nu$ be the message space, i.e., all bit strings of size ν. A one-time stegosystem consists of three probabilistic time algorithms $S = (SK, SE, SD)$, where:*

- *SK is the key generation algorithm; it has as input the parameter ν and outputs a key k of length κ (with κ a function of ν).*
- *SE is the embedding procedure, which can access the channel; its input is the security parameter κ, the key k, the message $m \in M$ to be embedded, and the history h of previously drawn covertexts. The output is the stegotext $s \in \Sigma^\lambda$ (note that $\ell(\nu) = \lambda$ will be the stretching of an appropriate error-correcting code).*
- *SD is the extracting procedure; its input is κ, k, and some $c \in \Sigma^*$. The output is a message $m \in M$ or fail.*

A function $\mu : \mathbb{N} \to \mathbb{R}$ is called *negligible* if for every positive polynomial $p(\cdot)$ there exists an N s.t., for all $n > N$, $\mu(n) < \frac{1}{p(n)}$. A stegosystem (SK, SE, SD) is *correct*, provided that

$$\forall m \in M, \Pr[SD(1^\kappa, k, SE(1^\kappa, k, h, m)) \neq m \mid k \leftarrow SK(1^\nu)] = \text{negligible}(\kappa) \ .$$

One-time stegosystem security is based on the indistinguishability between a transmission that contains a steganographically embedded message and a transmission that contains no embedded messages. An adversary $\mathcal{A}$ against a one-time stegosystem $S = (SK, SE, SD)$ is a pair of algorithms $\mathcal{A} = (SA_1, SA_2)$, that plays the following game, denoted as $G^{\mathcal{A}}(1^\kappa)$

1. A key k is generated by $SK(1^\nu)$.
2. Algorithm SA_1 gets as input κ the security parameter and public history h and outputs a message $(m^*, s, h_c) \in M \times \{0,1\}^*$, where s is some additional information. SA_1 can access $\mathcal{C}$, via an oracle $\mathcal{O}(h)$, which takes the history h as input. $\mathcal{O}(h)$ is defined as follows:
   - it gets a request of SA_1 that includes a suggested h.
   - it samples $c \xleftarrow{r} \mathcal{C}_h$.
   - it returns c to SA_1.
3. A bit b is chosen uniformly at random.
   - If $b = 0$ let $c^* \leftarrow SE(1^\kappa, k, m^*, h_c)$, so c^* is a stegotext.
   - If $b = 1$ let $c^* = c_1 || \ldots || c_\lambda$ where $c_i \xleftarrow{r} \mathcal{C}_{h_c || c_1 || \ldots || c_{i-1}}$.
4. The input for SA_2 is 1^κ, c^* and s. SA_2 outputs a bit b'. If $b' = b$ then output success else fail.

The advantage of the adversary $\mathcal{A}$ over a stegosystem S is defined as:

$$\mathbf{Adv}_S^{\mathcal{A}}(G(1^\kappa)) = \left| \Pr\left[G(1^\kappa) = \text{success}\right] - \frac{1}{2} \right| .$$

The probability includes the coin tosses of $\mathcal{A}$ and SE, as well as the coin tosses of $G(1^\kappa)$. The (information-theoretic) insecurity of the stegosystem is defined as

$$\mathbf{InSec}_S(\nu) = \max_{\mathcal{A}} \{ \mathbf{Adv}_S^{\mathcal{A}}(G(1^\kappa)) \} .$$

The maximum above is quantified over all (time unbounded) adversaries $\mathcal{A}$.

2.1   Error-Correcting Codes

Definition 2. *Let* $\mathsf{E} = (Enc, Dec)$ *be an error-correcting code for error rate* α, *where* $Enc(m) : \{0,1\}^\nu \mapsto \{0,1\}^{\ell(\nu)}$ *is the encoding function and* $Dec(\bar{m}) : \{0,1\}^{\ell(\nu)} \mapsto \{0,1\}^\nu$ *the corresponding decoding function. Specifically, we say that* E *is a* $(\nu, \ell(\nu), \alpha, \epsilon)$-*code if*

$$\Pr[Dec(Enc(m) \oplus e) = m] \geq 1 - \epsilon$$

where $e = (e_1, \ldots, e_{\ell(\nu)})$ *and each* e_i *is independently distributed in* $\{0,1\}$ *so that* $\Pr[e_i = 1] \leq \alpha$. *The error correcting code is said to incur a stretching of* $\ell(\nu) = \lambda$.

We remark that the error model adopted above is that of a binary symmetric channel with transition probability $3/8$. For such channels, there are constant rate codes for which the probability of error decays exponentially in the length of the codeword. See, e.g., [8,9] for a discussion of error-correcting coding over binary symmetric channels.

2.2   Function Families and Almost t-wise Independence

In this article, a *function family* will be a collection of functions from $\{0,1\}^n \to \{0,1\}$ denoted as $\mathcal{F}_\kappa$. We treat such families as indexed by a key k. In particular, $\mathcal{F}_\kappa = \{f_k \mid k \in \{0,1\}^\kappa\}$; note $|\mathcal{F}_\kappa| = 2^\kappa$. We will employ the notion of (almost) t-wise independent function families (cf. [7], [10]).

Definition 3. *The family $\mathcal{F}_\kappa$ of Boolean functions on $\{0,1\}^n$ is said to be ϵ-away from t-wise independent or (n,t,ϵ)-independent if for any t distinct domain elements $q_1, q_2, \ldots, q_t$ we have*

$$\sum_{\alpha \in \{0,1\}^t} \left| \Pr_{f_k}[f_k(q_1)f_k(q_2)\ldots f_k(q_t) = \alpha] - \frac{1}{2^t} \right| \le \epsilon \tag{1}$$

where f_k chosen uniformly from $\mathcal{F}_\kappa$.

The above is equivalent to the following formulation that is quantified over all computationally unbounded adversaries $\mathcal{A}$:

$$\left| \Pr_{f \xleftarrow{r} \mathcal{F}_\kappa}[G^{\mathcal{A}^{f[t]}}(1^\kappa) = 1] - \Pr_{f \xleftarrow{r} \mathcal{R}}[G^{\mathcal{A}^{f[t]}}(1^\kappa) = 1] \right| \le \epsilon \tag{2}$$

where $\mathcal{R}$ is the collection of *all* functions from $\{0,1\}^n$ to $\{0,1\}$ and $\mathcal{A}^{f[t]}$ is an unbounded adversary that is allowed to determine up to t queries to the function f before he outputs his bit. We employ the construction of almost t-wise independent sample spaces given by [10], [7].

Theorem 1. *There exist families of Boolean functions $\mathcal{F}_{t,\epsilon}^n$ on $\{0,1\}^n$ that are ϵ-away from t-wise independent, are indexed by keys of length $\kappa = 2(\frac{t}{2} + \log n + \log 1/\epsilon)$, and are computable in polynomial time.*

2.3   Rejection Sampling

A common method used in steganography employing a channel distribution is that of *rejection sampling* (cf. [1,4]). Assuming that one wishes to transmit a single bit m and employs a random function $f : \{0,1\}^d \times \Sigma \to \{0,1\}$ that is secret from the adversary he performs the following "rejection sampling" process:

$$
\begin{array}{|l|}
\hline
\texttt{rejsam}_h^{f,i}(m) \\
\hline
c \xleftarrow{r} \mathcal{C}_h \\
\text{if } f(i,c) \ne m \\
\text{then } c \xleftarrow{r} \mathcal{C}_h \\
\texttt{Output: } c \\
\hline
\end{array}
$$

Here Σ denotes the output alphabet of the channel, h denotes the history of the channel data at the start of the process, and $\mathcal{C}_h$ denotes the distribution on Σ given by the channel after history h. The receiver (that is also privy to the function f) applies the function to the received message $c \in \Sigma$ and recovers

m with probability higher than $1/2$. The sender and the receiver may employ a joint state denoted by i in the above process (e.g., a counter), that need not be secret from the adversary. Note that the above process performs only two draws from the channel with the *same* history (more draws could, in principle, be performed). These draws are typically assumed to be independent. One basic property of rejection sampling that we use is:

Lemma 1. *If f is drawn uniformly at random from the collection of all functions $\mathcal{R} = \{f : \{0,1\}^d \times \Sigma \rightarrow \{0,1\}\}$ and all $\mathcal{C}_h$ have at least one bit of min-entropy, then for all $i \in [1, 2^d]$ and all h,*

$$\Pr_{f \leftarrow \mathcal{R}}[f(i, \mathbf{rejsam}_h^{f,i}(m_i)) = m_i] \geq \frac{5}{8} \ .$$

See Appendix A for a proof.

3 The Construction

In this section we outline our construction for a one-time stegosystem as an interaction between Alice (the sender) and Bob (the receiver). Alice and Bob wish to communicate over a channel with distribution $\mathcal{C}$. We assume for all $h \in \Sigma^*$ that $\mathcal{C}$ has a minimum entropy of $H_\infty(\mathcal{C}_h) = \min \left\{ \log_2 \frac{1}{\Pr_{\mathcal{C}_h}[x]} \right\} \geq 1$. Without loss of generality we assume that the support of $\mathcal{C}_h$ is of size $|\Sigma| = 2^b$.

3.1 A One-Time Stegosystem

Fixing a message length ν and an alphabet Σ for the channel, Alice and Bob agree on the following:

An error-correcting code. Let $\mathsf{E} = (Enc, Dec)$ be a $(\nu, \lambda = \ell(\nu), 3/8, \epsilon_{enc})$-error-correcting code;

A pseudorandom function family. Let $\mathcal{F}_\kappa$ be a function family that is $(\log \lambda + \log |\Sigma|, 2\lambda, \epsilon_{\mathcal{F}})$-independent.

Note that each element of the family $\mathcal{F}_\kappa$ is a function $f_k : \{0, \dots, \lambda - 1\} \times \Sigma \rightarrow \{0, 1\}$ and that, in light of Theorem 1, such a function can be expressed with keys of length $2\lambda + 2(\log \lambda + \log |\Sigma| + \log 1/\epsilon_{\mathcal{F}})$. By the Shannon coding theorem, we may take $\lambda = O(\nu)$; thus the coin tosses for the SK algorithm consist of $O(\nu + \log |\Sigma| + \log(1/\epsilon_{\mathcal{F}}))$ bits. Alice and Bob communicate using the algorithm SE for embedding and SD for extracting described in Figure 1. In SE, after applying the error-correcting code E, we use $\mathbf{rejsam}_h^{f_k,i}(m)$ to obtain an element of the channel, denoted as c_i. We repeat this procedure for each bit m_i to obtain the complete embedding of the message, the stegotext, denoted as c_{stego}. In SD we parse the received stegotext block by block. Again the function f_k (the same one as used in SE) is queried with a block and the current counter and a message bit is received. After performing this for each received block, a message of size $\lambda = \ell(\nu)$ is received; by decoding the error-correcting code; we then obtain the

PROCEDURE SE:	PROCEDURE SD:
Input: Key k, hidden text m', history h	Input: Key k, stegotext c
let $m = Enc(m')$	
parse m as $m = m_0 \|m_1\| \ldots \|m_{\lambda-1}$	parse c_{stego} as $c = c_0, c_1, \ldots, c_{\lambda-1}$
for $i = 0$ to $\lambda - 1$ {	for $i = 0$ to $\lambda - 1$ {
$\quad\quad c_i =$rejsam$_h^{i,f_k}(m_i)$	$\quad\quad$ set $\bar{m}_i = f_k(i, c_i)$
$\quad\quad$ set $h \leftarrow h\|c_i$	$\quad\quad$ let $\bar{m} = \bar{m}_0, \bar{m}_1, \ldots, \bar{m}_{\lambda-1}$
}	}
Output: $c_{stego} = c_0, c_1, \ldots, c_{\lambda-1} \in \Sigma^\lambda$	Output: $Dec(\bar{m})$

Fig. 1. Encryption and Decryption algorithms for the one-time stegosystem of 3.1

original message size ν. Note that we sample at most twice from the channel for each bit we wish to send. The error-correcting code is needed to recover from the errors introduced by this process. The detailed security and correctness analysis follow in the next two sections.

3.2   Correctness

We focus on the mapping between $\{0,1\}^\lambda$ and Σ^λ ($\lambda = \ell(\nu)$) that is performed within the SE procedure of the one-time stegosystem of the previous section. In particular, for an initial history h and a function $f : \{0, \ldots, \lambda - 1\} \times \Sigma \to \{0,1\}$, consider the following: Recall that the key k determines a function f_k

$$P_h^f : \{0,1\}^\lambda \to \Sigma^\lambda \quad \left| \begin{array}{l} \text{input: } h, \; m_1, \ldots, m_\lambda \in \{0,1\} \\ \quad\quad \text{for } i = 0 \text{ to } \lambda - 1 \\ \quad\quad\quad c_i =\text{rejsam}_h^{i,f}(m_i) \\ \quad\quad\quad h \leftarrow h\|c_i \\ \text{output: } c_1, \ldots, c_\lambda \in \Sigma \end{array} \right.$$

for which the covertext of the message m is $P^{f_k}(m) = P_h^{f_k}(m)$, where h is the initial history. We remark now that the procedure defining P^f samples f at no more than 2λ points and that the family $\mathcal{F}$ used in SE is in fact $\epsilon_\mathcal{F}$-away from 2λ-wise independent. For a string $c = c_1, \ldots, c_\lambda \in \Sigma^\lambda$ and a function f, let $R^f(c) = (f(0, c_1), \ldots, f(\lambda - 1, c_\lambda)) \in \{0,1\}^\lambda$. By Lemma 1 above, each bit is independently recovered by this process with probability at least $5/8$. As E is an $(\nu, \lambda, 3/8, \epsilon_{enc})$-error-correcting code, we conclude that

$$\Pr_{f \leftarrow \mathcal{R}}[R^f(P_h^f(m)) = m] \geq 1 - \epsilon_{enc} \; .$$

This is a restatement of the correctness analysis of Hopper, et al [4]. Note, however, that the procedure defining $R^f(P_h^f(\cdot))$ involves no more than 2λ samples of f, and thus by the condition (2) following Definition 3,

$$\Pr_{f \leftarrow \mathcal{F}}[R^f(P_h^f(m)) = m] \geq 1 - \epsilon_{enc} - \epsilon_\mathcal{F} \tag{3}$$

so long as $\mathcal{F}$ is $(\log \lambda + \log |\Sigma|, 2\lambda, \epsilon_\mathcal{F})$-independent. (We remark that as described above, the procedure P_h^f depends on the behavior of channel; note, however, that if there were a sequence of channel distributions which violated (3) then there would be a fixed sequence of channel responses, and thus a deterministic process P^f, which also violated (3).) To summarize

Lemma 2. *With SE and SD described as above, the probability that a message m is recovered from the stegosystem is at least $1 - \epsilon_{enc} - \epsilon_\mathcal{F}$.*

3.3   Security

In this section we argue about the security of our one-time stegosystem. First we will show that the output of the rejection sampling function $\mathtt{rejsam}_h^{f,i}$, as employed here, is indistinguishable from the channel distribution $\mathcal{C}_h$, if we use a truly random function f. (This is a folklore result implicit in previous work.) In the second part we show that when we use $f_k \in \mathcal{F}_\kappa$, a function, that is $\epsilon_\mathcal{F}$-away from 2λ-wise independent, the advantage of an adversary $\mathcal{A}$ to distinguish between the output of the protocol and $\mathcal{C}_h$ is bounded by ϵ. Let $\mathcal{R} = \{f \mid \{0,1\}^{d+b} \rightarrow \{0,1\}\}$, where d is the size of the counter and $b = \log |\Sigma|$ is the number of bits required to express a channel element. First we characterize the probability distribution of the rejection sampling function:

Proposition 1. *The function $\mathtt{rejsam}_h^{f,i}(m)$ is random variable with probability distribution expressed by the following function: Let $c \in \Sigma$ and $m \in \{0,1\}$. Denote the failure probability as $\mathsf{fail} = \Pr_{c' \leftarrow \mathcal{C}_h}[f(i,c') \neq m]$. It holds that*

$$\Pr[\mathtt{rejsam}_h^{f,i}(m) = c] = \begin{cases} \Pr_{c' \leftarrow \mathcal{C}_h}[c' = c] \cdot (1 + \mathsf{fail}) & \text{if } f(i,c) = m \ , \\ \Pr_{c' \leftarrow \mathcal{C}_h}[c' = c] \cdot \mathsf{fail} & \text{if } f(i,c) \neq m \ . \end{cases}$$

Lemma 3. *For any h, i, m, the random variable $\mathtt{rejsam}_h^{f,i}(m)$ is perfectly indistinguishable from the channel distribution $\mathcal{C}_h$ when f is drawn uniformly at random from the space of all functions $\mathcal{R}$.*

The proofs these statements appear in Appendix A. Having established the behavior of the rejection sampling function when a truly random function is used, we proceed to examine the behavior of rejection sampling in our setting where the function is drawn from a function family that is ϵ-away from 2λ-wise independence. In particular we will show that the insecurity of the defined stegosystem is characterized as follows:

Theorem 2. *The insecurity of the stegosystem S of section 3.1 is bound by ϵ, i.e., $\mathbf{InSec}_S(\nu) \leq \epsilon$, where ϵ is the bias of the almost 2λ-wise independent function family employed; recall that $\lambda = \ell(\nu)$ is the stretching of the input incurred due to the error-correcting code.*

The proof appears in Appendix A.

3.4   Putting It All Together

Let us now turn to the following question: suppose that we want to transmit a number of bits ν so that the probability of transmission error is ϵ_{err} and the statistical distance from uniform we are willing to tolerate is ϵ_{sec}. *How long must be the key used in the one-time stegosystem?* Below we establish that we need $2\ell(\nu) + 2\log|\Sigma| + \mathsf{polylog}(\nu)$ bits where $\ell(\cdot)$ is the stretch due to error correction.

Theorem 3. *In order to transmit ν bits with transmission error ϵ_{err} and statistical distance from uniform ϵ_{sec} using the one-time stegosystem of section 3.1 over a covertext channel that has a support set Σ and using an error-correcting code that requires stretching $\ell(\cdot)$ and decoding error of ϵ_{ecc} the sender and the receiver need to share a key of length*

$$2\left(\ell(\nu) + \log\ell(\nu) + \log|\Sigma| + \ln(\epsilon_{err} - \epsilon_{ecc})^{-1} + \log\epsilon_{sec}^{-1}\right) \ .$$

Note that if a key of length $\ell(\nu) + \log|\Sigma| + \mathsf{polylog}(\nu)$ is used, then the insecurity of the system is a negligible function of $\ell(\nu)$. We remark that selecting $\epsilon_{ecc}, \epsilon_{err}, \epsilon_{sec}$ to be small constants (e.g. 2^{-80}) is sufficient for correctness and security in practice.

4   A Provably Secure Stegosystem for Longer Messages

In this section we show how to apply the "one-time" stegosystem of Section 3.1 together with a pseudorandom number generator so that longer messages can be transmitted.

Definition 4. *Let U_l denote the uniform distribution over $\{0,1\}^l$. A polynomial time deterministic program G is a pseudorandom generator (PRNG) if the following conditions are satisfied: 1. Variable output: For all seeds $x \in \{0,1\}^*$ and $y \in \mathbb{N}$, it holds that $|G(x,1^y)| = y$ and $G(x,1^y)$ is a prefix of $G(x,1^{y+1})$. 2. Pseudorandomness: For every polynomial p the set of random variables $\{G(U_l, 1^{p(l)})\}_{l\in\mathbb{N}}$ is computationally indistinguishable from the uniform distribution $U_{p(l)}$.*

Note that there is a procedure G' that if $z = G(x,1^y)$ it holds that $G(x,1^{y+y'}) = G'(x,z,1^{y'})$ (i.e., if one maintains z, one can extract the y' bits that follow the first y bits without starting from the beginning). For a PRNG G, if A is some statistical test, then we define the advantage of A over the PRNG as follows:

$$\mathbf{Adv}_G^A(l) = \left| \Pr_{\hat{\imath}\leftarrow G(U_l, 1^{p(l)})} [A(\hat{\imath}) = 1] - \Pr_{\hat{\imath}\leftarrow U_{p(l)}} [A(\hat{\imath}) = 1] \right|$$

The insecurity of the PRNG G is then defined

$$\mathbf{InSec}_G^{PRNG}(l) = \max_A \{\mathbf{Adv}_G^A(l)\} \ .$$

Note that typically in PRNGs there is a procedure G' as well as the process $G(x, 1^y)$ produces some auxiliary data aux_y of small length so that the rightmost y' bits of $G(x, 1^{y+y'})$ may be sampled directly as $G'(x, 1^{y'}, \mathsf{aux}_y)$. Consider now the following stegosystem $S' = (SE', SD')$ that can be used for arbitrary many and long messages and employs a PRNG G and the one-time stegosystem (SK, SE, SD) of Section 3.1. The two players Alice and Bob, share a key of length l denoted by x. They also maintain a state N that holds the number of bits that have been transmitted already as well the auxiliary information aux_N (initially empty). The function SE' is given input $N, \mathsf{aux}_N, x, m \in \{0, 1\}^\nu$ where m is the message to be transmitted. SE' in turn employs the PRNG G to extract a number of bits κ as follows $k = G'(x, 1^\kappa, \mathsf{aux}_N)$. The length κ is selected to match the number of key bits that are required to transmit the message m using the one-time stegosystem of section 3.1. Once the key k is produced by the PRNG the procedure SE' invokes the one-time stegosystem on input k, m, h. After the transmission is completed the history h, the count N, as well as the auxiliary PRNG information aux_N are updated accordingly. The function SD' is defined in a straightforward way based on SD.

Theorem 4. *The stegosystem $S' = (SE', SD')$ is provably secure in the model of [4] (universally steganographically secret against chosen hiddentext attacks); in particular $\mathbf{InSec}_{S'}^{SS}(t, q, l) \leq \mathbf{InSec}^{PRNG}(t + \gamma(\ell(l)), \ell(l) + \mathsf{polylog}(l))$ (where t is the time required by the adversary, q is the number of chosen hiddentext queries it makes, l is the total number of bits across all queries and $\gamma(v)$ is the time required to simulate the SE' oracle for v bits).*

4.1 Performance Comparison of the Stegosystem S' and the Hopper, Langford, von Ahn System

Let us fix an $(\nu, \lambda, 3/8, \epsilon_{\mathsf{enc}})$-error-correcting code E. Then the system of Hopper, et al. [4] correctly decodes a given message with probability at least ϵ_{enc} and makes no more than 2λ calls to a pseudorandom function family. Were one to use the pseudorandom function family of Goldreich, Goldwasser, and Micali [5], then this involves production of $\Theta(\lambda \cdot k \cdot (\log(|\Sigma|) + \log \lambda))$ pseudorandom bits, where k is the security parameter of the pseudorandom function family. Of course, the security of the system depends on the security of the underlying pseudorandom generator. On the other hand, with the same error-correcting code, the steganographic system described above utilizes $O(\lambda + \log |\Sigma| + \log(1/\epsilon_{\mathcal{F}}))$ pseudorandom bits, correctly decodes a given message with probability $\epsilon_{\mathsf{enc}} + \epsilon_{\mathcal{F}}$, and possesses insecurity no more than $\epsilon_{\mathcal{F}}$. In order to compare the two schemes, note that by selecting $\epsilon_{\mathcal{F}} = 2^{-k}$, both the decoding error and the security of the two systems differ by at most 2^{-k}, a negligible function in terms of the security parameter k. (Note also that pseudorandom functions utilized in the above scheme have security no better than 2^{-k} with security parameter k.) In this case our system uses $\Theta(\lambda + \log |\Sigma| + k)$ (pseudorandom) bits, a dramatic improvement over the $\Theta(\lambda k \log(|\Sigma|\lambda))$ bits of the scheme above.

References

1. Cachin, C.: An information-theoretic model for steganography. In: Information Hiding. (1998) 306–318
2. Zöllner, J., Federrath, H., Klimant, H., Pfitzmann, A., Piotraschke, R., Westfeld, A., Wicke, G., Wolf, G.: Modeling the security of steganographic systems. In: Information Hiding. (1998) 344–354
3. Mittelholzer, T.: An information-theoretic approach to steganography and watermarking. In: Information Hiding. (1999) 1–16
4. Hopper, N.J., Langford, J., von Ahn, L.: Provably secure steganography. In: CRYPTO. (2002) 77–92
5. Goldreich, O., Goldwasser, S., Micali, S.: How to construct random functions. J. ACM **33** (1986) 792–807
6. Naor, M., Reingold, O.: Number-theoretic constructions of efficient pseudo-random functions. J. ACM **51** (2004) 231–262
7. Alon, N., Goldreich, O., Håstad, J., Peralta, R.: Simple construction of almost k-wise independent random variables. Random Struct. Algorithms **3** (1992) 289–304
8. van Lint, J.: Introduction to Coding Theory. 3rd edition edn. Number 86 in Graduate Texts in Mathematics. Springer-Verlag (1998)
9. Gallager, R.G.: A simple derivation of the coding theorem and some applications. IEEE Transactions on Information Theory **IT-11** (1965) 3–18
10. Naor, J., Naor, M.: Small-bias probability spaces: Efficient constructions and applications. SIAM J. Comput. **22** (1993) 838–856

A   Proofs

Proof (of Lemma 1). To ease the notation let $f = f_k$. The event E_i can be defined as:

$$E_i = \begin{cases} [f(i, c_1) = m_i] \vee \\ [f(i, c_1) \neq m_i \wedge f(i, c_2) = m_i] \end{cases}$$

where c_1, c_2 are two independent random variables distributed according to the channel distribution C_h. Recall that $\Sigma = \{c_0, c_1, \ldots c_n\}$ is the support of the channel and each element $c_i \in \Sigma$ has assigned a probability p_i. We define two events:

- D: This is the event that two different symbols are drawn from the channel, i.e. $c_1 \neq c_2$
- $\bar{D}$: This event describes that twice the same symbol is drawn, i.e. $c_1 = c_2$

It follows easily that

$$\Pr[E_i = 1] = \Pr[f(i, c_1) = m_i] \\ + \Pr[(f(i, c_1) \neq m_i) \wedge (f(i, c_2) = m_i)] \ .$$

Now observe that $\Pr[f(i, c_1) = m_i] = \frac{1}{2}$, since it holds that f was selected uniformly at random from $\mathcal{R}$. For the second summand let the event A be $f(i, c_1) \neq m_i \wedge (f(i, c_2) = m_i)$. Now we have

$$\Pr[A] = \Pr[A|D]\Pr[D] + \Pr[A|\bar{D}] \Pr[\bar{D}] \ .$$

In this equation we see that the second addend $\Pr[A|\bar{D}]\Pr[\bar{D}] = 0$. Also,

$$\Pr[A|D]\Pr[D] = \frac{1}{4} \cdot \Pr[D] \ ,$$

since f is drawn uniformly at random from $\mathcal{R}$. So we get:

$$\Pr[E_i = 1] = \frac{1}{2} + \frac{1}{4} \cdot \Pr[D] \ .$$

To obtain $\Pr[D]$, let c_i be the symbol with the highest probability p_i, i.e. $\forall j$ $p_j \le p_i$, then

$$\Pr[\bar{D}] = p_0^2 + p_1^2 + \cdots + p_n^2 \le p_i(p_0 + p_1 + \cdots + p_n)$$
$$= p_i$$

Therefore $\Pr[D] \ge 1 - p_i$ and

$$\Pr[E_i = 1] \ge \frac{1}{2} + \frac{1}{4} \cdot (1 - p_i) \ .$$

Since we assume $H_\infty(\mathcal{C}) \ge 1$, we must have $p_i \le \frac{1}{2}$ so the success probability is

$$\Pr[E_i = 1] \ge \tfrac{1}{2} + \tfrac{1}{4} \cdot (1 - p_i)$$
$$> \tfrac{1}{2} + \tfrac{1}{8}$$
$$= \tfrac{5}{8} \ .$$

$\square$

Proof (of Proposition 1). Let c_1 and c_2 be the two (independent) samples drawn from $\mathcal{C}_h$ during rejection sampling. (For simplicity, we treat the process as having drawn two samples even in the case where it succeeds on the first draw.) Let $p_c = \Pr_{c' \leftarrow \mathcal{C}_h}[c' = c]$.

Note, now, that in the case where $f(i, c) \ne m$, the value c is the result of the rejection sampling process precisely when $f(i, c_1) \ne m$ and $c_2 = c$; as these samples are independent, this occurs with probability $\mathsf{fail} \cdot p_c$.

In the case where $f(i, c) = m$, however, we observe c whenever $c_1 = c$ or $f(i, c_1) \ne m$ and $c_2 = c$. As these events are disjoint, their union occurs with probability $p_c \cdot (\mathsf{fail} + 1)$, as desired. $\square$

Proof (of Lemma 3). Let f be a random function, as described in the statement of the lemma. Fixing the elements i, c, and m, we condition on the event $E_{\ne}$, that $f(i, c) \ne m$. In light of Proposition 1, for any f drawn under this conditioning we shall have that $\Pr[\mathbf{rejsam}_h^{f,i}(m) = c]$ is equal to

$$\Pr_{c' \leftarrow \mathcal{C}_h}[c' = c] \cdot \mathsf{fail}_f = p_c \cdot \mathsf{fail}_f \ ,$$

where we have written $\mathsf{fail}_f = \Pr_{c' \leftarrow \mathcal{C}_h}[f(i, c') \ne m]$ and $p_c = \Pr_{c' \leftarrow \mathcal{C}_h}[c' = c]$. Conditioned on $E_{\ne}$, then, the probability of observing c is

$$\mathbf{E}_f[p_c \cdot \mathsf{fail}_f \mid E_{\ne}] = p_c \left(p_c + \frac{1}{2}(1 - p_c) \right) \ .$$

Letting $E_=$ be the event that $f(i,c) = m$, we similarly compute

$$\mathbf{E}_f[p_c \cdot \mathtt{fail}_f \mid E_=] = p_c \left(1 + \frac{1}{2}(1 - p_c)\right) .$$

As $\Pr[E_=] = \Pr[E_{\neq}] = 1/2$, we conclude that the probability of observing c is exactly

$$\frac{1}{2}\left(p_c\left(p_c + \frac{1-p_c}{2}\right) + p_c\left(1 + \frac{1-p_c}{2}\right)\right) = p_c ,$$

as desired.   □

Proof (of Theorem 2). Let us play the following game $G(1^\kappa)$ with the adversary $\mathcal{A}$: In each round we either select $G_1^{\mathcal{A}}$ or $G_2^{\mathcal{A}}$:

$G_1^{\mathcal{A}}(1^\kappa)$	
1.	$k \leftarrow \{0,1\}^\kappa$
2.	$(m^*, s) \leftarrow SA_1^{\mathcal{O}(h)}(1^\kappa, h),\ m^* \in \{0,1\}^\nu$
3.	$b \xleftarrow{r} \{0,1\}$
4.	$c^* = \begin{cases} c_0, c_1, \ldots c_{\lambda-1} & c_i = \mathtt{rejsam}_h^{i,f_k}(m_i), h = h\|c & if\ b = 0 \\ \text{from the channel} & if\ b = 1 \end{cases}$
5.	$b^* \leftarrow SA_2(c^*, s)$
6.	if $b = b^*$ then success

$G_2^{\mathcal{A}}(1^\kappa)$	
1.	$f \leftarrow \mathcal{R}$
2.	$(m^*, s) \leftarrow SA_1^{\mathcal{O}(h)}(1^\kappa, h),\ m^* \in \{0,1\}^\nu$
3.	$b \xleftarrow{r} \{0,1\}$
4.	$c^* = \begin{cases} c_0, c_1, \ldots c_{\lambda-1} & c_i = \mathtt{rejsam}_h^{i,f_k}(m_i), h = h\|c & if\ b = 0 \\ \text{from the channel} & if\ b = 1 \end{cases}$
5.	$b^* \leftarrow SA_2(c^*, s)$
6.	if $b = b^*$ then success

$$\mathbf{Adv}_S^{\mathcal{A}}(G(1^\kappa)) = \left| \Pr[\mathcal{A}^{\mathcal{O}(h), c^* \leftarrow SE(k, \cdot, \cdot, \cdot)} = 1] - \Pr[\mathcal{A}^{\mathcal{O}(h), c^* \leftarrow \mathcal{C}_h} = 1] \right|$$
$$= \Pr_{f \leftarrow \mathcal{F}_\kappa}[G(1^\kappa) = 1] - \Pr_{f \leftarrow \mathcal{R}}[G(1^\kappa) = 1] \le \epsilon$$

And the lemma follows by the definition of insecurity.   □

Information-Theoretic Analysis of Security in Side-Informed Data Hiding

Luis Pérez-Freire, Pedro Comesaña, and Fernando Pérez-González*

Signal Theory and Communications Department,
University of Vigo, Vigo 36310, Spain
{lpfreire, pcomesan, fperez}@gts.tsc.uvigo.es

Abstract. In this paper a novel theoretical security analysis will be presented for data hiding methods with side-information, based on Costa's dirty paper scheme. We quantify the information about the secret key that leaks from the observation of watermarked signals, using the mutual information as analytic tool for providing a fair comparison between the original Costa's scheme, Distortion Compensated - Dither Modulation and Spread Spectrum.

1 Introduction

In this paper a novel theoretical security analysis of data hiding methods based on Costa's capacity-achieving scheme [1] is presented. Security in this schemes is introduced by parameterizing the codebook by means of a secret key Θ, in such a way that an unauthorized agent, who does not know that key, will not be able, for instance, to decode the embedded message, because he does not know what particular codebook has been used in the embedding stage. The motivation for the analysis we will present here is the fact that information about the secret key may leak from the observation of watermarked signals, and this information leakage can be exploited by an attacker to refine his knowledge about the key Θ, in order to gain access to the decoding of secret embedded messages, removal of the watermark with low attacking distortion, or even generation of forged watermarked signals. In this sense, our analysis is inspired by Shannon's work [2] in the field of cryptography. A previous security analysis in the field of data hiding following this rationale has been accomplished in [3], but only for spread spectrum methods, and using the Fisher Information Matrix as analytic tool. Instead, our approach relies on the framework presented in [4], using the mutual information to measure the information leakage about the secret key, which in

* This work was partially funded by *Xunta de Galicia* under projects PGIDT04 TIC322013PR and PGIDT04 PXIC32202PM; MEC project DIPSTICK, reference TEC2004-02551/TCM; FIS project G03/185, and European Comission through the IST Programme under Contract IST-2002-507932 ECRYPT. ECRYPT disclaimer: the information in this document reflects only the authors' views, is provided as is and no guarantee or warranty is given that the information is fit for any particular purpose. The user thereof uses the information at its sole risk and liability.

M. Barni et al. (Eds.): IH 2005, LNCS 3727, pp. 131–145, 2005.

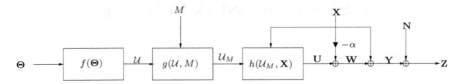

Fig. 1. Block diagram of Costa's schemes

turn can be used to calculate the *residual entropy* (*equivocation* in Shannon's nomenclature) or ignorance about the key for the attacker after a certain number of observations.

We will distinguish two different scenarios where the security will be assessed: in the first scenario, the attacker only has access to N_o signals watermarked with the same key, so the measure of information leakage will be given by the mutual information $I(\mathbf{Y}^1, \mathbf{Y}^2, \ldots, \mathbf{Y}^{N_o}; \boldsymbol{\Theta})$, where $\mathbf{Y}^i$ denotes the i-th watermarked vector observed (the superscript will be omitted when only one observation is considered, for simplicity of notation). In the second scenario, the attacker has also access to the embedded messages, hence the information leakage in this case is measured by $I(\mathbf{Y}^1, \mathbf{Y}^2, \ldots, \mathbf{Y}^{N_o}; \boldsymbol{\Theta}|\mathbf{M}^1, \mathbf{M}^2, \ldots, \mathbf{M}^{N_o})$. In the rest of this paper, capital letters will denote random variables, whereas its specific values will be denoted by italicized lowercase letters, and boldface letters will indicate vectors of length N_v. Both scenarios have already been considered in the analysis in [3] for spread spectrum, under the names of *Watermarked Only Attack* (WOA), and *Known Message Attack* (KMA), so we will adopt here the same terminology.

In the following section, the security analysis of Costa's scheme will be accomplished, whereas Section 3 will be devoted to the analysis of Distortion Compensated - Dither Modulation (DC-DM) [5], which is a practical (suboptimal) implementation of Costa's scheme using structured codebooks. In Section 4, a comparison between the two analyzed schemes and spread spectrum will be given, and the main conclusions will be summarized.

2   Random Codebooks (Costa's Construction)

In Fig. 1 the considered framework is represented. In Costa's construction, the codebook is random by definition; however, this randomness can be parameterized by a secret key $\boldsymbol{\Theta}$, resulting in a codebook $\mathcal{U} = f(\boldsymbol{\Theta})$. Depending on the sent message m, one coset in the codebook will be chosen, namely $\mathcal{U}_m = g(\mathcal{U}, m)$. Taking into account the host signal $\mathbf{X}$ and the distortion compensation parameter α (which belongs to the interval $[0,1]$) the encoder will look for a sequence $\mathbf{U} = h(\mathcal{U}_m, \mathbf{X})$ belonging to $\mathcal{U}_m$ such that $|(\mathbf{U} - \alpha\mathbf{X})^t\mathbf{X}| \leq \delta$, for some arbitrarily small δ. The watermark signal will be $\mathbf{W} = \mathbf{U} - \alpha\mathbf{X}$, and the watermarked signal $\mathbf{Y} = \mathbf{X} + \mathbf{W}$. Finally, the decoder will observe $\mathbf{Z} = \mathbf{X} + \mathbf{W} + \mathbf{N}$, where $\mathbf{N}$ is the channel noise, independent of both $\mathbf{X}$ and $\mathbf{W}$.

For the sake of simplicity, in this section we will focus on the analysis of this system when a single observation is available. We will also assume $\mathbf{X}$, $\mathbf{W}$ and $\mathbf{N}$ to be i.i.d. random vectors with distributions $\mathcal{N}(\mathbf{0}, \sigma_X^2 \mathbf{I}_{N_v})$, $\mathcal{N}(\mathbf{0}, P\mathbf{I}_{N_v})$ and

$\mathcal{N}(\mathbf{0}, \sigma_N^2 \mathbf{I}_{N_v})$, respectively, where $\mathbf{I}_{N_v}$ denotes the N_v-th order identity matrix. The embedding distortion is parameterized by the *Document to Watermark Ratio*, defined as DWR $= 10 \log_{10}(\sigma_X^2/P)$, and the distortion introduced by the attacking channel is parameterized by the *Watermark to Noise Ratio*, defined as WNR $= 10 \log_{10}(P/\sigma_N^2)$.

2.1 Known Message Attack

Since knowledge of the secret key and the sent symbol implies knowledge of the coset in the codebook (i.e., $\mathcal{U}_m$), we can write

$$I(\mathbf{Y}; \mathbf{\Theta}|M) = h(\mathbf{Y}) - I(\mathbf{Y}; M) - h(\mathbf{Y}|\mathcal{U}_M).$$

In App. A.1, we show that if $\alpha > 0.2$, then

$$I(\mathbf{Y}; \mathbf{\Theta}|M) = \frac{N_v}{2} \log \left[\frac{P + \sigma_X^2}{(1-\alpha)^2 \sigma_X^2} \right],$$

so

$$h(\mathbf{\Theta}|\mathbf{Y}, M) = h(\mathbf{\Theta}) - \frac{N_v}{2} \log \left[\frac{P + \sigma_X^2}{(1-\alpha)^2 \sigma_X^2} \right]. \qquad (1)$$

Since each component of each sequence $\mathbf{U}$ follows a Gaussian distribution with power $P + \alpha^2 \sigma_X^2$, and all of them are mutually independent, it follows that

$$h(\mathbf{\Theta}) = \frac{|\mathcal{U}| N_v}{2} \log \left[2\pi e(P + \alpha^2 \sigma_X^2) \right],$$

where $|\mathcal{U}| = e^{I(\mathbf{U}; \mathbf{Z})} = \left(\frac{[P+\sigma_X^2+\sigma_N^2][P+\alpha^2\sigma_X^2]}{P\sigma_X^2(1-\alpha)^2+\sigma_N^2(P+\alpha^2\sigma_X^2)} \right)^{N_v/2}$.

Eq. (1) shows that the higher the DWR is, the higher the residual entropy becomes, because the host signal is making difficult the estimation of the secret key. On the other hand, the larger α, the smaller the residual entropy will be, since the self-noise is reduced and the estimation becomes easier. In Fig. 2, theoretical results are plotted for different values of the DWR.

2.2 Watermarked Only Attack

Again, knowledge of the secret key and the sent symbol implies knowledge of the coset in the codebook (i.e., $\mathcal{U}_m$). Therefore, we can write

$$I(\mathbf{Y}; \mathbf{\Theta}) = h(\mathbf{Y}) - I(\mathbf{Y}; M|\mathbf{\Theta}) - h(\mathbf{Y}|\mathcal{U}_M). \qquad (2)$$

In App. A.2, it is shown that if $\alpha > 0.2$

$$I(\mathbf{Y}; \mathbf{\Theta}) = \frac{N_v}{2} \log \left[\frac{(P + \sigma_X^2) \left(P\sigma_X^2(1-\alpha)^2 + \sigma_N^2(P + \alpha^2\sigma_X^2) \right)}{P(P + \sigma_X^2 + \sigma_N^2)(1-\alpha)^2 \sigma_X^2} \right]. \qquad (3)$$

Be aware that we are assuming that the watermarker transmits at the maximum reliable rate allowed, thus the power of the channel noise will affect the

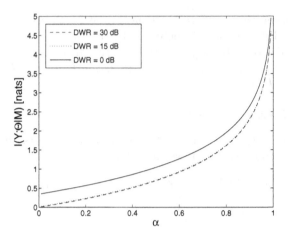

Fig. 2. $I(\mathbf{Y}; \Theta|M)$ for Costa in nats vs. α , for different values of DWR and $N_v = 1$

information leakage (this is further explained in App. A.2). For instance, when $\sigma_N^2 = 0$, the supremum of the maximum reliable rate is achieved, so the uncertainty about the sent symbol is also maximum, which complicates the attacker's work, yielding in this case $I(\mathbf{Y}; \Theta) = 0$ (*perfect secrecy* in the Shannon's sense [2]). In any case, using (3) we can write

$$h(\Theta|\mathbf{Y}) = h(\Theta) - \frac{N_v}{2} \log \left[\frac{(P + \sigma_X^2)\left(P\sigma_X^2(1 - \alpha)^2 + \sigma_N^2(P + \alpha^2\sigma_X^2)\right)}{P(P + \sigma_X^2 + \sigma_N^2)(1 - \alpha)^2\sigma_X^2} \right]. \quad (4)$$

Theoretical results are plotted in Fig. 3, showing their dependence on the DWR, the WNR and α. Since $I(\mathbf{Y}; \Theta)$ depends on the transmission rate and this depends in turn on the WNR, the WNR has been fixed in order to plot the results. Under the light of these plots, several conclusions can be drawn:

- The information leakage increases with α, because a smaller self-noise power is introduced.
- Conversely, the information leakage decreases for growing DWR's, because the uncertainty about the watermarked signal given the chosen **U** sequence is increased.
- The larger the WNR, the smaller the mutual information, because the embedder can achieve a higher reliable rate, thus increasing the uncertainty of the attacker about the sent symbol, which makes more difficult his job.

3   Distortion Compensated – Dither Modulation

We will focus on the scalar version of DC-DM [5] (also known as Scalar Costa Scheme, SCS [6]), for two reasons: first, for simplicity of the analysis, and second, because it provides the fundamental insights into structured quantization-based

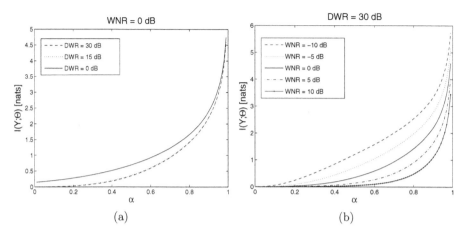

Fig. 3. $I(\mathbf{Y}; \mathbf{\Theta})$ vs. α in Costa, for different values of DWR and WNR $= 0$ dB (a), and for different values of WNR, setting DWR $= 30$ dB (b). In both plots, $N_v = 1$.

methods. In DC-DM, embedding is made component-wise, hence, following the notation of Fig. 1, the codebook for the k-th component in DC-DM is given by the lattice

$$\mathcal{U}_{t_k} = \bigcup_{l=0}^{|\mathcal{M}|-1} \left(\alpha \Delta \mathbb{Z} + \alpha l \frac{\Delta}{|\mathcal{M}|} + \alpha t_k \right), \tag{5}$$

being $|\mathcal{M}|$ the number of different symbols, $k = 0, \ldots, N_v - 1$, and t_k is the pseudo-random *dither signal* introduced to achieve randomization of the codebook. Each coset is chosen as a sublattice of (5), resulting in

$$\mathcal{U}_{m,t_k} = g(\mathcal{U}_{t_k}, m) = \alpha \Delta \mathbb{Z} + \alpha m \frac{\Delta}{|\mathcal{M}|} + \alpha t_k.$$

In DC-DM, αx_k is quantized to the nearest $u_k \in \mathcal{U}_{m,t_k}$, where x_k is the k-th component of $\mathbf{X}$, which is assumed to be independent and identically distributed (i.i.d.). Thus, the expression of the k-th component of the watermarked signal is $y_k = x_k + u_k - \alpha x_k$, which can be rewritten as $y_k = x_k + \alpha \left(Q_{\Lambda_{m,t_k}}(x_k) - x_k \right)$, where $Q_{\Lambda_{m,t_k}}(\cdot)$ is an Euclidean quantizer with uniform step size Δ with its centroids defined by the shifted lattice Λ_{m,t_k}, according to the to-be-transmitted message symbol m:

$$\Lambda_{m,t_k} = \Delta \mathbb{Z} + m \frac{\Delta}{|\mathcal{M}|} + t_k. \tag{6}$$

The dither signal $\mathbf{t}$ may be any deterministic function of the secret key $\boldsymbol{\theta}$, i.e. $\mathbf{t} = f(\boldsymbol{\theta})$. If function f is unknown, the only observation of watermarked vectors will not provide any information about $\boldsymbol{\theta}$, thus the target of the attacker is to disclose the dither signal used for embedding, or equivalently the location of the centroids. As it is usual in the analysis of quantization-based methods for data hiding [5], [6], we will assume a low-embedding-distortion regime, thus we can consider that the host pdf is uniform inside each quantization bin and all centroids occur with similar probabilities. This assumption (which we will refer to in the sequel as the *flat-host assumption*) implies that we can restrict our attention to the modulo-Δ version of Y_k without any loss of information, considerably simplifying the theoretical analysis. The security level of the system will depend, obviously, on the statistical distribution of the dither. We show in App. B that the entropy of the watermarked signal $\mathbf{Y}$ only depends on the modulo-Δ version of the dither, and furthermore the distribution which maximizes the residual entropy is the uniform over the quantization bin; thus, hereafter we will assume that $T_k \sim U(-\Delta/2, \Delta/2)$ with i.i.d samples.

3.1   Known Message Attack

This is the simplest case to analyze. When only one watermarked vector is observed ($N_o = 1$), the following equalities hold

$$I(\mathbf{Y}; \mathbf{T}|\mathbf{M}) = \sum_{i=1}^{N_v} \sum_{j=1}^{N_v} I(Y_i; T_j|Y_{i-1}, \ldots, Y_1, T_{j-1}, \ldots, T_1, \mathbf{M}) \qquad (7)$$

$$= \sum_{i=1}^{N_v} I(Y_i; T_i|M_i) = N_v I(Y_i; T_i|M_i), \qquad (8)$$

where Y_i denotes the i-th component of vector $\mathbf{Y}$, (7) follows from the chain rule for mutual informations [7], and (8) follows from the fact that the pairs Y_i, T_j and Y_i, M_j are independent $\forall\ i \neq j$, and furthermore $\{Y_i\}, \{T_i\}, \{M_i\}$ are i.i.d. processes. From the definition of mutual information we have

$$I(Y_i; T_i|M_i) = h(Y_i|M_i) - h(Y_i|T_i, M_i) \qquad (9)$$
$$= h(Y_i|M_i = 0) - h(Y_i|T_i = 0, M_i = 0), \qquad (10)$$

where (10) follows from the flat-host assumption introduced above. Furthermore, due to this assumption, the entropies of (10) can be easily calculated by considering one period of the watermarked signal. Finally, (8) results in

$$I(\mathbf{Y}; \mathbf{T}|\mathbf{M}) = N_v I(Y_i; T_i|M_i) = N_v \left(\log(\Delta) - \log((1 - \alpha)\Delta)\right)$$
$$= -N_v \log(1 - \alpha) \text{ nats }, \qquad (11)$$

so the residual entropy is

$$h(\mathbf{T}|\mathbf{Y}, \mathbf{M}) = h(\mathbf{T}|\mathbf{M}) - I(\mathbf{Y}; \mathbf{T}|\mathbf{M}) = N_v \log((1 - \alpha)\Delta) \text{ nats }. \qquad (12)$$

Fig. 4 shows the result for the mutual information when $N_v = 1$. For the general case of N_o observations one may be tempted to upper bound the mutual information by assuming that all observations will provide the same amount of information, but this bound will be too loose in most cases. For example, we can

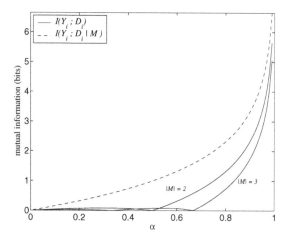

Fig. 4. Mutual informations for scalar DC-DM, in KMA and WOA cases with $N_v = 1$

calculate the exact mutual information when $\alpha \geq 0.5$, yielding (see Appendix C.1 for details)

$$I(\mathbf{Y}^1, \ldots, \mathbf{Y}^{N_o}; \mathbf{T}|\mathbf{M}^1, \ldots, \mathbf{M}^{N_o}) = N_v \left(-\log(1-\alpha) + \sum_{i=2}^{N_o} \frac{1}{i} \right) \text{ nats} . \quad (13)$$

It can be seen in Fig. 5-(a) that the first observations provide most of the information about the secret dither signal. In Fig. 5-(b), numerical results are shown for $\alpha < 0.5$ up to 10 observations, showing that the linear upper bound gets tighter (at least for a small number of observations) when α is decreased.

3.2 Watermarked Only Attack

In this case, the only information at hand for the attacker is the watermarked vector; hence, we must calculate the mutual information $I(\mathbf{Y}; \mathbf{T})$. By reasoning as in the KMA case we can write

$$I(\mathbf{Y}; \mathbf{T}) = N_v I(Y_i; T_i) = N_v \left(h(Y_i) - h(Y_i|T_i) \right). \quad (14)$$

Although it is always possible to obtain a theoretical expression for (14), we will calculate it here only for the case of binary signaling ($M_i = \{0, 1\}$), for the sake of simplicity. We have that $h(Y_i) = \log(\Delta)$, as in the KMA case, whereas for the term $h(Y_i|T_i)$ we have $h(Y_i|T_i) = h(Y_i|T_i = 0)$. Thus, we can write

$$I(Y_i; T_i) = \log(\Delta) - h(Y_i|T_i = 0),$$

For calculating $h(Y_i|T_i = 0)$ we must take into account that, for $\alpha < 0.5$, the pdf's associated to adjacent centroids overlap. It is easy to show that

$$h(Y_i|T_i = 0) = \begin{cases} \log(2(1-\alpha)\Delta) & \text{, for } \alpha \geq \frac{1}{2} \\ \log((1-\alpha)\Delta)\frac{(1-2\alpha)}{1-\alpha} + \log(2(1-\alpha)\Delta)\frac{\alpha}{(1-\alpha)} & \text{, for } \alpha < \frac{1}{2} \end{cases}$$

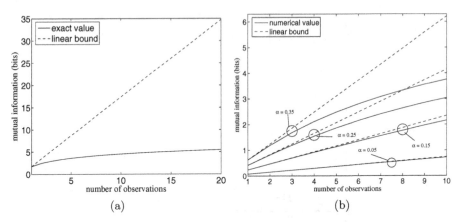

Fig. 5. Mutual information as a function of the number of observations for scalar DC-DM in the KMA case, for $N_v = 1$, and $\alpha = 0.7$ (a), and $\alpha < 0.5$ (b)

With the above expressions, derivation of the equivocation is straightforward. In Fig. 4, results for 2 and 3 transmitted symbols are shown. It can be seen that when $\alpha = 0.5$ (for the binary case, $|\mathcal{M}| = 2$) the information leakage is null [1], thus achieving *perfect secrecy*, in the sense that the attacker can not gain knowledge about the dither, regardless the number of observations; this is because the pdf of the host and that of the watermarked signal are the same. When $\alpha < 0.5$ the information leakage is very small due to overlaps between adjacent centroids. For the case of multiple observations and $\alpha \geq 0.75$ we have (see App. C.2 for details)

$$I(\mathbf{Y}^1, \ldots, \mathbf{Y}^{N_o}; \mathbf{T}) = N_v \left(-\log(1 - \alpha) - \log(2) + \sum_{i=2}^{N_o} \frac{1}{i} \right) \text{ nats .}$$

Then, the loss with respect to the KMA case is exactly $\log(2)$ nats (i.e. one bit), which is in accordance with the term $I(\mathbf{Y}; M|\boldsymbol{\Theta})$ of Eq. (2) obtained for Costa's scheme. For $\alpha < 0.75$, only numerical results have been obtained.

4   Comparison and Conclusions

Fig. 6-(a) shows a comparison between the information leakage in Costa and DC-DM, for several values of α. Notice that two different plots are shown for DC-DM: one with the theoretical results obtained in Section 3 under the flat-host assumption (DWR $= \infty$), and another plot with results obtained via numerical integration by considering finite DWR's [2]; it can be seen that both plots coincide

---

[1] It can be shown that for the general case of D-ary signalling, the values of $\alpha = k/D$, with $k = 0, \ldots, D - 1$ yield null information leakage.

[2] The exact pdf of the watermarked signal has been numerically computed for finite DWR's by following the guidelines given in [8].

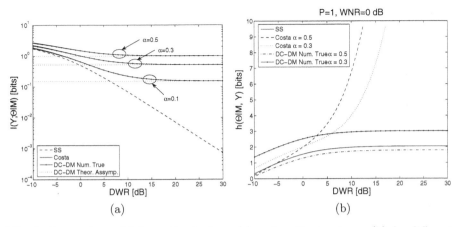

Fig. 6. Comparison of information leakage (a) and residual entropy (b) for different data hiding schemes, with $N_v = 1$ and $N_o = 1$

for any DWR of practical interest, thus supporting the validity of the flat-host assumption. The other remarkable result is the large resemblance between between Costa and DC-DM with finite DWR's.

An analysis similar to that carried out in Sections 2 and 3 is accomplished for spread spectrum data hiding in [4]; in this case, the secret parameter is the spreading sequence $\mathbf{s}$ used in the embedding stage, which will be assumed to be Gaussian with variance σ_S^2. The analysis for a single observation ($N_o = 1$) yields the mutual information $I(\mathbf{Y}; \mathbf{S}|\mathbf{M}) = \frac{N_v}{2} \log\left(1 + \sigma_S^2/\sigma_X^2\right)$ and the residual entropy $h(\mathbf{S}|\mathbf{Y}^1, \cdots, \mathbf{Y}^{N_o}, \mathbf{M}) = \frac{N_v}{2} \log\left(2\pi e \sigma_S^2 \sigma_X^2/(\sigma_X^2 + \sigma_S^2)\right)$.

Fig. 6-(a) shows that, when compared under the same conditions, the information leakage for the informed embedding methods is larger than those of spread spectrum. However, note that the security level is not only given by the information leakage but depends also on the entropy of the secret key, yielding values for the residual entropy which are compared in Fig. 6-(b), where we can see that the theoretical Costa's scheme provides much larger residual entropies for practical values of the DWR. Similar comparisons could be made for the WOA attack.

Summarizing, we have shown in this paper that an attacker can take advantage of the observation of watermarked signals to gain knowledge about the secret key (when all observations were generated with the same key), and that knowledge of the embedded messages can simplify the attacker's work. Theoretically, the attacker needs, in general, an infinite number of observations to achieve perfect knowledge of the secret key, but in practice this is not necessary, since he only may be interested in obtaining an estimate of that key; in this sense, one can exploit the relationship between the residual entropy and the estimation error in order to find appropriate thresholds which define a given security level, but this path will not be explored here due to lack of space.

References

1. Costa, M.H.M.: Writing on dirty paper. IEEE Transactions on Information Theory **29** (1983) 439–441
2. Shannon, C.E.: Communication theory of secrecy systems. Bell system technical journal **28** (1949) 656–715
3. Cayre, F., Fontaine, C., Furon, T.: Watermarking security: application to a WSS technique for still images. In Cox, I.J., Kalker, T., Lee, H., eds.: Third International Workshop on Digital Watermarking. Volume 3304., Seoul, Korea, Springer (2004)
4. Comesaña, P., Pérez-Freire, L., Pérez-González, F.: Fundamentals of data hiding security and their application to Spread-Spectrum analysis. In: 7th Information Hiding Workshop, IH05. Lecture Notes in Computer Science, Barcelona, Spain, Springer Verlag (2005)
5. Chen, B., Wornell, G.: Quantization Index Modulation: a class of provably good methods for digital watermarking and information embedding. IEEE Transactions on Information Theory **47** (2001) 1423–1443
6. Eggers, J.J., Bäuml, R., Tzschoppe, R., Girod, B.: Scalar Costa Scheme for information embedding. IEEE Transactions on Signal Processing **51** (2003) 1003–1019
7. Cover, T.M., Thomas, J.A.: Elements of Information Theory. Wiley series in Telecommunications (1991)
8. Pérez-Freire, L., Pérez-Gonzalez, F., Voloshinovskiy, S.: Revealing the true achievable rates of Scalar Costa Scheme. In: IEEE Int. Workshop on Multimedia Signal Processing (MMSP), Siena, Italy (2004) 203–206
9. Erez, U., Zamir, R.: Achieving $\frac{1}{2}\log(1+\text{SNR})$ over the Additive White Gaussian Noise Channel with Lattice Encoding and Decoding. IEEE Transactions on Information Theory **50** (2004) 2293–2314

Appendix

A   Mutual Information for a Single Observation in Costa's Scheme

A.1   Known Message Attack (KMA)

The mutual information between the received signal and the secret key when the sent message is known by the attacker can be written as

$$I(\mathbf{Y}; \Theta|M) = h(\mathbf{Y}|M) - h(\mathbf{Y}|\Theta, M) = h(\mathbf{Y}) - I(\mathbf{Y}; M) - h(\mathbf{Y}|\mathcal{U}_M). \quad (15)$$

Studying the second term, $I(\mathbf{Y}; M) = h(\mathbf{Y}) - h(\mathbf{Y}|M)$, it can be seen to be 0 whenever $f_{\mathbf{Y}}(\mathbf{y}) = f_{\mathbf{Y}|M}(\mathbf{y}|M = m)$ for all the possible values of m. Taking into account that $\mathbf{Y} = f_1(\Theta, M, \mathbf{X})$, this will be true in several cases. For example, if $\mathcal{U}_M$ is a lattice shifted by a random variable uniform over its Voronoi region (as in [9]); since the value of that random variable is not known by the attacker, the former equality is verified and $I(\mathbf{Y}; M) = 0$. This will be also the case when $\mathcal{U}_M$ is a random codebook [1]; the attacker could know exactly all the $\mathbf{u}$'s in $\mathcal{U}$, but if he does not know the value of M corresponding to each of them, the best he can do is to apply his a priori knowledge about $P(M = m)$, implying

$I(\mathbf{Y}; M) = 0$ again; this is the scenario studied here. Nevertheless, in the general case $0 \leq I(\mathbf{Y}; M) \leq I(\mathbf{Y}; M|\boldsymbol{\Theta})$.

To compute $h(\mathbf{Y}|\mathcal{U}_M)$ we will focus on the implementations using random codebooks. In those schemes every $\mathbf{u}$ in $\mathcal{U}_M$ has the same probability of being chosen. In order to facilitate the analysis, we will see $\mathbf{y}$ as the combination of a scaled version of $\mathbf{u}$ and a component orthogonal to $\mathbf{u}$, $\mathbf{y} = c\mathbf{u} + \mathbf{u}^\perp$; recalling that $\mathbf{u} = \mathbf{w} + \alpha\mathbf{x}$, we can write $\mathbf{u}^\perp = \mathbf{x} + \mathbf{w} - c\mathbf{w} - c\alpha\mathbf{x}$. Therefore, the value of c can be computed taking into account that $\sigma_X^2 + P = c^2(P + \alpha^2\sigma_X^2) + \sigma_X^2(1 - c\alpha)^2 + P(1 - c)^2$; after some trivial algebraic operations, one obtains

$$c = \frac{P + \alpha\sigma_X^2}{P + \alpha^2\sigma_X^2}.$$

Since all the variables are Gaussian, if N_v is large enough the samples of $\mathbf{y}$ will be very close to a sphere with radius $\sqrt{N_v \text{Var}\{\mathbf{U}^\perp\}}$ centered at some $c\mathbf{u}_o$; these spheres will be disjoint if[3] $\frac{\text{Var}\{\mathbf{U}^\perp\}}{c^2} < P$, which is true for any DWR if $\alpha > 0.2$. If this is the case, then we can write $h(\mathbf{Y}|\mathcal{U}_M) = h(\mathbf{Y}|\mathbf{U}) + \log(|\mathcal{U}_M|)$. Concerning $\log(|\mathcal{U}_M|)$, it is easy to see that

$$|\mathcal{U}_M| \approx e^{I(\mathbf{U};\mathbf{X})} = \left(\frac{P + \alpha^2\sigma_X^2}{P}\right)^{N_v/2}. \tag{16}$$

On the other hand,

$$h(\mathbf{Y}|\mathbf{U}) = h(\mathbf{U}^\perp) = \frac{N_v}{2}\log\left[2\pi e\frac{(1-\alpha)^2 P\sigma_X^2}{P + \alpha^2\sigma_X^2}\right], \tag{17}$$

so,

$$h(\mathbf{Y}|\mathcal{U}_M) = \frac{N_v}{2}\log\left[2\pi e\frac{(1-\alpha)^2 P\sigma_X^2}{P + \alpha^2\sigma_X^2}\right] + \frac{N_v}{2}\log\left[\frac{P + \alpha^2\sigma_X^2}{P}\right]$$

$$= \frac{N_v}{2}\log\left[2\pi e(1-\alpha)^2\sigma_X^2\right]. \tag{18}$$

Note that this value is just an upper bound when the spheres described above are not disjoint.

Finally, the information leakage is given by

$$I(\mathbf{Y};\boldsymbol{\Theta}|M) = \frac{N_v}{2}\log\left[2\pi e(P + \sigma_X^2)\right] - \frac{N_v}{2}\log\left[2\pi e(1-\alpha)^2\sigma_X^2\right]$$

$$= \frac{N_v}{2}\log\left[\frac{P + \sigma_X^2}{(1-\alpha)^2\sigma_X^2}\right]. \tag{19}$$

---

[3] It can be shown that this is a sufficient, but not necessary, condition.

A.2   Watermarked Only Attack (WOA)

In this case, the mutual information between the observations and the secret key is

$$I(\mathbf{Y};\boldsymbol{\Theta}) = h(\mathbf{Y}) - h(\mathbf{Y}|\boldsymbol{\Theta}) = h(\mathbf{Y}) - I(\mathbf{Y};M|\boldsymbol{\Theta}) - h(\mathbf{Y}|\boldsymbol{\Theta},M)$$
$$= h(\mathbf{Y}) - I(\mathbf{Y};M|\boldsymbol{\Theta}) - h(\mathbf{Y}|\mathcal{U}_M) = I(\mathbf{Y};\boldsymbol{\Theta}|M) - I(\mathbf{Y};M|\boldsymbol{\Theta}).$$

The only term that has not been analyzed yet is $I(\mathbf{Y};M|\boldsymbol{\Theta})$, which is the reliable rate that can be reached when the codebook is known. Note that the fact of not knowing the transmitted message produces a decrease in $I(\mathbf{Y};\boldsymbol{\Theta})$ equal to the transmission rate $I(\mathbf{Y};M|\boldsymbol{\Theta})$, since the increase in the uncertainty of the sent symbol complicates the attacker's work. In [1] it is shown that

$$I(\mathbf{Y};M|\boldsymbol{\Theta}) = \frac{N_v}{2}\log\left[\frac{P(P+\sigma_X^2+\sigma_N^2)}{P\sigma_X^2(1-\alpha)^2+\sigma_N^2(P+\alpha^2\sigma_X^2)}\right]. \tag{20}$$

So in this case, assuming again $\alpha > 0.2$, we can write

$$I(\mathbf{Y};\boldsymbol{\Theta}) = \frac{N_v}{2}\log\left[2\pi e(P+\sigma_X^2)\right] - \frac{N_v}{2}\log\left[\frac{P(P+\sigma_X^2+\sigma_N^2)}{P\sigma_X^2(1-\alpha)^2+\sigma_N^2(P+\alpha^2\sigma_X^2)}\right]$$
$$- \frac{N_v}{2}\log\left[2\pi e(1-\alpha)^2\sigma_X^2\right]$$
$$= \frac{N_v}{2}\log\left[\frac{(P+\sigma_X^2)\left\{P\sigma_X^2(1-\alpha)^2+\sigma_N^2(P+\alpha^2\sigma_X^2)\right\}}{P(P+\sigma_X^2+\sigma_N^2)(1-\alpha)^2\sigma_X^2}\right]. \tag{21}$$

B   Optimal Distribution for the Dither in DC-DM

First, we show that for scalar DC-DM

$$I(\mathbf{Y};\mathbf{T}) = I(\mathbf{Y};\mathbf{T} \bmod \Delta). \tag{22}$$

We will assume without loss of generality that $\mathbf{Y}$ and $\mathbf{T}$ are scalars. Let $f_T(t)$ and $f_Y(y|T=t)$ denote the pdf of the secret key and the pdf of the watermarked signal conditioned on the dither, respectively. Taking into account that, due to the periodicity of the embedding lattices (6), $f_Y(y|T=t) = f_Y(y|T=t+i\Delta)\ \forall\ i$, then it is possible to write

$$f_Y(y) = \int_t f_Y(y|T=t)f_T(t)dt = \int_0^\Delta f_Y(y|T=t)\sum_{i=-\infty}^{\infty} f_T(t+i\Delta)dt$$
$$= \int_0^\Delta f_Y(y|T=t)f_{T\bmod\Delta}(t)dt, \tag{23}$$

where $f_{T\bmod\Delta}(t)$ is the pdf of the modulo-Δ-reduced version of T, hence equality (22) inmediately follows, whatever the distribution of the host and the dither.

Now, we consider what is the best choice for the dither from a security point of view. For simplicity of notation we define the random variable $Z \triangleq T \bmod \Delta$. It is a known fact that the uniform distribution maximizes the entropy in an interval [7], but the watermarker is interested in maximizing the residual entropy

$$h(Z|Y) = h(Z) - h(Y) + h(Y|Z). \tag{24}$$

In the following discussion we will make use of the flat-host assumption introduced in Section 3, thus we will consider that $-\Delta/2 \leq Y < \Delta/2$. We have that $h(Y|Z) = h(Y|Z = z)\,, \forall\, z$, thus the rightmost term of (24) does not depend on the distribution of Z. Then, we must find $f_Z(z)$ such that $\{h(Z) - h(Y)\}$ is maximum. Let us define a random variable V such that $f_V(v) \triangleq f_Y(y|Z = 0)$. Under the flat-host assumption we have that $f_Y(y) = f_V(v) \circledast f_Z(z)$, where $\circledast$ denotes cyclic convolution over $[-\Delta/2, \Delta/2]$. Hence, the maximization problem can be written as

$$\max_{f_Z(z)} \{h(Z) - h(V \oplus Z)\},$$

where $\oplus$ denotes modulo-Δ sum. We have the following lemma:

Lemma 1. $h(Z) \leq h(V \oplus Z)$, with equality if $Z \sim U(-\Delta/2, \Delta/2)$.

Proof. Consider that $f_{\tilde{V}}(\tilde{v})$ is the periodic extension of $f_V(v)$ over n bins, properly scaled to ensure that $f_{\tilde{V}}(\tilde{v})$ is still a valid pdf, i.e.

$$f_{\tilde{V}}(\tilde{v}) = \frac{1}{n} \sum_{i=-n/2}^{n/2-1} f_V(v + i\Delta),$$

and that the same applies for $f_{\tilde{Z}}(\tilde{z})$. Now, define $\tilde{Q} \triangleq \tilde{V} + \tilde{Z}$. This way, $f_{\tilde{Q}}(\tilde{q})$ will be also periodic with period Δ in $n - 2$ bins. Notice that

$$h(\tilde{Z}) = h(Z) + \log(n). \tag{25}$$

Assuming that for sufficiently large n we can neglect the border effects, if we denote by Q the modulo-Δ version of $\tilde{Q}$, we have that

$$h(\tilde{Q}) = h(Q) + \log(n). \tag{26}$$

We know that $h(\tilde{Z}) \leq h(\tilde{Q})$ [7], hence by (25) and (26) we have $h(Z) \leq h(V \oplus Z)$. To achieve equality it is sufficient to choose Z such that $Z \sim U(-\Delta/2, \Delta/2)$. $\square$

The proof of the lemma shows that the uniform over the quantization bin maximizes the residual entropy.

C   Mutual Information for Multiple Observations in DC-DM

C.1   Known Message Attack (KMA)

Assuming that the flat-host assumption introduced in Section 3 is valid, we will use the modulo-Δ version of the pdf of Y_i, hence $-\Delta/2 \leq Y_i < \Delta/2$.

Without loss of generality, we consider that the transmitted symbol is the same $(M_i = 0)$ in the N_o observations. In the following, $\mathbf{Y}_k^{N_o}$ will denote a vector of N_o observations of the k-th component of $\mathbf{Y}$, and $Y_{k,i}$ will be the i-th observation of that component. The mutual information after N_o observations is given by

$$I(\mathbf{Y}_k^{N_o}; T_k | \mathbf{M}_k^{N_o}) = \sum_{i=1}^{N_o} I(Y_{k,i}; T_k | \mathbf{M}_k^{N_o}, Y_{k,i-1}, \ldots, Y_{k,1}) \tag{27}$$

$$= \sum_{i=1}^{N_o} \left(h(Y_{k,i} | \mathbf{M}_k^{N_o}, Y_{k,i-1}, \ldots, Y_{k,1}) - \log((1-\alpha)\Delta) \right) \tag{28}$$

The problem here is the calculation of the leftmost conditional entropy term in (28), since the pdf of the i-th observation depends on the previous ones. However, the observations are independent when the dither is known, so we can write [4]

$$f(y_1, y_2, \ldots, y_{N_o}) = \int_{t_{int}} \prod_{i=1}^{N_o} f_{Y_i}(y_i | T = t) f_T(t) dt$$

$$= \frac{1}{(1-\alpha)^{N_o-1}\Delta^{N_o}} \int_{t_{int}} f_{Y_{N_o}}(y_{N_o} | T = t) dt, \tag{29}$$

with $f_T(t) = U(-\Delta/2, \Delta/2)$, and t_{int} is the region of integration, given by

$$t_{int} = t \in (-\Delta/2, \Delta/2] \text{ such that } f(y_i | T = t) \neq 0 \,\forall\, i \leq N_o - 1, \tag{30}$$

which may be composed of disjoint intervals, in general. The obtention of the conditional pdf's by relying on (29) is straightforward, and the conditional entropy of (28) can be calculated as

$$h(Y_i | \mathbf{M}^{N_o}, Y_1, \ldots, Y_{i-1}) = \int h(Y_i | \mathbf{M}^{N_o}, Y_1 = y_1, \ldots, Y_{i-1} = y_{i-1}) dy_1 \ldots dy_{i-1}. \tag{31}$$

The integration limits in (30) can be specialized for $\alpha \geq 1/2$, resulting in

$$t_{int} = \begin{cases} \left[\max_i \{y_i - \mu\}, \min_i \{y_i + \mu\} \right), & \text{if } |y_i - y_j| < 2\mu \,\forall\, i, j < N_o \\ 0 & , \text{otherwise} \end{cases} \tag{32}$$

where $\mu = (1-\alpha)\Delta/2$. For $\alpha > 1/2$ there is no overlapping between adjacent centroids, and the pdf of Y_i conditioned on the previous observations can be analytically calculated, and the following conditional entropy is obtained

$$h(Y_i | \mathbf{M}^{N_o}, y_{i-1}, \ldots, y_1) = \frac{a}{(1-\alpha)\Delta} + \log\left((1-\alpha)\Delta\right) \text{ nats}, \tag{33}$$

where a is half the volume of t_{int}. Substituting (33) into (31), we obtain

$$h(Y_i | \mathbf{M}^{N_o}, Y_{i-1}, \ldots, Y_1) = \log((1-\alpha)\Delta) + \frac{1}{(1-\alpha)\Delta} E_{f(y_1, \ldots, y_{i-1})}[a], \tag{34}$$

---

[4] We will obviate subindex k in the following discussion, for simplicity of notation.

with

$$a = \frac{1}{2}((1 - \alpha)\Delta + \min\{y_1, \ldots, y_{i-1}\} - \max\{y_1, \ldots, y_{i-1}\}). \tag{35}$$

Hence, the conditional entropy depends on the mean value of the integration volume.

Analytical evaluation of (34) can be simplified by assuming that the received samples y_i are all independent but uniformly distributed around an unknown centroid [5] t: $Y_i \sim U(t - (1 - \alpha)\Delta/2, t + (1 - \alpha)\Delta/2)$. Under this assumption, let us define the random variable

$$X \triangleq \min(Y_1, Y_2, \ldots, Y_{N_o}) - \max(Y_1, Y_2, \ldots, Y_{N_o}).$$

The pdf of X for N observations can readily be shown to be

$$f_X(x) = N(N - 1)\frac{(-x)^{N-2}}{((1 - \alpha)\Delta)^N}[(1 - \alpha)\Delta + x],$$

with $x \in (-(1 - \alpha)\Delta, 0]$. Hence, the mean value of a results in

$$E_{f_X(x)}[a] = \frac{(1 - \alpha)\Delta}{2}\left(1 - \frac{N - 1}{N + 1}\right),$$

and substituting it in (34), after some algebra, we finally obtain the following expression for the conditional entropy

$$h(Y_i|\mathbf{M}^{N_o}, Y_{i-1}, \ldots, Y_1) = \log((1 - \alpha)\Delta) + \frac{1}{i} \text{ nats }, \text{ for } i > 1. \tag{36}$$

Substituting (36) in Eq. (28), we have the final expression for the mutual information

$$I(\mathbf{Y}_k^{N_o}; T|\mathbf{M}^{N_o}) = -\log(1 - \alpha) + \sum_{i=2}^{N_o} \frac{1}{i} \text{ nats }. \tag{37}$$

C.2   Watermarked Only Attack (WOA)

For the WOA case, we must take into account that the observations may be associated to any of the possible cosets; however, with binary signaling ($M = \{0, 1\}$) and $\alpha > 0.75$ there is no overlapping between the adjacent cosets, so the conditional pdf's can be calculated similarly to the case of KMA. Under these assumptions, it is possible to show that

$$h(Y_i|M_i, Y_{i-1}, \ldots, Y_1) = \log((1 - \alpha)\Delta) + \frac{1}{i} + \log(2) \text{ nats },$$

hence the mutual information in the WOA case for $\alpha > 0.75$ is given by

$$I(\mathbf{Y}_k^{N_o}; T) = -\log(1 - \alpha) - \log(2) + \sum_{i=2}^{N_o} \frac{1}{i} = I(\mathbf{Y}^{N_o}; T|\mathbf{M}^{N_o}) - \log(2) \text{ nats }.$$

---

[5] This simplification is possible since the chosen random variable yields the same mean value as the true distribution.

Fundamentals of Data Hiding Security and Their Application to Spread-Spectrum Analysis

Pedro Comesaña, Luis Pérez-Freire, and Fernando Pérez-González*

Signal Theory and Communications Department,
University of Vigo, Vigo 36310, Spain
{pcomesan, lpfreire, fperez}@gts.tsc.uvigo.es

Abstract. This paper puts in consideration the concepts of *security* and *robustness* in watermarking, in order to be able to establish a clear frontier between them. A new information-theoretic framework to study data-hiding and watermarking security is proposed, using the mutual information to quantify the information about the secret key that leaks from the observation of watermarked objects. This framework is applied to the analysis of a Spread-Spectrum data-hiding scheme in different scenarios. Finally, we show some interesting links between a measure proposed in previous works in the literature, which is based on Fisher Information Matrix, and our proposed measure.

1 Introduction

Although a great amount of the watermarking and data-hiding[1] literature deals with the problem of robustness, little has been said about security, and even in this time of relative maturity of watermarking research no consensus has been reached about its definition, and robustness and security continue to be often seen as overlapping concepts. The purpose of this first section is to give an overview of the evolution of research on watermarking security.

First, the notation and a general model for the evaluation of watermarking security will be introduced. The model is depicted in Figures 1-a and 1-b: a message $\mathbf{M}$ will be embedded in an original document $\mathbf{X}$ (the *host*), yielding a watermarked vector $\mathbf{Y}$. The embedding stage is parameterized by the embedding key Θ_e, and the resulting watermark is $\mathbf{W}$. In the detection/decoding stage, the detection key Θ_d is needed;[2] $\hat{\mathbf{M}}$ denotes the estimated message in the case of

---

* This work was partially funded by *Xunta de Galicia* under projects PGIDT04 TIC322013PR and PGIDT04 PXIC32202PM; MEC project DIPSTICK, reference TEC2004-02551/TCM; FIS project IM3, reference G03/185 and European Comission through the IST Programme under Contract IST-2002-507932 ECRYPT. ECRYPT disclaimer: The information in this paper is provided as is, and no guarantee or warranty is given or implied that the information is fit for any particular purpose. The user thereof uses the information at its sole risk and liability.

[1] In this paper we will use these both terms with no distinction.
[2] In symmetric watermarking $\Theta_e = \Theta_d$.

M. Barni et al. (Eds.): IH 2005, LNCS 3727, pp. 146–160, 2005.

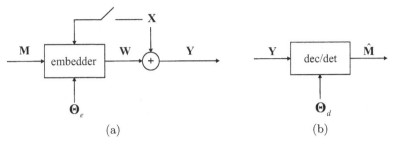

Fig. 1. General model for security analysis: embedding (a) and decoding/detection (b)

decoding, and the decision whether the received signal is watermarked or not in the case of detection. Capital letters denote random variables, and bold letters denote vectors.

During the first years, most of the literature deals with the problem of robustness, overlooking the meaning of security, in such a way that, at most, there was the notion of *intentional* and *non-intentional* attacks [1]. It could be said that the sensitivity attack [2] raised up the problem of security in watermarking, showing that a watermarking system could be broken in a number of iterations which is linear with the dimensionality of the host signal, but the first attempt at proposing a theoretical framework for assessing the security of a general watermarking scenario was [3]. The two main issues of this paper are the *perfect secrecy* (concept directly borrowed from the seminal work on cryptanalysis by Shannon in [4]) of the embedded message and the robustness of the embedding, characterizing both in terms of mutual information. However, this approach does not take into account that some information about the secret key may leak from the observations, giving advantage to the attacker. Thereafter, Kalker [5] shed some light on the concept of security in watermarking, giving definitions for *robust watermarking* and *security*, but perhaps they have the problem of being too general.

Another framework for watermarking security was proposed in [6], modeling watermarking as a game with some rules that determine which information (parameters of the algorithm, the algorithm itself, etc.) is public. According to this rules, attacks are classified as fair (the attacker only exploits publicly available information) or unfair (the attacker tries to access all the possible information which can be of help for him/her). The authors also define the *security level* as *"the amount of observation, the complexity, the amount of time, or the work that the attacker needs to gather in order to hack a system"*.

To the best of our knowledge, the most recent paper dealing with security is [7]. We agree with the authors about the difficulty of distinguishing between security and robustness. Kerckhoff's principle is also translated from cryptography to watermarking (it was introduced for the first time in [8]): all functions (encoding/embedding, decoding/detection, ...) should be declared as public except for a parameter called the secret key. An important contribution of [7] is the proposal of a security measure based on Fisher's Information Matrix [9]. In Section 4.2 it will be shown that the proposed measure is somewhat questionable since it is neglecting some important parameters as the uncertainty (differential entropy) in the secret key or in the watermarked signal. Finally, in [7] the security analysis of spread spectrum is performed and some practical methods for hacking systems are introduced.

After this brief overview the rest of the paper is organized as follows: In Sect. 2, definitions of *security* and *robustness* are proposed, and related issues are studied. In Sect. 3, a new information-theoretic measure is proposed for data-hiding security; this is applied to the study of Spread Spectrum watermarking security analysis in Sect. 4. Finally, in Sect. 5, the conclusions of this work are presented.

2   Fundamental Definitions

In this section, some thoughts about the concept of watermarking security are expounded and some definitions are proposed. First, in order to establish a clear line between robustness and security, the following definitions are put forward for consideration:

Definition 1. *Attacks to robustness are those whose target is to increase the probability of error of the data-hiding channel.*

Definition 2. *Attacks to security are those aimed at gaining knowledge about the secrets of the system (e.g. the embedding and/or detection keys).*

At first glance, in the definition of attacks to robustness we could have used the concept of channel capacity instead of the probability of error, but this entails some potential difficulties: for instance, an attack consisting on a translation or a rotation of the watermarked signal is only a desynchronization, thus the capacity of the channel is unaffected, but depending on the watermarking algorithm, the detector/decoder may be fooled. Another considerations about security, taking into account the above definitions, are the following:

About the intentionality of the attacks: attacks to security are obviously intentional, but not all intentional attacks are threats to security. For instance, an attacker may perform a JPEG compression to fool the watermark detector because he knows that, under a certain JPEG quality factor, the watermark will be effectively removed. Notice that, independently of the success of his attack, he has learned nothing about the secrets of the system. Hence, *attacks to security imply intentionality, but the converse is not necessarily true.*

About the blindness *of the attacks:* *blind* attacks are those which do not exploit any knowledge of the watermarking algorithm. Since attacks to security will try to disclose the secret parameters of the watermarking algorithm, it is easy to realize that they can not be blind. On the other hand, a *non-blind* attack is not necessarily targeted at learning the secrets of the system; for instance, in a data-hiding scheme based on binary scalar Dither Modulation (scalar DM), if an attacker adds to each watermarked coefficient a quantity equal to a quarter of the quantization step, the communication is completely destroyed because the bit error probability will be 0.5, although the attacker has learned nothing about the secrets of the systems. Hence, *security implies non-blindness, but the converse is not necessarily true.*

About the final purpose *of attacks:* many attacks to security constitute a first step towards performing attacks to robustness. This can be easily understood with a simple example: an attacker can perform an estimation of the secret pseudorandom sequence used for embedding in a spread-spectrum-based scheme (attack to security); with this estimated sequence, he can attempt to remove the watermark (attack to robustness).

About the distinction *between security and robustness:* a watermarking scheme can be extremely secure, in the sense that it is (almost) impossible for an attacker to estimate the secret key(s), but this does not necessarily affect the robustness of the system. For instance, the boundary of the detection region of watermarking algorithms whose decisions are based on linear correlation can be complicated by using, as a decision boundary, a fractal curve [10]; this way, security is highly improved since, for example, sensitivity-like attacks are no longer effective because the boundary of the detection region is extremely hard to describe. However, this countermeasure against security attacks does not improve anyway the robustness of the method. *Therefore, higher security does not imply higher robustness.*

About the measure of security itself: security must be measured separately from robustness. The following analogy with cryptography may be enlightening in this sense: in cryptography, the objective of the attacker is to disclose the encrypted message, so the security of the system is measured assuming that the communication channel is error-free; otherwise it makes no sense to measure security, since the original message was destroyed both for the attacker and fair users. By taking into account the definition of robustness given at the beginning of this section, the translation of this analogy to the watermarking scenario means that security must be measured assuming that no attacks to robustness occur.

The measure of security proposed here is a direct translation of Shannon's approach [4] to the case of continuous random variables, which was already hinted for watermarking by Hernández *et al.* in [11]. Furthermore, we will take into account Kerckhoff's principle [12], namely that the secrecy of a system must depend only on the secret keys. Security can be evaluated in the two scenarios of Figure 1.

1. For the scenario depicted in Figure 1-a, security is measured by the mutual information between the observations $\mathbf{Y}$ and the secret key $\boldsymbol{\Theta}$

$$
\begin{aligned}
I(\mathbf{Y}^1, \mathbf{Y}^2, \ldots, \mathbf{Y}^{N_o}; \boldsymbol{\Theta}) &= h(\mathbf{Y}^1, \mathbf{Y}^2, \ldots, \mathbf{Y}^{N_o}) - h(\mathbf{Y}^1, \mathbf{Y}^2, \ldots, \mathbf{Y}^{N_o} | \boldsymbol{\Theta}) \\
&= h(\boldsymbol{\Theta}) - h(\boldsymbol{\Theta} | \mathbf{Y}^1, \mathbf{Y}^2, \ldots, \mathbf{Y}^{N_o}),
\end{aligned}
\tag{1}
$$

where $h(\cdot)$ stands for differential entropy, and $\mathbf{Y}^n$ denotes the n-th observation.[3] Equivocation is defined as the remaining uncertainty about the key after the observations:

---

[3] The observations are independent signals watermarked with the same secret key $\boldsymbol{\Theta}$.

$$h(\boldsymbol{\Theta}|\mathbf{Y}^1, \mathbf{Y}^2, \ldots, \mathbf{Y}^{N_o}) = h(\boldsymbol{\Theta}) - I(\mathbf{Y}^1, \mathbf{Y}^2, \ldots, \mathbf{Y}^{N_o}; \boldsymbol{\Theta}). \qquad (2)$$

This scenario encompasses attacks concerning the observation of watermarked signals, where it is possible that additional parameters like the embedded message $\mathbf{M}$ or the host $\mathbf{X}$ are also known by the attacker. The model is valid for either side-informed and non-side-informed watermarking/data-hiding schemes.

2. The scenario depicted in Figure 1-b covers the so-called *oracle attacks*. In this case, the attacker tries to gain knowledge about the secret key $\boldsymbol{\Theta}$ by observing the outputs $\hat{\mathbf{M}}$ of the detector/decoder corresponding to some selected inputs $\mathbf{Y}$, so the information leakage is measured by

$$I(\hat{\mathbf{M}}^1, \ldots, \hat{\mathbf{M}}^{N_o}, \mathbf{Y}^1, \ldots, \mathbf{Y}^{N_o}; \boldsymbol{\Theta}),$$

where, in this case, $\mathbf{Y}^n$ are not necessarily watermarked objects but any arbitrary signal, for instance the result of the iterations of an attacking algorithm.

The translation of Shannon's approach to the continuous case is straightforward; we only must be careful with the concept of differential entropies, in order to redefine properly the *unicity distance* for continuous random variables: in this case, an attacker will have perfect knowledge of the key when $h(\boldsymbol{\Theta}|\mathbf{Y}^1, \mathbf{Y}^2, \ldots, \mathbf{Y}^{N_o}) = -\infty$. Hence, the security level is the number N_o of observations required to reach the unicity distance. However, since this number is ∞ in general, the security level could be measured by the growth-rate of mutual information with the number of observations N_o; another possibility is the establishment of a threshold in the value of the equivocation, which is directly related to the minimum error variance in the estimation of the key:

$$\sigma_E^2 \geq \frac{1}{2\pi e} e^{2h(\boldsymbol{\Theta}|\mathbf{Y})}, \qquad (3)$$

where σ_E^2 is the estimation error variance. For an attack based on the key estimate, its probability of success is given by the variance of the estimation error. This way, we can give the following definition:

Definition 3. *Given a required probability of success of an attack P_s, let σ_E^2 be the resulting variance of the secret key estimation error. Then, the security level is the minimum number of observations N_o^* needed to satisfy inequality (3).*

For the measure of security to be well defined, at least two of the three quantities involved in (2) must be given, because important information about the security of the system may be masked when only one of those quantities is available:

– The value of $h(\boldsymbol{\Theta})$ is only the a priori uncertainty about the key, so it does not depend on the system itself.
– The value of $I(\mathbf{Y}^1, \mathbf{Y}^2, \ldots, \mathbf{Y}^{N_o}; \boldsymbol{\Theta})$ shows the amount of information about the key that leaks from the observations, but a smaller information leakage

does not necessarily imply a higher security level: notice that, for example, a deterministic key would yield null information leakage, but the security is also null.
- The value of the equivocation $h(\Theta|\mathbf{Y}^1, \mathbf{Y}^2, \ldots, \mathbf{Y}^{N_o})$ is indicative of the remaining uncertainty about the key, but it does not reflect what is the a priori uncertainty.

3   Theoretical Evaluation of Security

In this section some theoretical measures about the residual entropy will be presented. The notation is borrowed from [7]: N_v will denote the length of the vectors (number of samples in each observation), N_o the number of observations, and N_c the number of carriers (or hidden symbols). After some modifications in the nomenclature described in [7], the following attacks will be analyzed:

- Known Message Attack (KMA): In this case the mutual information between the received signal and the secret key, when the sent message is known by the attacker, should be computed:

$$I(\mathbf{Y}^1, \cdots, \mathbf{Y}^{N_o}; \Theta|\mathbf{M}^1, \cdots, \mathbf{M}^{N_o}) = h(\mathbf{Y}^1, \cdots, \mathbf{Y}^{N_o}|\mathbf{M}^1, \cdots, \mathbf{M}^{N_o})$$
$$- h(\mathbf{Y}^1, \cdots, \mathbf{Y}^{N_o}|\Theta, \mathbf{M}^1, \cdots, \mathbf{M}^{N_o}),$$

so the residual entropy will be

$$h(\Theta|\mathbf{Y}^1, \cdots, \mathbf{Y}^{N_o}, \mathbf{M}^1, \cdots, \mathbf{M}^{N_o}) = h(\Theta) - h(\mathbf{Y}^1, \cdots, \mathbf{Y}^{N_o}|\mathbf{M}^1, \cdots, \mathbf{M}^{N_o})$$
$$+ h(\mathbf{Y}^1, \cdots, \mathbf{Y}^{N_o}|\Theta, \mathbf{M}^1, \cdots, \mathbf{M}^{N_o}). \quad (4)$$

- Watermarked Only Attack (WOA): The mutual information between the observations and the secret key is

$$I(\mathbf{Y}^1, \cdots, \mathbf{Y}^{N_o}; \Theta) = h(\mathbf{Y}^1, \cdots, \mathbf{Y}^{N_o}) - h(\mathbf{Y}^1, \cdots, \mathbf{Y}^{N_o}|\Theta)$$

and the residual entropy will be

$$h(\Theta|\mathbf{Y}^1, \cdots, \mathbf{Y}^{N_o}) = h(\Theta) - h(\mathbf{Y}^1, \cdots, \mathbf{Y}^{N_o}) + I(\mathbf{Y}^1, \cdots, \mathbf{Y}^{N_o}; \mathbf{M}^1, \cdots, \mathbf{M}^{N_o}|\Theta)$$
$$+ h(\mathbf{Y}^1, \cdots, \mathbf{Y}^{N_o}|\Theta, \mathbf{M}^1, \cdots, \mathbf{M}^{N_o}).$$

- Estimated Original Attack (EOA): In this case the following will be computed

$$I(\mathbf{Y}^1, \cdots, \mathbf{Y}^{N_o}; \Theta|\hat{\mathbf{X}}^1, \cdots, \hat{\mathbf{X}}^{N_o}) = h(\mathbf{Y}^1, \cdots, \mathbf{Y}^{N_o}|\hat{\mathbf{X}}^1, \cdots, \hat{\mathbf{X}}^{N_o})$$
$$- h(\mathbf{Y}^1, \cdots, \mathbf{Y}^{N_o}|\Theta, \hat{\mathbf{X}}^1, \cdots, \hat{\mathbf{X}}^{N_o}), (5)$$

where $\hat{\mathbf{X}}^i \triangleq \mathbf{X}^i + \tilde{\mathbf{X}}^i$ is an estimate of $\mathbf{X}^i$ and $\tilde{\mathbf{X}}^i$ is the estimation error; $\tilde{\mathbf{X}}^i$ is assumed to have power E and to be independent of $\mathbf{X}^i$. The Known Original Attack (KOA) proposed in [7] can be regarded to as a particular case of EOA, where the variance of the original host estimation error is set to 0. On the other hand, when the original host estimation error is σ_X^2, we are in the WOA case, so it can be also seen as particular case of EOA. The attacker could obtain this estimate by averaging several versions of the same host watermarked with different keys, but in order to ensure independence between the key and the estimate, the watermarked version with the to-be-estimated key should not be included in the averaging. Other alternative could be to filter the watermarked signal to compute the estimate of the original host (assuming the resulting signal is independent of the watermark). Taking into account (5), it is possible to write

$$h(\boldsymbol{\Theta}|\mathbf{Y}^1, \cdots, \mathbf{Y}^{N_o}, \hat{\mathbf{X}}^1, \cdots, \hat{\mathbf{X}}^{N_o}) = h(\boldsymbol{\Theta}) - h(\mathbf{Y}^1, \cdots, \mathbf{Y}^{N_o}|\hat{\mathbf{X}}^1, \cdots, \hat{\mathbf{X}}^{N_o})$$
$$+ h(\mathbf{Y}^1, \cdots, \mathbf{Y}^{N_o}|\boldsymbol{\Theta}, \hat{\mathbf{X}}^1, \cdots, \hat{\mathbf{X}}^{N_o}).$$

Finally, note that, depending on the method, the secret key could be related to the watermarking scheme parameters (i.e. the spreading sequence in spread-spectrum, the dither sequence in SCS or the codebooks in Costa schemes with random codebooks) through a deterministic function, constructing a Markov chain, in such a way that the attacker could be interested just in estimating the result of this function and not in the secret key itself. When $N_o = 1$, the superscript denoting the observation will be obviated for notation simplicity.

4   Security Analysis of Spread Spectrum Watermarking

For these methods, N_c random vectors (the spreading sequences), denoted by $\mathbf{U}_i$ are generated depending on the secret key $\boldsymbol{\Theta}$. In this way, the embedding function can be written as:

$$\mathbf{Y}^j = \mathbf{X}^j + \frac{1}{\sqrt{N_c}} \sum_{i=1}^{N_c} \mathbf{U}_i(-1)^{M_i^j}, \quad 1 \leq j \leq N_o, \tag{6}$$

with $\mathbf{Y}^j$, $\mathbf{X}^j$ and $\mathbf{U}_i$ N_v-dimensional vectors and $U_{i,j}$ is the j-th component of the i-th of the spreading sequence. The host is modeled as an i.i.d. Gaussian process, $\mathbf{X}^j \sim \mathcal{N}(0, \sigma_X^2 \mathbf{I}_{N_v})$, and the message letters $M_i^j \in \{0,1\}$, being $Pr\{M_i^j = 0\} = Pr\{M_i^j = +1\} = 1/2$. All of these quantities are assumed to be mutually independent. Since (6) is related with $\boldsymbol{\Theta}$ only through the $\mathbf{U}_i$'s, we will measure the security with respect to the $\mathbf{U}_i$'s.

4.1   Known Message Attack

To compute $I(\mathbf{Y}; \mathbf{U}_1, \mathbf{U}_2, \ldots, \mathbf{U}_{N_c}|\mathbf{M})$ (so $N_o = 1$) for a generic distribution of $\mathbf{U}_i$ numerical integration must be used. In Fig. 2 and Fig. 3 the results of this numerical integration are shown for $N_c = 1$ and both Gaussian and uniform distributions of $\mathbf{U}_1$ in the scalar case. Those figures show that the information the attacker can not learn (i.e., $h(\mathbf{U}_1|\mathbf{Y})$) is larger if $\mathbf{U}_1$ is chosen to be Gaussian. Taking this into account, we will focus on the case $\mathbf{U}_i \sim \mathcal{N}(0, \sigma_U^2 \mathbf{I}_{N_v})$. When the sent symbol is known to the attacker, the following result is derived in Appendix A.1 for $N_v > 1$, $N_c > 1$ and $N_o = 1$,

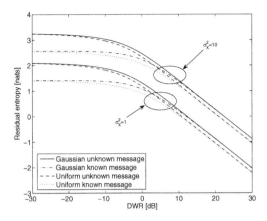

Fig. 2. Results of numerical integration for the equivocation $h(\mathbf{U}_1|\mathbf{Y})$ and $h(\mathbf{U}_1|M, \mathbf{Y})$ in spread-spectrum for Gaussian and uniform distributions of $\mathbf{U}_1$ and $N_v = 1$

$$I(\mathbf{Y}; \mathbf{U}_1, \mathbf{U}_2, \ldots, \mathbf{U}_{N_c}|\mathbf{M}) = \frac{N_v}{2} \log\left(1 + \frac{\sigma_U^2}{\sigma_X^2}\right), \tag{7}$$

yielding

$$h(\mathbf{U}_1, \mathbf{U}_2, \ldots, \mathbf{U}_{N_c}|\mathbf{Y}, \mathbf{M}) = \frac{N_v}{2} \log\left[\left(2\pi e \frac{\sigma_U^2}{N_c}\right)^{N_c} \cdot \frac{\sigma_X^2}{\sigma_X^2 + \sigma_U^2}\right].$$

The result in (7) says that the information that an attacker can obtain is the same whatever the number of carriers, although the entropy of the key is a linear function of this parameter (this result applies to a great variety of pdf's for the key, since by the central limit theorem, the sum of the carriers tends to a Gaussian). This result is also a consequence of the power normalization performed in (6); independently of the number of carriers, the power of the watermark stays constant.

In App. A.2, we analyze the case of one sent bit ($N_c = 1$), $N_v = 1$, when there are several available observations ($N_o > 1$), all of them watermarked with the same secret key. If $N_v > 1$ and the components are independent, the result is also valid, after multiplying it by N_v, so we can write

$$I(\mathbf{Y}^1, \cdots, \mathbf{Y}^{N_o}; \mathbf{U}_1|\mathbf{M}^1, \cdots, \mathbf{M}^{N_o}) = \frac{N_v}{2} \log\left(1 + \frac{N_o \sigma_U^2}{\sigma_X^2}\right), \tag{8}$$

which yields

$$h(\mathbf{U}_1|\mathbf{Y}^1, \cdots, \mathbf{Y}^{N_o}, \mathbf{M}^1, \cdots, \mathbf{M}^{N_o}) = \frac{N_v}{2} \log\left(2\pi e \frac{\sigma_U^2 \sigma_X^2}{N_o \sigma_U^2 + \sigma_X^2}\right) \tag{9}$$

This result shows that $I(\mathbf{Y}^1, \cdots, \mathbf{Y}^{N_o}; \mathbf{U}_1|\mathbf{M}^1, \cdots, \mathbf{M}^{N_o})$ grows non-linearly with the number of observations, although for large Document to Watermark

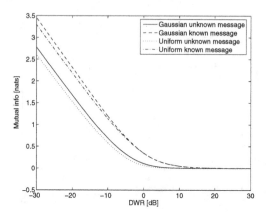

Fig. 3. Results of numerical integration for $I(\mathbf{Y}; \mathbf{U}_1)$ and $I(\mathbf{Y}; \mathbf{U}_1 | M)$ in spread-spectrum for Gaussian and uniform distribution of $\mathbf{U}_1$ and $N_v = 1$

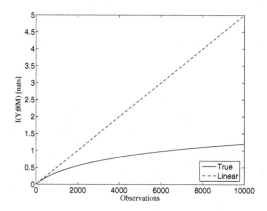

Fig. 4. $I(\mathbf{Y}^1, \cdots, \mathbf{Y}^{N_o}; \boldsymbol{\theta} | \mathbf{M}^1, \cdots, \mathbf{M}^{N_o})$ for spread-spectrum and Known Message Attack. DWR = 30 dB.

Ratios[4] (DWR >> 0) and low values of N_o it grows almost linearly. Moreover, (8) coincides with the capacity of a Gaussian channel with signal power σ_U^2 and noise power σ_X^2 / N_o. This suggests that the best method the attacker should follow for estimating $\mathbf{U}_1$ is just to average the observations $\mathbf{Y}^i$ (at least this is the case when both the host signal and the watermark are Gaussian distributed). In Fig. 4 the mutual information is compared with its linear version when DWR = 30 dB.

4.2   Comparison with the Result in [7]

In [7], the security level is defined as $O(N_o^\star)$, where $N_o^\star \triangleq N_o \mathrm{tr}(\mathrm{FIM}(\boldsymbol{\theta})^{-1})$ with $\mathrm{FIM}(\boldsymbol{\theta})$ the Fisher Information Matrix. In this section we try to link the result

---

[4]   The Document to Watermark Ratio is defined as $\mathrm{DWR} \triangleq 10 \log_{10} \left(\frac{\sigma_X^2}{\sigma_U^2} \right)$.

obtained in that paper with the one obtained here for spread-spectrum KMA when $N_c = 1$.

It is shown in App. B that the FIM obtained when a constant multiple (vectorial) parameter is estimated in the presence of i.i.d. Gaussian noise, taking into account N_o independent observations in the estimate, is $\frac{N_o}{\sigma_X^2} \mathbf{I}_{N_v}$, where σ_X^2 is the power of the interfering signal (the original host in our case). This is the only term considered in [7]. Nevertheless, an additional term should be taken into account, due to the random nature of the secret key (see [13]):

$$J_{P_{ij}} = \mathrm{E} \left[\frac{\partial \log f_{\mathbf{U}_1}(\mathbf{u}_1)}{\partial u_{1,i}} \cdot \frac{\partial \log f_{\mathbf{U}_1}(\mathbf{u}_1)}{\partial u_{1,j}} \right]. \tag{10}$$

If $\mathbf{U}_1$ is an i.i.d. Gaussian vector, it is easy to prove that $\mathbf{J}_P = \frac{1}{\sigma_U^2} \mathbf{I}_{N_v}$, so $\mathrm{FIM}(\mathbf{U}_1) = \left(\frac{N_o}{\sigma_X^2} + \frac{1}{\sigma_U^2} \right) \mathbf{I}_{N_v}$, yielding

$$N_o^\star = N_v \frac{\sigma_X^2 \sigma_U^2}{\sigma_U^2 + \sigma_X^2 / N_o},$$

which is obviously related with the proposed information-theoretic approach, since (9) is the differential entropy of a i.i.d. Gaussian random vector with co-variance matrix $N_o^\star / (N_o N_v) \mathbf{I}_{N_v}$.

On the other hand, if we considered only the FIM obtained when estimating a constant multiple parameter, the obtained $N_o^\star$ is $N_v \sigma_X^2$, which is obviously related with $h(\mathbf{Y}^1, \cdots, \mathbf{Y}^{N_o} | \mathbf{U}_1, \mathbf{M}^1, \cdots, \mathbf{M}^{N_o}) = \frac{N_v N_o}{2} \log(2\pi e \sigma_X^2)$; this was the methodology followed in [7]. Therefore, it does not take into account the entropy of the secret key neither the entropy of the watermarked signal. As stated in Sect. 2, both terms are relevant for the analysis of the system, so they should be considered. In fact, $h(\mathbf{Y}^1, \cdots, \mathbf{Y}^{N_o} | \mathbf{U}_1, \mathbf{M}^1, \cdots, \mathbf{M}^{N_o})$ for the KMA case grows linearly with the number of observations, while the mutual information will not increase linearly due to the dependence between observations. The linear approximation is actually an upper-bound; the larger the number of observations, the worse this approximation is.

4.3 Watermarked Only Attack

Due to the symmetry of the pdf's, it is possible to conclude that the components of the vector $\mathbf{Y}$ are still mutually independent, so for $N_c = 1$ and a single observation, we can write

$$I(\mathbf{Y}; \mathbf{U}_1) = N_v I(Y_i; U_{1,i}) = N_v \left(h(Y_i) - h(Y_i | U_{1,i}) \right) \tag{11}$$

$$= N_v \left(h(Y_i | \mathbf{M} = \mathbf{0}) - h(Y_i | U_{1,i}) \right). \tag{12}$$

In order to determine this for a generic distribution of $\mathbf{U}_1$, numerical integration should be used, whose results are plotted in Fig. 2. Once again, the information the attacker can not learn ($h(\mathbf{U}_1 | \mathbf{Y})$) is larger for the shown cases when $\mathbf{U}_1$ is chosen to be Gaussian. Therefore, assuming $\mathbf{U}_1$ to be Gaussian, we can write

$$I(\mathbf{Y};\mathbf{U}_1) = N_v \left(\frac{1}{2} \log \left(2\pi e (\sigma_X^2 + \sigma_U^2) \right) - h(Y_i|U_{1,i}) \right). \tag{13}$$

The rightmost term of (13) must still be numerically computed. When DWR $<<$ 0 we can easily analyze the asymptotic behavior of the mutual information taking into account $h(\mathbf{Y}) \approx h(\mathbf{U}_1)$ and $h(\mathbf{Y}|\mathbf{U}_1) \approx h(\mathbf{X}) + \log(2)$, yielding

$$I(\mathbf{Y};\mathbf{U}_1) \approx h(\mathbf{U}_1) - h(\mathbf{X}) - \log(2), \tag{14}$$
$$I(\mathbf{Y};\mathbf{U}_1|\mathbf{M}) \approx h(\mathbf{U}_1) - h(\mathbf{X}). \tag{15}$$

This explains and quantifies the gap between the WOA and KMA cases, which is exactly $\log(2) = 0.69$ nats. Nevertheless, note that a very small DWR is not practical, since it would yield unuseful watermarked images. This case has been introduced here only to shed some light into the general behavior of the mutual informations. On the other hand, to compute the gap between a Gaussian and a uniform distribution for $\mathbf{U}_1$, $h(\mathbf{U}_1)$ will be determined in both cases for a constant variance σ_U^2,

$$h(\mathbf{U}_{Gauss}) - h(\mathbf{U}_{unif}) = \frac{1}{2} \log(2\pi e \sigma_U^2) - \frac{1}{2} \log(12\sigma_U^2) = \frac{1}{2} \log \left(\frac{\pi e}{6} \right) = 0.1765,$$

which will be the asymptotic gap (in residual entropy terms) between the Gaussian and uniform cases for both known and unknown messages (see Fig. 2) when DWR $>> 0$, since for a large DWR both $I(\mathbf{Y};\mathbf{U}_1)$ and $I(\mathbf{Y};\mathbf{U}_1|\mathbf{M})$ are approximately 0.

For N_c carriers and $N_o = 1$ we have, similarly to the KMA case, the following mutual information:

$$\begin{aligned}
I(\mathbf{Y};\mathbf{U}_1,\mathbf{U}_2,\ldots,\mathbf{U}_{N_c}) &= N_v I(Y_i; U_{1,i}, U_{2,i}, \ldots, U_{N_c,i}) \\
&= N_v \left(h(Y_i) - h(Y_i|U_{1,i}, \ldots, U_{N_c,i}) \right) \\
&= N_v \left[\frac{1}{2} \log(2\pi e(\sigma_x^2 + \sigma_u^2)) - h(Y_i|U_{1,i}, \ldots, U_{N_c,i}) \right],
\end{aligned}$$

where the second term of the last equality must be numerically computed again.

The case of one sent bit ($N_c = 1$), $N_v = 1$, and several available observations ($N_o > 1$) needs very expensive numerical computations. Practical computations demand the reduction of the number of available observations to a very small value; in that case, the mutual information will be in the linear region, so no knowledge is available about the growth of the mutual information for large values of N_o.

4.4   Estimated Original Attack

In this case, the attacker will have access to an estimate of the original host signal, with some estimation error denoted by $\tilde{\mathbf{X}}$, which is assumed to be i.i.d. Gaussian with variance E, in such a way that for $N_o = 1$ we can write $I(\mathbf{Y};\mathbf{U}_1,\cdots,\mathbf{U}_{N_c}|$ $\mathbf{X} + \tilde{\mathbf{X}}) = N_v \left[h(Y_i|X_i + \tilde{X}_i) - h(Y_i|X_i + \tilde{X}_i, U_{1,i}, \cdots, U_{N_c,i}) \right]$. Assuming $\sigma_X^2 >> E$, $\tilde{X}_i$ will be almost orthogonal (and therefore independent) to $X_i + \tilde{X}_i$, so

$$I(\mathbf{Y}; \mathbf{U}_1, \cdots, \mathbf{U}_{N_c} | \mathbf{X} + \tilde{\mathbf{X}}) \approx N_v \left\{ h \left(\frac{1}{\sqrt{N_c}} \sum_{j=1}^{N_c} U_{j,i}(-1)^{M_j} - \tilde{X}_i \right) \right.$$

$$\left. - h \left(\frac{1}{\sqrt{N_c}} \sum_{j=1}^{N_c} U_{j,i}(-1)^{M_j} - \tilde{X}_i | U_{1,i}, \cdots, U_{N_c,i} \right) \right\}.$$

This situation is equivalent to that described in 4.3, but replacing σ_X^2 by E, so when $N_c = 1$ it is possible to use Fig. 2 for obtaining numerical results, using the *Estimation error to Watermark Ratio* (EWR), defined as $10 \log_{10} \left(\frac{E}{\sigma_U^2} \right)$, instead of the DWR, in the horizontal axis. When the estimate is perfect, i.e. $\sigma_{\tilde{x}}^2 = 0$, the mutual information approaches infinity.

5   Conclusions

In this paper, an overview of watermarking security has been introduced, showing the evolution of this concept in the last years. The frontier between *security* and *robustness* is rather fuzzy, so we have proposed some definitions in order to make a clear distinction between these two concepts, which in turn allows the isolation of the security analysis from the robustness issue. Based on these definitions, a new information-theoretic framework to evaluate watermarking security has been introduced based on the use of mutual information to measure the secret key leakage; this measure has been shown to be more complete than the measure proposed in [7], which was based on the FIM and did not take into account the term related with the variability of the secret key. Security of Spread Spectrum watermarking has been analyzed in different scenarios classified by the amount of information available to the attacker, quantifying the information leakage about the key as a function of the number of observations and the DWR.

References

1. Cox, I.J., Linnartz, J.P.M.G.: Some general methods for tampering with watermarks. IEEE Journal on Selected Areas in Communications **16** (1998) 587–593
2. Linnartz, J.P.M.G., van Dijk, M.: Analysis of the sensitivity attack against electronic watermarks in images. In Aucsmith, D., ed.: 2nd Int. Workshop on Information Hiding, IH'98. Volume 1525 of Lecture Notes in Computer Science., Portland, OR, USA, Springer Verlag (1998) 258–272
3. Mitthelholzer, T.: An information-theoretic approach to steganography and watermarking. In Pfitzmann, A., ed.: 3rd Int. Workshop on Information Hiding, IH'99. Volume 1768 of Lecture Notes in Computer Science., Dresden, Germany, Springer Verlag (1999) 1–17
4. Shannon, C.E.: Communication theory of secrecy systems. Bell system technical journal **28** (1949) 656–715
5. Kalker, T.: Considerations on watermarking security. In: IEEE Int. Workshop on Multimedia Signal Processing, MMSP'01, Cannes, France (2001) 201–206

6. Barni, M., Bartolini, F., Furon, T.: A general framework for robust watermarking security. Signal Processing **83** (2003) 2069–2084
7. Cayre, F., Fontaine, C., Furon, T.: Watermarking security part one: theory. In Edward J. Delp III, Wong, P.W., eds.: Security, Steganography, and Watermarking of Multimedia Contents VII. Volume 5681., San Jose, California, USA, SPIE (2005) 746–757
8. Furon, T., et al.: Security Analysis. European Project IST-1999-10987 CERTI-MARK, Deliverable D.5.5 (2002)
9. Fisher, R.A.: On the mathematical foundations of theoretical statistics. Philosophical Transactions of the Royal Society **222** (1922) 309–368
10. Barni, M., Bartolini, F.: Watermarking Systems Engineering. Signal Processing and Communications. Marcel Dekker (2004)
11. Hernández, J.R., Pérez-González, F.: Throwing more light on image watermarks. In Aucsmith, D., ed.: 2nd Int. Workshop on Information Hiding, IH'98. Volume 1525 of Lecture Notes in Computer Science., Portland, OR, USA, Springer Verlag (1998) 191–207
12. Kerckhoff, A.: La cryptographie militaire. Journal des sciences militaires **9** (1883) 5–38
13. van Trees, H.L.: Detection, Estimation, and Modulation Theory. John Wiley and Sons (1968)
14. Cover, T.M., Thomas, J.A.: Elements of Information Theory. Wiley series in Telecommunications (1991)

A   Calculation of Mutual Information for Spread Spectrum

A.1   Known Message Attack (KMA) for a Single Observation

For a single observation ($N_o = 1$) and $N_c = 1$, we have

$$I(\mathbf{Y}; \mathbf{U}_1 | \mathbf{M}) = \sum_{i=1}^{N_v} \sum_{j=1}^{N_v} I(Y_i; U_{1,j} | \mathbf{M}, Y_{i-1}, \ldots, Y_1, U_{1,j}, \ldots, U_{1,1}) \qquad (16)$$

$$= \sum_{i=1}^{N_v} I(Y_i; U_{1,i} | \mathbf{M}, Y_{i-1}, \ldots, Y_1) \qquad (17)$$

$$= \sum_{i=1}^{N_v} I(Y_i; U_{1,i} | \mathbf{M}) \qquad (18)$$

$$= N_v I(Y_i; U_{1,i} | \mathbf{M}), \qquad (19)$$

where (17) follows from the fact that Y_i and $U_{1,j}$ are independent $\forall\, i \neq j$; (18) follows from the independence between the components of $\mathbf{Y}$ given the message, and (19) follows from the fact that $\mathbf{Y}$ and $\mathbf{U}_1$ are i.i.d. processes. The theoretical expression for (19) is easy to calculate:

$$I(Y_i; U_{1,i} | \mathbf{M}) = I(Y_i; U_{1,i} | \mathbf{M} = \mathbf{0}) = h(Y_i | \mathbf{M} = \mathbf{0}) - h(Y_i | \mathbf{M} = \mathbf{0}, U_{1,i}),$$

where $h(Y_i|\mathbf{M} = \mathbf{0})$ will obviously depend on the distribution of $U_{1,i}$. Assuming $\mathbf{U}_1$ to be Gaussian, i.e. $\mathbf{U}_1 \sim \mathcal{N}(0, \sigma_U^2 \mathbf{I}_{N_v})$, we can write

$$I(Y_i; U_{1,i}|\mathbf{M}) = h(\mathcal{N}(0, \sigma_X^2 + \sigma_U^2)) - h(\mathcal{N}(0, \sigma_X^2)) = \frac{1}{2}\log\left(1 + \frac{\sigma_U^2}{\sigma_X^2}\right).$$

Next, the case of multiple carriers is analyzed. When $N_c > 1$, we can write

$$\begin{aligned}
I(\mathbf{Y}; \mathbf{U}_1, \mathbf{U}_2, \ldots, \mathbf{U}_{N_c}|\mathbf{M}) &= N_v I(Y_i; U_{1,i}, U_{2,i}, \ldots, U_{N_c,i}|\mathbf{M}) \\
&= N_v \left\{ h(Y_i|\mathbf{M}) - h(Y_i|U_{1,i}, \ldots, U_{N_c,i}, \mathbf{M}) \right\} \\
&= N_v \left\{ h\left(X_i + \sum_{j=1}^{N_c}(N_c)^{-1/2}U_{j,i}\right) - h(X_i) \right\} \\
&= N_v \left\{ h(\mathcal{N}(0, \sigma_X^2 + \sigma_U^2)) - h(\mathcal{N}(0, \sigma_X^2)) \right\} \\
&= \frac{N_v}{2}\log\left(1 + \frac{\sigma_U^2}{\sigma_X^2}\right). \tag{20}
\end{aligned}$$

A.2   Known Message Attack (KMA) for Multiple Observations

When $N_v = 1$, there are several available observations ($N_o > 1$) watermarked with the same secret key and there is one bit to be sent in each observation ($N_c = 1$) which we will assume without loss of generality to be the same for all the observations, it can be seen that the covariance matrix of $(\mathbf{Y}^1, \cdots, \mathbf{Y}^{N_o})$, denoted by $R_{\mathbf{Y}}$, becomes

$$R_{\mathbf{Y}} = \begin{pmatrix} \sigma_X^2 + \sigma_U^2 & \sigma_U^2 & \cdots & \sigma_U^2 \\ \sigma_U^2 & \sigma_X^2 + \sigma_U^2 & \cdots & \sigma_U^2 \\ \vdots & \vdots & \ddots & \vdots \\ \sigma_U^2 & \sigma_U^2 & \cdots & \sigma_X^2 + \sigma_U^2 \end{pmatrix},$$

so its entropy is (see [14])

$$h(\mathbf{Y}^1, \cdots, \mathbf{Y}^{N_o}) = \frac{1}{2}\log\left((2\pi e)^{N_o}|R_{\mathbf{Y}}|\right) = \frac{1}{2}\log\left((2\pi e)^{N_o}\left[\frac{N_o\sigma_U^2}{\sigma_X^2} + 1\right]\sigma_X^{2N_o}\right),$$

and we can write $I(\mathbf{Y}^1, \cdots, \mathbf{Y}^{N_o}; \mathbf{U}_1|\mathbf{M}^1, \cdots, \mathbf{M}^{N_o}) = \frac{1}{2}\log\left(1 + \frac{N_o\sigma_U^2}{\sigma_X^2}\right).$

B   Fisher Information Matrix for SS-KMA

In this section we will compute the Fisher Information Matrix of the estimate of the constant multiple parameter $\boldsymbol{\theta}$ taking into account the observations $\mathbf{Y}^1, \cdots, \mathbf{Y}^{N_o}$. Let us consider $\mathbf{Y}^j = \mathbf{X}^j + \boldsymbol{\theta}$, with $\mathbf{X}^j \sim \mathcal{N}(0, \sigma_X^2 \mathbf{I}_{N_V})$, and the $\mathbf{X}^j$'s to be mutually independent for $1 \leq j \leq N_o$ [5]. Following the definition of

---

[5] Be aware that this is the case described in Sect. 4.1 for $N_c = 1$, after multiplying the j-th observation by $(-1)^{M_1^j}$. In that case, the parameter to be estimated is $\mathbf{U}_1$.

Fisher Information Matrix ([13]), we can write

$$\text{FIM}_{ii}(\boldsymbol{\theta}) = \int f(\mathbf{y}^1, \cdots, \mathbf{y}^{N_o}|\boldsymbol{\theta}) \left(\frac{\partial}{\partial \theta_i} \log f(\mathbf{y}^1, \cdots, \mathbf{y}^{N_o}|\boldsymbol{\theta}) \right)^2 d\mathbf{y}^1 \cdots d\mathbf{y}^{N_o},$$

where $f(\mathbf{y}^1, \cdots, \mathbf{y}^{N_o}|\boldsymbol{\theta}) = \prod_{k=1}^{N_v} \prod_{j=1}^{N_o} \frac{1}{\sqrt{2\pi\sigma_X^2}} e^{\frac{-(y_k^j - \theta_k)^2}{2\sigma_X^2}}$, in such a way that

$$\frac{\partial}{\partial \theta_i} \log f(\mathbf{y}^1, \cdots, \mathbf{y}^{N_o}|\boldsymbol{\theta}) = \sum_{j=1}^{N_o} \frac{y_i^j - \theta_i}{\sigma_X^2} = \frac{\sum_{j=1}^{N_o} x_i^j}{\sigma_X^2},$$

and, finally, after a variable change,

$$\text{FIM}_{ii}(\boldsymbol{\theta}) = \int \left(\frac{\sum_{j=1}^{N_o} x_i^j}{\sigma_X^2} \right)^2 \prod_{j=1}^{N_o} \frac{1}{\sqrt{2\pi\sigma_X^2}} e^{\frac{-(x_i^j)^2}{2\sigma_X^2}} dx_i^1 \cdots dx_i^{N_o} = \frac{N_o}{\sigma_X^2}, \ 1 \le i \le N_v.$$

On the other hand,

$$\text{FIM}_{ik}(\boldsymbol{\theta}) = \int f(\mathbf{y}^1, \cdots, \mathbf{y}^{N_o}|\boldsymbol{\theta}) \left(\frac{\partial}{\partial \theta_i} \log f(\mathbf{y}^1, \cdots, \mathbf{y}^{N_o}|\boldsymbol{\theta}) \right)$$

$$\left(\frac{\partial}{\partial \theta_k} \log f(\mathbf{y}^1, \cdots, \mathbf{y}^{N_o}|\boldsymbol{\theta}) \right) d\mathbf{y}^1 \cdots d\mathbf{y}^{N_o}$$

$$= \left(\int \frac{\sum_{j=1}^{N_o} x_i^j}{\sigma_X^2} \prod_{j=1}^{N_o} \frac{1}{\sqrt{2\pi\sigma_X^2}} e^{\frac{-(x_i^j)^2}{2\sigma_X^2}} dx_i^1 \cdots dx_i^{N_o} \right)$$

$$\cdot \left(\int \frac{\sum_{l=1}^{N_o} x_k^l}{\sigma_X^2} \prod_{l=1}^{N_o} \frac{1}{\sqrt{2\pi\sigma_X^2}} e^{\frac{-(x_k^l)^2}{2\sigma_X^2}} dx_k^1 \cdots dx_k^{N_o} \right) = 0, \text{ for all } i \ne k,$$

so, we can conclude $\text{FIM}(\boldsymbol{\theta}) = \frac{N_o}{\sigma_X^2} \mathbf{I}_{N_v}$.

How to Combat Block Replacement Attacks?

Gwenaël Doërr and Jean-Luc Dugelay

Eurécom Institute, Multimedia Communications Department,
2229 route des Crêtes, B.P. 193, 06904 Sophia-Antipolis Cédex, France
{doerr, dugelay}@eurecom.fr
http://www.eurecom.fr/~image

Abstract. Block replacement attacks consist in exploiting the redundancy of the host signal to replace each signal block with another one or a combination of other ones. Such an attacking strategy has been recognized to be a major threat against watermarking systems e.g. additive spread-spectrum and quantization index modulation algorithms. In this paper, a novel embedding strategy will be introduced to circumvent this attack. The basic idea is to make the watermark inherit the self-similarities from the host signal. This can be achieved by imposing a linear structure on the watermark in a feature space e.g. the Gabor space. The relationship with existing multiplicative watermarking schemes will also be exhibited. Finally, experimental results will be presented and directions for future work will be discussed.

1 Introduction

Digital watermarking was initially introduced in the early 90's as a complementary protection technology [1] since encryption alone is not enough. Indeed, sooner or later, encrypted multimedia content is decrypted to be eventually presented to human beings. At this very moment, multimedia content is left unprotected and can be perfectly duplicated, manipulated and redistributed at a large scale. Thus, a second line of defense has to be added to address this issue. This is the main purpose of digital watermarking which basically consists in hiding some information into digital content in an imperceptible manner. Up to now, research has mainly investigated how to improve the trade-off between three conflicting parameters: imperceptibility, robustness and capacity. Perceptual models have been exploited to make watermarks less perceptible, benchmarks have been released to evaluate robustness, channel models have been studied to obtain a theoretical bound for the embedding capacity.

A lot of attention has focused on security applications such as Intellectual Property (IP) protection and Digital Rights Managements (DRM) systems. Digital watermarking was even thought of as a possible solution to combat illegal copying which was a forthcoming issue in the mid-90's. However the few attempts to launch watermarking-based copy-control mechanisms [2,3] have resulted in partial failures, which have significantly lowered the initial enthusiasm for this technology. These setbacks were mainly due to the claim that embedded

M. Barni et al. (Eds.): IH 2005, LNCS 3727, pp. 161–175, 2005.

watermarks would survive in a highly hostile environment even if very few works addressed this issue. Indeed, if the survival of the watermark against common signal processing primitives - filtering, lossy compression, global desynchronization - has been carefully surveyed, almost no work has considered that an attacker may exploit some knowledge on the watermarking systems to defeat it. Nevertheless, in applications such as copy control or fingerprinting, digital watermarking is usually seen as a disturbing technology. If content owners are glad to have means to protect their high valued multimedia items, customers on the other hand do not really appreciate that some hidden signal prevent them from freely copying digital material or that an invisible watermark identifies them as a source of leakage. Therefore, this protecting technology is likely to be submitted to strong hostile attacks when it is released to the public.

Security evaluation is now a growing concern in the watermarking community since recent studies have highlighted that most watermarking systems can be defeated by malicious attackers [4,5]. In particular, collusion attacks have often been mentioned as a possible mean to evaluate security [6,7]. Collusion consists in collecting several watermarked documents and combining them to obtain unwatermarked content. There are two basic cases. When different contents are watermarked with some kind of structure, colluders try to estimate this structure and exploit this knowledge in a second step to remove the watermark [8]. Alternatively, when similar contents carry uncorrelated watermarks, colluders can average them so that watermark samples sum to zero. Block Replacement Attacks (BRA) consist in replacing each signal block with another one or a combination of other ones and can thus be seen as an extension of this later strategy. BRA have been shown to defeat both additive Spread-Spectrum (SS) and Quantization Index Modulation (QIM) [9] and will thus be rapidly reviewed in Section 2. A novel embedding strategy is then designed in Section 3 to circumvent this attack by making the watermark inherit the self-similarities of the host signal. This is done by forcing a linear structure on the watermark in a feature space e.g. the Gabor space. At this point, an analogy between this new approach and previous multiplicative embedding schemes [10,11] can even be exhibited. Next, the resilience of these signal coherent watermarks against BRA is evaluated in Section 4 in comparison with standard additive SS watermarks. Finally, conclusions are drawn in Section 5 and tracks for future work are given.

2   Block Replacement Attacks

Multimedia digital data is highly redundant: successive video frames are highly similar in a movie clip, most songs contain some repetitive patterns, etc. An attacker can consequently exploit these similarities to successively replace each part of the signal with a *similar* one taken from another location in the same signal. In particular, such approaches have already been investigated to obtain efficient compression tools [12]. The signal to be processed is first partitioned into a set of blocks b_T of size S_T. Those blocks can either overlap or not. The asset of using overlapping blocks is that it prevents strong blocking artifacts on

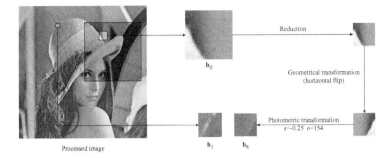

Fig. 1. BRA implementation using a fractal coding strategy: each block is replaced by the one in the search window which is the most similar modulo a geometrical and photometric transformation

the border of the blocks by averaging the overlapping areas. The attack processes then each one of these blocks sequentially. For each block, a search window is defined. It can be chosen in the vicinity of the target block $\mathbf{b}_T$ or randomly for security reasons. This search window is partitioned to obtain a codebook $\mathcal{Q}$ of blocks $\mathbf{b}_{Q_i}$ of size S_Q. Once again, these blocks can overlap or not. Next a candidate block for replacement $\mathbf{b}_R$ is computed using the blocks present in the codebook. Of course, the larger the codebook $\mathcal{Q}$ is, the more choices there are to compute a replacement block which is *similar* enough to the input block $\mathbf{b}_T$ so that they can be substituted without introducing strong visual artifacts. On the other hand, the larger the codebook $\mathcal{Q}$ is, the higher the computational complexity is and a trade-off has to be found. The Mean Square Error (MSE) can be used to evaluate how similar are two blocks with the following formula:

$$\mathrm{MSE}(\mathbf{b}_R, \mathbf{b}_T) = \frac{1}{S_T} \sum_{i=1}^{S_T} \left(\mathbf{b}_R(i) - \mathbf{b}_T(i) \right)^2, \tag{1}$$

where the summation index i can be one-dimensional (sound) or multidimensional (image, video). The lower the MSE is, the more similar are the two blocks. Thus, the original block $\mathbf{b}_T$ is substituted by the replacement block $\mathbf{b}_R$ associated with the lowest MSE.

There are many ways of computing the replacement block $\mathbf{b}_R$. One of the first proposed implementation was based on fractal coding [13] and is illustrated in Figure 1. The codebook is first artificially enlarged by also considering geometrically transformed versions of the blocks within the search window. For complexity reasons, a small number of transformations are considered e.g. downsampling by a factor 2 and 8 isometries (identity, 4 flips, 3 rotations). Next, the candidate replacement blocks are computed with a simple affine photometric compensation. In other terms, each block $\mathbf{b}_{Q_i}$ of the codebook is transformed in $s\mathbf{b}_{Q_i} + o\mathbf{1}$, where $\mathbf{1}$ is a block containing only ones, so that the MSE with the target block $\mathbf{b}_T$ is minimized. This is a simple least squares problem and the scale s and offset o can be determined as follows:

$$s = \frac{(\mathbf{b}_T - \mathrm{m}_T\mathbf{1}) \cdot (\mathbf{b}_{Q_i} - \mathrm{m}_{Q_i}\mathbf{1})}{|\mathbf{b}_{Q_i} - \mathrm{m}_{Q_i}\mathbf{1}|^2} \tag{2}$$

$$o = \mathrm{m}_T - s.\mathrm{m}_{Q_i} \tag{3}$$

where m_T (resp. m_{Q_i}) is the mean value of block $\mathbf{b}_T$ (resp. $\mathbf{b}_{Q_i}$), $\cdot$ is the linear correlation defined as:

$$\mathbf{b} \cdot \mathbf{b}' = \frac{1}{S_T} \sum_{i=1}^{S_T} \mathbf{b}(i)\mathbf{b}'(i) \tag{4}$$

and $|\mathbf{b}|$ is the norm defined as $\sqrt{\mathbf{b} \cdot \mathbf{b}}$. At this point, the transformed blocks $s\mathbf{b}_{Q_i} + o\mathbf{1}$ are sorted in ascending order according to their similarity with the target block $\mathbf{b}_T$ and the most similar one is retained for replacement. In the same fashion, an alternative approach consists in building iteratively sets of similar blocks and randomly shuffling their positions [14,9] until all the blocks have been replaced.

The baseline of the algorithm has then been improved to further enhance the performances of the attack. The main drawback of the previous implementation is that it is not possible to modify the strength of the attack. Furthermore, the computation of the replacement block is not properly managed: either it is too close from the target block $\mathbf{b}_T$ and the watermark is reintroduced, or it is too distant and strong visual artifacts appear. Optimally, one would like to ensure that the distortion $\Delta = \mathrm{MSE}(\mathbf{b}_R, \mathbf{b}_T)$ remains within two bounds τ_{low} and τ_{high}. To this end, several blocks $\mathbf{b}_{Q_i}$ can be combined to compute the replacement block instead of a single one as follows:

$$\mathbf{b}_R = \sum_{i=1}^{N} \lambda_i \mathbf{b}_{Q_i} \tag{5}$$

where the λ_i are mixing parameter chosen in such a way that Δ is minimized. This combination can take into account a fixed number of blocks [15] or also adapt the number of considered blocks for combination according to the nature of the block to be reconstructed [16]. Intuitively, approximating flat blocks require to combine fewer blocks than for highly textured ones. However, the computational load induced by computing optimal mixing parameters in Equation (5) for each candidate replacement block has motivated the design of an alternative implementation which is described in Table 1 [16]. First, for each block $\mathbf{b}_T$, the codebook $\mathcal{Q}$ is built and photometric compensation is performed. Next, a Principal Component Analysis (PCA) is performed considering the different blocks $\mathbf{b}_{Q_i}$ in the codebook. This gives a centroid $\mathbf{c}$ defined as follows:

$$\mathbf{c} = \frac{1}{|\mathcal{Q}|} \sum_{\mathbf{b}_{Q_i} \in \mathcal{Q}} \mathbf{b}_{Q_i} \tag{6}$$

and a set of eigenblocks $\mathbf{e}_i$ associated with their eigenvalues ϵ_i. These eigenblocks are then sorted by descending eigenvalues i.e. the direction $\mathbf{e}_1$ contains more information than any other one in the basis. Then, a candidate block for

Table 1. BRA procedure using block projection on a PCA-defined subspace

---

For each block $\mathbf{b}_T$ of the signal

| 1 | Build the block codebook $\mathcal{Q}$ |

| 2 | Perform photometric compensation |

| 3 | Performs the PCA of the blocks in $\mathcal{Q}$ to obtain a set of orthogonal eigenblocks $\mathbf{e}_i$ associated with their eigenvalues ϵ_i |

Set $N = 1$ and flag $= 0$

| 4 | While (flag $= 0$) AND ($N \leq S_T$) |

    (a) Build the optimal replacement block $\mathbf{b}_R$ using the eigenblocks $\mathbf{r}_i$ associated with the first N eigenvalues

    (b) Compute $\Delta = \mathrm{MSE}(\mathbf{b}_R, \mathbf{b}_T)$

    (c) If $\tau_{\mathrm{low}} \leq \Delta \leq \tau_{\mathrm{high}}$, set flag $= 1$

    (d) Else increment N

| 5 | Replace $\mathbf{b}_T$ by $\mathbf{b}_R$ |

---

replacement $\mathbf{b}_R$ is computed using the N first eigenblocks so that the distortion Δ is minimized. In other terms, the block $\mathbf{b}_T - \mathbf{c}$ is projected onto the subspace spanned by the N first eigenblocks and $\mathbf{b}_R$ can be written:

$$\mathbf{b}_R = \mathbf{c} + \sum_{i=1}^{N} \frac{(\mathbf{b}_T - \mathbf{c}) \cdot \mathbf{e}_i}{|\mathbf{e}_i|^2} \mathbf{e}_i \qquad (7)$$

Of course, the distortion Δ gracefully decreases as the number N of combined eigenblocks increases. Thus, an adaptive framework is introduced to identify which value N should have so that the distortion Δ falls within the range $[\tau_{\mathrm{low}}, \tau_{\mathrm{high}}]$. It should be noted that the underlying assumption is that most of the watermark energy will be concentrated in the last eigenblocks since the watermark can be seen as details. As a result, if a valid candidate block can be built without using the last eigenblocks, the watermark signal will not be reintroduced.

3   Signal Coherent Watermarks

As reminded in the previous section, for each signal block, BRA look for a linear combination of neighboring blocks resulting in a block which is similar enough to the current block so that a substitution does not introduce strong visual artifacts. Since watermarking systems do not perform today anything specific to ensure that the embedded watermark is coherent with the self-similarities of the host signal, most of them are defeated by such attacks. Intuitively, to ensure that the watermark will survive BRA, the embedding process should guarantee that *similar signal blocks carry similar watermarks* or alternatively that *pixels with similar neighborhood carry watermark samples with close values*. In this perspective, assuming that it is possible to characterize the neighborhood in each point with a feature vector, signal coherent watermarking can be achieved if watermark samples are considered as the output of a linear form in this feature space as it is theoretically demonstrated in Subsection 3.1. A practical implementation of this approach using Gabor features is then described in Subsection 3.2. Finally, a relationship with existing multiplicative watermarking scheme in the frequency space is exhibited in Subsection 3.3.

3.1   Linear Watermarking with Neighborhood Characteristics

Let us assume for the moment that it is possible to associate to each pixel position $\mathbf{p} = (x, y)$ with $1 \leq x \leq X$ and $1 \leq y \leq Y$ in the image $\mathbf{i}$ a feature vector $\mathbf{f}(\mathbf{i}, \mathbf{p})$ which characterizes *in some sense* the neighborhood of the image around this specific position. Thus, this function can be defined as follows:

$$\begin{aligned} \mathbf{f} : \mathcal{I} \times \mathcal{P} &\to \mathcal{F} \\ (\mathbf{i}, \mathbf{p}) &\mapsto \mathbf{f}(\mathbf{i}, \mathbf{p}) \end{aligned} \tag{8}$$

where $\mathcal{I}$ is the image space, $\mathcal{P} = [1 \ldots X] \times [1 \ldots Y]$ the position space and $\mathcal{F}$ the feature space. From a very low-level perspective, generating a digital watermark can be regarded as associating a watermark value $w(\mathbf{i}, \mathbf{p})$ to each pixel position in the image. However, if the embedded watermark is required to be immune against BRA, the following property should also be verified:

$$\mathbf{f}(\mathbf{i}, \mathbf{p}_0) \approx \sum_k \lambda_k \mathbf{f}(\mathbf{i}, \mathbf{p}_k) \Rightarrow w(\mathbf{i}, \mathbf{p}_0) \approx \sum_k \lambda_k w(\mathbf{i}, \mathbf{p}_k) \tag{9}$$

In other terms, if at a given position $\mathbf{p}_0$, the local neighborhood is similar to a linear combination of neighborhoods at other locations $\mathbf{p}_k$, then the watermark sample $w(\mathbf{p}_0)$ embedded at position $\mathbf{p}_0$ should be close to the linear combination (with the same mixing coefficients λ_k) of the watermark samples $w(\mathbf{p}_k)$ at these locations. A simple way to obtain this property is to make the watermarking process be the composition of a feature extraction operation and a linear form φ.

Hence, one can write $w = \varphi \circ \mathbf{f}$ where $\varphi : \mathcal{F} \to \mathbb{R}$ is a linear form which takes F-dimensional feature vectors in input. Next, to completely define this linear form, it is sufficient to set the values $\xi_f = \varphi(\mathbf{b}_f)$ for a given orthonormalized basis $\mathcal{B} = \{\mathbf{b}_f\}$ of the feature space $\mathcal{F}$. Without loss of generality, one can consider the canonical basis $\mathcal{O} = \{\mathbf{o}_f\}$ where $\mathbf{o}_f$ is a F-dimensional vector filled with 0's except the fth coordinate which is equal to 1. The whole secret of the algorithm is contained in the values ξ_f and they can consequently be pseudo-randomly generated using a secret key K. Now, if the values taken by the linear form on the unit sphere $\mathcal{U}$ of this subspace are considered, the following probability density function is obtained:

$$f_{\varphi|u}(w) = \frac{1}{\Xi\sqrt{\pi}} \frac{\Gamma\left(\frac{F}{2}\right)}{\Gamma\left(\frac{F-1}{2}\right)} \left[1 - \left(\frac{w}{\Xi}\right)^2 \right]^{\frac{F-3}{2}} \tag{10}$$

where $\Xi^2 = \sum_{f=1}^{F} \xi_f^2$ and $\Gamma(.)$ is the Gamma function. When the dimension F of the feature space $\mathcal{F}$ grows large, this probability density function tends towards a Gaussian distribution with zero mean and standard deviation $\Xi/\sqrt{F}$. Thus if the ξ_f's are chosen to have zero mean and unit variance, this ensures that the values of the linear form restricted to the unit sphere $\mathcal{U}$ are normally distributed with also zero mean and unit variance. Then, keeping in mind that φ is linear and that the following equation is valid,

$$w(\mathbf{i}, \mathbf{p}) = \varphi\left(\|\mathbf{f}(\mathbf{i}, \mathbf{p})\| \frac{\mathbf{f}(\mathbf{i}, \mathbf{p})}{\|\mathbf{f}(\mathbf{i}, \mathbf{p})\|}\right) = \|\mathbf{f}(\mathbf{i}, \mathbf{p})\| \varphi(\mathbf{u}(\mathbf{i}, \mathbf{p})) \quad \text{with } \mathbf{u}(\mathbf{i}, \mathbf{p}) \in \mathcal{U} \quad (11)$$

it is straightforward to realize that the obtained watermark is equivalent to a Gaussian watermark with zero mean and unit variance multiplied by some local scaling factors. The more textured is the considered neighborhood, the more complicated it is to characterize it and the greater the norm $\|\mathbf{f}(\mathbf{i}, \mathbf{p})\|$ is likely to be. Looking back at Equation 11, it results that the watermark is amplified in textured area whereas it is attenuated in smooth ones. This can be regarded as some kind of perceptual shaping [17].

3.2   A Practical Implementation Using Gabor Features

In order to impose a linear relationship between watermark samples with respect to some characteristics of the neighborhood, it is first necessary to define the features which will be used to differentiate between neighborhoods i.e. it is needed to define the feature extraction function $\mathbf{f}$ mentioned in Equation (8). In this perspective, Gabor features are among the most popular ones and have been now used for a long time for a broad range of applications including image analysis and compression [18], texture segmentation [19], face authentication [20] and facial analysis [21]. Images are classically viewed either as a collection of pixels (spatial domain) or as a sum of sinusoids of infinite extent (frequency domain). But these representations are just two opposite extremes in a continuum of possible joint space/frequency representations. Indeed, frequency can be viewed as a local phenomenon that may vary with position throughout the image. Moreover, Gabor wavelets have also received an increasing interest in image processing since they are particularly close to 2-D receptive fields profiles of the mammalian cortical simple cells [22].

A Gabor Elementary Function (GEF) $\mathbf{h}_{\rho,\theta}$ is defined by a radius ρ and an orientation θ and the response of an input image $\mathbf{i}$ to such a GEF can be computed as follows:

$$\mathbf{g}_{\rho,\theta} = \mathbf{i} * \mathbf{h}_{\rho,\theta} \quad (12)$$

where $*$ denotes convolution and $\mathbf{g}_{\rho,\theta}$ is the resulting filtered image. The GEF is a complex 2D sinusoid whose orientation and frequency are given by (θ, ρ) restricted by a Gaussian envelope. For computational complexity reasons, Gabor filtering is usually performed in the Fourier domain since it then comes down to a simple multiplication with the following filter:

$$\mathbf{H}_{\rho,\theta}(u, v) = \exp\left[-\frac{1}{2}\left(\left(\frac{u'-\rho}{\sigma_\rho}\right)^2 + \left(\frac{v'}{\sigma_\theta}\right)^2\right)\right]$$

$$\text{with } \begin{pmatrix} u' \\ v' \end{pmatrix} = \mathbf{R}_\theta \begin{pmatrix} u \\ v \end{pmatrix} = \begin{pmatrix} \cos\theta & \sin\theta \\ -\sin\theta & \cos\theta \end{pmatrix} \begin{pmatrix} u \\ v \end{pmatrix} \quad (13)$$

where σ_ρ and σ_θ characterize the bandwidth of the GEF. In other terms, $\mathbf{H}_{\rho,\theta}$ is a 2D Gaussian that is shifted ρ frequency units along the frequency u-axis and rotated by an angle θ. Thus, it acts as a bandpass filter with a center frequency controlled by ρ and θ and a bandwidth regulated by σ_ρ and σ_θ. To obtain real valued features $\mathbf{g}_{\rho,\theta}$ in the spatial domain, GEFs are paired as follows $\mathbf{H}_{\rho,\theta} \leftarrow \mathbf{H}_{\rho,\theta} + \mathbf{H}_{\rho,\theta+\pi}$.

A single GEF pair associates to each pixel $\mathbf{p}$ of the image a single feature value $\mathbf{g}_{\rho,\theta}(\mathbf{i}, \mathbf{p})$. As a result, the idea is now to design a filter bank of such GEF pairs to obtain for each pixel a multi-dimensional feature vector $\mathbf{g}(\mathbf{i}, \mathbf{p}) = \{\mathbf{g}_{\rho,\theta}(\mathbf{i}, \mathbf{p})\}$ with $1 \leq i \leq M$ and $1 \leq j \leq N$. Based on previous work [20], the different parameters of the GEF pairs are computed as follows:

$$\rho_{i,j} = \rho_{\min} + b\frac{(s+1)s^{i-1} - 2}{s-1} \tag{14}$$

$$\sigma_{\rho_{i,j}} = tbs^{i-1} \tag{15}$$

$$\theta_{i,j} = \frac{(j-1)\pi}{N} \tag{16}$$

$$\sigma_{\theta_{i,j}} = t\frac{\pi\rho_{i,j}}{2N} \tag{17}$$

$$b = \frac{\rho_{\max} - \rho_{\min}}{2}\left(\frac{s-1}{s^M - 1}\right) \tag{18}$$

The whole filter bank is specified by the 6 parameters M, N, $\rho_{\min}$, $\rho_{\max}$, s and t. The first two parameters determine respectively the number of orientations and frequencies in the filter bank. The next two ones specify the bandwidth within which the GEFs are bound. The parameter s controls how much the radial bandwidth increases when the radius increases. For instance, when it is set to

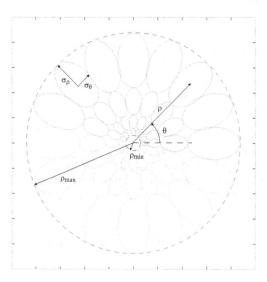

Fig. 2. Graphical representation in the Fourier domain of the GEFs levelset for value $1/e$ with $M = 8$, $N = 4$, $s = 2$ and $t = 1$

2, frequency bands are distributed in octave steps with a frequency bandwidth which doubles at each step. Finally, the parameter t sets the value at which neighboring filters intersect. As an example, with $t = 1$, they cross at equal value $1/e$ along their principal axis. Figure 2 depicts how GEFs are scattered throughout a specified frequency ring in the Fourier domain.

In each pixel position $\mathbf{p}$, the resulting MN-dimensional vector $\mathbf{g}(\mathbf{i}, \mathbf{p})$ can be regarded as the local power spectrum of the image and thus be used to characterize the neighborhood. It should be noted that if the Gabor filter bank is properly designed, it is possible to impose higher constraints. For instance, if the fractal approach depicted in Figure 1 is enforced, neighborhoods which are the same modulo a small set of geometrical operations, e.g. 8 isometries and downsampling by a factor 2, are required to carry the same watermark samples to achieve robustness [13]. Such constraints need to be taken into account to define the kernel of the linear form φ i.e. the non null vectors $\mathbf{v}$ for which $\varphi(\mathbf{v}) = 0$. However, more constraints induce a lower dimensional subspace for watermarking which can rapidly become critical.

3.3   Analogy with Multiplicative Watermarking Schemes

Since the values ξ_f of the linear form φ are defined on the canonical basis $\mathcal{O}$ when Gabor features are considered, the watermark sample obtained at position $\mathbf{p}$ is simply given by:

$$w(\mathbf{i}, \mathbf{p}) = \sum_{f=1}^{F} \xi_f \mathbf{g}_f(\mathbf{i}, \mathbf{p}) \tag{19}$$

where $\mathbf{g}_f(\mathbf{i}, \mathbf{p})$ is the fth coordinate of the F-dimensional Gabor feature vector $\mathbf{g}(\mathbf{i}, \mathbf{p})$. In other terms, the watermark is a linear combination of different Gabor responses $\mathbf{g}_f$. However, when M and N grow, more and more Gabor responses need to be computed which can be quickly computationally prohibitive. Hopefully, when the Fourier domain is considered, the watermark can be computed as follows:

$$\mathbf{W}(\mathbf{i}, \mathbf{q}) = \sum_{\mathbf{p} \in \mathcal{P}} \left(\sum_{f=1}^{F} \xi_f \, \mathbf{g}_f(\mathbf{i}, \mathbf{p}) \right) \omega_{\mathbf{p}, \mathbf{q}}$$

$$= \sum_{f=1}^{F} \xi_f \left(\sum_{\mathbf{p} \in \mathcal{P}} \mathbf{g}_f(\mathbf{i}, \mathbf{p}) \, \omega_{\mathbf{p}, \mathbf{q}} \right) = \sum_{f=1}^{F} \xi_f \, \mathbf{G}_f(\mathbf{i}, \mathbf{q})$$

$$= \sum_{f=1}^{F} \xi_f \, \mathbf{H}_f(\mathbf{q}) \, \mathbf{I}(\mathbf{q}) = \mathbf{H}(K, \mathbf{q}) \, \mathbf{I}(\mathbf{q}) \tag{20}$$

$$\text{with} \quad \mathbf{H}(K, \mathbf{q}) = \sum_{f=1}^{F} \xi_f \, \mathbf{H}_f(\mathbf{q})$$

where $\omega_{\mathbf{p}, \mathbf{q}} = \exp\left[-j2\pi \left((x-1)(u-1)/X + (y-1)(v-1)/Y \right) \right]$, capital letters indicate FFT-transformed variables and $\mathbf{q} = (u, v)$ denotes a frequency position with $1 \leq u \leq U$ and $1 \leq v \leq V$. In other terms, the watermark can be generated in one row in the Fourier domain by computing $\mathbf{H}$ and such an approach is likely to significantly reduce the computational cost.

Looking closely at Equation (20), it is straightforward to realize that the watermark generation process comes down to a simple multiplication between the image spectrum $\mathbf{I}$ and some pseudo-random signal $\mathbf{H}(K)$. In other terms, it really looks similar to basic well-known multiplicative embedding schemes in the frequency domain [10,11]. When the bandwidth of a GEF is close to 0, the 2D Gaussian in the Fourier domain tends toward a Dirac impulse centered at coordinates (ρ, θ) i.e. it tends toward an infinite sinusoid in the spatial domain. Therefore, multiplicative embedding in the FFT domain[1] is equivalent to imposing a linear relationship on the watermark samples according to the neighborhood which is characterized by its response to infinite sinusoids. Under this new light, FFT multiplicative watermarks can be seen as a special case of the Gabor watermarks introduced in Subsection 3.2 and are thus coherent with the host signal. Next, keeping in mind that DCT coefficients are simply FFT coefficients of some periodic image [23], it is immediate to assert that DCT multiplicative watermarks [10] are also signal coherent watermarks. At this point, it is interesting to note that multiplicative watermarking in the frequency domain was initially motivated by contrast masking properties: larger coefficients can convey a larger watermark without compromising invisibility [24]. This can be related with the natural perceptual shaping of signal coherent watermarks exhibited in Equation (11).

4   Experiments

The major claim in this paper is that a watermark whose samples have inherited the same linear relationships as the neighborhoods of the host signal should not be affected by BRA. An embedding scheme using Gabor features has been designed in Subsection 3.2 so that the generated watermark exhibits this property. Moreover, it has been shown in Subsection 3.3 that previous embedding schemes based on multiplicative embedding in the frequency space is also likely to resist BRA. It is now necessary to check whether or not these identified watermarks are degraded by such attacks in comparison with more current watermarks e.g. additive SS watermarks in the spatial domain. To this end, large-scale experiments have been conducted. The experimental protocol is detailed in Subsection 4.1 and the results are presented in Subsection 4.2.

4.1   Protocol

A watermark with zero mean and unit variance $\mathbf{w}(K, \mathbf{i})$ is embedded in the input image $\mathbf{i}$ to obtain a watermarked image $\mathbf{i}_{\mathrm{w}}$ according to the following embedding rule:

---

[1] In this paper, multiplicative embedding in the FFT domain means that the *complex* FFT coefficients are multiplied by pseudo-random values. It is slightly different from the algorithm described in [11] where only the *magnitude* of the FFT coefficients were watermarked.

$$\mathbf{i}_w = \mathbf{i} + \alpha \mathbf{w}(K, \mathbf{i}) \tag{21}$$

where K is a secret key used to generate the watermark and α an embedding strength equal to 3 so that the embedding process results in a distortion about 38.5 dB in terms of Peak Signal to Noise Ratio (PSNR). Four different watermark generation processes will be surveyed during the experiments:

SS: The embedded watermark is completely independent of the host content i.e. $\mathbf{w}(K, \mathbf{i}) = \mathbf{r}(K)$ where $\mathbf{r}(K)$ is a pseuso-random pattern which is generated using the secret key K and which is normally distributed with zero mean and unit variance.

Gabor: The generation process considers Gabor features to make the watermark inherit the self-similarities of the host signal. As discussed in Subsection 3.3, the watermark is generated in the Fourier domain using Equation (20) i.e. $\mathbf{W}(K, \mathbf{i}) = \mathbf{H}(K)\mathbf{I}$. Inverse FFT is then performed to come back to the spatial domain and the resulting watermark is scaled to have unit variance. In the reported experiments, the Gabor filter bank has been configured as follows: $M = 32$, $N = 16$, $\rho_{\min} = 0.01$, $\rho_{\max} = 0.45$, $s = 2$ and $t = 1.5$. Former investigations have demonstrated that the number MN of considered GEF pairs does not have a drastic impact on the performances of the algorithm with respect to the resilience against BRA [25].

FFT: The watermark is generated in the Fourier domain as follows $\mathbf{W}(K, \mathbf{i}) = \dot{\mathbf{r}}(K)\mathbf{I}$ where $\dot{\mathbf{r}}(K)$ is a pseudo-random pattern which is symmetric with respect to the center of the Fourier domain and which has value 0 at the DC coefficient position. This property has to be verified so that the resulting watermark is real-valued with zero mean after inverse transform. Once again, inverse FFT is performed to come back to the spatial domain and the resulting watermark is scaled to have unit variance. This algorithm can be regarded as an extension of the previous one when the GEFs are reduced to Dirac impulses in the frequency domain.

DCT: The watermark is generated in the frequency domain using the following formula $\hat{\mathbf{W}}(K, \mathbf{i}) = \mathbf{r}(K)\hat{\mathbf{I}}$ where "capital hat" denotes the DCT transform and $\mathbf{r}(K)$ is a normally distributed pseudo-random pattern which has value 0 at the DC coefficient position. Inverse DCT is then performed to come back to the spatial domain and the resulting watermark is scaled to have unit variance.

Next, the watermarked image $\mathbf{i}_w$ is attacked using the version of BRA described in Table 1. In the experiments, 8×8 blocks have been considered with an overlap of 4 pixels and the search window size has been set to 64×64. Furthermore, the two thresholds τ_{low} and τ_{high} have been set equal to the same value τ_{target}. As a result, the replacement block is obtained by considering more or less eigenblocks so that the distortion with the original signal block is as close as possible to the target value τ_{target}. This threshold can be used as an attacking strength which can be modified during experiments.

On the detector side, the only concern is to know whether or not the embedded watermark has survived. Therefore, non-blind detection can be considered and the residual correlation is computed as follows:

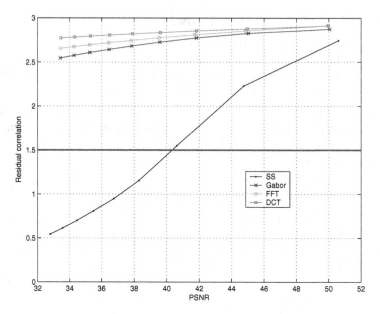

Fig. 3. Comparison of the impact of BRA with the 4 watermarking schemes under study: whereas non coherent watermarks (SS) are washed out when the attacking strength increases, coherent watermarks (Gabor/FFT/DCT) survive

$$d(\mathbf{i}, \tilde{\mathbf{i}}_w) = (\tilde{\mathbf{i}}_w - \mathbf{i}) \cdot \mathbf{w}(K, \tilde{\mathbf{i}}_w) \qquad (22)$$

where $\tilde{\mathbf{i}}_w$ is the attacked image and $\cdot$ denotes the linear correlation operation. To anticipate future blind detection, the detector generates the watermark using the attacked image instead of the original image. This has no impact for SS since it is content independent, but this may have one with signal coherent watermarks. The residual correlation should be equal to α if the watermark has survived while it should drop down to 0 when the watermark signal has been completely washed out. As a result, the presence of the watermark can be asserted by comparing the residual correlation $d(\mathbf{i}, \tilde{\mathbf{i}}_w)$ with a detection score τ_{detect} which can be set to $\alpha/2$ for equal false positive and false negative probabilities.

4.2 Experimental Results

A database of 500 images of size 512×512 has been considered for experiments. It contains snapshots, synthetic images, drawings and cartoons. All the images are first watermarked using one of the watermarking system under study i.e. SS, Gabor, FFT or DCT. This results in 4 collections of 500 watermarked images each. Then, each watermarked image is submitted to BRA with varying attacking strength τ_{target} to obtain a distortion vs. residual correlation curve. Finally, all the curves associated with a given watermarking method are averaged to depict the statistical behavior of this scheme against BRA. Those results have been gathered in Figure 3. It should be reminded that the goal of the attacker is to decrease the residual correlation while maintaining the image quality. First of all, experimental results clearly show that signal coherent watermarking has a strong impact on the efficiency of BRA. As a matter of fact, the residual correlation never goes below 2.5 with signal coherent watermarks (Gabor, FFT or DCT) while it already drops below the detection threshold $\tau_{\text{detect}} = 1.5$ for a distortion of 40 dB when SS watermarks are considered. Moreover, even if experiments at a larger scale should be carried out for a pertinent comparison, some kind of *ranking* appears amongst the signal coherent watermarking schemes. The observation that FFT behaves better than Gabor may be explained by the fact that the first algorithm is an extension of the second one. Therefore, the FFT curve would give some bound for the achievable performances with the Gabor scheme for different configurations. Finally, the superiority of DCT over FFT might be due to the properties of the DCT which ensure that the watermark will not be embedded in *fake* image frequencies revealed by the Fourier transform [24].

5 Conclusion

Security evaluation is now a growing concern in the watermarking community. Consumers are likely to attack the embedded watermark which they see as a disturbing signal and researchers have to anticipate these possible hostile behaviors. In this perspective, BRA are recognized to be among the most critical operations against watermarking systems today. Typically, these attacks exploit the fact that *similar blocks do not carry similar watermarks* to confuse the watermark detector. In this paper, a novel watermarking strategy has been investigated to remove this weak link. It basically aims at making the embedded watermark inherit the self-similarities of the host signal. Features are extracted in each pixel position to characterize the neighborhood and are exploited to export linear relationships between neighborhoods to watermark samples. A practical implementation using Gabor features has been presented and previous multiplicative embedding schemes in the frequency domain [10,11] have been shown to also produce signal-coherent watermarks even if, to the best knowledge of the authors, such a property has never been foreseen in previous works.

From a more general points of view, signal coherent watermarking can be seen as some kind of informed watermarking [1,26]. Digital watermarking can be seen as moving a point in a high dimensional media space to a nearby location i.e. introducing a small displacement in a random direction. The introduced framework only stipulates that the host signal self-similarities have to be considered to resist BRA and that in this case some of the possible directions are now prohibited. Future work will explore how former works [11,27] can be used to design a blind detector for signal coherent watermarks. Furthermore, security investigations will be conducted to determine whether or not an attacker can gain some knowledge about the imposed watermarking structure. Indeed, using a redundant watermarking structure has been demonstrated to lead to security pitfalls in the past [7,8].

Acknowledgment

This work has been supported in part by the European Commission through the IST Program under Contract IST-2002-507932 ECRYPT.

References

1. Cox, I., Miller, M., Bloom, J.: Digital Watermarking. Morgan Kaufmann Publishers (2001)
2. DVD Copy Control Association: ⟨http://www.dvdcca.org⟩
3. Secure Digital Music Initiative: ⟨http://www.sdmi.org⟩
4. Cayre, F., Fontaine, C., Furon, T.: Watermarking security, part I: Theory. In: Security, Steganography and Watermarking of Multimedia Contents VII. Volume 5681 of Proceedings of SPIE. (2005) 746–757
5. Cayre, F., Fontaine, C., Furon, T.: Watermarking security, part II: Practice. In: Security, Steganography and Watermarking of Multimedia Contents VII. Volume 5681 of Proceedings of SPIE. (2005) 758–768
6. Su, K., Kundur, D., Hatzinakos, D.: A novel approach to collusion resistant video watermarking. In: Security and Watermarking of Multimedia Contents IV. Volume 4675 of Proceedings of SPIE. (2002) 491–502
7. Doërr, G., Dugelay, J.-L.: Collusion issue in video watermarking. In: Security, Steganography and Watermarking of Multimedia Contents VII. Volume 5681 of Proceedings of SPIE. (2005) 685–696
8. Doërr, G., Dugelay, J.-L.: Security pitfalls of frame-by-frame approaches to video watermarking. IEEE Transactions on Signal Processing, Supplement on Secure Media **52** (2004) 2955–2964
9. Kirovski, D., Petitcolas, F.: Blind pattern matching attack on watermarking systems. IEEE Transactions on Signal Processing **51** (2003) 1045–1053
10. Cox, I., Kilian, J., Leighton, T., Shamoon, T.: Secure spread spectrum watermarking for multimedia. IEEE Transactions on Image Processing **6** (1997) 1673–1687
11. Barni, M., Bartolini, F., De Rosa, A., Piva, A.: A new decoder for optimum recovery of nonadditive watermarks. IEEE Transactions on Image Processing **10** (2001) 755–766
12. Fisher, Y.: Fractal Image Compression: Theory and Applications. Springer-Verlag (1994)
13. Rey, C., Doërr, G., Dugelay, J.-L., Csurka, G.: Toward generic image dewatermarking? In: Proceedings of the IEEE International Conference on Image Processing. Volume III. (2002) 633–636
14. Petitcolas, F., Kirovski, D.: The blind pattern matching attack on watermarking systems. In: Proceedings of the IEEE International Conference on Acoustics, Speech, and Signal Processing. Volume IV. (2002) 3740–3743
15. Kirovski, D., Petitcolas, F.: Replacement attack on arbitrary watermarking systems. In: Proceedings of the ACM Digital Rights Management Workshop. Volume 2696 of Lecture Notes in Computer Science. (2003) 177–189
16. Doërr, G., Dugelay, J.-L., Grangé, L.: Exploiting self-similarities to defeat digital watermarking systems - a case study on still images. In: Proceedings of the ACM Multimedia and Security Workshop. (2004) 133–142

17. Voloshynovskiy, S., Herrigel, A., Baumgärtner, N., Pun, T.: A stochastic approach to content adaptive digital image watermarking. In: Proceedings of the Third International Workshop on Information Hiding. Volume 1768 of Lecture Notes in Computer Science. (1999) 211–236

18. Daugman, J.: Complete discrete 2-D Gabor transforms by neural network for image analysis and compression. IEEE Transactions on Acoustics, Speech and Signal Processing **36** (1988) 1169–1179

19. Dunn, D., Higgins, W., Wakeley, J.: Texture segmentation using 2-D Gabor elementary functions. IEEE Transactions on Pattern Analysis and Machine Intelligence **16** (1994) 130–149

20. Duc, B., Fisher, S., Bigün, J.: Face authentication with Gabor information on deformable graphs. IEEE Transactions on Image Processing **8** (1999) 504–516

21. Donato, G., Bartlett, M., Hager, J., Ekman, P., Sejnowski, T.: Classifying facial actions. IEEE Transactions on Pattern Analysis and Machine Intelligence **21** (1999) 974–989

22. Ringach, D.: Spatial structure and symmetry of simple-cell receptive fields in macaque primary visual cortex. Journal of Neurophysiology **88** (2002) 455–463

23. Lim, J.: Two-Dimensional Signal and Image Processing. Prentice Hall International Editions (1989)

24. Foley, J., Legge, G.: Contrast masking in human vision. Journal of the Optical Society of America **70** (1980) 1458–1470

25. Doërr, G., Dugelay, J.-L.: A countermeasure to resist block replacement attacks. In: Accepted for publication in the IEEE International Conference on Image Processing. (2005)

26. Eggers, J., Girod, B.: Informed Watermarking. Kluwer Academic Publishers (2002)

27. Cheng, Q., Huang, T.: Robust optimum detection of transform domain multiplicative watermarks. IEEE Transactions on Signal Processing **51** (2003) 906–924

On the Intractability of Inverting Geometric Distortions in Watermarking Schemes[*]

Maciej Liśkiewicz[**] and Ulrich Wölfel

Institut für Theoretische Informatik, Universität zu Lübeck, Germany

Abstract. We examine the problem of watermarking schemes robust against geometric distortions from a complexity theoretic point of view. The main results presented are polynomial time reductions showing that the inversion of geometric distortions is computationally intractable.

1 Introduction

One of the great challenges in digital watermarking for the last years has been the development of systems robust against geometric distortions. Such a system should be robust against (1) deliberate attacks that have the intention of removing the watermark and (2) distortions that result from image processing operations as well as printing and scanning of images. Especially the problem of robustness against random local distortions is still considered difficult to solve.

As a standard way of benchmarking systems claiming robustness, stirmark [1,2] has been introduced and gained widespread acceptance in the watermarking community. For some time there was no watermarking system that was robust against the attacks of stirmark. Now that there are systems showing good results, it is an interesting question why they succeed where others fail.

In this paper we will discuss one approach to the problem of robustness against geometric distortions, namely inverting the geometric distortions. We take a closer look at specific methods and will analyse their computational complexities. We will present results based on complexity theory that show that this approach is intractable.

There are two main approaches of recovering watermarks in geometrically distorted images based on inverting the distortion, namely *exhaustive search* and *synchronisation and registration approaches*. We give short evaluations of both, but in the paper we will concentrate mainly on synchronisation and registration methods. Examples of these types of systems can be found e.g. in [3,4].

We analyse the approaches using NP-completeness as a measure for computational complexity of problems. First we introduce decision counterparts of the optimisation problems for inverting geometric distortions, then we give proofs for our NP-completeness results. One of the main results of this paper says that

---

[*] Supported by DFG research grant RE 675/5-1.
[**] On leave from Instytut Informatyki, Uniwersytet Wrocławski, Poland.

M. Barni et al. (Eds.): IH 2005, LNCS 3727, pp. 176–188, 2005.

inverting *arbitrary* geometric distortions by synchronisation or registration approaches is NP-complete. We also show that the problem remains NP-complete for some subclasses of geometric distortions like e.g. elastic transformations.

Being aware of the theoretical limits makes the construction of new schemes easier and more directed. Knowing that an approach is intractable, designers of new algorithms can choose their scheme accordingly, thus saving time and effort.

The paper is organised as follows. In Section 2 we give some definitions and notations used in the paper and formulate the basic decision problems. In Section 3 some subclasses of geometric distortions are discussed and the corresponding decision problems are given. In Section 4 we formally present our results and in Section 5 we give the proofs. In Section 6 we close the paper with conclusions and open problems.

2   Inverting Geometric Distortions

We start this section by giving a set of definitions and notations we will use throughout the rest of this paper. A watermarking scheme comprises a pair of embedder and detector defined as follows. Let $I \in \mathcal{X}^{N \times N}$ be an original cover image, where $\mathcal{X}$ is a set of pixel values and $N \times N$ the dimension of the data (without loss of generality we consider only grey images given as $N \times N$ square grids). Moreover, let $\mathcal{W}$ be the set of all watermarks and let W be an element of $\mathcal{W}$. The embedder consists of an embedding function $\mathcal{E} : \mathcal{X}^{N \times N} \times \mathcal{W} \rightarrow \mathcal{X}^{N \times N}$. The value $\hat{I} = \mathcal{E}(I, W)$, where I is the original cover data and W is a watermark shared with the decoder, is then transmitted via an attack channel to the detector. The detector consists of a detection function $\mathcal{D} : \mathcal{X}^{N \times N} \times \mathcal{W} \rightarrow \mathbb{R}$. In this setting we assume that the detector gets $\hat{I}^*$ from the attack channel. Knowing the watermark W he computes the response value $\mathcal{D}(\hat{I}^*, W)$ and decides that W is present in $\hat{I}^*$ by putting out 1 if the response is greater or equal to the threshold parameter $\tau \in \mathbb{R}$, respectively 0 otherwise. We assume that both functions $\mathcal{E}$ and $\mathcal{D}$ are computable in polynomial time with respect to N and the length of the watermark W. A reasonable constraint for the encoder is that the distortion between I and $\hat{I}$ is small. Speaking more formally, for a given embedding strength parameter $\alpha \in \mathbb{R}$ and for any watermark W we require that $d(I, \mathcal{E}(I, W)) \leq \alpha$, where d is a reasonable distortion function.

In this paper we restrict the attacker to arbitrary geometric distortions. Denote for short integers from the interval $[1, N]$ by $[N]$. We model a geometric distortion of an $N \times N$ image as a function

$$g : [N] \times [N] \rightarrow [N] \times [N].$$

For an image I define the value of pixels of a distorted image I^* as follows: $I_{i,j}^* = I_{g(i,j)}$. For short, we will denote such an image I^* by $g(I)$.

2.1   Exhaustive Search

Exhaustive search is a general method for recovering watermarks from geometrically distorted images. In this approach we search for a transformation g' which results in strong detection response when applied to the distorted watermarked image $g(\hat{I})$. More formally, we start with the identity transformation g' and then iteratively perform the following steps: (a) check whether the detection response $\mathcal{D}(g'(g(\hat{I})), W)$ is greater or equal to the detection threshold τ and stop if yes; (b) gradually modify g' and go to step a. This step can be done in such a way that in the combination of parameter values of g' we slightly modify one of the values.

In this process an inversion transformation to g (if such an inversion function exists) belongs to the solutions we are looking for. However, we can also obtain a transformation g' that is not related to g at all.

Two important issues concerning this approach are the high computational complexity and false positive probability of the method. Because the number of combinations of distortion parameter values is typically large, exhaustive search is computationally very expensive. The second issue is the high false positive probability: for an unwatermarked image I there is a high probability that when performing a large number of detection tests one obtains at least one response $\mathcal{D}(g'(I), W)$ of high value (see e.g. [5]).

Note that exhaustive search is a general method solving the following problem: for a given distorted image I^*, watermark W, and a detection threshold τ, find a geometric distortion $g \in \mathcal{G}$ such that $\mathcal{D}(g(I^*), W) \geq \tau$. Here, $\mathcal{G}$ denotes the searching space of the method, i.e. a subset of all geometric distortions that are tested in step (b). A decision counterpart of the problem for a concrete subclass $\mathcal{G}$ of all geometric distortions can be formulated as follows:

(ID) INVERTING DISTORTIONS for a watermarking scheme $(\mathcal{E}, \mathcal{D})$ and a subclass $\mathcal{G}$ of all geometric distortions:
INSTANCE: Distorted image I^*, watermark W, and detection threshold τ.
QUESTION: Is there a geometric distortion $g \in \mathcal{G}$ such that $\mathcal{D}(g(I^*), W) \geq \tau$?

It is obvious that the computational complexity of the decision counterpart of the exhaustive search, as defined above, depends on the subclass $\mathcal{G}$. For example, for many watermarking schemes $(\mathcal{E}, \mathcal{D})$ the problem can be solved very efficiently if $\mathcal{G}$ represents all geometric distortions. In Section 4 we discuss a specific scheme $(\mathcal{E}, \mathcal{D})$ and some other subclass $\mathcal{G}$ for which Problem ID can be solved fast. However, we leave open, whether the problem is feasible for more reasonable subclasses $\mathcal{G}$, e.g. for affine or elastic transformations (for a definition see Section 3).

2.2   Synchronisation and Registration Approaches

In contrast to exhaustive search, where varying geometric distortions are tested, the idea of this approach is, using a given reference image/pattern R, to invert the distortion by finding a transformation g' such that $\tilde{I} = g'(I^*)$ is close to the distorted image I^* and is detectable by $\mathcal{D}$.

One way of constructing a robust watermarking scheme based on this approach is depicted in Fig. 1. We start with a watermarking scheme $(\mathcal{E}, \mathcal{D})$ that is not robust against geometric distortions. A watermark W is embedded in

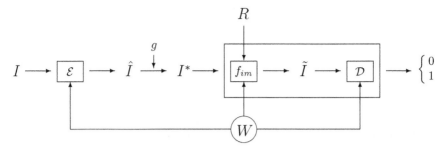

Fig. 1. Constructing a robust scheme by using an image matching function

an image I by means of the embedding function $\mathcal{E}$. The resulting watermarked image $\hat{I}$ is then distorted using a geometric distortion function g, yielding the image I^*. Using an image matching function f_{im} we get, for I^*, W and a given reference R, the image $\tilde{I}$, with $\tilde{I} \sim \hat{I}$. We finally detect the watermark using the detection function $\mathcal{D}$.

For a watermarking scheme $(\mathcal{E}, \mathcal{D})$ this approach can be considered as one of two optimisation problems: (1) for a given distorted image I^*, reference image R, watermark W and given error ϵ find a geometric distortion g transforming I^* to $g(I^*) = \tilde{I}$ such that the distortion between $\tilde{I}$ and the reference image R is at most ϵ and the detection response $\mathcal{D}(\tilde{I}, W)$ is maximal, or (2) for given I^*, R, and W as above and a detection threshold τ find a geometric distortion g transforming I^* to $g(I^*) = \tilde{I}$ such that $\mathcal{D}(\tilde{I}, W) \geq \tau$ and the distortion between $\tilde{I}$ and R is minimal.

This is a very general setting. In fact, the reference image R can be an unwatermarked cover image I or an image $\hat{I}$ watermarked with a different watermark W'. R can also be a synchronisation pattern and we can consider both problems as registration problems that additionally maximise the detection response (case 1) or have to additionally fulfill the constraint $\mathcal{D}(\tilde{I}, W) \geq \tau$ (case 2).

We investigate this approach using NP-completeness as a measure for the computational complexity of problems. We formulate the following decision problem that corresponds to the general optimisation problems above.

(IGD) INVERTING GEOMETRIC DISTORTIONS with a reference image for a watermarking scheme $(\mathcal{E}, \mathcal{D})$:
INSTANCE: Distorted image I^*, reference image R, watermark W, inversion error ϵ, and detection threshold τ.
QUESTION: Is there a geometric distortion g such that for $\tilde{I} = g(I^*)$ it holds:

$$d(\tilde{I}, R) \leq \epsilon \text{ and } \mathcal{D}(\tilde{I}, W) \geq \tau \text{ ?}$$

The first inequality guarantees that the detection probability is specified to contain only few false negatives. The second inequality makes sure that $\tilde{I}$ is in the detection region associated with watermarked versions of I. One of the main results of our paper says that the Problem IGD is NP-complete for some concrete watermarking scheme $(\mathcal{E}, \mathcal{D})$.

3   Some Subclasses of Geometric Distortions

In this section we discuss three subclasses of geometric distortions and formulate problems of inverting geometric distortions restricted to these subclasses.

Elastic distortions appear whenever the original data is continuously warped. Application areas where elastic distortions is a relevant problem include medical imaging, image recognition, etc. In digital watermarking the problem appears e.g. when watermarked images are printed and next scanned. These distortions are also simulated by the bending algorithms in stirmark [1].

Below we recall the definition of elastic distortions given in [7] and [6]. Recall, the distortion is modeled as $g : [N] \times [N] \to [N] \times [N]$. The strength of g is

$$S(g) = \sum_{\substack{i < N \\ j \leq N}} f_{dd}(g(i+1,j) - g(i,j) - (1,0)) + \sum_{\substack{i \leq N \\ j < N}} f_{dd}(g(i,j+1) - g(i,j) - (0,1)) \ ,$$

where $f_{dd} : \mathbb{Z} \times \mathbb{Z} \to \mathbb{R}$ is a function that charges the displacement differences of mapping g and expresses the deviation of g from the identity mapping in two dimensions. In the literature various functions f_{dd} have been used. In this paper we restrict ourselves to mappings the deviations of which may locally be at most one pixel. Formally we define

$$f_{dd}(x, y) = \begin{cases} 0 & \text{if } x^2 + y^2 \leq 2, \\ 1 & \text{otherwise} \end{cases}$$

and we call g with $S(g) = 0$ an *elastic geometric distortion*.

For all problems we formulate below, I^* denotes a distorted image, R a reference image, W a watermark, ϵ an inversion error, and τ a detection threshold.

(IED) INVERTING *ELASTIC* DISTORTIONS for $(\mathcal{E}, \mathcal{D})$:
INSTANCE: I^*, R, W, ϵ, and τ.
QUESTION: Is there an *elastic* geometric distortion g such that:

$$d(g(I^*), R) \leq \epsilon \text{ and } \mathcal{D}(g(I^*), W) \geq \tau \ ?$$

A natural restriction of arbitrary geometric distortions are bijective functions g. These can be viewed as permutations of the image pixels. We call this subclass *displacement* geometric distortions.

(IDD) INVERTING *DISPLACEMENT* DISTORTIONS for $(\mathcal{E}, \mathcal{D})$:
INSTANCE: I^*, R, W, ϵ, and τ.
QUESTION: Is there a *displacement* geometric distortion g such that

$$d(g(I^*), R) \leq \epsilon \text{ and } \mathcal{D}(g(I^*), W) \geq \tau \ ?$$

Another important subclass of all geometric distortions is the class of affine transformations, like e.g. rotations, translations, dilations, and shears.

Recall that a function $f : \mathbb{R}^2 \to \mathbb{R}^2$ is affine if there exists a 2×2 real matrix $A \in \mathbb{R}^{2 \times 2}$ and a vector $t \in \mathbb{R}^2$ such that for any $x \in \mathbb{R}^2$ we have:

$f(\boldsymbol{x}) = A\boldsymbol{x} + \boldsymbol{t}$. For the nearest neighbour interpolation method, we define the affine-transformed image I^* as follows. Let for i, j with $1 \le i, j \le N$

$$\begin{bmatrix} x_i \\ y_j \end{bmatrix} = f^{-1} \begin{bmatrix} i \\ j \end{bmatrix}$$

(we assume here that the inverse function f^{-1} exists) and let $\tilde{x}_i = \lfloor x_i + 0.5 \rfloor$ if $0.5 \le x_i < N + 0.5$ and otherwise let $\tilde{x}_i = 1$ if $x_i < 0.5$ and let $\tilde{x}_i = N$ if $x_i \ge N + 0.5$. Analogously we define $\tilde{y}_j$ from y_j. Then we require that $I^*_{i,j} = I_{\tilde{x}_i, \tilde{y}_j}$. Using our modeling of geometric distortions as functions $g : [N] \times [N] \to [N] \times [N]$, we define that g is affine if and only if there exists an affine function $f : \mathbb{R}^2 \to \mathbb{R}^2$ such that for all i, j with $1 \le i, j \le N$

$$g(i, j) = (\tilde{x}_i, \tilde{y}_j) .$$

(IAD) INVERTING *AFFINE* DISTORTIONS for $(\mathcal{E}, \mathcal{D})$:
INSTANCE: I^*, R, W, ϵ, and τ.
QUESTION: Is there an *affine* geometric distortion g such that

$$d(g(I^*), R) \le \epsilon \text{ and } \mathcal{D}(g(I^*), W) \ge \tau \text{ ?}$$

In our paper we prove NP-completeness of the first two problems and leave as an open question whether the last problem is NP-complete. We formally describe our results in the next section.

4   Our Results

We chose to use a simple correlation based watermarking scheme for our analysis [3, 50-51]. The embedding algorithm is additive, i.e. the watermark W is added to the original image I to obtain the watermarked image $\mathcal{E}(I, W) = I + W$. For the detection function we use linear correlation

$$\mathcal{D}(I^*, W) = \frac{1}{N^2} \sum_{1 \le i, j \le N} I^*_{i,j} \cdot W_{i,j} .$$

As our distortion measure we chose the L_1 distance

$$d(I^*, \tilde{I}) = \frac{1}{N^2} \sum_{1 \le i, j \le N} |I^*_{i,j} - \tilde{I}_{i,j}| .$$

Theorem 1. *The problem of inverting arbitrary geometric distortions with reference image (Problem IGD) for $(\mathcal{E}, \mathcal{D})$ is NP-complete. The problem remains NP-complete both for the classes of elastic and for the classes of displacement geometric distortions (Problems IED and IDD).*

We present the proofs of the theorem in the next section. Interestingly, if we omit the constraint $d(g(I^*), R) \le \epsilon$, the first problem can be solved in polynomial time. Speaking more formally we have:

Proposition 1. *For $(\mathcal{E}, \mathcal{D})$ specified as above and $\mathcal{G}$ – the class of all geometric distortions, the problem of inverting geometric distortions without reference image (Problem ID) can be solved in linear time. Moreover, restricting $\mathcal{G}$ to displacement distortions, Problem ID can be solved in time $O(N^2 \log N)$.*

Proof. For the first problem we determine the maximum pixel value v_{max} of I^*, resp. the minimum pixel value v_{min} of I^*. Then we get that $\max_g \mathcal{D}(g(I^*), W)$ is equal to $v_{max} \sum_{i=1}^{n_+} w_i^+ + v_{min} \sum_{i=1}^{n_-} w_i^-$, where we have two sets w^+ and w^- containing the positive, resp. negative, values of the watermark.

The algorithm solving the second problem works as follows: Sort the values of the watermark W and the image I^* in the increasing order. Let $w_1, w_2, \ldots, w_{N^2}$ and $v_1, v_2, \ldots, v_{N^2}$ be the sorted sequences of W, resp. I^*. This can be done in $cN^2 \log N$ time, for some constant c. Then $\max_g \mathcal{D}(g(I^*), W) = \sum_{i=1}^{N^2} v_i \cdot w_i$ and the problem has confirmative answer iff $\tau \leq \sum_{i=1}^{N^2} v_i \cdot w_i$. $\qquad\square$

We leave as an interesting open question whether Problem ID remains NP-complete for elastic and affine distortions.

5   Reductions

In this section we present polynomial-time reductions from some particular NP-complete problems to variants of inverting geometric distortions problems. Recall that a decision problem Π' is polynomial-time reducible to a decision problem Π if there is a function f that deterministically maps each instance x of Π' to an instance $f(x)$ of Π in polynomial time such that x is a *yes-instance* of Π' if and only if $f(x)$ is a *yes-instance* of Π. We write for this $\Pi' \propto \Pi$. If we choose the problem Π' to be complete for some complexity class C, we can prove that Π is also complete for C if $\Pi \in C$ and $\Pi' \propto \Pi$. This would mean that Π is at least as hard as the hardest problems in C. In our case the problem Π' will be *PARTITION* which is known to be NP-complete. For more information on the theory of NP-completeness, see [8].

PARTITION
INSTANCE: Finite sequence of positive integers $S = (s_1, s_2, \ldots, s_n)$.
QUESTION: Does there exist a partition $J_1, J_2 = [n] \setminus J_1$ of indices $[n]$ such that $\sum_{i \in J_1} s_i = \sum_{i \in J_2} s_i$?

PARTITION is a well known canonical NP-complete decision problem. It remains NP-complete if we require that n is even and $|J_1| = |J_2|$ or if for $S = (s_1, s_2, \ldots, s_{2n})$ we require that J_1 contains exactly one of $2i - 1, 2i$ for $i \in [n]$ ([8], Appendix A3). We formulate this modification of PARTITION as follows:

SEQUENCE PARTITION
INSTANCE: Finite sequence of positive integers $S = (s_1, s_2, \ldots, s_{2n})$.
QUESTION: Does there exist a sequence $(r_1, r_2, \ldots, r_n) \in \{0, 1\}^n$ such that $\sum_{i \in [n]} s_{2i-r_i} = \frac{1}{2} \sum_{j \in [2n]} s_j$?

5.1 Displacement Distortions

Proof. We first show a polynomial transformation of the partition problem to inverting *displacement* geometric distortions (Problem IDD).

1	2	6	7
3	5	8	13
4	9	12	14
10	11	15	16

Fig. 2. Zig-zag mapping π: value $\pi(i)$ is equal to the coordinates of the entry i

Let $S = (s_1, s_2, \ldots, s_n)$ be an input of the partition problem. Denote by $B := \frac{1}{2}\sum_{i\in[n]} s_i$. We construct an appropriate input I^*, R, W and thresholds ϵ and τ of the inverting problem as follows. Without loss of generality assume n has the form $\frac{1}{3}k^2$ for some integer k. We define pixel values of I^* and R based on values of the sequence S. To describe a mapping of S to I^* and R we use an arbitrary but fixed bijective function $\pi : [3n] \rightarrow [k]\times[k]$ that maps 1-1 indices of a sequence of length $3n = k^2$ to indices of a $k \times k$ matrix. An example for such a mapping π is a zig-zag function: $\pi(1) = (1,1)$, $\pi(2) = (1,2)$, $\pi(3) = (2,1)$, $\pi(4) = (3,1)$ and so on (see Fig. 2). Our reduction works for any polynomial time computable bijective function π. For every $i \in [n]$ we let

$$I^*_{\pi(3i-2)} := s_i , \quad R_{\pi(3i-2)} := 0 , \quad W_{\pi(3i-2)} := 0 ,$$
$$I^*_{\pi(3i-1)} := 0 , \quad R_{\pi(3i-1)} := s_i , \quad W_{\pi(3i-1)} := 0 ,$$
$$I^*_{\pi(3i)} := 0 , \quad R_{\pi(3i)} := 0 , \quad W_{\pi(3i)} := 1 .$$

We also define $\epsilon := \frac{2}{3n}B$ and $\tau := B$. For an illustration of this construction see Fig. 3. Obviously, for a given sequence S the reduction can can be done in polynomial time. Below we show that the reduction correctly transforms the partition problem to Problem IDD. Assume first that there exists a partition

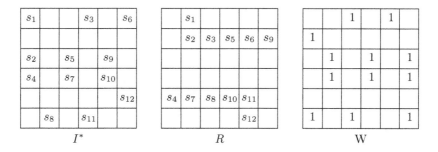

Fig. 3. Example construction of I^*, R and W and the zig-zag function π

J_1, J_2 of $[n]$ satisfying $\sum_{i \in J_1} s_i = \sum_{i \in J_2} s_i = B$. Then we transform I^* to $\tilde{I}$ such that for every $i \in J_1$ we switch pixels $\pi(3i - 2)$ and $\pi(3i)$ and for every $i \in J_2$ we switch pixels $\pi(3i - 2)$ and $\pi(3i - 1)$. As a result we get

$$
\text{for every } i \in J_1 \begin{cases} \tilde{I}_{\pi(3i-2)} := 0 , \\ \tilde{I}_{\pi(3i-1)} := 0 , \\ \tilde{I}_{\pi(3i)} := s_i , \end{cases} \text{and for every } i \in J_2 \begin{cases} \tilde{I}_{\pi(3i-2)} := 0 , \\ \tilde{I}_{\pi(3i-1)} := s_i , \\ \tilde{I}_{\pi(3i)} := 0 . \end{cases}
$$

Obviously there exists a bijective function g which describes the transformation. In fact, one can define g as follows: $g(\pi(3i-2)) := \pi(3i)$, $g(\pi(3i-1)) := \pi(3i-1)$, $g(\pi(3i)) := \pi(3i - 2)$, if $i \in J_1$ and $g(\pi(3i - 2)) := \pi(3i - 1)$, $g(\pi(3i - 1)) := \pi(3i-2)$, $g(\pi(3i)) := \pi(3i)$, if $i \in J_2$ (for an example of such a coding see Fig. 4). For such $\tilde{I}$ we get

$$
\begin{aligned}
d(\tilde{I}, R) &= \tfrac{1}{3n} \sum_{i \in [3n]} |\tilde{I}_{\pi(i)} - R_{\pi(i)}| \\
&= \tfrac{1}{3n} \sum_{i \in J_1} (|\tilde{I}_{\pi(3i-1)} - R_{\pi(3i-1)}| + |\tilde{I}_{\pi(3i)} - R_{\pi(3i)}|) \\
&= \tfrac{1}{3n} \sum_{i \in J_1} (s_i + s_i) = \tfrac{2B}{3n} = \epsilon , \\
\mathcal{D}(\tilde{I}, W) &= \sum_{i \in [3n]} \tilde{I}_{\pi(i)} \cdot W_{\pi(i)} = \sum_{i \in J_1} \tilde{I}_{\pi(3i)} \cdot W_{\pi(3i)} \\
&= \sum_{i \in J_1} s_i = B = \tau .
\end{aligned}
$$

Hence the inverting problem has a confirmative answer for the input $I^*, R, W, \epsilon, \tau$. Now assume that there exists a bijective function g such that for $\tilde{I} = g(I^*)$ the inequalities $\mathcal{D}(\tilde{I}, W) \geq \tau$ and $d(\tilde{I}, R) \leq \epsilon$ are true. Define:

$$
J_1 := \{i \in [n] : g(\pi(3j)) = \pi(3i - 2) \text{ for some } j \in [n]\}
$$
$$
J_2 := \{i \in [n] : g(\pi(3j - 1)) = \pi(3i - 2) \text{ for some } j \in [n]\} .
$$

It is easy to check that J_1 and J_2 is a partition of $[n]$. From the constraint $\mathcal{D}(\tilde{I}, W) \geq \tau = B$ we get

$$
\mathcal{D}(\tilde{I}, W) = \sum_{i \in J_1} I^*_{\pi(3i-2)} \geq B .
$$

Using the last inequality and the property $\epsilon \geq d(\tilde{I}, R)$ we obtain

$$
\begin{aligned}
\epsilon &= \tfrac{1}{3n} 2B \geq \tfrac{1}{3n} \left(\sum_{i \in J_1} I^*_{\pi(3i-2)} + \sum_{i \in [n]} R_{\pi(3i-1)} - \sum_{i \in J_2} I^*_{\pi(3i-2)} \right) \\
&\geq \tfrac{1}{3n} (B + 2B - \sum_{i \in J_2} I^*_{\pi(3i-2)})
\end{aligned}
$$

and one can conclude that $\sum_{i \in J_2} I^*_{\pi(3i-2)} \geq B$. From $\sum_{i \in J_1 \cup J_2} I^*_{\pi(3i-2)} = 2B$ we finally get that J_1 and J_2 is a positive solution of the partition problem. This completes the proof of completeness for the Problem IDD. $\square$

5.2   Elastic Distortions

Proof. To show that Problem IED is NP-complete we use SEQUENCE PARTITION and modify our previous construction to show an appropriate polynomial

$S = \{s_1, s_2, \ldots, s_{18}\}$

$U = \{s_1, s_4, s_5, s_7, s_8, s_{10}, s_{12}\}$

$V = \{s_2, s_3, s_6, s_9, s_{11}\}$

			s_5	
s_1	s_2	s_3		s_6	s_9
	s_4		s_8	
			s_{11}	
s_7		s_{10}		s_{12}

$$\tilde{I} = g(I^*)$$

Fig. 4. Example coding of a partition (U, V) of a base set S by a distorted image $\tilde{I}$

time reduction. Let $S = (s_1, s_2, \ldots, s_{2n})$ be an input of the sequence partition problem and denote by $B = \frac{1}{2} \sum_{i \in [2n]} s_i$. Without loss of generality assume n has a form k^2 for some integer k. We construct I^*, R, W and thresholds ϵ, τ of the inverting problem as follows.

The images and the watermark are $3k \times 3k$ matrices. We divide the matrices into k^2 square blocks each of 3×3 elements. In the i-th block of I^* and R we define two pixel values to be equal to s_{2i-1} and s_{2i} and the remaining pixel values are 0.

1	4	7	19	22	25
2	5	8	20	23	26
3	6	9	21	24	27
10	13	16	28	31	34
11	14	17	29	32	35
12	15	18	30	33	36

Fig. 5. Mapping π: a coordinate for value i corresponds to the value $\pi(i)$

In every 3×3 block of W the element in the middle of the block is of value 1 and the remaining elements are 0. For the reduction we use a bijective function $\pi : [9k^2] \to [3k] \times [3k]$ such that for every consecutive subsequence of integers of the form $9z+1, 9z+2, \ldots, 9z+9$, for some integer z, all values $\pi(9z+x)$ describe coordinates of the same block. The appropriate mapping π can be defined as follows: Every integer ℓ, with $1 \leq \ell \leq 9k^2$, can be represented uniquely by the quadruple i, j, x, y, with $1 \leq i, j \leq k$ and $1 \leq x, y \leq 3$. In fact, one can choose the representation in such a way that the equality

$$\ell = 9k(j - 1) + 9(i - 1) + 3(y - 1) + x$$

is true. Then for such a representation of ℓ we let

$$\pi(\ell) = \pi(9k(j - 1) + 9(i - 1) + 3(y - 1) + x) = (3(i - 1) + x, \ 3(j - 1) + y) \ .$$

For an illustration of such a function π for $k = 2$ see Fig. 5. Now for every $i \in [n]$ we let $I^*_{\pi(9(i-1)+1)}, R_{\pi(9(i-1)+1)} := s_{2i-1}, I^*_{\pi(9(i-1)+2)}, R_{\pi(9(i-1)+2)} := s_{2i}, W_{\pi(9(i-1)+5)} := 1$. Moreover let the remaining elements of I^*, R, and W be equal to 0. Finally we define $\epsilon := \frac{1}{9n}B$ and $\tau := B$ (compare Fig. 6). Obviously the construction can be done in polynomial time.

Assume that for $(s_1, s_2, \ldots, s_{2n})$ there exists a sequence $(r_1, r_2, \ldots, r_n) \in \{0,1\}^n$ with the property: $\sum_{i \in [n]} s_{2i-r_i} = B$. We define g in such a way that for $\tilde{I} = g(I^*)$ and for every $i \in [n]$ we have $\tilde{I}_{\pi(9(i-1)+5)} = s_{2i-r_i}$. The values of the remaining elements of $\tilde{I}$ coincide with the values of the corresponding elements in I^*. One can define the corresponding transformation as follows: for every $i \in [n]$ let $g(\pi(9(i-1)+5)) = \pi(9(i-1)+2-r_i)$ and for every (x, y) that does not coincide with $\pi(9(i-1)+5)$, for some $i \in [n]$, let $g(x,y) = (x,y)$. Obviously such a g is elastic. Moreover we get

$$d(\tilde{I}, R) = \tfrac{1}{9n} \sum_{i \in [n]} \tilde{I}_{\pi(9(i-1)+5)} \;=\; \tfrac{1}{9n} \sum_{i \in [n]} s_{2i-r_i} \;=\; \tfrac{1}{9n}B \;=\; \epsilon \ ,$$

$$\mathcal{D}(\tilde{I}, W) = \sum_{i \in [n]} \tilde{I}_{\pi(9(i-1)+5)} \cdot W_{\pi(9(i-1)+5)} \;=\; \sum_{i \in [n]} s_{2i-r_i} \;=\; B \;=\; \tau \ .$$

On the other hand if for an elastic g we obtain $\tilde{I} = g(I^*)$ such that the conditions $d(\tilde{I}, R) \leq \epsilon$ and $\mathcal{D}(\tilde{I}, W) \geq \tau$ are true then from the first condition we have $\sum_{i \in [n]} \tilde{I}_{\pi(9(i-1)+5)} \leq B$ and by the second condition we can conclude that $\sum_{i \in [n]} \tilde{I}_{\pi(9(i-1)+5)} \geq B$. Hence the equality holds. Moreover one can also conclude that for any pair of indices (x, y) which do not coincide with $\pi(9(i-1)+5)$, for some $i \in [n]$, it has to be true that $\tilde{I}_{x,y} = I^*_{x,y}$; otherwise the distortion exceeds the threshold ϵ. From the elasticity of g it follows that displacing s_{2i-1} more than two pixels (horizontally, vertically or diagonally) one has to displace s_{2i} at least one pixel, or vice versa. Therefore we can conclude that the only elastic transformation which fulfills all of these conditions is a transformation which for every 3×3 block containing s_{2i-1} and s_{2i} displaces to the middle of the block one of s_{2i-1} or s_{2i} (position $\pi(9(i-1)+5)$). $\qquad \square$

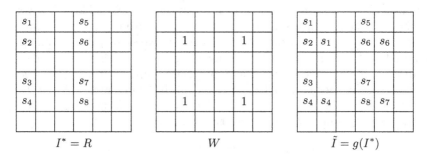

Fig. 6. Example construction of I^*, R and W and geometrically transformed image $\tilde{I}$. The transformation models the partition of the sequence $(s_1, s_2, \ldots, s_8)$ into two subsets: (s_1, s_4, s_6, s_7) and (s_2, s_3, s_5, s_8).

5.3   Arbitrary Geometric Distortions

Proof. Now we present the reduction for the Problem IGD. Again we use the sequence partition problem. Let $S = (s_1, s_2, \ldots, s_{2n})$ be an input of the problem and let B be half of the sum of all elements. Without loss of generality assume n has form $\frac{1}{3}k^2$ for some integer k and that for every $i \in [n]$ $s_{2i-1} \le s_{2i}$. For every $i \in [n]$ define $a_i := i \cdot B$

$$
\begin{aligned}
I^*_{\pi(i)} &:= a_i + s_{2i-1} , & R_{\pi(i)} &:= a_i , & W_{\pi(i)} &:= 1 , \\
I^*_{\pi(n+i)} &:= a_i + s_{2i-1} , & R_{\pi(n+i)} &:= a_i + s_{2i-1} , & W_{\pi(n+i)} &:= 0 , \\
I^*_{\pi(2n+i)} &:= a_i + s_{2i} , & R_{\pi(2n+i)} &:= a_i + s_{2i} , & W_{\pi(2n+i)} &:= 0 .
\end{aligned}
$$

Finally let $\epsilon := \frac{1}{3n}B$ and $\tau := \frac{n(n+1)}{2}B + B$.

Assume for $(s_1, s_2, \ldots, s_{2n})$ there exists a sequence $(r_1, r_2, \ldots, r_n) \in \{0,1\}^n$ such that $\sum_{i \in [n]} s_{2i-r_i} = B$. We define g in such a way that for $\tilde{I} = g(I^*)$ and for every $i \in [n]$ we have $\tilde{I}_{\pi(i)} = a_i + s_{2i-r_i}$ and the values of the remaining items of $\tilde{I}$ coincide with the values of the corresponding items in I^*. Obviously there exists such function g that realises the transformation. We get

$$
d(\tilde{I}, R) = \tfrac{1}{3n} \sum_{i \in [n]} (\tilde{I}_{\pi(i)} - R_{\pi(i)}) = \tfrac{1}{3n} \sum_{i \in [n]} s_{2i-r_i} = \tfrac{1}{3n}B = \epsilon ,
$$

$$
\mathcal{D}(\tilde{I}, W) = \sum_{i \in [n]} \tilde{I}_{\pi(i)} W_{\pi(i)} = \sum_{i \in [n]} (a_i + s_{2i-r_i}) = \tfrac{n(n+1)}{2}B + B = \tau .
$$

On the other hand assume that for some g the constraints $d(\tilde{I}, R) \le \epsilon$ and $\mathcal{D}(\tilde{I}, W) \ge \tau$ are true, with $\tilde{I} = g(I^*)$. Then without loss of generality we can assume that for all i, with $n < i \le 3n$, we have $\tilde{I}_{\pi(i)} = I^*_{\pi(i)} = R_{\pi(i)}$. If not then one can modify the transformation to the one fulfilling the property in such a way that we do not increase the distortion and do not change the strength of the watermark detector response. We can also assume that for every $i \in [n]$

$$
a_i + s_{2i-1} \le \tilde{I}_{\pi(i)} \le a_i + s_{2i} .
$$

If this is not the case then we obtain: $d(\tilde{I}, R) > \epsilon$, a contradiction. Hence for some sequence $(r_1, \ldots, r_n) \in \{0,1\}^n$ we have:

$$
\tfrac{1}{3n}B = \epsilon \ge d(\tilde{I}, R) = \tfrac{1}{3n} \sum_{i \in [n]} s_{2i-r_i} \text{ and}
$$

$$
\tfrac{n(n+1)}{2}B + B = \tau \le \mathcal{D}(\tilde{I}, W) = \sum_{i \in [n]} (a_i + s_{2i-r_i}) = \tfrac{n(n+1)}{2}B + \sum_{i \in [n]} s_{2i-r_i} .
$$

Combining both inequalities we get $\sum_{i \in [n]} s_{2i+2-r_i} = B$. This completes the proof. $\qquad \square$

6   Conclusions and Future Work

In this paper we have discussed different methods for designing watermarking schemes that are robust against geometric distortions. In particular we have looked at the problem of inverting geometric distortions. We have shown the problems *IDD*, *IED* and *IGD* to be NP-complete by giving polynomial time reductions from *PARTITION* and *SEQUENCE PARTITION*.

These results are consistent with previous research results. For example, Loo and Kingsbury propose the use of motion estimation based registration [9]. In their paper they get good results for a stirmark strength of up to 4. However, they also write that their algorithm cannot cope with large distortions, e.g. rotation, scaling, cropping.

There are still many open questions, e.g. whether *IAD* is NP-complete. Our future work will concentrate on answering these questions and extending the application of polynomial time reductions to different distortion functions and other watermarking schemes, such as spread spectrum watermarking.

References

1. Petitcolas, F.A.P., Anderson, R.J., Kuhn, M.G.: Attacks on copyright marking systems. In Aucsmith, D., ed.: Information Hiding, Second International Workshop, IH'98. Volume 1525 of LNCS., Portland, Oregon, U.S.A., Springer-Verlag (1998) 219–239
2. Petitcolas, F.A.P.: Watermarking schemes evaluation. IEEE Signal Processing **17** (2000) 58–64
3. Cox, I.J., Miller, M.L., Bloom, J.A.: Digital Watermarking. Academic Press (2002)
4. Dugelay, J.L., Petitcolas, F.A.: Possible counterattacks against random geometric distortions. In Delp, E.J., Wong, P.W., eds.: Security and Watermarking of Multimedia Contents II. Volume 3971 of Proc. SPIE. (2000) 338–345
5. Lichtenauer, J.F., Setyawan, I., Kalker, T.: Exhaustive geometrical search and the false positive watermark detection probability. In Delp, E.J., Wong, P.W., eds.: Security and Watermarking of Multimedia Contents V. Volume 5020 of Proc. SPIE. (2003) 203–214
6. Uchida, S., Sakoe, H.: A monotonic and continuous two-dimensional warping based on dynamic programming. In: ICPR '98: Proceedings of the 14th International Conference on Pattern Recognition-Volume 1, IEEE Computer Society (1998) 521
7. Keysers, D., Unger, W.: Elastic image matching is NP-complete. Pattern Recogn. Lett. **24** (2003) 445–453
8. Garey, M.R., Johnson, D.S.: Computers and Intractability; A Guide to the Theory of NP-Completeness. W. H. Freeman & Co., New York (1979)
9. Loo, P., Kingsbury, N.G.: Motion estimation based registration of geometrically distorted images for watermark recovery. In Delp, E.J., Wong, P.W., eds.: Security and Watermarking of Multimedia Contents III. Volume 4314 of Proc. SPIE. (2001) 606–617

Pre-processing for Adding Noise Steganography

Elke Franz and Antje Schneidewind

Dresden University of Technology, Dresden, Germany
{Elke.Franz, Antje.Schneidewind}@inf.tu-dresden.de

Abstract. This paper introduces and discusses an idea for utilizing noise introduced by scanning for steganography. In contrast to known approaches, we suggest a pre-processing step in order to reduce noise before embedding. This step shall enable us to embed by adding a noise signal without increasing local variances. The paper describes characteristic features of noise and possibilities to measure and consider them. Furthermore, we introduce a method to generate a noise signal that adheres to our simplified description. For embedding this signal, we consider the use of existing methods. Practical test results confirm the suitability of our approach, even if one must be aware of general limitations.

1 Introduction

Steganography as a method for confidential communication aims at hiding the existence of communication itself: The goal of a steganographic algorithm is to embed confidential messages by inconspicuously changing the cover material. Within this paper, we consider 8 bit gray scale images as cover data. Generally, stego images should have similar statistical properties as a steganographically unused image. In this case, an attacker would not be able to detect the use of steganography. However, successful attacks on steganographic systems have shown, that it is really a hard task to preserve the characteristics of the cover image while embedding. Even if some characteristics are preserved, others might be changed [1, 2, 5, 18]. Generally, it can be expected that attempts to reduce recognizable modifications of the characteristics of the cover data will finally decrease the embedding capacity unacceptably.

In order to prevent significant changes of the cover material, most steganographic algorithms try to utilize noise introduced by usual processes. Particularly, they try to detect noisy parts of the cover images in order to replace them with the secret message. A well known example is LSB steganography that replaces the least significant bits of the samples. However, this operation changes the statistics of the cover image. In order to overcome this problem, embedding by adding a noise signal is suggested in [7, 14, 21]. But simply adding a noise signal will also change statistical properties of the pixel values, e.g., increase their variance [9, 11]. This might be utilized for attacks.

The steganographic algorithm suggested in [8] utilizes knowledge about the cover data as side-information that is available only to the sender. Embedding is done during an information-reducing operation such as quantization. Therefore, the stego image is an information reduced variant of the cover image.

M. Barni et al. (Eds.): IH 2005, LNCS 3727, pp. 189–203, 2005.

We assume that the sender wants to use an image as cover without the necessity to apply an information-reducing operation. Our approach aims at mimicking noise introduced by scanning. Particularly, we want to embed by adding a noise signal under the condition that the variances of the gray scales do not increase. Resulting stego images should have characteristics of natural scans. This requires that the added noise signal has similar characteristics as noise introduced by a scanner. However, we also need side-information about the cover in order to not increase the variances. The suggested pre-processing step helps to estimate this information.

Within this paper, we discuss a possible realization of mimicking a scan process as suggested in [10]. Based on empirical evaluations of relevant characteristics of noise introduced by scanning, we derive a first simplified description of noise. We discuss an approach to generate a noise signal suitable for embedding which is based on this description. Particularly, we want to point out general limitations while trying to mimic the scan process.

The paper is structured as follows. Sec. 2 describes the basic approach. After pointing out preliminary ideas, we give an outline of the system and describe how to estimate the noise and an approximated original image. Afterwards, we discuss a possibility to generate an adapted noise signal. Sec. 3 gives an overview on our practical tests and summarizes their results. A possible optimization is introduced in Sec. 4. Finally, Sec. 5 concludes and gives an outlook.

2   Description of the Approach

2.1   Preliminary Ideas

Digital images are always affected by noise. We consider as noise the deviation of pixel values from the actual intensity at this point. Scanning can be seen as measuring the intensity of an analogue image. The CCD (charge coupled device) elements of the scanner are used for this measurement.

Each measurement is influenced by two different kinds of errors: systematic and random errors. Systematic errors describe systematic deviations of the measurement result, e.g., caused by a wrong calibration of the measuring device. Whenever detected, such errors can be eliminated. In contrast, random errors arise from various uncontrollable causes. Examples are thermic noise, quantization noise, or environmental conditions such as temperature, or humidity. We assume that each of these single causes has only a weak influence on the resulting measurement error which additively overlaps the original noise free signal [13]. Based on this assumption, we expect a normal distribution of our "measurement results", i.e., of the pixel values delivered by the CCD elements [15, 19].

If we subsequently scan an analogue image i times, we therefore expect that the gray scales at position (x, y), i.e., the pixels $p(x, y)_i$ of the scans S_i, are normally distributed. Furthermore, in case of an ideal homogeneous image, we expect that the gray scales within a column are normally distributed since they are delivered by one or at least the same CCD elements. Of course, in practice the analogue image will include some irregularities.

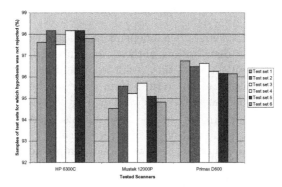

Fig. 1. Percent of samples of the test sets for which H_0 was not rejected

In order to verify our assumption regarding the normal distribution of the gray scales, we have scanned a homogeneous image and analyzed six test sets. Each test set consisted of samples of 100 subsequent pixels from each column, where the samples of a single test set were drawn starting at a fixed row. At an average, each scanned image contained 4700 columns, i.e., each test set contained 4700 samples. Altogether, we analyzed 28200 samples. We have applied a χ^2-test of goodness of fit [16] choosing a significance level of $\alpha = 0.05$ in order to test the hypothesis H_0, that the pixels adhere to a normal distribution. We performed this test for three different scanners: an HP ScanJet 6300C, a Mustek ScanExpress 12000P, and a Primax Colorado Direct/D600. For most of the samples, the hypothesis H_0 was not rejected (Fig. 1).

These results have confirmed our assumption that gray scales in a homogeneous area are normally distributed. Of course, it would be quite complex to describe the distribution of gray scales for each CCD element separately. Moreover, we have to consider the fact that noise in images consists of signal dependent and signal independent components [3]. Signal dependence implies, e.g., a dependence of the noise signal on image intensity. Consequently, it would be necessary to measure the distribution of pixels for each CCD element for different intensities of an image.

In order to be able to test the general idea, we hence used a simplified description. Therefore, we analyzed and described results of scanning homogeneous areas. To simplify matters, we assumed that as long as there is no defect CCD element, we can expect similar distributions of gray scales of pixels in homogeneous areas. For further tests, we have used a gray card containing 70 homogeneous blocks of different gray scales.

Since each scan S_i is affected by noise N_i due to the measurement error, we do not have access to an "original image" O without noise:

$$S_i = O + N_i \tag{1}$$

Hence, it is not possible to measure differences between a scan S_i and the original O, that means the noise N_i introduced by scanning, directly. We can only measure the differences N_{ij} resulting from subtracting S_i and S_j:

$$N_{ij} = S_i - S_j = (O + N_i) - (O + N_j) = N_i - N_j = N_{ij}. \qquad (2)$$

The distribution of the sum of two independent random variables corresponds to the convolution of the distributions of these random variables [16]. We assume N_i and N_j to be independent, since they result from random measurement errors. Therefore, the distribution of N_{ij} results from the convolution of the random variables N_i and N_j. Consequently, the variance σ_{ij}^2 of the differences N_{ij} is greater than the variances σ_i^2, σ_j^2 of the noise signals N_i, N_j. In case of zero-mean distributions of N_i and N_j, N_{ij} is also zero-mean.

This consideration also implies that we cannot simply add a noise signal to an image [6, 11]: The pixels of an image can be seen as realizations of a random variable. The noise signal, a sequence of positive and negative values, can also be seen as a random variable. Adding a noise signal to the pixels of an image means to add two random variables. The convolution increases the variances of the gray scales. For example, adding a random signal which has characteristics of measured differences N_{jk} to an image S_i would yield:

$$S_i' = S_i + N_{jk} = (O + N_i) + N_{jk} \qquad (3)$$

In contrast to a usual scan, the resulting image S_i' is additionally superimposed with a noise N_{jk}. Consequently, we would need the original version O of the image as well as a description of noise N_i in order to embed by mimicking the scan process. Obviously, we have to estimate O and N_i.

2.2   Characteristics of Noise Introduced by a Scanner

Differences between subsequently scanned images reflect these characteristics. Therefore, we have first evaluated difference images between subsequent scans of different test images in order to describe characteristic features of scanner noise. Of course, these subsequent scans were taken without changing any parameter. We have evaluated five different flatbed scanner types: HP ScanJet 6100C, HP ScanJet 6250C, HP ScanJet 6300C, Mustek ScanExpress 12000P (two different exemplars), and Primax Colorado Direct/D600. For these tests, we have evaluated about 600 scans and 600 difference images. A detailed description of the test results is given in [6]. Within this paper, we summarize only relevant features.

In order to evaluate the *dependence of noise on image intensity*, we have scanned a gray card containing 70 homogeneous blocks of different gray scales twice. Due to our simplifications, we have drawn a sample from a small area for each homogeneous block. Furthermore, we have drawn the corresponding samples from the difference image between two scans of the gray card. According to our expectations, the distribution of the differences depends on the level of intensity, i.e., the variances of the differences increase with growing intensity despite in saturation areas.

As mentioned in Sec. 2.1, we assume the gray scale values of the samples as well as the differences adhere to a *normal distribution*. Similar to the description in Sec. 2.1, we have applied a χ^2-test of goodness of fit [16] (hypothesis H_0 tested:

data adhere to a normal distribution). The results depend on the scanner type. For the samples of HP 6300C, the hypothesis was not rejected at all.

Based on this result, we are able to describe the distribution of the differences by estimating the parameters μ and σ for the 70 different intensity levels of the gray card. In this way, we can describe the signal dependence of noise.

Tests with a big homogeneous image that covers nearly the whole flat surface have pointed out *spacial non-uniformities* of the differences. However, a usual analogue image, e.g., a photograph, covers only a part of the flat surface. Therefore, we could exclude this influence since we have used an area of the surface which seems to produce similar differences.

However, a feature that must be considered is *mid-term stability*, which describes the stability of the output values of the scanner upon turning it on [4]. We have evaluated the average gray scale of a small homogeneous area. This area was scanned 30 times using fixed time intervals of one minute. Again, all parameters remain constant. The mid-term stability varies from scanner to scanner. The Primax D600 has shown a transient effect as it could be expected: The mean of the gray scales was quite high directly after turning on the scanner and swung into a lower value after about three minutes. However, the HP 6300C shows periodical peaks (Fig. 2).

Finally, our tests have confirmed that mechanical irregularities can cause quite strong *shifts* between the pixels of subsequently scanned images. The results differ from scanner to scanner. Generally, the shifts introduced by the tested HP scanners were negligible, while the Mustek scanners have caused big shifts.

Additionally to these possible influences, we also had to consider *correlations* between adjacent pixels. Evaluating this feature is work in progress.

To conclude, describing the characteristics of noise introduced by a scanner is quite complex. Furthermore, it is not easy to separate different influences. Since we do not have access to the original, unprocessed data and to the single processing steps, it is not easy to describe and mimic single noise components. We have to describe noise as a whole. For our first description, we have assumed a simplified model. Of course, like in every steganographic system, the quality of the model influences the security of the steganographic algorithm — if an attacker possesses a better model of scanning noise, he is able to distinguish between stego images and steganographically unused data.

Based on our empirical tests, we have derived a first simplified description of noise introduced by scanning. Thereby, we have chosen the HP 6300C due to its

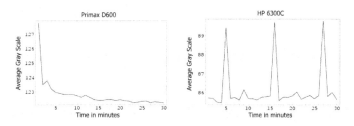

Fig. 2. Mid-term stability

preferable features. Our model considers the normal distribution of pixels as well as signal dependence of noise. Effects of mid-term stability are also considered. The description does not cover spatial non-uniformities, since we have selected a suitable surface area. Furthermore, our current description does not analyze possible shifts, because the chosen scanner produces only small shifts.

2.3   Outline of the Steganographic System

The steganographic system introduced within this paper contains three steps:

1. Since we cannot access the original image O, we have to calculate an estimation $\tilde{O}$ of the original for each cover image.
2. We have to determine characteristic features of noise N_i introduced by a scanner. This step needs to be performed only once. Since we cannot access N_i directly, we aim at an estimation $\widetilde{N_i}$.
3. Finally, we embed the secret message by adding a noise signal N_s (stego noise signal) to our estimated original $\tilde{O}$. N_s adheres to the distribution of $\widetilde{N_i}$ determined in the second step.

The basic idea of the whole system is to mimic noise introduced by scanning: Stego images should have same characteristics as usual scans. We clearly separate between determining an estimation $\tilde{O}$ and generating a noise signal N_s. Thereby, we aim at a general description for noise considering signal dependence.

Different approaches for the estimation of O will yield different results. Consequently, the description of N_i which is the basis for embedding describes not necessarily noise introduced by scanning. Actually, it describes the differences between our estimation and the scans. Even if our goal is to mimic noise introduced by scanning, this is currently the best we can achieve.

Fig. 3 illustrates the approach and points out the difference to usual steganographic algorithms that use one of the digitalized images as cover without a pre-processing step as suggested within this paper.

Estimating $\tilde{O}$. One possibility to determine $\tilde{O}$ is to scan an image n times and calculate the average of the resulting scans. By this, we use a set of input images in order to gain an estimation $\tilde{O}$. A set of covers instead of a single cover as

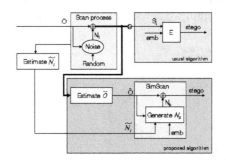

Fig. 3. Outline of the steganographic system

input is also considered in [20]. However, we do not select one of the images of the input set as actual cover in order to prevent cover-stego-attacks. Instead of this, we utilize the additional information delivered by the set of scans in order to calculate $\widetilde{O}$ which is not element of the set. The calculated estimation is used as cover for the actual embedding.

Currently, our solution needs access to a scanner. One could argue that scanning with a higher resolution and subsequently scaling down the resulting image is a better solution since it requires less effort. By this, we could directly apply the approach of [8]. However, our general goal is to mimic noise introduced by scanning. Perspectively, we aim at a solution for embedding without the necessity to really scan an analogue image.

Estimating $\widetilde{N_i}$. One possible way would be to estimate the parameters of the normal distribution of $\widetilde{N_i}$ from the parameters of the distribution of N_{ij}. Under the assumption that the noise is normally distributed, we can easily approximate the variance σ_i^2 of N_i by calculating σ_{ij}^2 divided by two. Another way is to measure the differences between the estimated original $\widetilde{O}$ and the scans S_i. In doing so, we calculate $\widetilde{N_i}$, an estimation of N_i, directly.

Calling the stego images that result from embedding N_s in $\widetilde{O}$ $stego(\widetilde{O})$, we can describe embedding in general as:

$$stego(\widetilde{O}) = \widetilde{O} + N_s, \text{where } \widetilde{O} = O + \epsilon \qquad (4)$$

The value ϵ describes the deviation of our estimation $\widetilde{O}$ from O. If ϵ would be very, very small, the two methods for estimating $\widetilde{N_i}$ were nearly equivalent. However, our estimation is not perfect.

Independent of the chosen method, we use $\widetilde{O}$ for embedding. The characteristics of the embedded signals N_s are different.

In the first method, $\widetilde{N_i}$ approximates the differences between O and S_i: $\widetilde{N_i} \approx S_i - O$, i.e., $stego(\widetilde{O}) \approx (O + \epsilon) + (S_i - O) \approx S_i + \epsilon$. The error of the estimation directly influences the result.

In contrast, in the second variant $\widetilde{N_i}$ describes the differences between our estimation $\widetilde{O}$ and the scans: $\widetilde{N_i} = S_i - \widetilde{O}$, i.e., $stego(\widetilde{O}) = \widetilde{O} + (S_i - \widetilde{O}) \approx S_i$.

Consequently, we realized the second possibility since this way seems to enable us to estimate noise tailored for our approach.

Generating N_s for embedding. Basically, there are two possibilities to realize a steganographic system that mimics noise introduced by scanning. First, the system could generate a further scan and subsequently embed the secret message into this scan. Strictly speaking, this case is equivalent to embedding according to the usual approach: The embedding must take care to maintain the characteristics of relevant features of the generated scan. The second approach would be to embed while mimicking the scan process. Within this paper, we investigate the second possibility.

The main challenge of this approach is to generate a suitable noise signal N_s which adheres to the distribution of $\widetilde{N_i}$. This noise signal can be added to the estimated original image $\tilde{O}$ according to known approaches for adding noise steganography [7]. The next sections discuss the single steps in detail.

2.4 Estimating $\tilde{O}$

In order to estimate $\tilde{O}$, we scanned the analogue image n times and calculated the average image as described above. Obviously, the number n of scans determines the accuracy of this estimation. *Confidence intervals* can be calculated in order to determine the interval in which the estimated parameter η lies with probability $\gamma = 1 - \delta$ [16]. The parameter γ is called *confidence coefficient*. In our case, we want to calculate the confidence interval of a sample with unknown variance. The variance is estimated by the sample variance s^2

$$s^2 = \frac{1}{n-1} \sum_{i=1}^{n} (p(x,y)_i - \overline{p(x,y)})^2$$

The confidence interval is calculated according to [16]:

$$\overline{p(x,y)} - t_{1-\frac{\delta}{2}} \frac{s}{\sqrt{n}} < \eta < \overline{p(x,y)} + t_{1-\frac{\delta}{2}} \frac{s}{\sqrt{n}}$$

where t means the quantile of the Student-t distribution with $n - 1$ degrees of freedom. A small confidence interval stands for a good estimation. For example, a value of 2 means the exact value may differ with probability γ by ± 1.

In order to determine the required number of scans, we have scanned the gray card 20 times and excluded outliers in order to consider mid-term stability. Within this test, there were two outliers. In the following evaluation, only the remaining $n' = 18$ images were used. For each gray block, we have drawn five samples containing the corresponding pixels $p(x,y)_i, i = 1, 2, ..., n'$ of all scans $S_i, i = 1, 2, ..., n'$ at one and the same position. We have calculated the confidence intervals using $\gamma = 0.95$ for each of the samples. Obviously, a greater sample size yields a more exact estimation. In our tests, we have achieved an average confidence interval of 1.59 for a sample size of 12 images. For practical reasons, this sample size should be sufficient.

For additional tests, we have scanned 200 different test images. Each test image was scanned 20 times. At this point, it is of interest how many outliers arise in practice. To exclude outliers, we have analyzed the MSEs between the scans S_i and $\tilde{O}$. The difference between the median of all MSEs and the MSE of S_i, $MSE_i = MSE(S_i, \tilde{O})$ determines whether S_i is an outlier. This evaluation has shown that 20 scans are sufficient for this scanner exemplar to get a set of at least 12 images which can be used to calculate $\tilde{O}$.

2.5 Estimating $\tilde{N_i}$

In order to estimate $\tilde{N_i}$, we have scanned the gray card 20 times. First, we have estimated an image $\tilde{O}$ by averaging all scans of the gray card. For each pixel $p(x,y)_{\tilde{O}}$ of $\tilde{O}$, the scans $S_1, S_2, ..., S_n$ yield a sample of size n: $\{p(x,y)_1, p(x,y)_2, ..., p(x,y)_n\}$.

The average $\overline{p(x,y)}$ of the sample was used as an estimation η of the mean which we assume to be the actual value of the appropriate pixel:

$$p(x,y)_{\widetilde{O}} = \overline{p(x,y)} = \frac{1}{n}\sum_{i=1}^{n}p(x,y)_i$$

Subsequently, we have determined the mean square error MSE between $\widetilde{O}$ and all scans S_i in order to be able to eliminate the outliers. The aim of this step was to describe the most likely characteristics and to consider mid-term stability.

Based on the calculated MSEs, we have selected one of the remaining scans as reference scan S_r and calculated the difference image $\widetilde{N}_r = S_r - \widetilde{O}$. For each gray block, we have drawn two samples containing 500 pixels in each case:

- $Sample_1$ was drawn from $\widetilde{O}$. The mean $m = E(Sample_1)$ of this sample determined the corresponding gray scale the noise $\widetilde{N}_r$ belongs to.
- $Sample_2$ was drawn from $\widetilde{N}_r$ (considering the same positions as in the first sample). This sample was used to determine the distribution of noise $\widetilde{N}_r$ w.r.t. the corresponding gray scale m.

We have estimated the parameters μ and σ for each of the 70 gray scales by calculating the mean and the standard deviation of $Sample_2$. The measured distribution was used as an estimation for $\widetilde{N}_i$.

2.6 Generating N_s for Embedding

Generally, we want to embed by adding a noise signal of appropriate distribution. That means, we always process the whole image independent of the actual message length.

The procedure described in Sec. 2.5 yields a first description of signal dependent noise: For the mean m of each block of the gray card, we have estimated the parameters of the noise signal. That means, we have a noise description for about 70 gray scales (we have not considered samples for which hypothesis of normal distribution was rejected). However, we need the parameters of noise for each of the 256 possible gray scales. Therefore, we have approximated the signal dependence of the gray scales g by polynomial functions $f_\mu(g), f_\sigma(g)$ of different degree based on our supporting points. As it could be expected, the higher the degree of the approximation function, the less the mean square error for the supporting points. However, the approximation function can be less suitable for the remaining gray scales. For our tests, we have used a polynomial function of sixth degree as approximation (Fig. 4).

In order to generate a suitable noise signal N_s, we first determine the parameters μ and σ of the noise distribution for the gray scale g of each pixel $p(x,y)_c$ of the cover by help of the approximation functions $f_\mu(p(x,y)_c), f_\sigma(p(x,y)_c)$.

For embedding by adding this noise signal, we suggest to use the approach described in [7]. This approach assumes that a pseudo random number generator (PRNG) produces the so called stego noise which shall be added to the pixels of the image according to the required distribution $N(\mu,\sigma)$.

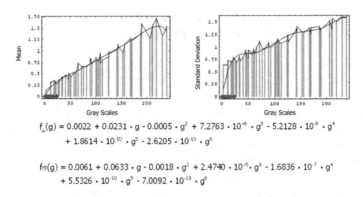

$f_\mu(g) = 0.0022 + 0.0231 \cdot g - 0.0005 \cdot g^2 + 7.2763 \cdot 10^{-6} \cdot g^3 - 5.2128 \cdot 10^{-8} \cdot g^4$
$+ 1.8614 \cdot 10^{-10} \cdot g^5 - 2.6205 \cdot 10^{-13} \cdot g^6$

$f\sigma(g) = 0.0061 + 0.0633 \cdot g - 0.0018 \cdot g^2 + 2.4740 \cdot 10^{-5} \cdot g^3 - 1.6836 \cdot 10^{-7} \cdot g^4$
$+ 5.5326 \cdot 10^{-10} \cdot g^5 - 7.0092 \cdot 10^{-13} \cdot g^6$

Fig. 4. Parameters of noise

Instead of parameterizing the PRNG for each pixel, it would also be possible to separate the stego noise signal. First, we have to add noise according to the estimated scanner noise (Sec. 2.5). However, the variances of this noise have to be decreased by a constant value σ_{emb}. In a second step, the message itself is embedded according to [7] as stego noise. Thereby, this stego noise would be normally distributed with $\mu = 0$, $\sigma = \sigma_{emb}$.

3   Practical Results

3.1   Evaluating the Suitability of Averaging

Obviously, averaging reduces noise inherent in images. Since we cannot get an original, noise free image, we cannot directly calculate the error of the estimation. Therefore, we used one of the scans as "original" S_O and generated 20 "scans" $S_i^*, i = 1, 2, ..., 20$ by adding a noise signal according to the description in Sec. 2.5. Subsequently, we have calculated $\widetilde{O}^*$ by averaging S_i^* and evaluated the differences between $\widetilde{O}^*$ and S_i^*.

In order to assess the suitability of averaging, we have calculated the ratio aq based on the simulated data:

$$aq = \frac{MSE(S_O, \widetilde{O}^*)}{Median(MSE(S_O, S_i^*))} \quad i = 1, 2, ..., n \tag{5}$$

which should be less than one for a suitable estimation. Within this test, we calculated $aq = \frac{0.224}{2.3997} = 0.093345$ what confirms our assumption. In practice, shifts are critical for averaging, since they influence the result on gray scale edges.

3.2   Evaluating Mimicking Noise

For first tests, we have processed scans of five photographs of different characteristics (big homogeneous areas, different degree of texture, edges of different strength) as described in Sec. 2. The resulting stego images are called $stego(\widetilde{O})$.

We have also embedded a uniformly distributed noise signal into these five scans. The stego images of this trial are called $stego(S_i)$. Thereby, we have used three different zero-mean noise signals with $\sigma_k = k$; $k = 1, 2, 3$.

As expected, adding a noise signal to an image without considering signal dependence holds the risk to destroy existing structures in the least significant bit plane. Since we have considered signal dependence while embedding into an estimated original, we could preserve existing structures.

Since our approach includes a pre-processing step which first tries to reduce noise, local variances should not be increased. We have calculated local variances for selected image blocks of our test images. We tried to select image blocks of different characteristics (range of gray scales, contrast). Tab. 1 summarizes our results, where $i.j$ references block j of image i. The tests confirm that noise reducing pre-processing and subsequently adding a signal dependent noise signal is a promising approach. However, there may be problems with texture rich images since we currently do not consider correlations between pixels. Effects of embedding by adding a signal independent noise are predictable: Without a noise reducing pre-processing, local variances increase approximately by the variance of the noise signal.

To summarize, these first test results show the suitability of the approach even if the approximation is still incomplete. In order to evaluate the detectability of the embedding, we performed steganalytical evaluations [12] for a large set of 200 test images. Since we have to scan each image 20 times, we have to evaluate 4000 scans. For each test image, we calculated 4 stego images:

- embedding in S_i by adding a zero-mean noise signal with $\sigma = 1$
- embedding in S_i by adding a zero-mean noise signal with $\sigma = 2$
- embedding an adapted noise signal in S_i ($stego(S_i)$) and
- embedding according to our approach ($stego(\widetilde{O})$).

Table 1. Local Variances

Block	Range	Contrast	S_i	$\widetilde{O}$	$stego(\widetilde{O})$
1.1	{54, 255}	medium	15.000	14.361	15.500
1.2	{66, 248}	medium	113.903	112.014	112.944
1.3	{19, 249}	many strong gray edges	131.722	127.431	133.014
1.4	{5, 255}	mainly homogeneous areas	12.778	3.778	13.250
2.1	{0, 154}	medium	25.611	9.361	18.250
2.2	{58, 255}	medium	141.194	138.528	139.347
3.1	{17, 244}	many strong gray edges	300.875	299.250	301.514
3.2	{54, 255}	mainly homogeneous areas	1.750	1.111	2.111
3.3	{21, 235}	many strong gray edges	406.444	407.111	412.264
4.1	{0, 129}	mainly homogeneous areas	22.111	6.944	15.861
4.2	{206, 253}	mainly homogeneous areas	3.444	2.528	3.500
4.3	{12, 251}	medium	11.000	3.778	10.500
4.4	{178, 255}	mainly homogeneous areas	4.278	3.194	3.778
5.1	{51, 218}	mainly homogeneous areas	12.111	10.250	11.500
5.2	{225, 255}	mainly homogeneous areas	0.778	0.250	1.361
5.3	{47, 232}	many strong gray edges	89.472	84.944	86.361
5.4	{226, 255}	mainly homogeneous areas	1.000	0.250	1.528

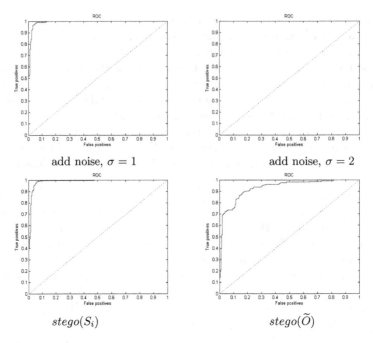

Fig. 5. Steganalytical results: ROC curves

Figure 5 summarizes the results of the steganalytical evaluations. As expected, embedding by simply adding a noise signal is detectable with an accuracy of 0.981 for $\sigma = 1$ and accordingly 1 for $\sigma = 2$. Embedding an adapted noise signal without a pre-processing step improves the results only a little bit (accuracy = 0.973). As we mentioned above, we use only a simplified noise description for the embedding scheme proposed within this paper. Therefore, as expected, it is also possible to detect stego images $stego(O)$ with an accuracy of 0.862. Nevertheless, the ROC curves show that our algorithm is a step forward to secure steganography, even if some improvement is necessary.

4   Optimizing the Approach

A remaining problem is still the required effort for repeated scanning. Even if this step is realized automatically by the steganographic system via TWAIN interface, there is some effort of time.

The problem of noise is well known in image processing. Therefore, it seems to be reasonable to investigate whether a noise reducing process can substitute averaging in order to reduce the required effort.

Digital image enhancement and restoration techniques are used to reduce effects of image quality degradation introduced by acquiring processes such as scanning. These operations can be thought of as two-dimensional filters. Filtering yields a smoothed image. The resulting gray scale $g'(x, y)$ is determined by evaluating adjacent pixels within a window $W_{x,y}$. For our tests, we have used a window size of 3x3 pixels. We have considered average filter, median filter, Wiener filter, and two variations of the peak-and-valley-filter discussed in [13] which basically performs the following evaluation:

$$g'(x,y) = \begin{cases} f_1(W_{x,y}) & \text{, if} \qquad g(x,y) \geq \max(W_{x,y}) + gap \\ f_2(W_{x,y}) & \text{, if} \qquad g(x,y) \leq \min(W_{x,y}) - gap \\ g(x,y) & \text{, otherwise} \end{cases} \qquad (6)$$

The first variation uses equal functions $f_1(), f_2()$: If necessary, the pixel is substituted by the average of $W_{x,y}$. For the second variation, $f_1()$ substitutes a pixel by the next maximum of $W_{x,y}$, and $f_2()$ substitutes a pixel by the next minimum of $W_{x,y}$. The parameter gap controls the strength of the substitution.

In order to assess the suitability of the investigated filters, we have applied them to the generated scans $\widetilde{O}_{f,i} = filter(S_i^*)$ (Sec. 3.1). We calculated $MSE(S_0, \widetilde{O}_f)$ for all filters in order to decide which filter converges best to averaging. The second variation of the peak-and-valley filter (using $gap = 1$) has produced the least MSEs. A visual evaluation has shown that this kind of filter also maintains image structures best. In contrast, applying a Wiener filter totally randomized the least significant bit plane in our tests.

We want to point out that there is an important difference between averaging and filtering. In case of averaging, we use a sample of gray scales of different scans in order to determine the gray scale of one pixel. In case of no shifts, our result lies within this sample. Using a filter implies to determine the pixels gray scale by evaluating its adjacent pixels. This procedure will work sufficiently within homogeneous areas. However, filtering introduces artifacts at edges. Finally, our description of noise must be adapted, since it describes the differences between $\widetilde{O}$ and S_i (Sec. 2.3).

5   Summary and Outlook

The main focus of this paper is to motivate the necessity of pre-processing for adding noise steganography. We discuss an approach to estimate an "original" image since simply adding a noise signal might also change statistical properties. Furthermore, we describe characteristic features of scanner noise that should be mimicked by our steganographic system. The paper also describes possibilities to measure these features and to generate a cover dependent noise signal that can be used for embedding. Actually our approach still requires significant effort.

Since the noise signal introduced by scanning is quite complex, we use only a simplified model for a first proof of concept. Currently, we do not consider dependencies of noise on image structures. Particularly, this can imply problems at edges. Correlations between pixels are a critical aspect that must be included in future descriptions. For a more sophisticated description, it is also necessary to consider possible shifts. The approximation function itself can be improved by using other functions than polynomials. Particularly, we consider the use of b-splines in order to enhance approximation between supporting points.

Finally, we have to reconsider our assumptions. An important aspect is the fact, that we have measured the parameters for the distribution from homogeneous blocks of a gray card. We have to keep in mind, that this could imply weaknesses which can be exploited by an attacker.

The paper has also discussed possibilities to improve the efficiency of the system. We have investigated several filters to reduce noise in order to determine an estimation $\widetilde{O}_f$ from a single cover. The results of first tests motivate to further investigate noise reducing algorithms, either as pre-processing step or as processing that can be utilized for steganography. By using filters as pre-processing, we have to reconsider our noise approximation.

We currently have a simplified description of noise introduced by one specific scanner. The results of the steganalysis confirm our assumption, that embedding while mimicking a natural process is a step forward to secure steganography, even if our approach needs some improvement. Further investigations have also to consider aging of physical devices what might imply simplifications of our approach. We expect that such considerations imply interesting aspects for digital forensics.

However, in our opinion there are still some general limitations. The first is the difficulty to model the noise signal. Since noise introduced by scanning is quite complex, one can expect that it is not possible at all to model it perfectly. Consequently, the security of the steganographic system is limited by the knowledge of an attacker: If he possesses a better description, he is able to distinguish between steganographically used and unused images. A second limitation are the two inherent error sources within our approach. Artifacts might be introduced due to the pre-processing and due to adding a noise signal in order to embed the secret message.

Acknowledgement

The work described in this paper has been supported in part by the European Commission through the IST Programme under Contract IST-2002-507932 ECRYPT.[1] The authors would like to thank Jochen Penne for his assistance and helpful discussions.

References

[1] R. Böhme, A. Westfeld: Exploiting Preserved Statistics for Steganalysis. In Proc. of 6th IHW, Canada, 2004, 8296.

[2] R. Böhme, A. Westfeld: Breaking Cauchy Model-Based JPEG Steganography with First Order Statistics. Proc. of 9th ESORICS, France, 2004, 125140.

[3] R. Brügelmann, W. Förstner: Estimation of Signal Dependent Noise Variance. Technical report TB-ipb 93/13, University Bonn, 1993.

---

[1] The information in this document reflects only the author's views, is provided as is and no guarantee or warranty is given that the information is fit for any particular purpose. The user thereof uses the information at its sole risk and liability.

[4] Comittee draft for IEC 61966-8: Colour measurement and management in multi-media systems and equipment. Part 8: Colour scanners. 1998.

[5] E. Franz: Steganography Preserving Statistical Properties. Proc. of 5th IHW, The Netherlands, 2002, 278-294.

[6] E. Franz: Steganographie durch Nachbildung plausibler Änderungen. Dissertation, TU Dresden, 2002.

[7] J. Fridrich, M. Goljan: Digital Image Steganography Using Stochastic Modulation. Proc. of EI SPIE, Canada, 2003, 191-202.

[8] J. Fridrich, M. Goljan, D. Soukal: Perturbed Quantization Steganography with Wet Paper Codes. Proc. of ACM Multimedia Workshop, Germany, 2004, 4-15.

[9] J. Fridrich: Feature-Based Steganalysis for JPEG Images and its Implications for Future Design of Steganographic Schemes. Proc. of 6th IHW, Canada, 2004.

[10] E. Franz, A. Pfitzmann: Steganography Secure Against Cover-Stego-Attacks. Proc. of 3rd IHW, Germany, 1999, 29-46.

[11] J.J. Harmsen, W.A. Pearlman: Steganalysis of additive noise modelable information hiding. Proc. of SPIE Electronic Imaging 5022, Canada, 2003.

[12] T. Holotyak, J. Fridrich, S. Voloshynovskiy: Blind Statistical Steganalysis of Additive Steganography Using Wavelet Higher Order Statistics. submitted to 9th IFIP TC-6 TC-11 Conference on Communications and Multimedia Security, 2005, Austria.

[13] M. Lückenhaus: Grundlagen des Wiener Filters und seine Anwendung in der Bildanalyse. Diplomarbeit, TU München, 1995.

[14] L.M. Marvel, C.G. Boncelet, C.T. Retter: Reliable Blind Information Hiding for Images. Proc. of 2nd IHW, USA, 1998, 4861.

[15] M.K. Ochi: Applied Probability and Stochastic Processes in Engineering and Physical Sciences. Wiley, 1990.

[16] A. Papoulis: Probability, Random Variables, and Stochastic Processes. 3rd Ed., New York, Mc Graw-Hill, 1991.

[17] I. Pitas:Digital Image Processing Algorithms and Applications. Wiley, 2000.

[18] P. Sallee: Model-Based Steganography. Proc. of International Workshop on Digital Watermarking, 2004, 154167.

[19] R. Storm: Wahrscheinlichkeitsrechnung, mathematische Statistik und statistische Qualitätskontrolle. Fachbuchverlag Leipzig - Köln, 1995.

[20] J. Zöllner et al.: Modeling the Security of Steganographic Systems. Proc. of 2nd IHW, USA, 1998, 344-354.

[21] Hide&Seek, http://www.rugeley.demon.co.uk/security/hdsk50.zip

Efficient Wet Paper Codes

Jessica Fridrich[1], Miroslav Goljan[1], and David Soukal[2]

[1] Dept. of Electrical and Computer Engineering,
[2] Dept. of Computer Science
SUNY Binghamton, Binghamton, NY 13902-6000, USA
{fridrich, mgoljan, dsoukal1}@binghamton.edu

Abstract. Wet paper codes were proposed as a tool for constructing steg-anographic schemes with an arbitrary selection channel that is not shared between the sender and the recipient. In this paper, we describe new approaches to wet paper codes that enjoy low computational complexity and improved embedding efficiency (number of message bits per embedding change). Some applications of wet paper codes to steganography and data embedding in binary images are discussed.

1 Introduction

The placement of embedding changes in the cover object is called the selection channel [1]. This channel is often constructed from a secret shared between the sender and the recipient (e.g., pseudo-random straddling [2]) and may also depend on the cover object itself (adaptive embedding [3]). In general, it is in the interest of both communicating parties not to reveal any information or as little as possible about the embedding changes as this knowledge can help an attacker [4]. Since the sender's main objective is to minimize the detectability of the hidden data, he may construct the selection channel using the knowledge of the cover and any other available side information, such as a high-resolution (or unquantized) version of the cover [5]. Another possibility is to determine the best selection channel by iteratively running known steganalysis algorithms on the stego object. An obvious problem here is that the recipient may not be able to determine the same selection channel and read the message because he does not have access to the cover object or any side information.

The non-shared selection channel in steganography has been called "writing on wet paper" [5–7]. To explain the metaphor, imagine that the cover object X is an image that was exposed to rain and the sender can only slightly modify the dry spots of X (the selection channel) but not the wet spots. During transmission, the stego image Y dries out and thus the recipient does not know which pixels the sender used (the recipient has no information about the dry pixels). Codes for writing on wet paper that are suitable for steganographic applications (in the sense explained below) are called wet paper codes (WPCs).

The problem of non-shared selection channels in steganography is equivalent to "writing in memory with defective cells" introduced by Tsybakov et al. [8]. A memory contains n cells out of which $n-k$ cells are permanently stuck at either 0 or 1. The writing device knows the locations and status of the stuck cells. The task is to write as many bits as possible into the memory (up to k) so that the reading device, that does

M. Barni et al. (Eds.): IH 2005, LNCS 3727, pp. 204–218, 2005.

not have any information about the stuck cells, can correctly read the data. Clearly, writing on wet paper is formally equivalent to writing in memories with stuck cell (stuck cells = wet pixels).

The defective memory is a special case of the Gelfand-Pinsker channel with informed sender [9]. The Shannon capacity of defective memory with $n-k$ stuck cells is asymptotically k/n per cell, a fact that is also easily established using random binning [10]. A generalized version of this channel that allows for randomly flipped cells in addition to stuck cells was studied by Heegard et al. [11,12] who proposed partitioned linear block codes, later recognized as instances of nested linear codes [10], and proved that these codes achieve Shannon capacity. However, in passive warden steganography, which is the subject of this paper, we will only need codes for the noise-free case.

For memory cells drawn from an alphabet of q symbols, maximum distance separable (MDS) codes, such as Reed-Solomon codes, can be used to construct a partitioned linear code achieving the channel capacity [10]. Each coset of a $[n, n-k, k+1]$ linear MDS code contains all symbol patterns of any $n-k$ stuck cells. Since this code contains q^k cosets, they can be indexed with all possible messages consisting of k symbols. One can then communicate k message symbols by first selecting an appropriate coset and finding in this coset a word with the same pattern of stuck $n-k$ cells as in the memory. Since this word is compatible with the memory defects, it can be written to the memory. The k message symbols are extracted from the index of the coset to which the word belongs. This approach, however, would be inefficient for our application. By grouping bits into q-ary symbols, the number of stuck *symbols* could drastically increase when the number of stuck *bits* is not small, which is often the case in steganographic applications.

There are three main differences in requirements between coding for defective memory and coding for wet paper steganography. First, the number of wet pixels can be quite large (e.g., 90% or more). Second, the number of wet pixels varies significantly with the stego method and for different instances of the cover object. This makes it difficult to assume an upper bound on the rate $r = k/n$ without sacrificing embedding capacity. Third, fortunately, steganographic applications are often run off line and do not require real time performance. It is quite acceptable to spend 2 seconds to embed a 10000-bit payload, but it is not acceptable to spend this time writing data into memory.

With these differences in mind, in [5,6] the authors proposed variable-rate random linear codes and showed that these codes asymptotically (and quickly) reach the channel capacity. They also described a practical implementation using Gaussian elimination on disjoint pseudo-random subsets of fixed size. We briefly summarize this approach to WPCs in Section 2. In the first method of this paper in Section 3, we follow the same approach but propose a different realization by imposing certain stochastic structure on the columns of the parity check matrix to be able to utilize the apparatus of LT codes [13]. This approach offers greatly simplified implementation, lower computational complexity, and improved embedding efficiency. In Section 4, we apply the method of Section 2 to very small blocks with a goal to further improve the embedding efficiency for short messages in a manner somewhat similar to matrix embedding [15]. A few applications of WPCs in steganography and fragile watermarking are discussed in Section 5. The paper is summarized in Section 6.

2 Random Linear Codes for Writing on Wet Paper

Let us assume that the cover object X consists of n elements $\{x_i\}_{i=1}^n$, $x_i \in J$, where J is the range of discrete values for x_i. For example, for an 8-bit grayscale image represented in the spatial domain, $J = \{0, 1, ..., 255\}$ and n is the number of pixels in X. The sender selects k *changeable elements* x_j, $j \in C \subset \{1, 2, ..., n\}$, $|C|=k$, which is the selection channel. The changeable elements may be used and modified independently from each other by the sender to communicate a secret message to the recipient, while the remaining elements are not modified during embedding.

It is further assumed that the sender and the recipient agree on a public symbol function S, which is a mapping $S: J \rightarrow \mathbb{F}$, where $\mathbb{F}$ is a finite field of q symbols. Although we do not consider it in this paper, S could in principle depend on the element position in X and a secret stego key shared by the sender and the recipient. For simplicity, the reader can assume that $\mathbb{F}$ is the Galois Field GF(2) and $S(x)$ the LSB of x (Least Significant Bit).

During embedding, the sender either leaves the changeable elements x_j, $j \in C$, unmodified or replaces x_j with some element y_j to modify its symbol from $S(x_j)$ to $S(y_j)$. The vector of cover object symbols $b_x = (S(x_1), ..., S(x_n))^{\mathsf{T}}$ changes to $b_y = (S(y_1), ..., S(y_n))^{\mathsf{T}}$, where "$\mathsf{T}$" denotes transposition. To communicate m symbols $s = (s_1, ..., s_m)^{\mathsf{T}}$, $s_i \in \mathbb{F}$, the sender modifies the changeable elements x_j, $j \in C$, so that

$$Db_y = s, \tag{1}$$

where D is an $m \times n$ matrix with elements from $\mathbb{F}$ shared by the sender and the recipient. Thus, similar to the coset coding approach by Heegard [11], the recipient reads the message as the syndrome of the received symbol vector b_y with the parity check matrix D. Heegard chose D to guarantee that (1) has a solution for any pattern of $n-k$ stuck cells. In [5,6], the authors showed that the high volatility of k among steganographic schemes and over different covers can be well handled by randomizing Heegard's approach and choosing D as a pseudo-random $m \times n$ matrix D generated from a stego key.

To study the solvability of (1) for pseudo-random matrices D, (1) is rewritten to

$$Dv = s - Db_x \tag{2}$$

using the variable $v = b_y - b_x$ with non-zero elements corresponding to the symbols the sender must change to satisfy (1). In (2), there are k unknowns v_j, $j \in C$, while the remaining $n - k$ values v_i, $i \notin C$, are zeros. Thus, on the left hand side, the sender can remove from D all $n - k$ columns i, $i \notin C$, and also remove from v all $n - k$ elements v_i with $i \notin C$. Keeping the same symbol for v, (2) now becomes

$$Hv = z, \tag{3}$$

where H is an $m \times k$ matrix consisting of those columns of D corresponding to indices C, v is an unknown $k \times 1$ vector, and $z = s - Db_x$ is the $k \times 1$ right hand side. Thus, the sender needs to solve a system of m linear equations with k unknowns in $\mathbb{F}$. The probability that (1) will have a solution for an arbitrary message s is equal to the probability that rank$(D)=m$. The rank of random rectangular matrices over finite fields was studied in [14]. In particular, the probability P(rank$(D)=m$) = $1-O(q^{m-k})$ with decreasing m, $m < k$, k fixed.

Let us assume that the sender always tries to embed as many symbols as possible by adding rows to D while (3) still has a solution. It can be shown [6] that for random binary matrices whose elements are iid realizations of a random variable that is uniformly distributed in $\{0,1\}$, the average maximum message length $m_{\max}$ that can be communicated in this manner is

$$m_{\max} = k + O(2^{-k/4}) \tag{4}$$

as k goes to infinity, $k < n$. A similar result can be established in the same manner for a finite field $\mathbb{F}$ with q symbols. Thus, this variable-rate random linear code asymptotically (and quickly) reaches the Shannon capacity of our channel.

The main complexity of this communication is on the sender's side, who needs to solve m linear equations for k unknowns in $\mathbb{F}$. Assuming that the maximal length message $m = k$ is sent, the complexity of Gaussian elimination for (3) is $O(k^3)$, which would lead to impractical performance for large payloads, such as $k > 10^5$. In [5], the authors proposed to divide the cover object into n/n_B disjoint random subsets (determined from the shared stego key) of a fixed, predetermined size n_B and then perform the embedding for each subset separately. The complexity of embedding is proportional to $n/n_B(kn_B/n)^3 = nr^3n_B^2$, where $r = k/n$ is the rate, and is thus linear in the number of cover object elements, albeit with a large constant.

By imposing a special stochastic structure on the columns of D, we show in the next section that it is possible to use the LT process to solve (3) in a much more efficient manner with a simpler implementation that fits well the requirements for steganographic applications formulated in the introduction.

3 Realization of Wet Paper Codes Using the LT Process

3.1 LT Codes

In this section, we briefly review LT codes and their properties relevant for our application, referring the reader to [13] for more details. LT codes are universal erasure codes with low encoding and decoding complexity that asymptotically approach the Shannon capacity of the erasure channel. For simplicity, we only use binary symbols noting that the codes can work without any modification with l-bit symbols. The best way to describe the encoding process is using a bipartite graph (see an example in Fig. 1) with w message bits on the left and W encoding bits on the right. Each encoding bit is obtained as an XOR of approximately $O(\ln(w/\delta))$ randomly selected message bits that are connected to it in the graph. The graph is generated randomly so that the degrees of encoding nodes follow so-called robust soliton distribution (RSD). The probability that an encoding node has degree i, is $(\rho_i + \tau_i)/\beta$, where

$$\rho_i = \begin{cases} \dfrac{1}{w} & i=1 \\[2mm] \dfrac{1}{i(i-1)} & i=2,...,w \end{cases}, \quad \tau_i = \begin{cases} R/(iw) & i=1,...,w/R-1 \\ R\ln(R/\delta)/w & i=w/R \\ 0 & i=w/R+1,...,w \end{cases}, \quad \beta = \sum_{i=1}^{w} \rho_i + \tau_i, \tag{5}$$

and $R = c \ln(w/\delta) \sqrt{w}$ for some suitably chosen constants δ and c. It is possible to uniquely determine all w message bits with probability better than $1-\delta$ from an arbitrary set of W encoding bits as long as

$$W > \beta w = w + O(\sqrt{w} \ln^2 (w/\delta)). \qquad (6)$$

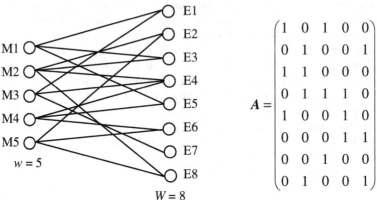

Fig. 1. Left: Bipartite graph with 5 message symbols and 8 encoding symbols. Right: Its bi-adjacency matrix.

The encoding bits can also be obtained from message bits using matrix multiplication in GF(2) with the bi-adjacency binary matrix A (Fig. 1). The decoding can be obviously done by solving a system of W linear equations with w unknowns – the message bits. The RSD allows solving the linear system by repeating the following simple operation (the LT process):

> Find an encoding bit that has only one edge (*encoding bit E7 in Fig. 1*). Its associated message bit (M3) *must be equal to this encoding bit. As the message bit is now known, we can XOR it with all encoding bits that are connected to it (E1 and E4) and remove it and all its edges from the graph. In doing so, new encoding nodes of degree one* (E1) *may be created. This process is repeated till all message bits are recovered.*

The decoding process fails if, at some point, there are no encoding bits of degree 1, while there are still some undetermined message bits. The RSD was derived so that the probability of failure of the LT process to recover all message bits is smaller than δ. The decoding requires on average $O(w \ln(w/\delta))$ operations.

3.2 Matrix LT Process

We can consider the LT process as a method for a fast solution of an *over-determined* system of equations $Ax = y$ with a random matrix A for which the Hamming weights of its rows follow the RSD. However, we cannot use it directly to solve (3) because (3) is *under-determined* and we are seeking one solution, possibly out of many solutions. In addition, because H was obtained from D by removing columns, H inherits the distribution of Hamming weights of columns from D but not the distribution of its rows. However, as explained in detail below, the LT process can be used to quickly bring H to the *upper* triangular form simply by permuting its rows and columns. Once in this form, (3) is solved using a back substitution.

The LT process on the bipartite graph induces the following row/column swapping process on its bi-adjacency matrix A. For an n-dimensional binary vector r, let $w_j(r)$ denote the Hamming weight of $(r_j, ..., r_n)$ (e.g., $w_1(r) \equiv w(r)$ is the usual Hamming weight of r). We first find a row r in A with $w_1(r) = 1$ (say, the 1 is in the j_1-th column) and exchange it with the first row. Then, we exchange the 1st and the j_1-th unknowns (swapping the 1st and j_1-th columns). At this point in the LT process, the value of the unknown No. 1 is determined from the first equation. In the matrix process, however, we do not evaluate the unknowns because we are only interested in bringing A to a *lower* triangular form by permuting its rows and columns. Continuing the process, we search for another row r with $w_2(r) = 1$ (say, the 1 is in the j_2-th column). If the LT process proceeds successfully, we must be able to do so. We swap this row with the second row and swap the 2nd and j_2-th columns. We continue in this way, now looking for a row r with $w_3(r) = 1$, etc. At the end of this process, the permuted matrix A will be lower diagonal with ones on its main diagonal.

Returning to the WPC of Section 2, we need to solve the system $Hv = z$ with m equations for k unknowns, $m < k$. By applying the above process of row and column permutations to H^T, we bring H to the form $[U, H']$, where U is a square $m \times m$ upper triangular matrix with ones on its main diagonal and H' is a binary $m \times (k-m)$ matrix. We can work directly with H if we replace in the algorithm above the word 'row' with 'column' and vice versa[1]. In order for this to work, however, the Hamming weights of *columns* of H must follow the RSD and the message length m must satisfy (from (6))

$$k > \beta m = m + O(\sqrt{m} \ln^2(m/\delta)). \tag{7}$$

This means that there is a small capacity loss of $O(\sqrt{m} \ln^2(m/\delta))$ in exchange for solving (3) quickly using the matrix LT process. This loss depends on the public parameters c and δ. Since the bounds in Luby's analysis are not tight, we experimented with a larger range for δ, ignoring its probabilistic interpretation. We discovered that it was advantageous to set δ to a much larger number (e.g., $\delta = 5$) and, if necessary, repeat the encoding process with a slightly larger matrix D till a successful pass through the LT process is obtained. For $c = 0.1$, the capacity loss was about 10% ($\beta = 1.1$) of k for $k=1500$ with probability of successful encoding about 50%. This probability increases and capacity loss decreases with increasing k (see Table 1).

To assess the encoding and decoding complexity, let us assume that the maximal length message is sent, $m \approx k/\beta$. The density of 1's in D (and thus in H) is $O(\ln(k/\delta)/k)$. Therefore, the encoding complexity of the WPC implemented using the LT process is $O(n \ln(k/\delta) + k \ln(k/\delta)) = O(n \ln(k/\delta))$. The first term arises from evaluating the product Db_x, while the second term is the complexity of the LT process. This

---

[1] To distinguish this process, which pertains to a binary matrix, from the original LT process designed for bi-partite graphs, we call it the "matrix LT process".

is a significant savings compared to solving (3) using Gaussian elimination. The decoding complexity is $O(n \ln(k/\delta))$, which corresponds to evaluating the product Db_y.

Table 1. Running time (in seconds) for solving $k \times k$ and $k \times \beta k$ linear systems using Gaussian elimination and matrix LT process ($c = 0.1$, $\delta = 5$); P is the probability of a successful pass

k	Gauss	LT	β	P
1000	0.023	0.008	1.098	43%
10000	17.4	0.177	1.062	75%
30000	302	0.705	1.047	82%
100000	9320	3.10	1.033	90%

The performance comparison between solving (3) using Gaussian elimination and the matrix LT process is shown in Table 1. The steeply increasing complexity of Gaussian elimination necessitates dividing the cover object into subsets as in [5]. The LT process, however, enables solving (3) for the whole object at once, which greatly simplifies implementation and decreases computational complexity at the same time. In addition, as will be seen in Section 4, the matrix LT process can modified to improve the embedding efficiency.

3.3 Communicating the Message Length

Note that for the matrix LT process, the Hamming weights of columns of H (and thus D) must follow the RSD that depends on m, which is unavailable to the decoder. Below, we show a simple solution to this problem, although other alternatives exist.

Let us assume that the parameter m can be encoded using h bits (in practice, $h \sim 20$ should be sufficient). Using the stego key, the sender divides the cover X into two pseudo-random disjoint subsets X_h and $X - X_h$ and communicates h bits using elements from X_h and the main message using elements from $X - X_h$. We must make sure that X_h will contain at least h changeable elements, which can be arranged for by requesting that $|X_h|$ be a few percent larger than h/r_{min}, where r_{min} is the minimal value of the rate $r = k/n$ that can be typically encountered (this depends on the specifics of the steganographic scheme and properties of the covers). Then, using the stego key the sender generates a pseudo-random $h \times |X_h|$ binary matrix D_h with density of 1's equal to ½. The sender embeds h bits in X_h by solving the WPC equations (3) with matrix D_h using a simple Gaussian elimination, which will be fast because D_h has a small number of rows. The message bits are hidden in $X - X_h$ using the matrix LT process with matrix D generated from the stego key using the parameter m.

The decoder first uses his stego key (and the knowledge of h and r_{min}) to determine the subset X_h and the matrix D_h. Then, the decoder extracts m (h bits) as the syndrome (1) with matrix D_h and the symbol vector obtained from X_h. Knowing m, the decoder now generates D and extracts the message bits as a syndrome (1) with matrix D and the symbol vector obtained from $X - X_h$.

4   Embedding Efficiency

The number of embedding changes in the cover object influences the detectability of hidden data in a major manner. The smaller the number of changes, the smaller the chance that any statistics used by an attacker will be disrupted enough to mount a successful attack. Thus, schemes with a higher embedding efficiency (number of random message bits embedded per embedding change) are less likely to be successfully attacked than schemes with a lower embedding efficiency.

The first general methodology to improving embedding efficiency of data hiding schemes was described by Crandall [15] who proposed an approach using covering codes (Matrix Embedding). This idea was later made popular by Westfeld in his F5 algorithm [2]. A formal equivalence between embedding schemes and covering codes is due to Galand and Kabatiansky [16]. From their work, we know that the number of messages that can be communicated by making at most l changes in a binary vector of length k is bounded from above by $2^{kh(l/k)}$, where $h(x) = -x\log_2(x) - (1-x)\log_2(1-x)$, assuming $k \to \infty$ and $l/k = const. < 1/2$. Additionally, they pointed out that embedding schemes based on random linear coverings asymptotically achieve this bound, which means that the bound is tight.

Using this result, we can now derive an upper bound on the embedding efficiency, which is defined as the ratio between the payload length m and the number of embedding changes l. Let $\mathbf{H}$ be the $m \times k$ binary matrix from (3). Assuming the Hamming weight of v is at most l (i.e., we perform up to l embedding changes out of k possible changes), we have for the payload length m, $m \le k\, h(l/k)$, or

$$\frac{m}{l} \le \frac{m/k}{h^{-1}(m/k)}, \tag{8}$$

where h^{-1} is the inverse of h on $[0, 1/2]$.

4.1   Block Minimal Method

In general, the problem of finding a solution to (3) with the minimum Hamming weight is an NP complete problem. For a very small m, however, it is possible to find the minimal Hamming weight solution quickly using brute force. This suggests applying the method of Section 2 on small blocks. The sender and receiver agree on a small integer p (e.g., $p < 20$) and using the stego key divide the cover object into $n_B = m/p$ disjoint random blocks of cardinality $n/n_B = pn/m$. Each block will contain on average $rpn/m = pk/m$ changeable elements (for simplicity we assume the quantities above are all integers). The sender will use a random binary $p \times pn/m$ matrix $\mathbf{D}_B$ for embedding up to p bits in each block as follows.

Let $\mathbf{H}_B$ be a submatrix of $\mathbf{D}_B$ with columns corresponding to changeable elements and C_1 be the set of *unique* columns of $\mathbf{H}_B$. Note that $\mathbf{H}_B$ will in general be different for different blocks. For two sets C, C' of binary vectors from $\{0,1\}^p$, we define $C \oplus C' = \{x \in \{0,1\}^p | x = c + c', c \in C, c' \in C'\}$, arithmetic in GF(2). Messages $s \in C_1$ can be communicated using one change, messages $s \in C_2 = C_1 \oplus C_1 - C_1$ using two changes, in general, messages $s \in C_i = C_{i-1} \oplus C_1 - (C_1 \cup \ldots \cup C_{i-1})$ using i changes[2]. If $\bigcup_{i=1}^{p} C_i = \{0,1\}^p$, which happens if and only if rank(H_B)=p, the system $H_B v = z$ will have a solution for all $z \in \{0,1\}^p$. The probability of this is $1 - O(2^{p(1-k/m)})$, which quickly approaches 1 with decreasing message length m (for p and k fixed) or with increasing p (for m and k fixed) because $m < k$.

The average number of changes, l_p, in each block can be obtained as

$$l_p(r,k,m) = E\{|v|\} = 2^{-p} \sum_{i=1}^{p} iE\{|C_i|\},$$ (9)

where the expected value is taken over random messages and $p \times pn/m$ matrices D_B from which columns are selected with probability r (to obtain H_B). Since the number of columns in H_B is approximately pk/m, l_p is mostly a function of the ratio k/m rather than the specific values of r, k, or m. From Fig. 2, we see that the embedding efficiency p/l_p increases with shorter messages (larger k/m) for a fixed p and it also increases in a curious non-monotonic manner with increasing p for k/m fixed. In general, one should use as large p as possible. In theory, when $p=m$, we would obtain the optimal solution with the smallest Hamming weight. However, a practical limit on the largest usable p is imposed by a rapidly increasing computational complexity. The most expensive operation in determining the set C_i is the term $C_{i-1} \oplus C_1$, which may require up to $p2^{2p-2}$ bit XOR operations. To obtain reasonable running times, we recommend $p \le 18$ (see Table 2 generated on a PC equipped with a 3.5GHz Pentium IV). We also note that the WPC based on random linear codes (Section 2) or LT process (Section3) achieves embedding efficiency of only about 2.

Table 2. Embedding time (in seconds) for $n=10^6$, $k=5 \times 10^4$ for Block Minimal method

k/m	2	3	4	5	6	7	8	9	10
p=16	2.86	1.72	1.24	0.92	0.76	0.64	0.52	0.42	0.43
p=17	8.80	5.38	3.78	3.01	2.50	2.18	1.60	1.53	1.45
p=18	27.92	17.53	12.41	9.67	7.87	7.54	5.87	5.66	4.83

For small k/m, the probability that rank(H_B)<p may become large enough to encounter a failure to embed in certain blocks. For example, for $p = 18$ and $k/m = 2$, Prob(rank(H_B)<18) ≈ 0.003. We note that this problem is not an issue for k/m>3 as this probability is very small. The encoder needs to communicate the number of bits embedded in each block. Let us assume k, n, and m are fixed. For the i-th block, let p_i be the largest integer for which the first p_i rows of H_B form a matrix of rank p_i. Furthermore, let $f(q)$, $q = p$, $p-1$, $\ldots$, 0, be the probability distribution of p_i over the blocks and random matrices H_B. The information necessary to communicate p_i is $H(f)$, the entropy[3] of f. The average number of bits that can be encoded per block is thus

---

[2] The symbol '–' stands for the set difference.

[3] In practice, the compressed bit-stream will be slightly larger than $H(f)$. Since f is not known to the decoder beforehand, adaptive coders, such as adaptive arithmetic coder, should be used.

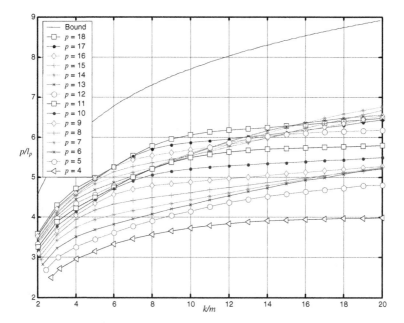

Fig. 2. Embedding efficiency for Block Minimal method as a function of k/m for various p and $r=1/20$. The upper bound is given by (8)

$E(f)-H(f) \leq p$ because $E(f) \leq p$. Thus, the pure payload $m' = m(E(f)-H(f))/p$ that can be embedded is slightly smaller than m. From Table 3, we see that this loss is negligible for $k/m \geq 2$. It also limits the Block Minimal method to cases with $k/m > 1.4$ (i.e., the method cannot be used when the payload is longer than roughly 70% of the maximal embeddable message).

Table 3. Capacity loss for $n=10^6$, $k=50000$, $p=18$, for Block Minimal method

k/m	1.1	1.2	1.3	1.4	1.5	1.6	1.7	1.8	1.9	2	3
k/m'	1.42	1.42	1.44	1.49	1.56	1.63	1.72	1.81	1.90	2.006	3.000

From the practical point of view, the sequence p_i should be compressed and then embedded, for example, one bit per block, as the first bit in each block. The decoder first extracts p bits from each block, decompresses the bit sequence formed by the first bits from each block, reads p_i for all blocks, and then discards $p-p_i$ bits from the end of each block message chunk.

In Fig. 3, we show the embedding efficiency p/l_p as a function of k/m for $p=18$ and compare the performance to other approaches. The graph takes into account the capacity loss discussed in the paragraph above.

We note that this approach can be considered as some stochastic form of matrix embedding. In matrix embedding, *all* cover elements can be modified, which means the encoder can for example choose $\boldsymbol{D}_B$ to be the $p \times (2^p-1)$ parity check matrix of a

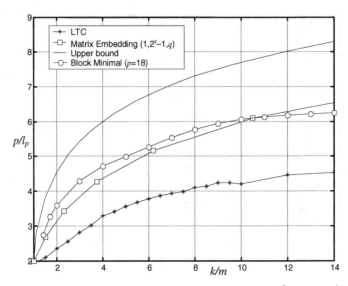

Fig. 3. Embedding efficiency as a function of the ratio k/m for $n = 10^6$, $k = 5 \times 10^4$. The curves show the upper bound (8), Matrix Embedding for $q = 1, \ldots, 6$ (assuming all n elements can be changed or $k = n$), Block Minimal, and the LTC algorithm (see Section 4.2).

binary Hamming code [2] and always have at most one embedding change ($C_1 = \{0,1\}^p$) to embed p bits in $2^p - 1$ pixels – matrix embedding $(1, 2^p - 1, p)$. In our application, however, we work with H_B, which is obtained as a submatrix of D_B defined by the selection channel. Thus, we cannot guarantee that $C_1 = \{0,1\}^p$ and have to allow more than one embedding change.

4.2 Improving Embedding Efficiency with LT Process (LTC Algorithm)

In this section, we present a few simple modification of the matrix LT process with the goal to decrease the Hamming weight of the obtained solution *without significantly increasing the computational complexity*. Recalling Section 3.2, if the columns of D follow the RSD, the system $Hv = z$ can be brought to the form $[U, H']\tilde{v} = \tilde{z}$, where U is an $m \times m$ upper triangular matrix, H' is a binary $m \times (k-m)$ matrix, and $\tilde{v}$, $\tilde{z}$ are correspondingly permuted vectors v and z. By setting $\tilde{v}_i = 0$ for $i > m$ and solving the rest using back substitution, we have $w(\tilde{v}) \approx m/2$ (assuming random message bits independent of the cover), which gives an embedding efficiency of roughly 2.

There are several avenues to be explored to improve the embedding efficiency. First, the shorter the message, the more choices will the encoder have for selecting the columns in the matrix LT process and thus "steer" the algorithm to decrease $w(\tilde{v})$.

Second, the RSD was derived for the case when $k = \beta m$. It is quite possible that for shorter messages, some other distribution will be more suitable for our goal. Note that this problem does not have any equivalent for the erasure codes because there is no need to collect more than the minimal necessary number of symbols for decoding. We postpone the question of the column weight distribution to our future research and in this section only briefly investigate the first option.

Recall that in the i-th step in the matrix LT process on H, we select a column c in H with $w_i(c) = 1$. The set of columns c with $w_i(c) = 1$ will be called *ripple* at the i-th step (note the difference in terminology as used in [13]). Note that if $\tilde{z}_i = 0$, for all $i > i_0$, the matrix LT process can be stopped after i_0 steps because we can set $\tilde{v}_i = 0$, $i > i_0$. Also, the smaller the index i_0, the more zeros there will be in $\tilde{v}$. Thus, in our choice of columns from the ripple we should prefer columns c, where the 1 is in row j for which $\tilde{z}_j = 1$. This way, all 1's in $\tilde{z}$ will hopefully be "depleted" sooner, producing a smaller i_0 and thus a solution with a smaller Hamming weight. To further utilize the remaining degree of freedom in our choice of columns from the ripple, it is advantageous to prefer denser columns in steps $i<i_0$, while preferring sparser columns in steps $i\geq i_0$. An explanation of this "recipe" is skipped due to lack of space in this paper.

Because the LT process has no effect on $w(\tilde{z}) = w(z)$, we must have $i_0 \geq w(z)$. In the best case when $i_0 = w(z)$, the expected value of $w(\tilde{v})$ will be approximately $w(z)/2$ (assuming U is random). Because the expected value of $w(z)$ taken over random messages is $m/2$, we cannot obtain better embedding efficiency than 4.

To further improve the efficiency, we observe that the smaller the $w(z)$, the smaller the $w(\tilde{v})$. Thus, it might be possible to reduce $w(z)$ before the LT process starts by adding selected columns of H to z. Keeping in mind that we need to preserve the low computational complexity of the matrix LT process, we propose the following simple and intuitive preprocessing step. Before starting the matrix LT process, we search for a column c in H such that $w(z-c) < w(z) - \log_2(m)$. If such columns exist, we choose the one leading to the smallest Hamming weight $w(z-c)$. We subtract c from z, remove it from H, assign 1 to the corresponding component of v, and search for another column. This is repeated until no such column can be found. The term $\log_2(m)$ is our ad hoc choice that gave us a good compromise between a small increase in computational complexity and performance improvement. Note that the embedding rate can now grow without a limit for increasing k/m because the probability of finding a well-fitting column increases with increasing k/m.

The embedding efficiency of the LTC algorithm, that includes some other minor improvements not described in this paper, is shown in Fig. 3. Its computational complexity is roughly comparable to the matrix LT process of Section 3.

We note that there are other simple measures that can be adopted to further improve the performance of the matrix LT process. For example, our preliminary experiments indicate that allowing occasional row adding during the matrix LT process has the potential to improve the embedding efficiency as well as significantly increase the probability of a successful pass. This issue is part of our future research.

We close this section with an observation that in steganography there is another possibility to minimize the impact of embedding changes different from increasing the embedding efficiency. Depending on the selection criteria applied by the sender, each changeable element can be assigned a numerical value, or changeability score, that somehow captures how undetectable the modification of that element is. For example, elements in highly textured areas of the cover image may have a higher score than elements in less textured areas. For short messages of length m, one may be better off (depending on the score distribution) narrowing the set of changeable elements from k to those $k' = \beta m$ elements with the highest score instead of maximizing the embedding efficiency with k changeable elements, $k \gg m$.

5 Applications in Steganography

Wet paper codes free the sender from having to consider the problem of communicating the selection channel to the recipient and thus they give him complete freedom in choosing the placement of embedding modifications. In adaptive steganography, for example, because the act of embedding itself modifies the cover, special care usually needs to be taken to make sure that the recipient identifies the same selection channel. WPCs not only solve this problem but also allow the sender to use selection channels that are *in principle* unavailable to the recipient and thus any attacker, such as channels determined from a high-resolution (or unquantized) version of the cover (see Perturbed Quantization Steganography [5] for more details).

Public key steganography [1] also benefits from WPCs because they enable message extraction without revealing any information about the selection channel. Thus, the matrix D can be made public to allow everybody to extract from the stego object a message potentially encrypted using an asymmetric cryptography without revealing any information about the placement of the embedding changes. Additionally, because each message bit is extracted as an XOR of many elements (e.g., $\ln(k/\delta)$ elements for the implementation using the matrix LT process), the "power of parity" [1] further helps mask the presence of secret message.

Another interesting application is the possibility to construct steganographic methods that cannot be subjected to brute force stego key searches of the type [17] because the embedding can contain an element of true randomness.

Lastly, we mention data hiding in binary images. In [18], the sender first identifies the set of "flippable" pixels that can be modified for embedding. Because the act of embedding itself modifies the pixel "flippability" status, the set of flippable pixels can not be shared with the recipient. To solve this problem, Wu proposed block embedding combined with random shuffling. The block embedding however, leaves most of the flippable pixels unused, leaving only a fraction of the embedding capacity for the payload. Because this situation exactly corresponds to writing on wet paper, the capacity of this data embedding method can be dramatically improved using WPCs [19]. In this application, the WPCs with improved embedding efficiency (Section 4) are particularly important as they help decrease the visual impact of embedding.

6 Summary

Wet paper codes enable steganography with non-shared (arbitrary) selection channels. In this paper, we describe a new approach (the matrix LT process) to wet paper codes using the apparatus developed for irregular low-density parity check erasure codes called LT codes. The new approach offers greatly simplified implementation and a substantially decreased computational complexity. We also present a few simple modifications of the matrix LT process to improve the embedding efficiency while preserving its low computational complexity. Additionally, we introduce another, different, approach to wet paper codes called Block Minimal embedding that provides significantly improved embedding efficiency and also enjoys low computational complexity suitable for steganographic applications. Finally, we briefly discuss a few applications to steganography and data embedding.

Acknowledgements

The work on this paper was supported by Air Force Research Laboratory, Air Force Material Command, USAF, under the research grants number FA8750-04-1-0112 and F30602-02-2-0093. The U.S. Government is authorized to reproduce and distribute reprints for Governmental purposes notwithstanding any copyright notation there on. The views and conclusions contained herein are those of the authors and should not be interpreted as necessarily representing the official policies, either expressed or implied, of Air Force Research Laboratory, or the U. S. Government. Special thanks belong to Petr Lisoněk for directing our attention to LT codes.

References

1. Anderson, R.J. and Petitcolas, F.A.P.: "On the Limits of Steganography". IEEE Journal of Selected Areas in Communications. Special Issue on Copyright and Privacy Protection, vol. **16**(4) (1998) 474–481
2. Westfeld, A. "High Capacity Despite Better Steganalysis (F5–A Steganographic Algorithm)". In: Moskowitz, I.S. (ed.): Information Hiding. 4th International Workshop. Lecture Notes in Computer Science, vol. 2137. Springer-Verlag, Berlin Heidelberg New York (2001) 289–302
3. Karahan, M., Topkara, U., Atallah, M., Taskiran, C., Lin, E., and Delp, E.: "A Hierarchical Protocol for Increasing the Stealthiness of Steganographic Methods". Proc. ACM Multimedia and Security Workshop. Magdeburg Germany (2004) 16–24
4. Westfeld, A. and Böhme, R.: "Exploiting Preserved Statistics for Steganalysis". In: Fridrich, J. (ed.): Information Hiding. 6th International Workshop. Lecture Notes in Computer Science, vol. 3200. Springer-Verlag, Berlin Heidelberg New York (2004) 67–81
5. Fridrich, J., Goljan, M., and Soukal, D.: "Perturbed Quantization Steganography with Wet Paper Codes". Proc. ACM Multimedia and Security Workshop. Magdeburg Germany (2004) 4–15
6. Fridrich, J., Goljan, M., Lisoněk, P., and Soukal, D.: "Writing on Wet Paper", (journal version) to appear in IEEE Trans. on Sig. Proc. Special Issue on Media Security (2005)
7. Fridrich, J., Goljan, M., Lisoněk, P., and Soukal, D.: "Writing on Wet Paper", Proc. SPIE, Electronic Imaging, Security, Steganography, and Watermarking of Multimedia Contents VII. San Jose (2005) 328–340
8. Kuznetsov, A.V. and Tsybakov, B.S.: "Coding in a Memory with Defective Cells". Probl. Inform. Transmission, vol. **10**. (1974) 132–138
9. Gelfand, S.I. and Pinsker, M.S.: "Coding for Channel with Random Parameters". Probl. Pered. Inform. (Probl. Inform. Transm.), vol. **9**(1). (1980) 19–31
10. Zamir, R., Shamai, S., and Erez, U.: "Nested Linear/Lattice Codes for Structured Multiterminal Binning". IEEE Trans. Inf. Th., vol. **48**(6). (2002) 1250–1276
11. Heegard, C.: "Partitioned Linear Block Codes for Computer Memory with 'Stuck-at' Defects". *IEEE Trans. Inf. Th.* vol. **29**. (1983) 831–842

12. Heegard, C. and El-Gamal, A.: "On the Capacity of Computer Memory with Defects". IEEE Trans. Inf. Th., vol. **29**. (1983) 731–739
13. Luby, M.: "LT Codes", Proc. The 43rd Annual IEEE Symposium on Foundations of Computer Science. (2002) 271–282
14. Brent, R.P., Gao, S., and Lauder, A.G.B.: "Random Krylov Spaces Over Finite Fields". SIAM J. Discrete Math. vol. **16**(2). (2003) 276–287
15. Crandall, R.: "Some Notes on Steganography". Posted on Steganography Mailing List. http://os.inf.tu-dresden.de/~westfeld/crandall.pdf (1998)
16. Galand, F. and Kabatiansky, G.: "Information Hiding by Coverings". Proc. ITW2003. Paris France (2003) 151–154
17. Fridrich, J., Goljan, M., Soukal, D., and Holotyak, T.: "Forensic Steganalysis: Determining the Stego Key in Spatial Domain Steganography". Proc. SPIE, Electronic Imaging, Security, Steganography, and Watermarking of Multimedia Contents VII. San Jose (2005) 631–642
18. Wu, M., Tang E., and Liu B., "Data Hiding in Digital Binary Image". Proc. Conf. on Multimedia & Expo (CD version). New York (2000)
19. Wu, M., Fridrich, J., Goljan, M., and Gou, H.: "Data Hiding in Digital Binary Images: A Revisit". Proc. SPIE, Electronic Imaging, Security, Steganography, and Watermarking of Multimedia Contents VII. San Jose (2005) 194–205

Translation-Based Steganography

Christian Grothoff, Krista Grothoff, Ludmila Alkhutova,
Ryan Stutsman, and Mikhail Atallah

CERIAS, Purdue University
{christian, krista}@grothoff.org,
{lalkhuto, rstutsma}@purdue.edu, mja@cs.purdue.edu

Abstract. This paper investigates the possibilities of steganographically embedding information in the "noise" created by automatic translation of natural language documents. Because the inherent redundancy of natural language creates plenty of room for variation in translation, machine translation is ideal for steganographic applications. Also, because there are frequent errors in legitimate automatic text translations, additional errors inserted by an information hiding mechanism are plausibly undetectable and would appear to be part of the normal noise associated with translation. Significantly, it should be extremely difficult for an adversary to determine if inaccuracies in the translation are caused by the use of steganography or by deficiencies of the translation software.

1 Introduction

This paper presents a new protocol for covert message transfer in natural language text, for which we have a proof-of-concept implementation. The key idea is to hide information in the noise that occurs invariably in natural language translation. When translating a non-trivial text between a pair of natural languages, there are typically many possible translations. Selecting one of these translations can be used to encode information. In order for an adversary to detect the hidden message transfer, the adversary would have to show that the generated translation containing the hidden message could not be plausibly generated by ordinary translation. Because natural language translation is particularly noisy, this is inherently difficult. For example, the existence of synonyms frequently allows for multiple correct translations of the same text. The possibility of erroneous translations increases the number of plausible variations and thus the opportunities for hiding information.

This paper evaluates the potential of covert message transfer in natural language translation that uses automatic machine translation (MT). In order to characterize which variations in machine translations are plausible, we have looked into the different kinds of errors that are generated by various MT systems. Some of the variations that were observed in the machine translations are also clearly plausible for manual translations by humans.

In addition to making it difficult for the adversary to detect the presence of a hidden message, translation-based steganography is also easier to use. The reason

M. Barni et al. (Eds.): IH 2005, LNCS 3727, pp. 219–233, 2005.

for this is that unlike previous text-, image- or sound-based steganographic systems, the cover does not have to be secret. In translation-based steganography, the original text in the source language can be publically known, obtained from public sources, and, together with the translation, exchanged between the two parties in plain sight of the adversary. In traditional image steganography, the problem often occurs that the source image in which the message is subsequently hidden must be kept secret by the sender and used only once (as otherwise a "diff" attack would reveal the presence of a hidden message). This burdens the user with creating a new, secret cover for each message.

Translation-based steganography does not suffer from this drawback, since the adversary cannot apply a differential analysis to a translation to detect the hidden message. The adversary may produce a translation of the original message, but the translation is likely to differ regardless of the use of steganography, making the differential analysis useless for detecting a hidden message.

To demonstrate this, we have implemented a steganographic encoder and decoder. The system hides messages by changing machine translations in ways that are similar to the variations and errors that were observed in the existing MT systems. An interactive version of the prototype is available on our webpage.[1]

The remainder of the paper is structured as follows. First, Section 2 reviews related work. In Section 3, the basic protocol of the steganographic exchange is described. In Section 4, we give a characterization of errors produced in existing machine translation systems. The implementation and some experimental results are sketched in Section 5. In Section 6, we discuss variations on the basic protocol, together with various attacks and possible defenses.

2   Related Work

The goal of both steganography and watermarking is to embed information into a digital object, also referred to as the cover, in such a manner that the information becomes part of the object. It is understood that the embedding process should not significantly degrade the quality of the cover. Steganographic and watermarking schemes are categorized by the type of data that the cover belongs to, such as text, images or sound.

2.1   Steganography

In steganography, the very existence of the secret message must not be detectable. A successful attack consists of detecting the existence of the hidden message, even without removing it (or learning what it is). This can be done through, for example, sophisticated statistical analyses and comparisons of objects with and without hidden information.

Traditional linguistic steganography has used limited syntactically-correct text generation [22] (sometimes with the addition of so-called "style templates") and semantically-equivalent word substitutions within an existing plaintext as a

---

[1] http://www.cs.purdue.edu/homes/rstutsma/stego/

medium in which to hide messages. Wayner [22,23] introduced the notion of using precomputed context-free grammars as a method of generating steganographic text without sacrificing syntactic and semantic correctness. Note that semantic correctness is only guaranteed if the manually constructed grammar enforces the production of semantically cohesive text. Chapman and Davida [4] improved on the simple generation of syntactically correct text by syntactically tagging large corpora of homogeneous data in order to generate grammatical "style templates"; these templates were used to generate text which not only had syntactic and lexical variation, but whose consistent register and "style" could potentially pass a casual reading by a human observer. Chapman et al [5], later developed a technique in which semantically equivalent substitutions were made in known plaintexts in order to encode messages. Semantically-driven information hiding is a relatively recent innovation, as described for watermarking schemes in Atallah et al [2]. Wayner [22,23] detailed text-based approaches that are strictly statistical in nature. However, in general, linguistic approaches to steganography have been relatively limited. Damage to language is relatively easy for a human to detect. It does not take much modification of a text to make it ungrammatical in a native speaker's judgement; furthermore, even syntactically correct texts can violate semantic constraints.

Non-linguistic approaches to steganography have sometimes used lower-order bits in images and sound encodings to hide the data, providing a certain amount of freedom in the encoding in which to hide information [23]. The problem with these approaches is that the information is easily destroyed (the encoding lacks robustness, which is a particular problem for watermarking), that the original data source (for example the original image) must not be disclosed to avoid easy detection, and that a statistical analysis can still often detect the use of steganography (see, e.g., [8,13,14,19,23], to mention a few).

2.2 Machine Translation

Most Machine Translation (MT) systems in use today are statistical MT systems based on models derived from a corpus, transfer systems that are based on linguistic rules for the translations, or hybrid systems that combine the two approaches. Other translation methodologies, such as semantic MT exist, but are not considered further as they are not commonly available at this time.

In statistical MT [1,3], the system is trained using a bilingual parallel corpus to construct a *translation model*. The translation model gives the translator statistical information about likely word alignments. A word alignment [17,18] is a correspondence between words in the source sentence and the target sentence. For example, for English-French translations, the system "learns" that the English word "not" typically corresponds to the two French words "ne pas". The statistical MT systems are also trained with a uni-lingual corpus in the target language to construct a *language model* which is used to estimate what constructions are common in the target language. The translator then performs an approximate search in the space of all possible translations, trying to maximize the likelihood of the translation to score high in both the translation model and the language model. The selection of the training data for the construction of the models is crucial for the quality of the statistical MT system.

3 Protocol

The basic steganographic protocol for this paper works as follows. The sender first needs to obtain a cover in the source language. The cover does not have to be secret and can be obtained from public sources - for example, a news website. The sender then translates the sentences in the source text into the target language using the steganographic encoder. The steganographic encoder essentially creates multiple translations for each sentence and selects one of these to encode bits from the hidden message. The translated text is then transmitted to the receiver, together with information that is sufficient to obtain the source text. This can either be the source text itself or a reference to the source. The receiver then also performs the translation of the source text using the same steganographic encoder configuration. By comparing the resulting sentences, the receiver reconstructs the bitstream of the hidden message. Figure 1 illustrates the basic protocol.

The adversary is assumed to know about the existence of this basic protocol and is also able to obtain the source text and to perform translations. It is not practical for the adversary to flag all seemingly machine-translated messages which do not correspond exactly to translations generated from the cover source by well-known MT systems. There are two reasons for this. First, there are too many variants of MT software out there (frequently produced by "tweaking" existing ones), many of which are not advertised or made public. Second, even if there was a single universal MT software copy that everyone uses, there are still wildly differing behaviors for it depending on the corpus on which it is trained – there are too many such potential corpora to track, especially as users seek better translation quality by using a corpus particularly suited to their application domain (e.g., news stories about home construction costs and markets).

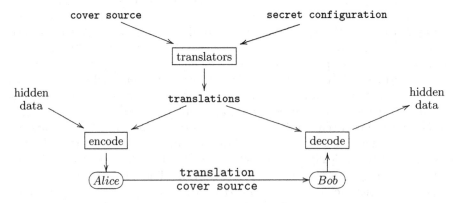

Fig. 1. Illustration of the basic protocol. The adversary can observe the public news and the message between Alice and Bob containing the selected translation and the (possibly public) cover source.

The adversary does not have access to the specific configuration of the steganographic encoder (which acts like a secret key). This configuration consists of everything that determines which translations are generated, such as the specific translation algorithms, the corpora used to train any user-generated translation systems which may be employed, rules, and dictionaries. It is assumed that the secret is transmitted using standard secret-sharing protocols and the specifics are not covered here. However, it should be noted that the size of the secret that is transmitted is flexible, based upon the user's choices; users can choose to simply share information about the settings of the encoder, or might choose to transmit entire corpora used to train a user-generated MT system. This varies based upon individual users' needs.

As with most steganographic systems, the hidden message itself can be encrypted with a secret key, making it harder for the adversary to perform guessing attacks on the secret configuration (as configurations of the steganographic system result in a random bitstream for the hidden message).

3.1   Producing Translations

The first step for both sender and receiver after obtaining the source text is to produce multiple translations of the source text using the same algorithm. The goal of this step is to deterministically produce multiple different translations of the source text. The simplest approach to achieve this is to apply (a subset of) all available MT systems on each sentence in the source text. If the parties have full access to the code of a statistical MT system, they can generate multiple MT systems from the same codebase by training it with different corpora.

In addition to generating different sentences using multiple translation systems it is also possible to apply post-processing on the resulting translations to obtain additional variations. Such post-processing includes transformations that mimic the noise inherent in any (MT) translation. For example, post-processors could insert common translation mistakes (as discussed in Section 4).

As translation quality differs between different engines and also depends on which post-processors were applied to manipulate the result, the translation system uses a heuristic to assign a probability to each translation that describes its relative quality compared to the other translations. The heuristic can be based on both experience with the generators and algorithms that rank sentence quality based on language models [6]. The specific set of translation engines, training corpora and post-processing operations that are used to generate the translations and their ranking are part of the secret shared by the two parties that want to carry out the covert communication.

3.2   Selecting a Translation

When selecting a translation to encode the hidden message, the encoder first builds a Huffman tree [12] of the available translations using the probabilities assigned by the generator algorithm. Then the algorithm selects the sentence that corresponds to the bit-sequence that is to be encoded.[2]

Using a Huffman tree to select sentences in accordance with their translation quality estimate ensures that sentences that are assumed to have a low translation quality are selected less often. Furthermore, the lower the quality of the selected translation, the higher the number of transmitted bits.

This reduces the total amount of cover text required and thus the amount of text the adversary can analyze. The encoder can use a lower limit on the relative translation quality to eliminate sentences from consideration where the estimated translation quality is below a certain threshold, in which case that threshold becomes part of the shared secret between sender and receiver.

3.3 Keeping the Source Text Secret

The presented scheme can be adapted to be suitable for watermarking where it would be desirable to keep the source text secret. This can be achieved as follows. The encoder computes a (cryptographic) hash of each translated sentence. It then selects a sentence such that the last bit of the hash of the translated sentence corresponds to the next bit in the hidden message that is to be transmitted. The decoder then just computes the hash codes of the received sentences and concatenates the respective lowest bits to obtain the hidden message.

This scheme assumes that sentences are long enough to almost always have enough variation to obtain a hash with the desired lowest bit. Error-correcting codes must be used to correct errors whenever none of the sentences produces an acceptable hash code. Using this variation reduces the bitrate that can be achieved by the encoding. More details on this can be found in our technical report [11].

4 Lost in Translation

Modern MT systems produce a number of common errors in translations. This section characterizes some of these errors. While the errors we describe are not a comprehensive list of possible errors, they are representative of the types of errors we commonly observed in our sample translations. An extended characterization of translation errors can be found in our technical report (omitted here due to space limitations). Most of these errors are caused by the reliance on statistical and syntactic text analysis by contemporary MT systems, resulting in a lack of semantic and contextual awareness. This produces an array of error types that we can use to plausibly alter text, generating further marking possibilities.

4.1 Functional Words

One class of errors that occurs rather frequently without destroying meaning is that of incorrectly-translated functional words such as articles, pronouns, and

---

[2] Wayner [22,23] uses Huffman trees in a similar manner to generate statistically plausible cover texts on a letter-by-letter basis.

prepositions. Because these functional words are often strongly associated with another word or phrase in the sentence, complex constructions often seem to lead to errors in the translation of such words. Furthermore, different languages handle these words very differently, leading to translation errors when using engines that do not account for these differences.

For example, many languages which use articles do not use them in front of all nouns. This causes problems when translating from languages whose article rules differ. For example, the French sentence "La vie est paralysée." translates to "Life is paralyzed." in English. However, translation engines predictably translate this as "The life is paralyzed."; "life" in the sense of "life in general" does not take an article in English. This is the same with many mass nouns like "water" and "money", causing similar errors.

Prepositions are also notoriously tricky; often, the correct choice of preposition depends entirely on the context of the sentence. For example, "J'habite à 100 mètres de lui" in French means "I live 100 meters from him" in English. However, [21] translates this as "I live *with* 100 meters of him", and [7] translates it as "In live *in* 100 meters of him." Both use a different translation of "à" ("with/in") which is entirely inappropriate to the context.

4.2 Blatant Word Choice Errors

Less frequently, a completely unrelated word or phrase is chosen in the translation. For example, "I'm staying home" and "I am staying home" are both translated into German by [21] as "Ich bleibe Haupt" ("I'm staying head") instead of "Ich bleibe zu Hause". These are different from semantic errors and reflect some sort of flaw in the actual engine or its dictionary, clearly impacting translation quality.

4.3 Additional Errors

Several other interesting error types were encountered which, for space reasons, we will only describe briefly.

- Basic grammar failures result in translations like "It do not work" [16,21].
- Word-for-word translations, in particular of idiomatic expressions, result in constructions such as "The pencils are at me."
- Words not in the source dictionary simply go untranslated, as with the translation of the registration for a Dutch news site which gives "These can contain no spaties or leestekens" for "Deze mag geen spaties of leestekens bevatten."
- Incorrect mapping of reflexive constructions between languages causes reflexive articles to be erroneously inserted in target translations (e.g. "Ich kämme mich" becomes "I comb myself").
- Proper names are sometimes unnecessarily translated; "Linda es muy Linda" ("Linda is very beautiful") is translated by [21] as "It is continguous is very pretty" and "Pretty it is very pretty" by [7]. Moving the capitalized name in the sentence does not always stop it from being erroneously translated.
- Verb tense is often inexact in translation, due to the lack of direct mapping between verb tenses in different languages.

4.4   Translations Between Typologically Dissimilar Languages

Typologically distant languages are languages whose formal structures differ radically from one another. These structural differences manifest themselves in many areas (e.g. syntax (phrase and sentence structure), semantics (meaning structure) and morphology (word structure)). Not surprisingly, because of these differences, translations between languages that are typologically distant (Chinese and English, English and Arabic, etc) are frequently so bad as to be incoherent or unreadable. We did not consider these languages for this work, since the translation quality is often so poor that exchange of the resulting translations would likely be implausible.

5   Implementation

This section describes some of the aspects of the implementation with focus on the different techniques that are used to obtain variations in the generated translations.

5.1   Translation Engines

The current implementation uses different translation services that are available on the Internet to obtain an initial translation. The current implementation supports three different services, and we plan on adding more in the future. Adding a new service only requires writing a function that translates a given sentence from a source language to the target language. Which subset of the available MT services should be used is up to the user to decide, but at least one engine must be selected.

A possible problem with selecting multiple different translation engines is that they might have distinct error characteristics (for example, one engine might not translate words with contractions). An adversary that is aware of such problems with a specific machine translation system might find out that half of all sentences have errors that match those characteristics. Since a normal user is unlikely to alternate between different translation engines, this would reveal the presence of a hidden message.

A better alternative is to use the same machine translation software but train it with different corpora. The specific corpora become part of the secret key used by the steganographic encoder; this use of a corpus as a key was previously discussed in another context (that of [2]) by Victor Raskin and Umut Topkara. As such, the adversary could no longer detect differences that are the result of a different machine translation algorithm. One problem with this approach is that acquiring good corpora is expensive. Furthermore, dividing a single corpus to generate multiple smaller corpora will result in worse translations, which can again lead to suspicious texts. That said, having full control over the translation engine may also allow for minor variations in the translation algorithm itself. For example, the GIZA++ system offers multiple algorithms for computing translations [9]. These algorithms mostly differ in how translation "candidate outcomes" are generated. Changing these options can also help to generate multiple translations.

After obtaining one or more translations from the translation engines, the tool produces additional variations using various post-processing algorithms. Problems with using multiple engines can be avoided by just using one high-quality translation engine and relying on the post-processing to generate alternative translations.

5.2 Semantic Substitution

Semantic substitution is one highly effective post-pass and has been used in previous approaches to hide information [2,5]. One key difference from previous work is that errors arising from semantic substitution are more plausible in translations compared to semantic substitutions in an ordinary text.

A typical problem with traditional semantic substitution is the need for substitution lists. A substitution list is a list of tuples consisting of words that are semantically close enough that subtituting one word for another in an arbitrary sentence is possible. For traditional semantic substitution, these lists are generated by hand. An example of a pair of words in a semantic substitution list would be `comfortable` and `convenient`. Not only is constructing substitution lists by hand tedious, but the lists must also be conservative in what they contain. For example, general substitution lists cannot contain word pairs such as `bright` and `light` since `light` could have been used in a different sense (meaning `effortless`, `unexacting` or even used as a noun).

Semantic substitution on translations does not have this problem. Using the original sentence, it is possible to automatically generate semantic substitutions that can even contain some of the cases mentioned above (which could not be added to a general monolingual substitution list). The basic idea is to translate back and forth between two languages to find semantically similar words. Assuming that the translation is accurate, the word in the source language can help provide the necessary contextual information to limit the substitutions to words that are semantically close in the current context.

Suppose the source language is German (d) and the target language of the translation is English (e). The original sentence contains a German word d_1 and the translation contains a word e_1 which is a translation of d_1. The basic algorithm is the following, as shown in Figure 2:

- Find all other translations of d_1 and call this set E_{d_1}. E_{d_1} is the set of candidates for semantic substitution. Naturally $e_1 \in E_{d_1}$.
- Find all translations of e_1; call this set D_{e_1}. This set is called the set of witnesses.
- For each word $e \in E_{d_1} - \{e_1\}$ find all translations D_e and count the number of elements in $D_e \cap D_{e_1}$. If that number is above a given threshold t, add e to the list of possible semantic substitutes for e_1.

A witness is a word in the source language that also translates to both words in the target language, thereby confirming the semantic proximity of the two

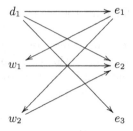

Fig. 2. Example of a translation graph produced by the semantic substitution discovery algorithm. Here two witnesses (w_1 and w_2) and the original word d_1 confirm the semantic proximity of e_1 and e_2. There is no witness for e_3, making e_3 an unlikely candidate for semantic substitution.

words. The witness threshold t can be used to trade more possible substitutions against a higher potential for inappropriate substitutions.

Examples: Given the German word "fein" and the English translation "nice", the association algorithm run on the LEO (http://dict.leo.org/) dictionary gives the following semantic substitutions: for three witnesses, only "pretty" is generated; for two witnesses, "fine" is added; for just one witness, the list grows by "acute", "capillary", "dignified" and "keen". Without witnesses (direct translations), the dictionary adds "smooth" and "subtle". The word-pair "leicht" and "light" gives "slight" (for three witnesses). However, "licht" and "light" gives "bright" and "clear". In both cases the given substitutions match the semantics of the specific German word.

5.3   Adding Plausible Mistakes

Another possible post-pass adds mistakes that are commonly made by MT systems to the translations. The transformations that our implementation can use are based on the study of MT mistakes from section 4. The current system supports changing articles and prepositions using hand-crafted, language specific substitutions that attempt to mimic the likely errors observed.

5.4   Results from the Prototype

Different configurations of the system produce translations of varying quality, but even quality degradation is not predictable. Sometimes our modifications actually (by coincidence) improve the quality of the translation. For example, a good translation of the original French sentence "Dans toute la région, la vie est paralysée." into English would be "In the entire region, life is paralysed." Google's translation is "In all the area, the life is paralysed." wheras LinguaTec returns "In all of the region the life is crippled.". Applying article substitution here can actually improve the translation: one of the choices generated by our implementation is "In all of the region, life is crippled." Even aggressive settings are still somewhat meaningful: "In all **an** area, **a** life is paralysed."

It should be noted that for simplicity that the engines currently used by the prototype are publically available free web engines, and that this is not demonstrative of the output of custom-generated engines or paid commercial software. The following slightly more extensive example is given for better illustration of the prototype system: The 24-bit string "lit" was encoded in a translation of a section of a movie review taken from the Deutsche Welle website. The text was translated from German to English using our prototype, with no semantic substitution, article and preposition replacement enabled, and no "badness threshhold". Source engines were Babelfish, Google and LinguaTec. The German text is the first part of a paragraph from a review about a Moroccan film called "Windhorse" [20], and reads as follows:

Der marokkanische Film "Windhorse" erzählt die Geschichte zweier, unterschiedlichen Generationen angehörender Männer, die durch Marokko reisen. Auf dem Weg suchen sie nach dem Einzigen, was ihnen wichtig ist: dem Sinn des Lebens.

Our prototype system gives the following translation:

The Moroccan film "Windhorse" tells story from men belonging by two, different generations who travel through Morocco. They are looking for the only one which is important to them on the way: the sense of a life.

For comparison, the source engine translations are also given:

Google: *The Moroccan film "Windhorse" tells the history of two, different generations of belonging men, who travel by Morocco. On the way they look for the none one, which is important to them: the sense of the life.*

LinguaTec: *The Moroccan film "Windhorse" tells the story of men belonging to two, different generations who travel through Morocco. They are looking for the only one which is important to them on the way: the meaning of the life.*

The Babelfish translation is identical to the Google translation except that "the none one" is replaced by "the only one". LinguaTec provides some different syntactic structures and lexical choices, but looks quite similar.

Clearly the addition of more engines would lead to more variety in the LiT version. Sometimes substitutions lead to quality degradation ("belonging by" vs. "belonging to"), and sometimes not ("sense of the life" vs. "sense of a life"). Sometimes the encoding makes the engine choose the better version of a section of text to modify: "They are looking for the only one" vs. "they look for the none one".

The original quality of the translations is not perfect. Furthermore, our version contains many of the same "differences" when compared to the source engines as the source engines have amongst themselves. Many of those differences are introduced by us ("story from men" vs. "story of men") as opposed to coming directly from the source engines. While none of the texts are particularly readable, our goal is to plausibly imitate machine-translated text, not to solve the problem of perfect translation.

The example has most of the prototype's transformations enabled in order to achieve a higher bitrate. In general, this results in more degradation of the translation; decreasing the number of transformations might improve the quality, but would also decrease the bitrate by offering fewer variations. More transformations and source engines may make the resulting text potentially more likely to be flagged as suspicious by an adversary. For this example, we achieve a bitrate of 0.0164 uncompressed and 0.0224 compressed (9.33 bits per sentence); different hidden texts would, due to the encoding scheme used, achieve slightly different bitrates. In general, we have found that for larger texts the prototype gives us average bitrates of between 0.00265 and 0.00641 (uncompressed), and 0.00731 and 0.01671 (compressed), depending upon settings.

6   Discussion

This section discusses various attacks on the steganographic encoding and possible defences against these attacks. The discussion is informal, as the system is based on MT imperfections that are hard to analyze formally (which is one of the reasons why MT is such a hard topic).

6.1   Future Machine Translation Systems

A possible problem that the presented steganographic encoding might face in the future is significant progress in machine translation. If machine translation were to become substantially more accurate, the possible margin of plausible mistakes might get smaller. However, one large category of current machine translation errors results from the lack of context that the machine translator takes into consideration.

In order to significantly improve existing machine translation systems, one necessary feature would be the preservation of context information from one sentence to the next. Only with that information will it be possible to eliminate certain errors. But introducing this context into the machine translation system also brings new opportunities for hiding messages in translations. Once machine translation software starts to keep context, it would be possible for the two parties that use the steganographic protocol to use this context as a secret key. By seeding their respective translation engines with k-bits of context they can make deviations in the translations plausible, forcing the adversary to potentially try 2^k possible contextual inputs in order to even establish the possibility that the mechanism was used. This is similar to the idea of splitting the corpus based on a secret key, with the difference that the overall quality of the per-sentence translations would not be affected.

6.2   Repeated Sentence Problem

A general problem with any approach to hiding messages in the translation is that if the text in the source language contains the same sentence twice, it might be translated into two different sentences depending on the value of the bit that was hidden. Since machine translation systems (that do not keep context) would always produce the same sentence, this would allow an attacker to suspect the use of steganography. The solution to this problem is to not use repeated sentences in the source text to hide data, and always output the translation that was used for the first occurence of the sentence.

This attack is similar to an attack used in image steganography. If an image is digitally altered, variations in the colors in certain implausible areas of the picture might reveal the existence of a hidden message. Solving this problem is easier for text steganography since it is easier to detect that two sentences are identical than to detect that a series of pixels in an image belong to the same digitally constructed shape and thus must have the same color.

6.3 Statistical Attacks

Statistical attacks have been extremely successful at defeating steganography of images, audio and video (see, e.g., [8,14,19]). An adversary may have a statistical model (e.g. a language model) that translations from all available MT systems obey. For example, Zipf's law [15] states that the frequency of a word is inversely proportional to its rank in the sorted-by-frequency list of all words. Zipf's law holds for English, and in fact holds even within individual categories such as nouns, verbs, adjectives, etc.

Assuming that all plausible translation engines generally obey such a statistical model, the steganographic encoder must be careful not to cause telltale deviations from such distributions. Naturally, this is an arms race. Once such a statistical law is known, it is actually easy to modify the steganographic encoder to eliminate translations that deviate significantly from the required distributions. For example, Golle and Farahat [10] point out (in the different context of encryption) that it is possible to extensively modify a natural language text without straying noticeably from Zipf's law. In other words, this is a very manageable difficulty, as long as the steganographic system is made "Zipf-aware".

We cannot preclude the existence of yet-undiscovered language models for translations that might be violated by our existing implementation. However, we expect that discovering and validating such a model is a non-trivial task for the adversary. On the other hand, given such a model (as we pointed out above) it is easy to modify the steganographic system so as to eliminate deviations by avoiding sentences that would be flagged.

6.4 Other Applications

While we have explored the possibility of using the inherent noise of natural language translation to hide data, we suspect that there may be other areas where transformation spaces exist which exhibit a similar lack of rigidity. For example, compilers doing source translation have a variety of possible output possibilities that still preserve semantics. Finding a way to hide information with these possibilities while still mimicking the properties of various optimization and transformation styles is a possibility for future work.

7   Conclusion

This paper introduced a new steganographic encoding scheme based on hiding messages in the noise that is inherent to natural language translation. The steganographic message is hidden in the translation by selecting between multiple translations which are generated by either modifying the translation process or by post-processing the translated sentences. In order to defeat the system, an adversary has to demonstrate that the resulting translation is unlikely to have been generated by any automatic machine translation system. A study of common mistakes in machine translation was used to come up with plausible modifications that could be made to the translations. It was demonstrated that the variations produced by the steganographic encoding are similar to those of various unmodified machine translation systems, demonstrating that it would be impractical for an adversary to establish the existence of a hidden message. The highest bitrate that our prototype could achieve with this new steganographic encoding is about 0.01671.

Acknowledgements

Portions of this work were supported by Grants IIS-0325345, IIS-0219560, IIS-0312357, and IIS-0242421 from the National Science Foundation, Contract N00014-02-1-0364 from the Office of Naval Research, by sponsors of the Center for Education and Research in Information Assurance and Security, and by Purdue Discovery Park's e-enterprise Center. We thank the anonymous reviewers for their helpful comments.

References

1. Y. Al-Onaizan, J. Curin, M. Jahr, K. Knight, J. Lafferty, I. D. Melamed, F. J. Och, D. Purdy, N. A. Smith, and D. Yarowsky. Statistical machine translation, final report, JHU workshop, 1999. http://www.clsp.jhu.edu/ws99/projects/mt/final_report/mt-final-report.ps.
2. M. Atallah, V. Raskin, C. Hempelmann, M. Karahan, R. Sion, and K. Triezenberg. Natural language watermarking and tamperproofing. In *Proceedings of the 5th International Information Hiding Workshop 2002*, 2002.
3. P. F. Brown, S. A. Della Pietra, V. J. Della Pietra, and R. L. Mercer. The mathematics of statistical machine translation: Parameter estimation. *Computational Linguistics*, 19(2):263–311, 1993.
4. M. Chapman and G. Davida. Hiding the hidden: A software system for concealing ciphertext in innocuous text. In *Information and Communications Security — First International Conference*, volume Lecture Notes in Computer Science 1334, Beijing, China, 11–14 1997.
5. M. Chapman, G. Davida, and M. Rennhard. A practical and effective approach to large-scale automated linguistic steganography. In *Proceedings of the Information Security Conference (ISC '01)*, pages 156–165, Malaga, Spain, 2001.
6. P. R. Clarkson and R. Rosenfeld. Statistical language modeling using the cmu-cambridge toolkit. In *Proceedings of ESCA Eurospeech*, 1997.

7. Smart Link Corporation. Promt-online. http://translation2.paralink.com/.

8. J. Fridrich, M. Goljan, and D. Soukal. Higher-Order Statistical Steganalysis of Palette. In *Proceedings of the SPIE International Conference on Security and Watermarking of Multimedia Contents*, volume 5020, pages 178–190, San Jose, CA, 21 – 24 January 2003.

9. U. Germann, M. Jahr, D. Marcu, and K. Yamada. Fast decoding and optimal decoding for machine translation. In *Proceedings of the 39th Annual Conference of the Association for Computational Linguistics (ACL-01)*, 2001.

10. P. Golle and A. Farahat. Defending email communication against profiling attacks. In *Proceedings of the 2004 ACM workshop on Privacy in the electronic society (WPES 04)*, pages 39–40, 2004.

11. C. Grothoff, K. Grothoff, L. Alkhutova, R. Stutsman, and M. Atallah. Translation-based steganography. Technical Report CSD TR 05-009, Purdue University, 2005. http://grothoff.org/christian/lit-tech.ps.

12. D. Huffman. A method for the construction of minimum redundancy codes. *Proceedings of the Institute of Radio Engineers*, 40:1098–1101, 1951.

13. N. F. Johnson and S. Jajodia. Steganalysis of images created using current steganography software. In *IHW'98 - Proceedings of the International Information hiding Workshop*, April 1998.

14. S. Lyu and H. Farid. Detecting Hidden Messages using Higher-Order Statistics and Support Vector Machines. In *Proceedings of the Fifth Information Hiding Workshop*, volume LNCS, 2578, Noordwijkerhout, The Netherlands, October, 2002. Springer-Verlag.

15. C. D. Manning and H. Schuetze. *Review of Foundations of Statistical Natural Language Processing*. MIT Press, Cambridge, MA, 1999.

16. B. Marx. Friedensverhandlungen brauchen ruhe. *Deutsche Welle Online*, Jan 2005.

17. F. J. Och and H. Ney. A comparison of alignment models for statistical machine translation. In *COLING00*, pages 1086–1090, Saarbrücken, Germany, August 2000.

18. F. J. Och and H. Ney. Improved statistical alignment models. In *ACL00*, pages 440–447, Hongkong, China, October 2000.

19. A. Pfitzmann and A. Westfeld. Attacks on steganographic systems. In *Third Information Hiding Workshop*, volume LNCS, 1768, pages 61–76, Dresden, Germany, 1999. Springer-Verlag.

20. S. Suren. Neue bilder der arabischen jugend. *Deutsche Welle Online*, March 2005.

21. Systran Language Translation Technologies. Systran. http://systransoft.com/.

22. P. Wayner. Mimic functions. *Cryptologia*, XVI(3):193–214, 1992.

23. P. Wayner. *Disappearing Cryptography: Information Hiding: Steganography and Watermarking*. Morgan Kaufmann, 2nd edition edition, 2002.

ID Modulation: Embedding Sensor Data
in an RFID Timeseries

Joshua R. Smith[1], Bing Jiang[2], Sumit Roy[2], Matthai Philipose[1],
Kishore Sundara-Rajan[1,2], and Alexander Mamishev[2]

[1] Intel Research Seattle, 1100 NE 45th Street, Seattle, WA 98105
Joshua.r.smith@intel.com
[2] Department of Electrical Engineering, Box 352500, University of Washington,
Seattle, WA 98195

Abstract. This paper reports the first use of *ID Modulation* to embed a
bitstream representing sensor information in a standards-compliant Radio
Frequency Identification (RFID) channel. Like other forms of information
hiding, ID Modulation embeds a new, lower bit-rate channel in a pre-existing
host channel, without requiring any changes to the protocols defining the host
channel. Like most other forms of information hiding, the embedded data is
represented as correlations introduced into the host channel data stream. Most
previous applications of information hiding have emphasized either secrecy (as
in steganography) or robustness to removal (as in watermarking). The benefit
of information hiding that is most important for the application reported here is
backward compatibility with pre-existing standards and hardware. It has
allowed us to build a new communication layer (for transmitting sensor data) on
top of current RFID infrastructure.

1 Introduction

Instrumenting the physical world with networked sensors is being recognized as an
intellectually and commercially important goal. [3, 5] The vision is that myriad tiny,
inexpensive networked sensor units, sometimes fancifully referred to as "smart dust"
[6], will make it possible to monitor environments such as buildings, civil structures,
manufacturing facilities, hospitals, natural ecosystems, or the home with
unprecedented detail, enabling a wide range of novel applications such as condition
monitoring, situational awareness, proactive maintenance, and in-home healthcare
[4,8].

However, the need to purchase, install, replace, and dispose of batteries is a severe
impediment to widespread and long term deployment of sensor networks as they have
been envisaged so far. To address this shortcoming of today's sensor networks, we
are developing a platform for battery-free wireless sensing called the Wireless
Identification and Sensing Platform (WISP). Wisps are passive Radio Frequency
Identification (RFID) tags that are augmented to support sensing in addition to
identification. Like ordinary passive RFID tags, Wisps do not have an on-board
power source; instead, an external reader device transmits power to the Wisp
electromagnetically.

M. Barni et al. (Eds.): IH 2005, LNCS 3727, pp. 234–246, 2005.

In developing Wisps, an information hiding approach has allowed us to create RFID tags that have new capabilities (notably sensing), and yet are still standards compliant and readable by conventional, off-the-shelf reader hardware. We call the technique of embedding additional application-layer data in a stream of RFID reads *ID Modulation.*

2 Background: α–Wisp

The α–Wisp, a battery-free wireless one bit accelerometer, was our first RFID-based ID-sensor.[1] It implements a primitive form of ID Modulation. The α–Wisp uses mercury switches both as sensors and as modulating elements that affect the ID it returns.

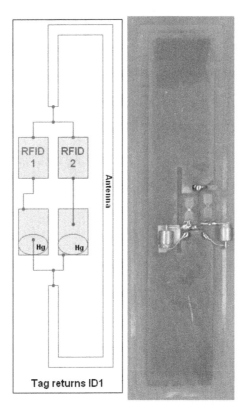

Fig. 1. Schematic diagram of α-Wisp battery-free one bit accelerometer (left); photograph of α-Wisp (right). The mercury switches are oriented anti-parallel, so that when one is open, the other is closed. In one acceleration / tilt state, RFID IC 1 is connected to the antenna, and the tag returns ID 1; in the other acceleration / tilt state, the tag returns ID 2. In α-Wisp, the mercury switches function as both sensor and modulating element. Later in the paper we split these logically distinct functions. (Figure reprinted from [1]).

236   J.R. Smith et al.

Fig. 2. The α-Wisp mounted on a coffee cup. One application of Wisp sensors is tracking human activity by object use. (Figure reprinted from [1].)

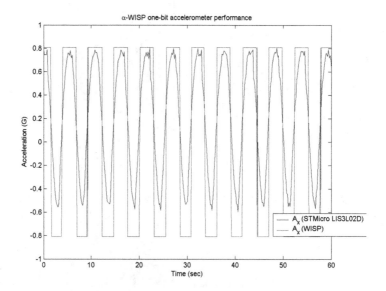

Fig. 3. α-Wisp in operation. The α-Wisp and the STMicroelectronics LIS3L02D, a conventional wired accelerometer, were mounted together and tilted periodically. The blue trace shows the x acceleration as measured by the wired accelerometer; the red trace shows the x acceleration as measured by α-Wisp, with no batteries or wires, via a conventional RFID reader. (Figure reprinted from [1].)

A mercury switch may be viewed as a simple, ultra low power inertial sensor with just one bit of dynamic range. If two mercury switches are mounted in a geometrically anti-parallel configuration, then they will in general experience acceleration that is identical in magnitude but opposite in sign. The state of the switches will therefore be anti-correlated: when one is open, the other will be closed. This enables a properly wired switch pair to function as a 2:1 multiplexer.

In the α–Wisp, geometrically anti-parallel mercury switches multiplex two RFID IC chips to one antenna. Each RFID IC is mounted in series with a mercury switch. The two IC – switch pairs are connected in parallel with one another to the antenna, as illustrated in the schematic diagram of Figure 1. (Other variants of this technique are also possible, as described in [1].) As explained above, the switch states are anti-correlated. Thus under positive acceleration (say), IC 1 will be connected to the antenna and IC 2 will be disconnected, causing the Wisp to return ID 1; under negative acceleration, the Wisp returns ID2.

To a decoder (or RFID reader, middleware system, database, warden, etc) that is unaware and uninterested in the special structure of the data stream generated by the α–Wisp, its responses look like an ordinary RFID timeseries. A decoder that is aware of the structure, however, can extract both identification and sensing data. In ordinary RFID systems, each ID is associated with a single physical object. With α-Wisp, two IDs are associated with each object. Consider the coffee cup of Figure 2, which is tagged with an α-Wisp. Seeing either ID1 or ID2 indicates that the coffee cup is present, which is what a single ordinary RFID read event conveys. But to an informed decoder, ID1 indicates that the cup is experiencing positive acceleration, and ID2 indicates negative acceleration. Seeing neither ID1 nor ID2 indicates that the coffee cup is absent.

Figure 3 shows the α-Wisp output as viewed by an informed decoder. The α-Wisp's one bit acceleration measurements were extracted by decoding the output of a conventional RFID reader according to the simple logic described above. In the figure, the α-Wisp's output is plotted against the output of a conventional wired accelerometer. The α-Wisp signal is clearly a one bit quantized version of the higher dynamic range acceleration measurement provided by the conventional accelerometer.

3   Bitstream Transmission Using ID Modulation

Transmitting a sequence of bits representing sensor data by ID Modulation is the main accomplishment in this work. As a working proof of concept, we will present a tri-axial accelerometer with one bit per axis of dynamic range that communicates its 3 bits of sensor data via ID Modulation.

3.1   Wisp Design and Implementation

Figure 4 shows a block diagram for a platform implementing bitstream ID modulation. Figure 5 is a photo of a the first working prototype. As in the original α-Wisp, this Wisp uses two RFID ICs and one RFID antenna. These original RFIDs are EPC class 1 compatible tags, the Alien Technologies ALL-9250. Unlike the original α-Wisp, this Wisp cleanly separates the sensing and modulating functions. Mercury switches are used for sensing, but no longer as modulating elements.

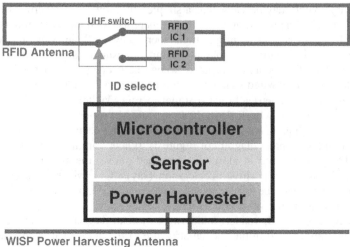

Fig. 4. Block Diagram of Wisp capable of supporting ID Modulation. The components are two RFID ICs, one RFID antenna, a GaAs switch capable of handling the 915MHz RF signal used by the base RFID system, an antenna and circuitry for harvesting power for the Wisp, a sensor, and an ultra-low power microcontroller for data acquisition and coding.

Fig. 5. Photograph of a prototype Wisp implementing the functions from the block diagram. At the top is an augmented RFID tag. The board at the bottom is our custom 915MHz power harvesting circuit. The sensor is at on the left: it is a mercury-switch-based three axis accelerometer with one bit per axis of dynamic range.

The modulation (or multiplexing) is now under electronic control, by the NEC UPG152TA SPDT GaAs switch, which is capable of switching high frequency signals (up to 2.5GHz), and offers low insertion loss.[9]

The heart (or brain) of the Wisp is a TI MSP430F1121 ultra low power microcontroller, which in its lowest power operating mode draws only 160µA at 1MHz and 2.2V, in standby mode only 0.7µA, and in off mode (with RAM retention), just 0.1µA.[7]

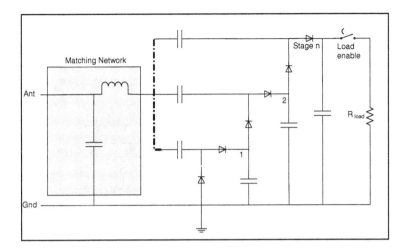

Fig. 6. The power harvesting circuit. The network highlighted in the rectangle matches the impedance of the antenna to that of the power harvesting circuit. This matching network is followed by n stages of voltage doubling. The Wisp described in this paper uses 4 stages of voltage doubling. The resistor at the right represents the load. The switch (labeled reset) indicates that the load is not always present, as the microcontroller may sleep for power conservation purposes.

Our custom-designed power harvesting unit appears at the bottom of the photo in Figure 5. Figure 6 is a schematic for the power harvesting unit. The unit consists of 4 cascaded voltage doublers, based on Agilent Technologies HSMS-2852 zero bias Schottky diodes. The size of the final filter capacitor determines how smooth the output power is, how quickly the unit powers up from zero, and how long the unit can operate in the absence of new power. At one extreme, we have experimented with using super capacitors on the order of 1F, which are able to store enough energy to enable usage models in which sensing can occur outside the field of view of the readers for substantial periods of time. A trade off is that the time to charge up the capacitor (from a current-constrained power harvester) becomes comparably long.

The sensor appears to the left of the development board. It consists of three orthogonally-mounted mercury switches. The orthogonal fixture for the mercury switches was fabricated by laser cutting acrylic. Each mercury switch is in series with a 150K resistor to ground. A "sensor enable" output pin on the microcontroller applies Vcc (the positive supply voltage) to the three switches. Three of the microcontroller's input pins are connected to the nodes between the resistors and switches. When a switch is closed, this node is pulled high; when the switch is open, it is pulled low.

3.2 Coding

For the initial experiments reported here, we have used a very simple coding scheme. The Wisp transmits packets that begin with a known synchronization sequence, and then codes the three bits using an interleaved repetition code.

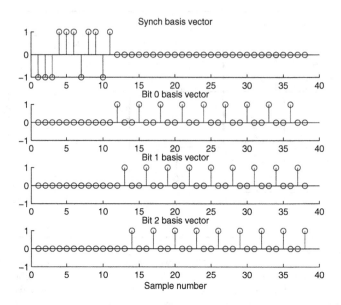

Fig. 7. Basis vectors used to encode and decode Wisp communications: Length 11 Barker Code (top subplot) for synchronization; interleaved length 9 repetition codes (subplots 2-4) for data bits.

The Wisp packets begin with a length-11 Barker sequence. The autocorrelation of a Barker sequence has the ideal "thumbtack" property for synchronization: it is sharply peaked at synchronization, and quickly becomes flat away from synchronization.[10, 2]. The Barker code is illustrated in the top subplot of Figure 7.

For these initial experiments, we have used an interleaved repetition code of rate 1/9. To improve robustness to burst errors, we have interleaved the codewords for each bit, i.e., we transmit bit 0, bit 1, and bit 2, and then repeat these 3 bits nine times. Subplots 2-4 of Figure 7 illustrates the coding of the sensor data. The figure shows stem plots of the basis functions corresponding to the synchronization signal, and for bit 0 – bit 2. Interleaving (as opposed to transmitting nine repetitions of bit 0, followed by nine repetitions of bit 1, and so on), should provide robustness to burst errors: sufficiently short burst errors will partially degrade all three bits, instead of completely erasing any single bit.

Each packet consists of 38 chips: 11 for the synchronization code, and 27 for the data. We used a chip time of 0.25s, thus the time to transmit a complete packet is 9.5s for an information bit rate of 0.3 bps.

3.3 Decoding

Decoding was performed by a host PC connected to an Alien Technologies 9RE-0001 Nanoscanner RFID reader. We implemented four simultaneous correlators in software, one for the synch signal, and one each for the data bits. Figure 7 shows the vectors that the correlators are convolving with the RFID timeseries. Because the synch pulse and the data pulses do not overlap, the target correlation sequences used by each correlator are non-overlapping. At the moment that a peak is detected in the synchronization signal (i.e. in the output of the correlator that is targeting the Barker sequence), the values on the other correlators are thresholded to determine the values for the data bits. (Even though the features that the correlators are seeking are offset from one another in time, this is handled automatically. The correlators are "loaded" with target sequences that represent the relative temporal positions of the features of interest. That is why we simply look a the correlator outputs at the moment the synch pulse is detected.) Decoding results will be presented in the next section.

4 Results

The antenna of the RFID reader was placed approximately one foot from the Wisp. For all the results and performance discussion in this paper, the Wisp was operated from harvested power.

Figure 8 illustrates ID Modulation from the Wisp's perspective. The top trace in each of the three oscilloscope screen shots shows the power supply voltage. The other two traces, which are microcontroller output pins under software control, serve as a differential signal that controls the GaAs switch. (Line 1 is set high and line 2 low to set the switch in its first state; line 1 and line 2 are reversed to place the switch in its second state).

The figure shows that the power supply voltage fluctuates dramatically, despite the final bypass capacitor. This is due to variations in the reader output. The reader signal has significant time-domain structure, such as quiet periods and amplitude modulation for downstream communication, that affect the harvested power levels. Also, the reader does not operate at a fixed frequency of 915MHz; instead it hops among 30 frequencies in the band spanning 902MHz to 928MHz. Using a network analyzer as a controlled frequency source, we verified that the Wisp's operating voltage was maximized at a drive frequency of 915MHz, and dropped about 7% (from 700mV to 650mV, for a fixed test antenna geometry) as the source was tuned down to 902MHz or up to 928MHz.

Figure 9 shows the outputs for all 4 correlators in operation for one minute. A peak in the synchronization signal is clearly visible with a period of 9.5 s as expected. Figure 10 shows a "zoomed in" look at the same trace. Beneath the synchronization pulse, one can see that the red (dashed) trace is positive, and the other two traces are negative. This is the correct result, as the red (dashed) trace represents bit 0, as the information being sent is bit 2 = 0, bit 1 = 0, and bit 0 = 1.

4.1 Performance and Characterization

The latest version of the three axis by one bit Wisp system, programmed to wake up every 150mS and toggle its ID if any sensor value has changed, draws only 7μA. The ID Modulation experiments reported here used an earlier version of the board that contained a voltage regulator. In the experiments, this earlier platform consumed 300uA to 500uA, depending on range to the reader. At higher voltages, more current was consumed.

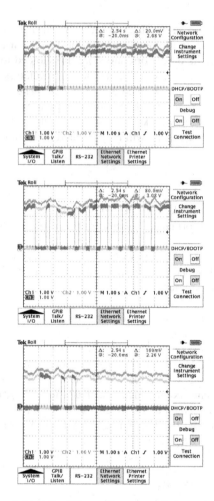

Fig. 8. Modulation viewed from the Wisp. The top trace in each figure shows the Wisp's power supply voltage. The other two traces represent the differential control signal for the multiplexer: when the darker trace voltage (input 1 to the multiplexer) is greater than the lighter trace voltage (input 2 to the multiplexer) RFID IC 1 is connected to the antenna and IC 2 is disabled; when the darker trace voltage is less than the lighter trace voltage, RFID IC 2 is enabled. The top figure corresponds to data 000; the middle figure is 001; and the bottom figure is 111. The Barker sequence is easily visible in the bottom image. The Barker sequence is also visible in the top and middle images, although the first, positive pulse in the Barker sequence is partially off the screen on the left side in these two images. The structure of the interleaved length 9 repetition code is easily visible in the middle figure.

The MSP430 requires at least 1.8V to operate. It appears that the voltage constraint, not the power constraint, is the factor that typically prevents Wisp microcontroller from operating. However, there is another factor that limits the operating range of the system. The GaAs switch negatively affects the range of the

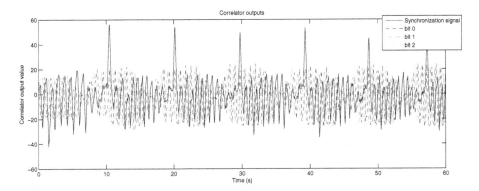

Fig. 9. Demodulated signals at the host. The RFID timeseries is feed into four simultaneous correlators. The signal that is seen spiking approximately every 10 seconds is the correlation with a length 11 Barker sequence used as a synch pulse. When a peak is detected on the synch signal, the values of the other correlators are thresholded to determine the data bit values.

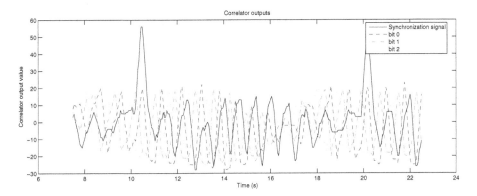

Fig. 10. Zoomed in view of demodulated signals at the host. To decode the data, the signals corresponding to the data bits are thresholded when there is a peak in the synch signal. In this case, the data value is 001 (bit 2 = 0, bit 1 = 0, bit 0 = 1).

base RFID system, so currently there is a range at which the WISP harvests enough power to run, and yet cannot be read by the reader. The full system can operate at distance range of 1 to 4 feet. From 4 to 5 feet, the microcontroller runs, but the IDs cannot be read. Beyond 5 feet, the microcontroller is not able to run.

The current end-to-end communication rate is about 0.3 bps. The underlying channel can be viewed as an erasure channel, since the probability of reading "No ID" when ID 1 or ID 2 are present is so much higher than the probability of reading ID 2 when ID 1 was transmitted (a substitution error). Thus the channel can be modeled as an erasure channel. The capacity of the erasure channel is well known to be 1-BER bits per use, where BER is the bit error rate for the underlying channel symbols. In the case of the Wisp, a BER = 0.13 was typical. This corresponds to a capacity of 0.87 bits per channel use. At 20 reads per second (a typical value using the Alien reader's fast Verify command), the theoretical capacity of the embedded sensor channel is 17.4 bits per second. Certainly it should be possible to make use of more intelligent coding schemes, in order to more closely approach the theoretical optimum.

Many of the key performance metrics of the Wisp described in this paper, such as rate and range, can be improved through various optimizations and engineering measures, a process we are currently engaged in.

5   Extensions and Future Work

Figure 11 shows a version of the ID Modulation scheme that uses just a single ID for communication. Rather than using ID1 and ID2 as channel symbols, ID1 and "no ID" would be used. The higher level channel model will no longer be an erasure channel, since a failure to read will correspond to a symbol substitution. This scheme will have a higher bit error rate, and therefore lower throughput. However, it has practical benefits as well: the one ID scheme offers an increased level of compatibility with legacy databases and business processes, since most of these systems assume that there is just one ID per object. It is also nice that no ID space is sacrificed in order to

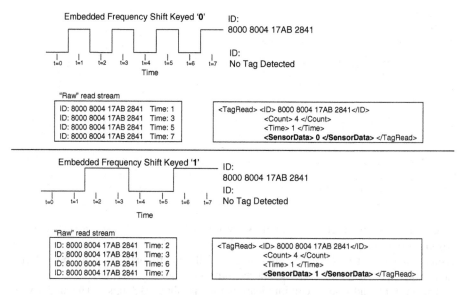

Fig. 11. ID Modulation using a single ID. In this example, a zero is encoded via an ID presence / absence transition frequency of 1.0 per unit time; a one is encoded as a transition frequency of 0.5 transitions per unit time. The achievable communication rate is lower using just a single ID, but this technique is more backward compatible with legacy databases and business processes, since these typically assume just one ID per physical object. It is also notable that this method does not require sacrificing any ID space to encode sensor data.

encode additional data. The single ID hiding scheme emphasizes that the additional sensor data is not encoded in the ID bits, but rather in the time structure of the RFID read stream. RFID systems typically treat ID reads as independent events. Our system encodes information in correlations among multiple events, and decodes the data by processing these events jointly. This extension will decrease sensor data communication rate, and increase backward compatibility.

Another direction we plan to take this work in the future will increase data throughput, but offer a lower degree of backward compatibility. The schemes reported in this paper encode less than one bit of sensor data per RFID read event, and rely on channel coding techniques to achieve robustness. The alternative approach that we will experiment with next is to use custom hardware to more properly implement RFID communication protocols. This will enable us to set all the ID bits to arbitrary values, which will allow us to encode more than one sensor bit per RFID read packet. This allows a larger number of sensor bits to be communicated per read event, while moving much further from the "one ID, one object" model.

An important issue that must be addressed in the future for any of the communication techniques discussed so far is that of combining the ID modulation-based sensing functionality with anti-collision protocols. The EPC specification requires support of certain primitives to perform anti-collision, but does not specify in detail how these primitives be used to support anti-collision. Those details are left to the RFID reader implementer. We believe that it is possible to create collision resolution protocols that support both ID Modulation and anti-collision, while maintaining compatibility with the EPC standard. These investigations may also suggest directions for the design of future protocols that can support the competing functions of identification (anti-collision) and sensor data communication, which both require the same scare resource, access to the reader channel.

6 Conclusion

It appears that Wisps can help deliver on the promise of sensor networks, by eliminating batteries in appropriate deployment scenarios. By using the fundamental principles of information hiding, we have been able to add a new capability---sensing---to RFID tags, while maintaining backward compatibility and preserving infrastructure investments. Most applications of information hiding thus far have focused on secrecy (steganography) or robustness to removal (watermarking). This paper highlights *standards extension* as another major benefit that information hiding can provide.

References

1. M. Philipose, J.R. Smith, B. Jiang, A. Mamishev, S. Roy, K. Sundara-Rajan "Battery-free Wireless Identification and Sensing." IEEE Pervasive Computing Magazine, Vol 4, No 1. pp. 10-18.
2. R.H. Barker, "Group Synchronizing of Binary Digital Sequences." In Communication Theory. London: Butterworth, pp. 273-287, 1953. As cited in [10].

3. D.E. Culler, H. Mulder, "Smart Sensors to Network the World," *Scientific American*, June 2004, pp. 85-91.
4. E. Dishman "Inventing Wellness Systems for Aging in Place," Computer, Vol 37, no. 5, 2004, pp. 34-41.
5. R. Poor, B. Hodges "Wireless Networks for Industrial Systems." Whitepaper available from http://www.ember.com/resources/whitepapers/request.html
6. J. M. Kahn, R. H. Katz, K. S. J. Pister. "Next century challenges: mobile networking for "Smart Dust", MobiCom 1999, pp. 271-278.
7. MSP430C11x1, MSP430F11x1A Mixed signal microcontroller, http://focus.ti.com/lit/ds/symlink/msp430f1121a.pdf
8. M. Philipose, K. Fishkin, D. Patterson, M. Perkowitz, D. Hahnel, D. Fox, and H. Kautz Inferring Activities from Interactions with Objects. IEEE Pervasive Computing Magazine, Vol 3, Issue 4, pp. 50-57.
9. NEC UPG152TA L,S Band SPDT GaAs MMIC Switch, http://www.qsl.net/n9zia/wireless/pdf/u152ta.pdf
10. E.W. Weisstein et al. "Barker Code." From MathWorld. http://mathworld.wolfram.com/BarkerCode.html

Embedding Covert Channels into TCP/IP

Steven J. Murdoch and Stephen Lewis

University of Cambridge, Computer Laboratory,
15 JJ Thomson Avenue, Cambridge CB3 0FD, United Kingdom
http://www.cl.cam.ac.uk/users/{sjm217, srl32}/

Abstract. It is commonly believed that steganography within TCP/IP is easily achieved by embedding data in header fields seemingly filled with "random" data, such as the IP identifier, TCP initial sequence number (ISN) or the least significant bit of the TCP timestamp. We show that this is not the case; these fields naturally exhibit sufficient structure and non-uniformity to be efficiently and reliably differentiated from unmodified ciphertext. Previous work on TCP/IP steganography does not take this into account and, by examining TCP/IP specifications and open source implementations, we have developed tests to detect the use of naïve embedding. Finally, we describe reversible transforms that map block cipher output onto TCP ISNs, indistinguishable from those generated by Linux and OpenBSD. The techniques used can be extended to other operating systems. A message can thus be hidden so that an attacker cannot demonstrate its existence without knowing a secret key.

1 Introduction

Steganographic covert channels based on modification of network protocol header values are best understood by considering a scenario with three actors; in keeping with the existing literature, we shall call them Alice, Bob and Walter. Alice can make arbitrary modifications to network packets originating from a machine within Walter's network. She wants to leak a message to Bob, who can only monitor packets at the egress points of this network. Alice aims to hide the message from Walter, who can see (but not modify) any packet leaving his network. This is analogous to a passive warden within the threat model introduced in [1].

In a practical instantiation of this problem, Alice and Bob may well be the same person. Consider a machine to which an attacker has unrestricted access for only a short amount of time, and which lies within a closely monitored network. The attacker installs a keylogger on the machine, and wishes to leak passwords to himself in such a way that the owner of the network does not observe that anything untoward is happening. An attacker might also want to watermark all transmissions from a particular machine; the steganography described in this paper can be used for this purpose.

Alice can choose which layer of the protocol stack she wishes to hide her message in. Each layer has its own characteristics, which indicate the scenarios in which it can best be used. In [2], the potential for embedding at all layers of the OSI model is discussed.

M. Barni et al. (Eds.): IH 2005, LNCS 3727, pp. 247–261, 2005.

At the bottom of the stack, in the Physical and Data-Link layers (e.g. Ethernet), there is some opportunity for embedding data. However, it requires low-level control of the hardware, which Alice may find difficult to obtain. Also, if she chooses to signal to Bob at this layer, her messages will be stripped out if they reach a device that connects networks at a higher layer (e.g. an IP router). This requires Bob to be on the same LAN. An example of a steganography system that relies on embedding at the Physical layer is described in [3].

Alice might also choose to embed data at the Presentation or Application layers of the network stack (e.g. in Telnet or HTTP/FTP traffic). If, however, she only has brief access to the machine from which she is leaking data, she needs to anticipate which applications are likely to be used on it; she can then modify them to carry her messages in the traffic they generate.

Similarly, the format of files sent over HTTP or FTP (such as JPEG or PDF) may also be viewed as protocols in which steganographic data can be embedded. These provide Alice with a high-bandwidth channel, but only if she is confident of being able to modify these files without arousing suspicion.

The only remaining layers to consider in the OSI model are Network, Transport and Session. TCP and IP (specified in [4] and [5]) fall within these layers, and are common to the vast majority of Internet applications. A message embedded in these protocols has the advantage that it will survive unchanged on its journey out of Walter's network. Here we consider only IPv4-based embedding; IPv6-based covert channels are discussed in [6].

In this paper we study a number of previously proposed schemes for embedding data within the TCP and IP protocol headers, thus creating a steganographic covert channel. We show how the use of these schemes can easily be detected by a passive warden. The algorithms used in the generation of some TCP/IP header fields are then looked at in detail, and our alternative method for embedding data, *Lathra*, is proposed. We show that a passive warden cannot detect the use of this method without knowledge of a secret key, subject to some realistic constraints. Our results will also be relevant to the field of operating system and physical device fingerprinting.

2   Threat Model

We have thus far assumed that the steganography can only be prevented by detection, not by attempting to remove any hidden information. This is known as the passive warden threat model. An active warden can modify traffic regardless of suspicion. As is shown in [7,8], an active warden can remove most, if not all, TCP/IP level steganography, and lower layer steganography will already have been removed by routing. He will, however, have difficulty removing steganography at higher layers (e.g. in JPEG images) without damaging the carrier.

In many scenarios, it may be infeasible for a warden to be active: the kind of filtering necessary to remove TCP/IP steganography can increase network latency, and might require a filtering router that can store large amounts of state. The warden may also wish to avoid the users being aware that the use of steganography is suspected.

In this paper, we assume that Alice operates in an environment with a passive warden and an unreliable network (permitting packet loss, duplication and reordering) and requires a TCP/IP based covert channel giving

- *indistinguishability*: Walter (a passive warden) should be unable to detect the presence of the data hidden in packets leaving Alice's machine; and
- *reliability*: she desires some indication of whether her messages to Bob have indeed arrived, so she can retransmit them if necessary.

3   Overview of TCP/IP Based Steganography

A common failing of existing proposals is the production of output from a different distribution to that which would be generated by unmodified TCP/IP implementations. In some cases, it is even outside the relevant specifications. For this reason, to design steganographic techniques or to detect their use, it is necessary to be familiar with the applicable standards and the details of their implementation. This section gives an overview of the TCP/IP standards and related work from a steganographic encoding perspective.

The basic TCP/IP protocol suite is specified in [4] and [5]. There are extensions to it (e.g. the TCP Extensions for High Performance [9]) that specify additional header options; these also give some scope for steganographic coding.

IP itself does not aim to provide any reliability guarantees, but rather allows client protocols on a host to transport blocks of data (datagrams) from a source to a destination, both specified by fixed length addresses. One noteworthy feature of IP for our purposes is that it allows fragmentation and reassembly of long datagrams, requiring certain extra header fields.

TCP, on the other hand, does aim to provide a reliable channel to its clients. It has a stream oriented interface, and keeps its reliability properties even within networks exhibiting packet loss, reordering and duplication. Its features for implementing reliability and flow control give scope for steganographic coding.

The TCP/IP header can serve as a carrier for a steganographic covert channel if a header field can take one of a set of values, each of which appears plausible to our passive warden. The warden should not be able to distinguish whether the header was generated by an unmodified TCP/IP stack or by a steganographic encoding mechanism. In this section we examine which header fields have more than one plausible value, and look at the amount of entropy available in each of them for use by a steganographic coding scheme.

TCP/IP steganography exploits the fact that few headers are altered in transit. As mentioned above, IP packets can be fragmented, but (unless we are hiding data in the fragmentation-related headers) no information is lost. The time-to-live field in the IP header is decremented each time the packet passes through a router, but the initial values used by IP stacks are well known, so this field gives little scope for steganography.

Figure 1 illustrates the base TCP/IP headers. The fields shown in italics are those that may be used to embed steganographic data. We now consider each of these fields in turn, assessing their potential for use as steganographic carriers.

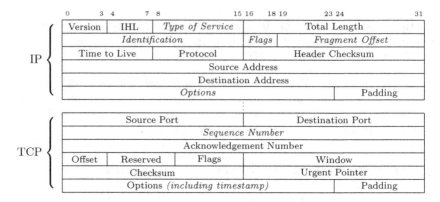

Fig. 1. Basic TCP/IP header structure

Type of Service: The eight Type of Service (ToS) bits in the IP header are used to indicate quality of service parameters to routers on a packet's path. They are now rarely used with their original semantics (as defined in [5]); they have been reused in, for example, the implementation of DiffServ.

There is potential for using the bits in this field as a steganographic carrier, as described in [2], because many networks never use them. However, this would be easily detected by the warden in our threat model, as the field is set to zero in almost all default operating system configurations.

IP Identification: As described in [5], the IP Identification field (IP ID) is 'an identifying value assigned by the sender to aid in assembling the fragments of a datagram', and is allocated 16 bits of the IP header. Because the IP ID is used to distinguish fragments making up one packet from fragments making up another, the only constraints on its value are uniqueness over the length of time that fragments of a packet might reasonably remain in a network, and unpredictability.

IP IDs that are unique within a given time window are necessary to ensure that fragments of different packets are not reassembled into one packet on the receiving host. Unpredictability prevents 'idle scanning' [10], whereby an attacker can portscan a host without ever sending a packet directly to it.

A scheme for embedding data in this field is described in [11]. It uses a pseudo-random sequence, generated by a Toral Automorphism System, to ensure that the modified field is random. However this can be detected since IP ID fields are not random, as shown in Section 5.1.

IP Flags: IP packets include two flags, *Do Not Fragment* (DF), indicating that the packet should be discarded if it cannot be sent without fragmentation, and *More Fragments* (MF) which is 0 if the packet contains the last fragment, or if a packet has not been fragmented. In [11] the use of the DF bit for steganographic signalling is proposed. If this is used on packets smaller than the maximum segment size the DF flag has no effect on the packets' behaviour. However, the normal state of DF can be predicted from the packet's context, so the warden in our threat model can detect the use of this technique.

IP Fragment Offset: When IP packets are fragmented, the individual fragments contain an offset field; this allows the receiving host to reconstruct the fragments in the correct positions in its receive buffers. Information can be transmitted covertly by modulating the size of the fragments originated by a host, and thus the fragment offsets. As with the IP identification and ToS fields, this method of steganographic encoding is easily detected. In environments where path MTU discovery [12] is routinely used, fragmented packets are unusual.

IP Options: IP packets very rarely contain 'options', so their steganographic potential is limited. In [2] the use of the IP Timestamp option is described (not to be confused with the TCP Timestamp discussed in Section 3), but in addition to being easily detectable, packets with this option present can travel at most 20 hops, so it is of little use in the open Internet.

TCP Sequence Number: TCP sequence numbers support the reliability features provided by TCP (and to some extent, the flow control features). Each octet of data transmitted over a TCP stream is assigned a sequence number. In TCP, a connection (defined by a pair of sockets) can be reused, and hence the host must be able to detect whether a segment is from a current or previous incarnation of a connection.

When a connection is established, both hosts must choose an *initial sequence number* (ISN). Careful design of the algorithm for generating these initial sequence numbers ensures that overlap in sequence number space between different incarnations of a connection is prevented.

There are other properties required of the algorithm used for initial sequence number generation. For a given connection, the ISNs used must be hard to guess for those not involved in the connection [13]. To allow a connection in the TIME_WAIT state to be restarted, the sequence numbers for a given socket pair should also be monotonically increasing.

A prototype implementation of steganography using TCP ISNs (and also the IP ID), Covert_TCP, is described in [14]. It simply replaces the chosen field with the data to be sent, so can be detected either by observing that the field does not meet the required overlap and uniqueness constraints, or by comparing the data observed with statistical patterns of suspected plaintext.

A passive warden using a Support Vector Machine (SVM) is presented in [15]. It is designed to detect the use of Covert_TCP within the IP ID and TCP ISN. A SVM is a machine learning technique that is suitable for automatically identifying features which are not well understood. In the case of IP IDs and ISNs, the algorithm for generating them is well understood and precisely described in source code, so it is not necessary to use a machine learning technique. The SVM can only identify simple features, so it cannot detect the complex structure present in these fields and their interdependencies.

The design and implementation of *Nushu*, an improvement to Covert_TCP for Linux 2.4, is described in [16]. Nushu uses TCP ISNs for encoding information and encrypts outgoing ISNs to hide the use of steganography, however it still may be detected. Firstly, the output will not exhibit the structure of TCP ISNs expected from Linux. Secondly, a flaw in the use of DES for encryption allows the recovery of statistical information on the plaintext. These techniques will be further discussed in Section 5.3.

TCP Timestamp: The TCP timestamp option allows a host to accurately measure the round trip time of a path, and also mitigates problems associated with sequence number wrap-around in networks with large bandwidth × delay products. For our purposes, it is only necessary to understand the constraints on the values of TCP timestamps; more details about the features based on them can be found in [9].

The timestamp option consists of two 32 bit fields, TS Value and TS Echo Reply. The TS Value field is set based on the 'timestamp clock' of the sender, and it is into this field that hidden data can be embedded. The only constraints on the timestamp clock are that its tick frequency be between 1 Hz and 1 kHz, and that it be strictly monotonic.

A covert channel based on modulating the least significant bit of the TCP timestamps transmitted by a host, `devcc`, is described in [17]. The scheme works by incrementing the timestamp associated with a packet (and delaying it accordingly) in order to transmit a '1' bit of ciphertext. The use of TCP timestamps is not universal, but it is deployed as standard on newer versions of Linux and other Unix-like operating systems, so the observation of timestamps from an operating system which does not support them would be suspicious. As described in Section 5.3, the distribution of values in the timestamp field is modified from the expected one, in a detectable manner, by the use of this covert channel.

Packet Order: In addition to the content of the packet, the ordering of packets can be used to carry information, as is described in [11]. This relies on being used on an IPSec network to recover the original order, limiting its applicability. Since packets are seldom reordered by the transmitting host, a warden who is close to Alice will undoubtedly notice the unusually large amount of re-ordering.

4   IP ID and TCP ISN Implementations

The passive warden considered in this paper has knowledge of both the TCP/IP standards and particular implementations. He can check whether the values he observes could have been generated by an unmodified operating system, or even by the operating system he knows to be installed on the originating host.

Two fields which are commonly used to embed steganographic data are the IP ID and TCP ISN. A sufficiently precise description of their generation cannot be found within the public literature, so details of the implementation are included here. Due to their construction, these fields contain some structure, but as mentioned in Section 3, they must also be partially unpredictable. This is achieved by having randomly generated, per-host, secrets and by the use of cryptographic functions. We assume that the warden is aware of the implementation, but does not have access to these secrets and is not able to exploit vulnerabilities in the cryptographic primitives.

4.1 Linux

The Linux 2.0 ISN generator (shown in Figure 2) is based on RFC1948 [18]. It uses SHA-1 to hash a block of 16 32-bit words, with words 9–11 set to the source and destination IP address and port, and the remaining 13 words filled with a cryptographically secure, random secret, initialised on boot. Rather than using the values defined in the SHA-1 standard for the initial state, the first 5 words of the block are used. To obtain the ISN, the second word of the hash is selected and the current time (in microseconds) added. This achieves the goals of RFC1948, but calculation of a SHA-1 hash is slow, and hence this algorithm causes a significant delay in the TCP connection establishment process.

The algorithm used in Linux 2.2 (shown on the left in Figure 3) was modified to reduce the time needed to calculate each ISN. Rather than using SHA-1, a reduced block-size variant of MD4 was used, which reads 8 32-bit blocks per iteration, rather than the 16 in the original, and so it also reduces the steps per round from 16 to 8. This is used in a similar way to SHA-1 in Linux 2.0, except it limits the reuse of random data. Since even the full size MD4 algorithm is known to be insecure, the random data is rekeyed every 300 seconds (5 minutes) to limit the impact of secret compromise. To avoid this resulting in repeated ISNs, after the hash is calculated, the most significant byte is replaced with a counter incremented on rekeying and initialised to the current time divided by 300. Finally, as with Linux 2.0, the time in microseconds is added.

Early versions of Linux 2.4 contained the same ISN generator as Linux 2.2. It was also used (up to the hashing step) with a different secret to initialise the per-destination counters for IP IDs on packets which may be fragmented. A global counter was previously used, but this was vulnerable to idle scanning. In later versions of Linux 2.4 and in Linux 2.6 the algorithm was changed slightly, as shown on the right of Figure 3, mainly to improve performance on multiprocessor systems. The difference from a detection perspective is that the rekey counter is initialised to zero on boot. The use of MD4 is changed, and the same secret is used for both ISN and IP ID generation (exploiting this for detection would require finding a vulnerability in MD4). Packets which will not be fragmented,

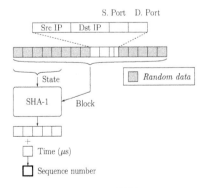

Fig. 2. Linux 2.0 ISN generator

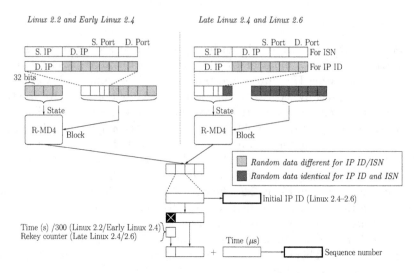

Fig. 3. Linux 2.2–2.6 ISN generator and Linux 2.4–2.6 IP ID generator

due to the DF bit being set, are assigned a predictable IP ID. For TCP this is
a per-socket counter initialised to the sequence number xored with a timer, for
UDP a per-socket counter initialised with a timer; for other protocols, with zero.

4.2 OpenBSD

The algorithm used for ISN generation in OpenBSD was introduced in December 2000; Figure 4 shows its operation. It is initialised by keying a block cipher
with 1024 bits of random data and setting the most significant bit of the generated ISNs to be zero. It is rekeyed every 2 hours, or every 30,000 connections,
whichever is sooner. On rekeying, the MSB of the generated ISNs is toggled: this
prevents collisions between ISNs generated in adjacent rekey intervals. When a
new TCP connection is made, the ISN is generated as follows:

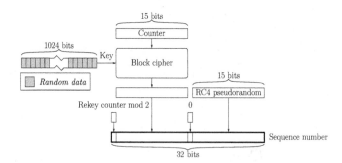

Fig. 4. OpenBSD ISN generator

- The MSB set to either '1' or '0', depending on whether the operating system is in an 'odd' or 'even' rekey interval.
- The next 15 bits are set to the output of a custom block cipher run in counter mode; the counter is updated each time an ISN is generated.
- The next bit is *always* zero.
- The final 15 bits are generated by an RC4 based pseudorandom number generator (PRNG).

The result of running the block cipher in counter mode is that a different pseudorandom sequence is defined in each rekey interval. The 15-bit values in this sequence are then inserted into the ISNs, followed by a zero bit: this ensures that no two ISNs within a given rekey interval are closer together than 2^{15} octets. The scheme thus satisfies all of the constraints described in Section 3 apart from per socket pair monotonicity.

The IP ID algorithm in OpenBSD uses a linear congruential generator, described in [19], rekeyed every 3 minutes (or after 30,000 IDs have been generated, whichever is sooner). It uses the same MSB-toggling mechanism as the sequence number generator to prevent collisions between rekey intervals.

5   Detection of TCP/IP Steganography

As described above, each operating system exhibits well defined characteristics in generated TCP/IP fields. These can be used to identify any anomalies that may indicate the use of steganography. We have therefore defined a suite of tests which may be applied to network traces and used to identify whether the results are consistent with known operating systems (and in particular, with the operating system believed to be installed on the source host). However these are not intended as acceptance tests for proposed steganographic schemes.

5.1   IP ID Characteristics

1. *Sequential Global IP ID.* Some operating systems, particularly older ones (e.g. Linux <2.4), use a global counter for the IP ID. If connections to different hosts have sequentially increasing IP IDs then it is likely that this strategy is in use.
2. *Sequential Per-host IP ID.* Others (e.g. Linux ≥2.4) use a per-host counter for packets which may be fragmented. The warden can test whether connections to different hosts use apparently unrelated IP IDs, but connections to the same host have a sequentially increasing IP ID.
3. *IP ID MSB Toggle.* OpenBSD toggles the most significant bit of the IP ID every rekey interval (3 minutes or 30,000 IP IDs), so the MSB is examined to check if it matches this pattern.
4. *IP ID Permutation.* Within a rekey interval, the OpenBSD IP ID is non-repeating; the presence of any duplicates eliminates the possibility that this strategy is in use.

5.2   TCP ISN Characteristics

5. *Rekey Timer.* In Linux 2.2 (and early 2.4) the most significant byte of the ISN is initialised to the current time since the epoch, divided by 300. The system time in microseconds is then added. The rekey timer can be recovered by subtracting the host time, in microseconds, from each ISN and verifying that the top byte increases by one every 5 minutes. This requires a clock synchronised to 8 seconds accuracy ($2^{23}/1,000,000$), which seems a reasonable assumption, since many systems use NTP synchronisation. The host time can even be queried directly, for example by using the daytime service, or indirectly, by observing patterns in the ISNs.

6. *Rekey Counter.* In Linux 2.6 (and late 2.4) the MSB of the ISN is set to the time since system startup (in seconds) divided by 300. The system time in microseconds is added, as before, and hence the rekey counter can be recovered using the same method as in Test 5.

7. *Zero bit 15.* All ISNs generated by OpenBSD will have bit 15 cleared.

8. *ISN MSB Toggle.* As with the IP ID, OpenBSD toggles the MSB of the generated ISN every rekey interval (2 hours or 30,000 IP IDs).

9. *ISN Permutation.* Bits 16 to 30 within OpenBSD ISNs are non-repeating within a rekey interval.

10. *Full TCP Collisions.* In Linux 2.0–2.6, and other RFC1948 inspired systems, the hash used for ISN generation is based on the socket pair, so collisions may be encountered. For Linux 2.0 there is no rekeying, so all 32 bits will be identical (subject to clock skew), after subtracting the time. This test and the following one can also be used to estimate clock skew between Alice and the warden and hence identify the physical device without the use of TCP timestamps [20].

11. *Partial TCP Collisions.* For Linux 2.2–2.6 it would be expected that collisions within a rekey period will have the same least significant 24 bits (subject to clock skew), after subtracting the time.

5.3   Explicit Steganography Detection

12. *Nushu Cryptography.* As covered in Section 3, Nushu encrypts data before including it in the ISN field. This will result in a distribution unlike that normally generated by Linux and so will be detected by the other TCP tests. However due to a flaw in the way that encryption is used, Nushu also exhibits characteristics of its own which may be exploited. The encryption operates by DES encrypting the IV (source port$\oplus$destination port $\parallel$ source IP address$\oplus$ destination IP address) with a shared key, then xoring the first 32 bits of the resulting keystream with the hidden data. When IV collisions occur, the ISNs can be xored to remove the key-stream; the result is the xor of two plaintexts. If these plaintexts are the same, as is the case when data is not being sent, the result would be zero, and in other cases redundancy in encoding would be apparent.

13. *TCP Timestamp.* The scheme used in `devcc`, described in [17], can be detected using the methods outlined in [21]. If a low bandwidth TCP connection is being used to leak information, a randomness test can be applied to the least significant bits of the timestamps in the TCP packets. If "too much" randomness is detected in the LSBs, it can be deduced that a steganographic covert channel is in use.

   For a high bandwidth TCP connection (where segment transmission rate $\gg$ timestamp update rate), a warden can merely calculate the ratio of the number of distinct timestamp values seen to the difference between the start and end timestamp values. If the covert channel described in [17] is in use, this ratio will be close to 0.75; if not, it will be very close to 1.

14. *Other Anomalies.* Features which would indicate the use of steganography include: unusual flags (e.g. DF when not expected, ToS set), excessive fragmentation, use of IP options, non-zero padding, unexpected TCP options (e.g. timestamps from operating systems which do not generate them) and excessive re-ordering.

5.4 Accuracy

Table 1 shows which tests detect which operating systems/steganographic techniques. All of these tests (except Test 13) are based directly on the original implementations, and make no assumptions about the probabilistic effects. Hence, they will not suffer from false negatives. False positives are possible, so in this section we consider the number of packets required to avoid these.

IP ID. Test 1 will reach an error probability of $1/2^{16}$ after only 2 packets, as will Test 2 for 2 fragmentable packets directed to the same host within a rekey interval. Due to the prevalence of path MTU discovery, fragmentable packets are

Table 1. Expected results of tests on unmodified operating systems and TCP/IP steganography systems. A matching test is indicated by '•'. The last three columns are tests for the presence of steganography, the others test for the absence. Nushu and `devcc` were written for early Linux 2.4 and are assumed to share the characteristics of all fields which are not explicitly modified. `Covert_TCP` creates all fields itself. Our improved TCP/IP steganography scheme, Lathra, is described in Section 6.

Software	\	1	2	3	4	5	6	7	8	9	10	11	\	12	13	14
								Tests								
Linux 2.0		•									•					
Linux 2.2		•				•						•				
Early Linux 2.4				•		•						•				
Late Linux 2.4/2.6				•			•					•				
OpenBSD			•	•				•	•	•						
Covert_TCP														•		
Nushu				•												
devcc				•		•						•			•	•
Lathra/Linux				•			•					•				
Lathra/OpenBSD			•	•				•	•	•						

rare, however this test will still be effective in the normal case where sockets are used to send several packets, due to the per-socket IP ID counters used in TCP and UDP. The probability of error in Test 3 halves with every packet after the first one is observed. From the 'birthday paradox', after around 181 packets a collision would be expected which would match Test 4.

TCP ISN. Test 5 needs one packet to achieve a $1/2^8$ error probability; Test 6 needs 2 packets to get the same. Test 7 halves the error probability with every SYN packet, as does Test 8 after the first packet. As with the equivalent IP ID check, Test 9 needs around 181 SYN packets within a rekey interval. Tests 10 and 11 depend on the randomness of the source port selection, but on a heavily loaded machine, our experiments show these collisions occur approximately every 1,000 SYN packets for a fixed destination port.

Steganography. Test 12 also depends on port selection randomness, but our experiments show collisions every 1,000 SYN packets (even with random destination ports). Test 13 relies on observation of consecutive TCP timestamps: if n timestamps are seen without discontinuity, the probability that the devcc scheme is in use is $1/2^{n-1}$. The accuracy of Test 14 depends on the steganography being used, but for naïve implementations only one packet is needed.

6   Detection-Resistant TCP Steganography Schemes

Our aim in this section is to develop a robust scheme, Lathra, using the TCP ISNs generated by OpenBSD and Linux as a steganographic carrier. We achieve this by following the implementation of the real ISN generators, so OpenBSD and Linux are discussed as separate cases. This discussion only considers the content of the steganographic channel, but to be protected from timing attacks, care must also be taken to ensure that the generation algorithms have the same response time as the original implementations.

6.1   OpenBSD

The MSB of our output must exactly mimic the output of the real OpenBSD TCP stack: it must toggle every 2 hours (or 30,000 connections). The next 15 bits, when extracted in turn from each ISN generated within a rekey interval, must resemble a pseudorandom sequence.

The functions in Figure 5 encode (and decode) the integer n as a permutation of the sequence $(0, 1, 2, \ldots, m)$, with x-times redundancy (i.e. Bob only needs to receive one in x ISNs transmitted by Alice). In order to remove patterns in our permutation, Alice must choose a key, K, for each rekey interval, and transmit it to Bob in, for example, the least significant 15 bits of the first ISN.

These functions allow us to encode the 16 MSBs of the ISN. The 17th bit must be zero, and we encode data into the remaining 15 bits using a block cipher. The output of the cipher is analogous to the PRNG in the genuine implementation. We xor a hash of other header fields with the input data to give freshness. If this yields the same value more than once, we skip that packet.

PERMUTATION-CODE(m, n, x)

1   $base \leftarrow m$
2   $output\_symbols \leftarrow (0, 1, 2, \ldots, m)$
3   **while** $n \neq 0$
4   **do** $index \leftarrow n \bmod base$
5       $n \leftarrow \lfloor n/base \rfloor$
6   **for** $i \leftarrow 0$ **to** $x - 1$
7   **do output** ENCIPHER$(output\_symbols[index] + i \times m, K)$
8       $output\_symbols \leftarrow output\_symbols \setminus output\_symbols[index]$
9       $base \leftarrow base - 1$

PERMUTATION-DECODE(m, x)

1   $base \leftarrow m$
2   $multiplicand = 1$
3   $input\_symbols \leftarrow (0, 1, 2, \ldots, m)$
4   $n \leftarrow 0$
5   **while input** $symbol$
6   **do** $symbol \leftarrow$ DECIPHER$(symbol, K)$
7       $symbol \leftarrow symbol \bmod m$
8   **if seen** $symbol$
9   **then skip**
10      $n \leftarrow n +$ INDEX-OF$(symbol$ in $input\_symbols) \times multiplicand$
11      $input\_symbols \leftarrow input\_symbols \setminus symbol$
12      $multiplicand \leftarrow multiplicand \times base$
13      $base \leftarrow base - 1$
14 **return** n

Fig. 5. OpenBSD permutation coding and decoding functions

6.2   Linux

Simply encoding our data within the least significant 24 bits of the ISN could be detected by the warden, because he can detect the absence of a uniform distribution after subtraction of the time. Our generated ISN thus needs to have the carry into the top byte set correctly. We must add one to the top byte of our generated ISN if, and only if, the value that we place into the the bottom 24 bits (our encrypted data) is strictly less than the least significant 24 bits of the time.

To ensure reliability, Alice can check if she receives an ACK for each ISN and resend if not, then use a standard reliability protocol, for example that used in Nushu, to reassemble the data. So that the data cannot be differentiated from random numbers, it must be encrypted. To achieve freshness, while allowing each packet to be decrypted independently, the plaintext is xored with a hash of other header fields (not including the IP ID, which is derived from the ISN), then encrypted with a variable length block cipher. Half of the space of plaintexts is reserved specifically to avoid duplications in the space of ciphertext (if the same data is to be sent, and the hash of other header fields is the same, one of these dummy values is encoded and transmitted). Due the the RFC1948 based design, if Alice encounters a packet with the same source and destination IP address and port as one already used, within a rekey interval, it must be skipped.

7   Conclusion

In this paper, we have provided an overview of the opportunities for using TCP/IP header fields as a carrier for a steganographic covert channel. A detailed description of the ISN and IP ID generation schemes in Linux and OpenBSD was presented, and a number of previously proposed schemes for TCP/IP-based steganography were described.

We have shown that a passive warden can detect use of these schemes because the modified headers that they produce can easily be distinguished from those generated by a genuine TCP/IP stack.

Finally, we have outlined two schemes for encoding data with ISNs generated by OpenBSD and Linux. Both schemes generate ISNs that are almost indistinguishable from those generated by a genuine TCP stack, except by wardens with knowledge of a shared secret key or who can exploit vulnerabilities in the underlying cryptography used in Lathra and the original ISN generation algorithms. In particular, for the Lathra/Linux case we assume that the warden cannot tell that two adjacent sequence numbers could not have been generated by an instance of MD4 with the same partial input. In Lathra/OpenBSD we make a similar assumption about the counter mode output of the block cipher and the use of RC4.

Acknowledgements. Thanks are due to Joanna Rutkowska, George Danezis, Richard Clayton and Markus Kuhn for their helpful contributions.

References

1. Simmons, G.J.: The prisoners' problem and the subliminal channel. In Chaum, D., ed.: Crypto '83. Advances in Cryptography, Plenum Press (1983) 51–67
2. Handel, T., Sandford, M.: Hiding data in the OSI network model. In Anderson, R., ed.: Information Hiding. Volume 1174 of Lecture Notes in Computer Science., Springer-Verlag (1996) 23–38
3. Szczypiorski, K.: HICCUPS: Hidden communication system for corrupted networks. In: International Multi-Conference on Advanced Computer Systems. (2003) 31–40 http://krzysiek.tele.pw.edu.pl/pdf/acs2003-hiccups.pdf.
4. Postel, J.: STD7: Transmission control protocol. IETF (1981)
5. Postel, J.: STD5: Internet protocol. IETF (1981)
6. Lucena, N.B., Lewandowski, G., Chapin, S.J.: Covert channels in IPv6. In: 5th Privacy Enhancing Technologies Workshop. (2005)
7. Fisk, G., Fisk, M., Papadopoulos, C., Neil, J.: Eliminating steganography in Internet traffic with active wardens. In Petitcolas, F., ed.: Information Hiding. Volume 2578 of Lecture Notes in Computer Science., Springer-Verlag (2002) 18–35
8. Handley, M., Paxson, V., Kreibich, C.: Network intrusion detection: Evasion, traffic normalization, and end-to-end protocol semantics. In: 10th Usenix Security Symposium. (2001)

9. Jacobson, V., Braden, R., Borman, D.: RFC1323: TCP extensions for high performance. IETF (1992)
10. Fyodor: Idle scanning and related IPID games (2001) `http://www.insecure.org/nmap/idlescan.html`.
11. Ahsan, K., Kundur, D.: Practical data hiding in TCP/IP. In: ACM Workshop on Multimedia and Security. (2002) `http://ee.tamu.edu/~deepa/pdf/acm02.pdf`.
12. Mogul, J., Deering, S.: RFC1191: Path MTU discovery. IETF (1990)
13. Bellovin, S.M.: Security problems in the TCP/IP protocol suite. Computer Communication Review **19** (1989) 32–48
14. Rowland, C.H.: Covert channels in the TCP/IP protocol suite. First Monday **2** (1997) `http://www.firstmonday.org/issues/issue2_5/rowland/`.
15. Sohn, T., Seo, J., Moon, J.: A study on the covert channel detection of TCP/IP header using support vector machine. In Perner, P., Qing, S., Gollmann, D., Zhou, J., eds.: Information and Communications Security. Volume 2836 of Lecture Notes in Computer Science., Springer-Verlag (2003) 313–324
16. Rutkowska, J.: The implementation of passive covert channels in the Linux kernel. In: Chaos Communication Congress, Chaos Computer Club e.V. (2004) `http://www.ccc.de/congress/2004/fahrplan/event/176.en.html`.
17. Giffin, J., Greenstadt, R., Litwack, P., Tibbetts, R.: Covert messaging in TCP. In Dingledine, R., Syverson, P., eds.: Privacy Enhancing Technologies. Volume 2482 of Lecture Notes in Computer Science., Springer-Verlag (2002) 194–208
18. Bellovin, S.: RFC1948: Defending against sequence number attacks. IETF (1996)
19. de Raadt, T., Hallqvist, N., Grabowski, A., D. Keromytis, A., Provos, N.: Cryptography in OpenBSD: An overview. In: USENIX Annual Technical Conference (FREENIX Track). (1999) 93–102
20. Kohno, T., Broido, A., claffy, k.: Remote Physical Device Fingerprinting. In: 2005 IEEE Symposium on Security and Privacy, Oakland, California, IEEE CS (2005) 211–225
21. Hintz, A.: Covert channels in TCP and IP headers. Presentation at DEFCON 10 (2002) `http://guh.nu/projects/cc/`.

Steganalysis Based on Multiple Features Formed by Statistical Moments of Wavelet Characteristic Functions

Guorong Xuan[1], Yun Q. Shi[2], Jianjiong Gao[1], Dekun Zou[2], Chengyun Yang[1],
Zhenping Zhang[1], Peiqi Chai[1], Chunhua Chen[2], and Wen Chen[2]

[1] Tongji University, Shanghai, China
grxuan@public1.sta.net.cn
[2] New Jersey Institute of Technology, Newark, NJ, USA
shi@njit.edu

Abstract. In this paper[1], a steganalysis scheme based on multiple features formed by statistical moments of wavelet characteristic functions is proposed. Our theoretical analysis has pointed out that the defined n-th statistical moment of a wavelet characteristic function is related to the n-th derivative of the corresponding wavelet histogram, and hence is sensitive to data embedding. The selection of the first three moments of the characteristic functions of wavelet subbands of the three-level Haar wavelet decomposition as well as the test image has resulted in total 39 features for steganalysis. The effectiveness of the proposed system has been demonstrated by extensive experimental investigation. The detection rate for Cox et al.'s non-blind spread spectrum (SS) data hiding method, Piva et al.'s blind SS method, Huang and Shi's 8×8 block SS method, a generic LSB method (as embedding capacity being 0.3 bpp), and a generic QIM method (as embedding capacity being 0.1 bpp) are all above 90% over all of the 1096 images in the CorelDraw image database using the Bayes classifier. Furthermore, when these five typical data hiding methods are jointly considered for steganalysis, i.e., when the proposed steganalysis scheme is first trained sequentially for each of these five methods, and is then tested blindly for stego-images generated by all of these methods, the success classification rate is 86%, thus pointing out a new promising approach to general blind steganalysis. The detection results of steganalysis on Jsteg, Outguess and F5 have further demonstrated the effectiveness of the proposed steganalysis scheme.

1 Introduction

Steganalysis is the science and art to detect if an image contains hidden message, what the data embedding method is, what the used key is, and finally, if possible, what the hidden message is. It is the opposite side of steganography, which is also sometimes referred to as data hiding, or watermarking. Therefore, steganalysis also provides an effective way to evaluate the security performance of a data hiding

[1] This research is supported partly by National Natural Science Foundation of China (NSFC) on the project "The Research of Theory and Key Technology of Lossless Data Hiding (90304017)", and by New Jersey Commission of Science and Technology via New Jersey Center of Wireless Networking and Internet Security (NJWINS).

M. Barni et al. (Eds.): IH 2005, LNCS 3727, pp. 262–277, 2005.
© Springer-Verlag Berlin Heidelberg 2005

method. That is, it can be used to improve the security of a data hiding algorithm. Thus, a good data hiding method should be able to hide data imperceptibly not only to human eyes, but also to computer analysis.

Steganalysis seems a prohibitive task because of the diversity of cover images, the variety of data hiding methods and the infinite possibility of hidden messages. The basis of steganalysis is that there exists difference between the images before and after data hiding, and the difference is detectable. Normally, natural images tend to be continuous and smooth. The correlation between adjacent pixels is strong. Often, the hidden data will be independent to the cover media. The watermarking process may change the continuity because it incurs random variation. As a result, it may reduce the correlation among adjacent pixels, bit-planes and image blocks. Discovering the difference of some statistical characteristics between the cover and stego media becomes the key issue in steganalysis.

In [1], the first four statistical moments of wavelet coefficients and their prediction errors of nine high frequency subbands are used to form a 72-dimensional (72-D) feature vector for steganalysis. However, as shown and analyzed later in this paper, the performance in terms of detection rate is not satisfactory, because the selected features are not sensitive to data hiding process. The steganalysis method based on the mass center of histogram characteristic function has shown improved effectiveness in steganalysis [2]. The performance is however still not high enough because the rather limited number of features cannot achieve high detection rate.

In this paper, the statistical moments of characteristic functions (CF's) of wavelet subbands are proposed to form multi-dimensional (M-D) feature vector for steganalysis. We analyze why these features are effective to steganalysis. The substantially superior performance in steganalysis over the prior arts [1, 2] has been demonstrated by extensive experimental investigation.

The rest of this paper is organized as follows: Section 2 discusses the features proposed for steganalysis. In Section 3, our new effective steganalysis system is proposed. Experimental evaluation of the proposed steganalysis system is presented in Section 4. Finally, conclusion is drawn and discussion is made in Section 5.

2 Features Using Moments of Wavelet Characteristic Functions

In this section, we focus on the proposed M-D feature vector based on statistical moments of wavelet characteristic functions.

2.1 Steganalysis as a Task of Pattern Recognition

Based on whether an image contains hidden message, images can be classified into two classes: the image with no hidden message and the corresponding stego-image (the same image with message hidden in it). Steganalysis can thus be considered as a task of pattern recognition to decide which class a test image belongs to. The key issue for steganalysis just like for pattern recognition is feature selection. The features should be sensitive to the data hiding process. In other words, the features should be rather different for the image without hidden message and for the corresponding stego-image. The larger the difference, the better the features are. The features should be as general as possible, i.e., they are effective to all different types of images and different data hiding schemes. Often in practice it is very hard to achieve a high recognition rate with a single feature when the classification such as steganalysis is complicated in nature. Therefore, M-D feature vectors should be used under the circumstances. Each image is a sample point in the M-D feature space. Steganalysis has thus become a pattern classification process in the M-D feature space. It is desirable to have features in individual dimensions of the feature vector independent to one another. Just like for pattern recognition, in addition to feature selection, classifier design is another key issue for steganalysis; and the performance of a steganalysis scheme, both feature selection and classifier design, is evaluated by its classification success or error rate.

2.2 Moments of Wavelet Characteristic Functions for Steganalysis

As introduced in Section 1, an effective feature is proposed in [2], which is the mass center of histogram characteristic function (defined as the Fourier transform of the histogram). It has been proved that after a message is embedded into an image the mass center will decrease under the assumption that the hidden data are Gaussian distributed, additive to, and independent to the cover image.

It is well-known that the histogram of a digital image or a wavelet subband is essentially the probability mass function (pmf), if the image grayscale values or the wavelet coefficient values are treated as a random variable. Furthermore, if each component of the histogram is multiplied by a correspondingly shifted unit impulse, we then have the probability density function (pdf). According to [3], one can consider the characteristic function and the pdf (here, histogram) are similar to a Fourier transform pair (with the sign in the exponential reversed). Denote histogram by $h(x_j)$, and characteristic function (CF) by $H(f_k)$, both j and k are allowed to vary from 0, 1, up to N-1. Then they form a pair of discrete Fourier transform (DFT). That is, the mass center defined in [2] is essentially the first moment of the characteristic function of the image.

On the other hand, because of the de-correlation capability of wavelet transform, the coefficients of different subbands at the same level are kind of independent to each other. Therefore, the features generated from different wavelet subbands at the same level are kind of independent to each other as well. This is suitable for steganalysis (a particular type of pattern recognition as discussed in Section 2.1).

Motivated by these considerations, we propose to use the statistical moments of the characteristic functions of wavelet subbands as features for steganalysis. The n-th statistical moment of a characteristic function, M_n, is defined as follows.

$$M_n = \left(\sum_{k=0}^{N/2} f_k^n |H(f_k)|\right) \Big/ \left(\sum_{k=0}^{N/2} |H(f_k)|\right) \tag{1}$$

where $|H(f_k)|$ is the magnitude of the characteristic function, which is the DFT of the histogram.

According to the Fourier transform theory, since the histogram is real-valued, the magnitude of CF, $|H(f_k)|$, is even symmetric, while the CF's phase angle is odd symmetric. Therefore, only a half of points need to be used in the moment calculation for steganalysis.

In most of additive data hiding schemes, the to-be-embedded data obey Gaussian-like distribution. That is, the magnitude of the DFT of the hidden data is decreasing as the frequency index changes from 1, 2, up to N/2. Clearly, the sequence of $|H(f_k)|$ is non-negative. Therefore, by using the discrete Chebyshev inequality [2, 4(pp.239-240)], it can be shown that the defined moments will decrease after the data hiding process is applied, indicating that the defined features are sensitive to data hiding.

Next an analysis is provided to show that moments in characteristic function domain are more sensitive to data hiding than moments in histogram domain. In Table 2.1, the first three order absolute moments calculated in histogram domain and that calculated in characteristic function domain are listed for comparison, where the histogram is assumed to obey Gaussian distribution. It is shown that the n-th moment of CF is proportional to $(1/\sigma)^n$, while the n-th moment of histogram is proportional to σ^n. The histogram of a natural image can often be modeled as a mixture of several Gaussian distributions. In fact, the histogram of wavelet subband coefficients is generally modeled as Laplace-like, which can be modeled as the mixture of two Gaussian distributions with large variance difference. Since the moment of CF is proportional to $(1/\sigma)^n$, it is mainly determined by the distribution with the smaller variance; and the moment of histogram is proportional to σ^n, so it is mainly determined by the distribution with the larger variance. Or, we can say the moment of CF reflects the status on the peak of the histogram while the moment of histogram reflects the overall status of the histogram. In the process of data hiding, the distribution with smaller variance changes much more obviously than that with larger variance. In other words, the status on the peak of the histogram is impacted more greatly by the process of data hiding than the overall status of the histogram. So we can observe that the moment of CF is more sensitive to the process of data hiding.

Table 2.1. Moments in histogram domain and in characteristic function domain

n-th order absolute moment	$n=1$	$n=2$	$n=3$
in histogram domain $$\int_{-\infty}^{\infty}|x|^n\{h(x)\}dx$$ under Gaussian distribution $h(x)=\dfrac{1}{\sigma\sqrt{2\pi}}e^{-\frac{x}{2\sigma^2}}$	$\dfrac{\sigma\sqrt{2}}{\sqrt{\pi}}$	σ^2	$\dfrac{2\sigma^3\sqrt{2}}{\sqrt{\pi}}$
in characteristic function domain $$\left(\int_{-\infty}^{\infty}|f|^n|H(f)|df\right)\Big/\left(\int_{-\infty}^{\infty}|H(f)|df\right)$$ under characteristic function of Gaussian distribution $H(f)=e^{-\frac{\sigma^2 f^2}{2}}$	$\dfrac{\sqrt{2}}{\sigma\sqrt{\pi}}$	$\dfrac{1}{\sigma^2}$	$\dfrac{2\sqrt{2}}{\sigma^3\sqrt{\pi}}$

2.3 Proposed 39-D Feature Vector for Steganalysis

To facilitate the discussion, the proposed 39-D feature vector is presented here first. Some more discussions will be presented in Section 3. In our proposed steganalysis scheme we apply a three-level Haar discrete wavelet transformation (DWT) to a test image. Therefore there are 12 subbands, denoted by LL_i, HL_i, LH_i, HH_i, and $i=1,2,3$. The first three moments for each of these 12 subbands and the test image, denoted by LL_0, result in 39 features, or, equivalently a 39-D feature vector.

2.4 N-th Moments of Wavelet Subbands Versus N-th Moments of Characteristic Functions of Wavelet Subbands

As described in Section 1, the statistical moments of wavelet subbands have been proposed as features for steganalysis in [1]. In Section 2.2 we proposed to use statistical moments of characteristic functions (CF's) of wavelet subbands as features for steganalaysis. In this subsection, we compare these two different sets of features, and shall show why the moments of CF's of wavelet subbands are more effective.

In doing so, we use mathematical derivation in the analogue domain for the sake of format simplicity. As pointed in [3], the inverse transform of characteristic function produces the pdf (here, the histogram) as follows.

$$h(x) = \int_{-\infty}^{\infty} H(f) e^{-j2\pi f x} df \qquad (2)$$

Furthermore, we can derive the n-th derivative of the histogram evaluated at the origin, $x=0$, as follows.

$$\frac{d^n}{dx^n} h(x) \bigg|_{x=0} = \frac{d^n}{dx^n} \int_{-\infty}^{\infty} H(f) e^{-j2\pi f x} df \bigg|_{x=0}$$

$$= (-j2\pi)^n \int_{-\infty}^{\infty} f^n H(f) df \qquad (3)$$

$$= \begin{cases} (-1)^{n/2} 2(2\pi)^n \int_0^{\infty} f^n \, \mathrm{Re}(H(f)) df, & n \in even \\ (-1)^{(n-1)/2} 2(2\pi)^n \int_0^{\infty} f^n \, \mathrm{Im}(H(f)) df, & n \in odd \end{cases}$$

Straightforwardly, Formula (4) can be obtained from Equation (3).

$$\left| \left(\frac{d^n}{dx^n} h(x) \bigg|_{x=0} \right) \right| \leq 2(2\pi)^n \int_0^{\infty} f^n |H(f)| df \qquad (4)$$

We then observe that the right hand of the above inequality is the moments of CF's, M_n, multiplied by a scalar, which is dependent to the energy of an image or a wavelet subband, from which the moment is generated. This indicates that the features we defined actually are the upper bound (up to a scalar) of the magnitude of the n-th derivative of the histogram evaluated at the origin of the histogram, i.e., $x=0$. Furthermore, this observation can easily be extended to the case when $x \neq 0$ by using the translation property of the Fourier transform theory. That is, the defined n-th moment of a CF is closely related to the n-th derivative of the corresponding histogram. We have already showed at the end of Section 2.2 that the n-th moments defined will decrease after data embedding. This decrease lowers the upper bound of the magnitude of the n-th derivative of the histogram. This implies that the moments of CF's defined in our method can sensitively catch the changes caused by data hiding.

On the one hand, as shown above, the n-th moments of wavelet CF's have been shown closely related to the n-th derivative of the corresponding histogram. On the other hand, the n-th moments of wavelet subbands, selected features for steganalysis in [1], calculated through integration, are actually the statistical average of the n-th power of wavelet coefficients in the wavelet subbands. Under the assumption that the hidden data obey Gaussian distribution and are additive to the cover image, the histogram of the stego-image, the convolution of the histogram of the original image and the histogram of the hidden data (Gaussian distributed), will obviously become more flat than before data embedding. Obviously, the moments of wavelet CF's, which are related to the n-th derivatives of the histogram, will be able to catch this change. On contrary, the moments of wavelet subbands will average the change, and, consequently, are less sensitive to data hiding than the moments of CF's of wavelet subbands. Compared with that obtained by applying the proposed method, the experimental results obtained by applying the 72-D feature vector exactly the same as proposed in [1], shown in Section 4, have verified this analysis.

2.5 Differentiation Versus Integration

It is observed from Section 2.4 that, roughly speaking, one set of features for steganalysis (the moments of wavelet subbands [1]) perceives the histogram change caused by data hiding via integration, another set of features (the moments of characteristic functions of wavelet subbands) perceives the histogram change caused by data hiding via differentiation. The latter is expected to be more sensitive to the changes caused by data hiding. This has been verified by experimental works presented in Section 4.

Although it has been proved in [2] that the first moment of histogram characteristic function will decrease after data hiding, and it has been said in [2] that the histogram of the stego-image will be flatter than that of the original image, the following question has not been answered in [2] yet. That is, the histogram's becoming flatter owing to data hiding should also be able to be measured by the statistical moments of the test image. Why do we need the moments of the histogram characteristic function to catch this change in histogram? The mathematical relation between the n-th derivative of the histogram and the n-th moment of the corresponding CF shown in Section 2.4 has provided an answer.

2.6 Further Discussion and Graphical Illustration

We have assumed the noise introduced by data hiding is additive and Gaussian, and is independent to the cover image. These assumptions are valid for all of three major types of data hiding techniques, i.e., the spread spectrum (SS) method, the least significant bit-plane (LSB) method, and the quantization index modulation (QIM) method. It is well-known that the pdf of the sum of two independent random signals is the convolution of the individual pdf of these two signals.   Because of the assumptions made above, obviously, the pdf, hence the histogram, of the stego-image is expected to be more flat than that of the original image. This type of change is expected to be perceived in steganalysis. Now, according to Formula (4), the n-th moments defined and used in the proposed method is related to the magnitude of the n-th derivative of the histogram at the origin ($x=0$). As said, this observation can be extended to other points as $x \neq 0$. Therefore, we expect the features defined can catch the changes in the flatness of the histogram resulted from the data embedding. To facilitate the discussion, let us consider the cases, which cover all of subbands involved in the steganalysis. Two cases are discussed separately.

Case 1. For high frequency subbands, i.e., LH_i, HL_i, HH_i, $i=1,2,3$, the DWT coefficients in these subbands have mean values around at $x=0$. The histograms are known to be Laplacian-like. As shown by Formula (4), the n-th moment of the characteristic function is the upper bound of the magnitude of the n-th derivative of the histogram at $x=0$ (up to a scalar). This is to say that the moments, our features, can catch the changes occurring with the peak of the histogram. We shall show this peak point is very sensitive to data embedding, thus making our steganalysis effective.

Case 2. The second case consists of LL_i, $i=0,1,2,3$. That is, not only the test image, but also all of LL subbands in the three-level DWT decomposition are included. The LL_i subbands as $i=1,2,3$ are essentially the low frequency pass filtered version of the test image. In Case 2, Formula (4) is still valid. That is, the magnitude of the n-th derivatives of the histogram evaluated at the origin $x=0$ and other points are upper bounded by the n-th moment of CF defined (up to a scalar quantity).

Now, let us take a look into the histogram from the moments of characteristic functions. That is, we use some graphs to illustrate what we analyzed above. Due to the space limitation, we show only the first level of four Haar wavelet subbands of a given test image. Furthermore, the graph size is rather limited. To view these graphs clearly, readers are suggested to zoom them up to 500%. Figure 2.1 (a) shows one of CorelDraw [5] images with the order No. 18093. Figure 2.1 (b) is its grayscale image obtained by using the irreversible color transformation (ICT) [6]. Figure 2.1(c) is the stego-image of the grayscale image, using Cox et al.'s SS embedding method. In Figure 2.2, the histograms of the four subbands at the first level Haar wavelet transform of this grayscale image are displayed. Figure 2.3 provides a magnified view of these four histograms around the small interval containing $x=0$. In Figure 2.4, the graphs of characteristic functions of these four subbands of the image No. 18093 are shown. In the legend field of all figures, "Orig" denotes the original image, while "Cox" denotes the watermarked image is generated with Cox et al.'s spread spectrum data hiding method [7]. The numbers in the legend field are the first moment of the characteristic function of the corresponding subbands of the image.

It is observed from Figure 2.2 and, more clearly, from Figure 2.3, that the histograms of the wavelet subbands of the stego-image tend to be flatter than their counterparts of the original image as discussed. And, from observing the first order moments (listed in each graph), it appears that the first order moment of the stego-image (in this example, generated by using Cox et al.'s SS data hiding method) is smaller than the first moment of the original image. That is, after data hiding process, the upper bound of the magnitude of the first order derivative of histogram of the stego-image at *x=0* reduces from that of the original image, which agrees with what depicted in Figure 2.3. With this simple graph illustration, we have partially verified our analysis made above. This is true in general in our experimental works with all of the 1096 images in the CorelDraw image database.

(a) Original color image   (b) Grayscale image   (c) Stego-image (Cox et al.'s SS)

Fig. 2.1. CorelDraw image No.18093

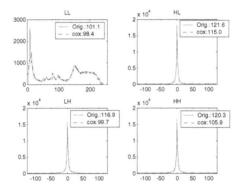

Fig. 2.2. Histogram of the first level wavelet subbands of image No. 18093

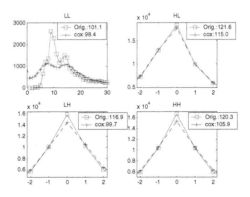

Fig. 2.3. Zoom in of Figure 2.2

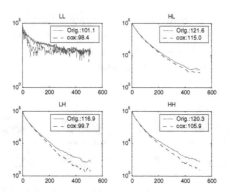

Fig. 2.4. Characteristic function of the first-level wavelet subbands of image No. 18093

3   Proposed Steganalysis Scheme

In this section, the M-D feature vector based on moments of CF's of wavelet subbands of a test image, and the Bayes classifier used in our steganalysis scheme are presented.

3.1   39-D Feature Vector

As discussed above, the proposed 39-D feature vector includes, in its components, the 1st, 2nd and 3rd moments of the characteristic function of 13 subbands (the image itself, LL_1, HL_1, LH_1, HH_1, LL_2, HL_2, LH_2, HH_2, LL_3, HL_3, LH_3, HH_3).

Note that we choose to include the moments of CF's generated from the DWT subbands, LL_i, $i=1,2,3$, into feature vector for steganalysis as well. Our experimental works have shown that these features also make contributions towards the success of steganalysis. Readers are referred to Table 4.2 in Section 4.

We select the three-level DWT decomposition, and we use the first three order moments of the characteristic functions as features because our experimental investigation have shown that it does not improve performance further if we use more than three-level decomposition and/or use more than the first three order moments.

3.2   Bayes Classifier

In addition to feature selection, the design of classifier is another key element in steganalysis. It affects the classification performance in terms of classification success rate as well as computational complexity and, hence, implementation speed. Therefore, the classifier plays an important role in steganalysis.

In this paper, the Bayes classifier under the condition of Gaussian distribution is adopted to steganalyze test images, each represented by a 39-D feature vector, denote by X_i, where i is the index of the test image. The notations of ω_1, ω_2 are used to denote the class of original images and the class of stego-images, respectively. Assume that both image classes obey Gaussian distribution. The mean vectors and covariance matrixes of ω_1 and ω_2 are denoted by μ_1, μ_2 and Σ_1, Σ_2, respectively. The Bayes classifier can be stated as follows [8].

A. Maximum posterior decision:

if

$$P(\omega_1 / X_i) \geq P(\omega_2 / X_i), \quad X_i \in \omega_1 \qquad (5)$$

else

$$X_i \in \omega_2 \qquad (6)$$

where:

$$P(\omega_k / X_i) = \frac{P(\omega_k) p(X_i / \omega_k)}{\sum\limits_{m=1}^{2} P(\omega_m) p(X_i / \omega_m)}, k = 1, 2 \qquad (7)$$

and

$$p(X_i / \omega_1) = N(X_i, \mu_1, \Sigma_1), \qquad p(X_i / \omega_2) = N(X_i, \mu_2, \Sigma_2) \qquad (8)$$

where N stands for normal (Gaussian) distribution.

B. Decision function:

$$\text{If } g_1(X_i) \geq g_2(X_i), X_i \in \omega_1 \text{ else } X_i \in \omega_2 \qquad (9)$$

$$\text{where, } g_k(X_i) = -\frac{1}{2} X_i^T \Sigma_k^{-1} X_i + \left(\Sigma_k^{-1} \mu_k \right)^T X_i - \frac{1}{2} \mu_k^T \Sigma_k^{-1} \mu_k - \frac{1}{2} \ln |\Sigma_k| \qquad (10)$$

4 Evaluation of the Proposed Steganalysis Method

To evaluate the proposed steganalysis scheme based on the multiple moments of wavelet characteristic function, we use the CorelDraw image database [5] as the experimental image set. This database contains 1096 images in total, including images of various kinds, say, architecture, place, leisure, ocean, animal, food and so on. In the experiments, we randomly choose 5/6 of the 1096 CorelDraw images (specifically, 896 images in our experiments) for training purpose, following the common practice in the automatic recognition of Arabic numerals [9]. The remaining 1/6 of the 1096 images (specifically, the remaining 200 images) are used for testing purpose. The successful classification rate in steganalysis is referred to as detection rate in this paper. To be reliable, the detection rates are reported by averaging the rates obtained in multiple times (specifically 30 times) of such types of randomly conducted experiments.

In the first set of experiments, data are embedded into images by using the following five typical data embedding methods, i.e., the non-blind spread spectrum (SS) method by Cox et al. [7], the blind SS method by Piva et al. [10], the 8x8 block based SS method by Huang and Shi [11], a generic quantization index modulation (QIM) method by Chen et al. [12], and a generic least significant bit-plane method (LSB). The non-blind SS method by Cox et al. is noted for its strong robustness. The hidden data are a random number sequence obeying Gaussian distribution with zero mean and unit variance. The data are embedded into the 1000 coefficients of global discrete cosine transform (DCT) coefficients of the largest magnitudes except the DC coefficient. The original cover image is needed for hidden data extraction. The SS method by Piva et al. is blind. That is, it does not need the original cover image for hidden data extraction. It embeds data into some 16,000 selected middle frequency DCT coefficients. The block SS method by Huang Shi is also blind. Data are hidden in the low frequency block DCT coefficients. Note that the LSB is one type of methods widely used by many steganographic algorithms. A generic LSB data hiding method with embedding rate as 0.3 bpp (bit per pixel) is used in this experiment. For the QIM data hiding, some selected middle frequency of 8x8 block DCT coefficients are quantized to embed data. Here a typical JPEG quantization table is used. The quantization step size used in the QIM scheme is 5. The data embedding capacity is set to be 0.1 bpp.

The consideration that various data hiding methods, in particular the SS methods, are included in our experimental investigation is justified as follows. Although it may not carry as many information bits as the LSB methods in general, the SS methods can still serve for the covert communication purpose. For example, a terrorist command may need only to send a 'GO' command to his cell members for an attack. By the way, some newly developed SS methods can hide a large amount of data. For instance, a data embedding rate from 0.5 bpp (bits per pixel) to 0.75 bpp can now be easily achieved [e.g., 13]. In addition, the SS methods are known more robust than the LSB. Therefore, it is necessary to consider the SS methods for steganalysis.

In the second set of experiments, data are embedded into color images by using some steganographic tools, i.e., Jsteg [14], Outguess [15] and F5 [16], respectively.

4.1 Experimental Results with Five Typical Data Hiding Methods

For each of these five data hiding methods, 1096 stego-images are generated from the 1096 CorelDraw images. For each method, now we have 1096 pairs of images, one is the original image, another is the stego-image generated by the data hiding method. Then the 39-D feature vector as defined above is extracted from each of these 1096 pairs of images. The detection rate is reported by averaging over 30 times randomly conducted experiments. The test results are shown in the right-most column of Table 4.1. There TP stands for true positive, FP for false positive, and the average is the arithmetic average of TP and TN (true negative).

Table 4.1. Detection rate in the unit of % (averaged over 30 times experiments)

Data hiding methods	Harmsen's [2]			Farid's [1]			Proposed		
	TP	FP	average	TP	FP	average	TP	FP	average
Cox et al.'s SS	54.1	15.6	69.2	77.6	47.9	64.9	95.7	5.4	95.1
Piva et. al's SS	91.8	45.9	73.0	86.5	10.9	87.8	96.1	10.8	92.6
Huang and Shi' block SS	96.7	33.6	81.5	92.0	39.7	76.1	98.3	7.0	95.7
Generic QIM (0.1 bpp)	90.2	46.6	71.8	99.5	0.00	99.7	98.9	2.8	98.0
Generic LSB (0.3 bpp)	79.7	56.9	61.4	89.9	46.1	71.9	94.4	6.2	94.1
5 methods combined	85.9	62.1	77.9	67.6	20.4	69.6	84.5	8.4	85.7

To compare the performance of the proposed method with Farid's method [1], we use the exactly same 72-D feature vector as proposed in [1], the same Bayes classifier used above, and the 1096 CorelDraw images to conduct the similar steganalysis experiments. The test results are shown in the middle column of Table 4.1.

We also use the features proposed in [2], the Bayes classifier introduced above, and the 1096 CorelDraw images to conduct the same experiments as described above. The corresponding results are shown in the left column of Table 4.1.

It is obvious from Table 4.1 that the proposed steganalysis scheme outperforms both of the prior arts proposed in [1,2].

By the combination of the five methods, it is meant that all the stego-images associated with the five methods and the original images are used together in experiments. Concretely, we now have 1096 6-tuple images with each 6-tuple having one original CorelDraw image, and five stego-images generated by these five data hiding methods, respectively. Again, 896 6-tuples are randomly selected for training and the remaining 200 6-tuples are used for testing. The purpose of this experiment is to examine if our proposed method can successfully detect stego-images from original images when all of these five data hiding methods are jointly considered. From Table 4.1, we can see the average detection rate is 86%. It is reasonable to see the combined detection rate is somehow lower than that obtained for each individual data hiding method. However, the detection rate of 86% indicates that our proposed scheme has some blind steganalysis capability. In other words, the proposed method has made a significant step towards establishment of a blind and powerful steganalysis system.

Table 4.2 contains the average detection rates obtained by applying each individual statistical moment alone for the non-blind spread spectrum (SS) data hiding method by Cox et al. [7]. The moments in the right-most three columns (referred to as the right side below) are the moments of CF's of wavelet subbands (our proposed method), while the left side columns (from the 2nd to 4th columns in Table 4.2) are moments of wavelet subbands, which, excluding LL_i, $i=0,1,2,3$, are proposed for steganalysis in [1]. It is clearly that each individual detection rate in the right side is higher than its counterpart in the left side, indicating that the proposed wavelet CF's moments are more effective to steganalsysi than the moments of wavelet subbands. Furthermore, as pointed out in Section 3.1, the utilization of the moments of wavelet CF's, specifically, LL_i, $i=0,1,2,3$, has been justified. It is clearly observed that these moments do make relatively strong contribution to steganalysis.

Table 4.2. Average detection rate in unit of % by applying each feature alone

	1st moment of histogram	2nd moment of histogram	3rd moment of histogram	1st moment of CF	2nd moment of CF	3rd moment of CF
LL_0	50.4	50.1	50.3	63.4	65.8	54.0
LL_1	50.5	50.3	50.2	63.8	62.9	54.9
LH_1	50.1	50.0	50.0	54.7	54.9	54.7
HL_1	50.1	50.0	50.0	54.4	54.9	54.6
HH_1	50.2	50.0	50.0	55.2	54.9	55.2
LL_2	50.5	50.4	50.5	64.2	56.2	53.6
LH_2	50.1	50.0	50.0	55.5	55.4	55.3
HL_2	50.2	50.0	50.0	55.8	55.6	55.6
HH_2	50.1	50.0	50.1	51.7	52.3	53.0
LL_3	50.5	50.5	50.5	56.6	52.9	54.2
LH_3	50.5	50.1	50.0	62.3	61.6	59.9
HL_3	50.3	50.1	50.0	61.5	59.2	55.9
HH_3	50.1	50.0	50.0	51.6	52.1	51.3

4.2 Experimental Results in the Reduced Feature Space

In order to facilitate the visualization of steganalysis, we apply the Bhattacharyya distance technique [17] developed and utilized in the pattern recognition field to reduce the M-D (M=39 in our case) feature vectors to r-D (r=3 in our case) feature vectors. According to [17], the matrix A in the dimensionality reduction is obtained by minimizing the upper bound of the detection error rate in the M-D space, i.e., $\varepsilon_m = \min_A \varepsilon(A)$, where $A = (A)_{m \times r}$ is the dimensionality reduction matrix.

With respect to all of the 1096 CorelDraw images, and the corresponding 1096 stego-images generated by applying the generic LSB data hiding method (data embedding rate is 0.3 bpp as described above), we apply the steganalysis methods in [1], [2] and the proposed method, respectively, to produce feature vectors according to [1], [2], and this paper. Then, all of the 2192 features vectors of 72-D [1] and 39-D (our proposed) are reduced to 3-D by using the above-mentioned Bhattacharyya distance technique. Note that the 2192 feature vectors generated by [2] are 3-D vectors already. Figures 4.1 (a),(b),(c) display, respectively, the distribution of these 3-D feature vectors. There the red points denote the feature vectors of the original images, while the blue pints the feature vectors of the stego-images.

As shown in Figure 4.1, the detection rate of the proposed steganalsyis method with the 39-D feature vectors is 94.0%. When applying the Bhattacharyya distance technique to reduce the 39-D feature vectors to the 3-D feature vectors, the detection rate is 87.0%, indicating the detection rate does not lower much. With the steganalysis method in [2] is applied, the 3-D feature vectors are produced, the detection rate is 54.7%. With the steganalysis method in [1], the detection rate is 71.8% for 72-D feature vectors, and is 50.1% for the reduced 3-D feature vectors.

It is observed from Figure 4.1 that the distribution of the 3-D feature vectors between the original and the stego-images with the proposed steganalysis method are most clearly separable among these three steganalysis methods. This agrees with the difference among the detection rates reported in Table 4.1.

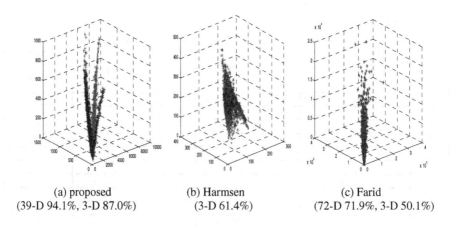

(a) proposed	(b) Harmsen	(c) Farid
(39-D 94.1%, 3-D 87.0%)	(3-D 61.4%)	(72-D 71.9%, 3-D 50.1%)

Fig. 4.1. Distribution of 3-D feature vectors (CorelDraw image database, LSB data hiding)

4.3 Experimental Results with Three Staganographic Algorithms

Jsteg, OutGuess and F5 algorithms have been, respectively, applied to each of the 1096 color CorelDraw images to generate stego-images. Similar to [1], the central portions of some randomly selected CorelDraw images with sizes of $20\times20,40\times40,80\times80$ are embedded. For both original and stego color images, the ICT has been applied to produce corresponding gray-scale images. Features are then generated from the gray-scale images for steganalysis. Bayes classifier has been used as classifier. The test results are shown in Table 4.3. Note that OutGuess sometimes cannot be applied to some color images to generate stego-images. As a result, only about half of 1096 CorelDraw images can hide a central portion of color image of size 80×80. Therefore, there are no test results of 80×80 data hiding for OutGuess.

Note that though the Bayes classifier is optimum when the priori probabilities obey Gaussian distribution, non-linear classifiers such as neural network and SVM can generally provide better performance in pattern classification [8]. In addition, it is noted that detection rates can be improved significantly by collecting statistics from within and across all three color components [1]. These tasks are on our agenda of future work. Here by using the same Bayes classifier and the same procedure to collect features from converted gray-scale images, it is desired to compare the effectiveness of different feature sets in steganalysis. Table 4.3 indicates that our proposed feature set outperforms that proposed in [1] in general.

Table 4.3. Test results on several steganographic algorithms

Method	JSteg				F5				OutGuess		
Payload	10x10	20x20	40x40	80x80	10x10	20x20	40x40	80x80	10x10	20x20	40x40
Farid	51.9%	58.8%	80.3%	99.4%	49.7%	50.5%	51.1%	68.7%	59.8%	60.0%	75.4%
Ours	54.6%	64.0%	75.5%	87.9%	50.1%	50.8%	56.1%	74.3%	77.1%	78.2%	82.7%

5   Conclusion

In this paper, we have proposed to use statistical moments of wavelet characteristic functions as features for steganalysis. In theoretical analysis and in extensive experiments, the superiority of the proposed features over statistical moments of wavelet subbands, which is discussed in [1], has been shown. Specifically, we show that the n-th moments of wavelet characteristic function are related to the magnitude of the n-th derivative of the histogram at different values, x, in the histogram. Note that when the $x=0$, the peak points of histograms of high frequency subbands are considered. Therefore, the proposed features are sensitive to the changes of the histogram of wavelet subbands caused by data hiding. Equivalently, the differentiation of histogram is more effective than integration of histogram for steganalysis. Graphs and experiment results support this observation.

We have also shown that, owing to the de-correlation property of wavelet decomposition, the wavelet based feature vector, i.e., adding the statistical moments of characteristic function of wavelet subbands is much more effective than the features extracted from image in spatial domain alone as proposed in [2].

39-D feature vectors are proposed for steganalysis. It includes the 1st, 2nd and 3rd moments of characteristic function of the subbands with the 3-level Haar wavelet decomposition. Bayes classifier is adopted to classify the testing images.

Extensive experimental works have demonstrated that the proposed steganalysis system based on the proposed M-D feature vector is rather effective. For the non-blind spread spectrum data hiding method by Cox et al. which is the tough method for steganalysis, the detection rate reaches 95%, while the steganalysis schemes in [1] and in [2] implemented by us can only reach 65% and 69%, respectively.

Besides, a fit-in-for-all system is tested with the stego-images generated by all the five typical data hiding methods. The average correct classification rate is 86%. This promising result has pointed out a new and practical way towards blind and powerful steganalysis for future research. The test results on Jsteg, OutGuess and F5 have further demonstrated the effectiveness of the proposed steganalysis scheme.

In addition, all of these experiments are conducted over a set of images with a large size, which is considered necessary for steganalysis.

References

1. S. Lyu and H. Farid: Detecting hidden messages using higher-order statistics and support vector machines. Proc. of 5th International Workshop on Information Hiding, Noordwijkerhout, The Netherlands, 2002.
2. J. J. Harmsen: Steganalysis of Additive Noise Modelable Information Hiding. Master Thesis of Rensselaer Polytechnic Institute, Troy, New York , advised by Professor W. A. Pearlman, (2003)
3. A. Leon-Garcia: Probability and Random Processes for Electrical Engineering. 2nd Ed., Addison-Wesley (1994)
4. D. S. Mitrinovic, J. E. Pecaric and A. M. Fink: Classical and New Inequalities in Analysis. The Netherlands. Kluwer Academic Publishers (1993)
5. CorelDraw Software, www.corel.com.
6. C. Christopoulos, A. Skodras, and T. Ebrahimi: The JPEG2000 Still Image Coding Sysyem: An Overview. IEEE Transactions on Consumer Electronics, vol. 46. (Nov. 2000) 1103-1127
7. I. J. Cox, J. Kilian, T. Leighton and T. Shamoon: Secure Spread Spectrum Watermarking for Multimedia. IEEE Trans. on Image Processing, Vol.6 (1997) 1673-1687
8. K. Fukunaga: Introduction to Statistical Pattern Recognition, 2nd Edition, Academic Press Inc.. Boston. (1990)
9. The MNIST DATABASE of handwritten digits. Yann LeCun, NEC Research Institute. http://yann.lecun.com/exdb/mnist/
10. A. Piva, M. Barni, E Bartolini, V. Cappellini: DCT-based Watermark Recovering without Resorting to the Uncorrupted Original Image. Proc. of the 1997 International Conference on Image Processing vol. 1 (1997) 520
11. J. Huang and Y. Q. Shi: An adaptive image watermarking scheme based on visual masking. IEE Electronic Letters, vol. 34, (1998)748-750
12. B. Chen and G. W. Wornell: Digital watermarking and information embedding using dither modulation. Proc. of IEEE Second Workshop of Multimedia Signal Processing. Los Angeles, CA. (Dec. 1998) 273-278

13. G. Xuan, Y. Q. Shi, Z. Ni, "Reversible data hiding using integer wavelet transform and companding technique," IWDW04, Korea, October 2004.
14. Jsteg V4, by Derek Upham, is available at ftp.funet.fi
15. OutGuess, by Niels Provos, is available at www.outguess.org
16. F5, by A. Westfeld, is available at wwwrn.inf.tu-dresden.de/~westfeld/f5.html.
17. G. Xuan, P. Chai, M. Wu, "Bhattacharyya distance feature selection," Proceedings of the 13th International Conference on Pattern Recognition, pp. 195-199, Aug. 25-29, 1996, Vienna, Austria.

Assessment of Steganalytic Methods
Using Multiple Regression Models

Rainer Böhme

Technische Universität Dresden, Institute for System Architecture,
01062 Dresden, Germany
rainer.boehme@inf.tu-dresden.de

Abstract. This paper proposes multiple regression models as a method
for quantitative evaluation of the accuracy in steganalysis with respect to
various moderating factors, such as parameter choice of the detector and
properties of the carrier object. The case for multivariate statistical inference in steganalysis is particularly relevant: recent findings suggest that
type and characteristics of carrier do matter, but the precise relations
remain still opaque. In this paper we provide an exemplary comparison between two length-estimating attacks against LSB steganography.
Extensions and applications for improved steganalysis are addressed.

1 Motivation

Steganography is the art and science of hiding information such that its presence
cannot be detected. Unlike cryptography, where anybody on the transmission
channel notices the flow of information but cannot read its content, steganography aims to embed a confidential message in unsuspicious data, such as image
or audio files [21].

Attempts to attack steganographic systems are referred to as *steganalysis*.
For passive attacks it is sufficient if an adversary detects the existence of a hidden message even if she cannot decrypt its content [1]. By the weakest definition,
a steganographic algorithm is considered as broken if there exists a method that
can determine whether or not a medium contains hidden information with a
success rate better than random guessing. For practical steganalysis the performance of detection methods is usually expressed in terms of detection rate, the
probability that a stego object is identified, and false positive rate, the probability that a clean carrier is incorrectly considered as stego object.

Since it is obvious that the detectability of a secret message depends on its
length as a proportion to the total capacity of a given carrier object, the continuous chase between steganography and steganalysis can be merely considered as
process that ultimately converges in revealing an upper bound for conditional
secure steganography. Apart from the message length, recent research in image
steganography showed two additional sources of influence: adjustment of the detection method and properties of the carrier object (i. e., source, storage format,
etc.) [13,14,15]. Even though systematic evidence for these factors is still sparse

M. Barni et al. (Eds.): IH 2005, LNCS 3727, pp. 278–295, 2005.

and exists in a merely isolated manner, we have to assume that all types of moderating factors are mutually dependent.

Hence, a scientifically rigorous evaluation of the entirety of intervening factors requires a methodology, which is suitable for the identification and quantification of individual factors and their interaction with other variables. The capability to infer statistical sound evidence from experimental data rather than from demanding formal analyses would be considered as advantageous.

This paper proposes regression analysis as an appropriate tool to evaluate steganalytic performance and its interdependence with moderating variables. Therefore we demonstrate the effectiveness with an example comparison of two well-understood methods for the detection of data embedded by overwriting the least significant bits (LSB) of a carrier signal: *Regular-Singular* (RS) [7] and *Weighted Stego Image* (WS) analysis [6]. The ideas behind both methods and their variations are briefly addressed in Section 2. Section 3 elaborates on an operable notion of steganalytic accuracy. Further, the methodology to assess the accuracy in dependence of influencing factors is outlined, before it is applied to study the influence of image properties in Section 4. Finally, Section 5 concludes with a discussion of possible applications of the proposed methodology for improved steganalysis.

2   Related Work

There are two categories of steganalytic methods, namely targeted attacks and so-called "blind" or "universal" attacks. The former are designed to detect stego objects stemming from one specific steganographic algorithm by exploiting its characteristic artefacts, while the latter rely on the discriminatory power of machine learning algorithms fed with a number of features computed from large training sets of both clean carrier and stego objects [20]. This paper is restricted to targeted attacks, because they are more reliable and their mode of operation is transparent. In particular, we will focus on quantitative attacks, which output an estimation of the secret message length [8], in contrast to solely a binary decision whether a given object contains a stego message or not [24]. This restriction is reasonable because pure binary attacks tend to have very limited reliability if only a fraction of the steganographic capacity is used. Moreover, the majority of current targeted attacks belongs to the quantitative class.

Algorithms for image steganography can be classified by the embedding domain, and the embedding function employed. In the frequency domain, there exist quantitative attacks for the embedding functions of *JSteg*, *OutGuess* and *F5* [8]. There is a whole arsenal of quantitative attacks against the ubiquitous embedding function of randomised LSB flipping in the spatial domain [4,6,7,9,19,25,26], and recent efforts to attack the still hard-to-detect $\pm K^1$ embedding function also pursue a length estimation approach [10,12].

Regarding the actively researched area of LSB flipping attacks, there is no common methodology to compare different methods or different variations of one

---

[1] Also referred to as *LSB matching* [15] or *additive noise steganography*.

method. When introducing their new WS method, Fridrich and Goljan [6] compare mean and variance of the new estimation with results from RS and conclude that WS is more reliable for very short messages. So do Zhang and Ping when evaluating their detector based on difference histograms with *Sample Pairs* and RS [25]. The probably most comprehensive evaluation of LSB detection methods is given in [13,14]. However, the methods and variations are judged by their discriminatory power to tell stego objects and carrier apart, without regarding additional information, such as length estimation. In the same papers, different variations of the detection methods (for instance the group size and selection rule in RS analysis) are compared in *Receiver Operating Characteristics* (ROC) diagrams. These graphs show the relationship between detection rate and false positive rate for different operating points. When proposing a recursive method for pixel selection to improve the reliability of *Pairs Analysis* [9], Westfeld [23] reports area-based measures derived from the ROC diagram in addition to the graphical presentation.

In order to avoid time-consuming simulations, Dabeer et al. [2] propose analytical derivation of bounds for binary detectors of LSB replacement steganography in a framework of statistical hypothesis tests. However, by the nature of the approach and the difficulty in specifying a proper image model, the bounds obtained are rather loose. Furthermore, the analyses solely cover memoryless attacks, which are confined to first-order statistics. By contrast, as this paper aims to evaluate the most sophisticated attacks published, we accept the computational complexity and deliberately choose the simulation approach.

Concerning influences of image properties, Ker compares ROC curves for different image sizes [14] and previous compression type [13], respectively. For some hypotheses, non-parametric tests are computed to identify statistical significant differences. The analyses of image properties in [8] merely rely on the interpretation of outliers in the test set. To sum it up, rigorous quantification and statistically strong evidence (in terms of hypothesis tests and confidence intervals) in the literature is sparse. However, we consider this as a prerequisite for a sound comparison of different methods, especially when a number of exogenous factors are to be examined.

To demonstrate the methodology proposed in this paper, we selected two well-known length-estimating attacks, RS and WS, for a regression-based assessment. Therefore we summarise the ideas behind both methods. However, for a detailed discussion the reader is referred to the original publications.

RS analysis [7] measures the amount of embedding changes by observing the proportion of *regular* and *singular* groups of pixels before and after two types of flipping operations: the first works exactly like the embedding function $(0 \leftrightarrow 1, 2 \leftrightarrow 3, \ldots)$, while the other one swaps the opposite pairs of values $(1 \leftrightarrow 2, 3 \leftrightarrow 4, \ldots)$. Groups are counted as *regular* if a noisiness measure increases after flipping, otherwise as *singular*. The fraction of LSB flipped bits can be computed by solving a quadratic equation over statistics of the groups. The way pixels are grouped, the group size, and a mask vector used for the noisiness measure, are subject to experimental fine tuning.

In contrast to RS analysis, WS analysis [6] computes its estimator on statistics of individual pixels, rather than on pre-aggregated groups. The secret message length is computed from the difference between the stego image and an estimate of the cover image generated from the neighbourhood pixels. The fact that the accuracy of the cover image estimation depends on the local variance is reflected by a weighting mechanism, which can be adjusted with a parameter α. The charm of this attack lies in the elegant closed-form equation, and compared to this simplicity the achievable performance is remarkably good.

In the experiments described below, we use RS with constant group size 4 and mask $(0, 1, 1, 0)$. For WS we set $\alpha = 1$, as recommended in the initial paper. All analyses were implemented and processed in R [22,11], using the generalised nonlinear regression functions from the package *gnlm* [17].

3   Measuring the Accuracy of Steganalytic Methods

Regression analysis fits models specified as equation systems to multivariate data. Apart from few exceptions where special data was needed, the models in this paper are fitted to data generated in the following experimental setup: 304 never-compressed source images taken from different digital cameras were obtained from the beta version of the *Digital Forensic Image Library* database [5], then converted into 8-bit grayscale and downsized to four different bounding boxes of 800, 400, 200, and 100.[2] From the set of images with longer edge of 800 pixels we create smaller images by cropping the central area to, again, 400, 200, and 100. This procedure ensures that we have images in the sample where the dimension is not correlated with spatial characteristics, such as noise or local energy. From each of the resulting 2,128 carrier images, 18 independent stego objects were simulated and then evaluated with both RS and WS, leading to a total sample of 76,608 attacks. The 18 cases split up into 14 fixed embedding ratios $q \in \{0.0, 0.01, 0.03, 0.05, 0.1, 0.2, \ldots, 0.9, 1.0\}$ and four uniformly random q in the intervals $[0, 0.125]$, $[0, 0.25]$, $[0, 0.5]$, and $[0, 1]$. Hence, small embedding ratios are over-represented in the data set. Random sub-samples of results from *different* images are drawn for all parameter estimations used for inference to avoid undue dependence between error terms and over-interpretation of the relatively small core set of images.

3.1   Analysis of Error Distribution

To model the accuracy of the length estimation we have to consider the error distributions. Therefore we fitted the deviation of the estimate from the actual embedding ratio $\hat{q} - q$ to different symmetric two-parameter distributions. As shown in Figure 1 for $q = 0.2$, the Cauchy distribution fits best for RS and WS. We can confirm that this is valid independent of q (cases where the quadratic equation in RS has no root were censored).

---

[2] We use *Netpbm*'s `pnmscale` utility with default settings. Its *Pixel Mixing* downsizing algorithm is described at `http://netpbm.sourceforge.net/doc/pamscale.html`

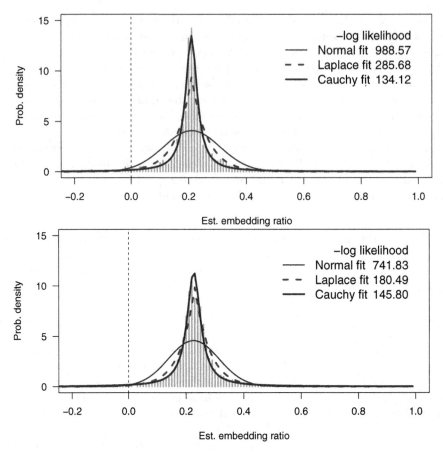

Fig. 1. Error distribution of RS analysis (top) and WS analysis (bottom) from 2000+ stegotexts of varying size. Exactly 20 % of each image's capacity was used.

The probability density function of the Cauchy distribution is given as

$$d(x, \mu, \lambda) = \frac{1}{\pi} \frac{\lambda}{\lambda^2 + (x - \mu)^2} \quad , \tag{1}$$

where π is the radial constant, μ is the median, and λ is a scale parameter so that $2 \cdot \lambda$ is the width of the distribution at half of the maximum density. Known for its fat tails, this distribution is employed for extreme value tests in Monte Carlo simulations. Since current length-estimating attacks also face a high number of outliers, we may assume that the errors for length estimations follow a Cauchy distribution. A validation of 500 randomly drawn residuals with the more sensitive Kolmogorov-Smirnov goodness-of-fit test leads to the same result, as reported in Table 1 (a p-value above 0.1 is accepted as decision criterion).

The distribution assumption can be further supported by the argument that a division of two Gaussian random variables yields a Cauchy distribution. Accord-

Table 1. One-sample Kolmogorov-Smirnov tests

	Goodness of fit			
	RS analysis		WS analysis	
Distribution	D	Test statistic	D	Test statistic
Normal	0.3036	$p < 0.001$	0.3018	$p < 0.001$
Laplace	0.2502	$p < 0.001$	0.3031	$p < 0.001$
Cauchy	0.0388	$p = 0.44$	0.0438	$p = 0.29$

ingly, at least for those length-estimating attacks solving quadratic equations, it seems plausible that the Cauchy error characteristic can be explained analytically from the computation rules for the estimate of the secret message length. However, this is beyond the scope of this paper.

The finding that both length-estimating attacks follow a Cauchy distribution is a surprising result. At the same time, it is cautionary because no moments are defined for this distribution. This implies that mean and variance are unsuitable for comparisons between estimation results, and researchers are recommended to report scale and location parameters of the Cauchy distribution! If necessary, quantiles and other non-parametric measures could serve as alternatives.

The importance of this finding is illustrated in Figure 2, where Gaussian variance and Cauchy scale are plotted as measures of accuracy of RS and WS. In the left chart, the sample variance σ^2 is estimated for 2000 simulation trials at each step of embedding ratio q. The relation appears shaky and unstable because the moments do not converge and the outliers push it in arbitrary directions. Hence, there is no visible difference between the two attack strategies and both show a notable decrease in (absolute) accuracy for embedding ratios above 0.75. The Cauchy estimates of the same data, in turn, provide a much clearer picture. The

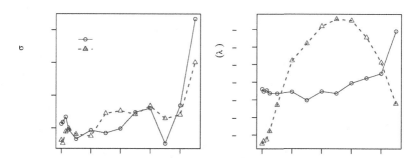

Fig. 2. Fallacy of Gaussian moments: compared to sample variance estimates (left) the Cauchy scale parameters (right) appear more stable and show different pattern for both methods ($N \approx 2200$ simulated attacks per data point)

accuracy of RS decreases gradually whereas WS shows a nonlinear relationship with superior accuracy for very low and very high embedding ratios.[3] These clear dependency structures provide a good starting point for regression models.

3.2   Estimation and Interpretation of Nonlinear Regression Models

An error distribution different from Gaussian also complicates the case for regression analysis. Instead of linear models with their fast *Ordinary Least Squares* (OLS) parameter estimation and straightforward test statistic, we have to resort to generalised nonlinear regression models, which employ a *Maximum Likelihood* (ML) estimation. For response distributions outside the exponential dispersion family, such as the Cauchy distribution, parameter estimation requires an iterative numerical procedure [3,16]. In turn, this procedure leaves more flexibility in the design of the model. So we use linear regression terms to explain both parameters of the distribution of the dependent variable, i. e., the secret message length estimate $\hat{q}$, with one or more predictor variables $\mathbf{x} = (x_1, x_2, \ldots, x_n)$. Each model consists of two equations, one for each parameter of the Cauchy distribution:

$$\hat{q} \sim \mathbf{Cau}(\mu, \lambda) : \begin{cases} \mu & = a_0 + a_1 \cdot x_1 + a_2 \cdot x_2 + \ldots + a_n \cdot x_n \\ \log(\lambda^2) = b_0 + b_1 \cdot x_1 + b_2 \cdot x_2 + \ldots + b_n \cdot x_n \end{cases} \quad (2)$$

The log transformation of the scale parameter effectively forms a non-negativity constraint without modifying the solver.

After estimating the coefficient vectors $\mathbf{a} = (a_0, \ldots, a_n)$ and $\mathbf{b} = (b_0, \ldots, b_n)$ from data, the coefficients can be interpreted as weights indicating the direction of influence and importance of each predictor for the location μ and the scale λ of the resulting Cauchy random variable.

In the stego-detection case, μ is closely linked to q, the embedding ratio. Further influences on μ we call *bias*. The value of λ determines the amount of outliers so that we can interpret this parameter as best proxy for the *accuracy* of the secret message length estimation. Hereby, larger λ imply broader distributions, and smaller values lead to sharper peaks. In the following, our definition of accuracy will always refer to the shape parameter: positive coefficients b_i denote that predictor x_i decreases the accuracy, whereas negative coefficients b_i indicate better precision with increasing x_i. However, we should refrain from over-interpreting very small coefficients. As a rule of thumb, we may consider a predictor term as influential if the absolute value of its coefficient is at least two standard errors greater than zero. The relative impact of predictors with comparable units of measurement can be ranked according to the coefficients' absolute values.

Apart from individual coefficients, it is also important to inspect the overall model fitting indicators. The negative log likelihood is a basic criterion to rate the goodness of fit to the data. The smaller the value (i. e., the higher the likelihood) the more appropriate is the model. However, this value is highly dependent on

---

[3] For the low range, this is consistent with the findings reported in [6].

the number of observations N, so that this indicator cannot be used to compare across different samples. Models with multiple terms can be compared to nested smaller models with the *Likelihood Ratio Test* (LRT). Usually the *default model* with solely constant terms (a_0 and b_0) is used as reference. The higher the LRT value the greater the improvement between the default and the tested model. Again, LRT should not be used to compare models of different samples. There is also a method to compute a p value for the test statistic of the null hypothesis that both models explain equally well. Finally, the proportion of variance R^2 explained by the model is a popular indicator for the Gaussian case. In the nonlinear case, the literature contains a number of proposals for pseudo-R^2 measures. The values displayed in the following tables are computed according to the McFadden method [18].

As a first concrete example, we investigate the accuracy of RS and WS in dependence of the embedding ratio q with the following models.

$$\textbf{Model } Q^0: \quad \begin{aligned} \mu &= a_0 + 1 \cdot q \\ \log(\lambda^2) &= b_0 \end{aligned} \tag{3}$$

$$\textbf{Model } Q^1: \quad \begin{aligned} \mu &= a_0 + a_1 \cdot q \\ \log(\lambda^2) &= b_0 \end{aligned} \tag{4}$$

$$\textbf{Model } Q^2: \quad \begin{aligned} \mu &= a_0 + a_1 \cdot q \\ \log(\lambda^2) &= b_0 + b_1 \cdot q \end{aligned} \tag{5}$$

$$\textbf{Model } Q^3: \quad \begin{aligned} \mu &= a_0 + a_1 \cdot q \\ \log(\lambda^2) &= b_0 + b_1 \cdot q + b_2 \cdot q^2 \end{aligned} \tag{6}$$

Q^0 serves as a reference (or default) model for the model comparisons. Q^1 is suitable to identify relative linear deviation from the true embedding ratio (for an ideal detector, a_1 should not differ significantly from one). Finally, Q^2 and Q^3 model the relationship between embedding ratio and scale parameter. The inclusion of the quadratic term was motivated by the pattern of Figure 2. The estimation results are shown in Table 5 in the appendix.

Regarding the positive intercept of the location parameter a_0, we see that both detection methods constantly overestimate the hidden message length. While this bias is below 1 % for RS, WS outputs on average two percentage points more hidden bits than actually embedded. Q^1_{WS} further tells us that the bias increases proportionally with the message length q from $a_{0,\text{WS}} = 0.013$ (for $q = 0$) up to $a_{0,\text{WS}} + a_{1,\text{WS}} - 1 = 0.036$ (for $q = 1$). As a_1 in Q^1_{RS} is very close to 1, the model does not differ significantly from Q^0_{RS} (LRT $= 0.3, p = 0.61$). There is no evidence for a linear dependency between q and the (small) bias of RS.

However, it is not primarily the bias that makes steganalysis unreliable, but the extent of outliers that is reflected in the scale parameter of the fitted models. Interpreting the scale parameters, we see that RS achieves on average a tighter distribution and thus a higher accuracy than WS ($b_{0,\text{RS}} < b_{0,\text{WS}}$ in Q^0). The coefficients of Q^2 and Q^3 describe the functions that fit the right graphs in Figure 2 best. The fact that the RS models still have an appreciable error probability ($p > 0.01$) supports an interpretation that RS detects small, medium, and large messages almost equally accurate. WS, however, has an important negative weight for the quadratic predictor b_2. This reflects its relative advantage for hidden message lengths q close to zero and one. Over the whole range of q, RS estimates are less sensitive in both bias and accuracy.

Up to now, we discussed the detection accuracy in relation to q separately for each attack. Since both models were fitted on different data, we cannot tell whether the numerical differences in the coefficients do statistically matter. To build a family of models for performance *comparison*, we define a joint default model that is fitted to the results of both methods:

$$\textbf{Model } C^0: \quad \begin{aligned} \mu &= a_0 + 1 \cdot q \\ \log(\lambda^2) &= b_0 \end{aligned} \tag{7}$$

$$\textbf{Model } C^1: \quad \begin{aligned} \mu &= a_0 + 1 \cdot q + a_1 \cdot m \\ \log(\lambda^2) &= b_0 \end{aligned} \tag{8}$$

$$\textbf{Model } C^2: \quad \begin{aligned} \mu &= a_0 + 1 \cdot q \\ \log(\lambda^2) &= b_0 + b_1 \cdot m \end{aligned} \tag{9}$$

$$\textbf{Model } C^3: \quad \begin{aligned} \mu &= a_0 + 1 \cdot q + a_1 \cdot m \\ \log(\lambda^2) &= b_0 + b_1 \cdot m \end{aligned} \tag{10}$$

Then we add an indicator variable **m** to the joint data set, which takes a value of $m_i = 1$ if the element of the dependent variable $\hat{q}_i$ is a result of RS analysis. Otherwise (WS) we set $m_i = 0$. After fitting two more models C^1 and C^2 which

Table 2. Model with indicator variable: test differences between RS and WS

Parameter[†]	Model			
	C^0	C^1	C^2	C^3
Location $[\mu]$				
Intercept	0.013 (0.001)	0.019 (0.001)	0.013 (0.001)	0.019 (0.001)
RS Analysis		−0.011 (0.002)		−0.011 (0.002)
Scale $[\log(\lambda^2)]$				
Intercept	−7.281 (0.061)	−7.300 (0.061)	−7.247 (0.086)	−7.253 (0.085)
RS Analysis			−0.070 (0.124)	−0.096 (0.122)
Model fit				
−log likelihood	11996	11973	11996	11973
R^2 (in %)		0.19	0.00	0.20
LRT		46.2 $p < 0.001$	0.3 $p = 0.57$	46.9 $p < 0.001$
$N = 2128$				[†]std. error in brackets

include the indicator variable as predictor for bias and scale, respectively, we can interpret the coefficients of the indicator variable a_1 and b_1 as average difference in performance between both methods.

The logic of inference goes as follows. If the improvement of explanatory power of the models including the indicator variable is significantly better—in terms of the LRT test—than the joint default model, then we accept the hypothesis that both methods differ in performance.

The estimated values from our test data are displayed in Table 2. The results show that model C^1, capturing the difference in bias, adds significant explanatory power (LRT $= 46.2, p < 0.001$), whereas the differences in scale in C^2 do not (even if we control for bias as in model C^3). Ceteris paribus, RS and WS differ significantly in bias: WS on average overestimates the actual message length by 1.1 percentage point more than RS. Note that this example comparison does not control for q, where we identified a quadratic relationship for the scale parameter of WS in previous analyses.

In the next section we use the same methodology to analyse the influences of image properties, such as image size and macro characteristics.

4 Exploring the Influence of Image Properties

4.1 Influence of Image Size

Due to the logic of statistical attacks—namely the law of large numbers—it is quite intuitive that the number of observations determines the detection power. Nevertheless the bulk of detection schemes has been evaluated with constant image sizes, which often range around or above the upper end of our sample. Again, the most systematic analyses of image size to date are given in [13,14]. The author shows evidence for the direction of influence and describes the type of influence as "not proportional" [14, p. 103].

Further investigations of this relationship can be achieved with the regression model approach. To increase the reliability when choosing the appropriate link function, a particular data set has been generated. It consists of about 18,000 attacks on 1,500 images with dimensions randomised in the range between 6 K and 500 K pixels. From this data, we estimated models for six types of possible relationship between the image size n (measured in the number of pixels, i.e., the product of the dimensions) and the scale parameter of the Cauchy distribution: log to the bases 10 and e, square root, linear, quadratic, exponential. As a result, the log-proportional model scored the highest R^2 values, the square root ranked second. A tabulation of scale estimates fitted to subsets of the random dimension data reveals that the detection accuracy keeps its level almost constant for large images, and sharply declines when the number of observations falls below a method-specific threshold. So any concave function should fit this relationship reasonably well.

With the link function obtained, the following models were formulated (the normalisation of n shifts the coefficients to meaningful ranges):

$$\text{Models } S: \quad \mu \quad = a_0 + q \tag{11}$$

Table 3. Influence of image size on the accuracy of RS and WS estimation

Parameter[†]	Model					
	S_{RS}^1	S_{RS}^2	S_{RS}^3	S_{WS}^1	S_{WS}^2	S_{WS}^3
Scale $[\log(\lambda^2)]$						
Intercept	−9.819	−8.620	−10.235	−8.855	−8.043	−9.210
	(0.111)	(0.094)	(0.116)	(0.114)	(0.091)	(0.122)
No. of pixel (log)	−1.093		−0.933	−0.717		−0.626
	(0.040)		(0.042)	(0.041)		(0.043)
Local variance		0.847	0.512		0.547	0.366
		(0.045)	(0.045)		(0.045)	(0.045)
Model fit						
−log likelihood	11779	11954	11717	11861	11934	11829
R^2 (in %)	2.88	1.43	3.39	1.23	0.61	1.49
LRT	698.6	347.9	822.4	295.1	147.5	358.5
	$p < 0.001$	$p < 0.001$	$p < 0.001$	$p < 0.001$	$p < 0.001$	$p < 0.001$

$N = 2128$ [†]std. error in brackets

(Models S^0 omitted due to space limitations; compare Q^0 in Table 5)

$$\text{Model } S^0 : \quad \log(\lambda^2) = b_0 \tag{12}$$

$$\text{Model } S^1 : \quad \log(\lambda^2) = b_0 + b_1 \cdot \log \frac{n}{n_{\max}} \tag{13}$$

$$\text{Model } S^2 : \quad \log(\lambda^2) = b_0 + b_2 \cdot v_{\text{loc}} \tag{14}$$

$$\text{Model } S^3 : \quad \log(\lambda^2) = b_0 + b_1 \cdot \log \frac{n}{n_{\max}} + b_2 \cdot v_{\text{loc}} \tag{15}$$

The results are given in Table 3, where the location coefficients are omitted because they were negligible in all models. The interpretation of the b_1 coefficients between S^0 and S^1 suggests that the image size is a slightly more important predictor for the accuracy of RS than of WS. This is plausible because RS computes its estimate on the already aggregated number of groups, which is a fraction of the number of individual pixels evaluated by WS. Hence, with a concave relationship between observations and accuracy, RS suffers more from a low number of observations.

S^2 and S^3 are defined to further explore the reasons why small images are harder to estimate than large ones: apart from the already mentioned statistical argument (law of large numbers), smaller images tend to have higher local variance v_{loc} since the size reduction concentrates the image's energy to smaller space.[4] Multiple regression is the method to tell apart, which portion of the accuracy loss results from the reduced number of observations and which from the higher local variance. The estimated coefficients suggest that local variance contributes between 13 % (WS) and 15 % (RS) to the performance loss for small

---

[4] We measure local variance as the normalised square sum of differences between adjacent pixels in both horizontal and vertical direction.

images. The values are given as differences in $|b_1|$ between the single predictor models S^1 and the multi predictor models S^3. Moreover, local variance alone—it usually goes along with image size, but we separate the effects here—has larger impact on RS than on WS (see b_2 of models S^2). This seems plausible because WS inherently employs a variance criterion as weighting mechanism.

4.2 Influence of Macro Characteristics

The last family of models in this paper was motivated by an explorative analysis of the joint distribution of both attacks. In the complete set of simulation results we found a moderate correlation of errors between RS and WS estimates (Spearman's $\rho = 0.30$, Kendall's $\tau = 0.21$, Pearson's product-moment correlation is inappropriate for Cauchy random variables). This means that there exists a systematic component in the error distribution. After estimating Cauchy scale parameters for all cases simulated from the same source image, we could identify the depicted scenery of the source photograph as (part of the) systematic component. With heuristic means, basically manual inspection of extreme realisations in the joint accuracy distribution, we found that images with noisy textures yield the least accurate stego detection for both RS and WS. Conversely, images with flat regions and soft gradients worked best for both methods. Interestingly, images with high contrast and distinct edges yield average accuracy with WS whereas inferior precision when analysed with RS. Finally, images with a large proportion of saturated pixels caused a high number of outliers in WS.

As a consequence of these observations we tried to capture the visually perceived characteristics of the source photographs with a set of image macro characteristics to include them in regression models. For this purpose, a vector $\mathbf{c}$ of five basic image statistics is computed from each carrier and stego object, namely mean and median of intensity, histogram entropy, proportion of saturated pixels (i.e., maximum or minimum intensity) and local variance (cf. footnote 4 for a definition). This selection of image metrics has been used as predictor in models M (where $1 \leq k \leq 5$). Table 4 reports the coefficients and predictor ranges.

$$\textbf{Model } M^0 \quad : \qquad \begin{aligned} \mu \quad &= a_0 + q \\ \log(\lambda^2) &= b_0 \end{aligned} \qquad\qquad (16)$$

$$\textbf{Model } M^k \quad : \qquad \begin{aligned} \mu \quad &= a_0 + q + a_1 \cdot c_k \\ \log(\lambda^2) &= b_0 + b_1 \cdot c_k \end{aligned} \qquad (17)$$

The results indicate that local variance is indeed the most important predictor for the detection accuracy of both RS ($R^2 = 1.44$) and WS ($R^2 = 0.62$). Note that local variance may be confounded with image size since we do not control for this factor. An obvious difference between the two methods is the influence of saturated areas. This ratio is quite important for WS ($R^2 = 0.59$) while its influence on RS is much smaller ($R^2 = 0.07$) and in the opposite direction. The accuracy of WS analysis suffers from a high proportion of saturated pixels. RS, however, gains accuracy in terms of sharper distributions but looses precision since saturation causes a systematic bias (towards overestimating the actual message length).

Table 4. Model summary: image properties influencing detection accuracy

Predictor	Sample range $c_{\min}$ $c_{\max}$		Coefficients of independent models M^k attack: RS carrier	stego	attack: WS carrier	stego
Mean	0.06 1.00	b_1			0.252 (0.058)	...
Median	0.05 1.00	b_1			0.237 (0.059)	...
Hist. entropy	0.57 7.88	b_1			−0.175 (0.058)	−0.168 (0.059)
Saturation	0.00 0.94	a_1	0.056 (0.012)	0.062 (0.009)	0.017 (0.002)	...
		b_1	−2.282 (1.434)	−2.614 (1.447)	0.150 (0.060)	0.200 (0.057)
Local variance	0.00 10.20	b_1	0.845 (0.045)	...	0.736 (0.061)	...

$N = 2128$ (for each model)   (values from models with LRT $p > .01$ left blank)

The remaining metrics, namely mean, median, and entropy, show significant but weak effects on the accuracy of WS. These tendencies must not be over-interpreted because we suspect that these variables are confounded with saturation in our sample: saturation largely occurs at maximum intensity, which directly affects the mean ($R^2 = 0.19$), and—albeit in a more indirect way—the median ($R^2 = 0.07$). Since saturation shows up as peak in the histogram, the inverse effect on histogram entropy can be explained as well ($R^2 = 0.05$). The fact that standard errors soar in multi-factor models—including saturation and its related metrics—supports the hypothesis that it is an artifact of collinearity.

Though still limited by the naive selection of image metrics, these results are interesting for steganalysis research for two reasons. First, the findings stimulate directions for research on possible correction mechanisms to counterbalance the identified factors of influence. Second, an evaluation of macro characteristics prior to the actual attack enables the steganalyst to choose the most reliable attack for a given suspect image. This raises the question whether it is possible to construct a powerful *meta-attack* from the set of existing LSB detection schemes in the literature. However, this requires as prerequisite that macro characteristics computed from the stego image only yield comparable explanatory power. To verify this on the basis of our data, we computed the models separately for image properties extracted from the clean carrier images and from the stego images. Since the differences are close to zero (equal values are printed as dots in Table 4), we see that at least this set of macro characteristics is mostly invariant to LSB embedding.

Table 5. Accuracy of RS and WS depending on message size: sample of independent cases for inference

Parameter[†]	Model							
	Q_{RS}^0	Q_{RS}^1	Q_{RS}^2	Q_{RS}^3	Q_{WS}^0	Q_{WS}^1	Q_{WS}^2	Q_{WS}^3
Location $[\mu]$								
Intercept	0.007	0.008	0.007	0.007	0.020	0.013	0.012	0.012
	(0.001)	(0.001)	(0.001)	(0.001)	(0.001)	(0.001)	(0.001)	(0.001)
Emb. ratio		0.999	0.999	1.000		1.023	1.029	1.024
		(0.003)	(0.003)	(0.003)		(0.003)	(0.003)	(0.003)
Scale $[\log(\lambda^2)]$								
Intercept	−7.390	−7.389	−7.553	−7.451	−7.206	−7.256	−7.682	−8.067
	(0.062)	(0.062)	(0.091)	(0.112)	(0.059)	(0.060)	(0.092)	(0.113)
Emb. ratio			0.542	−0.662			1.270	5.502
			(0.220)	(0.795)			(0.207)	(0.758)
(Emb. ratio)^2				1.514				−5.185
				(0.961)				(0.893)
Model fit								
−log likelihood	12014	12014	12011	12010	11985	11951	11932	11915
R^2 (in %)		0.00	0.03	0.04		0.28	0.44	0.58
LRT		0.3	6.3	8.8		67.4	105.1	139.7
		$p=0.61$	$p=0.04$	$p=0.03$		$p<0.001$	$p<0.001$	$p<0.001$

$N = 2128$

[†]std. error in brackets

5   Discussion

After the introduction of regression analysis as a methodology to assess steganalytic techniques and to study multi-factor influence on the detection accuracy, we will use the remaining section to discuss the bottom line profits for steganalysis, as well as limitations and directions for future research.

The most apparent application is in benchmarking steganalysis. The method is suitable for performance evaluations and comparisons between stego detection schemes against different types of data. The required setup is described in Section 3. However, with its capability to quantify accuracy, to identify sources of influence, to rank moderating factors, and to tell substantial from statistically negligible improvements apart, the range of possible applications goes far beyond benchmarking. It is also a tool for the steganalyst, because it enables him or her to explore relationships between properties of the carrier and phenomena with security implications. More insight into the carrier is presumably one key to more reliable steganalysis.

Once a set of important predictors has been identified, the integration of a calibrated regression model into stego detectors can improve reliability even further. For example, it is evident how to make steganalysis adaptive with a regression model. The optimal detection strategy is automatically chosen depending on an evaluation of image properties. This can be considered as side information for the steganalyst. Moreover, not only the detection method or its parameters, but also the decision criterion can be modulated with knowledge from image properties. In a simple case, the alarm threshold is adjusted to an appropriate quantile of the error distribution for very small images. Preliminary results with detectors already show a notable reduction of the false positive rate.

From a statistical point of view, it is evident that the knowledge of a stationary error distribution for quantitative steganalysis yields confidence intervals for the estimated secret message length and enables the derivation of meaningful p-values for binary hypothesis tests. For example, a $5\% \pm 10$ estimation is quite likely a false positive and thus should not trigger alarm, whereas $5\% \pm 1$ is definitely suspect. Confidence bands can also make comparisons of ROC curves more convincing, because statistical significant improvements show up clearly.

Regarding the limitations, we distinguish between general limitations of the method itself and specific uncertainty of the results presented in this paper. The regression approach is genuinely confirmatory. Its strength lies in testing hypotheses about multivariate relationships rather than generating new insight. It is data driven, thus the quality of the results heavily depends on the quality of the data, especially on the availability of a large number of observations covering the whole range of values of all predictor variables. There are also two operational drawbacks worth mentioning. First, the amount of model data demands careful selection and interpretation. Second, the results are difficult to communicate, especially if interaction terms are involved.

The results presented in this paper were generated with a limited data base and a naive selection of possible predictors. It is merely for demonstration purpose and must not be generalised before the findings are validated with data from larger image stocks. This implies that the exact values of coefficients given in the paper are subject to further revision after more and more diverse data has been processed. However, we are confident that the directions of influence (the signs) and the order of magnitude is likely to remain stable. (More prudently, we hope that we can at least explain divergence if it occurs).

Topics for future research include a more comprehensive comparison of quantitative LSB steganalysis, e. g., by covering *Pairs Analysis* [9] and SPA with its cubic variation [4,19], together with a much broader and more heterogeneous image base. Here we must consider the possibility that new methods show a different error distribution than Cauchy, which would require a more general formulation of the notion of accuracy. One step further, we plan to examine more advanced macro characteristics and image pre-processing steps. For example, previous JPEG compression of varying degree seems to affect the detection result considerably. Desirable extensions for the methodology include robust regression methods and better regression diagnostic. Here, dealing with multicollinearity and extending the method to binary steganalysis are promising research areas. Of course, the whole procedure can be transferred to study steganalysis of other embedding functions—particularly $\pm K$ steganalysis suffers from a strong influence of image characteristics—or eventually to different carrier media, such as raw and compressed audio files.

To conclude, this paper is intended to motivate the community to rely further on a statistical sound methodology for multivariate effects. Multiple regression models are just one possible approach, and we are eagerly awaiting alternative proposals.

Acknowledgements

The work on this paper was supported by the Air Force Office of Scientific Research under the research grant number FA8655-04-1-3036. The U. S. Government is authorised to reproduce and distribute reprints for Governmental purposes notwithstanding any copyright notation there on. The views and conclusions contained herein are those of the author and should not be interpreted as necessarily representing the official policies, either expressed or implied, of the Air Force Office of Scientific Research, or the U. S. Government. The travel to the Information Hiding Workshop has been supported in part by the European Commission through the IST Programme under contract IST-2002-507932 ECRYPT. The author wants to thank Andrew Ker, Jessica Fridrich and Miroslav Goljan for their helpful comments.

References

1. Anderson, R., Petitcolas, F. A. P.: On the Limits of Steganography. *IEEE Journal of Selected Areas in Communications* **16** (1998) 474–481
2. Dabeer, O., Sullivan, K., Madhow, U., Chandrasekaran, S., Manjunath, B. S.: Detection of Hiding in the Least Significant Bit. *IEEE Trans. on Signal Processing* **52** (2004) 3046–3058

3. Dennis, J. E., Schnabel, R. B.: Numerical Methods for Unconstrained Optimization and Nonlinear Equations. Prentice Hall, New York (1983)
4. Dumitrescu, S., Wu, X., Wang, Z.: Detection of LSB Steganography Via Sample Pair Analysis. *IEEE Trans. on Signal Processing* **51** (2003) 1995–2007
5. Farid, H., Johnson, M.: The Digital Forensic Image Library (DFIL). Beta version (2004)
6. Fridrich, J., Goljan, M.: On Estimation of Secret Message Length in LSB Steganography in Spatial Domain. In: Delp, E. J., Wong, P. W. (eds.): Security, Steganography and Watermarking of Multimedia Contents VI, *Proc. of SPIE*, San Jose, CA (2004)
7. Fridrich, J., Goljan, M., Du, R.: Reliable Detection of LSB Based Image Steganography. *Proc. of the ACM Workshop on Multimedia and Security* (2001) 27–30
8. Fridrich, J., Goljan, M., Hogea, D., Soukal, D.: Quantitative Steganalysis of Digital Images: Estimating the Secret Message Length. *ACM Multimedia Systems Journal* **9** (2003) 288–302
9. Fridrich, J., Goljan, M., Soukal, D.: Higher-order Statistical Steganalysis of Palette Images. In: Delp, E. J., Wong, P. W. (eds.): Security and Watermarking of Multimedia Contents V, *Proc. of SPIE* (2003) 178–190
10. Fridrich, J., Soukal, D., Goljan, M.: Maximum Likelihood Estimation of Length of Secret Message Embedded Using $\pm K$ Steganography in Spatial Domain. In: Delp, E. J., Wong, P. W. (eds.): Security, Steganography and Watermarking of Multimedia Contents VII, *Proc. of SPIE*, San Jose, CA (2005) 595–606
11. Ihaka, R., Gentlemen, R.: R – A Language for Data Analysis and Graphics. *Journal of Computational Graphics and Statistics* **5** (1996) 299–314
12. Holotyak, T., Fridrich, J., Soukal, D.: Stochastic Approach to Secret Message Length Estimation in $\pm K$ Embedding Steganography. In: Delp, E. J., Wong, P. W. (eds.): Security, Steganography and Watermarking of Multimedia Contents VII, *Proc. of SPIE*, San Jose, CA (2005) 673–684
13. Ker, A. D.: Quantitative Evaluation of Pairs and RS Steganalysis. In: Delp, E. J., Wong, P. W. (eds.): Security, Steganography and Watermarking of Multimedia Contents VI, *Proc. of SPIE*, San Jose, CA (2004)
14. Ker, A. D.: Improved Detection of LSB Steganography in Grayscale Images. In: Fridrich, J. (ed.): Information Hiding. Sixth International Workshop, LNCS 3200, Springer-Verlag, Berlin Heidelberg (2004) 97–115
15. Ker, A. D.: Resampling and the Detection of LSB Matching in Colour Bitmaps. In: Delp, E. J., Wong, P. W. (eds.): Security, Steganography and Watermarking of Multimedia Contents VII, *Proc. of SPIE*, San Jose, CA (2005) 1–15
16. Lindsey, J. K.: Nonlinear Models in Medical Statistics. Oxford University Press (2001)
17. Lindsey, J. K.: Nonlinear Regression and Repeated Measurements Libraries, http://popgen0146uns50.unimaas.nl/~jlindsey/rcode.html (2001)
18. Long, J. S.: Regression Models for Categorial and Limited Dependent Variables. Sage Publications, Thousand Oaks (1997)
19. Lu, P., Luo, X., Tang, Q., Shen, L.: An Improved Sample Pairs Method for Detection of LSB Embedding. In: Fridrich, J. (ed.): Information Hiding. Sixth International Workshop, LNCS 3200, Springer-Verlag, Berlin Heidelberg (2004) 116–127
20. Lyu, S., Farid, H.: Detecting Hidden Messages Using Higher-Order Statistics and Support Vector Machines. In: Petitcolas, F. A. P. (ed.): Information Hiding. Fifth International Workshop, LNCS 2578, Springer-Verlag, Berlin Heidelberg (2003) 340–354

21. Petitcolas, F. A. P., Anderson, R. J., Kuhn, M. G.: Information Hiding—A Survey. *Proc. of the IEEE* **87** (1999) 1062–1078
22. The R Project for Statistical Computing, `http://www.r-project.org/`.
23. Westfeld, A.: Space Filling Curves in Steganalysis. In: Delp, E. J., Wong, P. W. (eds.): Security, Steganography and Watermarking of Multimedia Contents VII, *Proc. of SPIE*, San Jose, CA (2005) 28–37
24. Westfeld, A., Pfitzmann, A.: Attacks on Steganographic Systems. In: Pfitzmann, A. (ed.): Information Hiding. Third International Workshop, LNCS 1768, Springer-Verlag, Berlin Heidelberg (2000) 61–76
25. Zhang, T., Ping, X.: A New Approach to Reliable Detection of LSB Steganography in Natural Images. *Signal Processing* **83** (2003) 2085–2093
26. Zhang, X., Wang, S., Zhang, K.: Steganography with Least Histogram Abnormality. In: Gorodetsky et al. (eds.): MMM-ACNS 2003, LNCS 2776, Springer-Verlag, Berlin Heidelberg (2003) 395–406

A General Framework for Structural Steganalysis of LSB Replacement

Andrew D. Ker

Oxford University Computing Laboratory, Parks Road, Oxford OX1 3QD, England
adk@comlab.ox.ac.uk

Abstract. There are many detectors for simple Least Significant Bit (LSB) steganography in digital images, the most sensitive of which make use of structural or combinatorial properties of the LSB embedding method. We give a general framework for detection and length estimation of these hidden messages, which potentially makes use of *all* the combinatorial structure. The framework subsumes some previously known structural detectors and suggests novel, more powerful detection algorithms. After presenting the general framework we give a detailed study of one particular novel detector, with experimental evidence that it is more powerful than those previously known, in most cases substantially so. However there are some outstanding issues to be solved for the wider application of the general framework.

1 Introduction

Spatial domain Least Significant Bit (LSB) replacement is a popular and simple type of steganography. It combines high capacity with extreme ease of implementation (see [1] for a 2-line embedding program) and, in digital images, is visually imperceptible. Many of the steganography tools available on the internet use some form of LSB replacement, but in fact it is highly vulnerable to statistical analysis. The literature is replete with such detectors, the most sensitive of which make use of *structural* or combinatorial properties of the LSB algorithm [2,3,4,5,6].

In this paper we present a general framework for structural detectors, which potentially includes *all* the combinatorial properties of LSB replacement, by considering effects of LSB changes on arbitrary groups of samples. As such we will present it as a generalisation of something akin to Sample Pairs Analysis (SPA) [3]. In fact, many previously known structural detectors are special cases of this general framework, although we will only make explicit the connection with the Sample Pairs method. The value of the framework is both to place the older methods into a common context and also to provide new, more powerful, detectors. Because it makes full use of the structural information, in some sense this framework should be the last word on the detection of LSB replacement, although many practical questions remain open.

We give a brief re-presentation of the SPA method, slightly modified in detail and exposition to make the subsequent generalisation work tidily (Sect. 2). The

M. Barni et al. (Eds.): IH 2005, LNCS 3727, pp. 296–311, 2005.

general framework is presented in Sect. 3. The optimal implementation of the method is still unclear, but in Sect. 4 we present a case study of the technique applied to 3-tuples of pixel groups (we call this *Triples Analysis*). Despite some outstanding issues which mean that the method is not applicable to large hidden messages, experimental results show that it provides detection (and length estimation) of LSB steganography which is generally much more sensitive than the previously known methods.

There is still work to be done apply the framework to larger groups of pixels effectively, and to avoid potential problems with very large hidden messages, and we discuss these issues briefly in Sect. 5.

1.1   LSB Steganography and Steganalysis

The LSB embedding method is simple. The secret message consists of a stream of bits, and the cover medium is expressed as a stream of bytes (typically the grayscale or RGB pixel values of a bitmap image). The least significant bits of the cover bytes are overwritten by the secret message. For security, and to spread the stego noise, the cover is usually traversed in a pseudorandom order.

Despite many detectors for LSB steganography it remains of interest because it is one of the few embedding methods simple enough to require no special software [1]. Furthermore it is still possible to use it for secure communication, if the hidden message is kept very short in relation to the capacity of the cover. The aim of the steganalyst must be to refine the detection methods so that reliable detection of smaller messages is possible.

There are, broadly, two approaches to the detection of LSB steganography. One is to use signal processing techniques to extract feature vectors for a learning machine of some sort; literature on this ranges from very simple noise detectors such as [7] to the more sophisticated wavelet methods of [8]. Such detectors are likely to work for a wide range of embedding methods in addition to LSB Replacement, but do not provide any information on the nature of the hidden message and are generally less sensitive than specialised methods.

Other detectors make use of "structural" or combinatorial properties specific to the LSB embedding method. Such detectors appear to have much in common. In each case we assume that a cover image is fixed and a random hidden message, of bit rate p, is embedded. The "Sample Pairs" technique of [3] (discovered independently by this author who called it "Couples"), the "Pairs" method of [4], and the "Difference Histogram" method of [6] all consider pairs of pixels (although they differ in which pairs are selected) and use some macroscopic quantity $F(p)$ which depends on the secret bit rate p; in each case there is a claim or proof that $F(p)$ is a quadratic in p, although key parameters of the quadratic are unknown without the cover image; where necessary, one derives or estimates $F(1)$ by considering maximal embedding, and an assumption about natural cover images provides $F(0)$; now there is enough information to determine the missing parameters and it is possible, given an image with unknown hidden data, to solve for (an estimate of) p.

The method of "RS" [2] is more general in that it uses groups of two or more pixels, but there is a still a quadratically varying quantity, similar algebraic manipulation, and an assumption about cover images sufficient to solve for the length of hidden data. The general framework above is explained in [2], in which similarities between the Sample Pairs method and the RS method are noted[1].

The detection framework we propose here is different: there is still a macroscopic property of images which depends on the length of hidden data, in this case a vector $\mathbf{F}(p)$; we will prove thoroughly how $\mathbf{F}(p)$ depends on p along with some unknown parameters; instead of trying to estimate the latter, we will *invert* the process: given an image we hypothesise a value for p and compute what this would imply for $\mathbf{F}(0)$. The other novelty is a model for cover images (or, more precisely, for the macroscopic properties of cover images). Then we can find the value of p which leads to a value of $\mathbf{F}(0)$ closest to the model: this is the estimator for p. The novel technique is suggested by the detector of [5], and this paper can be seen as a substantially generalised version of that work (which, like almost all other detectors, only considers pairs of pixels). The most important difference between the techniques presented here and most previous detectors is that g-tuples of pixels are considered in full generality. The functional form of $\mathbf{F}(p)$ will be a vector of polynomials of degree g.

This new framework includes the framework of [2] as a special case, and also subsumes the steganalysis methods of [3,4,5,6]. We do not give all the details here; briefly, the connection is made by collapsing the vector $\mathbf{F}(p)$ to a single quantity (by taking a certain linear function of its components, for example). With an appropriate selection of pixel groups and an appropriate linear function of $\mathbf{F}(p)$, each of the LSB steganography detectors in [2,3,4,5,6] are expressible in the new framework: their assumptions about the functional form of the relevant macroscopic property can be justified (and sometimes exposed as approximations), and an equation for the estimate of p derived. In some cases the derived equation is not quite identical to the original, but in each case it is possible to explain why the solutions are approximately equal. The case of RS is particularly interesting, because our new framework predicts a polynomial of degree g when the mask size is g pixles. It can be shown that, if the parameters of the RS method are chosen carefully, the higher coefficients vanish to leave a quadratic equation for p (just as in the standard RS method). However, the collapsing of the vector $\mathbf{F}(p)$ leads to less robust behaviour which our novel detector will avoid.

2   An Extensible Presentation of Sample Pairs

There are a number of equivalent ways to present the general framework, and we will do so using terminology somewhat similar to Sample Pairs Analysis in [3].

---

[1] There is some evidence in [1] that, despite the potentially more general form, the method of RS is slightly inferior to, or at best only as reliable as, that of Sample Pairs. But in any case the performance of the two methods is extremely close, so too for the methods of Pairs and Difference Histogram.

For clarity we will slightly alter some of the notation: we will use throughout caligraphic letters ($\mathcal{X}$) for sets, upper-case letters (X) for random variables, lower-case letters (x) for constants and realisations of random variables, and will make a clear distinction between nonrandom properties of a cover image and random properties of stego images based on that cover image (the randomness coming from the content and location of the hidden payload).

Suppose that a digital image consists of a series of samples $s_1, s_2, \ldots, s_N$ taking values in the range $0 \ldots 2M + 1$ (typically $M = 127$). A *sample pair* is a pair (s_i, s_j) for some $1 \le i \ne j \le N$. Let $\mathcal{P}$ be a set of sample pairs; in [3] it is all pairs which come from horizontally or vertically adjacent pixels. Write $\mathcal{C}_m$ for the subset of $\mathcal{P}$ consisting of sample pairs where the sample values differ by exactly m after right-shifting by one bit (i.e. dividing by 2). Also write $\mathcal{X}_m$ for the sample pairs of $\mathcal{P}$ which differ in value by m with the higher value even and $\mathcal{Y}_m$ for those which differ by m but with the higher value odd. In this way, $\mathcal{P}$ is partitioned into subsets $\mathcal{C}_m$, $0 \le m \le M$, and each $\mathcal{C}_m$ is partitioned into $\mathcal{X}_{2m-1}, \mathcal{X}_{2m}, \mathcal{Y}_{2m}, \mathcal{Y}_{2m+1}$. In [3] $\mathcal{C}_m$ is referred to as a "submultiset", and $\mathcal{X}_m$ and $\mathcal{Y}_m$ as "trace submultisets"; we will use the simpler terminology "trace set" and "trace subset", respectively. Altering LSBs cannot affect which trace set a sample pair lies in, but it can move sample pairs between trace subsets as samples in the pair have their LSB flipped.

Suppose that a random hidden message of length $2pN$, where $0 \le p \le 0.5$ is unknown to the detector, is embedded using LSB replacement of a random selection of samples independent of the content of the cover or hidden message[2]. Suppose that a sample pair lies in trace set $\mathcal{C}_m$ with $m > 0$. The probability that neither sample is altered is $(1-p)^2$, the probabilities that either sample is altered is $p(1-p)$, and the probability that both are altered is p^2; each of these events moves the sample pair amongst the trace subsets of $\mathcal{C}_m$ according to the transition diagram Fig. 1 (transitions are labelled with their probabilities). $m = 0$ leads to a special case.

Let c_m, d_m, x_m, y_m be the cardinalities of the sets $\mathcal{C}_m$, $\mathcal{D}_m$, $\mathcal{X}_m$, $\mathcal{Y}_m$ in a particular cover image (they are nonrandom properties of the cover, but unknown to the detector), and let C'_m, D'_m, X'_m, Y'_m be the random variables representing the cardinalities of those sets after LSB embedding of a random message of length $2pN$. We know that $C'_m = c_m$ because $\mathcal{C}_m$ is closed under LSB operations. By considering the probabilistic transition systems in Fig. 1, Dumitrescu *et al.* derive the equations analogous to the following:

$$E\left[p^2 c_m - p(D'_{2m} + 2X'_{2m-1}) + X'_{2m-1}\right] = x_{2m-1}(1 - 2p)^2 \qquad (1)$$
$$E\left[p^2 c_m - p(D'_{2m} + 2Y'_{2m+1}) + Y'_{2m+1}\right] = y_{2m+1}(1 - 2p)^2 \qquad (2)$$

(In [3] the expectation is implicit.) x_m and y_m cannot be observed by a detector which only has access to the stego image but there is a plausible assumption:

$$x_{2m+1} = y_{2m+1} \text{ for all } m; \qquad (3)$$

---

[2] In [3] calculations are performed assuming that pN is the hidden message length. The use of $2pN$ instead makes the following algebra somewhat simpler.

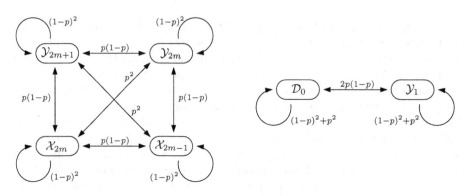

Fig. 1. Transitions between the subsets of $\mathcal{C}_m$, and the probability of each. Left, for all $m \geq 1$. Right, for $m = 0$, where $\mathcal{D}_0 = \mathcal{X}_0 \cup \mathcal{Y}_0$.

in [3] this assumption is cast as an expectation but the quantities involved are nonrandom if the cover image is fixed. It is plausible because sample pairs in a continuous tone image should not have any particular parity structure. Assuming that the observed values from the random variables are close to their expectations, (1), (2), and (3) give enough information to form quadratic equations for p, one for each m. In [3] these equations are summed to give a single quadratic, which is solved for an estimator $\hat{p}$ of p.

Our aim is to extend the sample pairs method to groups of pixels of more than two. For example, consider 3-tuples of adjacent samples, and trace sets $\mathcal{C}_{m,n}$ where the successive sample values differ by m and n, after right-shifting one bit. This does work, giving trace subsets and transition diagrams analogous to Fig. 1. But there are a number of awkward corners. Firstly, special cases proliferate: whereas for sample pairs there is the special transition diagram for $m = 0$, for 3-tuples we reach one special case for $m = 0, n \neq 0$, one for $m \neq 0, n = 0$ and another for $m = n = 0$. For g-tuples with $g \geq 4$ there are even more special cases. Secondly, the ad-hoc process by which Dumitrescu *et al.* derive (1) and (2) is difficult to generalise when the number of trace subsets rises. We will solve these problems by using a slightly modified version of the sample pairs technique.

2.1   A Modified, Extensible, Presentation

To remove the special case at $m = 0$ we have to take slightly finer distinctions in the trace sets and subsets:

$$\mathcal{C}_m = \{(j, k) \in \mathcal{P} \mid \lfloor k/2 \rfloor = \lfloor j/2 \rfloor + m\}$$
$$\mathcal{E}_m = \{(j, k) \in \mathcal{P} \mid k = j + m, \text{ with } j \text{ even}\}$$
$$\mathcal{O}_m = \{(j, k) \in \mathcal{P} \mid k = j + m, \text{ with } j \text{ odd}\}$$

with m now able to take negative values. $\mathcal{E}_m$ and $\mathcal{O}_m$ are analogous to $\mathcal{X}_m$ and $\mathcal{Y}_m$ but the new definitions break reflectional symmetry: no longer do we have (j, k) and (k, j) always belonging to the same set. The new transition diagram (probabilities included) is shown in Fig. 2. There are no special cases.

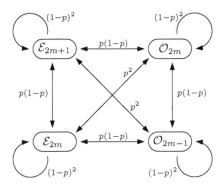

Fig. 2. Transitions between subsets of $\mathcal{C}_m$, in the modified presentation

Consider the random variable E'_{2m}, the cardinality of $\mathcal{E}_{2m}$ after a random message of length $2pN$ is embedded. It is actually the sum of four multinomial distributions, but we can reason about its expectation in an elementary manner. Sample pairs can enter $\mathcal{E}_{2m}$ in four ways: either having been in $\mathcal{E}_{2m}$ before and remaining there (and on average a proportion $(1-p)^2$ of the e_{2m} pairs in this position should remain), having been in $\mathcal{O}_{2m-1}$ before and moving to $\mathcal{E}_{2m}$ ($p(1-p)$ of the o_{2m-1} will do so), having been in $\mathcal{E}_{2m+1}$ ($p(1-p)$ of e_{2m+1} will do so), or having been in $\mathcal{O}_{2m}$ (p^2 of o_{2m} will do so). Thus,

$$E[E'_{2m}] = (1-p)^2 e_{2m} + p(1-p)o_{2m-1} + p(1-p)e_{2m+1} + p^2 o_{2m}.$$

We can repeat this for each of $O'_{2m-1}, E'_{2m+1}, O'_{2m}$ to get four linear equations which we express in vector form as

$$\begin{pmatrix} E[E'_{2m}] \\ E[O'_{2m-1}] \\ E[E'_{2m+1}] \\ E[O'_{2m}] \end{pmatrix} = \begin{pmatrix} (1-p)^2 & p(1-p) & p(1-p) & p^2 \\ p(1-p) & (1-p)^2 & p^2 & p(1-p) \\ p(1-p) & p^2 & (1-p)^2 & p(1-p) \\ p^2 & p(1-p) & p(1-p) & (1-p)^2 \end{pmatrix} \begin{pmatrix} e_{2m} \\ o_{2m-1} \\ e_{2m+1} \\ o_{2m} \end{pmatrix}. \quad (4)$$

The 4-by-4 matrix is the transition matrix of the transition system in Fig. 2 and it is invertible as long as $2p \neq 1$. If we make the assumption that the observed realisations of the random variables e'_{2m}, etc, are close to their expectations, we can form estimators for the unknown cover image quantities e_{2m}, etc.:

$$\begin{pmatrix} \hat{e}_{2m} \\ \hat{o}_{2m-1} \\ \hat{e}_{2m+1} \\ \hat{o}_{2m} \end{pmatrix} = \frac{1}{(1-2p)^2} \begin{pmatrix} (1-p)^2 & -p(1-p) & -p(1-p) & p^2 \\ -p(1-p) & (1-p)^2 & p^2 & -p(1-p) \\ -p(1-p) & p^2 & (1-p)^2 & -p(1-p) \\ p^2 & -p(1-p) & -p(1-p) & (1-p)^2 \end{pmatrix} \begin{pmatrix} e'_{2m} \\ o'_{2m-1} \\ e'_{2m+1} \\ o'_{2m} \end{pmatrix} \quad (5)$$

This has enabled us to hypothesise a value for p and then *undo* the effect of embedding a hidden message of length $2pN$. Certainly we could not expect to recover the cover image itself, but macroscopic properties of the cover, such as the cardinalities of the trace subsets, can be estimated in this way.

At this stage we must use some sort of "model" of cover images. The analogy to the sample pairs method would be $e_{2m+1} = o_{2m+1}$ for each m. Setting $\hat{e}_{2m+1} = \hat{o}_{2m+1}$ and using the relevant components of (5) (with m and with $m+1$) gives

$$(c_m - c_{m+1})p^2 + (e'_{2m+2} + o'_{2m+2} + 2o'_{2m+1} - e'_{2m} - o'_{2m} - 2e'_{2m+1})p + e'_{2m+1} - o'_{2m+1} = 0$$

for each m, which is analogous to Dumitrescu's equation. One can sum all these equations to reach an estimator for p: it is almost identical to the Sample Pairs estimator, the minor difference being due to the split between $\mathcal{C}_{-m}$ and $\mathcal{C}_m$.

Alternatively, we can consider deviations from $\hat{e}_{2m+1} = \hat{o}_{2m+1}$ to be "errors", and solve for p to find the closest image to our model by minimising the sum-square error $\sum(\hat{e}_{2m+1} - \hat{o}_{2m+1})^2$. Treating deviations from the assumptions as errors is a technique described in [5]. We will prefer this paradigm in the generalisation which follows, because it extends to more complex cover assumptions.

Note that we have not used an assumption that $e_{2m} = o_{2m}$. Although as plausible as $e_{2m+1} = o_{2m+1}$ it is not helpful in estimating p. It is easy to check, using (4), that when $e_{2m} = o_{2m}$ the same holds for stego images too. Therefore it does not provide any discrimination between cover and stego images.

3   Generalised Framework

We now generalise by considering g-tuples of sample values, for arbitrary g. The same overall method will be used: determination of the probabilities of transition between trace subsets, hypothesising a value for p, inverting the formula to express the cardinalities of the cover image trace subsets in terms of those of the stego image, using a model for cover images, and solving for p. Further investigation is needed to decide how optimally to apply the last step.

Suppose that a set of g-tuples of sample values $\mathcal{T}$ is selected (e.g. the intensities of all horizontal rows of g adjacent pixels). The trace sets and subsets are:

$$\mathcal{C}_{m_1,\ldots,m_{g-1}} = \{(s_1,\ldots,s_g) \in \mathcal{T} \mid \lfloor s_{i+1}/2 \rfloor = \lfloor s_i/2 \rfloor + m_i \text{ for each } 1 \leq i < g\}$$
$$\mathcal{E}_{m_1,\ldots,m_{g-1}} = \{(s_1,\ldots,s_g) \in \mathcal{T} \mid s_{i+1} = s_i + m_i, \text{ with } s_1 \text{ even}\}$$
$$\mathcal{O}_{m_1,\ldots,m_{g-1}} = \{(s_1,\ldots,s_g) \in \mathcal{T} \mid s_{i+1} = s_i + m_i, \text{ with } s_1 \text{ odd}\}$$

Changing LSBs of samples cannot affect which of the trace sets the tuples inhabit, but they are moved between the trace subsets according to a 2^g-state transition process. It is convenient to write $\mathcal{A}_{0,m_1,\ldots,m_{g-1}}$ for $\mathcal{E}_{m_1,\ldots,m_{g-1}}$ and $\mathcal{A}_{1,m_1,\ldots,m_{g-1}}$ for $\mathcal{O}_{m_1,\ldots,m_{g-1}}$, and to abbreviate the subscripts using sequence notation (we write $\boldsymbol{s}$ for a sequence of integers and $\boldsymbol{s}.t$ for concatenation). We write $P(\mathcal{A}_{\boldsymbol{s}}, \mathcal{A}_t)$ for the probability of transition between $\mathcal{A}_{\boldsymbol{s}}$ and $\mathcal{A}_t$.

We specify the trace subsets each set $\mathcal{C}_{m_1,\ldots,m_{g-1}}$ is divided into using induction on g, as follows. The base case is $g = 1$: there is a single trace set $\mathcal{C}$ (all individual samples) divided into two subsets $\mathcal{A}_0$ and $\mathcal{A}_1$, and $P(\mathcal{A}_0, \mathcal{A}_0) = P(\mathcal{A}_1, \mathcal{A}_1) = 1 - p$, $P(\mathcal{A}_0, \mathcal{A}_1) = P(\mathcal{A}_1, \mathcal{A}_0) = p$. If $\mathcal{C}_t$ divides into trace subsets $\mathcal{A}_{\boldsymbol{s}_1}, \ldots, \mathcal{A}_{\boldsymbol{s}_n}$ then $\mathcal{C}_{t.k}$ divides into

$$\mathcal{A}_{\boldsymbol{s}_1.(2k+\alpha_1)}, \ldots, \mathcal{A}_{\boldsymbol{s}_n.(2k+\alpha_n)}, \quad \mathcal{A}_{\boldsymbol{s}_1.(2k+\alpha_1+1)}, \ldots, \mathcal{A}_{\boldsymbol{s}_n.(2k+\alpha_n+1)}$$

where α_i is zero if the sum of components in s_i is even, and minus one otherwise. The transition probabilities are given by

$$P(\mathcal{A}_{s_i.(2k+\alpha_i)}, \mathcal{A}_{s_j.(2k+\alpha_j)}) = (1 - p)P(\mathcal{A}_{s_i}, \mathcal{A}_{s_j})$$
$$P(\mathcal{A}_{s_i.(2k+\alpha_i+1)}, \mathcal{A}_{s_j.(2k+\alpha_j)}) = pP(\mathcal{A}_{s_i}, \mathcal{A}_{s_j})$$
$$P(\mathcal{A}_{s_i.(2k+\alpha_i)}, \mathcal{A}_{s_j.(2k+\alpha_j+1)}) = pP(\mathcal{A}_{s_i}, \mathcal{A}_{s_j})$$
$$P(\mathcal{A}_{s_i.(2k+\alpha_i+1)}, \mathcal{A}_{s_j.(2k+\alpha_j+1)}) = (1 - p)P(\mathcal{A}_{s_i}, \mathcal{A}_{s_j})$$

If the trace subsets are considered in the order given, the transition probabilities can be expressed concisely as matrices. The matrices, and their inverses, are g-fold Kronecker tensor products:

$$T_1 = \begin{pmatrix} 1 - p & p \\ p & 1 - p \end{pmatrix} \qquad\qquad T_1^{-1} = \frac{1}{1 - 2p}\begin{pmatrix} 1 - p & -p \\ -p & 1 - p \end{pmatrix}$$

$$T_{g+1} = \left(\begin{array}{c|c} (1-p)T_g & pT_g \\ \hline pT_g & (1-p)T_g \end{array}\right) \qquad T_{g+1}^{-1} = \frac{1}{1-2p}\left(\begin{array}{c|c} (1-p)T_g^{-1} & -pT_g^{-1} \\ \hline -pT_g^{-1} & (1-p)T_g^{-1} \end{array}\right)$$

Given a trace set $\mathcal{C}_t$ divided into trace subsets $\mathcal{A}_{s_1}, \ldots, \mathcal{A}_{s_n}$, write a_i for the size of $\mathcal{A}_{s_i}$ in the cover image, and A_i' for the size of the subset under random embedding of a message of length $2pN$. Just as with (4) we have

$$E[\mathbf{A}'] = T_g\mathbf{a}.$$

Observing the stego image we can count the realisations of the random variables A_i, say a_i'. Assuming that the realisations are close to their expectations, we can form estimators for the unknown values a_i:

$$\hat{\mathbf{a}} = T_g^{-1}\mathbf{a}'.$$

Note that T_g depends on p. Finally, we need a model for cover images, the analogue of (3); this may include $e_s = o_s$, although (as in Sect. 2) not all s will provide a useful discrimination between cover and stego images. We estimate p by finding the value which makes our estimate of $\hat{\mathbf{a}}$ the closest fit to the model. How best to do this depends on the cover image assumptions, but the technique of [5] (in which deviations are treated as errors and the sum-square error minimised) should generally be applicable.

4   Case Study: $g = 3$

The case $g = 1$ is degenerate. We have seen that the case $g = 2$ is very similar to the Sample Pairs method or the more robust modification of [5], depending on the cover image model used. We now consider the case $g = 3$, which we call *Triples Analysis* (by analogy with our name for SPA, "Couples"), showing in detail how the general framework can be used for steganalysis. Experimental

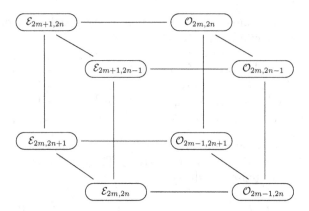

Fig. 3. The 8 trace subsets of $\mathcal{C}_{m,n}$. Subsets connected by an edge are related by the flipping of the LSB of exactly one sample in the 3-tuple.

results are included to demonstrate that the extension to 3-tuples provides a substantially more sensitive detector.

Fix a trace set $\mathcal{C}_{m,n}$; it is divided into 8 trace subsets. The full transition diagram contains a lot of information and we do not display all of it. Instead, in Fig. 3 we show how 3-tuples are moved amongst the trace subsets when a single sample has the LSB altered. In general, the probability of transition from one trace subset to another is $p^i(1-p)^{3-i}$, where i is the length of the shortest path between them in Fig. 3. If the trace subsets are enumerated in the order $\mathcal{E}_{2m,2n}$, $\mathcal{O}_{2m-1,2n}$, $\mathcal{E}_{2m+1,2n-1}$, $\mathcal{O}_{2m,2n-1}$, $\mathcal{E}_{2m,2n+1}$, $\mathcal{O}_{2m-1,2n+1}$, $\mathcal{E}_{2m+1,2n}$, $\mathcal{O}_{2m,2n}$ then the transition matrix is

$$
T_3 = \begin{pmatrix}
(1-p)^3 & p(1-p)^2 & p(1-p)^2 & p^2(1-p) & p(1-p)^2 & p^2(1-p) & p^2(1-p) & p^3 \\
p(1-p)^2 & (1-p)^3 & p^2(1-p) & p(1-p)^2 & p^2(1-p) & p(1-p)^2 & p^3 & p^2(1-p) \\
p(1-p)^2 & p^2(1-p) & (1-p)^3 & p(1-p)^2 & p^2(1-p) & p^3 & p(1-p)^2 & p^2(1-p) \\
p^2(1-p) & p(1-p)^2 & p(1-p)^2 & (1-p)^3 & p^3 & p^2(1-p) & p^2(1-p) & p(1-p)^2 \\
p(1-p)^2 & p^2(1-p) & p^2(1-p) & p^3 & (1-p)^3 & p(1-p)^2 & p(1-p)^2 & p^2(1-p) \\
p^2(1-p) & p(1-p)^2 & p^3 & p^2(1-p) & p(1-p)^2 & (1-p)^3 & p^2(1-p) & p(1-p)^2 \\
p^2(1-p) & p^3 & p(1-p)^2 & p^2(1-p) & p(1-p)^2 & p^2(1-p) & (1-p)^3 & p(1-p)^2 \\
p^3 & p^2(1-p) & p^2(1-p) & p(1-p)^2 & p^2(1-p) & p(1-p)^2 & p(1-p)^2 & (1-p)^3
\end{pmatrix}
$$

The inverse of T_3 consists of third order rational polynomials in p. A very convenient substitution is $q = 1/(1-2p)$; then we have (after some simplification)

$$
T_3^{-1} = \frac{1}{8}\begin{pmatrix}
(1+q)^3 & (1-q)(1+q)^2 & (1-q)(1+q)^2 & (1-q)^2(1+q) & \cdots \\
(1-q)(1+q)^2 & (1+q)^3 & (1-q)^2(1+q) & (1-q)(1+q)^2 & \cdots \\
(1-q)(1+q)^2 & (1-q)^2(1+q) & (1+q)^3 & (1-q)(1+q)^2 & \cdots \\
(1-q)^2(1+q) & (1-q)(1+q)^2 & (1-q)(1+q)^2 & (1+q)^3 & \cdots \\
(1-q)(1+q)^2 & (1-q)^2(1+q) & (1-q)^2(1+q) & (1-q)^3 & \cdots \\
(1-q)^2(1+q) & (1-q)(1+q)^2 & (1-q)^3 & (1-q)^2(1+q) & \cdots \\
(1-q)^2(1+q) & (1-q)^3 & (1-q)(1+q)^2 & (1-q)^2(1+q) & \cdots \\
(1-q)^3 & (1-q)^2(1+q) & (1-q)^2(1+q) & (1-q)(1+q)^2 & \cdots
\end{pmatrix}.
\tag{6}
$$

(Only half of T_3^{-1} is displayed, but the rest can be deduced by rotational symmetry). Given a stego image we consider each trace set $\mathcal{C}_{m,n}$ in turn and count the trace subsets to make a vector $\mathbf{x}'$. Then we can hypothesise a value of p and form estimates for the sizes of the trace subsets of the cover image using:

$$\hat{\mathbf{x}} = T_3^{-1}\mathbf{x}'.$$

In the case $g = 2$ there was just one property which we assumed that cover images have: $e_{2m+1} = o_{2m+1}$ for each m. In the case $g = 3$ there is an analogous property, which we will refer to as *parity symmetry*:

$$e_{m,n} = o_{m,n}$$

for each m and n. However, there are also some other plausible symmetries which might enrich our cover image model. One is *order symmetry*:

$$e_{m,n} = e_{n,m}$$

for each m and n (similarly $o_{m,n} = o_{n,m}$), and another is *reflectional symmetry*:

$$e_{m,n} = \begin{cases} e_{-n,-m}, & \text{if } m+n \text{ is even} \\ o_{-n,-m}, & \text{if } m+n \text{ is odd} \end{cases}$$

(and similarly for $o_{m,n}$ with even and odd swapped). Between them, the assumptions of order and reflectional symmetry state that pixels within groups can be considered in any order without changing the size of the trace subsets.

Recall, from Sect. 2, that some cover assumptions may not distinguish covers from stego images: this lead us to discard $e_{2m} = o_{2m}$ when $g = 2$. Here, it is routine to check that parity symmetry, if true for covers, is also true for stego images when m and n are both even, or $m = n$, and that order symmetry, if true for covers, is also true for stego images when *either* m or n is even, or $m = n$. Finally, reflectional symmetry never gives discrimination between covers and stego images.

Consider just one case of parity symmetry, $e_{2m+1,2n+1} = o_{2m+1,2n+1}$. To use the generalised framework to make an estimate of p, we compute "error terms" for each m and n, $\epsilon_{m,n} = \hat{e}_{2m+1,2n+1} - \hat{o}_{2m+1,2n+1}$. Then we find the value of p which minimises the sum-square of the errors. First, write

$$d_0 = e'_{2m+1,2n+1} - o'_{2m+1,2n+1}$$
$$d_1 = e'_{2m+1,2n+2} + e'_{2m,2n+2} + o'_{2m,2n+1} - o'_{2m+1,2n} - o'_{2m+2,2n} - e'_{2m+2,2n+1}$$
$$d_2 = e'_{2m,2n+3} + o'_{2m-1,2n+2} + o'_{2m,2n+2} - o'_{2m+2,2n-1} - e'_{2m+2,2n} - e'_{2m+3,2n}$$
$$d_3 = o'_{2m-1,2n+3} - e'_{2m+3,2n-1}$$

(each d_i also depends on m and n, but in the interests of readability we will leave these parameters implicit.) Then, using (6) and gathering similar terms,

$$\epsilon_{m,n} = \tfrac{1}{8}(d_0(1+q)^3 + d_1(1-q)(1+q)^2 + d_2(1-q)^2(1+q) + d_3(1-q)^3)$$
$$= \tfrac{1}{8}((d_0 + d_1 + d_2 + d_3) + q(3d_0 + d_1 - d_2 - 3d_3)+$$
$$q^2(3d_0 - d_1 - d_2 + 3d_3) + q^3(d_0 - d_1 + d_2 - d_3))$$

We will find the value of q to minimise $S(q) = \sum_{m,n} \epsilon^2_{m,n}$. Writing

$$c_0 = d_0 + d_1 + d_2 + d_3, \qquad c_1 = 3d_0 + d_1 - d_2 - 3d_3,$$
$$c_2 = 3d_0 - d_1 - d_2 + 3d_3, \qquad c_3 = d_0 - d_1 + d_2 - d_3,$$

(again leaving m and n implicit) we have

$$S(q) = \tfrac{1}{64} \sum_{m,n} c_0^2 + q(2c_0c_1) + q^2(2c_0c_2 + c_1^2) + q^3(2c_0c_3 + 2c_1c_2) +$$
$$q^4(c_2^2 + 2c_1c_3) + q^5(2c_2c_3) + q^6(c_3^2). \tag{7}$$

so that

$$S'(q) = \tfrac{1}{64} \sum_{m,n} 2c_0c_1 + q(4c_0c_2 + 2c_1^2) + q^2(6c_0c_3 + 6c_1c_2) +$$
$$q^3(4c_2^2 + 8c_1c_3) + q^4(10c_2c_3) + q^5(6c_3^2). \tag{8}$$

(To include other instances of parity symmetry or order symmetry in the cover model, the above calculations are repeated with the appropriate $\epsilon_{m,n}$ and included in the sum.) There will always be at least one real root of the quintic (8), but it could lead to up to 5 roots for q. We can discard implausible roots inside the range $(-10, 10/11)$ (because these would give obviously wrong estimates of p outside $(-0.05, 0.55)$) and substitute the remaining roots back into (7) to determine the location of the minimum $\hat{q}$. Finally, $\hat{p} = \tfrac{1}{2}(1 - \tfrac{1}{\hat{q}})$.

4.1   Experimental Results

Triples Analysis was implemented and widely tested. We comment on some implementation choices: we used all triples of horizontally adjacent pixels for $\mathcal{T}$ (some basic experiments indicate that it makes negligible difference if vertical groups are also included). For colour images the red, green and blue components were initially considered separately, and the trace subsets for each channel added together. After some initial experiments we found that it was marginally most accurate to use *only* the assumption $e_{2m+1,2n+1} = o_{2m+1,2n+1}$, although further research is needed to determine why this would be the case. Finally, we used only m, n in the range -5 to $+5$, because the trace sets are very small outside of this range.

Further initial experiments also indicate that the Triples estimator has a flaw: when the hidden message is long, the estimator gives wildly inaccurate results. In fact this can be explained theoretically, but for reasons of space we do not do so here. It is not a substantial problem: we can "screen" the method by first applying the standard SPA estimate, and proceeding to the Triples estimate only when the SPA estimate is below, say, 0.5^3. In any case, our main interest is in the difficult case of detection when p is small.

---

[3] Here and hereafter we use p in the more usual way, to represent the proportionate length of the hidden message (previously this quantity was called $2p$). For screening, it seemed best to use a modification of the detector in [5] (which, as published, contains a few bugs) and proceed to the Triples estimate only for $\hat{p} < 0.3$.

Triples Analysis was compared with the standard methods of RS[4] and SPA. LSB Steganography was simulated on a number of sets of cover images, and detection statistics computed. To avoid overspecialisation, and in view of the wide variation in results depending on the cover image type noted in [1], we used a variety of sets of cover images:

Bitmap images: 3000 uncompressed bitmaps downloaded from `http://photo gallery.nrcs.usda.gov`, very high resolution images apparently scanned from film, reduced in size to approximately 640×450.

JPEG images: three digital stock photo libraries: one of 5000 "high-quality" images, stored at quality factor 75, all sized 900×600; one of 10000 "medium-quality" images, stored at quality factors between 50 and 75, of similar size; and one of 20000 smaller "low-quality" images, 640×400, quality factor 58.

The experiments were repeated with each set of covers separately, and also with the bitmap images subject to JPEG compression prior to use as a bitmap cover image (to examine in isolation the effect of JPEG compression). Note that we have restricted our experiments to colour covers.

4.2   Reliability as an Estimator

We used the methods of RS, Sample Pairs and Triples to estimate the value of p, for each image in each set. This was repeated with the true value of p varying from 0 to 1, at intervals of 0.05. As with RS and Sample Pairs, the Triples estimator is approximately unbiased: for example, over the set of 3000 bitmaps the average error was observed to be between -0.016 and 0.009, depending on the true value of p.

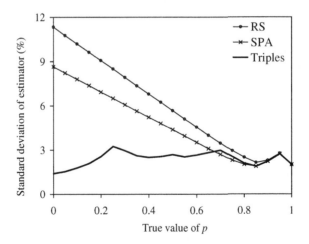

Fig. 4. Standard deviation of estimators, observed from a set of 3000 cover images subject to JPEG compression at quality factor 75, as p varies.

---

[4] The RS "mask" used was the standard $[0, 1, 1, 0]$, from [2].

Table 1. Standard deviation[5] of estimators ($\times 10^2$) when the true value of p is zero

Detector	3000 Uncompressed Bitmaps				Other sets of JPEG images		
	Unaltered	JPEG q.f.			5000 high quality	10000 med. quality	20000 low quality
		90	75	50			
RS	2.67	10.94	11.38	10.64	3.63	4.34	9.51
SPA	2.56	8.56	8.64	7.87	2.62	3.31	7.17
LSM	2.96	3.90	2.71	2.49	1.29	1.41	2.63
Triples	2.36	2.08	1.40	1.20	0.55	0.35	1.35

We compare the estimators by their sample standard deviation: one graph is shown in Fig. 4. We observe that, for this set of cover images, the Triples estimator is very substantially more accurate than the RS or SPA estimators in the case of small hidden messages. Indeed, it is surprising quite how unreliably the standard estimators performed – this is due to JPEG compression artefacts which cause the RS or SPA cover image assumptions to fail, whereas the Triples method treats errors in the cover assumption more robustly. Note that the poor performance of RS and SPA is mitigated as the hidden message length increases.

Rather than repeat such charts for every set of cover images, we merely compare the estimators when the true value of p is zero, i.e. for cover images. This gives a reasonable summary of relative performance, because the graph shapes are broadly similar in all cases, with the methods converging to similar performance near $p = 1$, and because small hidden messages are of particular interest (their detection being difficult). Table 1 shows this information for each cover image set, also including the robust modified SPA estimator of [5].

In the case of uncompressed bitmaps the Triples estimator is somewhat more accurate than RS or SPA. In the case of JPEG compressed covers it is very substantially more accurate: whereas the RS and SPA methods lose accuracy because of compression artefacts, the Triples method actually gains accuracy. Our conclusion is that the Triples method is more reliable and very much more robust to artefacts in the cover images.

4.3 Reliability as a Discriminator

A different question is how well the detector discriminates between the case $p = 0$ and $p = p_1$, for fixed p_1. In [1] it is shown that the discrimination problem is not necessarily optimally solved by an estimator for p. Following the methodology of [1] we should use a discriminator which shows how well an image under analysis matches the cover assumptions. This would simply be $S(0)$. However, $S(0)$ does not make a good discriminator because cover images vary (a lot!) in how well they meet the cover assumptions. A better discriminator is $S(0)/S(\hat{p})$ – this

---

[5] According to [9] the sample standard deviation is not a consistent estimator for measuring magnitude of error; subsequent experiments using a robust scale estimator yielded comparable results.

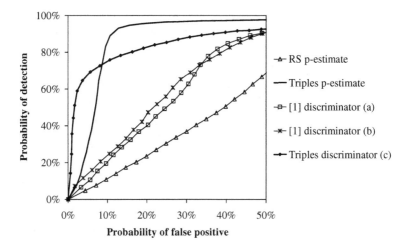

Fig. 5. Receiver Operating Characteristic curves, observed for the set of 3000 cover images subject to JPEG compression at quality factor 75. Random messages of length 2% of the maximum have been embedded. Detectors shown are the RS and Triples estimator of p, two discriminators from [1], and the Triples quantity $S(0)/S(\hat{p})$.

statistic should be near 1 for cover images and higher for stego images. We emphasise that this value is not merely testing whether $\hat{p} = 0$: it is a measure of *how certain* we are that $p \neq 0$; when the function S has a low gradient near $\hat{p}$ we should have correspondingly lower confidence in the estimate, and this is reflected in the quotient discriminator[6].

Performance of the discriminators, in the case $p_1 = 0.02$ and for one particular set of cover images, is displayed in Fig. 5. We have included the RS and Triples estimators of p, along with three discriminators which do not estimate p:

(a) from [1]: compute the estimate for p by applying the standard SPA calculation separately to each trace set C_i, call it p_i; take the minimum of p_0, p_1 and p_2.
(b) from [1]: compute the relative difference of x_1' and y_1', these quantities as defined by the standard SPA method [3].
(c) novel: the ratio $S(0)/S(\hat{p})$ (including all four useful cover assumptions).

The embedding rate of 0.02 is below reliable detectability by the standard methods. In this case the Triples method is superior, and the discriminator which does not estimate p has even better performance at low false positive rates.

Again, it is impossible to include such graphs for each cover set and each value of p_1. Instead, we follow [1] by showing the lowest value of p_1 for which a certain (fairly arbitrary) level of reliability is achieved. This data is shown

---

[6] Some initial experiments suggested that, for discrimination, it was best to include all three useful cases of parity symmetry, and the one useful case of order symmetry, in the computation of S. This is in contrast to the case of simple estimation and some further work should be undertaken to investigate this.

Table 2. The lowest embedding rate p_1 for which "reliable" discrimination from $p = 0$ is achieved. Here, "reliable" is taken to mean a false positive rate of 5% and a false negative rate of 50%. Figures above 0.1 are accurate to 0.01; figures between 0.01 and 0.1 are accurate to 0.002; figures below 0.01 are accurate to 0.001.

Detector	3000 Uncompressed Bitmaps				Other sets of JPEG images		
	Unaltered	JPEG q.f.			5000 high quality	10000 med. quality	20000 low quality
		90	75	50			
RS	0.054	0.26	0.28	0.27	0.072	0.080	0.22
SPA	0.052	0.21	0.22	0.20	0.052	0.058	0.17
LSM	0.062	0.098	0.072	0.060	0.024	0.024	0.060
Triples	**0.042**	**0.040**	**0.026**	**0.018**	**0.010**	**0.005**	**0.016**
(a)	**0.028**	0.090	0.068	0.052	0.022	0.020	0.050
(b)	0.12	0.13	0.064	0.046	0.022	0.012	0.032
(c)	0.054	**0.016**	**0.012**	**0.018**	**0.006**	**0.003**	**0.009**

in Tab. 2. The Triples method is vastly superior in every case except for simple uncompressed covers, in which case discriminator (a) from [1] is most sensitive. This suggests that further improvements to the final stage of the Triples method may be possible, if a number of uncorrelated estimates for p can be produced.

5   Conclusions and Further Work

We have described a general framework for steganalysis of LSB Replacement, which can consider arbitrary tuples of pixels. It involves a new paradigm for detection, in which the effects of embedding a message of known length can be inverted, and a cover image model against which a best fit is found. The framework can include many of the previously known detectors, although we have not, in this paper, given the mathematical details of such relationships.

To demonstrate that the framework is worthwhile, we have tested one case, called Triples Analysis, which is a generalisation of the Sample Pairs/Couples method to include 3-tuples of pixels. It is necessary to screen the Triples method by first applying a standard estimator, because of inaccurate results when the hidden message length is high. A range of experiments verify that this makes for a reliable detector and estimator of hidden messages, performing somewhat better than the standard detectors on uncompressed covers, and very much better on images where the cover has artefacts. We conclude that it is a more robust detector, less prone to floods of false positive results caused by the cover type. (Although for reasons of space we have not included further experimental results, we observed that Triples Analysis maintains superior performance when the cover images are JPEGs which have been reduced in size – even when the reduction is as much as a factor of 5.)

Although the general framework uses all the structure of the LSB embedding method, it does not close the book on LSB detectors. We should apply it to tuples of pixels larger than 3, in the hope that even further improvements will result. However there are problems: increasing the group size g divides the set of tuples $\mathcal{T}$ into ever-smaller trace sets, and the assumption that random variables are close to their expectations causes errors when the law of large numbers cannot be relied upon (indeed, Triples Analysis already suffers with poor performance on very small images). It will be necessary to combine some of the trace sets, but to do so in a way which does not reduce the method back to the case of lower g. Further work is needed to identify how best to do this, how to produce the results at the final stage (i.e. whether minimising the sum-square error is optimal), and whether there are better ways to select $\mathcal{T}$ than simply horizontal rows of pixels.

Finally, we might hope to use denoising techniques to determine further information about the cover image, combining the best attributes of the structural detectors with those based on signal processing.

Acknowledgements

The author is a Royal Society University Research Fellow.

References

1. Ker, A.: Improved detection of LSB steganography in grayscale images. In: Proc. 6th Information Hiding Workshop. Volume 3200 of Springer LNCS. (2004) 97–115
2. Fridrich, J., Goljan, M., Du, R.: Reliable detection of LSB steganography in color and grayscale images. Proc. ACM Workshop on Multimedia and Security (2001) 27–30
3. Dumitrescu, S., Wu, X., Wang, Z.: Detection of LSB steganography via sample pair analysis. In: Proc. 5th Information Hiding Workshop. Volume 2578 of Springer LNCS. (2002) 355–372
4. Fridrich, J., Goljan, M., Soukal, D.: Higher-order statistical steganalysis of palette images. In Delp III, E.J., Wong, P.W., eds.: Security and Watermarking of Multimedia Contents V. Volume 5020 of Proc. SPIE. (2003) 178–190
5. Lu, P., Luo, X., Tang, Q., Shen, L.: An improved sample pairs method for detection of LSB embedding. In: Proc. 6th Information Hiding Workshop. Volume 3200 of Springer LNCS. (2004) 116–127
6. Zhang, T., Ping, X.: A new approach to reliable detection of LSB steganography in natural images. Signal Processing **83** (2003) 2085–2093
7. Harmsen, J., Pearlman, W.: Steganalysis of additive noise modelable information hiding. In Delp III, E.J., Wong, P.W., eds.: Security and Watermarking of Multimedia Contents V. Volume 5020 of Proc. SPIE. (2003) 131–142
8. Lyu, S., Farid, H.: Steganalysis using colour wavelet statistics and one-class vector support machines. In Delp III, E.J., Wong, P.W., eds.: Security, Steganography, and Watermarking of Multimedia Contents VI. Volume 5306 of Proc. SPIE. (2004) 35–45
9. Böhme, R.: Assessment of steganalytic methods using multiple regression models. In: Proc. 7th Information Hiding Workshop. Springer LNCS (2005)

New Steganalysis Methodology: LR Cube Analysis for the Detection of LSB Steganography

Kwangsoo Lee, Changho Jung, Sangjin Lee, and Jongin Lim

Center for Information Security Technologies, Korea University, Korea
kslee@cist.korea.ac.kr

Abstract. In this paper, we present a new steganalytic technique to detect the use of LSB steganography in the gray-scale images. We are motivated by a need to research the high-dimensional joint characteristics of locally correlated samples. In the development, we used the successively adjacent n-pixel chains in the horizontal and vertical directions as the basic units of our steganalysis. The experimental results of the proposed method are described and compared with those of previous steganalytic methods. At the results, the proposed method outperformed the previous steganalytic methods and highly detected the low-rate embedding, even if any false detection were not occurred.

1 Introduction

Steganography is the art of hiding secret messages into innocuous looking cover-signals for the purpose of invisible communication. Secure steganographic systems must not leave any discernable traces in stego-signals that are in potential use for the detection of hidden messages. On the other hand, steganalysis is the science of breaking steganographic systems. It takes advantage of statistical or perceptual distinction of the stego-signals from the cover-signals so that it can determine whether a given signal is in the steganographic use.

Digital images are frequently used as the cover-signals for steganography because they are proliferated through the internet and contain a lot of redundancies that could be modulated without having any significant impacts on the perceptual and statistical properties of the images. Earlier steganographers observed that the least significant bits (LSBs) of image data are extremely random and can be substituted by the random message bits unsuspiciously. The substituting method is called the LSB embedding or the LSB steganography. In this paper, we focus on the detection of the LSB steganography in the gray-scale images.

Recently, we proposed a steganalytic technique to detect the use of LSB steganography in RGB color images [12]. In that, we used the RGB color vectors as the basic units for the consideration of the joint characteristics of three color components of the color vectors, and took advantage of the local correlation of the neighboring RGB color vectors. We presented a new concept of the set complexities on the three-dimensional lattice space Z^3 of the RGB color space, and designed the two types of special sets, named the left δ-cube and the right

M. Barni et al. (Eds.): IH 2005, LNCS 3727, pp. 312–326, 2005.

δ-cube, having the contrast effects by the LSB steganography. The steganalytic technique is based on a new model, named the LR cube model, that will be discussed in generalized form in this paper.

In this paper, we present a new steganalytic technique to detect the use of LSB steganography in the gray-scale images. We are inspired by our recent work [12] and are motivated by a need to investigate the high-dimensional joint characteristics of the locally correlated samples. Firstly, we generalize the LR cube model to the n-dimensional lattice space Z^n and develop the steganalysis algorithm based on the model for the LSB steganalysis in the n-dimensional vector signals. This method will be named the LR cube analysis. So far, we have been working on the task of how to apply the LR cube analysis to the gray-scale images. This paper shows just one of the possible methods showing the good detecting performances. In this one, we use the successively adjacent n-pixel chains in the horizontal and vertical directions as the n-dimensional vectors that are the basic units in the LR cube analysis.

The proposed method can detect the stego-images generated by the LSB steganography as well as by the PSP steganography [9]. To demonstrate the detection efficiency of our method, we will compare the experimental results of our method with those of the previous LSB steganalytic methods such as the regular-singular analysis [5] and the sample pair analysis [8]. In conclusion, the proposed method outperformed the previous steganalytic methods and has highly detected the low-rate embedding such as 5% and 10% in bpp (bits-per-pixels), even if any false detection were not occurred.

In section 2, we discuss the previous works in our concern. In section 3, we describe our approach for the steganalysis. We describe the general framework of the LR cube analysis in section 4 and explain how to draw the n-dimensional vectors from the gray-scale images in section 5. We display the experimental results of the LR cube analysis in section 6 and conclude this paper in section 7.

2   Previous Works

For the development of steganalysis, it is necessary to find the core properties of natural signal which does not hold if any artificial modifications are occurred in the signal. There are several steganalytic methods to detect the use of LSB steganography. In this section, we discuss the previous works in our concern for steganalysis and those assumptions of signal properties.

2.1   First-Order Statistical Steganalysis

The signal noise are frequently assumed to be normally distributed. Fig. 1 shows the ideally expected sample distributions before and after the LSB embedding. Westfeld and Pfitzmann [2] presented the chi-square attack that analyzes the first-order statistic such as the histogram of pixel values. They used the observation that those frequencies of both values of each PoVs (pair of values which only differ in the LSBs) tend to be equalized after the LSB embedding. The chi-square attack is the way of measuring the similarity between the observed

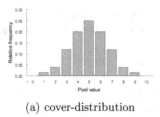

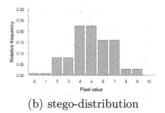

(a) cover-distribution   (b) stego-distribution

Fig. 1. Ideally expected sample distributions before and after the LSB embedding

sample distribution and its theoretically expected stego-distribution by using a χ^2-test (e.g., [1]).

There are, however, some drawbacks in the first-order statistical steganalysis. Their method is efficient for the detection of the sequentially embedded hidden messages, but not for the detection of the randomly scattered hidden messages. Some improvements [4,7] of the chi-square attack can detect the use of LSB steganography with the random scattering. But, these methods still fail in the detection of the low-rate embedding by the LSB steganography with random scattering. The reason is that the histogram distortion by the low-rate embedding is relatively small and the equalization of the PoVs characteristics is too insufficient for the detection. In fact, the first-order statistical steganalyses fail often in the detection of the low-rate embedding such as 10% embedding in bpp (bits-per-pixel).

2.2   Second-Order Statistical Steganalysis

There are another types of steganalytic methods. Fridrich et al. [5] introduced the regular-singular (RS) analysis that uses a dual statistics such as the correlation of adjacent samples. Later, Dumitrescu et al. [8] provided the mathematical modelling to the RS analysis and proposed the sample pair (SP) analysis. These methods take advantage of second-order statistic such as the spatial correlation of adjacent pixels and have merit to estimate the hidden message lengths in gray-scale images. These second-order statistical steganalyses have outperformed the first-order statistical steganalyses. The reason is seemed to be originated from the advantage of their classification models that use the dependencies such as the adjacency.

The SP analysis is based on the assumption that, for the cover-signals, a pair of adjacent samples having the $2m + 1$ difference has an equal probability to be $(2k - 2m - 1, 2k)$ or $(2k - 2m, 2k + 1)$, and also equal probability to be $(2k, 2k - 2m - 1)$ or $(2k + 1, 2k - 2m)$, if m is not too large. They modelled the effect of LSB embedding by a finite-state machine whose states are selected multisets of sample pairs, called trace multisets (refer the literature [8]). The assumption of the SP analysis is plausible by the symmetrical property of the quantization noise distribution like in AWGN channel. For instance, see Fig. 1 again and consider all of the possible sample pairs, then you can check easily the assumption of the SP analysis.

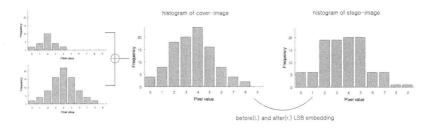

Fig. 2. An example of the interference of the two ideal sample distributions

For the usual gray-scale images, the sample distributions are the results of the statistical interferences from the uncorrelated parts of the images. The statistical interferences influence the detecting performance of these steganalytic methods. Fig. 2 represents an example of interference from two ideal sample distributions before and after the LSB embedding. We can see that the symmetrical property does not hold in the cover-distribution. This will cause the initial bias of the statistics assumed by the above two methods. The initial bias indicates that the methods does not free from the false positive for detecting the low-rate embedding such as 5% and 10% in bpp (bits-per-pixel). Ker [10] presented an improvement of the two methods by segmentation of an image into correlated parts.

3   Our Approach

We have maintained the another viewpoint on the sample pair analysis. The sample pairs can be regarded as two-dimensional vectors. The two-dimensional vectors can contain the various information such as the spatial correlation more than the one-dimensional histogram bins. For the gray-scale images with 256 gray-level, the two-dimensional vector bins can contain $256^2 = 65536$ different vectors, while the one dimensional histogram bins can contain only the 256 values. The two-dimensional vector approach for the steganalysis can take advantage of the various information such as the spatial correlation by putting the information data into the affluent vector bins.

In this paper, we present a new steganalytic technique to detect the use of LSB steganography in the gray-scale images. We are motivated by a need to research the higher-dimensional joint characteristics of the spatially correlated samples via the higher-dimensional vector approach. The higher-dimensional vector approach can make use of the strengthened pixel dependencies. It is our opinions that this approach can diminish the interferences of the uncorrelated statistics of an image and give a good separation of the uncorrelated statistics of itself.

How to use these vectors? We are inspired by our recent work [12] that use the three-dimensional RGB vectors of the RGB color images and are based on the new steganalytic model, named the LR cube model. We generalized the LR model with the dimensional extension for n-dimensional vector signals. The

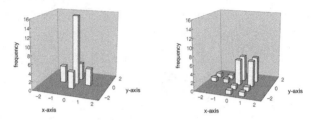

Fig. 3. Histograms of 2-D vectors before(left) and after(right) the LSB embedding

developed LR cube analysis has been highly sensitive to the small changes of the image data by the LSB embedding.

4   Principle of LR Cube Analysis

In this section, we describe the principle of the LR cube analysis (LRCA) in generalized form so that can be universally used for many types of digital signals.

4.1   The Space of Sample Points

The digital signal can be represented by the succession of samples $s_1, s_2, \cdots, s_N$, where the samples s_i are integers and the indices i represent the times in the discrete-time domain. A *sample point* means an n-tuple $(s_{i_1}, s_{i_2}, \cdots, s_{i_n})$, where $1 \leq i_j \leq N$. The sample points will be used as basic units for analyzing the higher order statistic, such as sample correlation. Let S be a set of sample points drawn from a digital signal. We will come back to the issue of how these sample points should be extracted from the gray-scale image data in section 3.

The sample points are treated as the points of the n-dimensional lattice space Z^n, and the set of sample points S as a subset of Z^n. A function $f_S : Z^n \to \{0, 1\}$, called the *state function with S*, is defined as follows: for every $p \in Z^n$,

$$f_S(p) = \begin{cases} 1 & \text{if } p \in S \text{ ,} \\ 0 & \text{otherwise .} \end{cases} \tag{1}$$

A point $p \in Z^n$ is said to be *filled with S* if $f_S(p) = 1$, and the point p is said to be *empty with S* otherwise.

Let $\mathcal{F}$ be the collection of subsets of Z^n. For a set of sample points S, a measure $\gamma_S : \mathcal{F} \to [0, \infty]$, called the the *complexity measure with S*, is defined as follows: for every $A \in \mathcal{F}$,

$$\gamma_S(A) = \sum_{s \in A} f_S(s) . \tag{2}$$

A set $A \in \mathcal{F}$ is said to be *m-complex with S* if $\gamma_S(A) = m$. From the definition, it follows that $0 \leq \gamma_S(A) \leq |A|$ for every $A \in \mathcal{F}$. In the model, the ratio $\gamma(A)/|A|$ is viewed as the complex level of S in the set A.

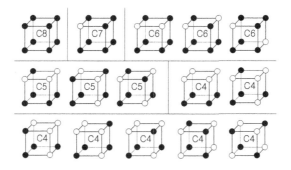

Fig. 4. Patterns inventory of δ-cubes in Z^3

For a positive integer δ, the δ-cube is defined by the set of the form,

$$Q(a;\delta) = \{s \in Z^n \colon \sigma_i = \alpha_i \ \text{or} \ \sigma_i = \alpha_i + \delta, \ 1 \le i \le n\} \ . \tag{3}$$

Here, $a = (\alpha_1, \cdots, \alpha_n) \in Z^n$ and $s = (\sigma_1, \cdots, \sigma_n) \in Z^n$. Since every δ-cube has 2^n points, it can show 2^n-complexity to the maximum. Fig. 4 shows the pattern inventory of δ-cubes in Z^3 with different complexities in unoriented figure (floating in three dimension). The black and white points represent the filled and empty states of the points, respectively. If the colors are changed to each other, C8, C7, C6, and C5 become C0, C1, C2, and C3, respectively.

Given a set of sample points S, the δ-cubes can be classified into their complexities with S. Let Ω_δ be the collection that consists of δ-cubes in Z^n, and let $\Omega_\delta(m)$ be the sub-collection of Ω_δ that contains the δ-cubes which are m-complex with S. Then, the collection Ω_δ is partitioned into the sub-collections $\Omega_\delta(m)$:

$$\Omega_\delta = \Omega_\delta(0) \cup \Omega_\delta(1) \cup \cdots \cup \Omega_\delta(2^n) \ . \tag{4}$$

4.2 LR Cube Model

From now on we will assume that δ is fixed to a positive *odd* integer. Let P be the set of the points a of Z^n whose coordinates α_i are *even* integers. For a point $a \in P$, the set

$$Q_L(a;\delta) = \{s \in Z^n : \sigma_i = \alpha_i \ \text{or} \ \sigma_i = \alpha_i - \delta, \ 1 \le i \le n\} \tag{5}$$

is called the *left δ-cube with corner at a*, and the set

$$Q_R(a;\delta) = \{s \in Z^n : \sigma_i = \alpha_i \ \text{or} \ \sigma_i = \alpha_i + \delta, \ 1 \le i \le n\} \tag{6}$$

is called the *right δ-cube with corner at a* (refer Fig. 5).

It is clear that every point of Z^n is contained in exactly one of the left δ-cubes. So the left δ-cubes are pairwise disjoint, and their union cover the lattice space Z^n. The same is true for right δ-cubes:

$$Z^n = \dot{\bigcup}_{a \in P} Q_L(a;\delta) \ \text{and} \ Z^n = \dot{\bigcup}_{a \in P} Q_R(a;\delta) \ . \tag{7}$$

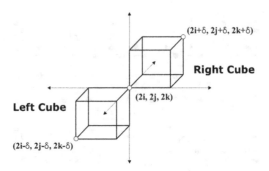

Fig. 5. Three-dimensional left and right δ-cubes

Let $\mathcal{L}_\delta$ be the collection of left δ-cubes with corners in P, and let $\mathcal{R}_\delta$ be the collection of right δ-cubes with corners in P:

$$\mathcal{L}_\delta = \{Q_L(a;\delta) : a \in P\} \text{ and } \mathcal{R}_\delta = \{Q_R(a;\delta) : a \in P\} . \tag{8}$$

For a set of sample points S, let $\mathcal{L}_\delta(m)$ be the sub-collection of $\mathcal{L}_\delta$ that contains the left δ-cubes which are m-complex with S, and let $\mathcal{R}_\delta(m)$ be the sub-collection of $\mathcal{R}_\delta$ that contains the right δ-cubes which are m-complex with S. Then $\mathcal{L}_\delta$ and $\mathcal{R}_\delta$ are partitioned as follows:

$$\mathcal{L}_\delta = \mathcal{L}_\delta(0) \cup \mathcal{L}_\delta(1) \cup \cdots \cup \mathcal{L}_\delta(2^n), \text{ and } \mathcal{R}_\delta = \mathcal{R}_\delta(0) \cup \mathcal{R}_\delta(1) \cup \cdots \cup \mathcal{R}_\delta(2^n) . \tag{9}$$

We assumes that the following statement is hold:

LR cube assumption: Given a cover-signal I, there exists a set of sample points S drawn from I and a positive odd integer δ such that

$$E\left[\left|\mathcal{L}_\delta[m]\right|\right] = E\left[\left|\mathcal{R}_\delta[m]\right|\right] , \tag{10}$$

for all $m = 0, 1, 2, \cdots, 2^n$, where $E[\cdot]$ denotes the expected value.

This is a key observation for our steganalysis. The expected cardinalities of $\mathcal{L}_\delta[m]$ and $\mathcal{R}_\delta[m]$ are the same for sample points drawn from cover-signals if δ is not too large.

4.3   Statistical Measuring

The LRCA is to measure the distortion level of the LR cube distribution. We assume that a set of sample points S is given and the δ value is set by a positive odd integer. One can induce the state function $f_S(\cdot)$ with S by Eq. (1) and accumulate the collections $\mathcal{L}_\delta - \mathcal{L}_\delta(0)$ and $\mathcal{R}_\delta - \mathcal{R}_\delta(0)$ of left and right δ-cubes with corners in P that are not 0-complex with S. Then one can take part the collections $\mathcal{L}_\delta - \mathcal{L}_\delta(0)$ and $\mathcal{R}_\delta - \mathcal{R}_\delta(0)$ into $L_\delta(m)$ and $R_\delta(m)$ of the complexities $m = 0, 1, 2, \cdots, 2^n$, with S, respectively and can obtain the two distributions $|\mathcal{L}_\delta(m)|$ and $|\mathcal{R}_\delta(m)|$ for $m = 1, 2, \cdots, 2^n$. Here, we do not consider the case of

$m = 0$ for the statistical measurement because it cannot give any information of the state changes of sample points from signal distortions.

We use a χ^2-test to determine whether the set of sample points S shows the distortion of the two distributions of the left and right δ-cubes. The expected distribution $E_\delta^*(m)$ for the χ^2-test can be computed from those two distributions. We assume that the two distributions are similar to a cover signal. As results, we can take the arithmetic mean,

$$E_\delta^*(m) = \frac{|\mathcal{L}_\delta(m)| + |\mathcal{R}_\delta(m)|}{2} \; , \tag{11}$$

to determine the expected distribution. The expected distribution is compared with the observed distribution

$$E_\delta(m) = |\mathcal{L}_\delta(m)| \; . \tag{12}$$

The χ^2 value for the difference between the two distributions is given as

$$\chi^2 = \sum_{m=1}^{\nu+1} \frac{(E_\delta(m) - E_\delta^*(m))^2}{E_\delta^*(m)} \; , \tag{13}$$

where ν is the degrees of freedom, that is the maximal complexity with S of the left and right δ-cubes minus one. The p-value is then given by the cumulative distribution function

$$p = \int_0^{\chi^2} \frac{t^{(\nu-2)/2}e^{-t/2}}{2^{\nu/2}\Gamma(\nu/2)} dt \; . \tag{14}$$

In the application of LRCA to detection of hidden messages, the p-value will be used for discrimination between cover-signals and stego-signals: for a given decision threshold T_p, if $p > T_p$, then the signal I will be regarded as a stego-signal.

4.4   Impact of LSB Embedding on the Distribution

LSB embedding in a digital signal changes the sample points drawn from the signal. In a lattice space Z^n, it can alter the point states; an empty point can a filled point or a filled point can be an empty point. In fact, a point state can be altered when the point has a small frequency such as $0, 1, 2, \cdots$. However, the points with large frequencies maintain the filled states. After LSB embedding, in a δ-cube, if the newly generated *filled* (or *empty*) points are increased (decreased) more than the newly generated empty (or filled) points, then the δ-cube becomes more complex (or simpler).

It is clear that the right 1-cube is closed under LSB embedding. Assume that the message bits are uniformly distributed, and are embedded in a signal by LSB embedding. If an empty point is contained in a heavy-weighted right 1-cube (in which total sum of the point frequencies are large), the point tends to be filled from some other sample points with large frequencies because of the histogram equalization of LSB embedding. Consequently, the right 1-cube will be more complex after LSB embedding.

For the convenience of description, we define the terms, "inner" and "outer". The inner point of $Q(a; \delta)$ means the point s of Z^n such that $\alpha_i \leq \sigma_i \leq \alpha_i + \delta$ for all $i = 1, \cdots, n$. The inner cube of $Q(a; \delta)$ is the cube whose points are totally inner points of $Q(a; \delta)$. For example, $Q(a; 1)$ is the unique inner 1-cube of itself and $Q(a; \delta)$ has 2^n inner 1-cubes with common points when δ is larger than 2. On the other hand, an outer point of $Q(a; \delta)$ means a point s of Z^n that is not an inner point of $Q(a; \delta)$. The outer cube of $Q(a; \delta)$ is the cube whose points are outer points of $Q(a; \delta)$ with an exception of one point.

Assuming that the distribution of sample points on a lattice space Z^n has an n-dimensional bell-shaped curve, we discuss the complexity changes of δ-cubes by LSB embedding, according to their locations in the distribution as follows:

Center: If a δ-cube is located at the center of the distribution, all the points of the δ-cube have large frequency values. The points of the δ-cube will maintain the filled state with high probability after LSB embedding. Consequently, the complexities of the δ-cubes will not be changed. This case can hardly affect the LR cube distribution.

Tail: If a δ-cube is located at the tail of the distribution, many of the points of the δ-cube have 0 frequency values and few points of the δ-cube have small frequency values. The complexity changes in both of the left and right δ-cubes are negligible. This case can also hardly affect the LR cube distribution.

Slope: If a δ-cube is located at the slope of the distribution, some of the points of the δ-cube can have small frequency such as $0, 1, 2, \cdots$, where the points are located in the low position of the slope.

In a right δ-cube $Q_R(a; \delta)$, a point s with small frequency is contained an adjacent inner right 1-cube $Q_R(s; 1)$ in which some points have larger frequency than the point s with high probability. The histogram equalization of $Q_R(a; 1)$ by LSB embedding results in an increment of the frequency of the point s. In particular, the empty points of $Q_R(a; \delta)$ can becomes filled with high probability. As the result, the right δ-cubes will be more complex after LSB embedding.

On the contrary, in a left δ-cube $Q_L(a; \delta)$, a point s with small frequency is contained an adjacent outer right 1-cube $Q_L(s; 1)$ in which most of other points have smaller frequencies than or equal to the frequency of the point s with high probability. The histogram equalization of $Q_L(a; 1)$ by LSB embedding results in a decrement of the frequency of the point s. In particular, it is possible that the filled points of $Q_R(a; \delta)$ with the small frequency, such as $1, 2$, can becomes empty with high-probability. As the result, the left δ-cubes will be simpler after LSB embedding.

In summary, LSB embedding causes the numerical difference between the numbers of left and right δ-cubes having the same complexity with the stego-signal.

5   Applying the LRCA to Gray-Scale Images

In this section, we present a sampling method for the application of LRCA to gray-scale images and discuss how the δ values should be set. The issue on the dimension of the sample points will be discussed in the next section with the experimental results .

For a principle steganalysis, an efficient sampling method can give an improvement of the steganalysis. For example, Dumitrescu et al. pointed out the effect of sampling method (see [8]). Furthermore, some improvements of the RS and SP analysis are introduced in [10,11].

In this paper, leaving the issue on optimal sampling, we restrict to show the possibility of applying the LRCA to gray-scale images. In [12], we used the RGB colors themselves as the 3-dimensional sample points of the basic units on LRCA, and investigate local correlations between the colors of an image. For a gray-scale image, we use the sample points whose components are drawn from the successive n pixels in the image, unlike in [12]. Each of these sample points will have some information of a local correlation in an image.

In a formalized description, let $g(i,j)$ denote an NxM gray-scale image, where $i = 0, 1, \cdots, N - 1$, and $j = 0, 1, \cdots, M - 1$. Given a dimension n of sample points, let $s_v(i,j)$ denote the vertical sample point at the pixel position (i,j), where the components $\sigma_k = g(i + k - 1, j)$ for $k = 1, 2, \cdots, n$. Then, the set of vertical sample points is the set of the form,

$$S_v = \{s_v(i,j) : 0 \le i \le N - n \text{ and } 0 \le j \le M - 1\} . \tag{15}$$

In the similar way, let $s_h(i,j)$ denote the horizontal sample point at the pixel position (i,j), where the components $\sigma_k = g(i, j + k - 1)$ for $k = 1, 2, \cdots, n$. Then, the set of horizontal sample points is the set of the form,

$$S_h = \{s_h(i,j) : 0 \le i \le N - 1 \text{ and } 0 \le j \le M - n\} . \tag{16}$$

We will use their union set $S = S_v \cup S_h$ as the set of n-dimensional sample points for LRCA.

How should the δ-value be set? This is also an issue with SP analysis. For the convenience of an explanation, let $d(x, y)$ be a distance in the space Z^n defined by

$$d(x, y) = \max_{1 \le i \le n} |x_i - y_i| \tag{17}$$

Intuitively, if the two sample points x and y are drawn in the locally correlated parts of an image, then the component-wise differences $|x_i - y_i|$ will be small, and $d(x, y)$ is small. Inversely, if $d(x, y)$ is large, the two sample points can be regarded as being contained in uncorrelated regions. This suggests that the δ values should not be set by large value. We have seen that the δ values larger than 7 resulted in the irregular statistic of LRCA. Furthermore, δ with a value 1 does not have any effect on the detection by LRCA. For our experiments, we set the δ value by 3.

6   Experimental Results

6.1   Test Images

We used our image database consisting of 1332 RGB color images. Those images were initially obtained from scanners by anonymous photographic experts. All of them has the size 1296x960. In our experiment, we converted the true-color images to the gray-scale, and resize them to 324x240, by using an executable program[1]. We embedded the random messages in the gray-scale images by both of LSB steganography and PSP steganography, where the message lengths are chosen by 5%, 10%, 15%, 20%, 25%, and 30% bpp (bits per pixel). Some images showed the small limited capacities with PSP steganography. We excluded such images from the stego-image sets by PSP steganography. Tab. 1 depicts the number of stego-images generated by PSP steganography.

Table 1. The number of stego-images generated by PSP steganography

cover-images	5%	10%	15%	20%	25%	30%
1332	1301	1234	1166	1084	995	907

Although the lossy compressed images such as jpeg format are proliferated, there are many uncompressed images in the internet. Some of detection algorithms [3,6] can discriminate between the cover-images and the stego-images if their initial sources are jpeg format, but they fail in discriminating between stego-images from the jpeg sources and cover-images from the scanned sources. So, the methods do the false alarm to many scanned cover-images. Generally, the detection for images from the scanned sources is more difficult task than for images from the jpeg sources [10]. That is the reason of why we chose the scanned sources.

6.2   Simulations on the Sampling Dimension

In the experiments, δ was fixed in 3 because LRCA have been well-performed in the δ value. When the sampling dimensions are less than 4, LRCA was not sensitive to LSB embedding. The reason for the low dimension is explained in previous sections. For the higher dimension n, the space Z^n can have the different 256^n sample points with 256 gray-scale. This is an enormous number. Although the local correlation can limit the number of different sample points, the limits will be enormous too. Consequently, most of sample points will have low frequencies such as 1. This case is similar to the property of the tail of bell-shaped curves. So LSB embedding cannot give significant impacts on the LR cube distribution. When the dimension is greater than 7, LRCA have been resulted in incorrect detections of the cover and stego images.

---

[1] ACDSee 3.0, http://www.acdsystems.com

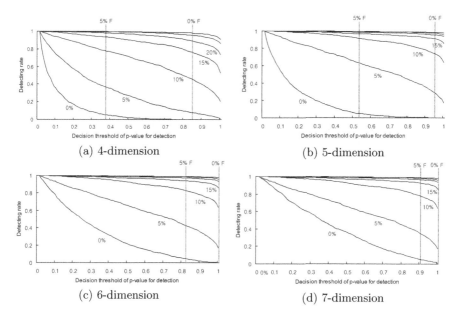

Fig. 6. Detecting performances of LRCA for LSB steganography

Fig. 6 depicts the simulation results of the LRCA on the parameters of the dimension 4, 5, 6, and 7 for the stego-images generated by LSB steganography. The graphs display the detecting rates of the LRCA according to the decision threshold of the p-value. In the figure, the dotted lines indicate the decision thresholds of their statistics with the false positives about 0% and 5%. When the dimension is increased, the statistics of cover-images become more irregular. From the figure. the case of the dimension 5 shows the better performance than the other cases.

6.3   Comparison of LRCA with RS and SP Analysis

Fig. 7 depicts the experimental results of LRCA, RS analysis, and SP analysis, with our 1332 cover-images and their stego-images generated by both of LSB and PSP steganography. The graphs depict the detecting rates according to the decision thresholds of the statistic for each of the algorithms. In this experiments, we use the sampling dimension 5 and the δ value 3 for LRCA, the mask [0 1;1 0] for RS analysis, and m in the range from 0 to 15 for SP analysis. Also Tab. 2 summarizes the comparison of the performances of those algorithms for some specific thresholds. You can see that the LRCA outperformed the RS and SP analysis. One of the most interesting features at the results is that LRCA highly detected the low-rate embedding such as 5% and 10% in bpp by the LSB steganography as well as by the PSP steganography, even if any false detections were not occurred. It seems that the LSB substitution principle itself is not good for the secure steganographic model.

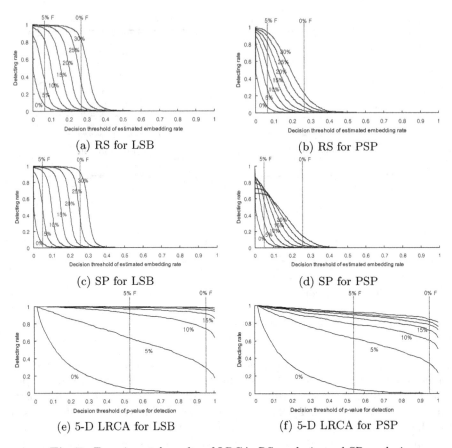

Fig. 7. Experimental results of LRCA, RS analysis, and SP analysis

7   Conclusion

We introduced a new steganalysis algorithm for the detection of LSB steganography in gray-scale images. We generalized our recent work into n-dimensional LR cube analysis and showed how to apply it to gray-scale images. We also discussed the issues on the input parameters such as sampling dimension and the δ values. From experimental results, we showed that the LRCA can be applied to gray-scale images. Furthermore, those results suggest that the dimensional extension technique by using locally correlated samples can provide the good separation of uncorrelated parts of a signal. LRCA outperformed the RS and SP analysis. It is interesting that the LRCA highly detected the low-rate embedding such as 5% and 10% in bpp by both of LSB steganography and PSP steganography, even when any false detections were not occurred. We conclude that the LSB replacement principle itself is not good for the secure steganographic model.

Table 2. Comparison of the detecting performances of RS and SP analysis and LRCA on the specific decision thresholds for both of LSB and PSP steganography

Statistic		decision threshold	embedding method	embedding rate in bpp						
				0%	5%	10%	15%	20%	25%	30%
RS		0.277	LSB	0.000	0.002	0.007	0.014	0.045	0.247	0.772
			PSP	0.000	0.002	0.003	0.017	0.057	0.104	0.193
		0.076	LSB	0.049	0.252	0.750	0.938	0.980	0.988	0.994
			PSP	0.049	0.197	0.422	0.640	0.763	0.859	0.922
SP		0.266	LSB	0.000	0.001	0.003	0.005	0.026	0.211	0.876
			PSP	0.000	0.001	0.002	0.008	0.025	0.064	0.130
		0.049	LSB	0.052	0.503	0.936	0.984	0.992	0.996	0.997
			PSP	0.052	0.322	0.576	0.703	0.724	0.701	0.657
LRCA	5-D	0.95	LSB	**0.000**	**0.291**	**0.741**	**0.913**	**0.957**	**0.976**	**0.983**
			PSP	**0.000**	**0.344**	**0.606**	**0.720**	**0.781**	**0.817**	**0.843**
		0.53	LSB	0.048	0.633	0.915	0.967	0.987	0.995	0.993
			PSP	0.048	0.627	0.789	0.860	0.896	0.910	0.925

Acknowledgements

This research was supported by the MIC(Ministry of Information and Communication), Korea, under the ITRC(Information Technology Research Center) support program supervised by the IITA(Institute of Information Technology Assessment)

References

1. Maurer, U. M.: A Universal Statistical Test for Random Bit Generators. *Journal of Cryptology,* 5(2): 89–105, (1992)
2. Westfeld, A. and Pfitzmann, A.: Attacks on steganographic systems. Information Hiding. 3rd International Workshop. Lecture Notes in Computer Science, vol. 1768. Springer-Verlag, Berlin Heidelberg New York(1999) pp. 61–76,
3. Fridrich, J., Du, R., and Meng, L.: Steganalysis of LSB Encoding in Color Images. Proceedings IEEE International Conference on Multimedia and Expo ICME 2000. New York (2000)
4. Provos, N. and Honeyman, P.: Detecting Stegnaographic Content on the Internet. CITI Technical Report 03–11. (2001)
5. Fridrich, J., Goljan, M., and Du, R.: Detecting LSB stegangoraphy in color and gray-scale images. Magazine of IEEE Multimedia. Special Issue on Security, October-November issue. (2001) pp. 22–28
6. Westfeld, A.: Detecting Low Embedding Rates. Information Hiding. 5th International Workshop. Lecture Notes in Computer Science, Vol.2578. Springer-Verlag, Berlin Heidelberg New York (2002) pp. 324–339.
7. Fridrich, J., Goljan, M., and Soukal, D.: Higher-Order Statistical Steganalysis of Palette Images. in Proc. EI SPIE Santa Clara, CA, Jan 2003, pp. 178-190.

8. Dumitrescu, S., Wu, X., and Wang, Z.: Detection of LSB Steganography via Sample Pair Analysis. In: Peticolas, F.A.P. (Ed.): Information Hiding. 5th International Workshop. Lecture Notes in Computer Science, vol. 2578. Springer-Verlag, Berlin Heidelberg (2003). pp. 355–372.

9. Franz, E.: Steganography Preserving Statistical Properties. In: Peticolas, F.A.P. (Ed.): Information Hiding. 5th International Workshop. Lecture Notes in Computer Science, vol. 2578. Springer-Verlag, Berlin Heidelberg (2003). pp. 278–294.

10. Ker, A. D.: Improved Detection of LSB Steganography in Grayscale Images. In: Fridrich, J. (Ed.): Information Hiding. 6th International Workshop. Lecture Notes in Computer Science, vol. 3200. Springer-Verlag, Berlin Heidelberg (2004). pp. 97–115

11. Westfeld, A.: Space Filling Curves in Steganalysis. In: Edward J. Delp III, Ping Wah Wong (Eds.): Security, Steganography, and Watermarking of Multimedia Contents VII. Proceedings of SPIE, San Jose, CA, (2005). pp. 28–37

12. Lee, K., Jung, C., Lee, S., and Lim, J.: Color Cube Anlysis for Detection of LSB Steganography in RGB Color Images. ISH 05, in conjunction with ICCSA 2005. Lecture Notes in Computer Science, vol. 3481. Springer-Verlag, Berlin Heidelberg (2005). pp. 537–546

An Analysis of Empirical PMF Based Tests for Least Significant Bit Image Steganography

Stark Draper, Prakash Ishwar, David Molnar, Vinod Prabhakaran,
Kannan Ramchandran, Daniel Schonberg, and David Wagner*

University of California, Berkeley
infohide@taverner.eecs.berkeley.edu

Abstract. We consider here the class of probability mass-function (PMF) based detectors of least significant bit (LSB) embedded steganography. That is, in this paper we investigate the use of frequency counts of pixel intensities as a statistic for tests detecting the presence of hidden messages. We focus on LSB replacement (though we briefly consider LSB matching) embedding as it is a simple technique where the effect on the true PMF of the resulting image can be understood mathematically. We begin our study by considering the existing tests of Westfeld and Pfitzmann [11] and Dabeer et al. [1]. These tests assume that pixel intensities are random values that are independent and identically distributed (i.i.d.). We generalize these tests by considering PMFs of neighboring pixel intensities. We argue that consideration of higher order of correlations provide only diminishing marginal returns, and thus we can make general statements on the value of PMF based detectors. We measure the performance of our tests by calculation of receiver operating curves (ROC) over a corpus of 350 digital images. We then proceed to compare to a non-PMF based test, in particular the RS tests of Fridrich et al [3]. Although our generalized tests outperform existing PMF based predecessors, they are outperformed by the RS tests. This indicates that using PMFs as a statistic for detecting hidden messages is inherently insufficient.

1 Introduction

Steganography is the practice of hiding a message in a covertext. Figure 1 shows an example of least significant bit (LSB) image steganography. While the images appear the same, the LSBs of each pixel in the image on the right have been replaced with a hidden message. Figure 2 depicts a block diagram in which message MSG is encoded into a string of length N (the length of the covertext in pixels). Random variable $\mathbf{M}^N$ denotes the encoded message. A stegoencoder takes $\mathbf{M}^N$, a covertext image denoted $\mathbf{X}^N$, and outputs a stegotext denoted $\mathbf{Y}^N$. The aim of *steganalysis* is to distinguish images with hidden messages from those without. Specifically, given a sample image $\mathbf{z}^N$ from either $\mathbf{X}^N$ or $\mathbf{Y}^N$, we want to decide whether $\mathbf{z}^N$ contains a hidden message or not.

* This research was supported by NSF under grant CCR-0325311.

M. Barni et al. (Eds.): IH 2005, LNCS 3727, pp. 327–341, 2005.

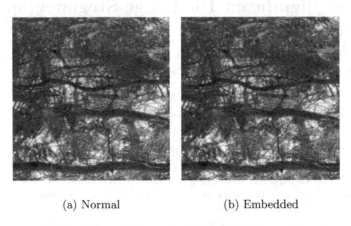

(a) Normal   (b) Embedded

Fig. 1. Example Photograph With LSB Embedding

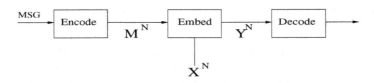

Fig. 2. Embedding message MSG into covertext $\mathbf{X}$ to obtain stegotext $\mathbf{Y}$

In this paper we consider the class of probability mass function (PMF) based steganography detectors for LSB embedding. We restrict ourselves to PMF-based detectors of LSB embedding because it is possible to develop mathematically how the embedding impacts the PMF. By considering existing tests, and then generalizing new tests, we are able to make statements about the entire class of such detectors. Existing LSB PMF-based tests rely on an i.i.d. assumption about the observation. Our new tests use a first-order memory model in order to capture spatial correlations between neighboring pixels of the covertext. The advantage of considering memory is that it allows for greater separation between the embedded and covertext distributions. It is natural to believe that the greatest advantage in considering memory would be seen by this first-order generalization, and that further order increases would produce diminishing marginal gains. Note that this paper primarily focuses on LSB replacement embedding, though we briefly consider LSB matching.

Our main contribution is to develop intuitions of how a higher order covertext model affects PMF-based steganalytic performance. To this end, we develop a first order memory generalization of the PMF covertext model and present three new tests based on our model. The first test is a generalization of the χ_2 test proposed by Westfeld and Pfitzmann and used by Provos and Honeyman in StegDetect [11] [8]. This test has the advantages of being simple and intuitive. Our next two tests are generalizations of the memoryless tests of Dabeer et al.

[1]. The first of these generalizations is a *blind* test using the Kullback-Leibler (KL) divergence. The test is *blind* in that the test makes no assumptions about the specific the covertext. Our final test is an *informed* test, also based on the KL divergence. The informed test assumes knowledge (possibly only partial) of the covertext statistics. We build on the hypothesis testing framework of Dabeer et al. to obtain our tests. By developing this framework, we are able to show that our blind test is optimal for the class of first order memory models.

Our empirical results suggest that first order memory can lead to significant gains in the case of χ_2 tests, but only minor gains in the case of our blind tests. Since the gains from the consideration of the correlation are only marginal, this suggests that PMF based tests are inherently limited. When further comparing our tests against a non-PMF based test (the RS test of [3]), we see that the non-PMF based test exhibits far superior results, further discouraging the use of PMF based tests.

This paper is organized as follows. We begin by discussing simple PMF image models, define LSB replacement, and outline the hypothesis testing framework in Section 2. In Section 3 we discuss our higher order empirical PMFs and we introduce our covertext model and derive our new tests. Then, in Section 4, we empirically evaluate our tests, the test of Westfeld and Pfitzmann, the tests of Dabeer et al., and RS steganalysis. Finally, in Section 5 we consider LSB matching embedding and provide an extension of our framework to this embedding technique.

2   Background

In this paper, uppercase letters, such as X, refer to random variables, while lowercase letters, such as x, refer to instances of the corresponding random variable. Boldface letters, such as $\mathbf{p}$, refer to either vectors or matrices, with the meaning clear from context. A superscript on a character indicates vector length. For example, $\mathbf{X}^N$ is a vector-valued random variable of length N, $X^N = (x_1, \ldots, x_N)$.

Throughout this work, we assume that images are 8-bit grayscale throughout, with a set of pixel values from the alphabet $\mathcal{A} := \{0, 1, \ldots, 255\}$. Let $\mathcal{P}^0$ be the set of all probability mass functions (PMF) on $\mathcal{A}$. Let $\mathcal{P}'$ be the set of all joint PMFs on $\mathcal{A} \times \mathcal{A}$. Thus

$$\mathcal{P} := \left\{ \mathbf{p} = (p_0, p_1, \ldots, p_{255}) \in \mathbb{R}^{256} : p_i \geq 0, \sum_{i=0}^{255} p_i = 1 \right\}$$

$$\mathcal{P}' := \left\{ \mathbf{p} = \begin{pmatrix} p_{0,0} & \cdots & p_{0,255} \\ \vdots & \ddots & \vdots \\ p_{255,0} & \cdots & p_{255,255} \end{pmatrix} \in \mathbb{R}^{256 \times 256} : p_{i,j} \geq 0, \sum_{i=0}^{255} \sum_{j=0}^{255} p_{i,j} = 1 \right\}$$

We will often speak of the *empirical PMF* $\mathbf{q}(\mathbf{z}^N)$ of a vector $\mathbf{z}^N \in \mathcal{A}^N$. The empirical PMF $\mathbf{q}(\mathbf{z}^N)$ on $\mathcal{A}$ is just the normalized histogram of the pixel values in $\mathbf{z}^N$. Thus $q_i = \frac{n_i}{\sum n_j}$ where n_j is the number of occurrences of value j in $\mathbf{z}^N$, i.e. $n_j = \#\{k \in \{1, \ldots, N\} : z_k = j\}$. Given a matrix $\mathbf{z}^N \in \mathcal{A}^N \times \mathcal{A}^N$, the first order empirical PMF $\mathbf{q}(\mathbf{z}^N)$ on $\mathcal{A} \times \mathcal{A}$ is the normalized histogram of $\frac{(N)(N-1)}{2}$ pairs of pixel values in $\mathbf{z}^N$. We will omit the $\mathbf{z}^N$ and write $\mathbf{q}$ when the meaning is clear from context.

2.1 LSB Replacement

We now proceed to define LSB replacement embedding. While an image with LSB replacement and the original image may be indistinguishable to the human eye, the empirical statistics vary. One can see visual evidence of this by comparing the histograms of pixel values between an original and a modified image; the modified image displays a pronounced "stair-step" effect. Example histograms for LSB replacement in which all pixels of an image have the least significant bit replaced with message data are shown in Figure 3.

When the LSB plane of the pixels are replaced with bits equally likely to be 0 or 1 (true at high rates), the probability of seeing the two pixel intensities whose other bit planes are equivalent are averaged. This is responsible for the "stair-step" character of embedded images. Though less pronounced at rates below one embedded bit per pixel, the effect is still prominent enough to allow detection. Below, we make this notion more precise by first defining LSB embedding of a message and then giving properties that must hold for an embedded image.

Let $\mathbf{m}^N$ be an encoded message, with $m_i \in \{0, 1, \emptyset\}$. The special $\emptyset$ symbol indicates a location of the message where no embedding is performed. For LSB replacement embedding at *rate* R, we define an encoding function $F_R : \{0,1\}^{NR} \rightarrow \{0, 1, \emptyset\}^N$; this function "expands" an arbitrary message to N symbols with an expected fraction $1 - R$ of $\emptyset$ symbols. Let $\mathbf{x}^N$ be an instance from the covertext

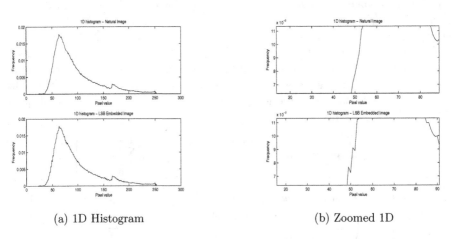

(a) 1D Histogram   (b) Zoomed 1D

Fig. 3. Histograms showing effect of LSB embedding at rate 1 in an 8-bit grayscale image. Histograms from the original image are on the top row and histograms from the embedded image are on the bottom row. The plateaus giving the "stair-step" effect its name are pronounced in the embedded image.

distribution $\mathbf{X}^N$. We then define the embedding function $\mathbf{y}^N := E(\mathbf{m}^N, \mathbf{x}^N)$. In the definition of this function below, we define only for the LSB plane, since all other bit planes of $\mathbf{y}^N$ are set equal to those of $\mathbf{x}^N$.

$$LSB(y_i) = \begin{cases} 1 & \text{if } m_i = 1 \\ 0 & \text{if } m_i = 0 \\ x_i & \text{if } m_i = \emptyset \end{cases}$$

If $\mathbf{X}^N$ has PMF $\mathbf{p} \in \mathcal{P}$ and we apply embedding $\mathbf{y}^N = E(\mathbf{m}^N, \mathbf{x}^N)$ at rate R, then $\mathbf{Y}$ will have the PMF $\mathbf{p}_R \in \mathcal{P}_R$ given by

$$\begin{aligned} p_{R,2l} &= (1 - \tfrac{R}{2})p_{2l} + \tfrac{R}{2}p_{2l+1} \\ p_{R,2l+1} &= \tfrac{R}{2}p_{2l} + (1 - \tfrac{R}{2})p_{2l+1} \end{aligned}, \quad \text{for } l = 0, 1, \ldots, 127 \qquad (1)$$

Notice that the larger the embedding rate R, the "smaller" the set of possible PMFs $\mathcal{P}_R$ (as shown by Dabeer et al. [1]). An alternative view of averaging over groups of consecutive pixel intensities is to see that it limits the ratio between those PMF values. The following relationships are derived.

$$\frac{R}{2 - R} \leq \frac{p_{R,2l}}{p_{R,2l+1}} \leq \frac{2 - R}{R}, \quad \text{for } l = 0, 1, \ldots, 127 \qquad (2)$$

Thus we see that for all $p_R \in \mathcal{P}_R$ the ratio of pixel pairs is bounded. These bounds explain the "stair-step" effect observed in the histograms, since they limit how much pixels intensities within a group can deviate.

2.2   Hypothesis Testing

We now set up a hypothesis testing framework for tests to detect steganographic embedding. First we define the hypothesis that data is not embedded as $\mathcal{H}_0$ and the hypothesis that data is embedded at rate R as $\mathcal{H}_1$.

$$\mathcal{H}_0 : \mathbf{p} \in \mathcal{P} \setminus \mathcal{P}_R, \quad \mathcal{H}_1 : \mathbf{p} \in \mathcal{P}_R$$

A detector d_N is characterized by the acceptance region $A \subseteq \mathcal{A}^N$:

$$d(\mathbf{z}^N) = \begin{cases} \mathcal{H}_0 & \text{if } \mathbf{z}^N \in A, \\ \mathcal{H}_1 & \text{otherwise.} \end{cases}$$

We denote the false negative probability of a detector by P_1 and the false positive probability by P_2. These probabilities are defined as follows

$$\begin{aligned} P_1 &:= \Pr[\mathbf{x}^N \leftarrow \mathbf{X}^N, \mathbf{Y}^N = E(\mathbf{x}^N, \mathbf{m}^N), \mathbf{z}^N \leftarrow \mathbf{Y}^N : d(\mathbf{z}^N) = \mathcal{H}_0] \\ P_2 &:= \Pr[\mathbf{z}^N \leftarrow \mathbf{X}^N : d(\mathbf{z}^N) = \mathcal{H}_1] \end{aligned}$$

Notice that the random variable $\mathbf{M}^N$ depends on the message encoding used. For detection to be nontrivial, the distribution over $\mathbf{X}^N$ must not be in the set $\mathcal{P}_R$. We do not model $\mathbf{X}^N$ as a "random" distribution, thus we do not need to consider a distribution over distributions; instead we assume that the distribution of $\mathbf{X}^N$

is not in $\mathcal{P}_R$. This assumption is one we must make for this class of tests to work, and empirical results indicate that it is reasonable.

Now fix a constant $\lambda > 0$ and consider a sequence of detectors $\{d_1, d_2, \ldots\}$. The value of λ represents the false negative probability we are willing to tolerate, while simultaneously wishing to minimize the false positive probability.

We seek a sequence of detectors that minimizes $\liminf_{N \to \infty} -\frac{1}{N} \log(P_2)$ subject to the constraint $\liminf_{N \to \infty} -\frac{1}{N} \log(P_1) \geq \lambda$. Let $\mathbf{q}$ be the empirical PMF of a sample $\mathbf{z}^N$. Let $D(\mathbf{q}||\mathbf{p})$ be the Kullback-Leibler divergence between PMFs $\mathbf{p}$ and $\mathbf{q}$. Define $D(\mathbf{q}||\mathcal{P}_R) := \min_{\mathbf{p} \in \mathcal{P}_R} D(\mathbf{q}||\mathbf{p})$. We consider a sequence of detectors because by a result of Hoeffding we can specify a test which is asymptotically optimal as N goes to infinity [5]. The optimal test is the following

$$d_{OPT(\lambda)}(\mathbf{q}) = \begin{cases} \mathcal{H}_0 & \text{if } D(\mathbf{q}||\mathcal{P}_R) \geq \lambda, \\ \mathcal{H}_1 & \text{otherwise.} \end{cases}$$

where $\mathbf{q}$ is the empirical PMF derived from a sample $\mathbf{z}^N$.

3   Steganography Tests

In this section we present both existing tests and our extensions of them, a summary is given in Figure 4. Note that each of these tests compares a derived statistic to a threshold value λ. Specifically, in the following tests we compute a statistic $\alpha \in \mathbb{R}$. Given a statistic α, the derived test d_λ works as follows:

$$d_\lambda = \begin{cases} \mathcal{H}_0 & \text{if } \alpha \geq \lambda, \\ \mathcal{H}_1 & \text{otherwise.} \end{cases}$$

Name	Threshold Condition	PMF Type
Memoryless blind	$D(\mathbf{q}||\mathcal{P}_R) \geq \lambda$	Derived
StegDetect	$\chi_2(\mathbf{q}||\mathcal{P}_1) \geq \lambda$	Derived
Memoryless informed	$D(\mathbf{q}||\mathbf{p}_R) - D(\mathbf{q}||\mathbf{p}) \geq \lambda$	Provided
RS Steganalysis	See [3]	Not Applicable

(a) Existing Tests

Name	Threshold Condition	PMF Type
First-order blind	$D(\mathbf{q}||\mathcal{P}_R) \geq \lambda$	Derived
First-order χ_2	$\chi_2(\mathbf{q}||\mathcal{P}_1) \geq \lambda$	Derived
First-order informed	$D(\mathbf{q}||\mathbf{p}_R) - D(\mathbf{q}||\mathbf{p}) \geq \lambda$	Provided

(b) New Tests

Fig. 4. Summary of tests. In the charts above, the middle column gives the threshold condition under which the tests outputs $\mathcal{H}_0$. In the last column in the charts above, an explanation of which type of PMF the input is compared to is given.

Each of the tests below takes the empirical PMF $\mathbf{q}$ as an input. Further note throughout this section we define $0/0 = 1$ for convenience.

3.1 Properties of Neighboring Pixel PMFs

Before proceeding to the tests, we present background on first order memory PMFs. The relation between a first order PMF $\mathbf{p} \in \mathcal{P}'$ and an embedded first order $\mathbf{p}_R \in \mathcal{P}'_R$ is

$$
\begin{aligned}
p_{R,2l,2k} &= (1 - \tfrac{R}{4})p_{2l,2k} + \tfrac{R}{4}p_{2l,2k+1} + \tfrac{R}{4}p_{2l+1,2k} + \tfrac{R}{4}p_{2l+1,2k} \\
p_{R,2l,2k+1} &= \tfrac{R}{4}p_{2l,2k} + (1 - \tfrac{R}{4})p_{2l,2k+1} + \tfrac{R}{4}p_{2l+1,2k} + \tfrac{R}{4}p_{2l+1,2k} \\
p_{R,2l+1,2k} &= \tfrac{R}{4}p_{2l,2k} + \tfrac{R}{4}p_{2l,2k+1} + (1 - \tfrac{R}{4})p_{2l+1,2k} + \tfrac{R}{4}p_{2l+1,2k} \\
p_{R,2l+1,2k+1} &= \tfrac{R}{4}p_{2l,2k} + \tfrac{R}{4}p_{2l,2k+1} + \tfrac{R}{4}p_{2l+1,2k} + (1 - \tfrac{R}{4})p_{2l+1,2k}
\end{aligned}
\tag{3}
$$

$$
\text{for } l = 0, 1, \ldots, 127, \quad k = 0, 1, \ldots, 127
$$

As in the memoryless case (Eq. (1)), where pixel intensities were considered in groups of two, from Eq. (3) it is clear we now consider pixel intensities in blocks of four (2×2). As with the memoryless case, bounds on the ratios between pixel intensity frequencies can be generated for PMFs residing in $\mathcal{P}_R$.

$$
\begin{aligned}
\tfrac{R}{4-3R} \leq \tfrac{p_{R,2l,2k+1}}{p_{R,2l,2k}} \leq \tfrac{4-3R}{R} \qquad & \tfrac{R}{4-3R} \leq \tfrac{p_{R,2l+1,2k}}{p_{R,2l,2k+1}} \leq \tfrac{4-3R}{R} \\
\tfrac{R}{4-3R} \leq \tfrac{p_{R,2l+1,2k}}{p_{R,2l,2k}} \leq \tfrac{4-3R}{R} \qquad & \tfrac{R}{4-3R} \leq \tfrac{p_{R,2l+1,2k+1}}{p_{R,2l,2k+1}} \leq \tfrac{4-3R}{R} \\
\tfrac{R}{4-3R} \leq \tfrac{p_{R,2l+1,2k+1}}{p_{R,2l,2k}} \leq \tfrac{4-3R}{R} \qquad & \tfrac{R}{4-3R} \leq \tfrac{p_{R,2l+1,2k+1}}{p_{R,2l+1,2k}} \leq \tfrac{4-3R}{R}
\end{aligned}
\tag{4}
$$

As in the memoryless case, examining histograms of images with high rate LSB embedding gives visual evidence that empirical statistics differ. Figure 5 exhibits the "blockiness" induced by the PMF averaging of high rate embedding.

3.2 Chi-squared Tests

In order to obtain a PMF for the basis of comparison, χ_2 tests calculate $\mathbf{p}^*$. $\mathbf{p}^*$ is by applying Equations 1 and 3 (respective of PMF dimension) at rate $R = 1$. Once $\mathbf{p}^*$ is generated, a χ_2 distance from the empirical PMF is measured. The formula for a χ_2 distance is

$$
\chi_2(\mathbf{p}, \mathbf{q}) = \sum_{i=0}^{255} \frac{(q_i - p_i^*)^2}{p_i^*}
$$

In this section, we also discuss the Westfeld and Pfitzmann statistic used by StegDetect here [11] [8]. StegDetect does not explicitly generate a comparison PMF but, as we show, is equivalent to the χ_2 test.

The StegDetect test of Westfeld and Pfitzmann[8] is defined here.

$$
\alpha = \sum_{k=0}^{127} \frac{(q_{2k+1} - q_{2k})^2}{q_{2k+1} + q_{2k}}
$$

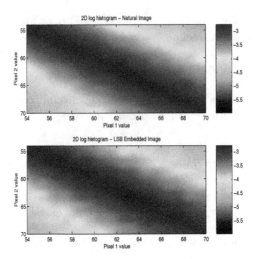

Fig. 5. Two-dimensional histograms of normal and embedded images. Note the "blockiness" effect in the histogram for the embedded image.

The memoryless χ_2 test is defined as follows.

$$\alpha = \chi_2(\mathbf{p}^*, \mathbf{q}) = \sum_{i=0}^{255} \frac{(q_i - p_i^*)^2}{p_i^*}$$

$$p_{2k}^* = p_{2k+1}^* = \frac{q_{2k+1} + q_{2k}}{2}, \quad \text{for } k = 0, 1, \ldots, 127$$

Finally, the first order χ_2 test is as follows.

$$\alpha = \chi_2(\mathbf{p}^*, \mathbf{q}) = \sum_{i=0}^{255} \sum_{j=0}^{255} \frac{(q_{i,j} - p_{i,j}^*)^2}{p_{i,j}^*}$$

$$p_{2l,2k}^* = p_{2l+1,2k}^* = p_{2l,2k+1}^* = p_{2l+1,2k+1}^* = (q_{2l,2k} + q_{2l+1,2k} + q_{2l,2k+1} + q_{2l+1,2k+1})/4$$
$$\text{for } l = 0, 1, \ldots, 127, \quad k = 0, 1, \ldots, 127$$

As can be seen above, the first order χ_2 test is the natural extension of its memoryless χ_2 counterpart. All three tests have the advantage of being computationally simple and easy to implement. Since these tests do not consider rate, however, they suffer when lower embedding rates are employed.

The StegDetect and the memoryless χ_2 test are in fact the same test, as proven mathematically below.

$$\chi_2(\mathbf{p}^*, \mathbf{q}) = \sum_{i=0}^{255} \frac{(q_i - p_i^*)^2}{p_i^*} = \sum_{k=0}^{127} \left(\frac{(q_{2k} - p_{2k}^*)^2}{p_{2k}^*} + \frac{(q_{2k+1} - p_{2k+1}^*)^2}{p_{2k+1}^*} \right) \quad (5)$$

$$= \sum_{k=0}^{127} \frac{(q_{2k} - \frac{q_{2k} + q_{2k+1}}{2})^2 + (q_{2k+1} - \frac{q_{2k} + q_{2k+1}}{2})^2}{\frac{q_{2k} + q_{2k+1}}{2}} \quad (6)$$

$$= \sum_{k=0}^{127} \frac{(q_{2k} - q_{2k+1})^2 + (q_{2k+1} - q_{2k})^2}{2(q_{2k} + q_{2k+1})} = \sum_{k=0}^{127} \frac{(q_{2k} - q_{2k+1})^2}{q_{2k+1} + q_{2k}} \quad (7)$$

3.3   Blind Tests

Unlike the test above, our "blind" tests (blind of the covertext PMF) require knowledge of the rate R. Following our hypothesis testing framework, this test finds the distance between the observed PMF and the set of rate R embedded PMFs $\mathcal{P}_R^i$. Our memoryless Blind tests uses the statistic $\alpha = D(\mathbf{q}||\mathcal{P}_R)$ while our first order Blind test uses $\alpha = D(\mathbf{q}||\mathcal{P}_R')$.

The difficulty of computing these statistics efficiently lies in finding the PMF $\mathbf{p} \in \mathcal{P}_R$ (or $\mathbf{p} \in \mathcal{P}_R'$) that is closest to the observed PMF in $\mathcal{P}_R$ or $\mathcal{P}_R$ respectively. For the memoryless case, Dabeer et al. gave an algorithm for calculating the PMF $\mathbf{p}^*$ that minimizes this distance [1]. Pseudocode is given in Figure 6. Intuitively, this algorithm checks each set of PMF values to see if they violate Eq. (2). In the case that the conditions are not violated, the values of $\mathbf{p}^*$ are set equal to $\mathbf{q}$. If the conditions are violated though, the ratio of the two values are set equal to the violated bound while their sum is held constant.

For the first order memory test, the algorithmics become more involved. Let $\mathbf{q}$ denote the observed first order PMF. Pseudocode for computing $\mathbf{p}^*$ is shown in Figure 7.

Algorithm 3.1: FINDPSTARMEMORYLESS($\mathbf{q}$)

for $l \leftarrow 0$ **to** 127
if $\frac{q_{2l+1}}{q_{2l}} > \frac{2-R}{R}$
    then $p_{2l}^* = \frac{R}{2}(q_{2l} + q_{2l+1})$ and $p_{2l+1}^* = (1 - \frac{R}{2})(q_{2l} + q_{2l+1})$
    else if $\frac{q_{2l+1}}{q_{2l}} < \frac{R}{2-R}$
    then $p_{2l}^* = (1 - \frac{R}{2})(q_{2l} + q_{2l+1})$ and $p_{2l+1}^* = \frac{R}{2}(q_{2l} + q_{2l+1})$
    else $p_{2l}^* = q_{2l}$ and $p_{2l+1}^* = q_{2l+1}$

Fig. 6. Algorithm for computing $\mathbf{p}^*$ for memoryless sources

Algorithm 3.2: FINDPSTARMEMORY($\mathbf{q}$):
for $l \leftarrow 0$ **to** 127
for $k \leftarrow 0$ **to** 127
    $Q \leftarrow \{q_{2l,2k}, q_{2l,2k+1}, q_{2l+1,2k}, q_{2l+1,2k+1}\}$
    $\{w_1, w_2, w_3, w_4\} \leftarrow SortHighToLow(Q)$
    if $\frac{w_1}{w_4} > \frac{4-3R}{R}$ **then**
        $\tilde{w}_i \leftarrow 4\left(\frac{w_i - w_4}{w_1 - w_4}\right)\left(\frac{1-R}{R}\right) + 1$
        $\hat{w}_i \leftarrow \tilde{w}_i \frac{\sum_{j=1}^4 w_j}{\sum_{j=1}^4 \tilde{w}_j}$
        $\tilde{W} \leftarrow \{w_1, w_2, w_3, w_4\}$
        $\{p_{2l,2k}^*, p_{2l,2k+1}^*, p_{2l+1,2k}^*, p_{2l+1,2k+1}^*\} \leftarrow InvertOrderOfSortOperation(\tilde{W})$
    else $\{p_{2l,2k}^*, p_{2l,2k+1}^*, p_{2l+1,2k}^*, p_{2l+1,2k+1}^*\} \leftarrow \{q_{2l,2k}, q_{2l,2k+1}, q_{2l+1,2k}, q_{2l+1,2k+1}\}$

Fig. 7. Algorithm for computing $\mathbf{p}^*$ for first-order sources

In this code, if a 2×2 block of pixels does not violate the conditions of Eq. (4), then the block is transferred to the $\mathbf{p}^*$. If the conditions of Eq. (4) are violated, then the values of $\mathbf{q}$ are scaled so that the block satisfies those conditions while maintaining the same summation and relative scale. By following this procedure, the distance between the observed PMF $\mathbf{q}$ and the set $\mathcal{P}_R$ is found.

These tests have two significant advantages over the simple χ_2 tests presented earlier. First, they are able to exploit knowledge of the rate R. This allows for strong performance at all rates. Second, the KL divergence is a more complete "distance" then the χ_2 metric.

3.4   Informed Tests

In addition to the empirical PMF and target rate, "informed" tests take in information on the covertext PMF $\mathbf{p}$. These tests compare the KL distances from both the given distribution and the rate R expected embedded distribution. For the memoryless case, the test takes in an input PMF $\mathbf{p}$ and observed PMF $\mathbf{q}$ and then runs as follows.

- Calculate the PMF $\mathbf{p}_R \in \mathcal{P}_R$ which would result if we applied rate R embedding (with a random message) to a covertext with PMF $\mathbf{p} \in \mathcal{P}$. This can be done according to Equation 1.
- Calculate $\alpha = D(\mathbf{q}\|\mathbf{p}_R) - D(\mathbf{q}\|\mathbf{p})$.

The first order memory case can be described similarly to the memoryless case. The test takes in an input PMF $\mathbf{p}$ and observed PMF $\mathbf{q}$ and then runs as follows.

- Calculate the PMF $\mathbf{p}_R \in \mathcal{P}'_R$ which would result if we applied rate R embedding (with a random message) to a covertext with PMF $\mathbf{p} \in \mathcal{P}'$. This can be done according to Equation 3.
- Calculate $\alpha = D(\mathbf{q}\|\mathbf{p}_R) - D(\mathbf{q}\|\mathbf{p})$.

Note that these tests opperate even if $\mathbf{p}$ is only an approximation to the true distribution of the covertext. The tests are robust to small errors in $\mathbf{p}$; however, the quality of the test is limited by the quality of the supplied distribution. Careful choice of distribution is crucial when using an informed test.

4   Empirical Results for LSB Replacement

We calculated these tests on a set of 350 images chosen from a larger corpus of 2977 Portable Network Graphics (png) images obtained from Sullivan et al. [2]. We embed at 3 rates; $R = 0.05$, $R = 0.5$, and $R = 1.0$. The messages were generated randomly according to a Bernoulli$(1/2)$ i.i.d. random process. We ran each of the tests given in Section 3 on the embedded images.

Based on this data, receiver operating curves (ROC) were generated by calculating false negative and positive rates from a variety of thresholds. We provide the resulting ROCs in Figure 9. In the ROC plots, the results for the χ_2 tests (on the left) and the blind tests (on the right) at Rates 0.5 and 0.05 are presented.

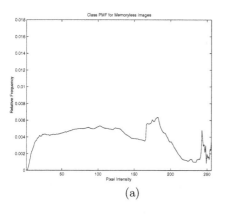
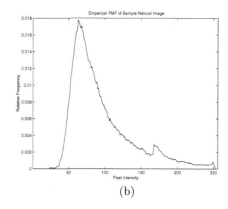

(a)   (b)

Fig. 8. Comparison of PMF used for informed test (a) and a sample PMF for a natural image (b). As can be seen in the image on the left, by averaging over the entire corpus of images a roughly flat PMF is achieved, significantly differing from the empirical PMF of any actual image.

The memoryless tests are plotted with solid lines while the memory model tests are plotted with dashed lines. The $R = 0.05$ results are always higher in the plot. For every test on the rate $R = 1$ embedded data, the ROC curves are nearly ideal. Since these would be difficult to see in the plots, they have been omitted.

As expected, StegDetect and the memoryless χ_2 tests resulted in the same parameter value. As a result, the StegDetect lines are omitted below. Further, we see that the memory version of the χ_2 square test outperforms the memoryless version at rate $R = 0.5$. Since $R = 0.05$ is such a low rate both tests perform very poorly, though moderate performance gain from the memory test is observed.

The memory blind test outperforms the memoryless blind test at rate $R = 0.5$. Here, the improvement in performance is less significant though, and they perform nearly identically for large false negative rates. As with the χ_2 tests, both blind tests perform nearly identically for $R = 0.05$, with the memoryless test slightly outperforming the memory test. Both tests perform poorly though due to the low rate. Note that at each rate, the blind tests outperform the χ_2 tests. This agrees with intuitions, since the χ_2 tests assume rate $R = 1$ embedding.

The prior distributions we chose were obtained by averaging all the PMFs within our image corpus. Unfortunately, because our corpus is large, the resulting prior PMF did not match any single image well. In Figure 8 we show histograms of the prior distribution used for the informed test and the histogram of a particular image file to illustrate these differences. As a result of the choice of prior distribution we made (though it was the natural choice), each informed tests performed very poorly at every rate. Each time, the test results were nearly equivalent to random guessing. This suggests that proper choice of prior distribution for the informed test is essential.

Finally, we comment on the results of RS steganalysis. Our results showed RS steganalysis performing well in all cases, showing ideal or near ideal performance. We were able to draw two tentative conclusions from this result. First, the RS

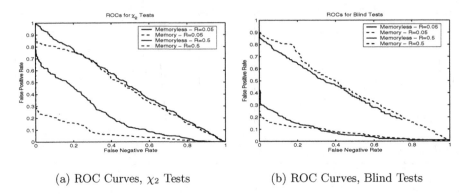

(a) ROC Curves, χ_2 Tests   (b) ROC Curves, Blind Tests

Fig. 9. ROC Curves for our tests applied to LSB replacement, over 350 digital camera images. In each of these plots, the rate $R = 0.5$ are plotted in a darker shade while the rate $R = 0.05$ are plotted in a lighter shade (and are consistently higher in the plot). In addition, memoryless tests are plotted with solid lines while memory tests are plotted in dashed lines. Results for all other tests are omitted for clarity.

test has an advantage by trying to estimate the rate at which the embedding occurred as opposed to a parameter off which to make a decision. Second, there seems to be an advantage in working off the true data instead of the PMF as a summary statistic. This would suggest that a better model for steganalysis would be to include even higher order relationships, as the RS test does.

5   LSB Matching

Above, we have focused exclusively on LSB replacement embedding. An alternate form of LSB embedding is LSB matching [7]. In this section we briefly describe LSB matching and describe some results of our steganalysis framework against LSB matching on a corpus of digital camera images. As before, we encode a message MSG into $\mathbf{m}^N$ at rate R with $m_i \in \{0, 1, \emptyset\}$. LSB matching is defined as follows:

$$y_i = \begin{cases} x_i \pm 1 & \text{if } LSB(y_i) \neq m_i \\ x_i & \text{if } LSB(y_i) = m_i \\ x_i & \text{if } m_i = \emptyset \end{cases}$$

Whenever x_i is not one of the extreme values (i.e., $x_i \in \{0, 255\}$) the choice between addition and subtraction is made at random (each option being equally likely).

The effect of LSB matching on the PMF of an image contrasts with that of LSB replacement. Instead of the "stair-step" effect induced by replacement, LSB matching has a smoothing effect. Ignoring the "edge-effects" due to the embedding rule at the extreme values of the PMF, we can write $\mathbf{p}_R$ as a filtered version of $\mathbf{p}$.

$$
\begin{array}{lll}
\text{For memoryless PMFs} & \mathbf{p}_R = \mathbf{p} * \mathbf{f} \\
\text{For neighboring pixel PMFs} & \mathbf{p}_R = \mathbf{p} * \mathbf{f} * \mathbf{f}^T \\
\text{where} & \mathbf{f} = (R/4, 1 - R/2, R/4)
\end{array}
$$

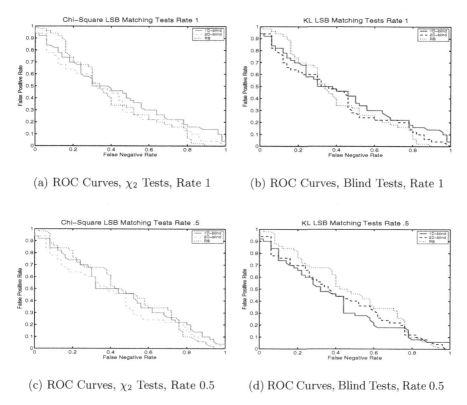

(a) ROC Curves, χ_2 Tests, Rate 1   (b) ROC Curves, Blind Tests, Rate 1

(c) ROC Curves, χ_2 Tests, Rate 0.5   (d) ROC Curves, Blind Tests, Rate 0.5

Fig. 10. ROC Curves for our tests on LSB matching, over 50 digital camera images. All embedding was performed at rate 1 and rate 0.5. Memoryless tests are plotted with solid lines while memory tests are plotted in dashed lines. The RS test curve for each rate is included on all graphs.

In these equations, the symbol $*$ denotes convolution and the superscript $\mathbf{f}^T$ indicates transpose. Since embedding is done on a pixel by pixel basis, the neighboring pixel PMF equation consists of a convolution on each dimension. As can be seen by examining this filter, the filter is a moving average filter and thus has a smoothing effect. As with LSB replacement, as the rate increases the space of possible PMFs shrinks.

It is clear that simply applying the tests above designed for LSB replacement will be sub-optimal. In Figure 10 we demonstrate the results of applying our tests to 50 digital camera images. We note that the RS steganalysis offers no performance advantage at rate 1 and performs slightly worse than our tests at rate 0.5. This is because RS steganalysis takes advantage of structural properties that are present only with LSB replacement and not LSB matching. Ker gives a more detailed overview of these properties [6]. Developing optimal tests for LSB matching (particularly in the blind case) is a part of ongoing work.

6   Related Work

Early work in detection of LSB embedding was done by Westfeld and Pfitzmann, who proposed a χ_2 test for detection [11]. Later, Westfeld introduced a generalization of the χ_2 test that succeeds even at low embedding rates; this test works by "hashing" parts of the image into different combinations, then running a test on each individual combination [10]. Westfeld also pointed out the possibility of estimating the *length* of embedded data, which our tests do not provide.

Provos and Honeyman created the StegDetect system and searched millions of pictures from the Internet looking for steganographic embedding using the Westfeld and Pfitzmann test [8]. Dabeer et al. introduced the hypothesis testing framework and proved the KL divergence test is the optimal LSB detector for memoryless covertext distributions [1]. Fridrich et al. analyzed the RS test, which takes into account spatial correlations of individual pixels [3]. Fridrich and Goljan later proposed another method based on local estimators that has similar performance to the RS test, but admits a cleaner theoretical derivation [4].

7   Conclusions and Future Directions

The gains achieved by considering the first order memory model over a memoryless assumption suggest that the extensions to higher-order memory models for images would be of only limited value. Although offering the advantage of a rigorous mathematical framework, PMF based steganalysis seems inferior to RS steganography, at least on the class of test images we have considered. One area to explore would be other cover text models, such as the graphical Wainwright-Simoncelli-Willsky wavelet tree model [9]. Such a model may offer advantages in generating sufficient statistics for steganography since the model is not restricted to pixel intensity frequency counts.

Acknowledgments

We would like to thank Martin Wainwright for his valuable discussions on this topic. We also thank Jessica Fridrich, Miroslav Goljan, Andrew Ker, the other attendees, and the anonymous reviewers of the Information Hiding Workshop for feedback and suggestions. Finally, we thank the UCSB Vision Group for graciously allowing us to use their digital camera image set.

References

1. O. Dabeer, K. Sullivan, U. Madhow, S. Chandrasekaran, and B. S. Manjunath. Detection of hiding in the least significant bit. In *IEEE Trans. on Signal Processing*, volume 52, pages 3046–3058, Oct. 2004.
2. UCSB Vision Group; Sullivan et al., 2004. Collection of 2977 digital camera images.
3. J. Fridrich and M. Goljan. Practical steganalysis of digital images - state of the art. In *Proceedings of SPIE*, volume 4675, 2002.

4. J. Fridrich and M. Goljan. On estimation of secret message length in LSB steganography in spatial domain. In *SPIE*, 2004.
5. W. Hoeffding. Asymptotically optimal tests for multinomial distributions. *Ann. Math. Statist.*, 36:369–408, 1965.
6. A. Ker. A general framework for structural steganalysis of LSB replacement. In *IHW 2005*, 2005.
7. A. Ker. Steganalysis of LSB matching in grayscale images. *IEEE Signal Processing Letters*, 12(6), June 2005.
8. N. Provos and P. Honeyman. Hide and seek: An introduction to stegangography. *IEEE Security & Privacy Magazine*, May 2003.
9. M. J. Wainwright, E. P. Simoncelli, and A. S. Willsky. Random cascades on wavelet trees and their use in analyzing and modeling natural images. *Applied Computational and Harmonic Analysis*, 11:89–123, 2001.
10. A. Westfeld. Detecting low embedding rates. In *IHW 2002*, 2002.
11. A. Westfeld and A. Pfitzmann. Attacks on steganographic systems. In *IHW 1999*, 1999.

Self-validating Branch-Based Software Watermarking

Ginger Myles and Hongxia Jin

Computer Science Division, IBM Almaden Research Center,
San Jose, CA 95120
{gmyles, jin}@us.ibm.com

Abstract. Software protection is an area of active research in which a variety of techniques have been developed to address the issue. Examples of such techniques are software watermarking, code obfuscation, and tamper detection. In this paper we present a novel dynamic software watermarking algorithm which incorporates ideas from code obfuscation and tamper detection. Our technique simultaneously provides proof of ownership and the capability to trace the source of the illegal redistribution. It additionally provides a solution for distributing pre-packaged, fingerprinted software which is linked to the consumer. Our technique is specific to programs compiled for the x86 Intel architecture, however, we have proposed an extension for use on Java bytecode.

1 Introduction

The problem of protecting software from illegal copying and redistribution has been the focus of considerable research motivated by billions of dollars in lost revenue each year [1]. The growing concern regarding software piracy can be attributed to a variety of factors such as the distribution of software in architectural neutral formats and the ease of sharing over the Internet. In previous years piracy was limited by the necessity to physically transfer a piece of software on a floppy disc or CD-ROM. With the increases in bandwidth, physical transfer is no longer necessary.

In the unfortunate event that software is illegally redistributed or an important algorithmic secret is stolen, an owner would like to be able to take action against the theft. This requires demonstration of ownership and/or identification of the source of the illegal redistribution. A technique which enables such action is *software watermarking*.

Software watermarking is used to embed a unique identifier in a piece of software in order to encode identifying information. While this technique does not prevent piracy, it does provide a way to prove ownership of pirated software. In some cases it is even possible to identify the original purchaser. However, for software watermarking to be useful it must be resilient against a variety of attacks, e.g. semantics-preserving code transformations and program analysis tools.

In this paper we propose a novel dynamic software watermarking algorithm, *branch-based watermarking*, which incorporates ideas from code obfuscation (to aid in preventing reverse engineering) and software tamper detection (to thwart

M. Barni et al. (Eds.): IH 2005, LNCS 3727, pp. 342–356, 2005.

attacks such as the application of semantics-preserving transformations). The heart of the algorithm is centered around redirecting branch instructions to a specifically constructed fingerprint branch function. This function is responsible for computing the program's fingerprint and regulating execution. Through the use of this function automated attacks will result in non-functional software.

The branch-based software watermarking algorithm makes several improvements over previously proposed techniques:

1. Simultaneously provides proof of authorship and the ability to trace the source of the illegal distribution.
2. Demonstrates a significantly higher level of resilience to attack without significant overhead.
3. Provides a means for distributing pre-packaged, fingerprinted software which is linked to the consumer.

2   Software Watermarking

Software watermarking takes the approach of discouraging piracy through a program transformation which embeds a message (the "watermark") into the program. The most basic software watermarking system consists of two functions: $\text{embed}(P, w, k) \rightarrow P'$ and $\text{recognize}(P', k) \rightarrow w$. Using the secret key k, the embed-function incorporates the watermark w into a program P, yielding a new program P'. The recognize-function uses the same key k to extract the watermark from a suspected pirated copy.

Each software watermarking algorithm is categorized based on a set of characteristics. These include whether the code is analyzed as a static or dynamic object, the type of recognizer used, the embedding technique, and the type of mark embedded.

Static/Dynamic. Strictly static watermarking algorithms only use features available at compile-time for embedding and recognition. On the other hand, strictly dynamic watermarking algorithms use information gathered during the execution of the program. Abstract watermarking algorithms are neither strictly static or dynamic. Instead, such techniques are static in that recognition does not require execution of the program. However, they are dynamic since the watermark is hidden in the semantics of the program.

Recognition Type. A watermark recognizer is categorized based on the information needed to identify the watermark. Both blind and informed watermarking algorithms require the watermarked program and the secret key to extract the watermark. An informed technique additionally requires an unwatermarked version of the program and/or the embedded mark.

Embedding Technique. To incorporate a watermark, a program has to be manipulated through semantics-preserving transformations. Such transformations can be categorized as follows:
  - Reorder or rename code sections.
  - Insert new (non-functional and/or never executed) code .

– Manipulate the program's statistical properties such as instruction frequencies.

Mark Type. An *authorship mark* (AM) is a watermark in which the same mark is embedded in every copy of the program. An AM is used to identify the author and is in essence a copyright notice. On the other hand, a *fingerprint mark* (FM) is unique for each copy distributed and is normally used to identify the purchaser. Through the use of a FM it is possible to identify the source of an illegal distribution.

Previous watermarking algorithms use one of the above embedding techniques. In this paper we introduce a new embedding technique in which a section of code is added to the program. The new code both calculates the fingerprint as the program executes and directs program execution.

3   Related Work

A variety of software watermarking algorithms have been proposed. Due to the relative ease of static watermarking there are far more static than dynamic algorithms. A few examples of static watermarking algorithms are those proposed by Venkatesan et al. [2], Stern et al. [3], and Qu and Potkonjak [4]. Venkatesan et al. embed the watermark through an extension to a method's control flow graph. The watermark is encoded in a subgraph which is incorporated into the original graph. Stern et al. modify the instruction frequencies of the original program to embed the watermark. Qu and Potkonjak proposed a very stealthy, but fragile, algorithm which makes use of the graph coloring problem to embed the watermark in the register allocation of the method. In each of these cases, as well as all other static watermarking algorithms, the watermark can be destroyed by basic code optimization or obfuscation techniques.

The first dynamic software watermarking algorithm was proposed by Collberg and Thomborson [5]. This technique embeds the watermark in the structure of a graph, built on the heap at runtime, as the program executes on a particular input. A second dynamic technique proposed by Collberg et al. [6] is path-based and relies on the dynamic branching behavior of the program. To embed the watermark the sequence of branches taken and not taken on a particular input is modified. Two variations for this algorithm were developed to target the varied capabilities of Java bytecode and native executables. A final dynamic technique was developed by Nagra and Thomborson [7]. This technique leverages the ability to execute blocks of code on different threads. The watermark is encoded in the choice of blocks executed on the same thread. Cousot and Cousot [8] developed an abstract watermarking algorithm. The technique uses an abstract interpretation framework to embed a watermark in the values assigned to integer local variables during program execution.

4   Branch Based Software Watermarking

The heart of the branch-based software watermarking algorithm is centered around the use of a branch function specifically designed to generate the program's fingerprint as the program executes. If the branch function is properly designed the branch-based algorithm can simultaneously embed authorship and fingerprint marks. Additionally, tamper detection can be incorporated. In the following algorithm description we will provide an example as to how these three features can be incorporated in a single branch function.

The embed function for the branch-based algorithm deviates from the standard definition in that it has four inputs and two outputs.

$$\texttt{embed}(P, AM, key_{AM}, key_{FM}) \rightarrow P', FM$$

Using the two secret keys, key_{AM} and key_{FM}, the embed function incorporates the authorship mark AM and the fingerprint generating code into the program P, yielding a new program P' and the fingerprint mark FM. Since the algorithm can simultaneously embed an authorship and a fingerprint mark, two secret keys are required. This is in contrast to the usual single key. key_{AM} is tied to the authorship mark and is the same for every copy of the program. key_{FM} is required for the fingerprint mark and should be unique for each copy. A fingerprint mark for a particular instance of a program is based on the fingerprint key and the program execution. Thus, the actual fingerprint mark is generated during embedding and is an output of the embed function.

Similarly, the recognize function is non-standard with three inputs and two outputs.

$$\texttt{recognize}(P', key_{AM}, key_{FM}) \rightarrow AM, FM$$

Because the branch-based watermarker uses a blind recognizer, AM and FM can be obtained from the watermarked program by providing only the two secret keys.

Additionally, the branch-based watermarker is classified as dynamic, thus one of the secret keys, key_{AM}, is actually an input sequence to the program. By executing the program with the secret input, a trace consisting of a set of functions F is identified. The set F consists of those functions which will participate in the fingerprint calculation. During watermark recovery, if the program is executed with the input sequence, the same set of functions used for embedding will be executed. This will make it possible to identify both AM and FM.

4.1   Fingerprint Branch Function

A branch function is a special function originally proposed as part of an obfuscation technique used to disrupt static disassembly of native executables [9]. It was also used by Collberg et al. [6] in watermarking native executables, however, it was used in a manner different than in our branch-based watermark. The original obfuscation technique converted unconditional branch instructions to a call to a branch function inserted in the program. The sole purpose of a branch function is to transfer the control of execution to the instruction which was the target of the unconditional branch. Figure 1 illustrates the general idea of the branch function. To increase the versatility of the branch function we have devised an extension which makes it possible to convert conditional branches as well.

$$j_1: \text{jump } t_1 \qquad j_1: \text{call } b \rightarrow$$

$$\cdots \qquad\qquad \cdots \qquad\qquad\qquad\qquad\qquad \rightarrow t_1$$

$$j_2: \text{call } t_2 \quad\Longrightarrow\quad j_2: \text{call } b \rightarrow \boxed{\begin{array}{c}\text{branch} \\ \text{function } b\end{array}} \begin{array}{c}\rightarrow t_2 \\ \rightarrow t_3\end{array}$$

$$\cdots \qquad\qquad \cdots$$

$$j_3: \text{jump } t_3 \qquad j_3: \text{call } b \rightarrow$$

Fig. 1. Unconditional branch instructions are converted to calls to a branch function. The branch function transfers execution to the original branch target.

The FM for a program is generated as the program executes through the use of a specifically designed branch function. We call this branch function a *fingerprint branch function* (FBF). The original branch function was designed simply to transfer execution control to the branch target. In addition to the transfer of control, the FBF is also responsible for evolving a key. Each time the FBF is called a new key, k_i, is calculated. k_i is then used to aid in identifying the original branch target. The FBF performs the following tasks:

- An integrity check which produces the value v_i.
- Generation of the next function key, k_i, through the use of a one-way function, the integrity check value, and the previous key; $k_i = g(k_{i-1}, v_i)$.
- k_i is used to eventually transfer execution to the original branch target.

Within the FBF, an authorship mark and tamper detection can be incorporated. From a legal perspective, to prove ownership, it is not sufficient to simply recover a mark from a program. It is also necessary to show the watermark was intentionally embedded, i.e. recognition is not by chance. Choosing AM such that $AM = pq$ where p and q are two large primes is one possible example of a strong watermark. Since factoring is a hard problem, only the person who embedded such a watermark would be able to identify the factors p and q. To embed such an authorship mark in the FBF, the AM is encoded in the one-way function used to generate the next function key. A possible example is:

$$k_i = SHA1[(k_{i-1} \oplus AM) \parallel v_i]$$

Through the incorporation of an integrity check the FBF can detect tampering throughout the entire program. An integrity check is a section of code inserted in the program to verify the integrity of the program. The integrity checks are capable of identifying if a program has been subjected to semantics-preserving transformations or even if a debugger is present. For example, an integrity check could calculate a checksum over a block of code. If an attacker inserts breakpoints or makes some other modification to the code, the checksum will be different. We have developed a variety of different types of integrity checks. The integrity check will produce some value v_i which is then used as an additional input to the one-way function responsible for the key generation.

4.2   Embedding

The embedding of the authorship and fingerprint marks occur by injecting the FBF into the program. Selected branch instructions are then converted to calls to the FBF. The embedding process consists of three phases. The first phase is to execute the program using the secret input sequence, key_{AM}, to obtain a trace of the program. The trace will identify the set of functions F through which execution passes. These functions will be used in the watermarking.

In the second phase of the algorithm, the branches in each function $f \in F$ are replaced by calls to the FBF. Additionally, a mapping is created between the calculated key and the replaced branch instruction. The key, branch mapping is used in phase three to construct a structure, such as a table or array, which is added to the program. The structure is accessed during execution to obtain information relating to the replaced branch instruction. This information is necessary for proper program execution. Key evolution is linked to proper program execution through the organization of the structure. Using a perfect hash function, each key is mapped to a unique location in the structure.

$$h : \{k_i, k_2, ..., k_n\} \to \{1, 2, ..., m\}, n \leq m$$

If a minimal perfect hash function is used the table size can be minimized.

Unlike the authorship mark, the fingerprint mark is not embedded in the program. Instead it is generated as the program is executed. Each function in the set F, obtained by executing the program with the secret input sequence, will produce a final function key. Each of these keys are combined in a commutative way to produce the fingerprint mark for the program. The variation in FM is obtained through the fingerprint key, key_{FM}, which is unique for each copy of the program. key_{FM} is used to begin the key evolution process in each fingerprinted function. Based on the unique key, the fingerprint for each program will evolve differently. Since the key is used to access the inserted structure, each program will contain a differently organized structure.

4.3   Recognition

As with embedding, the first step in recognizing the embedded marks is to execute the program using the secret input sequence. Execution will identify the set of functions F which have been fingerprinted, as well as the FBF itself. Once the FBF has been identified, the one-way function can be isolated to extract AM. To extract FM we have to access the location where the final function key is stored for each $f \in F$ while the program is executing. The final function keys are combined to form the FM.

4.4   Highlighted Features

The branch-based watermarking algorithm includes two features which should be highlighted. First, because the inserted structure is customized to a particular fingerprint generation, the program will only execute with the specific user key. This has the desired effect of the use of a dongle, but without the drawback of dongle distribution. In addition, the fingerprint key does not have to be stored in the program, but instead could be distributed with the program and required every time the program is executed. It is currently a concern that an attacker could obtain the initial key and use that information in an attack. One possible solution is to leverage features of secure computing devices such as the Trusted Platform Module (TPM) available in the IBM ThinkPad laptop.

The second feature relates to the static variation between differently fingerprinted instances of a program. Because the static variation occurs only in the inserted structure, a higher level of resistance to collusive attacks can be achieved. This advantage will be further discussed in Section 6.1. Additionally, this feature can be used to enable software companies to produce and distribute fingerprinted software in the traditional manner. The program purchased would be non-functional until the user installs the software and registers it with the company. Upon registration, the user key and structure will be distributed creating a fully functioning program. Previously, if a software company wanted to tie a specific fingerprint mark to a purchaser, the user had to purchase the software directly from the company. At the time of purchase the program was fingerprinted. By using the branch-based watermark, distribution of fingerprinted software can be accomplished through pre-packaged software sold at retail stores. Installation of a fully functioning copy does require an initial Internet connection, however, this does not appear to be a drawback since most software now requires an initial registration.

5   Native Code Implementation

Our implementation of the branch-based watermarking algorithm for native code is accomplished by disassembling a statically linked binary, modifying the instructions, and then rewriting the instructions to a new executable file. The current prototype is designed to watermark Windows executable files. It provides the capability to embed an authorship mark, a fingerprint mark, and tamper detection.

As was described in Section 4.2, the embedding procedure is accomplished in three phases. In the first phase, an execution trace of the program is obtained based on the secret input sequence. Currently, identification of the set of functions used in watermarking requires manual monitoring. The program is preprocessed and a break point is inserted at the beginning of each function. As the program is executed using a debugger, information about each function encountered is recorded in a file.

During the second phase, instructions in each of the selected functions are modified. Special care must be taken in selecting which branch instructions are converted since the branch is tied to a particular key value. To ensure proper program behavior, branches are selected such that they reside on a deterministic path through the function. Without imposing this constraint, irregular key evolution will occur, resulting in the transfer of execution to an incorrect instruction. For each branch replaced, a mapping between the calculated key and the branch, target displacement is maintained.

$$\theta = \{k_1 \rightarrow d_1, k_2 \rightarrow d_2, \cdots, k_n \rightarrow d_n\}$$

θ is used in phase three to construct a table T which is stored in the data section of the binary. The table is used to store the branch, target displacement for each branch in the program which has been replaced. The first step in laying out the table is to construct a hash function such that each key maps to a unique slot in the table.

$$h = \{k_1, k_2, \cdots, k_n\} \rightarrow \{1, 2, \cdots, n\}$$

The displacements are stored in the table such that $T[h(k_i)] = d_i$.

The fingerprint branch function is a new function inserted in the program during embedding. The inserted FBF performs the following tasks:

- An integrity check which produces the value v_i.
- Generation of the next function key, k_i, through the use of a one-way function, the integrity check value, and the previous key; $k_i = g(k_{i-1}, v_i)$.
- Identification of the displacement to the next instruction via $d_i = T[h(k_i)]$, where T is a table stored in the data section and h is a hash function.
- Computation of the return location by adding the displacement d_i to the return address.

5.1   Strength Enhancing Features

Two additional features can be incorporated in the branch-based watermarking algorithm to increase the strength: integrity check branch functions and additional indirection. Each of these increases the amount of analysis required to remove the authorship and fingerprint marks.

Integrity check branch functions (ICBF) are based on the same principle as the FBF. The ICBFs are called by replaced branch instructions not used in the fingerprint generation, i.e. branches not on a deterministic path or branches in a function which is not part of the secret input. The important feature of the ICBFs is that each performs a different type of integrity check. This makes it possible to establish a check and guard system similar to that proposed by Chang and Atallah [10]. For instance the ICBFs could be used to verify that the FBF or other integrity checks have not been altered or removed.

Within the ICBFs, the integrity check value, v_i, and the branch instruction offset are used as inputs to generate a key for displacement look up. The displacements for the ICBFs are stored in the same table used by the FBF. The one-way function used to generate the key in the ICBF could be the same as that used by the FBF. If so, the authorship mark would appear in multiple locations throughout the program. If instead, different one-way functions are used, additional authorship marks could be embedded in the program, further strengthening the proof of ownership.

The second strength enhancing feature is to increase the level of indirection. Additional levels of indirection increase confusion and require more extensive analysis for an attacker. Further indirection can be incorporated in the branch-based watermarking algorithm by rerouting all calls to the ICBFs and the FBF through a single super branch function which transfers execution to the proper branch function.

6 Experimental Results

In this section we provide an evaluation of the branch-based watermarking scheme with respect to its robustness against attack and the overhead incurred. We have created a prototype implementation for watermarking Windows executable files. The current prototype only provides watermarking capabilities and does not include any of the strength enhancing features.

The evaluation was performed using the SPECint-2000 benchmark suite applications. We were unable to use *eon* and *perlbmk* because they would not build. Our experiments were run on a 1.8 GHz Pentium 4 System with 512 MB of main memory running Windows XP Professional. The programs were compiled using Microsoft's VisualStudio C++ 6.0 with optimizations disabled.

6.1 Resilience

We examined four categories of attacks to evaluate the robustness of the branch-based watermarking algorithm.

Additive Attack. In an additive attack an adversary embeds an additional watermark so as to cast doubt on the origin of the intellectual property. An attacker is successful even if the original mark remains intact, however, it is more desirable to damage the original mark. For an additive attack to be successful the program has to continue to function properly after the embedding of the second watermark. To simulate an additive attack we double watermarked the benchmark applications using the branch-based watermarking algorithm. In each case the result was an improperly functioning application. The double watermark attack fails because the integrity check detects the program alteration. A simple checksum integrity check will detect that a call to FBF1 is now a call to FBF2 or that FBF2 has been added to the program. So the attack is detected when FBF2 transfers execution control to FBF1. We believe that a similar result would be obtained if any of the currently known watermarking algorithms were used as the second watermark, however, this hypothesis is untested.

Distortive Attack. In a distortive attack, a series of semantics-preserving transformations are applied to the program in an attempt to render the watermark useless. It is the goal of the attacker to distort the software in such a way that the watermark becomes unrecoverable, yet the program's functionality and performance remain intact. To verify our hypothesis that the branch-based watermarking algorithm would be resistant to distortive attacks we subjected the benchmark applications to five different obfuscations:

1. Conversion of unconditional jumps to conditional jumps through the use of opaque predicates.
2. Conversion of unconditional jumps to calls to a branch function [9].
3. Conversion of function calls to calls to a branch function [9].
4. Basic block reordering.
5. Merging of two functions into 1 function whose control flow is regulated through opaque predicates.

In each case the resulting application was non-functional because the integrity checks detected the modification.

Collusive Attack. The most crucial attack on a fingerprinted application is the collusive attack. This occurs when an adversary obtains multiple differently fingerprinted instances of a program and is able to compare them to isolate the fingerprint. With previous watermarking algorithms, prevention of a collusive attack is often addressed through the use of code obfuscation. The general idea is to apply different sets of obfuscations to the fingerprinted programs. This will make the programs differ everywhere. This is a viable option to thwart a collusive attack, however, it may not always be feasible due to the size and/or performance overhead incurred through obfuscation.

The branch-based watermarking scheme is resistant to the collusive attack without the use of obfuscation. The only difference between two fingerprinted programs is the order of the values in the table. Thus, an attacker would have to examine the data section in order to even notice a difference.

The algorithm is still susceptible to dynamic collusive attacks, but some of those attacks can be warded off through the use of integrity checks which recognize the use of a debugger and cause the program to fail. In a dynamic attack, the only difference the adversary might notice is the value of the key that is generated at each stage, which will ultimately yield a different table slot. In order for an adversary to launch a successful collusive attack, extensive manual analysis in the form of a subtractive attack will be required to remove the fingerprint.

Subtractive Attack. In a subtractive attack, the attacker attempts to remove the watermark from the disassembled or decompiled code. If the watermark has poor transparency, an attacker may be able to discover the location of the watermark after manual or automated code inspection and then remove it from the program without destroying the software. Baring the use of a completely secure computing device, guaranteed protection against subtractive attacks is not possible. All that we can hope is that the analysis required to remove the watermark is extensive enough that an attacker finds it too costly.

The robustness against reverse engineering is partially based on the number of converted branches which contribute to the fingerprint calculation. Since the algorithm requires the branches to be on a deterministic path, the number of usable branches is being limited. During preliminary development there was question if there would be enough branches on the deterministic path to make the technique a viable option. Through analysis of a variety of different applications, we found a satisfactory number of conditional and unconditional branch instructions. Table 1 shows the total number of branches and the number of usable branches in the SPECint-2000 benchmark applications. By additionally using conditional branches we are able to significantly increase the number of usable branches. This makes the algorithm a viable option. Additionally, the data indicates that even after embedding the watermark, many branches are still available for use in the integrity check branch functions.

Table 1. Total number of branches versus the number of usable branches in the SPECint-2000 benchmark suite applications

Program	Total Branches	Usable including conditionals	Usable excluding conditionals
gzip	2843	464	170
vpr	5814	1153	674
gcc	28136	4886	3056
mcf	2028	290	89
crafty	3340	496	178
parser	5628	864	522
gap	18999	1942	1027
vortex	16144	3462	1049
bzip2	2354	457	211
twolf	4397	729	429

From our analysis, we believe that if the strength enhancing features are incorporated into the algorithm the removal of the code which generates the fingerprint will be prohibitively difficult. If the attacker is able to identify which sections of code are generating the fingerprint, he will have to manually analyze the program to identify the call instructions which are converted branch instructions. He will then have to identify the correct target instruction and replace the call with the correct branch and displacement. If the adversary only converts those branches responsible for the fingerprint generation and does not also convert the other branches, the program will fail to execute properly. This is because the integrity check branch functions are designed as a check and guard system. One of their duties is to verify that the fingerprint generating branch function has not been altered or removed. Thus, removal of the fingerprint branch function also requires removal of the integrity check branch functions. While this is not entirely impossible, the manual analysis required to accomplish such a task is extensive.

6.2   Cost

To evaluate the cost we used the SPECint-2000 benchmark suite. The overall performance of the watermarked program was evaluated using the SPEC reference inputs. The execution times reported were obtained through five runs. The highest and lowest values were discarded and the average was computed for the remaining three runs.

As can be seen in Table 2 very little performance overhead is incurred by the additional calls and integrity checks. The unwatermarked benchmark application gcc did not execute properly on the reference inputs so we were unable to obtain performance information suitable for comparison with the other results. However, when run using the test data no significant slowdown was observed.

The majority of the space cost incurred by the branch-based watermark is based on the size of the fingerprint branch function and the displacement table. Since the fingerprint is generated as the program executes, the size of the fingerprint does not impact the size of the watermarked program. Additionally, any difference between the converted branch and the call instruction sizes will

Table 2. Effect of watermarking on execution time

Program	Branches Used	Execution Time (sec)		
		Original (T_0)	Watermarked (T_1)	Slowdown (T_1/T_0)
gzip	79	435.52	435.52	1.00
vpr	405	479.12	480.62	1.00
mcf	24	563.07	562.55	1.00
crafty	94	326.96	326.40	1.00
parser	239	519.31	588.34	1.13
gap	742	292.20	292.01	1.00
vortex	477	316.22	316.66	1.00
bzip2	135	743.18	739.82	0.99
twolf	233	912.43	922.84	1.01

Table 3. Effect of watermarking on program size

Program	Branches Used	Program Size (KB)		
		Original (S_0)	Watermarked (S_1)	Increase (S_1/S_0)
gzip	79	100	104	1.04
vpr	405	212	252	1.19
gcc	2124	1608	2604	1.62
mcf	24	64	68	1.06
crafty	94	316	320	1.01
parser	239	184	188	1.02
gap	742	660	780	1.18
vortex	477	608	660	1.09
bzip2	135	88	96	1.09
twolf	233	316	332	1.05

contribute to the size of the watermarked application. Table 3 shows the effect watermarking had on the size of the benchmark applications. For most of the applications the size increase was minimal. gcc was most significantly impacted but it was also the application in which the greatest number of branches were converted. A technique to minimize the size impact is to use a minimal perfect hash function in assigning the slots in the displacement table. Our implementation did not use such a hash function, thus the results could be improved.

7   Extension to Java Bytecode

Due to restrictions placed on the Java language, a straight forward implementation of the previously described watermarking algorithm is not possible. The most limiting aspect is the difficulty in modifying the program counter register which would be analogous to the return address modification in native code. This makes it impossible to implement the branch function as it is described. However, we have devised a technique for watermarking Java applications which maintains the essence of the idea through the use of the Java interface and explicitly thrown exceptions.

The Java implementation diverges from the native code version in the second phase of the embedding. The Java FBF (JFBF) uses a completely different mechanism for transferring execution control to the branch target. The JFBF makes use of an interface A which gets added to the application during embedding. Additionally, n classes A1, A2, ..., An are added which each implement the interface A. The interface A defines a method branch which is then implemented by each of the n subclasses. The main purpose of branch is to explicitly throw an exception. Within each of the n subclasses, branch will throw a different exception. Once the exception is thrown, it will be propagated up to the method which invoked JFBF. When this occurs the invoking method will find the exception in its exception table and transfer control to the instruction specified. This instruction is the target of the converted branch.

In the second phase, certain branch instructions along the deterministic path are replaced by instructions which invoke the fingerprint branch function. In the native code version we were able to replace jmp, jcc, and call instructions. With the Java version we are only able to replace goto and conditional branches. We are unable to replace invoke instructions because of the restrictions placed on the exception table entries. The target listed in the exception table must be an instruction within the method.

As the branch instructions are modified, two mappings are maintained. The first mapping ϕ, maps the branch target to the exception type which will be used in transferring execution control to the target instruction. The second mapping θ, maps the current key k_i to that same exception type.

$$\theta = \{k_1 \rightarrow e_1, k_2 \rightarrow e_2, ..., k_n \rightarrow e_n\}$$

ϕ is used to modify the method's exception table. For each target a new exception table entry is added. One key aspect of the Java branch-based watermarker is that for each converted branch, n entries must be added to the exception table. One of the entries is the correct target and $n-1$ are decoys. If the decoy exception entries are omitted, the branch, target pairs become obvious. Prior to execution, a Java application must pass the verification process. Verification involves checking that the class file and the bytecode meet certain constraints. Examples of the constraints include checking for consistent stack height or that local variables have been initialized. During verification, an exception edge is considered a possible execution path. Thus the targets of the decoy exceptions must be chosen such that the bytecode will still pass the Java verifier.

θ is used during phase three. In the Java version, an array is used to store objects instead of a displacement table. The array T stores objects which are subclasses of A, so a combination of objects A1, A2, ..., An. The array is constructed again using a hash function which uniquely maps each key to a slot in the array. The objects are stored such that $T[h(k_i)] = A_j$, where A_j's branch method throws the exception e_i.

To regulate execution control and generate the fingerprint the JFBF performs the following tasks:

- An integrity check producing v_i.
- Generation of the next method key, k_i, through the use of a one-way function; $k_i = g(k_{i-1}, v_i)$.

- Object look up through the use of an array, the key, and a hash function, A a = $T[h(k_i)]$.
- Call the method branch using the object a, a.branch().

Currently, we only have a preliminary implementation of the branch-based software watermarking algorithm for Java bytecode. Because the implementation only includes minimal functionality we have yet to perform a thorough experimental evaluation. As our future work we plan to carry out such an evaluation.

8 Conclusion

In this paper we described a novel approach to software watermarking, branch-based watermarking, which incorporates ideas from code obfuscation and tamper detection to increase robustness against determined attempts at discovery and removal. Our technique simultaneously provides proof of ownership and the capability to trace the source of the illegal redistribution. This is an improvement over previous techniques which required the developer to choose between embedding an authorship mark or a fingerprint mark. Additionally, the branch-based watermarker provides a solution for distributing pre-packaged, fingerprinted software which is uniquely linked to the purchaser.

The branch-based watermark prototype demonstrates that the technique can successfully thwart both additive and distortive attacks. The technique also demonstrates a higher level of resistance to subtractive and collusive attacks. Previous fingerprinting techniques addressed the prevention of collusive attacks through the use of code obfuscation which introduces additional overhead. The only static variation introduced by the branch-based watermark is in the table. This makes it more highly resilient to collusive attacks even without the use of obfuscation. Additionally, the overhead associated with the technique is quite minimal and should be tolerable for most applications. By eliminating automated attacks, such as semantics-preserving transformations, and many of the common manual attacks, attackers are forced to use more complex and costly techniques. Thus, attackers who lack the necessary skill or find the required attacks to be too expensive will be eliminated.

References

1. International Planning and Research Corporation: Sixth annual BSA global software piracy study (2001)
2. Venkatesan, R., Vazirani, V., Sinha, S.: A graph theoretic approach to software watermarking. In: Information Hiding Workshop. (2001)
3. Stern, J.P., Hachez, G., Koeune, F., Quisquater, J.J.: Robust object watermarking: Application to code. In: Information Hiding Workshop. (1999)
4. Qu, G., Potkonjak, M.: Hiding signatures in graph coloring solutions. In: Information Hiding Workshop. (1999)
5. Collberg, C., Thomborson, C.: Software watermarking: Models and dynamic embeddings. In: Symposium on Principles of Programming Languages. (1999)

6. Collberg, C., Carter, E., Debray, S., Huntwork, A., Kececioglu, J., Linn, C., Stepp, M.: Dynamic path-based software watermarking. In: Conference on Programming Language Design and Implementation. (2004)
7. Nagra, J., Thomborson, C.: Threading software watermarks. In: Information Hiding Workshop. (2004)
8. Cousot, P., Cousot, R.: An abstract interpretation-based framework for software watermarking. In: Symposium on Principles of Programming Languages. (2004)
9. Linn, C., Debray, S.: Obfuscation of executable code to improve resistance to static disassembly. In: ACM Conference on Computer and Communications Security. (2003)
10. Chang, H., Atallah, M.J.: Protecting software code by guards. In: ACM DRM workshop. (2001)

Data Hiding in Compiled Program Binaries for Enhancing Computer System Performance

Ashwin Swaminathan[1], Yinian Mao[1], Min Wu[1], and Krishnan Kailas[2]

[1] Department of ECE, University of Maryland, College Park, MD 20742, USA
{ashwins, ymao, minwu}@eng.umd.edu*
[2] IBM T.J. Watson Research Center, Yorktown Heights, NY 10598, USA
krish@watson.ibm.com

Abstract. Information hiding has been studied in many security applications such as authentication, copyright management and digital forensics. In this work, we introduce a new application where successful information hiding in compiled program binaries could bring system-wide performance improvements. Our goal is to enhance computer system performance by providing additional information to the processor, *without* changing the instruction set architecture. We first analyze the statistics of typical programs to demonstrate the feasibility of hiding data in them. We then propose several techniques to hide a large amount of data in the operand fields with very low computation and storage requirements during the extraction process. The data embedding is made reversible to recover the original instructions and to ensure the correct execution of the computer program. Our experiments on the SPEC CPU2000 benchmark programs show that up to 110K bits of information can be embedded in large programs with as little as 3K bits of additional run-time memory in the form of a simple look-up table.

1 Introduction

The machine instructions in a compiled computer program, as specified by the Instruction Set Architecture (ISA) of a processor [1], are the primary means for exchanging information between the programmer and the computer hardware. An instruction set consisting of fixed width instructions is one of the key aspects of the reduced instruction set computing (RISC) architecture principles employed by several modern processors [1,2]. This is because fixed width instructions are easy to fetch, decode and execute; thus greatly help simplify the fetch and decode stages of processor pipeline. However, the fixed width RISC instruction sets make it difficult to expand the instruction encoding space in the future for adding more information to the existing instructions, or for adding more instructions to an existing ISA.

It has been shown by several microarchitecture studies in the past that if a small amount of side information could be added to instructions, it would

---

* This work was supported in part by the U.S. National Science Foundation under CAREER Award CCR-0133704.

M. Barni et al. (Eds.): IH 2005, LNCS 3727, pp. 357–371, 2005.

help improve the performance of processors. For example, the accuracy of data value prediction techniques can be greatly improved if one could embed an extra bit of information to each instruction of interest. This would help to classify them based on the predictability criteria, resulting in improved instruction-level parallelism opportunity as well as better utilization of prediction tables [3]. In the multiprocessor systems, it has been shown that more relaxed memory consistency models can be easily supported for obtaining better performance on multiprocessor workloads if one can classify the load/store instructions with an extra bit of information [4]. In general, even though adding 1-2 extra bits of information to existing instructions could improve performance or simplify the hardware structures, it is not practical to re-design the instruction set architecture (ISA). This is mainly because changing the ISA is a major effort, and it cannot easily support backward compatibility – making it difficult for older versions of binary programs to run on the new versions of the processor. It is clear from the above discussion that embedding additional information to the instructions of a program binary without modifying the ISA has the potential for providing system-wide performance improvements.

In this work, we investigate the feasibility and techniques to store and extract additional information for computer programs in an ISA-independent way and without inserting extra instructions. We also study the cost for such data embedding and extraction, which can be quantified in several aspects including the amount of computation and storage needed during embedding and extraction. Our contribution in this paper is three fold. First, we show that such invertible embedding is possible for most programs. Second, we propose algorithms to find embeddable program segments and introduce schemes that can achieve data embedding and extraction transparent to the program execution. Third, we optimize the embedding/extraction algorithms under stringent practical constraints in terms of computation complexity and storage limitations.

This paper is organized as follows. In Section 2, we discuss the proposed data hiding framework. The details of the proposed algorithms are explained in Section 3 along with their simulation results. An improvement to the proposed schemes to reduce the memory overhead is examined in Section 4 and the related works are discussed in Section 5. The final conclusions are drawn in Section 6.

2   Challenges, Feasibility, and the Proposed Framework

In this section, we examine the constraints and challenges in hiding data in program binaries, in order for the processor to take advantage of the hidden data to enhance the execution performance. We then discuss the feasibility of hiding data in program binaries and present the proposed data hiding framework to meet these stringent constraints.

2.1   Challenges and Constraints

Embedding data into program binaries is a challenging task because of the numerous stringent constraints at the decoding side in the Central Processing Unit

(CPU). Given the high sophistication and performance requirement in modern processor design, the extra on-chip logic and memory have to be kept minimum for extracting the hidden data in parallel with the program execution. It is also not desirable to introduce extra instructions in the program for data hiding, as it consumes more cycles and slows down the program execution. Compared with data extraction, the data embedding process can be performed off-line and only once for a program. Thus, we can afford relatively more computation and memory resource during data embedding. Another important constraint in hiding data in program binaries is that the data hiding scheme should not interfere with the normal program execution. This requires the data embedding be reversible (or lossless), so that both the original program (host data) and the embedded data can be recovered at the decoder side without any errors.

Reversible data hiding has been studied in the context of multimedia data [5,6]. Typically, the host data is first losslessly compressed and the extra information is then appended to the compressed host data. At the decoder side, the appended extra information is read out and the host data is recovered using a lossless decoding method. The main challenge in compressing a program binary without interfering normal program execution arises from the fact that the order of execution of all instructions in a program can be unpredictable. Due to the data dependent control flows and branches in a program, instructions are not always executed in the same sequence as they appear in the program binary. The instruction execution order is often dynamically determined at the program execution time and some instructions might not be executed at all. Additionally, all modern processors use speculative execution of instructions [1]. The most common form of control flow speculation involves executing instructions after a branch (along a predicted path) before the branch instruction completes its execution. When the branch condition is resolved and a mis-prediction is indicated, the processor will have to roll-back to the branch. As such, the data embedding scheme cannot presume a certain execution order to use the previous instruction(s) to hide information for subsequent instruction(s). Hence it is very difficult to employ common lossless data compression schemes such as the Lempel-Ziv and the arithmetic coding [7], where the decoding result depends on the preceding codes. In other variable-length coding schemes, such as the Huffman coding [7], the length of some codewords that appear infrequently may well exceed the length of an instruction (32 bits) and would not suit our purpose. These common compression schemes also require a non-trivial amount of static or run-time memory, which is expensive to accommodate in the CPU design.

To satisfy the stringent computation and memory constraints on the processor side and the considerations discussed above, we choose to use individual instruction as the basic data embedding unit as opposed to using a block of code segments. We also choose to use fixed-length compression techniques through simple table lookup operations as opposed to variable-length ones. Next, we discuss the feasibility of hiding data in program binaries and present the proposed data hiding framework.

2.2 A Lossless Data Hiding Framework for Program Binaries

We use IBM PowerPC ISA as an example to demonstrate the feasibility of hiding data in program binaries. The principle of our scheme can be extended to other ISAs. The IBM PowerPC ISA is a typical RISC ISA with fixed-width instruction encoding [8]. A typical PowerPC instruction contains 4 bytes of information, including 6 bits for the opcode (which indicates the type of operation) and the remaining 26 bits for the operand (which indicates the parameters to use). The 26-bit operand suggests a total of 2^{26} possible combinations. While using 26 bits to represent these combinations makes it easy for the computer hardware to process, information theory suggests that it is possible to use fewer than 26 bits if the 2^{26} combinations are not equally likely to appear [7].

To understand the distribution of the operand combinations in computer programs, we examine the SPEC CPU2000 benchmark programs [9]. SPEC CPU2000 are a collection of representative programs widely used in computer

Table 1. Statistics of SPEC programs and the data hiding results by applying the Exhaustive Search algorithm to all instructions

Program Name	Total # of instructions in the program (N)	# of distinct combinations appearing in operand field (X)	n	Memory for LUT (S bits)	Relative overhead (η) Memory req. / Data Hidden
SWIM	2937	1800	9	2330	79.33 %
ART	5985	2564	9	2330	38.93 %
WUPWISE	8218	3807	9	2330	28.35 %
EQUAKE	9589	4500	10	5146	53.66 %
LUCAS	12449	6430	10	5146	41.34 %
APPLU	15936	8992	10	5146	32.29 %
MCF	18351	6738	10	5146	28.04 %
FACEREC	19044	9015	10	5146	27.02 %
GZIP	28727	10443	11	11290	39.30 %
BZIP2	28632	9838	11	11290	39.43 %
APSI	43244	18538	12	24602	56.89 %
AMMP	46346	15682	12	24602	53.08 %
GALGEL	57971	19990	12	24602	42.44 %
PARSER	62807	15194	11	11290	17.98 %
CRAFTY	72486	23876	11	11290	15.58 %
TWOLF	85981	23876	12	24602	28.61 %
EON	121012	23787	11	11290	9.33 %
MGRID	151202	31492	13	53274	35.23 %
VORTEX	167056	29951	11	11290	6.76 %
VPR	182039	36942	13	53274	29.27 %
PERLBMK	192898	35929	12	24602	12.75 %
MESA	209986	39538	13	53274	25.37 %
GAP	220308	39085	13	53274	24.18 %
FMA3D	235383	80849	13	53274	22.63 %
SIXTRACK	360292	84514	14	114714	31.84 %
CC1	571820	86355	14	114714	20.06 %

DATA EMBEDDING PROCESS   **DATA EXTRACTION PROCESS**

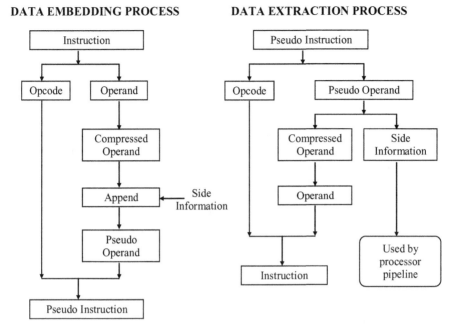

Fig. 1. A lossless data hiding framework for program binaries

system research. A brief description of the SPEC programs can be found in the Appendix of this paper. By analyzing the operands of these representative programs, we observe that only a very small portion of the 2^{26} combinations in the operand field actually appear in a program. The number of unique combinations of the operands that occur at least once in each of the SPEC programs are shown in Table 1. The table shows that less than one percent of the 2^{26} possible combinations are used in these programs. This important observation suggests that the operand information can be represented in fewer than 26 bits, and there is a considerable amount of room to compress the operands and hide data.

As a general framework for reversible data hiding in program binaries, we first losslessly compress the compiled program binaries and embed the side information into them. The details of the embedding and the extraction processes are shown in Fig. 1. Since each instruction in the program binary usually contains a short opcode and a longer operand field, we focus on the operand field and compress them in a lossless manner to represent them in fewer bits. We then use the resulting space to store the desired extra information. The data extraction is performed during program execution. In this stage, the operand field is decompressed and side information is extracted. The opcode along with the decompressed operand field is executed the normal way. The extracted side information may be used by the processor pipeline for a variety of applications.

In principle, if X distinct combinations appear in the operand field, we can represent the operands uniquely in $y = \lceil \log_2(X) \rceil$ bits with a one-to-one reversible mapping. The mapping table can be stored in program header and used to establish a look-up table (LUT) in the data extractor, as long as its size is very small compared to the number of bits gained. The $(26 - y)$ bits per instruction that are obtained in this process can be used to store the side information. At the data extraction side, the y-bit compressed operand is replaced by the matching 26-bit operand found in the LUT. Once the hidden data is extracted and the original instruction is recovered, the extracted side information can be utilized without affecting the normal program execution.

For large programs such as the CC1 (GNU C++ compiler), we have $X = 86355$ and $y = 17$ from Table 1, suggesting that we would save $26 - y = 9$ bits per instruction to store the side information. However, if we build a mapping table for these 86355 instructions, its size would be at least $X \times 26 = 2245230$ bits. Clearly, this is a large overhead for gaining 9-bit side information per instruction. Moreover, it is difficult to store such a large table in the on-chip memory for fast access. Therefore, instead of trying to embed many bits into each instruction, we consider a more practical objective, namely, to embed only one or a few bits into each instruction using as small LUT as possible. In the next section, we will discuss how to design data hiding schemes that can achieve fast and resource-efficient data extraction.

3   The Proposed Data Hiding Algorithms

Computer architecture research has suggested that even one-bit side information per instruction would be very advantageous to enhance system performance. As such, we focus on designing efficient techniques to embed one bit of extra information per instruction. These techniques can easily be extended to embed more than one bit per instruction at an added cost of a larger LUT.

Considering the challenges and constrains posed in Section 2.1, we propose the following practical method for embedding information into a program. We search for the smallest n so that there exists a subset of n operand bits (out of the 26 bits), for which no more than 2^{n-1} distinct operand combinations have appeared in the program. We can then losslessly represent this subset of n bits using $(n - 1)$ bits and thus provide one bit per instruction for data hiding. To facilitate the discussion, we say that the operands set has a *Negative Redundancy* of n in this case. A lower value of negative redundancy implies more redundancy in the program, and in turn a smaller LUT for data embedding and extraction.

As far as data extraction is concerned, if we have M combinations of n-bit pattern appearing, we would require a LUT of size $M \times n$ for the inverse mapping. Additionally, we would require up to 26 bits to specify the subset of bits involved in the mapping. Thus, the total cost in terms of memory usage is upper bounded by $(Mn + 26)$ bits. As mentioned earlier, this LUT can be stored in the program header, and will be loaded into run-time memory to initialize the data extractor at the beginning of program execution. To reduce the overhead in program storage and in run-time memory, we would prefer this LUT to be as small as possible. The data embedding can be performed by searching through the LUT, and the computation and memory requirement for embedding are much less stringent than for extraction. These considerations lead us to propose the following encoding and decoding algorithms.

3.1 Exhaustive Search Algorithm

As indicated before, the size of the look-up table (S) is upper bounded by $(Mn + 26)$ bits where $M \leq 2^{n-1}$. To minimize the memory and computation overhead at the decoding end, we would like to find the smallest subset of bits for which we start to see at most 2^{n-1} distinct combinations appear. We denote this optimal value of n by n_{opt} and the optimal subset that gives this mapping by Ω_{opt}. One way to find n_{opt} and Ω_{opt} is by exhaustively searching over every possible subset. The worst case complexity of the search over the 26-bit operand is $\binom{26}{1} + \binom{26}{2} + \cdots + \binom{26}{26} = 2^{26} - 1$ on the embedder side. The *Exhaustive Search* algorithm is described in Algorithm 1.

Algorithm 1 Exhaustive Search Algorithm

Input: Compiled Static Instruction file
Output: Possible Mapping
for $n = 1, 2, \ldots, 26$ **do**
   Initialize: Γ - set of all possible n-bit combinations
   for k = 1, 2, ..., $\binom{26}{n}$ **do**
      Choose as P, the kth n-tuple in Γ.
      Count the number of distinct combinations that appear in P. Call it X
      if $X \leq 2^{n-1}$ **then**
         {One possibility found}
         return *Obtained Position* (P)
      end if
   end for
end for

The exhaustive search algorithm for finding the bit positions was tested on the standard SPEC CPU2000 benchmark program suite [9]. In this experiment, we consider all the instructions in a program and try to find a bit-position combination that can be used for embedding. The experiment results are summarized in Table 1. We list the number of instructions (N) in the program (excluding all the relocatable instructions that will be modified by the OS loader); the number of unique combinations of the bit positions, out of the possible 2^{26}, in the operand fields (X); the negative redundancy of the operand bits (n); the memory required to store the inverse mapping table (S); and its ratio (η) with respect to the amount of data hidden (D), where D is equal to the number of instructions with one hidden bit per instruction. From the results, we observe that the negative redundancy n is usually in the range of 9 to 15 and therefore the size of the LUT, S, is not small. Moreover, the ratio η is above 20% in most cases and this indicates a relatively high overhead in obtaining data hiding payload. Another disadvantage for the exhaustive search is the high computational complexity in finding the bit positions. However, it provides a basis for comparison with other search algorithms.

3.2 Consecutive Search Algorithm

The exhaustive search algorithm has two problems - large memory requirement in data extraction and high computational complexity in data embedding. To address these problems, we introduce the consecutive search algorithm. We also observe through experiments that n can be greatly reduced if we choose to embed data in only a subset of instructions (e.g. load/store instructions) that appear frequently in static programs.

To speed up the search for the bit positions, we propose a modified approach to find the sub-optimal value of n by considering only consecutive bit positions in the search. This would speed up the encoding process exponentially. The number of iterations required to find a mapping reduces from $\binom{26}{n}$ to $(26 - n) + 1$ for a particular n. We denote this sub-optimal value of n by $n_{sopt}^{(c)}$ to reflect the positions being consecutive. While we have $n_{sopt}^{(c)} \geq n_{opt}$, our experiments show that it is close to the optimal solution in most cases. The *Consecutive Search* algorithm is described in detail in Algorithm 2.

Algorithm 2 Consecutive Search Algorithm

Input: Compiled Static Instruction file
Output: Possible Mapping
for $n = 1, 2, \ldots, 26$ **do**
  Initialize:
  Γ - set of all possible n-bit combinations, where $|\Gamma| = 27 - n$
  $\Gamma = \{(1, 2, \ldots, n), (2, 3, \ldots, n+1), \ldots, (26 - n + 1, \ldots, 26)\}$
  for k = 1, 2, ..., $26 - n + 1$ **do**
    Choose as P, the kth n-tuple in Γ
    Count the number of distinct combinations that appear in P. Call it X
    if $X \leq 2^{n-1}$ **then**
      {One possibility found}
      return *Obtained Position* (P)
    end if
  end for
end for

This method of choosing consecutive bit positions was tested with the SPEC CPU2000 benchmark suite [9]. In this experiment, we selected the Load/Store instructions for data hiding, as the memory access are often the performance bottleneck in program execution [1]. For comparison, the results for the exhaustive and consecutive search are shown in Table 2. We note that in most programs, about one third of the instructions are load/store instructions. Therefore, there is still a substantial amount of space for hiding data. From the table we can see that n_{opt} is usually around 5–9, while $n_{sopt}^{(c)}$ is greater than n_{opt} by 1 or 2 bits; and the total memory required for data extraction is usually no more than 2500 bits. Furthermore, the computation complexity is greatly reduced when consecutive search is employed. We also observe that by restricting our data hiding scheme to only load/store instructions, the ratio $\eta = S/D$ is only around 5%, which indicates that we can hide more data for a fixed amount of memory usage.

Table 2. Data hiding results of the Consecutive and Exhaustive Search algorithms on Load/Store instructions. One bit is embedded in each load/store instruction.

Program Name	Total # instr. in the prog. (N)	# of embeddable Load/Store instructions (N_{ls})	# of unique combinations of Ld/St instr. appearing in operands(X_{ls})	n_{opt}	$n_{sopt}^{(c)}$	LUT size (bits)	Overhead (sub-opt) $\frac{mem.req.}{datahidden} \times 100\%$	Overhead (opt) $\frac{mem.req.}{datahidden} \times 100\%$
SWIM	2937	854	515	4	5	58	12.41 %	6.79 %
ART	5985	1611	544	5	6	106	13.53 %	6.57 %
WUPWISE	8218	2682	1255	5	5	106	3.95 %	3.95 %
EQUAKE	9589	3581	1526	5	6	106	6.09 %	2.96 %
LUCAS	12449	3755	2059	5	5	106	2.82 %	2.82 %
APPLU	15936	5846	3563	7	7	474	8.11 %	8.11 %
MCF	18351	5272	1976	5	7	106	8.99 %	2.01 %
FACEREC	19044	6215	3506	4	5	58	1.71 %	0.93 %
GZIP	28727	7546	2627	5	8	106	13.91 %	1.40 %
BZIP2	28632	7604	2163	6	8	218	13.80 %	2.87 %
APSI	43244	16380	6429	7	7	474	2.89 %	2.89 %
AMMP	46346	15338	4830	6	8	474	6.84 %	3.09 %
GALGEL	57971	20062	7405	8	8	1050	5.23 %	5.23 %
PARSER	62807	17182	3482	5	8	106	6.11 %	0.61 %
CRAFTY	72486	18213	5710	5	8	106	5.76 %	0.58 %
TWOLF	85981	26965	6204	6	8	218	3.89 %	0.81 %
EON	121012	43185	7646	7	8	474	2.43 %	1.09 %
MGRID	151202	39662	7299	9	10	2330	12.98 %	5.87 %
VORTEX	167065	43696	5346	5	8	106	2.40 %	0.24 %
VPR	182039	42880	7238	9	10	2330	12.00 %	5.43 %
PERLBMK	192898	57535	5733	7	8	474	1.82 %	0.82 %
MESA	209986	67305	14037	9	9	2330	3.46 %	3.46 %
GAP	220308	58038	6855	7	9	474	4.01 %	0.81 %
FMA3D	235383	98215	41437	8	8	1050	1.07 %	1.07 %
SIXTRACK	360292	101848	26804	11	11	11290	11.08 %	11.08 %
CC1	571820	138792	13373	9	10	2330	3.70 %	1.67 %

Table 3. Operand positions obtained for data hiding using the Exhaustive Search and the Consecutive Search algorithms

Program Name	Exhaustive Search		Consecutive Search	
	n_{opt}	operand bits selected	$n_{sopt}^{(c)}$	operand bits selected
MCF	5	(1,2,11,12,13)	7	(10,11,12,13,14,15,16)
PARSER	5	(2,3,11,12,13)	8	(6,7,8,9,10,11,12,13)
TWOLF	6	(1,2,3,11,12,13)	8	(6,7,8,9,10,11,12,13)
EON	7	(2,3,7,8,11,12,13)	8	(7,8,9,10,11,12,13,14)
VORTEX	5	(1,2,11,12,13)	8	(7,8,9,10,11,12,13,14)

3.3   Iterative Search Algorithm

In this part, we introduce the Iterative Search algorithm to mitigate the disadvantages of both the exhaustive search and the consecutive search algorithms discussed before. The Iterative Search algorithm is based on the observation shown in Table 3, that the exhaustive and consecutive search algorithms often produce bit position subsets that have a large overlap. So we first run the Consecutive Search algorithm to find an initial guess for the solution with a negative redundancy of $n_{sopt}^{(c)}$, and then proceed with an iterative algorithm to find the optimal solution.

Algorithm 3 Iterative Search Algorithm

Input: Compiled Static Instruction file (F)
Output: Possible Mapping
Initialize: $P_1 = Consecutive\_Search(F)$
$n_{sopt}^{(c)} = |P_1|$
for i = 1, 2, ..., 26 **do**
    {*Use P_i to find P_{i+1} of a lower negative redundancy*}
    $\Gamma_i = Generate\_Ordered\_Positions\ (P_i)$
    for k = 1, 2, ..., $|\Gamma_i|$ **do**
        Choose as p_k, the kth (n-1)-tuple in Γ_i
        Count the number of distinct combinations that appear in p_k. Call it X
        if $X \leq 2^{n-2}$ **then**
            {*One possibility found*}
            $P_{i+1} \leftarrow p_k$
            break **for loop** and *goto* **flag:**
        end if
    end for
    if $X > 2^{n-2}$ for all positions in Γ_i **then**
        {*P_i is the best solution*}
        return P_i
    end if
    flag:
end for

Generate_Ordered_Positions
Input: Initial Guess (p)
Output: Ordered set (Γ) to run search
Initialize: $n = |p| - 1$
for $j = n, n - 1, ..., 0$ **do**
    Obtain a subset p_1 by choosing j components from the vector p
    Obtain a subset p_2 by choosing $n - j$ components from the vector $\{1, 2, ..., 26\} - p$
    Concatenate p_1 and p_2 to form a search vector g
    Add the search vector g to the set Γ
end for
return Γ

Suppose the solution in the i-th iteration has a negative redundancy of r and the set of bit positions is P_i. In the $(i + 1)$-th iteration, we use P_i to find a solution of negative redundancy $r - 1$ by a systematic search. In this search, we form a new set of bit positions by choosing j ($j = r - 1, r - 2, \ldots, 1, 0$) positions out of the solution P_i and remaining $(r - 1 - j)$ positions from the set $\{1, 2, \ldots, 26\} - P_i$. The basic idea behind this ordering is the resemblance of the final optimal solution (obtained using exhaustive search) and the sub-optimal solution (obtained using the consecutive search), as indicated by Table 3. We then check if this set of bit positions is a possible solution. We initially start our iteration from $j = r - 1$ and proceed to lower values of j. If we are able to find a mapping of negative redundancy $(r - 1)$, we update P_{i+1} to the set of new bit positions and proceed on to the next iteration. It is to be noted that if P_{i+1} is a solution, then adding any extra bit to P_{i+1} set still remains a solution. Therefore, if we are not able to find any mapping of negative redundancy $(r - 1)$, we conclude that there is no mapping with a negative redundancy less than r and declare P_i to be the optimal solution. The details are presented in Algorithm 3.

We note that the Iterative Search algorithm in the worst case corresponds to the Exhaustive Search algorithm and in the best case would correspond to the Consecutive Search algorithm in terms of computational requirements. By this ordered search, we can expect to reach the optimal solution n_{opt} in fewer iterations than the exhaustive search.

4   Improved Data Hiding Through Program Partitioning

In this section, we reduce the storage overhead of the basic data hiding algorithm introduced in the previous section by program partitioning. We divide the main program into several parts and find a mapping table for each part. Each table would have smaller size than without the partitioning. These tables can be stored together in the program header and loaded to the on-chip memory sequentially during program execution. The storage overhead in the static program is the total size of all LUTs, but the run-time memory overhead is determined only by the size of the largest LUT.

We use the program $SIXTRACK$ to illustrate this principle. From Table 2, we see that the size of the LUT for $SIXTRACK$ is more than 11K bits without program partitioning. When we split the program into several segments and embed data into each segment, we can reduce the mapping table size by a factor of two to four. These results are shown in Table 4. Similar experiments were conducted on some other SPEC program files to find out the minimum number of partitions required to limit the size of each LUT to be less than a given value S. Table 5 presents the results for three different values of S. We can see that program partitioning can help reduce the size of each LUT to a manageable extent. This is achieved at the cost of reloading the corresponding LUT prior to the execution of each partition. Such cost can be reduced by carefully designing the partitions based on program flow models.

Table 4. Data hiding results using program partitions for the *SIXTRACK* program

	Negative Redundancy	Total # bits hidden	Memory overhead (LUT size in bits)
(a) FULL PROCESSING	11	101848	11290
(b) BLOCK PROCESSING - 3 BLOCKS			
First Set (100K instructions)	6	27005	218
Second Set (100K instructions)	9	27155	2330
Third set (160K instructions)	9	47688	2330
Total		101848	4878
(c) BLOCK PROCESSING - 4 BLOCKS			
First Set (100K instructions)	6	27005	218
Second Set (90K instructions)	8	24722	1050
Third set (90K instructions)	7	26677	474
Fourth set (80K instructions)	8	23444	1050
Total		101848	2792

Table 5. Results on program partition for selected SPEC programs: showing here are the number of partitions required to limit the size of each LUT to be less than a given value S

Program Name	$S = 1$ Kbits	$S = 12$ Kbits	$S = 24$ Kbits
SWIM	2	1	1
APPLU	5	1	1
APSI	11	4	1
GALGEL	14	6	3
TWOLF	20	5	2
VORTEX	37	8	1
PERLBMK	42	10	2
MESA	45	12	2
GAP	47	14	2

5   Related Work

In this paper, we investigate the possibility of data hiding in complied program binaries for enhancing system performance in RISC ISAs. The related prior art mostly falls in four main categories:

Steganography for program binaries has been studied in [18], where side information is inserted into a selected set of binary instructions by choosing one out of two (or more) different forms of the instruction that are functionally identical. Such an embedding scheme requires an equal amount of computation both at the embedding side and at the decoding side. To achieve reversibility, the effective embedding payload will be substantially reduced.

In the computer architecture field, there are works on instruction abbreviation techniques for embedded DSPs. In [10], the authors present a technique for entropy bounded encoding of the ISA, where the primary concern is on variable size instructions which frequently occur in DSP architecture. In [11] and [12], the authors present an instruction set synthesis technique for configurable ASIPs and variable instruction set architectures. As these techniques require changes to the ISA, they cannot be applied in fixed-width RISC instruction sets.

Software watermarking techniques have been proposed for intellectual property protection. Early software watermarking schemes re-organize basic blocks in complied codes to embed a hidden mark [13]. Later, it was proposed to incorporate graph theoretical approaches in software watermarking [14]. In this case, the mark is embedded by inserting extra instructions and re-structuring existing instructions in a given program; and the watermark is formed by the control flow of the program. Dynamic path-based software watermarking was proposed in [15]. It uses the run-time trace of a program and a particular program input (the secret key) to carry hidden information. An analogous approach was proposed to watermark HDL code for ASIC and FPGA design [16]. All these schemes aim at preventing software piracy, where hostile adversaries have strong incentives to remove the embedded watermark. In our application of enhancing computer system performance, such adversarial environment does not exist and our focus is to provide side information to the processor at the lowest cost. In most software watermarking schemes, usually after watermark embedding, the number of instructions will be increased and the execution of the program will be slowed down. In contrast, our scheme aims at speeding up the program execution while maintaining the number of instructions.

In the field of multimedia signal processing, various techniques for reversible data hiding and lossless compression have been proposed for multimedia data [5,6]. Some algorithms use additive spread spectrum techniques [17] and some others hide data by modifying selected features (such as the LSB) of the host signal [5]. These techniques cannot be directly extended for hiding data in program binaries because of the inherent differences in the host data. As discussed in Section 2.1, compression techniques such as the Lempel-Ziv and the arithmetic coding require the knowledge of the execution order of the instructions and are not suitable for our purpose. To our best knowledge, the current paper presents the first work that applies information hiding techniques to program binaries of fixed-width instruction set processors, whereby extra information is transparently embedded and can be extracted with very low cost by the processor to enhance computer system performance.

6   Conclusions

In this work, we have investigated data hiding in computer programs for transparently embedding additional information that may be used by the processor for a variety of applications. We have shown that it is feasible to achieve efficient data hiding and fast data extraction using minimal additional logic and memory resources. We present a framework to achieve ISA-independent data hiding that is transparent to program execution. Under this framework, we introduce three algorithms to find bit positions in the operands of instructions that can be losslessly compressed to embed data. In addition, we propose improvement techniques through program partition to reduce the cost in data embedding and extraction. The effectiveness of our approaches are demonstrated through experimental results on the SPEC benchmark programs. Our experiments show that in most cases the proposed schemes can achieve linear time complexity in data embedding and require less than 3K bits of run-time memory overhead.

References

1. D. A. Patterson and J. L. Hennessy, *Computer Architecture A Quantitative Approach.* Morgan Kaufmann Publishers, Inc., 1996.
2. G. Radin, "The 801 minicomputer," in *Symposium on Architectural Support for Programming Languages and Operating Systems (1st ASPLOS'82), Computer Architecture News,* (Palo Alto, CA), pp. 39–47, 1982.
3. F. Gabbay and A. Mendelson, "Can program profiling support value prediction?," in *Proceedings of the 30th Annual International Symposium on Microarchitecture,* pp. 270–280, IEEE Computer Society TC-MICRO and ACM SIGMICRO, 1997.
4. K. Gharachorloo, D. Lenoski, L. Laudon, P. Gibbons, A. Gupta, and H. Hennessy, "Memory consistency and event ordering in scalable shared-memory multiprocessors," *Proceedings of the 17th Annual International Symposium on Computer Architecture, published in ACM SIGARCH,* vol. 18, pp. 15–26, May 1990.
5. J. Fridrich, M. Goljan, and R. Du, "Lossless data embedding - new paradigm in digital watermarking," *EURASIP Journal on Applied Signal Processing,* vol. 2002, no. 2, pp. 195–196, 2002.
6. M. U. Celik, G. Sharma, A. M. Tekalp, and E. Saber, "Reversible data hiding," in *Proc. of IEEE Intl. Conference on Image Processing,* vol. 2, pp. 157–160, 2002.
7. T. M. Cover and J. A. Thomas, *Elements of Information Theory.* John Wiley & Sons, 1991.
8. IBM Corporation, *Book I: PowerPC User Instruction Set Architecture, Version 2.01,* 2003.
9. Standard Performance Evaluation Corporation (SPEC). http://www.spec.org.
10. G. G. Pechanek, S. Lorin, and T. Conte, "Any-size Instruction Abbreviation Technique for Embedded DSPs," *15th IEEE Intl. ASIC/SOC Conf.,* pp. 8–12, 2002.
11. J. Lee, K. Choi, and N. Dutt, "Efficient Instruction Encoding for Automatic Instruction Set Design of Configurable ASIPs," *Proceedings of the IEEE/ACM international conference on Computer-aided design,* pp. 649–654, 2002.
12. J. Liu, T. Kong, and F. C. Chow, "Effective compilation support for variable instruction set architecture," in *IEEE International Conference on Parallel Architectures and Compilation Techniques,* pp. 56–67, 2002.
13. R. L. Davidson and N. Myhrvold, "Method and system for generating and auditing a signature for a computer program," *US Patent 5,559,884,* 1996.
14. R. Venkatesan, V. Vazirani, and S. Sinha, "A graph theoretic approach to software watermarking," in *Proc. of 4th Intl. Workshop on Info. Hiding,* pp. 157–168, 2001.
15. C. Collberg, E. Carter, S. Debray, H. Huntwork, J. Kececioglu, C. Linn, and M. Stepp, "Dynamic path-based software watermarking," *ACM SIGPLAN Notices,* vol. 39, pp. 107–118, May 2004.
16. L. Yuan, P. R. Pari, and G. Qu, "Soft IP protection: Watermarking HDL codes," in *Proc. of 6th International Workshop on Information Hiding,* pp. 224–238, 2004.
17. C. W. Honsineger, P. W. Jones, M. Rabbani, and J. C. Stoffel, "Lossless recovery of an original image containing embedded data," in *US Patent 6,278,791,* 2001.
18. R. El-Khalil, and A. Keromytis, "Hydan: Hiding information in program binaries," in *International Conf. on Information and Communications Security,* ICICS 2004.

Appendix – Description of the SPEC Benchmarks [9]

Program Name	Program Type	Language	Description
SWIM	float	Fortran 77	Shallow water modelling software.
ART	float	C	Adaptive Resonance Theory (ART) neural network - used to recognize objects in a thermal image
WUPWISE	float	Fortran 77	Wuppertal Wilson Fermion Solver - a program in quantum chromodynamics
EQUAKE	float	C	Simulates seismic wave propagation
LUCAS	float	C	Lucas-Lehmer test for primality check
APPLU	float	Fortran 77	Computational fluid dynamics and physics
MCF	integer	C	Combinatorial optimization
FACEREC	float	Fortran 90	Implementation of a face recognition system
GZIP	integer	C	GNU zip for data compression
BZIP2	integer	C	Compression program
APSI	float	Fortran 77	Program used in weather prediction
AMMP	float	C	Program used in computational chemistry to model large systems of molecules
GALGEL	float	Fortran 90	Program used in computational fluid dynamics
PARSER	integer	C	Program used for word processing
CRAFTY	integer	C	A high-performance computer chess program
TWOLF	integer	C	Used in computer aided design
EON	integer	C++	A probabilistic ray tracer based computer visualization program
MGRID	float	Fortran 77	A simple multi-grid solver in computing three dimensional potential field
VORTEX	integer	C	A single-user object-oriented database transaction benchmark
VPR	integer	C	Versatile Place and Route (VPR) is a FPGA circuit placement and routing program
PERLBMK	integer	C	A cut-down version of Perl v5.005_03 program
MESA	float	C	A free OpenGL work-alike 3D graphics library
GAP	integer	C	Implements a language and library designed mostly for computing in groups
FMA3D	float	Fortran 90	A finite element method computer program designed for Mechanical Response Simulation
SIXTRACK	float	Fortran 77	High energy nuclear physics accelerator design
CC1	integer	C	C++ language compiler

Dither Modulation Watermarking of Dynamic Memory Traces

Alan J. Larkin*, Félix Balado, Neil J. Hurley**, and Guenolé C.M. Silvestre**

Department of Computer Science, University College Dublin,
Belfield, Dublin 4, Ireland
{alan, fiz, neil.hurley, guenole.silvestre}@ihl.ucd.ie
http://www.ihl.ucd.ie

Abstract. We describe a dynamic software watermark embedded in the memory trace of an executing Java program. Our approach is a generalisation of the spread–transform watermarking technique developed for use in the multimedia domain. We show how the spread–transform paradigm enables the embedding of dither modulation watermarks in a Java program and report its robustness to realistic additive noise attacks.

1 Introduction

Recent years have witnessed an hitherto unseen level of concern about the issue of software piracy and intellectual property (IP) protection, among commercial and non–commercial software developers alike.

The advent of the Internet has radicalised software business models. It has now become common practice for vendors to make *trial* versions of even the most costly and sophisticated software freely available for download. Although such trial programs are typically time limited or partially disabled, they necessarily contain most of the developer's code and IP. This constitutes a major risk to the developer as this software is now vulnerable to attack by *crackers*, who attempt to disable the protection techniques, and plagiarism by competitors. Furthermore, the Internet has made possible the rapid mass distribution of derived or cracked software, enabling virtually any computer user to become a significant threat to even heavyweight developers.

Another related, although distinct, contributing factor has been the remarkable rise of the Java programming language. One of the principal reasons for Java's popular success has been its *"write once, run anywhere"* paradigm. In attaining this goal the language developers devised a compiled Java format (byte-code), which is effectively isomorphic to the original source code. As a consequence, Java software is easily reverse engineered, which makes it an insecure medium for algorithms and other IP.

---

* Supported by Irish Research Council for Science Engineering and Technology grant RS/2002/798–2.
** Supported by Enterprise Ireland Basic Research Grant SC/2002/178.

M. Barni et al. (Eds.): IH 2005, LNCS 3727, pp. 372–386, 2005.

A final development which is threatening software creators is the marked increase in interest in decompilation and other reverse engineering tools and techniques. As reverse engineering becomes ever more sophisticated, software developers are finding it increasingly difficult to conceal their IP, even by choosing to work in languages that are traditionally more difficult to reverse engineer than Java, such as C++.

Many tools exist for combating these problems, from the legal to the technical. One technical solution is remote execution, whereby the most intellectually valuable sections of a program reside only on secure servers [19]. A registered client program utilises the server as an oracle; sending input and receiving output, but never being exposed to the internals of the computation. Such an approach can be highly effective for detecting illegal software use (by an unlicensed user) and preventing IP theft. However remote execution is generally unattractive to legitimate customers for efficiency, reliability and privacy reasons.

Other approaches have been based on the use of hardware tokens such as *dongles*. These devices were typically plugged into a computer's serial port. The correct execution of a program was reliant on the presence of its dongle. More recently this concept has been advanced through the use of smart cards [10], which enable small portions of a program's computation to be performed by the token. Both techniques complicate piracy since the hardware devices are not readily reproducible. However this approach is not compatible with modern lightweight web–based business practices.

The most widely used software based protection technique is *obfuscation* [4] — the process of transforming one program into an equivalent one, which is more difficult to reverse engineer and understand. Obfuscation has the advantage that it is cheap and non–intrusive and can be quite effective. However it is only an impediment to theft. Obfuscation is not useful for identifying a theft, nor resolving the true *owner* of a given piece of software. These are the functions of a *software watermark*.

1.1   Software Watermarking

A software watermark is a piece of information that is embedded within a program. The presence of the watermark does not change the functionality of the program, and, generally, its presence should only be detectable through the use of an authorised detector. When used to encode ownership information, watermarking may be employed to both deter and detect theft of the host program, and in the event of such a theft, help resolve rightful ownership over it. Consequently, a would–be thief is required to destroy any watermarks present in the code they intend to steal, or risk detection and prosecution. Software watermarks must be resilient to such deliberate *attacks*.

Digital watermarking originally evolved in the multimedia domain. It has been the subject of much research and has become a formal and mature discipline [12, 14]. Multimedia, such as images and audio, have natural representations as vectors in numeric spaces. These vectors can be manipulated to encode a watermark without introducing any humanly perceptible changes.

The application of watermarking protection techniques to software is a relatively recent development, and although a number of techniques have been devised, the art remains in its infancy. Despite being conceptually similar, multimedia and software watermarking are in practice quite different. The smooth and natural mappings from objects to vectors employed in the multimedia domain, are not naturally present in the software domain. Instead, software watermarks tend to be embedded at a more abstract level; for example in the topology of dynamically created heap structures [3], or in a program's control–flow–graph [18].

A limited amount of work has been carried out in which a concerted effort is made to view the software watermarking problem as one to which multimedia solutions can be adapted [16, 7, 6, 15]. In each of these cases, an additive *spread–spectrum* algorithm [5] was applied to a feature vector extracted from the host program.

In this paper we too seek to exploit results from the multimedia domain to improve software watermarking, however our approach differs significantly from the others. We describe a novel approach for watermarking the collective run–time memory consumption of the set of Java methods comprising a program. In our case, the feature vector extraction process can be seen as an extension of the *spread–transform* technique (a more general method of spreading watermark information over a host signal than spread–spectrum) that is frequently employed on multimedia but, to date, has never applied to software. To this feature vector we apply a quantisation based watermarking algorithm [1]. Again the advantages of such algorithms over simple additive ones have not yet been exploited by the software watermarking community. We describe in particular how *dither modulation* watermarking is well suited to our problem.

This paper is organised as follows: In Section 2 we introduce the notion of a memory trace of a Java program, and show how the general process of watermarking a program's memory consumption may be viewed in terms of the spread–transform. Section 3 describes dither modulation watermarking, in particular its application to memory traces, and in Section 4 we present a statistical attack model against which we evaluate our proposal.

Notation: In this paper we will employ the following notational conventions;

- Lowercase bold roman letters ($\mathbf{x}$) denote vectors. All vectors are assumed to be column vectors. Row vectors are denoted with the use of a T superscript, meaning *transpose*. The ith element of a vector $\mathbf{x}$ is denoted by x_i.
- Matrices are set in bold uppercase roman letters ($\mathbf{A}$). The (i, j) element of a matrix $\mathbf{A}$ is denoted by a_{ij}.
- $\mathbb{N}$, $\mathbb{Z}$, and $\mathbb{R}$ represent the set of natural, integer and real numbers respectively. An additional scalar superscript, for example $\mathbb{R}^N$, denotes the N–dimensional cartesian product of that set. Unless otherwise specified, a $+$ superscript denotes the subset of positive numbers.
- $\lceil \cdot \rceil$ denotes rounding up to the next integer. $\| \cdot \|$ denotes a Euclidean norm. $\mathrm{E}\{\cdot\}$ denotes expectation.

2 Memory Trace Spread–Transform Watermarking

We define the N–dimensional memory trace (MT) of a Java program as the N–element vector corresponding to the total dynamic memory allocation performed during each of the N equal length time intervals $T_1, \ldots, T_N$, of an execution of that program;

$$x_i^{\text{ST}} = \text{memory allocated during } T_i.$$

This signal is of course inherently *keyed* upon the program input, or more generally upon the context of the execution.

If the program is comprised of K methods $\{m_1, \ldots, m_K\}$, we can consider the dynamic trace of the sequence of method invocations, and express x_i^{ST} as

$$x_i^{\text{ST}} = \sum_{j=1}^{K} a_{ij} \bar{x}_{ji},$$

where a_{ij} denotes the number of invocations of method m_j during interval T_i, and $\bar{x}_{ji}$ denotes the *average* number of bytes consumed over all executions of m_j during interval T_i. Define $\mathbf{A} = \{a_{ij}\} \in \mathbb{N}^{N,K}$ to be the *method execution frequency matrix* and $\overline{\mathbf{X}} = \{\bar{x}_{ji}\} \in \mathbb{R}^{K,N}$. The preceeding equation then becomes

$$\mathbf{x}^{\text{ST}} = \text{diag}(\mathbf{A}\overline{\mathbf{X}}).$$

Modulating a watermark vector $\mathbf{w}$ onto the MT vector $\mathbf{x}^{\text{ST}}$ leads to the problem of solving

$$\mathbf{x}_w^{\text{ST}} = \mathbf{x}^{\text{ST}} + \mathbf{w} \tag{1}$$
$$= \text{diag}(\mathbf{A}(\overline{\mathbf{X}} + \Delta\overline{\mathbf{X}}), \tag{2}$$

for matrix $\Delta\overline{\mathbf{X}}$, whose (i,j) component represents the amount by which the *average* memory consumption of m_j during T_i must be modified in order to embed $\mathbf{w}$.

Note that modifying a method's memory consumption by an amount that varies with the current interval of execution requires complicated dynamic control flow analysis and/or unstealthy modifications (conditional statements pertaining to the context in which the method is being invoked) to be applied to the program source. To avoid these problems we seek instead a solution which is *context–free*, that is, one in which the overhead added to each method's memory consumption is independent of the time interval. Thus we reformulate (2) as

$$\mathbf{x}_w^{\text{ST}} = \text{diag}(\mathbf{A}\overline{\mathbf{X}}) + \mathbf{A}\Delta\bar{\mathbf{x}} \tag{3}$$

where $\Delta\bar{x}_j$ represents the *constant* memory overhead that must be added to method m_j.

From (3) it becomes clear at this point that watermarking the MT vector $\mathbf{x}^{\text{ST}}$ with watermark vector $\mathbf{w}$, is analogous to Chen and Wornell's [1] spread–transform (ST) watermarking of $\overline{\mathbf{X}}$, in which the ith element of the vector $\mathbf{A}\Delta\bar{\mathbf{x}}$ is embedded in the linear projection of $\overline{\mathbf{X}}$ onto the ith row of $\mathbf{A}$.

An important difference between standard ST and our application is the structure of $\mathbf{A}$. In standard ST, $\mathbf{A}$ has the form,

$$\mathbf{A} = \text{block diag}(\mathbf{t}^T) = \begin{pmatrix} \mathbf{t}^T & & 0 \\ & \ddots & \\ 0 & & \mathbf{t}^T \end{pmatrix}, \tag{4}$$

for some *spreading–vector* $\mathbf{t} \in \mathbb{R}^{\lceil \frac{K}{N} \rceil}$. In our case, the ST must be generalised to projection matrices without this particular shape. The significance of this difference becomes apparent when solving (3) for $\Delta \overline{\mathbf{x}}$.

When $\mathbf{A}$ is of the form in Equation (4), the inversion of the projection onto $\mathbf{A}$ can be performed for each row of (3) independently of the others, making the computation trivial. In our generalised case however, the projection must be reversed for all of the rows *simultaneously*.

$$\begin{aligned} \Delta \overline{\mathbf{x}} &= \mathbf{A}^+ (\mathbf{x}_w^{\text{ST}} - \text{diag}(\mathbf{A}\overline{\mathbf{X}})) \\ &= \mathbf{A}^+ (\mathbf{x}^{\text{ST}} + \mathbf{w} - \text{diag}(\mathbf{A}\overline{\mathbf{X}})) \\ &= \mathbf{A}^+ (\text{diag}(\mathbf{A}\overline{\mathbf{X}}) + \mathbf{w} - \text{diag}(\mathbf{A}\overline{\mathbf{X}})) \\ &= \mathbf{A}^+ \mathbf{w}, \end{aligned} \tag{5}$$

where $\mathbf{A}^+$ denotes the Moore–Penrose pseudo–inverse of $\mathbf{A}$, given by $\mathbf{A}^+ \triangleq \mathbf{A}(\mathbf{A}^T\mathbf{A})^{-1}$.

2.1 Watermarking Embedding

The above discussion suggests the following general procedure for embedding a ST watermark in the MT of a Java program;

1. Use some *profiling* process to extract the memory trace $\mathbf{x}^{\text{ST}}$ and method execution frequency matrix $\mathbf{A}$ from the program as it executes under some *special* input (the key)[1].
2. Obtain a watermark $\mathbf{w}$ for the given information to be embedded, and compute $\Delta \overline{\mathbf{x}}$ (5).
3. Modify each of the program's K methods, so that the new method m_j allocates, on average, $\Delta \overline{x}_j$ more bytes on the heap per execution than the original method.

Several of the practical issues which arise with this embedding process are worth noting at this point;

1. Real–valued solutions to (5) are not desirable, since memory cannot be allocated in fractions of bytes in Java code.

---

[1] Note that (5) is independent of $\mathbf{x}^{\text{ST}}$, and as such this technique does not strictly require access to the original memory trace, however in the following section we exploit access to it for watermark message encoding.

2. Furthermore, the solution space is made discrete by the target Java Virtual Machine's (JVM) memory manager. For example, on the Sun JVM [11], memory is allocated in blocks of 8 bytes with a minimum of 2 blocks, implying $\Delta\overline{\mathbf{x}} = 8\mathbf{y}, \mathbf{y} \neq \mathbf{1} \in \mathbb{Z}^m$.
3. Negative elements in $\Delta\overline{\mathbf{x}}$ imply that the corresponding method must be optimised to use a certain number of bytes less memory than before. Performing such targeted optimisation is a hard problem.
4. Finally, a method's memory consumption may be affected by its context of execution, requiring care to be taken to ensure method modifications have the desired effects.

The first two of these issues can be addressed by reformulating (5) as an optimisation problem,

$$\min_{\Delta\overline{\mathbf{x}}} \|\mathbf{A}\Delta\overline{\mathbf{x}} - \mathbf{w}\| \quad \text{s.t.} \quad \Delta\overline{\mathbf{x}} = 8\mathbf{y}, \quad \mathbf{y} \neq \mathbf{1} \in \mathbb{Z}^m, \tag{6}$$

thus suitably constraining the solution space. Point 4 is most simply dealt with by making all modifications in the first basic block[2] of each method's bytecode, thus removing the effects of execution context, although more sophisticated, stealthy approaches may be developed. We postpone discussion of the remaining issue of negative solutions until the next section.

2.2 Watermarking Detection

Having developed an embedding process we now turn our attention to decoding. In ST watermarking, watermark decoding must be performed on the projection of the received signal $\widehat{\overline{\mathbf{X}}}$, a distorted version (due to attacks or other interference) of $\overline{\mathbf{X}}$;

$$\widehat{\mathbf{x}}^{\text{ST}} = \text{diag}(\mathbf{A}\widehat{\overline{\mathbf{X}}}). \tag{7}$$

Recall that, in practice, this amounts to extracting the MT $\widehat{\mathbf{x}}^{\text{ST}}$ from the received program via profiling of an execution under the key program input. Once obtained, the MT is subjected to the detection routine counterpart of the watermark message coding method used at the embedder.

Equation (7) fails to highlight another important difference between our application of ST to software and its standard use in the multimedia domain; the projection matrix $\mathbf{A}$ is part of the object being transmitted, and as such may be subjected to distortion. The previous equation should read,

$$\widehat{\mathbf{x}}^{\text{ST}} = \text{diag}(\widehat{\mathbf{A}}\widehat{\overline{\mathbf{X}}}),$$

where $\widehat{\mathbf{A}}$ denotes the received program's method execution frequency matrix. Even an undistorted program is likely to yield mildly differing method execution frequency matrices from one execution to the next due to chaotic processes such as IO blocking, or thread interleaving within the JVM. However we assume that the time interval is suitably large (N is small) so that $\mathbf{A} \simeq \widehat{\mathbf{A}}$.

---

[2] A basic block is a sequence of one or more consecutive instructions having only one entry point and one exit point.

3   Dither–Modulation in the Memory Trace Domain

In Equation (1), a vector **w** was modulated onto the ST of the host signal. At this point any watermarking algorithm may be applied to determine the value of **w**. Similarly to previous work in the multimedia domain [1], we employ the Dither Modulation (DM) algorithm. In this section we describe the approach and discuss its particular merits with respect to Java MT watermarking.

DM is a form of Quantisation Index Modulating (QIM) watermark [1], a class of algorithms in which information is embedded via the choice of one *quantiser* from a set, and the application of that quantiser to the original signal.

A scalar quantiser $\mathcal{Q}$ is a mapping from a one dimensional space, to a discrete subset of that space. For example,

$$\mathcal{Q} : \mathbb{R} \to \{c_i : c_i \in \mathbb{Z}\}.$$

Normally, a minimum–distance mapping is employed.

In QIM, a set of quantisers $Q = \{\mathcal{Q}_1, \ldots, \mathcal{Q}_l\}$ is defined. At the embedder, the watermark message $\mathbf{b} \in \{0, \ldots, l-1\}^N$ is chosen. The ith element of the original signal, in our case $\mathbf{x}^{\text{ST}}$, is then quantised using the quantiser in Q indexed by b_i;

$$x_{w_i}^{\text{ST}} = \mathcal{Q}_{b_i}\left(x_i^{\text{ST}}\right).$$

In conjunction with Equation (1) this implies that

$$w_i = \mathcal{Q}_{b_i}\left(x_i^{\text{ST}}\right) - x_i^{\text{ST}}. \tag{8}$$

This encoding of the watermark message is then added to the projected signal in (1).

During the (blind) watermark extraction phase, the elements of the signal received at the decoder $\widehat{\mathbf{x}}_w^{\text{ST}}$, are quantised using each quantiser in Q. The received message $\widehat{\mathbf{b}}$ is reconstructed from the indices of the sequence of quantisers which contain the reconstruction points closest (in a Euclidean sense) to the elements of $\widehat{\mathbf{x}}_w^{\text{ST}}$;

$$\widehat{b}_i = \arg\min_k \left\| \mathcal{Q}_k\left(\widehat{x}_{w_i}^{\text{ST}}\right) - \widehat{x}_{w_i}^{\text{ST}} \right\|.$$

The Binary DM (Fig. 1) algorithm which we utilise in the remainder of this paper is a specialisation of QIM, in which two uniform quantisers $Q = \{\mathcal{Q}_0, \mathcal{Q}_1\}$ are employed. $\mathcal{Q}_0$ and $\mathcal{Q}_1$ are both of step size $\Delta \in \mathbb{R}$ and are mutually shifted, or *dithered*, by $\Delta/2$.

Our motivation for selecting the DM algorithm over spread–spectrum (as has been the trend in the software domain) is two–fold. The first is an inherent property of QIM watermarking termed *host signal interference rejection*. QIM's exploitation of knowledge of the host signal $\mathbf{x}^{\text{ST}}$ at the encoder (c.f. footnote [3]), prevents the host signal from acting as interference in the transmission of the watermark message from the embedder to the detector, thus improving the watermark's robustness to distortion/capacity. The second is a practical advantage which we contrive from the properties of the MT domain.

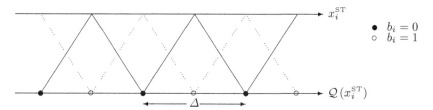

Fig. 1. Binary Dither Modulation in the ith dimension. The ith element of the original signal $\mathbf{x}^{\text{ST}}$ (upper line) is *quantised* to either a • or a ∘ (lower line) if $b_i = 0$ or $b_i = 1$, respectively. With a quantiser step size of Δ, the maximum distortion that it will be necessary to introduce per dimension of $\mathbf{x}^{\text{ST}}$ is $\frac{\Delta}{2}$. After embedding, the maximum tolerable amplitude distortion per dimension before an error is introduced is $\frac{\Delta}{4}$.

First we note that quantising to *any* reconstruction point in the appropriate quantiser is enough to encode a given watermark element. For image and audio data, relatively low limits on the acceptable level of distortion introduced due to watermarking and attacking alike, are naturally defined by the human sensory systems. Consequently, quantising to the *nearest* quantisation point is important in order to preserve the imperceptibility of the watermark. In the MT domain however, the imperceptibility of the embedded information is not of overriding importance. Although it may be considered undesirable for a watermark to significantly increase the memory footprint of a given piece of software, the principal concern and only strict requirement is the preservation of the functionality of the program.

This realisation enables us to address the outstanding practical issue raised in the previous section; that of negative values in $\Delta\bar{\mathbf{x}}$. By always quantising *up* to the nearest quantisation point, we can ensure that non–negative solutions to Equation (6) can be generated. Thus our DM quantisers are of the form;

$$\mathcal{Q}_0(x) = \left\lceil \tfrac{x}{\Delta} \right\rceil \Delta \quad \text{and} \quad \mathcal{Q}_1(x) = \left(\left\lceil \tfrac{x - \frac{\Delta}{2}}{\Delta} \right\rceil + \tfrac{1}{2} \right) \Delta. \tag{9}$$

Additionally we note that when Δ is chosen to be divisible by 16, simple manipulation of (6) using (8) and (9) reduces the problem to an optimisation of a natural number linear system, thus permitting natural solutions.

4   Experimental Results

4.1   Experimental Framework

Implementation of a system illustrated in Fig. 2 has been undertaken in order to facilitate experimentation and analysis of the proposed watermark. The embedding process consists of three principle stages; 1) feature extraction or profiling, 2) formulation and solution of Equation (6), and 3) realisation of the required program modifications.

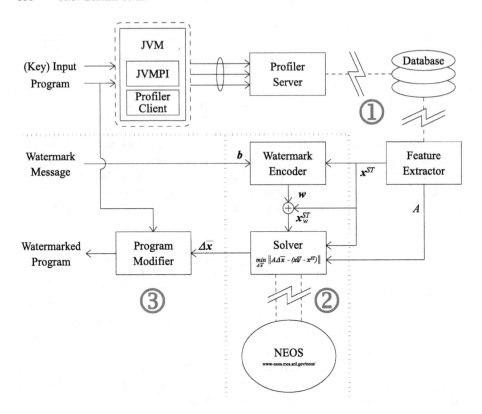

Fig. 2. Memory Trace Watermarking Framework

Table 1. Test Program

Name: Java Tree Builder (JTB) [17]
Description: JavaCC Grammar annotater, composed of 1447 methods
Input: Java1.2-a.jj

---

1. The extraction of the MT vector and method execution frequency matrix is achieved through the use of a purpose built profiling tool. Constructed as client–server pair, our Java profiler is built upon the Java Virtual Machine Profiling Interface (JVMPI) [9]. The profiling client resides in the same process as the JVM. User–specified statistics of interest are gathered on a per–thread basis, and with minimal client–side processing are sent to the server. This minimal processing, per–thread profiling ensures the least possible distortion of the extracted signals due to the presence of the profiler. The server receives the raw data, re–synchronises it, and processes it in a user–specified manner into a database describing the execution of the program. Generating such a database enables the user to create many different views of a single execution.

2. For the MT watermarking application, the features of interest are the MT itself and the method execution frequency matrix. These are extracted during stage 2, and are used to formulate a representation of Equation (6). This optimisation problem is non–trivial, and so we employ the NEOS Server [8] to generate solutions. NEOS is a free web–server which offers access to a large number of mathematical optimisation suites. Specifically, we send our problem to NEOS for solution using the XPRESS–MP Mixed Integer Linear Programmer [13]. (Note that we are restricted to solving Equation (6) as an L_1–norm minimisation problem, rather than the more desirable L_2–norm). Frequently, exact solutions to our problems do not exist, and so there is normally some embedding error inherent in our process. Indeed, on occasion, no solutions are found or the problem is determined to be infeasible. In such cases we have no recourse other than to re–profile under a different program input.
3. Assuming an acceptable solution can be computed, we proceed with the final step, modifying the program's methods so that they allocate extra memory as dictated by NEOS. This can be as trivial as the insertion of superfluous `byte` array allocation instructions at the start of each method, although more sophisticated approaches involving the use of opaque predicates could and should be used. In what follows this last step is simulated.

We now report results from simulated embedding and attacking of the watermarking scheme. Our early results are restricted to simulations on a single Java program shown in Table 1. Experiments were performed on the Sun JVM (version 1.4.2–02), running under GNU Linux on a dual Intel Xeon 2.8 GHz machine, with 2.5 Gb RAM.

4.2   Attack Model

Proper analysis of a watermarking scheme's robustness requires a model of the attacks to which the watermarked signal may be subjected. In this paper we employ an additive noise model derived from experimentation on a set of automated attacks from the SANDMARK system [2] (Table 2).

The amplitude distortions introduced into the watermark channel (the average method memory consumptions, $\overline{\mathbf{X}}$) by application of these attacks to the test program were measured. Under the assumption that these noise samples are independent and identically distributed, the Central Limit Theorem predicts that they should follow Normal distributions. Empirical evidence in fact shows that they are drawn from peaked distributions. We conclude that the independence assumption does not hold, due to correlations existing amongst both the rows of the execution frequency matrix (as a result of *the principle of locality*), and its columns (as a result of inter–method dependencies).

Using maximum likelihood estimation, the noise signals due to the considered attacks were in fact all found to be well approximated by the Laplacian distribution;

$$f_X(x; \mu, \lambda) = \frac{\lambda}{2} e^{-\lambda|x-\mu|}.$$

The estimated parameters for each attack are listed in Fig. 4.

382 A.J. Larkin et al.

Table 2. Considered Attacks from the SANDMARK System

Name	Description
Array Folder	"Folds" a 1–dimensional array into a multi–dimensional array.
Array Splitter	Splits 1–dimensional array fields into 2 array fields.
Block Marker	Randomly marks all basic blocks in a program with either a 0 or 1.
Constant Pool Reorderer	Reorders the constants in the constant pool and assigns random indices to them.
False Refactor	Two classes C1 and C2 that have no common behavior are refactored forming a class C3.
Field Assignment	Inserts bogus fields into a class and makes assignments to that field in specific locations throughout the code.
Insert Opaque Predicates	Inserts an opaque predicate into every boolean expression.
Integer Array Splitter	Splits a local variable array into two arrays.
Overload Names	Renames methods so that as many as possible have the same name.
Publicize Fields	Makes the fields of a class public.
Rename Registers	Renames local variables to random identifiers.
Reorder Parameters	Shuffles the argument orders for all methods.

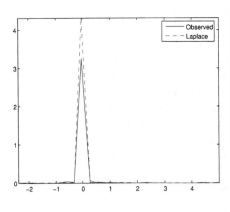

Attack	μ	λ
Array Splitter	81.1735	0.0020650
Constant Pool Reorderer	51.3785	0.0026051
Overload Names	-23.1289	0.0030382
Array Folder	48.5469	0.0030583
Integer Array Splitter	58.8219	0.0036680
False Refactor	57.0828	0.0037142
Block Marker	56.2616	0.0037221
Insert Opaque Predicates	74.3434	0.0041431
Publicize Fields	60.3178	0.0045263
Field Assignment	64.1785	0.0046936
Reorder Parameters	57.2756	0.0047845
Rename Registers	57.9861	0.0048702

Fig. 3. Laplacian Model of Array Splitter Attack

Fig. 4. Parameters of Laplacian Model of SANDMARK Attacks

4.3   Robustness

–4 Hamming error–correction–coded (ECC) watermarks were embedded in the $N = 32$–dimensional MT of the test program[3]. At this dimension, the correlation between the original matrix $\mathbf{A}$ and each of the attacked frequency matrices $\widehat{\mathbf{A}}$, bar one[4], was found to be in the range $[0.899, 0.993]$. In these experiments $N = 32$ was thus considered sufficiently small so that $\mathbf{A} \simeq \widehat{\mathbf{A}}$ (Section 2.2).

We measure the robustness of the transmission of the watermark message from the embedder to the detector as the proportion of erroneously transmitted bits, or the *bit–error–rate* (BER). Fig. 5 shows the simulated BER against the *watermark–to–noise–ratio* (WNR) for JTB under attack with Laplacian noise. The WNR in decibels is defined as,

$$\text{WNR} = 10 \log_{10} \frac{\text{E}\{\|\mathbf{A}\Delta\overline{\mathbf{x}}\|^2\}}{\text{E}\{\|\mathbf{A}\mathbf{d}\|^2\}},$$

where $\mathbf{d}$ is the noise vector, and provides a fair measure of the strength of a watermark in relation to an attack. Note that we compute the WNR in the projection domain (the runtime memory consumption per interval), arguing that for our application it is in this domain that the presence of the watermark may become apparent.

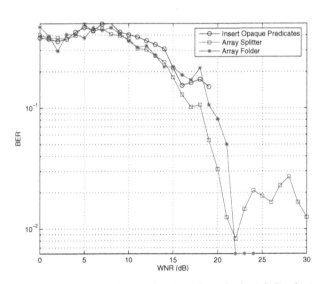

Fig. 5. Bit–Error–Rate *vs.* WNR for JTB Attacked with Laplacian Noise

It is clear from Fig. 5 that our scheme requires significantly greater WNR than classical ST–DM. This fact can be attributed to the difficulty of satisfying

---

[3] For these experiments, $N = 32$ implied interval widths of 485 ms, real time.
[4] Correlation after the Array Splitter attack was found to be 0.795.

all the constraints of Equation (6). As noted earlier however, notions of perceptibility are not clearly defined in the MT domain, and as long as the presence of the watermark does not render the program unusable, in this case by grossly over inflating the program's memory footprint, the watermark may be considered acceptable.

5   Summary and Conclusions

In this paper we have described a new form of dynamic Java watermarking, which is unique both in terms of the feature vector used to carry the watermark, and in its application of ST–DM principles. The watermark has a high degree of stealth, with simple and isolated pieces of *watermark generating code* pervading the entire program. We have also seen that with appropriate embedding strength the watermark is robust to a number of realistic attacks.

Additionally, we have modelled of a set of attacks to which this watermark may be subjected. Within the software watermarking community the term *attack model* is frequently used in an informal manner, often being applied to what are little more than lists of program transformations. Such *models* are of poor use for forecasting the performance of a watermarking system. Our model on the other hand, is mathematical, and has enabled us to make predictions about the robustness of our watermark.

This model does however remain modest. As yet we have considered only a narrow band of the full spectrum of automated transformations to which software may be subjected. Further experimentation may expose the additive noise model to be unsuitable for describing processes such as optimisation, decompilation, or multiple obfuscations applied in series. These attacks may prove to be more *desynchronsing* than additive in nature.

Future work must focus on expansion of our attack model, and more complete evaluation of this watermark's robustness. Beyond this, an interesting direction for future research is the embedding of the watermark in a frequency domain, such as the Fourier Transform, of the MT. Again such techniques have long been employed on multimedia, but are yet to make the crossover to software. We hypothesise that embedding in the low frequency components (corresponding to the global shape of the MT) of such a transformed signal, will improve resilience to attacks, which appear to introduce noise primarily at the local level.

Acknowledgements

The authors wish to gratefully acknowledge the support of Enterprise Ireland (grant SC/2002/178) and the Irish Research Council for Science Engineering and Technology (grant RS/2002/798–2).

We also wish to thank Julian Keenaghan for his helpful contribution.

References

1. B. Chen and G. W. Wornell. Quantization Index Modulation: A Class of Provably Good Methods for Digital Watermarking and Information Embedding. In *ISIT: Proceedings IEEE International Symposium on Information Theory, sponsored by The Information Theory Society of The Institute of Electrical and Electronic Engineers*, volume 47, pages 1424–1443, May 2000.
2. C. S. Collberg. SANDMARK *User's Guide*, Jan 2003. www.cs.arizona.edu/sandmark.
3. C. S. Collberg and C. D. Thomborson. Software Watermarking: Models and Dynamic Embeddings. In *Principles of Programming Languages 1999, (POPL'99)*, pages 311–324, Jan 1999.
4. C. S. Collberg, C. D. Thomborson, and D. Low. A Taxonomy of Obfuscating Transformations. Technical Report TR98–148, Department of Computer Science, The University of Auckland, Jul 1997.
5. I. J. Cox, J. Kilian, T. Leighton, and T. Shamoon. A Secure, Robust Watermark for Multimedia. In *Workshop on Information Hiding*, pages 175–190, May 1996.
6. D. M. Curran, N. J. Hurley, and M. Ó Cinnéide. Securing Java Through Software Watermarking. In *Principles and Practice of Programming in Java (PPPJ'03)*, Jun 2003.
7. G. Hachez. *A Comparative Study of Software Protection Tools Suited for E-Commerce with Contributions to Software Watermarking and Smart Cards*. PhD thesis, Universite Catholique de Louvain, Mar 2003.
8. Argonne National Laboratory. NEOS Optimization Server. www-neos.mcs.anl.gov/neos.
9. S. Liang and D. Viswanathan. Comprehensive Profiling Support in the Java Virtual Machine. In *5th USENIX Conference on Object-Oriented Technologies and Systems (COOTS'99)*, May 1999.
10. A. Maña and E. Pimentel. An Efficient Software Protection Scheme. In M. Dupuy and P. Paradinas, editors, *Trusted Information: The New Decade Challenge, IFIP TC11 Sixteenth Annual Working Conference on Information Security (IFIP'01)*, volume 193 of *IFIP Conference Proceedings*, pages 385–402. Kluwer, Jun 2001.
11. Sun Microsystems. Java Virtual Machine. java.sun.com.
12. M. Miller, I. J. Cox, J. P. Linnartz, and T. Kalker. A Review of Watermarking Principles and Practices. *Digital Signal Processing in Multimedia Systems*, 1999.
13. Dash Optimization. Xpress–MP. www.dashoptimization.com.
14. F. A. P. Peticolas, R. J. Anderson, and M. G. Kuhn. Information Hiding — A Survey. In *Proceedings of the IEEE*, volume 87, pages 1062–1078, Jul 1999.
15. T. Sahoo and C. Collberg. Software Watermarking in the Frequency Domain: Implementation, Analysis, and Attacks. Technical Report TR04–07, Department of Computer Science, The University of Arizona, Mar 2004.
16. J. P. Stern, G. Hachez, F. Koeune, and J.–J. Quisquater. Robust Object Watermarking: Application to Code. In A. Pfitzmann, editor, *Information Hiding: 3rd International Workshop (IH'99)*, volume 1768 of *Lecture Notes in Computer Science (LNCS)*, pages 368–378, Germany, 2000. Springer.
17. UCLA Compilers Group. Java Tree Builder. compilers.cs.ucla.edu/jtb.

18. R. Venkatesan, V. Vazirani, and S. Sinha. A Graph Theoretic Approach to Software Watermarking. In I. S. Moskowitz, editor, *Information Hiding Workshop (IH'01)*, volume 2137 of *Lectures Notes in Computer Science (LNCS)*, pages 157–168, Pittsburgh, PA, USA, 2001. Springer–Verlag.

19. X. Zhang and R. Gupta. Hiding Program Slices for Software Security. In *International Symposium on Code Generation and Optimization (CGO'03)*, page 325, Mar 2003.

A Family of Collusion 2-Secure Codes

Josep Cotrina-Navau, Marcel Fernandez, and Miguel Soriano*

Department of Telematics Engineering, Universitat Politècnica de Catalunya,
C/ Jordi Girona 1 i 3, Campus Nord, Mod C3, UPC, 08034 Barcelona, Spain
{jcotrina, marcelf, soriano}@mat.upc.es

Abstract. We present systematic strategy for collusions attacking a fingerprinting scheme. As a particular case, this strategy shows that linear codes are not good fingerprinting codes. Based on equidistant codes, we construct a family of fingerprinting codes in which the identification of guilty users can be efficiently done using minimum distance decoding.

1 Introduction

The fingerprinting technique consists in making the copies of a digital object unique by embedding a different set of marks in each copy. Having unique copies of an object clearly rules out plain redistribution, but still a coalition of dishonest users can collude, compare their copies and by changing the marks where their copies differ, they are able to create a pirate copy that tries to disguise their identities. Thus, the fingerprinting problem consists in finding, for each copy of the object, the right set of marks that help to prevent collusion attacks.

The construction of collusion secure codes was first addressed in [2]. In that paper, Boneh and Shaw obtain $(c > 1)$-secure codes, where N is the number of words and ϵ the probability of failing to identify a guilty user. The construction composes an inner binary code with an outer random code. Therefore, the identification algorithm involves decoding of a random code, that is known to be a NP-hard problem [1].

Barg *et al.* in [1] present a construction based on the composition of two codes, an inner binary (c, c)-separable code and an outer non-binary code. Dual binary Hamming codes are used in the work by Domingo-Ferrer and Herrera in [4].

Most of fingerprinting codes base their security on the fact that any coalition of $c > 1$ users, that know c codewords, does not have enough information to construct a copy with a new false fingerprint that frames an innocent user, or that does not unveil any member of the coalition.

The security of such codes is normally based on the fact that the coalition can not use any pre-established strategy, and therefore, the only possibility is to construct the new false fingerprint in an random way. In this case, the probability of framing an innocent user is lowered. The only possible strategy that

---

* This work has been supported in part by the Spanish Research Council (CICYT) Project TIC2002-00818 (DISQET) and TIC2003-01748 (RUBI) and by the IST-FP6 Project 506926 (UBISEC).

M. Barni et al. (Eds.): IH 2005, LNCS 3727, pp. 387–397, 2005.

is assumed in all fingerprinting schemes is the majority strategy, so all existing fingerprinting codes are robust against this strategy. Here we show a new possible strategy. Moreover, we show how to construct families of 2-secure codes from binary linear equidistant codes. The proposed construction has the particularity that an innocent user is never framed and the probability of identifying at least one coalition member is $1 - \epsilon$ for any $\epsilon > 0$.

The paper is organized as follows. In Section 2 we provide some definitions on fingerprinting, as well as some previous results. Section 3 presents an arithmetic attack to fingerprinting codes. Section 4 discusses the use of equidistant binary linear codes as fingerprinting codes. In Section 5 we present a new construction of fingerprinting codes based on equidistant binary linear codes, in which, besides being robust to the arithmetic attack, identifying the guilty users can be done using minimum distance decoding as shown in Section 5.1.

2   Previous Results and Definitions

Let $\mathcal{Q}$ be a finite alphabet of size Q. We define $\mathcal{Q}^n = \{x = x_1 x_2 \cdots x_n | x_i \in \mathcal{Q}\}$. The elements of $\mathcal{Q}^n$ are called words. For any set X, $|X|$ denotes the cardinality of X.

Following [1][2] (we refer readers to these papers for a more detailed exposition), given a subset $X \subseteq \mathcal{Q}^n$, we define the *envelope* $\mathcal{E}(X) \subseteq \mathcal{Q}^n$ of X as a set of words than can be derived from X using the rules that we detail below.

If $y \in \mathcal{E}(X)$ then y is a *descendant* of X and any $x \in \mathcal{E}(X)$ is a *parent* of y. A position i is *undetectable* for X if $x_i^r = x_i^s, \forall x^r, x^s \in X$. The undetectable positions form a set denoted by $\mathcal{Z}(X)$.

Given X, to determine $\mathcal{E}(X)$, by the marking assumption, the positions in $\mathcal{Z}(X)$ can not be modified, thus if $y \in \mathcal{E}(X)$ then $y_i = x_i^r, \forall i \in \mathcal{Z}(X), \forall x^r \in X$. For the rest of positions, *detectable* positions, there are several options to choose from.

The *narrow-sense* envelope

$$e(X) = \{y \in \mathcal{Q}^n | y_i \in \cup_{x \in X} x_i\}.$$

The *wide-sense* envelope

$$E(X) = \{y \in \mathcal{Q}^n | y_i = x_i^1 \forall i \in \mathcal{Z}(X)\}.$$

These two definitions can be generalized in a natural way if unreadable (or erased) symbols are allowed.

With the above notation, the fingerprinting problem can be summarized as follows. Let us consider a code C and a coalition with fingerprints (codewords) $U = \{u_1, u_2, \ldots, u_t\}$. The coalition creates a new false fingerprint $y \in \mathcal{E}(U)$ and the distributor D needs to determine which codewords can produce y, that is, D determines a set $X = \{x_1, \ldots, x_f\}$ such that $y \in \mathcal{E}(X)$. Finally using some (good) criteria, D determines a possible guilty between the members of X.

Obviously if $X \nsubseteq U$, depending on the criteria used by D, other users, not in the coalition, can be framed.

Usually the criteria used by D is based on the Hamming distance. That is, the distributor D sets as guilty one of the users whose codeword is within Hamming distance less than some value δ from the fingerprint y.

Thus, if we define $X_\delta = \{x \in X | d(x, y) < \delta\}$, where $d(,)$ represents the Hamming distance, in order to avoid framing users not in the coalition we need to show that there exists a value δ such that $X_\delta \subseteq U$, or that the probability $p(X_\delta \not\subseteq U) < f(C)$, where $f(C) \geq 0$ is an arbitrary small value that depends on some of the code parameters.

For a fixed-code family C we define the error probability of the distributor D in identifying a guilty user as

$$p_e(\mathcal{C}) = \min_{C \in \mathcal{C}} \min_{D_s} \max_{U \subset C, |U| = t} p_e(U)$$

where D_s represents all possible strategies used by D and $p_e(U)$ the error probability under the optimal strategy of a coalition U.

Barg et al, in [1], establish some useful bounds on the value of $p_e(\mathcal{C})$. In [1] it is always assumed that the code family $\mathcal{C}$ is known by the coalition. Under this assumption they show that a single code is not useful for fingerprinting schemes. For example using a single code C, $p_e(C) \geq (t-1)/(2t-1)$ where t is the coalition size, and for a non (t,t)-separable code $p_e(C) \geq 1/2$.

Therefore, they state that the only possibility is to use a family of codes (known by the coalition) and allowing the distributor to choose randomly a member of the family to implement the fingerprinting scheme. Now, the coalition does not know which member of the family it is used, thus an uncertainty about the used code exists. For this case $p_e(C) \geq |C|^{-1}(t-1)/(2t-1)$

Moreover, once the code and the tracing strategy used by D are fixed (this represents a practical case), the error probability we are interested on is

$$p_e = \max_{U \subset C, |U| = t} p_e(U).$$

That is, the goal of any fingerprinting scheme is to minimize p_e, that represents the maximal error-probability achievable by the scheme.

In practical constructions, the alphabet $\mathcal{Q}$ is a finite field (or it has some algebraic structure). If this is not the case, we can define a bijective map $Op : \mathcal{Q} \to \mathbb{Z}_{|\mathcal{Q}|}$ and let $\mathcal{Q}$ have a group structure. Thus, from now we assume that $(\mathcal{Q}, +)$ is a group. Obviously, the subtraction operation $(-)$ is also defined on $\mathcal{Q}$.

We define the *envelope-subtraction*, represented by $\ominus$, of two elements $y^1, y^2 \in E(X)$, as $y = y^1 \ominus y^2$, where $y = y_1 \cdots y_n$, $y_i = x_i^1 \forall i \in \mathcal{Z}(X), x^1 \in X$, and $y_i = y_i^1 - y_i^2 \forall i \notin \mathcal{Z}(X)$.

For the binary case, $\mathcal{Q} = \{0, 1\} = \mathbb{F}_2$, $y_i = x_i^1 \forall i \in \mathcal{Z}(X), x^1 \in X$, and $y_i = 1$ otherwise.

If we assume that users know $\mathcal{Q}$ then we must assume that users also know the group structure, because the users can deduce the group structure of $\mathcal{Q}$ by defining all the bijections between $\mathcal{Q}$ and $\mathbb{Z}_{|\mathcal{Q}|}$ (remember that p_e is determined considering the optimal strategy of any coalition).

Obviously, for the binary case we must assume that users know $\mathcal{Q}$.

3   Arithmetic Attack to Fingerprinting Codes

In this section we present our attack, that we call *arithmetic-attack*. This attack
determines some necessary conditions that must satisfy fingerprinting codes. As
a consequence of these conditions we prove that linear codes are not useful for
fingerprinting schemes.

Remember that we suppose that the code C used in the fingerprinting scheme
is unknown by the colluders (hypothesis that benefices the distributor), and
that the distributor D uses the Hamming distance strategy as the identification
assumption.

Then if C is a linear code we show that the probability p_e of framing a user
is $p_e \geq 1/3$.

This not means that linear codes can not be used to construct fingerprinting
codes, but we need to be careful that the resulting code is not linear.

Theorem 1. *Let C be any fingerprinting code defined over an alphabet $\mathcal{Q}$. We
assume that coalitions know $(\mathcal{Q}, +)$. If for some pair of different code words
(fingerprints) $u, v \in C - \{0\}$ we have that $u - v$ and $v - u$ are also in C, then
$p_e \geq 1/3$.*

Proof. Given two code words (fingerprints) $U = \{u, v\} \subset C - \{0\}$, we consider
coalitions $U_1 = \{u, v\}$, $U_2 = \{u, u - v\}$ and $U_3 = \{v, v - u\}$. Each coalition
$U_i = \{x^{i_1}, x^{i_2}\}$ produces a false fingerprinting y^i as $y^i = x^{i_1} \ominus x^{i_2}$.

In what follows we show that the false fingerprinting produced by one of these
coalitions can frame a user not in the same coalition, thus in this case $p_e \geq 1/3$.

A necessary condition to avoid framing the user with fingerprint $x^{i_1} - x^{i_2}$,
not a member of U_i, is

$$d(x^{i_1} - x^{i_2}, y^i) > d(x^{i_j}, y^i), \tag{1}$$

for $i = 1, 2, 3$ and $j = 1$ or $j = 2$. But, in what follows, we will show that this is
contradictory.

First note that

$$d(x^{i_1} - x^{i_2}, y^i) = d(x^{i_1} - x^{i_2}, x^{i_1} \ominus x^{i_2}) = \\ = |\{z | x_z^{i_1} = x_z^{i_2} \neq 0\}|. \tag{2}$$

Moreover if $x^{j_k} = x^{i_1} - x^{i_2} \in U_j$, $i \neq j$, and we define

$$\{x^j\} = U_j - \{x^{j_k}\} \tag{3}$$

then $\{x^j, -x^j\} \cap U_i \neq \emptyset$.

Now consider $x^{i_1} - x^{i_2} = x^{j_k} \in U_j$. We show that

$$d(x^{j_k}, y^j) \geq d(x^{i_1} - x^{i_2}, y^i). \tag{4}$$

By equation (2) we only need to show that coordinates z such that $x_z^{i_1} = x_z^{i_2} \neq 0$
satisfy

$$x_z^{j_k} \neq y_z^j,$$

but $x_z^{j_k} = 0$, and following the notation used in equation (3) we see that $y_z^j = \pm x_z^j$, but we know that $\{x^j, -x^j\} \cap U_i \neq \emptyset$ thus $x_z^j \neq 0$.

Finally, using equation (4) it is an easy combinatorial problem to show that inequalities in equation (1) are impossible.

Thus we can conclude that $p_e \geq 1/3$. □

Corollary 1. *Let C be any linear code, with $|C| > 2$, defined over any alphabet Q. If coalitions know $(Q, +)$ then $p_e \geq 1/3$.*

Proof. There exist $u, v \in C - \{0\}$, therefore $u - v$ and $v - u$ are also words of C. □

Corollary 2. *Let C be any linear binary code, with $|C| > 2$, then $p_e \geq 1/3$.*

Proof. In this case $Q = \mathbb{F}_2$ thus any coalition can deduce $(Q, +)$. □

A more restrictive result for the case of linear codes can be stated.

Proposition 1. *Let C be a linear code over a finite field, with $|C| > 2$. Let $U = \{u, v\} \subset C$ represents any arbitrary 2-coalition that produces the false fingerprinting $y = u \ominus v$. Then the probability p of framing an innocent user, not in the coalition, satisfies $p \geq 1/9$.*

Proof. From theorem 1, for each pair $\{u, v\}$ that does not frame any user (*good-pair*), we know how to construct a pair that frames other users (*bad-pair*). Moreover, given two good-pairs $\{u, v\}$ and $\{u', v'\}$, without loss of generality, relabeling the fingerprints (code words) if necessary, we can construct two bad-pairs $U_1 = \{u - v, u\}$ and $U_2 = \{u' - v', u'\}$. It can happen that $U_1 = U_2$, but in this case $u' = u - v$ and $v' = -v$. Moreover, if the bad-pair associated to another good pair $\{u'', v''\}$ is $U_3 = \{u'' - v'', u''\}$, and $U_3 = U_2 = U_1$ then $v'' = -v$ and $v'' = -v'$ so $v = v' = v'' = 0$, and $u'' = u' = u$.

Therefore, in the worst case, two good-pairs generate the same bad-pair, thus the probability that an arbitrary coalition is a bad-pair is $p \geq 1/3$. □

Remember that for the binary case, $Q = \{0, 1\} = \mathbb{F}_2$, the operation $y = x^1 \ominus x^2$ consists on set $y_i = x^1$ if $i \in \mathcal{Z}(X)$, and $y_i = 1$ otherwise. Thus the strategy of the coalition on this case is to set the detectable positions of the fingerprinting to the value 1.

4   Equidistant Binary Linear Codes as Fingerprinting Codes

In this section we discuss some of the properties about equidistant binary linear codes related to the fingerprinting problem.

Equidistant binary codes are $(2, 2)$-separable, equidistant codes, with all codewords except the all zero codewords have the same Hamming weight.

We first show that considering an equidistant code C, a 2-coalition c cannot generate any false fingerprint that is closer (in the Hamming sense) to a codeword $w \in C - c$ than to the own coalition codewords, that is

$$\min\{d(x, y)|x \in c\} \leq d(w, y), \quad \forall w \in C - c$$

where $d(,)$ represents the Hamming distance.

Proposition 2. *Let C be an equidistant binary $C = C[n, k, d]$ code. Let $c = \{u, v\} \subset C$ be a coalition, and let y be a false fingerprint generated by c.*
Then, we always have that

$$d(w, y) \geq \frac{d}{2} \quad i \quad \min\{d(x, y)|x \in c\} \leq \frac{d}{2},$$

where w is any codeword, $w \in C - c$.

Proof. Given the coalition $c = \{u, v\} \subset C$, since the code is equidistant then $d(u, v) = d$. This coalition can only detect, and therefore decide which will be, d positions of the false fingerprint. Reordering the codeword positions we can assume that the detectable positions are the first d positions. To simplify the notation, we represent the codewords $x \in C$ as $x = (x_d, x_{n-d})$, where x_d represents the first d positions.

Given a codeword $w \in C - c$, since $u_{n-d} = v_{n-d}$, there always exists an $\alpha \in \mathbb{N}$, with $0 \leq \alpha \leq d$ such that

$$d(w_{n-d}, u_{n-d}) = d(w_{n-d}, v_{n-d}) = \alpha.$$

Then, since $d(w, u) = d$ we have that

$$d(w_d, u_d) = d(w_d, v_d) = d - \alpha. \tag{5}$$

But $d(u_d, v_d) = d$, because they are precisely the positions where they do not agree, $u_d = 1 + v_d$ and therefore

$$d(w_d, u_d) + d(w_d, v_d) = d. \tag{6}$$

Substituting the values of (5) into (6) we obtain

$$d - \alpha + d - \alpha = d,$$

where

$$\alpha = \frac{d}{2}$$

Therefore, let $y = (y_d, y_{n-d})$ any false fingerprint generated by the coalition. Recalling that $y_{n-d} = u_{n-d} = v_{n-d}$, we have that

$$d(w, y) \geq d(w_{n-d}, y_{n-d}) = d(w_{n-d}, u_{n-d}) = \frac{d}{2}. \tag{7}$$

Moreover, assuming that

$$d(u, y) = d(u_d, y_d) \geq \frac{d}{2},$$

then

$$d(v, y) = d(v_d, y_d) = d - d(u_d, y_d) \leq \frac{d}{2},$$

and so

$$\min\{d(x, y)|x \in c\} \leq \frac{d}{2}.$$

$\square$

From the Proposition 2 it follows that the worst situation for the distributor is when

$$d(y, w) = d(y, u) = d(y, v) = \frac{d}{2}, \tag{8}$$

for some $w \in C - c$.

Note that the $(2, 2)$-separability of the equidistant codes, determines that there can only exist a single codeword w with this property. Moreover, for this to happen, the false fingerprint y_d must have exactly $d/2$ symbols from u_d and $d/2$ symbols from v_d.

Next proposition gives the necessary conditions, so (8) is satisfied.

Proposition 3. *Let C be an equidistant binary $C = C[n, k, d]$ code. Let $c = \{u, v\} \subset C$ be a coalition and let y be a false fingerprint generated by the coalition c. Then*

$$d(y, w) = d(y, u) = d(y, v) = \frac{d}{2}, \tag{9}$$

only if

$$d(y_d, u_d) = d(y_d, v_d) = \frac{d}{2},$$

and therefore the Hamming weight of the false fingerprint y, denoted by $w(y)$, satisfies $w(y) \mod 2 = 0$.

Moreover, if $w(y) \mod 2 \neq 0$, then we can obtain the coalition c using minimum distance decoding.

Proof. A necessary condition to satisfy (9) is that $w(y)$ is even. Note that $d/2 = d(y, w) = w(y + w)$ is even. Then, $w(y + w)$ is even if and only if $w(y)$ and $w(w)$ have the same parity, but $w(w)$ is always even and therefore $w(y)$ must be even.

Moreover, if $w(y)$ is odd, then $d(y, x) \neq d/2, \forall x \in C$, and therefore

$$\min\{d(x, y) | x \in \{u, v\}\} \leq t = \frac{d}{2} - 1,$$

where t is the correcting capacity of the code, in other words, we can decode considering the correcting capacity of the code. $\qed$

Assuming that (9) is satisfied, there is still a chance to unveil the coalition as is shown in the following proposition.

Proposition 4. *Let C be an equidistant binary $C = C[n, k, d]$ code. Let $c = \{u, v\} \subset C$ be a coalition and y a false fingerprint generated by the coalition c, such that*

$$d(y, w) = d(y, u) = d(y, v) = \frac{d}{2}. \tag{10}$$

Then the probability p_C of recovering the coalition satisfies

$$p_C = \frac{2^k - 2}{2^d}.$$

Proof. If (10) is satisfied, then $d(w_d, y_d) = 0$, since due to Proposition 2 (equation (7)) we know that $d(w_{n-d}, y_{n-d}) = d/2$.

Considering all the codewords, $x^i = (x_d^i, x_{n-d}^i) \in C$, then $x_d^i \neq x_d^j$ for $i \neq j$, since in any other case $d(x^i, x^j) \leq n - d < d$. Therefore, the space C_d generated by $\{x_d^i | x^i \in C\}$ of dimension k (can be seen as a code subspace, where the code is a space of dimension k).

Since in this case the false fingerprint y satisfies $d(y_d, w_d^i) = 0$ for some codeword, this means that k free positions in the false fingerprint, but the remaining $d - k$ positions are fixed.

Now, assuming that all false fingerprints have the same probability, the probability p_c that $y_d \in C_d$

$$p_c = \left(\frac{1}{2}\right)^{d-k},$$

and therefore the probability p_C that $d(y_d, w_d^i) = 0$ for some codeword $w^i \in C - c$

$$p_C = \frac{2^k - 2}{2^k} \left(\frac{1}{2}\right)^{d-k} = \frac{2^k - 2}{2^d}. \tag{11}$$

Using the results in [3] we have that for equidistant codes $d \geq 2^{k-1}$.   □

Note that in this case, we exceed the correcting capacity of the code and we will have to use decoding algorithms such as the ones discussed in [5].

5   Construction of Fingerprinting Codes

Equidistant linear codes cannot be used as fingerprinting codes as shown above, since the 2-coalition has enough information about the codeword symbols, so they can construct a false fingerprint deterministically that satisfies $d(y_d, w_d^i) = 0$ for some codeword $w^i \in C - c$, taking $d/2$ symbols from each codeword.

However, equidistant linear codes can be used in a concatenated scheme, so the probability that the coalition is able to determine *correctly* $d/2$ symbols from each codeword can be made as small as we seek.

In order to create a family $\mathcal{C}$ of 2-secure codes we consider an equidistant linear binary code C, mappings $\psi_i : \mathbb{F}_2 \to \mathbb{F}_2^m$, with $\psi_i(0) = 1 + \psi_i(1)$, chosen uniformly at random among all possible ones, for $i = 1, \ldots, n$, where $m > 0$ is an integer.

To generate the C_k code of the family, we choose uniformly a random permutation $\pi_k : \mathbb{F}_2^{mn} \to \mathbb{F}_2^{mn}$ and we define the codewords through the mapping

$$\pi_k \circ (\psi_1, \ldots, \psi_n) : C \to C_k$$

Note that in this construction, when a coalition generates a false fingerprint does not have any information that helps them reconstruct the symbols (they have to do it at random), and therefore they can generate *symbols* that do not correspond to any one of the symbols used in the encoding process, that is, the distributor can detect positions that have been modified, and of course take advantage of it, as is shown in the following theorem.

Theorem 2. *Let $C = C[n, k, d]$ be an equidistant binary linear code. Let $\mathcal{C}$ the family of codes created according to the above paragraph. Let $c = \{u, v\}$ be a coalition and let $y = (y_1, \ldots, y_{mn})$ be the false fingerprint generated by c. If any of the symbols of y is not valid, that is, $y_i \notin \{\psi_i(0), \psi_i(1)\}$, for some $1 \leq i \leq n$, then the coalition can be identified.*

Proof. Taking the invalid symbols y_i', and replacing them by valid symbols y_i', we can always construct a new false fingerprint y', in such a way that $w(y')$ is odd.

Obviously c can generate y' and since $w(y')$ is odd, by Proposition 2 it can be seen that

$$\min\{d(x, y') | x \in \{u, v\}\} < \frac{d}{2} < d(w, y'), \ \forall w \in C - c,$$

that is, the false fingerprint y' is closer to some coalition codeword than to any other codeword. Moreover, the false fingerprint is also within the error correcting capability of the code. $\square$

Taking into account the previous result, it is clear that the only way of not being able to decode correctly, is that the coalition c constructs a false fingerprint with $d/2$ (correct) symbols from each codeword, and also that $d(y_d, w_d) = 0$ for some codeword $w \in C - c$ (Propositions 3 and 4).

Next proposition evaluates the probability that, considering that the coalition has taken $d/2$ symbols from each codeword, the false fingerprint is erroneous.

Proposition 5. *Let $C[n, k, d]$ be an equidistant binary linear code. Let $\mathcal{C}$ be the family of codes created according to the previous paragraph. Let $c = \{u, v\}$ be a coalition and let y be the false fingerprint generated by c, in such a way that y contains $md/2$ bits from u and $md/2$ bits from v. Then, the probability p_v that y is a correct false fingerprint (all the symbols of the false fingerprint are correct) is*

$$p_v = \frac{\binom{d}{d/2}}{\binom{md}{md/2}}.$$

Proof. The coalition knows md bits of each codeword. Using this knowledge, they want to construct a false fingerprint that contains $d/2$ correct symbols of each codeword.

Since the coalition does not know neither the symbol encoding nor the bit position of each symbol among the md known bits, we can assume that the election of the $md/2$ has to be done in a totally random way.

In this case the number of possible elections is

$$\binom{md}{md/2}$$

On the other hand, the correct elections (the symbols that have been correctly reconstructed) are precisely the ones in which the chosen bots correspond exactly to $d/2$ symbols among the available d symbols, in other words there are

$$\binom{d}{d/2}$$

possible ways of choosing them correctly.   □

Using the previous proposition and the fact the minimum distance of the code increases with the same order of magnitude as the code length [3], the relationship between the probability p_v of not being able to identify any member of the coalition using minimum distance decoding, and the code length satisfies

$$p_v = \frac{\binom{d}{d/2}}{\binom{md}{md/2}} < \frac{2^d}{2^{\frac{3md}{4}}} = 2^{-d(\frac{3m}{4}-1)}.$$

5.1   Decoding

In the decoding process, there is only one situation in which we will not be able to find any member of the coalition, and this will be when the false fingerprint satisfies $d(y, u) = d(y, v) = d(y, w) = d/2$, for some codeword $w \in C - c$.

This case has probability $p_C p_v$ and we will be able to detect it, since the decoding algorithm does not return any codeword.

A different situation is encountered when the false fingerprint y satisfies $d(y, u) = d(y, v) = d/2$ and $d(y, w) > d/2$, for all $w \in C - c$. This situation is also detected, since again the decoding algorithm does not return any codeword. The probability of this case is $(1 - p_C)p_v$. Note that applying the algorithm in [5] we are able to find the coalition.

Finally, if the false fingerprint is not correct, and this happens with probability $1 - p_v$, we are always able to identify the coalition. Note that this means that we will never frame an innocent user, and also that with probability as close to 1 as desired, we will be able to trace a coalition member.

6   Conclusions

We have presented an attack to fingerprinting codes that shows that linear codes are not good fingerprinting codes. Taking this attack into account we discuss the construction of a new family of fingerprinting codes based on equidistant binary linear codes. One of the strong points of our construction is that the identification of guilty users can be done using minimum distance decoding.

References

1. A. Barg, G. R. Blakley, and G. Kabatiansky. Digital fingerprinting codes: Problem statements, constructions, identification of traitors. *IEEE Trans. Inform. Theory*, 49(4):852–865, 2003.

2. D. Boneh and J. Shaw. Collusion-secure fingerprinting for digital data. *IEEE Trans. Inform. Theory*, 44(5):1897–1905, 1998.
3. A. Bonisoli. Every equidistant linear code is a sequence of dual hamming codes. *Ars Combinatoria*, 18:181–196, 1984.
4. J. Domingo-Ferrer and J. Herrera-Joancomartí. Simple collusion-secure fingerprinting schemes for images. *Electronics Letters*, 38:1697–1699, 2000.
5. M. Fernandez and M. Soriano. Fingerprinting concatenated codes with efficient identification. In *Information Security Conference–ISC, LNCS*, volume 2433, pages 459–470, 2002.

Best Security Index for Digital Fingerprinting

(Extended Abstract)

Kozo Banno[1], Shingo Orihara[2], Takaaki Mizuki[3], and Takao Nishizeki[1]

[1] Graduate School of Information Sciences, Tohoku University,
Aramaki-Aza-Aoba 6-6-05, Aoba-ku, Sendai 980-8579, Japan
[2] NTT Information Sharing Platform Laboratories,
Midori-Cho 3-9-11, Musashino-Shi, Tokyo 180-8585, Japan
[3] Information Synergy Center, Tohoku University,
Aramaki-Aza-Aoba 6-3, Aoba-ku, Sendai 980-8578, Japan
tm-paper@rd.isc.tohoku.ac.jp

Abstract. Digital watermarking used for fingerprinting may receive a collusion attack; two or more users collude, compare their data, find a part of embedded watermarks, and make an unauthorized copy by masking their identities. In this paper, assuming that at most c users collude, we give a characterization of the fingerprinting codes that have the best security index in a sense of "$(c, p/q)$-secureness" proposed by Orihara *et al.* The characterization is expressed in terms of intersecting families of sets. Using a block design, we also show that a distributor of data can only find asymptotically a set of c users including at least one culprit, no matter how good fingerprinting code is used.

1 Introduction

Various kinds of data such as documents, music, movies, etc. are digitized, and are processed as digital contents. The digital data can be sent to millions of people instantly through the Internet, and copyright violation is now a serious social problem. One of the key techniques for the problem is digital watermarking. It embeds a secret mark in the digital contents so that the secret mark cannot be detected when the resulting contents are conventionally replayed. The digital watermarking usually embeds either "author's ID" or "user's ID" as a secret mark. In the former case, the author of the contents can insist that the contents are produced by himself/herself. In the latter, a distributor of the contents can identify a user from his/her contents. The latter is called fingerprinting.

Digital watermarking used for fingerprinting may receive a collusion-attack; two or more users collude, compare their data, find a part of embedded watermarks, and make an unauthorized copy by masking their identities. In this paper we assume that at most c users collude for some number c. The "$(c, p/q)$-secureness" has been proposed as an index to measure the resilience of fingerprinting codes for such a collusion attack; a code for fingerprinting is $(c, p/q)$-*secure* for integers $p \geq 0$ and $q \geq 1$ if a distributor can find a set of q users such that at least p of them are surely collusive [5]. The largest fraction p/q among all

M. Barni et al. (Eds.): IH 2005, LNCS 3727, pp. 398–412, 2005.
© Springer-Verlag Berlin Heidelberg 2005

fingerprinting codes is called the *best security index* and denoted by $s(c)$. Some upper and lower bounds on $s(c)$ are given, and it is known that $s(1) = 1/1$, $s(2) = 2/3$ and $s(3) = 3/7$ [5]. However, it has been remained open to determine accurately the value of $s(c)$ for $c \geq 4$.

In this paper, we first characterize the fingerprinting codes that have the best security index $s(c)$, and then show that $s(c)$ is determined by the intersecting families of sets. Using a block design, we furthermore show that $s(c) \leq c/(c^2 - c + 1)$ for an infinite number of c and hence $s(c) = 1/c$ holds asymptotically. Thus a distributor can only find a set of c users including at least one culprit, no matter how good fingerprinting code is used.

The remainder of the paper is organized as follows. In Sect. 2, we formally describe a model of watermarking and define the "$(c, p/q)$-secureness" and the best security index $s(c)$. In Sect. 3, we present a characterization of fingerprinting codes that have the best security index $s(c)$. In Sect. 4, we show that $s(c) = 1/c$ holds asymptotically. Finally, in Sect. 5, we conclude with discussions.

2   Preliminaries

In this section, we first present a model of watermarking used in the paper, and then define some terms.

2.1   The Model of the Watermark

Assume that there are a number n of (legal) *users*, $u_1, u_2, \cdots, u_n$, and a *distributor* of contents. A *watermark* w is a binary sequence of length $l \geq 1$: $w \in W = \{0, 1\}^l$. The distributor chooses a watermark $w_i \in W$ for each user u_i, $1 \leq i \leq n$. The watermarks $w_1, w_2, \cdots, w_n$ are distinct with each other, and are called the *legal watermarks*. The set $\Gamma = \{w_1, w_2, \cdots, w_n\}$ is called an (l, n)-*code* or simply a *code*. The distributor embeds a watermark w_i in the contents, and distributes the resulting contents to each user u_i. The i-th bit of a watermark $w \in W$ is denoted by $\langle w \rangle_i$.

We make the following assumption throughout the paper.

Assumption 1 (Marking Assumption [3]). *Any single user cannot find out where his/her watermark is embedded in the contents. However, if two or more users collude, then, since their watermarks are different from each other, they can realize some of the bit positions of their contents in which their watermarks are embedded by comparing their data and finding some differences in their data. These discovered bits cannot be deleted, but can be arbitrarily changed to either 0 or 1.*

We call a nonempty subset $C \subseteq \Gamma$ a *coalition* of a code Γ. Let $r = |C|$, and let $C = \{w_{c_1}, w_{c_2}, \cdots, w_{c_r}\}$. Thus the r users $u_{c_1}, u_{c_2}, \cdots, u_{c_r}$ are collusive. If all the i-th bits of their watermarks are same, i.e. $\langle w_{c_1} \rangle_i = \langle w_{c_2} \rangle_i = \cdots = \langle w_{c_r} \rangle_i$, then the users in coalition C cannot change the i-th bits of their watermarks because they cannot know where their i-th bits are embedded in the contents.

Otherwise, the users in C can change the i-th bits of their watermarks to either 0 or 1 arbitrarily because they can know where the i-th bits of their watermarks are embedded. The set of all watermarks that are obtained in this way is called the set of *falsified watermarks* by coalition C, and is denoted by $F(C)$. Thus, each falsified watermark $w \in F(C)$ satisfies

$$\langle w \rangle_i = \begin{cases} 0 & \text{if } \langle w_{c_1} \rangle_i = \langle w_{c_2} \rangle_i = \cdots = \langle w_{c_r} \rangle_i = 0; \\ 1 & \text{if } \langle w_{c_1} \rangle_i = \langle w_{c_2} \rangle_i = \cdots = \langle w_{c_r} \rangle_i = 1; \\ 0 \text{ or } 1 & \text{otherwise} \end{cases}$$

for each bit position i, $1 \le i \le l$. We hence have

$$F(C) = \{w \in W \mid \text{for each } i, \ 1 \le i \le l,$$
$$\text{there is } w' \in C \text{ with } \langle w \rangle_i = \langle w' \rangle_i\}. \tag{1}$$

One can observe from Eq. (1) that the set $F(C)$ of bit sequences can be represented by a sequence of characters $0, 1$ and $*$ of length l; the i-th character $\langle F(C) \rangle_i$ of $F(C)$, $1 \le i \le l$, satisfies

$$\langle F(C) \rangle_i = \begin{cases} 0 \text{ if } \langle w_{c_1} \rangle_i = \langle w_{c_2} \rangle_i = \cdots = \langle w_{c_r} \rangle_i = 0; \\ 1 \text{ if } \langle w_{c_1} \rangle_i = \langle w_{c_2} \rangle_i = \cdots = \langle w_{c_r} \rangle_i = 1; \\ * \text{ otherwise}, \end{cases} \tag{2}$$

where $*$ means DON'T CARE. It should be noted that $C \subseteq F(C)$ for any coalition $C \subseteq \Gamma$.

When a distributor finds an unauthorized copy, he/she detects an illegal watermark $w \in (W - \Gamma)$ embedded in the copy and finds a coalition C such that $w \in F(C)$. We assume that a bounded number of users, say at most c users, take part in the coalition C.

An illegal watermark $w \in (W - \Gamma)$ may be contained in $F(C)$ for several coalitions C of at most c users. So we define a set $\mathcal{S}(c, w; \Gamma)$ of coalitions as follows.

Definition 1. *For a code Γ, a watermark $w \in W$ and an integer $c \ge 1$, we define a* suspected family *for w as*

$$\mathcal{S}(c, w; \Gamma) = \{C \subseteq \Gamma \mid 1 \le |C| \le c, \ w \in F(C)\}.$$

We often denote $\mathcal{S}(c, w; \Gamma)$ simply by $\mathcal{S}(c, w)$.

Thus $\mathcal{S}(c, w; \Gamma) \subseteq 2^\Gamma$. If $\mathcal{S}(c, w; \Gamma) = \emptyset$, then there is no coalition of at most c users that can make the watermark w. From Definition 1 and Eq. (2) we immediately have the following lemma.

Lemma 1. *Let $w \in W$, $C \subseteq \Gamma$, $1 \le |C| = r \le c$ and $C = \{w_{c_1}, w_{c_2}, \cdots, w_{c_r}\}$. Then $C \notin \mathcal{S}(c, w; \Gamma)$ if and only if there exists a bit position i, $1 \le i \le l$, such that*

$$\langle w_{c_1} \rangle_i = \langle w_{c_2} \rangle_i = \cdots = \langle w_{c_r} \rangle_i \ne \langle w \rangle_i. \tag{3}$$

A distributor can find $\mathcal{S}(c, w; \Gamma)$ as follows.

- First, the distributor considers a family $\mathcal{E}_0^w = \{C \mid C \subseteq \Gamma, 1 \leq |C| \leq c\}$.
- Then, for each bit-position i, $1 \leq i \leq l$, the distributor removes from $\mathcal{E}_0^w$ all sets $C \in \mathcal{E}_0^w$ such that

$$\langle w_{c_1} \rangle_i = \langle w_{c_2} \rangle_i = \cdots = \langle w_{c_r} \rangle_i \neq \langle w \rangle_i.$$

By Lemma 1, the resulting family is the suspected family $\mathcal{S}(c, w; \Gamma)$.

The *c-coalition detection problem* is to detect a coalition that made the unauthorized copy, assuming that at most c users collude.

2.2   Secureness of Codes

Various research has been done on the secureness of codes (e.g. [3,4,5,6,7,8]). Boneh and Shaw defined "*c-secureness*" as an index to measure the resilience of watermarks for collusion attacks [3]; a code is *c-secure* if a distributor can detect at least one of the collusive users when at most c users collude. However, they showed that there is indeed no c-secure code [3]. They also defined "*ϵ-error c-secureness*"; a code is *ϵ-error c-secure* if a distributor can detect at least one of the collusive users with probability at least $1 - \epsilon$ when at most c users collude. They constructed an example of an ϵ-error c-secure code [3]. If a code is ϵ-error c-secure, then a distributor can detect at least one of the collusive users with small error, but cannot surely detect a definitely collusive user. Orihara *et al.* introduced the "*$(c, p/q)$-secureness*" as an index to measure the quality of a code; if a code is $(c, p/q)$-secure, then the distributor may not detect all the collusive users, but can detect a group of q users including at least p collusive users [5]. Yoshioka *et al.* [7,8] investigated the relationships among c-secureness, ϵ-error c-secureness, $(c, p/q)$-secureness, c-frameproofness [3], c-secure frameproofness [6], and so on. Note that the more basic collusion problem was discussed first by Blakley, Meadows and Purdy [2].

In the remainder of this section, we explain $(c, p/q)$-secureness.

We first define some terms.

Definition 2. *For integers $p \geq 0$ and $q \geq 1$, we call $[p/q]$ an index. For a set V, we say that a family $\mathcal{S} \subseteq 2^V$ is $[p/q]$-detectable if there exists a set $X \subseteq V$ such that $|X| = q$ and $|C \cap X| \geq p$ for any set $C \in \mathcal{S}$.*

If a suspected family $\mathcal{S}(c, w)$ is $[p/q]$-detectable, then there is a set X of q suspicious users and a distributor can insist that at least p of them are surely culprits.

For a family $\mathcal{S} \subseteq 2^V$, there are many pairs of integers p and q for which $\mathcal{S}$ is $[p/q]$-detectable. For example, if $V = \{w_1, w_2, w_3, w_4\}$ and

$$\mathcal{S} = \{\{w_1, w_2\}, \{w_2, w_3\}, \{w_3, w_1\}\},$$

then $\mathcal{S}$ is $[1/2]$-detectable and $[2/3]$-detectable. So we wish to specify a pair of integers p and q best to describe the feature of $\mathcal{S}$. We thus define a total order "$\preceq$" on the set of indices as follows.

Definition 3. *Let $p \geq 0$ and $q \geq 1$. If either $\frac{p}{q} < \frac{r}{s}$, or $\frac{p}{q} = \frac{r}{s}$ and $q < s$, then $[p/q] \prec [r/s]$. If $p = r$ and $q = s$, then $[p/q] = [r/s]$. If $[p/q] \prec [r/s]$ or $[p/q] = [r/s]$, then $[p/q] \preceq [r/s]$.*

For example, we have $[0/4] \prec [1/4] \prec [1/3] \prec [1/2] \prec [2/4] \prec [2/3] \prec [3/4] \prec [1/1] \prec [2/2] \prec [3/3] \prec [4/4]$.

We then define the "detectable index" of a family $\mathcal{S} \subseteq 2^V$ as follows.

Definition 4. *For a set V and a nonempty family $\mathcal{S} \subseteq 2^V$, we define a detectable index $d(\mathcal{S})$ of $\mathcal{S}$ to be the "best" index $[p/q]$ such that the $\mathcal{S}$ is $[p/q]$-detectable, that is*

$$d(\mathcal{S}) = \max\left\{[p/q] \mid \mathcal{S} \text{ is } [p/q]\text{-detectable}\right\}$$

where $\max(\preceq)$ is taken over all indices. We define $d(\mathcal{S}) = [\infty/\infty]$ if $\mathcal{S} = \emptyset$, and define $[p/q] \preceq [\infty/\infty]$ for any indices $[p/q]$.

We now define a $(c, p/q)$-secureness as follows.

Definition 5. *Let Γ be a code and let c is a natural number. We say that Γ is $(c, p/q)$-secure if $d(\mathcal{S}(c, w; \Gamma)) \succeq [p/q]$ for any watermark $w \in W$.*

If a code Γ is $(c, p/q)$-secure, then for any (illegal) watermark $w \in W$ there is a set X of q suspicious users such that at least p of them are surely culprits, under an assumption that at most c users collude.

We now define a "security index" $s(\Gamma, c)$ of a code Γ as follows.

Definition 6. *For a natural number c, a security index $s(\Gamma, c)$ of a code Γ is*

$$s(\Gamma, c) = \min\left\{d\left(\mathcal{S}(c, w; \Gamma)\right) \mid w \in W\right\}$$

where $\min(\preceq)$ is taken over all watermarks $w \in W$.

The security index $s(\Gamma, c)$ is the minimum detectable index $d(\mathcal{S}(c, w; \Gamma))$ for all watermarks $w \in W$. Clearly, $s(\Gamma, c)$ is also the maximum one for all indices $[p/q]$ such that a code Γ is $(c, p/q)$-secure.

We now define the best security index $s(c)$ as follows.

Definition 7. *The best security index $s(c)$ for collusions of at most c users is*

$$s(c) = \max\{s(\Gamma, c) \mid \Gamma \text{ is a code}\}$$

where $\max(\preceq)$ is taken over all codes Γ.

3 c-Intersecting Code

In this section, we present a characterization of fingerprinting codes that have the best security index $s(c)$.

We first define some terms.

Definition 8. *A family S of sets is* intersecting *if $C \cap C' \neq \emptyset$ for any sets $C, C' \in S$. An intersecting family S is c-intersecting if $|C| \leq c$ for every set $C \in S$.*

Definition 9. *A code Γ is c-intersecting if the suspected family $S(c, w; \Gamma)$ is intersecting for every watermark $w \in W$.*

The code Γ_c in Sect. 4, the c-secure frameproof code in [6], and the (c,c)-separating code in [4] are examples of c-intersecting codes.

For a set V, we denote by $\mathcal{F}(V, c)$ the set of all c-intersecting families $\mathcal{E} \subseteq 2^V$:

$$\mathcal{F}(V, c) = \{\mathcal{E} \subseteq 2^V \mid \mathcal{E} \text{ is } c\text{-intersecting}\}.$$

We define an index $d(n, c)$ as follows:

$$d(n, c) = \min\{d(\mathcal{E}) \mid \mathcal{E} \in \mathcal{F}(V, c)\}$$

where V is a set of n elements, i.e., $|V| = n$. The index $d(n, c)$ is determined only by n and c, and does not depend on the set V. For example, $d(3, 2) = [2/3]$, because $d(\mathcal{E}) = [2/3]$ for a 2-intersecting family

$$\mathcal{E} = \{\{w_1, w_2\}, \{w_2, w_3\}, \{w_3, w_1\}\} \in \mathcal{F}(V, 2)$$

and $d(\mathcal{E}') = [1/1] \succ [2/3]$ for any other 2-intersecting family $\mathcal{E}' \in \mathcal{F}(V, 2)$ where $V = \{w_1, w_2, w_3\}$. Note that $d(\mathcal{E}') = [1/1]$ for $\mathcal{E}' = \{\{w_1, w_2\}, \{w_1, w_3\}\} \in \mathcal{F}(V, 2)$.

A main result of this section is the following theorem.

Theorem 1. *If a code Γ is c-intersecting, then $s(\Gamma, c) = s(c) = d(n, c)$ and hence the $s(\Gamma, c)$ is the maximum among all codes.*

We give a proof of Theorem 1 in the remainder of this section. For a Boolean value $x \in \{0, 1\}$, we define $\overline{x}$ as follows:

$$\overline{x} = \begin{cases} 1 & \text{if } x = 0; \\ 0 & \text{if } x = 1. \end{cases}$$

We then have the following lemma, the proof of which is omitted in this extended abstract due to the page limitation.

Lemma 2. *A code Γ is c-intersecting if and only if, for any coalitions $C_1, C_2 \subseteq \Gamma$ such that $C_1 \cap C_2 = \emptyset$ and $|C_1| = |C_2| = c$, there exists a bit position i, $1 \leq i \leq l$, such that $\langle F(C_1) \rangle_i = x$ and $\langle F(C_2) \rangle_i = \overline{x}$, $x \in \{0, 1\}$.*

If $S(c, w; \Gamma)$ is intersecting, then $C \cap C' \neq \emptyset$ for any coalitions $C, C' \in S(c, w; \Gamma)$. For a legal watermark $w_i \in \Gamma$,

$$\{w_i\} \in S(c, w_i; \Gamma)$$

and hence $\bigcap \{C \mid C \in S(c, w_i; \Gamma)\} = \{w_i\}$. Thus every coalition that can make a legal watermark w_i includes w_i. On the other hand, if a coalition $C \in \Gamma$

could make a legal watermark $w_i \in (\Gamma - C)$, then an innocent user u_i would be suspected. However, if Γ is c-intersecting, then such a false charge would not occur.

The fewer coalitions included in a suspected family are, the more accurate information a distributor obtains about the collusive users. However, we have the following lemma.

Lemma 3. *For any code Γ and any c-intersecting family $\mathcal{E} \subseteq 2^\Gamma$, there is a watermark $w \in W$ such that $\mathcal{E} \subseteq \mathcal{S}(c, w; \Gamma)$.*

Proof. If $\mathcal{E} = \emptyset$, then clearly $\emptyset = \mathcal{E} \subseteq \mathcal{S}(c, w; \Gamma)$ for any watermark $w \in W$. One may thus assume that $|\mathcal{E}| = m \geq 1$ and $\mathcal{E} = \{C_1, C_2, \cdots, C_m\}$. Since $\mathcal{E}$ is c-intersecting,

$$C_i \cap C_j \neq \emptyset \tag{4}$$

for any indices i and j, $1 \leq i < j \leq m$. If

$$\bigcap_{i=1}^{m} F(C_i) \neq \emptyset \tag{5}$$

then there is a watermark $w' \in W$ such that $w' \in \bigcap_{i=1}^{m} F(C_i)$, and $\mathcal{E} = \{C_1, C_2, \cdots, C_m\} \subseteq \mathcal{S}(c, w'; \Gamma)$. It thus suffices to verify Eq. (5).

Suppose for a contradiction that $\bigcap_{i=1}^{m} F(C_i) = \emptyset$. Since $C_1 \subseteq F(C_1) \neq \emptyset$, there is an integer r, $1 < r \leq m$, such that $\bigcap_{i=1}^{r-1} F(C_i) \neq \emptyset$ and $\bigcap_{i=1}^{r} F(C_i) = \emptyset$. Thus there exists a bit position k, $1 \leq k \leq l$, such that $\langle \bigcap_{i=1}^{r-1} F(C_i) \rangle_k = x$ and $\langle F(C_r) \rangle_k = \bar{x}$, where $x \in \{0, 1\}$. Since $\langle \bigcap_{i=1}^{r-1} F(C_i) \rangle_k = x$, we have $\langle F(C_j) \rangle_k = x$ for some index j, $1 \leq j \leq r-1$. Therefore by Eq. (2) we have $\langle w \rangle_k = x$ for every watermark $w \in C_j$. On the other hand, since $\langle F(C_r) \rangle_k = \bar{x}$, we have $\langle w \rangle_k = \bar{x}$ for every watermark $w \in C_r$. We thus have $C_j \cap C_r = \emptyset$, contrary to Eq. (4). $\square$

If, for any watermark $w \in W$, $\mathcal{S}(c, w; \Gamma)$ is intersecting and is of a *star type* in particular, that is, there is a legal watermark $w_i \in \Gamma$ which is included in every coalition $C \in \mathcal{S}(c, w; \Gamma)$, then a distributor can surely detect the user u_i as one of the collusive users. However, when $n \geq 3$ and $c \geq 2$, there is no code Γ such that $\mathcal{S}(c, w; \Gamma)$ is of a star type for every watermark $w \in W$, because $\mathcal{E} = \{\{w_1, w_2\}, \{w_2, w_3\}, \{w_3, w_1\}\}$ is intersecting but is not of a star type, and by Lemma 3 there is a watermark $w \in W$ such that $\mathcal{E} \subseteq \mathcal{S}(c, w; \Gamma)$.

The following lemma is known [5].

Lemma 4 ([5]). *If $\mathcal{S}_1 \subseteq \mathcal{S}_2 \subseteq 2^\Gamma$, then $d(\mathcal{S}_1) \succeq d(\mathcal{S}_2)$.*

Using Lemmas 2, 3 and 4, we now prove the following Lemma 5 on the secureness of an intersecting code.

Lemma 5. *If Γ is a c-intersecting code and $|\Gamma| = n$, then $s(\Gamma, c) = d(n, c)$.*

Proof. Let $\Gamma = \{w_1, w_2, \cdots, w_n\}$. One may assume that

$$d(n, c) = d(\mathcal{E}_{\min}) \tag{6}$$

for a c-intersecting set $\mathcal{E}_{\min} \in \mathcal{F}(\Gamma, c)$. Then,

$$d(\mathcal{E}_{\min}) \preceq d(\mathcal{E}) \tag{7}$$

for every $\mathcal{E} \in \mathcal{F}(\Gamma, c)$. It should be noted that the value $d(\mathcal{E}_{\min})$ is determined only by n and c and does not depend on what bit-sequence each watermark $w_i \in \Gamma$ is.

We first verify $d(n, c) \preceq s(\Gamma, c)$. By Definition 6,

$$s(\Gamma, c) = \min_{w \in W} \{d(\mathcal{S}(c, w; \Gamma))\}.$$

One may assume that a watermark $w_{\min} \in W$ attains the minimum above. Then

$$s(\Gamma, c) = d(\mathcal{S}(c, w_{\min}; \Gamma)) \preceq d(\mathcal{S}(c, w; \Gamma)) \tag{8}$$

for every watermark $w \in W$. Since the code Γ is c-intersecting, $\mathcal{S}(c, w_{\min}; \Gamma)$ is c-intersecting and hence

$$\mathcal{S}(c, w_{\min}; \Gamma) \in \mathcal{F}(\Gamma, c). \tag{9}$$

By Eqs. (6) – (9), we have

$$d(n, c) = d(\mathcal{E}_{\min}) \preceq d(\mathcal{S}(c, w_{\min}; \Gamma)) = s(\Gamma, c).$$

We then verify $d(n, c) \succeq s(\Gamma, c)$. Since $\mathcal{E}_{\min}$ is c-intersecting, by Lemma 3 there is a watermark $w' \in W$ such that

$$\mathcal{E}_{\min} \subseteq \mathcal{S}(c, w'; \Gamma).$$

Therefore, by Lemma 4, we have

$$d(\mathcal{E}_{\min}) \succeq d(\mathcal{S}(c, w'; \Gamma)),$$

and hence

$$d(n, c) = d(\mathcal{E}_{\min}) \succeq d(\mathcal{S}(c, w'; \Gamma))$$
$$\succeq \min_{w \in W} \{d(\mathcal{S}(c, w; \Gamma))\} = s(\Gamma, c),$$

as desired. □

We are now ready to prove Theorem 1.

Proof of Theorem 1. Let $\Gamma = \{w_1, w_2, \cdots, w_n\}$. By Lemma 5 $s(\Gamma, c) = d(n, c)$. Therefore it suffices to verify $s(\Gamma, c) = s(c)$.

Suppose for a contradiction that there is a code $\Gamma_a = \{w_1^a, w_2^a, \cdots, w_n^a\}$ such that $s(\Gamma_a, c) \succ s(\Gamma, c)$. Let l_a be the length of the code Γ_a, and let l be the length of the code Γ. From Γ_a and Γ we construct a new code $\Gamma_b = \{w_1^b, w_2^b, \cdots, w_n^b\}$ of length $l_b = l_a + l$ where $w_i^b = w_i^a \parallel w_i$, $1 \leq i \leq n$, that is, the bit-sequence w_i^b is a concatenation of w_i^a and w_i.

We claim that $\varGamma_b$ is c-intersecting. Let $w \in \{0,1\}^{l_b}$ be an arbitrary watermark of length l_b. Let $\mathcal{E}_0^w = \{C \mid C \subseteq \varGamma_b, 1 \le |C| \le c\}$. Compare the i-th bits of w and $w_i^b \in \varGamma_b$ for each i, $l_a + 1 \le i \le l_b$, and remove C from $\mathcal{E}_0^w$ if Eq. (3) holds for C. (See Lemma 1.) The resulting family is intersecting, because the bit-subsequences of $\varGamma_b$ from the $(l_a + 1)$-th position to the l_b-th correspond to the bit-sequences of a c-intersecting code $\varGamma$. $\mathcal{S}(c, w; \varGamma_b)$ can be obtained from the resulting intersecting family by repeating the operation above from the first position to the l_a-th, and hence $\mathcal{S}(c, w; \varGamma_b)$ is a subset of the resulting intersecting family. Thus $\mathcal{S}(c, w; \varGamma_b)$ is intersecting, and hence $\varGamma_b$ is c-intersecting.

Let $\mathcal{E}_{l_a}^w$ be a family obtained from $\mathcal{E}_0^w$ by repeating the operation for the watermark $w \in \{0,1\}^{l_b}$ and each watermark $w_i^b \in \varGamma_b$ from the first position to the l_a-th, and let $\mathcal{E}_{l_b}^w$ be the family obtained from $\mathcal{E}_{l_a}^w$ by repeating the operation from the $(l_a + 1)$-th position to the l_b-th. Then $\mathcal{E}_{l_b}^w = \mathcal{S}(c, w; \varGamma_b)$, and hence $d(\mathcal{E}_{l_b}^w) = d(\mathcal{S}(c, w; \varGamma_b))$. Since $\mathcal{E}_{l_b}^w \subseteq \mathcal{E}_{l_a}^w$, by Lemma 4 we have

$$d\big(\mathcal{S}(c, w; \varGamma_b)\big) = d(\mathcal{E}_{l_b}^w) \succeq d(\mathcal{E}_{l_a}^w). \tag{10}$$

Let w' be the first l_a bits sequence of w. Let $\mathcal{E}_{l_a}^{w'}$ be the family obtained from $\mathcal{E}_0^{w'} = \{C \mid C \subseteq \varGamma_a, 1 \le |C| \le c\}$ by repeating the operation for w' and $w_i^a \in \varGamma_a$ from the first position to the l_a-th. Then $\mathcal{E}_{l_a}^{w'} = \mathcal{S}(c, w'; \varGamma_a)$. Although $\mathcal{E}_{l_a}^{w'} \subseteq 2^{\varGamma_a}$ and $\mathcal{E}_{l_a}^w \subseteq 2^{\varGamma_b}$, the families $\mathcal{E}_{l_a}^{w'}$ and $\mathcal{E}_{l_a}^w$ are isomorphic. We therefore have

$$d(\mathcal{E}_{l_a}^w) = d(\mathcal{E}_{l_a}^{w'}) = d\big(\mathcal{S}(c, w'; \varGamma_a)\big). \tag{11}$$

By Eqs. (10) and (11), for an arbitrary watermark $w \in \{0,1\}^{l_b}$ and the watermark w' that is the first l_a bits sequence of w, we have

$$d\big(\mathcal{S}(c, w; \varGamma_b)\big) \succeq d(\mathcal{E}_{l_a}^w) = d\big(\mathcal{S}(c, w'; \varGamma_a)\big). \tag{12}$$

Let $\hat{w}$ be a watermark $w \in \{0,1\}^{l_b}$ that minimizes the index $d\big(\mathcal{S}(c, w; \varGamma_b)\big)$. Then

$$d\big(\mathcal{S}(c, \hat{w}; \varGamma_b)\big) = \min_{w \in \{0,1\}^{l_b}} \big\{ d\big(\mathcal{S}(c, w; \varGamma_b)\big) \big\}$$
$$= s(\varGamma_b, c). \tag{13}$$

Let $\hat{w}'$ be the watermark that is the first l_a bits sequence of $\hat{w}$, then by Eq. (12) we have

$$d\big(\mathcal{S}(c, \hat{w}; \varGamma_b)\big) \succeq d\big(\mathcal{S}(c, \hat{w}'; \varGamma_a)\big). \tag{14}$$

By Eqs. (13) and (14) we have

$$s(\varGamma_b, c) \succeq d\big(\mathcal{S}(c, \hat{w}'; \varGamma_a)\big)$$
$$\succeq \min_{w' \in \{0,1\}^{l_a}} \big\{ d\big(\mathcal{S}(c, w'; \varGamma_a)\big) \big\}$$
$$= s(\varGamma_a, c). \tag{15}$$

Since both Γ and Γ_b are c-intersecting, by Lemma 5

$$s(\Gamma, c) = s(\Gamma_b, c) = d(n, c). \tag{16}$$

By Eqs. (15) and (16) we have

$$s(\Gamma, c) \succeq s(\Gamma_a, c).$$

However, this contradicts to the assumption $s(\Gamma_a, c) \succ s(\Gamma, c)$. $\square$

4   The Best Security Index

In this section, using theory of block designs, we show that $s(c) = [1/c]$ holds asymptotically.

Orihara *et al.* obtained the following Theorems 2 and 3 for the upper bound on the security index $s(\Gamma, c)$ [5].

Theorem 2 ([5]). *If $c \le (n+1)/2$, then $s(\Gamma, c) \preceq [c/(2c-1)]$ for every code Γ. If $n \ge 7$ and $c \ge 3$, then $s(\Gamma, c) \preceq [3/7]$ for every code Γ.*

A code $\Gamma_c = \{w_1, w_2, \cdots, w_n\}$ is defined by the following $n \times l$ binary matrix

$$\Gamma_c = \begin{array}{c} w_1 \\ w_2 \\ \vdots \\ w_n \end{array} \underbrace{\begin{bmatrix} 1000\cdots0110\cdots & & 0 \\ 0100\cdots0100\cdots & & 0 \\ \vdots & \cdots\cdots & \vdots \\ 0000\cdots1000\cdots & & 1 \end{bmatrix}}_{\binom{n}{1} \quad \binom{n}{2} \quad \cdots \quad \binom{n}{c}},$$

where $l = \binom{n}{1} + \binom{n}{2} + \cdots + \binom{n}{c}$. The i-th row represents w_i for each i, $1 \le i \le n$. Each column corresponds to a set $C \subseteq \Gamma$ such that $1 \le |C| \le c$. The first $\binom{n}{1} = n$ columns list all bit patterns of length n, each having exactly one 1. The succeeding $\binom{n}{2}$ columns list all bit patterns, each having exactly two 1's, and so on. The last $\binom{n}{c}$ columns list all bit patterns, each having exactly c 1's. Thus each watermark has length l. The following theorem is known for $s(c)$ and $s(\Gamma_c, c)$ [5].

Theorem 3 ([5]). *For any natural number c, $s(c) \succeq s(\Gamma_c, c) \succeq [1/c]$. If $n \ge 3$ then $s(2) = s(\Gamma_2, 2) = [2/3]$, and if $n \ge 8$ then $s(3) = s(\Gamma_3, 3) = [3/7]$.*

Thus a lower bound $[1/c]$ on $s(c)$ is known, but the exact value of $s(c)$ has not been known for $c \ge 4$. We now have the following theorem on $s(c)$.

Theorem 4. *If $1 \le c \le n/2$, then $s(c) = s(\Gamma_c, c) = d(n, c)$.*

Proof. Let $C_1, C_2 \subseteq \Gamma_c$ be any coalitions such that $C_1 \cap C_2 = \emptyset$ and $|C_1| = |C_2| = c$. Then there exists a bit position i such that every watermark $w \in \Gamma_c$ satisfies

$$\langle w \rangle_i = \begin{cases} 1 \text{ if } w \in C_1 \\ 0 \text{ otherwise} \end{cases}$$

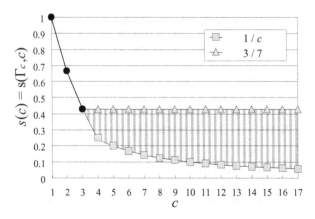

Fig. 1. The best security index $s(c) = s(\Gamma_c, c)$

and

$$\binom{n}{1} + \binom{n}{2} + \cdots + \binom{n}{c-1} < i \leq \binom{n}{1} + \binom{n}{2} + \cdots + \binom{n}{c}.$$

Since $\langle w \rangle_i = 1$ for every watermark $w \in C_1$, we have $\langle F(C_1) \rangle_i = 1$. Since $\langle w \rangle_i = 0$ for every watermark $w \in C_2$, we have $\langle F(C_2) \rangle_i = 0$. Thus Γ_c is c-intersecting by Lemma 2, and hence $s(c) = s(\Gamma_c, c) = d(n, c)$ by Theorem 1.   □

The results in Theorems 2, 3 and 4 are illustrated in Figure 1. Note that $s(c) = s(\Gamma_c, c)$, $c \geq 4$, takes some value in the shaded region in Fig. 1.

We then give a new upper bound on $s(c)$. Remember that $s(c) = d(n, c)$, and that

$$d(n, c) = \min \{d(\mathcal{E}) \mid \mathcal{E} \in \mathcal{F}(\Gamma, c)\} \tag{17}$$

for an arbitrary set Γ with $|\Gamma| = n$. Therefore a detectable index $d(\mathcal{E})$ for any family $\mathcal{E} \in \mathcal{F}(\Gamma, c)$ is an upper bound on $s(c)$. We thus wish to find a family $\mathcal{E} \in \mathcal{F}(\Gamma, c)$ for which $d(\mathcal{E})$ is as smaller as possible in order to obtain a good upper bound on $s(c)$. For the purpose, we use "block designs."

Definition 10. *Let $V = \{x_1, x_2, \cdots, x_v\}$ be a set of v elements $x_1, x_2, \cdots, x_v$. We call a family $\mathcal{E} = \{B_1, B_2, \cdots, B_b\}$ of b subsets $B_1, B_2, \cdots, B_b$ of V a block design on V with parameters (b, v, r, k, λ) or a (b, v, r, k, λ)-block design if*

(1) each block B_i, $1 \leq i \leq b$, contains exactly k elements;
(2) each element x_i, $1 \leq i \leq v$, belongs to exactly r blocks; and
(3) any two distinct elements x_i and x_j, $i \neq j$, belong to exactly λ blocks.

The parameters b, v, r, k and λ must satisfy the following two equations [1]:

$$vr = kb \tag{18}$$

and

$$(k - 1)r = (v - 1)\lambda. \tag{19}$$

If $b = v$, $r = k$ and $\lambda \geq 1$, then any two distinct blocks B_i and B_j, $i \neq j$, in a (v, v, k, k, λ)-block design $\mathcal{E} = \{B_1, B_2, \cdots, B_v\}$ have exactly λ common elements [1], and hence a family $\mathcal{E} = \{B_1, B_2, \cdots, B_v\}$ is intersecting.

We have the following lemma.

Lemma 6. *Let $\mathcal{E} = \{B_1, B_2, \cdots, B_v\}$ be a (v, v, k, k, λ)-block design. If $d(\mathcal{E}) = [p/q]$ for integers $p \geq 0$ and $q \geq 1$, then*

$$p \leq \begin{cases} \left\lfloor \dfrac{kq}{v} \right\rfloor & \text{if} \quad 1 \leq q \leq v \\ k & \text{if} \quad v < q. \end{cases}$$

Proof. Let $V = \bigcup_{i=1}^{v} B_i$. We shall consider only the case of $1 \leq q \leq v$, because the case of $v < q$ is similar (and easier).

Let $1 \leq q \leq v$. Suppose for a contradiction that $p > \left\lfloor \dfrac{kq}{v} \right\rfloor$. Then

$$p \geq \left\lfloor \frac{kq}{v} \right\rfloor + 1.$$

Since $d(\mathcal{E}) = [p/q]$, there exists a set $X \subseteq V$ such that $|X| = q$ and

$$|B_i \cap X| \geq p \geq \left\lfloor \frac{kq}{v} \right\rfloor + 1$$

for every block $B_i \in \mathcal{E}$. We thus have

$$\sum_{i=1}^{v} |B_i \cap X| \geq pv \geq \left(\left\lfloor \frac{kq}{v} \right\rfloor + 1 \right) v > kq. \qquad (20)$$

Since $|X| = q$, one may assume that $X = \{x_1, x_2, \cdots, x_q\}$. Then we have

$$\sum_{i=1}^{v} |B_i \cap X| = \sum_{i=1}^{v} \sum_{j=1}^{q} |B_i \cap \{x_j\}|$$

$$= \sum_{j=1}^{q} \sum_{i=1}^{v} |B_i \cap \{x_j\}|. \qquad (21)$$

Since each element in V belongs to exactly k blocks, we have

$$\sum_{i=1}^{v} |B_i \cap \{x_j\}| = k. \qquad (22)$$

Thus, by Eqs. (21) and (22), we have

$$\sum_{i=1}^{v} |B_i \cap X| = \sum_{j=1}^{q} k = kq,$$

contrary to Eq. (20). $\qquad \qquad \square$

We can prove the following Lemma 7 by Lemma 6.

Lemma 7. *Let Γ be a set, and let $\mathcal{E} = \{B_1, B_2, \cdots, B_v\}$ be a (v, v, k, k, λ)-block design on $V \subseteq \Gamma$. Then $d(\mathcal{E}) = [k/v]$.*

Proof. $V = \bigcup_{i=1}^{v} B_i$, $|V| = v$, and $|B_i \cap V| = k$ for each block $B_i \in \mathcal{E}$. Therefore $\mathcal{E}$ is $[k/v]$-detectable, and hence $d(\mathcal{E}) \succeq [k/v]$. Thus it suffices to verify that $d(\mathcal{E}) \preceq [k/v]$, that is, $[p/q] \preceq [k/v]$ for any index $[p/q]$ such that $\mathcal{E}$ is $[p/q]$-detectable.

We first consider the case where $1 \leq q \leq v$. In this case $p \leq \left\lfloor \dfrac{kq}{v} \right\rfloor$ by Lemma 6, and hence

$$\frac{p}{q} \leq \frac{\left\lfloor \frac{kq}{v} \right\rfloor}{q} \leq \frac{\frac{kq}{v}}{q} = \frac{k}{v}.$$

We thus have $[p/q] \preceq [k/v]$.

We then consider the case where $q > v$. In this case $p \leq k$ by Lemma 6, and hence

$$\frac{p}{q} \leq \frac{k}{q} < \frac{k}{v}.$$

We thus have $[p/q] \prec [k/v]$.   □

If there exists a (v, v, c, c, λ)-block design $\mathcal{E} = \{B_1, B_2, \cdots, B_v\}$ on a set V such that $V \subseteq \Gamma$ and $|\Gamma| = n$, then $\mathcal{E} \in \mathcal{F}(\Gamma, c)$ and hence $d(\mathcal{E})$ is an upper bound on $s(c)$ and $d(\mathcal{E}) = [c/v] \succeq s(c)$ by Lemma 7. By Eq. (19), the parameter v of a (v, v, c, c, λ)-block design satisfies

$$v = \frac{c^2 - c}{\lambda} + 1. \tag{23}$$

We thus have

$$s(c) \preceq d(\mathcal{E}) = [c/v] = \left[c \Big/ \left(\frac{c^2 - c}{\lambda} + 1 \right) \right].$$

We wish to make the index $d(\mathcal{E}) = [c/v]$ as smaller as possible in order to obtain a good upper bound on $s(c)$. We thus wish to make v bigger and hence λ smaller by Eq. (23). Hence we let $\lambda = 1$, because by Eq. (19) $\lambda \geq 1$ when $c \geq 2$. Then

$$v = c^2 - c + 1,$$

and we have

$$s(c) \preceq d(\mathcal{E}) = [c/(c^2 - c + 1)].$$

There does not always exist a $(c^2 - c + 1, c^2 - c + 1, c, c, 1)$-block design for every natural number c. However, there exists a $(c^2 - c + 1, c^2 - c + 1, c, c, 1)$-block design if $c - 1$ is a prime power: $c - 1 = p^q$ for some prime p and natural number q [1]. We thus have the following theorem.

Theorem 5. *Let n be any natural number. If c is a natural number such that $c^2 - c + 1 \leq n$ and $c - 1$ is a prime power, then $s(c) \preceq [c/(c^2 - c + 1)]$.*

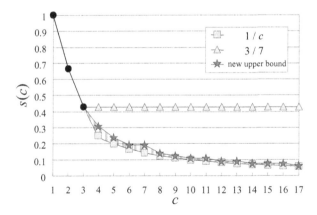

Fig. 2. The best security index $s(c)$

Proof. Since $c - 1$ is a prime power, there exists a $(c^2 - c + 1, c^2 - c + 1, c, c, 1)$-block design $\mathcal{E} = \{B_1, B_2, \cdots, B_{c^2-c+1}\}$ [1]. By Lemma 7, $d(\mathcal{E}) = [c/(c^2-c+1)]$. Since $\mathcal{E} \in \mathcal{F}(\Gamma, c)$ for a set Γ with $|\Gamma| = n$, we have $s(c) = d(n, c) \preceq d(\mathcal{E}) = [c/(c^2 - c + 1)]$ by Eq. (17). $\qquad\square$

We immediately have the following corollary on $s(c)$ for every natural number c.

Corollary 1. *Let n be any natural number, and let c be any natural number such that $3 \leq c \leq n$. If c' is a natural number such that*

$$c' = \max\{c'' \mid c'' \leq c,\ c'' - 1 \text{ is a prime power},\ c''^2 - c'' + 1 \leq n\},$$

then $s(c) \preceq [c'/(c'^2 - c' + 1)]$.

The results of Theorem 5 and Corollary 1 are illustrated in Figure 2. If $c \geq 4$, then $s(c)$ takes some value in the shaded region in Fig. 2. Theorem 5 and Corollary 1 imply that $s(c) = [1/c]$ holds asymptotically when c becomes large. Hence, a distributor can only find a set of c users including at least one culprit, no matter how good fingerprinting code is used.

5   Conclusions

This paper deals with the problem of fingerprinting codes for collusion attacks. We presented a characterization of fingerprinting codes that have the best security index $s(c)$, that is, we showed that every c-intersecting code has the best security index $s(c)$. We also showed that the value $s(c)$ depends only on the number c of collusive users and the number n of users, and that $s(c) = [1/c]$ holds asymptotically. Thus a distributor can find only a set of c users such that at least one of them is surely collusive, regardless of how good code is used.

Stinson *et al.* introduced a "c-secure frameproof code" [6], and Cohen *et al.* studied a "(t, u)-separating code" [4]. One can easily know that the following (a), (b) and (c) are equivalent with each other:

(a) Γ is a c-intersecting code;

(b) Γ is a c-secure frameproof code; and

(c) Γ is a (c, c)-separating code.

Acknowledgment

We thank the anonymous referees whose comments and suggestions helped us to improve the presentation of the paper.

References

1. T. Beth, D. Jungnickel and H. Lenz, "Design Theory, Second edition," Cambridge University Press, 1999.

2. G. R. Blakley, C. Meadows, and G. B. Purdy, "Fingerprinting long forgiving messages," Proc. CRYPTO '85, Lecture Notes in Computer Science, vol. 218, pp. 180–189, Springer-Verlag, 1986.

3. D. Boneh and J. Shaw, "Collusion secure fingerprinting for digital data," IEEE Trans. on Information Theory, vol. 44, no. 5, pp. 1897–1905, 1998.

4. G. D. Cohen and H. G. Schaathun, "Upper bounds on separating codes," IEEE Trans. on Information Theory, vol. 50, no. 6, pp. 1291–1294, 2004.

5. S. Orihara, T. Mizuki, and T. Nishizeki, "New security index for digital fingerprinting and its bounds," IEICE Trans. Fundamentals, vol. E86-A, no. 5, pp. 1156–1163, 2003.

6. D. R. Stinson, T. van Trung, and R. Wei, "Secure frameproof codes, key distribution patterns, group testing algorithms and related structures," Journal of Statistical Planning and Inference, vol. 86, no. 2, pp. 595–617, 2000.

7. K. Yoshioka, J. Shikata, and T. Matsumoto, "Collusion secure codes: Systematic security definitions and their relations," IEICE Trans. Fundamentals, vol. E87-A, no. 5, pp. 1162–1171, 2004.

8. K. Yoshioka, J. Shikata, and T. Matsumoto, "On collusion security of random codes," IEICE Trans. Fundamentals, vol. E88-A, no. 1, pp. 296–304, 2005.

Author Index

Lecture Notes in Computer Science

For information about Vols. 1–3712

please contact your bookseller or Springer

Vol. 3762: R. Meersman, Z. Tari, P. Herrero (Eds.), On the Move to Meaningful Internet Systems 2005: OTM 2005 Workshops. XXXI, 1228 pages. 2005.

Vol. 3761: R. Meersman, Z. Tari (Eds.), On the Move to Meaningful Internet Systems 2005: CoopIS, DOA, and ODBASE, Part II. XXVII, 653 pages. 2005.

Vol. 3760: R. Meersman, Z. Tari (Eds.), On the Move to Meaningful Internet Systems 2005: CoopIS, DOA, and ODBASE, Part I. XXVII, 921 pages. 2005.

Vol. 3759: G. Chen, Y. Pan, M. Guo, J. Lu (Eds.), Parallel and Distributed Processing and Applications - ISPA 2005 Workshops. XIII, 669 pages. 2005.

Vol. 3758: Y. Pan, D.-x. Chen, M. Guo, J. Cao, J.J. Dongarra (Eds.), Parallel and Distributed Processing and Applications. XXIII, 1162 pages. 2005.

Vol. 3757: A. Rangarajan, B. Vemuri, A.L. Yuille (Eds.), Energy Minimization Methods in Computer Vision and Pattern Recognition. XII, 666 pages. 2005.

Vol. 3756: J. Cao, W. Nejdl, M. Xu (Eds.), Advanced Parallel Processing Technologies. XIV, 526 pages. 2005.

Vol. 3754: J. Dalmau Royo, G. Hasegawa (Eds.), Management of Multimedia Networks and Services. XII, 384 pages. 2005.

Vol. 3753: O.F. Olsen, L.M.J. Florack, A. Kuijper (Eds.), Deep Structure, Singularities, and Computer Vision. X, 259 pages. 2005.

Vol. 3752: N. Paragios, O. Faugeras, T. Chan, C. Schnörr (Eds.), Variational, Geometric, and Level Set Methods in Computer Vision. XI, 369 pages. 2005.

Vol. 3751: T. Magedanz, E.R. M. Madeira, P. Dini (Eds.), Operations and Management in IP-Based Networks. X, 213 pages. 2005.

Vol. 3750: J.S. Duncan, G. Gerig (Eds.), Medical Image Computing and Computer-Assisted Intervention – MICCAI 2005, Part II. XL, 1018 pages. 2005.

Vol. 3749: J.S. Duncan, G. Gerig (Eds.), Medical Image Computing and Computer-Assisted Intervention – MICCAI 2005, Part I. XXXIX, 942 pages. 2005.

Vol. 3748: A. Hartman, D. Kreische (Eds.), Model Driven Architecture – Foundations and Applications. IX, 349 pages. 2005.

Vol. 3747: C.A. Maziero, J.G. Silva, A.M.S. Andrade, F.M.d. Assis Silva (Eds.), Dependable Computing. XV, 267 pages. 2005.

Vol. 3746: P. Bozanis, E.N. Houstis (Eds.), Advances in Informatics. XIX, 879 pages. 2005.

Vol. 3745: J.L. Oliveira, V. Maojo, F. Martín-Sánchez, A.S. Pereira (Eds.), Biological and Medical Data Analysis. XII, 422 pages. 2005. (Subseries LNBI).

Vol. 3744: T. Magedanz, A. Karmouch, S. Pierre, I. Venieris (Eds.), Mobility Aware Technologies and Applications. XIV, 418 pages. 2005.

Vol. 3742: J. Akiyama, M. Kano, X. Tan (Eds.), Discrete and Computational Geometry. VIII, 213 pages. 2005.

Vol. 3740: T. Srikanthan, J. Xue, C.-H. Chang (Eds.), Advances in Computer Systems Architecture. XVII, 833 pages. 2005.

Vol. 3739: W. Fan, Z.-h. Wu, J. Yang (Eds.), Advances in Web-Age Information Management. XXIV, 930 pages. 2005.

Vol. 3738: V.R. Syrotiuk, E. Chávez (Eds.), Ad-Hoc, Mobile, and Wireless Networks. XI, 360 pages. 2005.

Vol. 3735: A. Hoffmann, H. Motoda, T. Scheffer (Eds.), Discovery Science. XVI, 400 pages. 2005. (Subseries LNAI).

Vol. 3734: S. Jain, H.U. Simon, E. Tomita (Eds.), Algorithmic Learning Theory. XII, 490 pages. 2005. (Subseries LNAI).

Vol. 3733: P. Yolum, T. Güngör, F. Gürgen, C. Özturan (Eds.), Computer and Information Sciences - ISCIS 2005. XXI, 973 pages. 2005.

Vol. 3731: F. Wang (Ed.), Formal Techniques for Networked and Distributed Systems - FORTE 2005. XII, 558 pages. 2005.

Vol. 3729: Y. Gil, E. Motta, V. R. Benjamins, M.A. Musen (Eds.), The Semantic Web – ISWC 2005. XXIII, 1073 pages. 2005.

Vol. 3728: V. Paliouras, J. Vounckx, D. Verkest (Eds.), Integrated Circuit and System Design. XV, 753 pages. 2005.

Vol. 3727: M. Barni, J. Herrera-Joancomartí, S. Katzenbeisser, F. Pérez-González (Eds.), Information Hiding. XII, 414 pages. 2005.

Vol. 3726: L.T. Yang, O.F. Rana, B. Di Martino, J.J. Dongarra (Eds.), High Performance Computing and Communications. XXVI, 1116 pages. 2005.

Vol. 3725: D. Borrione, W. Paul (Eds.), Correct Hardware Design and Verification Methods. XII, 412 pages. 2005.

Vol. 3724: P. Fraigniaud (Ed.), Distributed Computing. XIV, 520 pages. 2005.

Vol. 3723: W. Zhao, S. Gong, X. Tang (Eds.), Analysis and Modelling of Faces and Gestures. XI, 4234 pages. 2005.

Vol. 3722: D. Van Hung, M. Wirsing (Eds.), Theoretical Aspects of Computing – ICTAC 2005. XIV, 614 pages. 2005.

Vol. 3721: A.M. Jorge, L. Torgo, P.B. Brazdil, R. Camacho, J. Gama (Eds.), Knowledge Discovery in Databases: PKDD 2005. XXIII, 719 pages. 2005. (Subseries LNAI).

Vol. 3720: J. Gama, R. Camacho, P.B. Brazdil, A.M. Jorge, L. Torgo (Eds.), Machine Learning: ECML 2005. XXIII, 769 pages. 2005. (Subseries LNAI).

Vol. 3719: M. Hobbs, A.M. Goscinski, W. Zhou (Eds.), Distributed and Parallel Computing. XI, 448 pages. 2005.

Vol. 3718: V.G. Ganzha, E.W. Mayr, E.V. Vorozhtsov (Eds.), Computer Algebra in Scientific Computing. XII, 502 pages. 2005.

Vol. 3717: B. Gramlich (Ed.), Frontiers of Combining Systems. X, 321 pages. 2005. (Subseries LNAI).

Vol. 3716: L. Delcambre, C. Kop, H.C. Mayr, J. Mylopoulos, Ó. Pastor (Eds.), Conceptual Modeling – ER 2005. XVI, 498 pages. 2005.

Vol. 3715: E. Dawson, S. Vaudenay (Eds.), Progress in Cryptology – Mycrypt 2005. XI, 329 pages. 2005.

Vol. 3714: H. Obbink, K. Pohl (Eds.), Software Product Lines. XIII, 235 pages. 2005.

Vol. 3713: L.C. Briand, C. Williams (Eds.), Model Driven Engineering Languages and Systems. XV, 722 pages. 2005.